Ford Escort Owners Workshop Manual

John S Mead

Models covered

Ford Escort front-wheel-drive Hatchback, Cabriolet, Estate, Van and Combi, including XR3, XR3i, RS Turbo and special/limited editions
1117 cc, 1296 cc, 1297 cc, 1392 cc & 1597 cc petrol engines

Does not cover Diesel engine or RS 1600i models

(686 – 1T6)   ^

Haynes Publishing Group
Sparkford Nr Yeovil
Somerset BA22 7JJ England

Haynes Publications, Inc
861 Lawrence Drive
Newbury Park
California 91320 USA

Acknowledgements

Thanks are due to the Champion Sparking Plug Company Limited who supplied the illustrations showing the spark plug conditions, and to Duckhams Oils who provided lubrication data. Certain other illustrations are the copyright of the Ford Motor Company Limited, and are used with their permission. Thanks are also due to Sykes-Pickavant Limited who supplied some of the workshop tools, and all those people at Sparkford who assisted in the production of this manual.

© **Haynes Publishing Group 1991**

A book in the **Haynes Owners Workshop Manual Series**

Printed by J. H. Haynes & Co. Ltd, Sparkford, Nr Yeovil, Somerset BA22 7JJ, England

ISBN 1 85010 585 5

British Library Cataloguing in Publication Data
Mead, John S. *1950–*
Ford Escort (fwd) owners workshop manual. – 3rd ed.
1. Cars. Maintenance & repair – Amateurs' manuals
I. Title   II. Series
629.28'7222
ISBN 1-85010-585-5

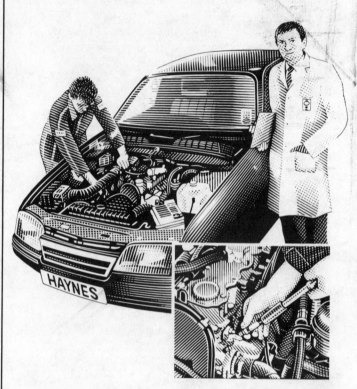

Contents

Ford Escort Ghia

Ford Escort 5-door Estate

About this manual

Its aim

The aim of this manual is to help you get the best·value from your vehicle. It can do so in several ways. It can help you decide what work must be done (even should you choose to get it done by a garage), provide information on routine maintenance and servicing, and give a logical course of action and diagnosis when random faults occur. However, it is hoped that you will use the manual by tackling the work yourself. On simpler jobs it may even be quicker than booking the car into a garage and going there twice, to leave and collect it. Perhaps most important, a lot of money can be saved by avoiding the costs a garage must charge to cover its labour and overheads.

The manual has drawings and descriptions to show the function of the various components so that their layout can be understood. Then the tasks are described and photographed in a step-by-step sequence so that even a novice can do the work.

Its arrangement

The manual is divided into 13 Chapters, each covering a logical sub-division of the vehicle. The Chapters are each divided into Sections, numbered with single figures, eg 5; and the Sections into paragraphs (or sub-sections), with decimal numbers following on from the Section they are in, eg 5.1, 5.2, 5.3 etc.

It is freely illustrated, especially in those parts where there is a detailed sequence of operations to be carried out. There are two forms of illustration: figures and photographs. The figures are numbered in sequence with decimal numbers, according to their position in the Chapter – eg Fig. 6.4 is the fourth drawing/illustration in Chapter 6. Photographs carry the same number (either individually or in related groups) as the Section or sub-section to which they relate.

There is an alphabetical index at the back of the manual as well as a contents list at the front. Each Chapter is also preceded by its own individual contents list.

References to the 'left' or 'right' of the vehicle are in the sense of a person in the driver's seat facing forwards.

Unless otherwise stated, nuts and bolts are removed by turning anti-clockwise, and tightened by turning clockwise.

Vehicle manufacturers continually make changes to specifications and recommendations, and these, when notified, are incorporated into our manuals at the earliest opportunity.

Whilst every care is taken to ensure that the information in this manual is correct, no liability can be accepted by the authors or publishers for loss, damage or injury caused by any errors in, or omissions from, the information given.

Project vehicles

The vehicles used in the preparation of this manual, and appearing in many of the photographic sequences were a Ford Escort 1.3 L, Escort 1.4 GL and Escort RS Turbo.

Introduction to the Ford Escort

Introduced in September 1980, the Ford Escort soon established itself as Britain and Europe's best selling car.

The cars feature front-wheel-drive from a transverse engine/transmission arrangement with independent front and rear suspension on Saloon and Estate models, dual circuit brakes and four or five-speed manual or three-speed automatic transmission.

The model range is extensive including three or five-door Hatchback Saloon, Estate, soft-top Cabriolet and Van versions, available with overhead valve or overhead camshaft engines. High performance models in the range are the Escort XR3, XR3i with fuel-injection, and RS Turbo with fuel-injection and turbocharger.

Extensive modifications to all models were introduced in 1986, with changes to engine sizes and specification, revised body styling and interior, and a number of steering, suspension, and transmission improvements. 1986 also saw the introduction of Ford's unique Anti-lock Braking System as standard equipment on RS Turbo models and a low cost option on certain other models.

All the cars in the range have been designed with the emphasis on economical motoring, ease of maintenance and a high standard of handling, performance and comfort.

Ford Escort Cabriolet

Ford Escort RS Turbo (1985 model)

Ford Escort L (1986 model)

Ford Escort XR3i (1986 model)

General dimensions, weights and capacities

Dimensions

Overall length:
  Pre-1986 models:
    Saloon and Cabriolet .... 4068 mm (160.2 in)
    Estate .... 4131 mm (162.6 in)
    Van .... 4129 mm (166.6 in)
  1986 models onwards:
    Saloon (except XR3i and RS Turbo) .... 4049 mm (159.4 in)
    Cabriolet, XR3i and RS Turbo .... 4061 mm (159.9 in)
    Estate .... 4107 mm (161.7 in)
    Van .... 4181 mm (164.6 in)

Overall width:
  Pre-1986 models (except RS Turbo) .... 1640 mm (64.6 in)
  Pre-1986 RS Turbo .... 1656 mm (65.2 in)
  1986 models onwards .... 1743 mm (68.6 in)

Overall height:
  Pre-1986 models:
    Saloon (except XR3i), Estate and Cabriolet .... 1400 mm (55.1 in)
    XR3i .... 1389 mm (54.7 in)
    Van .... 1568 mm (61.7 in)
  1986 models onwards:
    Saloon (except XR3i and RS Turbo), and Cabriolet .... 1371 mm (54.0 in)
    XR3i and RS Turbo .... 1349 mm (53.1 in)
    Estate .... 1389 mm (54.7 in)
    Van .... 1594 mm (62.8 in)

Wheelbase:
  Saloon, Estate and Cabriolet .... 2402 mm (94.6 in)
  Van .... 2501 mm (98.5 in)

Front track:
  Pre-1986 models:
    Saloon, Estate and Cabriolet .... 1400 mm (55.1 in)
    Van .... 1390 mm (54.7 in)
  1986 models onwards:
    Saloon (except XR3i and RS Turbo) Estate and Van .... 1404 mm (55.3 in)
    XR3i, RS Turbo and Cabriolet .... 1423 mm (56.0 in)

Rear track:
  Pre-1986 models:
    Saloon, Estate and Cabriolet .... 1423 mm (56.0 in)
    Van .... 1384 mm (54.5 in)
  1986 models onwards:
    Saloon (except XR3i and RS Turbo) and Estate .... 1427 mm (56.2 in)
    XR3i, RS Turbo and Cabriolet .... 1439 mm (56.7 in)
    Van .... 1384 mm (54.5 in)

Weights

Nominal kerb weight:

	Saloon	Estate	Cabriolet	Van
1.1 litre 3-door	855 kg (1885 lb)	885 kg (1951 lb)	–	860 kg (1896 lb)
1.1 litre 5-door	875 kg (1929 lb)	905 kg (1996 lb)	–	
1.3 litre 3-door	870 kg (1918 lb)	895 kg (1973 lb)	–	870 kg (1918 lb)
1.3 litre 5-door	890 kg (1962 lb)	915 kg (2018 lb)	–	–
1.4 litre 3-door	885 kg (1951 lb)	900 kg (1985 lb)	930 kg (2051 lb)	875 kg (1929 lb)
1.4 litre 5-door	905 kg (1996 lb)	920 kg (2029 lb)		
1.6 litre 3-door (except fuel-injection and RS Turbo)				
Manual transmission	895 kg (1973 lb)	910 kg (2007 lb)	940 kg (2073 lb)	885 kg (1951 lb)
Automatic transmission	925 kg (2040 lb)	945 kg (2084 lb)		
1.6 litre 5-door:				
Manual transmission	915 kg (2018 lb)	930 kg (2051 lb)		
Automatic transmission	945 kg (2084 lb)	965 kg (2129 lb)		
1.6 litre:				
Fuel-injection	960 kg (2117 lb)	–	995 kg (2194 lb)	–
RS Turbo	980 kg (2161 lb)	–		–

Maximum trailer weight:
- 1.1 litre models .... 245 kg (540 lb)
- All other models .... 408 kg (900 lb)

Van payloads:
- 35 Van .... 491 kg (1083 lb)
- 55 Van .... 772 kg (1592 lb)

Maximum roof rack load .... 75 kg (165 lb)

Capacities

Engine oil (drain and refill):
- OHV engine:
  - With filter change .... 3.25 litres (5.7 pints)
  - Without filter change .... 2.75 litres (4.8 pints)
- CVH engine:
  - Carburettor engines with filter change:
    - Pre-July 1982 .... 3.75 litres (6.6 pints)
    - July 1982 onwards .... 3.50 litres (6.2 pints)
  - Carburettor engines without filter change:
    - Pre-July 1982 .... 3.50 litres (6.2 pints)
    - July 1982 onwards .... 3.25 litres (5.7 pints)
  - Fuel-injected engines with filter change .... 3.85 litres (6.8 pints)
  - Fuel-injected engines without filter change .... 3.60 litres (6.3 pints)

Fuel tank:
- All models (except XR3i and Van) pre-May 1983 .... 40 litres (8.8 gallons)
- All other models (except Van) .... 48 litres (10.6 gallons)
- Van .... 50 litres (11.0 gallons)

Cooling system:
- 1.1 litre OHV engine .... 6.7 litres (11.8 pints)
- 1.1 litre CVH engine:
  - With small radiator .... 6.2 litres (11.0 pints)
  - With large radiator .... 7.2 litres (12.6 pints)
- 1.3 litre OHV engine .... 7.1 litres (12.5 pints)
- 1.3 litre CVH engine:
  - Pre-1986 .... 7.1 litres (12.5 pints)
  - 1986 onwards .... 7.6 litres (13.3 pints)
- 1.4 litre CVH engine .... 7.6 litres (13.3 pints)
- 1.6 litre CVH engine:
  - Pre-1986 .... 6.9 litres (12.1 pints)
  - 1986 onwards .... 7.8 litres (13.7 pints)

Transmission:
- 4-speed manual .... 2.8 litres (4.9 pints)
- 5-speed manual .... 3.1 litres (5.5 pints)
- Automatic transmission .... 7.9 litres (13.9 pints)

Jacking and towing

Jacking

The jack supplied in the vehicle tool kit should only be used for emergency roadside wheel changing unless it is supplemented with axle stands.

The jack supplied with Saloon, Cabriolet and Estate versions is of half scissors type, while the jack supplied with the Van is of full scissors type.

Use the jack at the mounting points on either side of the vehicle just below the sill.

When using a trolley or other type of workshop jack, it can be placed under the front lower crossmember (provided a shaped block of wood is used as an insulator) to raise the front of the vehicle.

To raise the rear of a Saloon (except fuel-injected variants) or Estate, place the jack under the right-hand suspension lower arm mounting bracket using a rubber pad as an insulator.

To raise the rear of a Van, place the jack under the centre of the axle tube, taking care not to contact the brake pressure regulating valve or the hydraulic lines.

Axle stands should only be located under the double-skinned sections of the side members at the front of the vehicle, or under the sill jacking points. At the rear of the vehicle (Saloon or Estate), place the stands under the member to which the tie-bar is attached. On Vans, place the stands under the leaf spring front attachment body bracket.

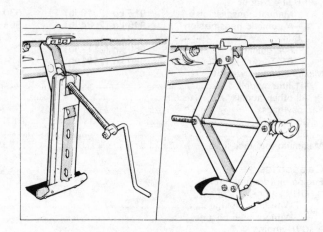

Owner jacks as supplied on Saloon and Estate models (left) and Van models (right)

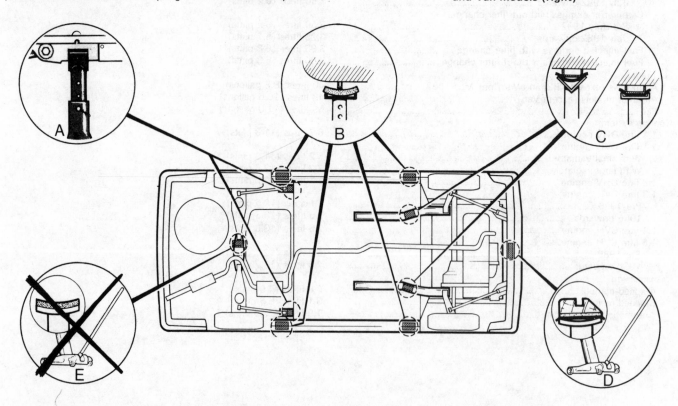

Jacking and support points on vehicle underside (Saloon and Estate models)

A   Axle stand positions (rear)
B   Axle stand positions under sills (with wooden or rubber pad)
C   Axle stand positions (front)

D   Trolley jack position for raising front of car (use shaped wooden block as shown on pre-1986 models)
E   Trolley jack position for raising rear of car on carburettor engine models only (not to be used on fuel-injection versions due to fuel pump location)

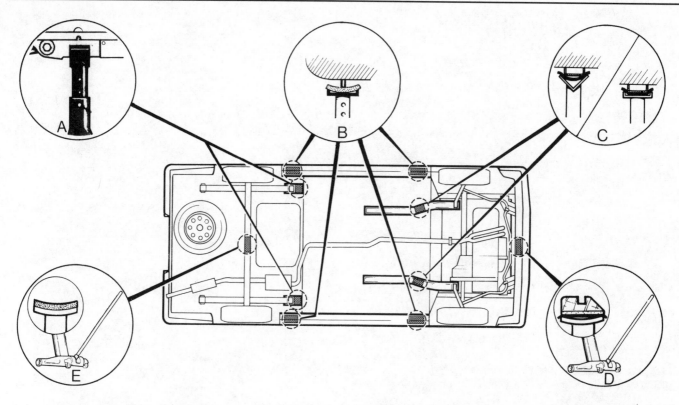

Jacking and support points on vehicle underside (Van models)

A   Axle stand positions (rear)
B   Axle stand positions under sills (with wooden or rubber pad)
C   Axle stand positions (front)

D   Trolley jack position for raising front of vehicle (use shaped wooden block as shown on pre-1986 models)
E   Trolley jack position for raising rear of vehicle

Provided only one wheel at the rear of the vehicle is to be raised, the Saloon and Estate may be jacked up under the rear spring seat, or the Van under the leaf spring-to-axle tube mounting plate.

Never work under, around or near a raised car unless it is adequately supported in at least two places with axle stands or suitable sturdy blocks.

Towing

Towing eyes are fitted to the front and the rear of the vehicle for attachment of a tow rope.

Always unlock the steering column if being towed by another vehicle. If servo-assisted brakes are fitted, remember that the servo is inoperative if the engine is not running.

If automatic transmission is fitted the selector lever must be set in the 'N' position when being towed. The maximum towing distance should not exceed 12 miles (20 km) and the towing speed must be kept down to a maximum of 19 to 25 mph (30 to 40 kph).

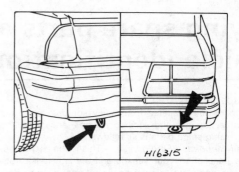

Vehicle towing eyes

Buying spare parts and vehicle identification numbers

Buying spare parts

Spare parts are available from many sources, for example: Ford garages, other garages and accessory shops, and motor factors. Our advice regarding spare parts is as follows:

Officially appointed Ford garages – This is the best source of parts which are peculiar to your vehicle and are otherwise not generally available (eg; complete cylinder heads, internal gearbox components, badges, interior trim etc). It is also the only place at which you should buy parts if your vehicle is still under warranty – non-Ford components may invalidate the warranty. To be sure of obtaining the correct parts it will always be necessary to give the storeman your vehicle's engine and chassis number, and if possible, to take the 'old' part along for positive identification. Remember that many parts are available on a factory exchange scheme – any parts returned should always be clean! It obviously makes good sense to go straight to the specialists on your vehicle for this type of part for they are best equipped to supply you.

Other garages and accessory shops – These are often very good places to buy materials and components needed for the maintenance of your vehicle (eg; spark plugs, bulbs, drivebelts, oils and greases, touch-up paint, filler paste etc). They also sell general accessories, usually have convenient opening hours, charge lower prices and can often be found not far from home.

Motor factors – Good factors will stock all of the more important components which wear out relatively quickly (eg brake cylinders/pipes/hoses/seals/shoes and pads etc). Motor factors will often provide new or reconditioned components on a part exchange basis – this can save a considerable amount of money.

Vehicle identification numbers

The *Vehicle Identification Number* is located on the plate found under the bonnet above the radiator. The plate also carries information concerning paint colour, final drive ratio etc.

The engine number is located in one of the following places, according to engine type:

Front right-hand side of engine block
Front face of cylinder block
Front left-hand side of engine block
Cylinder block above clutch bellhousing

A tuning decal will also be found under the bonnet. This illustrates graphically the basic tuning functions, typically plug gap, ignition timing, idle speed and CO level, and (where applicable) valve clearances, points gap and dwell angle.

Additionally, on later models a chassis number is stamped on the floor panel between the driver's seat and door, and is covered by a fold back plastic flap.

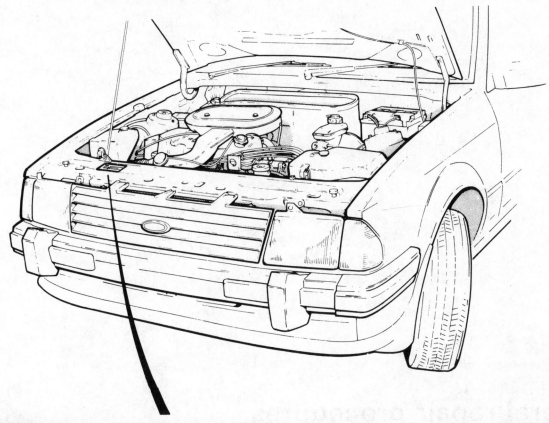

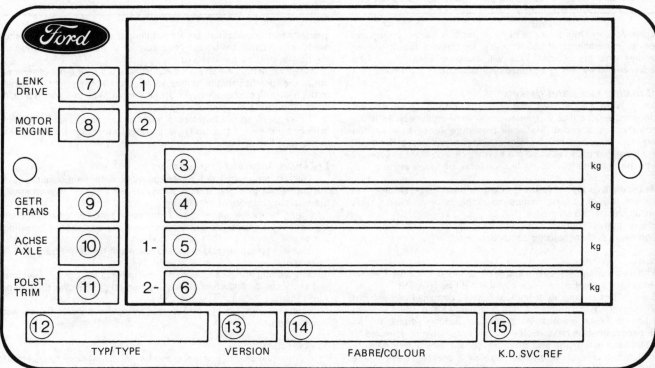

Ford				
LENK DRIVE	⑦	①		
MOTOR ENGINE	⑧	②		
○		③		kg
GETR TRANS	⑨	④		kg
ACHSE AXLE	⑩	1- ⑤		kg
POLST TRIM	⑪	2- ⑥		kg

⑫	⑬	⑭	⑮
TYP/ TYPE	VERSION	FABRE/COLOUR	K.D. SVC REF

Vehicle identification plate location

1 Type Approval Number
2 Vehicle Identificaton Number
3 Gross vehicle weight
4 Gross train weight
5 Permitted front axle loading
6 Permitted rear axle loading
7 Steering (LHD/RHD)
8 Engine
9 Transmission
10 Axle (final drive ratio)
11 Trim (interior)
12 Body type
13 Special territory version
14 Body colour
15 KD reference (usually blank)

General repair procedures

Whenever servicing, repair or overhaul work is carried out on the car or its components, it is necessary to observe the following procedures and instructions. This will assist in carrying out the operation efficiently and to a professional standard of workmanship.

Joint mating faces and gaskets

Where a gasket is used between the mating faces of two components, ensure that it is renewed on reassembly, and fit it dry unless otherwise stated in the repair procedure. Make sure that the mating faces are clean and dry with all traces of old gasket removed. When cleaning a joint face, use a tool which is not likely to score or damage the face, and remove any burrs or nicks with an oilstone or fine file.

Make sure that tapped holes are cleaned with a pipe cleaner, and keep them free of jointing compound if this is being used unless specifically instructed otherwise.

Ensure that all orifices, channels or pipes are clear and blow through them, preferably using compressed air.

Oil seals

Whenever an oil seal is removed from its working location, either individually or as part of an assembly, it should be renewed.

The very fine sealing lip of the seal is easily damaged and will not seal if the surface it contacts is not completely clean and free from scratches, nicks or grooves. If the original sealing surface of the component cannot be restored, the component should be renewed.

Protect the lips of the seal from any surface which may damage them in the course of fitting. Use tape or a conical sleeve where possible. Lubricate the seal lips with oil before fitting and, on dual lipped seals, fill the space between the lips with grease.

Unless otherwise stated, oil seals must be fitted with their sealing lips toward the lubricant to be sealed.

Use a tubular drift or block of wood of the appropriate size to install the seal and, if the seal housing is shouldered, drive the seal down to the shoulder. If the seal housing is unshouldered, the seal should be fitted with its face flush with the housing top face.

Screw threads and fastenings

Always ensure that a blind tapped hole is completely free from oil, grease, water or other fluid before installing the bolt or stud. Failure to do this could cause the housing to crack due to the hydraulic action of the bolt or stud as it is screwed in.

When tightening a castellated nut to accept a split pin, tighten the nut to the specified torque, where applicable, and then tighten further to the next split pin hole. Never slacken the nut to align a split pin hole unless stated in the repair procedure.

When checking or retightening a nut or bolt to a specified torque setting, slacken the nut or bolt by a quarter of a turn, and then retighten to the specified setting.

Locknuts, locktabs and washers

Any fastening which will rotate against a component or housing in the course of tightening should always have a washer between it and the relevant component or housing.

Spring or split washers should always be renewed when they are used to lock a critical component such as a big-end bearing retaining nut or bolt.

Locktabs which are folded over to retain a nut or bolt should always be renewed.

Self-locking nuts can be reused in non-critical areas, providing resistance can be felt when the locking portion passes over the bolt or stud thread.

Split pins must always be replaced with new ones of the correct size for the hole.

Special tools

Some repair procedures in this manual entail the use of special tools such as a press, two or three-legged pullers, spring compressors etc. Wherever possible, suitable readily available alternatives to the manufacturer's special tools are described, and are shown in use. In some instances, where no alternative is possible, it has been necessary to resort to the use of a manufacturer's tool and this has been done for reasons of safety as well as the efficient completion of the repair operation. Unless you are highly skilled and have a thorough understanding of the procedure described, never attempt to bypass the use of any special tool when the procedure described specifies its use. Not only is there a very great risk of personal injury, but expensive damage could be caused to the components involved.

Tools and working facilities

Introduction

A selection of good tools is a fundamental requirement for anyone contemplating the maintenance and repair of a motor vehicle. For the owner who does not possess any, their purchase will prove a considerable expense, offsetting some of the savings made by doing-it-yourself. However, provided that the tools purchased meet the relevant national safety standards and are of good quality, they will last for many years and prove an extremely worthwhile investment.

To help the average owner to decide which tools are needed to carry out the various tasks detailed in this manual, we have compiled three lists of tools under the following headings: *Maintenance and minor repair, Repair and overhaul,* and *Special.* The newcomer to practical mechanics should start off with the *Maintenance and minor repair* tool kit and confine himself to the simpler jobs around the vehicle. Then, as his confidence and experience grow, he can undertake more difficult tasks, buying extra tools as, and when, they are needed. In this way, a *Maintenance and minor repair* tool kit can be built-up into a *Repair and overhaul* tool kit over a considerable period of time without any major cash outlays. The experienced do-it-yourselfer will have a tool kit good enough for most repair and overhaul procedures and will add tools from the *Special* category when he feels the expense is justified by the amount of use to which these tools will be put.

It is obviously not possible to cover the subject of tools fully here. For those who wish to learn more about tools and their use there is a book entitled *How to Choose and Use Car Tools* available from the publishers of this manual.

Maintenance and minor repair tool kit

The tools given in this list should be considered as a minimum requirement if routine maintenance, servicing and minor repair operations are to be undertaken. We recommend the purchase of combination spanners (ring one end, open-ended the other); although more expensive than open-ended ones, they do give the advantages of both types of spanner.

Combination spanners - 10, 11, 12, 13, 14 & 17 mm
Adjustable spanner - 9 inch
Set of Torx type keys or socket bits
Spark plug spanner (with rubber insert)
Spark plug gap adjustment tool
Set of feeler gauges
Screwdriver - 4 in long x $^1/4$ in dia (flat blade)
Screwdriver - 4 in long x $^1/4$ in dia (cross blade)
Combination pliers - 6 inch
Hacksaw (junior)
Tyre pump
Tyre pressure gauge
Oil can
Fine emery cloth (1 sheet)
Wire brush (small)
Funnel (medium size)

Repair and overhaul tool kit

These tools are virtually essential for anyone undertaking any major repairs to a motor vehicle, and are additional to those given in the *Maintenance and minor repair* list. Included in this list is a comprehensive set of sockets. Although these are expensive they will be found invaluable as they are so versatile - particularly if various drives are included in the set. We recommend the ½ in square-drive type, as this can be used with most proprietary torque wrenches. If you cannot afford a socket set, even bought piecemeal, then inexpensive tubular box spanners are a useful alternative.

The tools in this list will occasionally need to be supplemented by tools from the *Special* list.

Sockets (or box spanners) to cover range in previous list
Reversible ratchet drive (for use with sockets)
Extension piece, 10 inch (for use with sockets)
Universal joint (for use with sockets)
Torque wrench (for use with sockets)
'Mole' wrench - 8 inch
Ball pein hammer
Soft-faced hammer, plastic or rubber
Screwdriver - 6 in long x $^5/16$ in dia (flat blade)
Screwdriver - 2 in long x $^5/16$ in square (flat blade)
Screwdriver - 1$^1/2$ in long x $^1/4$ in dia (cross blade)
Screwdriver - 3 in long x $^1/8$ in dia (electricians)
Pliers - electricians side cutters
Pliers - needle nosed
Pliers - circlip (internal and external)
Cold chisel - $^1/2$ inch
Scriber
Scraper
Centre punch
Pin punch
Hacksaw
Valve grinding tool
Steel rule/straight-edge
Allen keys
Selection of files
Wire brush (large)
Axle-stands
Jack (strong trolley or hydraulic type)

Special tools

The tools in this list are those which are not used regularly, are expensive to buy, or which need to be used in accordance with their manufacturers' instructions. Unless relatively difficult mechanical jobs are undertaken frequently, it will not be economic to buy many of these tools. Where this is the case, you could consider clubbing together with friends (or joining a motorists' club) to make a joint purchase, or borrowing the tools against a deposit from a local garage or tool hire specialist.

The following list contains only those tools and instruments freely available to the public, and not those special tools produced by the vehicle manufacturer specifically for its dealer network. You will find occasional references to these manufacturers' special tools in the text of this manual. Generally, an alternative method of doing the job without the vehicle manufacturers' special tool is given. However, sometimes, there is no alternative to using them. Where this is the case and the relevant tool cannot be bought or borrowed, you will have to entrust the work to a franchised garage.

> *Valve spring compressor (where applicable)*
> *Piston ring compressor*
> *Balljoint separator*
> *Universal hub/bearing puller*
> *Impact screwdriver*
> *Micrometer and/or vernier gauge*
> *Dial gauge*
> *Stroboscopic timing light*
> *Dwell angle meter/tachometer*
> *Universal electrical multi-meter*
> *Cylinder compression gauge*
> *Lifting tackle*
> *Trolley jack*
> *Light with extension lead*

Buying tools

For practically all tools, a tool factor is the best source since he will have a very comprehensive range compared with the average garage or accessory shop. Having said that, accessory shops often offer excellent quality tools at discount prices, so it pays to shop around.

There are plenty of good tools around at reasonable prices, but always aim to purchase items which meet the relevant national safety standards. If in doubt, ask the proprietor or manager of the shop for advice before making a purchase.

Care and maintenance of tools

Having purchased a reasonable tool kit, it is necessary to keep the tools in a clean serviceable condition. After use, always wipe off any dirt, grease and metal particles using a clean, dry cloth, before putting the tools away. Never leave them lying around after they have been used. A simple tool rack on the garage or workshop wall, for items such as screwdrivers and pliers is a good idea. Store all normal wrenches and sockets in a metal box. Any measuring instruments, gauges, meters, etc, must be carefully stored where they cannot be damaged or become rusty.

Take a little care when tools are used. Hammer heads inevitably become marked and screwdrivers lose the keen edge on their blades from time to time. A little timely attention with emery cloth or a file will soon restore items like this to a good serviceable finish.

Working facilities

Not to be forgotten when discussing tools, is the workshop itself. If anything more than routine maintenance is to be carried out, some form of suitable working area becomes essential.

It is appreciated that many an owner mechanic is forced by circumstances to remove an engine or similar item, without the benefit of a garage or workshop. Having done this, any repairs should always be done under the cover of a roof.

Wherever possible, any dismantling should be done on a clean, flat workbench or table at a suitable working height.

Any workbench needs a vice: one with a jaw opening of 4 in (100 mm) is suitable for most jobs. As mentioned previously, some clean dry storage space is also required for tools, as well as for lubricants, cleaning fluids, touch-up paints and so on, which become necessary.

Another item which may be required, and which has a much more general usage, is an electric drill with a chuck capacity of at least 5/16 in (8 mm). This, together with a good range of twist drills, is virtually essential for fitting accessories such as mirrors and reversing lights.

Last, but not least, always keep a supply of old newspapers and clean, lint-free rags available, and try to keep any working area as clean as possible.

Spanner jaw gap comparison table

Jaw gap (in)	Spanner size
0.250	1/4 in AF
0.276	7 mm
0.313	5/16 in AF
0.315	8 mm
0.344	11/32 in AF; 1/8 in Whitworth
0.354	9 mm
0.375	3/8 in AF
0.394	10 mm
0.433	11 mm
0.438	7/16 in AF
0.445	3/16 in Whitworth; 1/4 in BSF
0.472	12 mm
0.500	1/2 in AF
0.512	13 mm
0.525	1/4 in Whitworth; 5/16 in BSF
0.551	14 mm
0.563	9/16 in AF
0.591	15 mm
0.600	5/16 in Whitworth; 3/8 in BSF
0.625	5/8 in AF
0.630	16 mm
0.669	17 mm
0.686	11/16 in AF
0.709	18 mm
0.710	3/8 in Whitworth; 7/16 in BSF
0.748	19 mm
0.750	3/4 in AF
0.813	13/16 in AF
0.820	7/16 in Whitworth; 1/2 in BSF
0.866	22 mm
0.875	7/8 in AF
0.920	1/2 in Whitworth; 9/16 in BSF
0.938	15/16 in AF
0.945	24 mm
1.000	1 in AF
1.010	9/16 in Whitworth; 5/8 in BSF
1.024	26 mm
1.063	11/16 in AF; 27 mm
1.100	5/8 in Whitworth; 11/16 in BSF
1.125	11/8 in AF
1.181	30 mm
1.200	11/16 in Whitworth; 3/4 in BSF
1.250	11/4 in AF
1.260	32 mm
1.300	3/4 in Whitworth; 7/8 in BSF
1.313	15/16 in AF
1.390	13/16 in Whitworth; 15/16 in BSF
1.417	36 mm
1.438	17/16 in AF
1.480	7/8 in Whitworth; 1 in BSF
1.500	11/2 in AF
1.575	40 mm; 15/16 in Whitworth
1.614	41 mm
1.625	15/8 in AF
1.670	1 in Whitworth; 11/8 in BSF
1.688	111/16 in AF
1.811	46 mm
1.813	113/16 in AF
1.860	11/8 in Whitworth; 11/4 in BSF
1.875	17/8 in AF
1.969	50 mm
2.000	2 in AF
2.050	11/4 in Whitworth; 13/8 in BSF
2.165	55 mm
2.362	60 mm

Conversion factors

Length (distance)
Inches (in)	X	25.4	= Millimetres (mm)	X 0.0394	= Inches (in)
Feet (ft)	X	0.305	= Metres (m)	X 3.281	= Feet (ft)
Miles	X	1.609	= Kilometres (km)	X 0.621	= Miles

Volume (capacity)
Cubic inches (cu in; in³)	X	16.387	= Cubic centimetres (cc; cm³)	X 0.061	= Cubic inches (cu in; in³)
Imperial pints (Imp pt)	X	0.568	= Litres (l)	X 1.76	= Imperial pints (Imp pt)
Imperial quarts (Imp qt)	X	1.137	= Litres (l)	X 0.88	= Imperial quarts (Imp qt)
Imperial quarts (Imp qt)	X	1.201	= US quarts (US qt)	X 0.833	= Imperial quarts (Imp qt)
US quarts (US qt)	X	0.946	= Litres (l)	X 1.057	= US quarts (US qt)
Imperial gallons (Imp gal)	X	4.546	= Litres (l)	X 0.22	= Imperial gallons (Imp gal)
Imperial gallons (Imp gal)	X	1.201	= US gallons (US gal)	X 0.833	= Imperial gallons (Imp gal)
US gallons (US gal)	X	3.785	= Litres (l)	X 0.264	= US gallons (US gal)

Mass (weight)
Ounces (oz)	X	28.35	= Grams (g)	X 0.035	= Ounces (oz)
Pounds (lb)	X	0.454	= Kilograms (kg)	X 2.205	= Pounds (lb)

Force
Ounces-force (ozf; oz)	X	0.278	= Newtons (N)	X 3.6	= Ounces-force (ozf; oz)
Pounds-force (lbf; lb)	X	4.448	= Newtons (N)	X 0.225	= Pounds-force (lbf; lb)
Newtons (N)	X	0.1	= Kilograms-force (kgf; kg)	X 9.81	= Newtons (N)

Pressure
Pounds-force per square inch (psi; lbf/in²; lb/in²)	X	0.070	= Kilograms-force per square centimetre (kgf/cm²; kg/cm²)	X 14.223	= Pounds-force per square inch (psi; lbf/in²; lb/in²)
Pounds-force per square inch (psi; lbf/in²; lb/in²)	X	0.068	= Atmospheres (atm)	X 14.696	= Pounds-force per square inch (psi; lbf/in²; lb/in²)
Pounds-force per square inch (psi; lbf/in²; lb/in²)	X	0.069	= Bars	X 14.5	= Pounds-force per square inch (psi; lbf/in²; lb/in²)
Pounds-force per square inch (psi; lbf/in²; lb/in²)	X	6.895	= Kilopascals (kPa)	X 0.145	= Pounds-force per square inch (psi; lbf/in²; lb/in²)
Kilopascals (kPa)	X	0.01	= Kilograms-force per square centimetre (kgf/cm²; kg/cm²)	X 98.1	= Kilopascals (kPa)
Millibar (mbar)	X	100	= Pascals (Pa)	X 0.01	= Millibar (mbar)
Millibar (mbar)	X	0.0145	= Pounds-force per square inch (psi; lbf/in²; lb/in²)	X 68.947	= Millibar (mbar)
Millibar (mbar)	X	0.75	= Millimetres of mercury (mmHg)	X 1.333	= Millibar (mbar)
Millibar (mbar)	X	0.401	= Inches of water (inH₂O)	X 2.491	= Millibar (mbar)
Millimetres of mercury (mmHg)	X	0.535	= Inches of water (inH₂O)	X 1.868	= Millimetres of mercury (mmHg)
Inches of water (inH₂O)	X	0.036	= Pounds-force per square inch (psi; lbf/in²; lb/in²)	X 27.68	= Inches of water (inH₂O)

Torque (moment of force)
Pounds-force inches (lbf in; lb in)	X	1.152	= Kilograms-force centimetre (kgf cm; kg cm)	X 0.868	= Pounds-force inches (lbf in; lb in)
Pounds-force inches (lbf in; lb in)	X	0.113	= Newton metres (Nm)	X 8.85	= Pounds-force inches (lbf in; lb in)
Pounds-force inches (lbf in; lb in)	X	0.083	= Pounds-force feet (lbf ft; lb ft)	X 12	= Pounds-force inches (lbf in; lb in)
Pounds-force feet (lbf ft; lb ft)	X	0.138	= Kilograms-force metres (kgf m; kg m)	X 7.233	= Pounds-force feet (lbf ft; lb ft)
Pounds-force feet (lbf ft; lb ft)	X	1.356	= Newton metres (Nm)	X 0.738	= Pounds-force feet (lbf ft; lb ft)
Newton metres (Nm)	X	0.102	= Kilograms-force metres (kgf m; kg m)	X 9.804	= Newton metres (Nm)

Power
Horsepower (hp)	X	745.7	= Watts (W)	X 0.0013	= Horsepower (hp)

Velocity (speed)
Miles per hour (miles/hr; mph)	X	1.609	= Kilometres per hour (km/hr; kph)	X 0.621	= Miles per hour (miles/hr; mph)

Fuel consumption*
Miles per gallon, Imperial (mpg)	X	0.354	= Kilometres per litre (km/l)	X 2.825	= Miles per gallon, Imperial (mpg)
Miles per gallon, US (mpg)	X	0.425	= Kilometres per litre (km/l)	X 2.352	= Miles per gallon, US (mpg)

Temperature

Degrees Fahrenheit = ($°C \times 1.8$) + 32   Degrees Celsius (Degrees Centigrade; °C) = ($°F - 32$) x 0.56

*It is common practice to convert from miles per gallon (mpg) to litres/100 kilometres (l/100km), where mpg (Imperial) x l/100 km = 282 and mpg (US) x l/100 km = 235

Safety first!

Professional motor mechanics are trained in safe working procedures. However enthusiastic you may be about getting on with the job in hand, do take the time to ensure that your safety is not put at risk. A moment's lack of attention can result in an accident, as can failure to observe certain elementary precautions.

There will always be new ways of having accidents, and the following points do not pretend to be a comprehensive list of all dangers; they are intended rather to make you aware of the risks and to encourage a safety-conscious approach to all work you carry out on your vehicle.

Essential DOs and DON'Ts

DON'T start the engine without first ascertaining that the transmission is in neutral.

DON'T suddenly remove the filler cap from a hot cooling system – cover it with a cloth and release the pressure gradually first, or you may get scalded by escaping coolant.

DON'T attempt to drain oil until you are sure it has cooled sufficiently to avoid scalding you.

DON'T grasp any part of the engine, exhaust or silencer without first ascertaining that it is sufficiently cool to avoid burning you.

DON'T allow brake fluid or antifreeze to contact the machine's paintwork or plastic components.

DON'T syphon toxic liquids such as fuel, brake fluid or antifreeze by mouth, or allow them to remain on your skin.

DON'T inhale dust – it may be injurious to health (see *Asbestos* heading).

DON'T allow any spilt oil or grease to remain on the floor – wipe it up straight away, before someone slips on it.

DON'T use ill-fitting spanners or other tools which may slip and cause injury.

DON'T attempt to lift a heavy component which may be beyond your capability – get assistance.

DON'T rush to finish a job, or take unverified short cuts.

DON'T allow children or animals in or around an unattended vehicle.

DON'T inflate a tyre to a pressure above the recommended maximum. Apart from overstressing the carcase and wheel rim, in extreme cases the tyre may blow off forcibly.

DO ensure that the machine is supported securely at all times. This is especially important when the machine is blocked up to aid wheel or fork removal.

DO take care when attempting to slacken a stubborn nut or bolt. It is generally better to pull on a spanner, rather than push, so that if slippage occurs you fall away from the machine rather than on to it.

DO wear eye protection when using power tools such as drill, sander, bench grinder etc.

DO use a barrier cream on your hands prior to undertaking dirty jobs – it will protect your skin from infection as well as making the dirt easier to remove afterwards; but make sure your hands aren't left slippery. Note that long-term contact with used engine oil can be a health hazard.

DO keep loose clothing (cuffs, tie etc) and long hair well out of the way of moving mechanical parts.

DO remove rings, wristwatch etc, before working on the vehicle – especially the electrical system.

DO keep your work area tidy – it is only too easy to fall over articles left lying around.

DO exercise caution when compressing springs for removal or installation. Ensure that the tension is applied and released in a controlled manner, using suitable tools which preclude the possibility of the spring escaping violently.

DO ensure that any lifting tackle used has a safe working load rating adequate for the job.

DO get someone to check periodically that all is well, when working alone on the vehicle.

DO carry out work in a logical sequence and check that everything is correctly assembled and tightened afterwards.

DO remember that your vehicle's safety affects that of yourself and others. If in doubt on any point, get specialist advice.

IF, in spite of following these precautions, you are unfortunate enough to injure yourself, seek medical attention as soon as possible.

Asbestos

Certain friction, insulating, sealing, and other products – such as brake linings, clutch linings, gaskets, etc – contain asbestos. *Extreme care must be taken to avoid inhalation of dust from such products since it is hazardous to health.* If in doubt, assume that they *do* contain asbestos.

Fire

Remember at all times that petrol (gasoline) is highly flammable. Never smoke, or have any kind of naked flame around, when working on the vehicle. But the risk does not end there – a spark caused by an electrical short-circuit, by two metal surfaces contacting each other, by careless use of tools, or even by static electricity built up in your body under certain conditions, can ignite petrol vapour, which in a confined space is highly explosive.

Always disconnect the battery earth (ground) terminal before working on any part of the fuel or electrical system, and never risk spilling fuel on to a hot engine or exhaust.

It is recommended that a fire extinguisher of a type suitable for fuel and electrical fires is kept handy in the garage or workplace at all times. Never try to extinguish a fuel or electrical fire with water.

Note: *Any reference to a 'torch' appearing in this manual should always be taken to mean a hand-held battery-operated electric lamp or flashlight. It does **not** mean a welding/gas torch or blowlamp.*

Fumes

Certain fumes are highly toxic and can quickly cause unconsciousness and even death if inhaled to any extent. Petrol (gasoline) vapour comes into this category, as do the vapours from certain solvents such as trichloroethylene. Any draining or pouring of such volatile fluids should be done in a well ventilated area.

When using cleaning fluids and solvents, read the instructions carefully. Never use materials from unmarked containers – they may give off poisonous vapours.

Never run the engine of a motor vehicle in an enclosed space such as a garage. Exhaust fumes contain carbon monoxide which is extremely poisonous; if you need to run the engine, always do so in the open air or at least have the rear of the vehicle outside the workplace.

The battery

Never cause a spark, or allow a naked light, near the vehicle's battery. It will normally be giving off a certain amount of hydrogen gas, which is highly explosive.

Always disconnect the battery earth (ground) terminal before working on the fuel or electrical systems.

If possible, loosen the filler plugs or cover when charging the battery from an external source. Do not charge at an excessive rate or the battery may burst.

Take care when topping up and when carrying the battery. The acid electrolyte, even when diluted, is very corrosive and should not be allowed to contact the eyes or skin.

If you ever need to prepare electrolyte yourself, always add the acid slowly to the water, and never the other way round. Protect against splashes by wearing rubber gloves and goggles.

Mains electricity and electrical equipment

When using an electric power tool, inspection light etc, always ensure that the appliance is correctly connected to its plug and that, where necessary, it is properly earthed (grounded). Do not use such appliances in damp conditions and, again, beware of creating a spark or applying excessive heat in the vicinity of fuel or fuel vapour. Also ensure that the appliances meet the relevant national safety standards.

Ignition HT voltage

A severe electric shock can result from touching certain parts of the ignition system, such as the HT leads, when the engine is running or being cranked, particularly if components are damp or the insulation is defective. Where an electronic ignition system is fitted, the HT voltage is much higher and could prove fatal.

Routine maintenance

For modifications, and information applicable to later models, see Supplement at end of manual

Maintenance is essential for ensuring safety and desirable for the purpose of getting the best in terms of performance and economy from your vehicle. Over the years the need for periodic lubrication has been greatly reduced if not totally eliminated. This has unfortunately tended to lead some owners to think that because no such action is required, the items either no longer exist, or will last forever. This is certainly not the case; it is essential to carry out regular visual examination as comprehensively as possible in order to spot any possible defects at an early stage before they develop into major expensive repairs.

The following service schedules are a list of the maintenance requirements and the intervals at which they should be carried out, as recommended by the manufacturers. Where applicable these procedures are covered in greater detail throughout this manual, near the beginning of each Chapter.

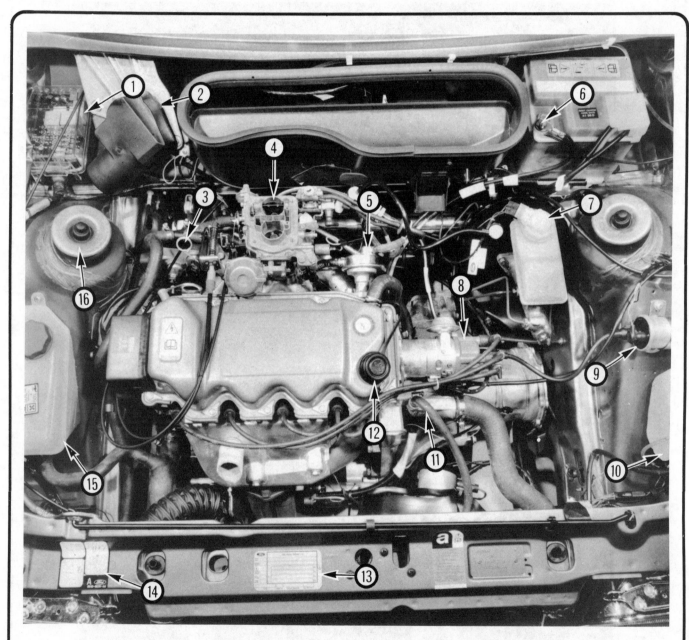

Engine and under bonnet component location on 1986 1.4 litre models (air cleaner removed for clarity)

1	Fuse and relay box	5	Fuel pump
2	Windscreen wiper motor	6	Battery negative terminal
3	Engine oil dipstick	7	Brake master cylinder
4	Carburettor		reservoir

8	Distributor
9	Ignition coil
10	Washer reservoir
11	Thermostat housing
12	Oil filler cap

13	Vehicle identification plate
14	Engine tuning decal
15	Cooling system expansion tank
16	Suspension strut top mounting

Engine and under bonnet component locations on 1986 RS Turbo models

1 Fuse and relay box
2 Windscreen wiper motor
3 Crankcase emission control filter
4 Engine oil dipstick
5 Throttle housing
6 Inlet manifold
7 Throttle position sensor
8 Charge air temperature sensor
9 Distributor
10 Brake master cylinder reservoir
11 Battery negative terminal
12 Ignition coil
13 Fuel filter
14 Washer reservoir
15 Air cleaner
16 Fuel distributor
17 Intake air hose
18 Turbocharger
19 Vehicle identification plate
20 Engine tuning decal
21 Cooling system expansion tank
22 Suspension strut top mounting

**Front underbody view of a
1986 1.4 litre Saloon model**

1 Anti-roll bar clamp
2 Anti-roll bar
3 Front suspension lower arm
4 Steering tie-rod
5 Transmission support
   crossmember
6 Gearchange rod
7 Gearchange stabiliser
8 Driveshaft
9 Engine oil drain plug
10 Brake caliper
11 Alternator
12 Exhaust front pipe
13 Starter motor

22

Rear underbody view of a
1986 1.4 litre Saloon model

1 Fuel filler pipe
2 Suspension lower arm
3 Tie-bar
4 Tie-bar front mounting
5 Fuel tank
6 Handbrake cable adjuster
7 Exhaust mounting
8 Exhaust intermediate
   silencer
9 Exhaust rear silencer
10 Rear towing eye

Every 250 miles (400 km) or weekly

Engine, cooling system and brakes
Check the oil level and top up if necessary
Check the coolant level and top up if necessary
Check the brake fluid level in the master cylinder and top up if necessary

Lights and wipers
Check the operation of all interior and exterior lights, wipers and washers
Check and, if necessary, top up the washer reservoir adding a screen wash such as Turtle Wax Tech Screen wash

Tyres
Check the tyre pressures and adjust if necessary
Visually examine the tyres for wear or damage

Every 6000 miles (10 000 km) or 6 months – whichever comes first

Engine (Chapter 1)
Renew the engine oil and filter
On OHV engines remove and clean the oil filler cap

Cooling system (Chapter 2)
Check the hoses, hose clips and visible joint gaskets for leaks and any signs of corrosion or deterioration
Check and if necessary top up the cooling system

Fuel, exhaust and emission control systems (Chapter 3)
Visually check the fuel pipes and hoses for security, chafing, leaks and corrosion
Check the fuel tank for leaks and any sign of damage or corrosion
On RS Turbo models check the tightness of the exhaust manifold retaining nuts
Check and if necessary adjust the idle speed and mixture settings

Ignition system (Chapter 4)
Remove, clean and reset the spark plugs
Clean the distributor cap, coil tower and HT leads and check for tracking
On contact breaker point distribution lubricate the distributor shaft and cam
On contact breaker point distributors check and if necessary adjust the points gap (dwell angle), then check the ignition timing
On RS Turbo models renew the spark plugs

Braking system (Chapter 9)
Check the front disc pad and rear brake shoe lining thickness
Check the condition and security of all brake pipes, hoses and unions including the servo vacuum hose (where fitted)

Suspension and steering (Chapter 10)
Check the tyres for damage, tread depth and uneven wear
Check and adjust the tyre pressures
Check the steering components for any signs of damage

Bodywork (Chapter 11)
Check the seat belt webbing for cuts or damage and check the seat belt operation
Carefully inspect the paintwork for damage and the bodywork for corrosion

Electrical system (Chapter 12)
Check the function of all lights, electrical equipment and accessories
Check the condition and adjustment of the alternator drivebelt

Every 12 000 miles (20 000 km) or 12 months – whichever comes first

In addition to all the items in the 6000 mile (10 000 km) service, carry out the following:

Engine (Chapter 1)
On OHV engines check and if necessary adjust the valve clearances

Fuel, exhaust and emission control systems (Chapter 3)
Check the underbody for signs of fuel or exhaust leaks and check the exhaust system condition and security
On RS Turbo models check the tightness of the turbocharger-to-manifold nuts

Ignition system (Chapter 4)
Renew the spark plugs
On contact breaker point distributors renew the contact breaker points

Manual transmission (Chapter 6)
Visually check for oil leaks around the transmission joint faces and oil seals
Check and if necessary top up the transmission oil

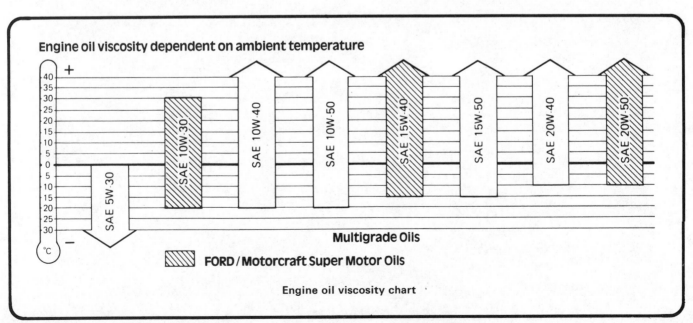

Engine oil viscosity chart

Automatic transmission (Chapter 7)
  Visually check for fluid leaks around the transmission joint faces and seals
  Check and if necessary top up the automatic transmission fluid
  Check the operation of the selector mechanism

Driveshafts (Chapter 8)
  Check the driveshafts for damage or distortion and check the condition of the constant velocity joint bellows

Suspension and steering (Chapter 10)
  Check the condition and security of all steering gear components, front and rear suspension joints and linkages, and steering gear bellows condition
  Check the front and rear shock absorbers for fluid leaks
  Inspect the roadwheels for damage
  Check the tightness of the roadwheel bolts
  Check the wheel bearings for wear

Bodywork (Chapter 11)
  Lubricate all hinges, door locks, check straps and the bonnet release mechanism
  Check the operation of all door, tailgate, bonnet release and window regulator components

Road test
  Check the operation of all instruments and electrical equipment
  Check for any abnormalities in the steering, suspension, handling or road feel
  Check the performance of the engine, clutch and transmission
  Check the operation and performance of the braking system

Every 24 000 miles (40 000 km) or 2 years – whichever comes first

  In addition to all the items in the 12 000 (20 000 km) and 6000 (10 000 km) services, carry out the following:

Cooling system (Chapter 2)
  Renew the antifreeze in the cooling system

Fuel, exhaust and emission control systems (Chapter 3)
  Renew the air cleaner air filter element
  On CVH engines renew the crankcase emission control filter
  On fuel-injected engines renew the fuel filter
  On OHV engines clean the oil filler cap

Every 36 000 miles (60 000 km) or 3 years – whichever comes first

  In addition to all the items listed in the previous services, carry out the following:

Engine (Chapter 1)
  On CVH engines renew the timing belt

Braking system (Chapter 9)
  Make a thorough inspection of all brake components and rubber seals for signs of leaks, general deterioration and wear
  Drain and refill the hydraulic system with fresh fluid

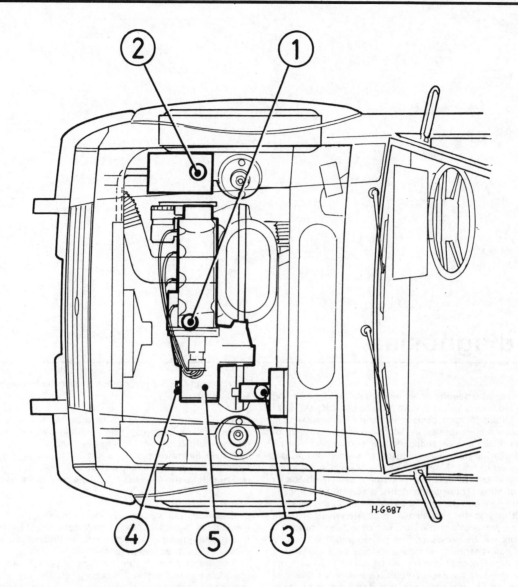

H.G887

Recommended lubricants and fluids

Component or system	Lubricant type/specification	Duckhams recommendation
1 Engine	Multigrade engine oil, viscosity SAE 10W/30 or multigrade engine oil with a viscosity rating suitable for the environmental temperature in which the vehicle is operated – see viscosity chart	Duckhams QXR, Hypergrade, or 10W/40 Motor Oil
2 Cooling system	Antifreeze to Ford specification SSM-97B-9103-A	Duckhams Universal Antifreeze and Summer Coolant
3 Braking system	Brake fluid to Ford specification SAM-6C 9103-A	Duckhams Universal Brake and Clutch Fluid
4 Manual transmission	Hypoid gear oil, viscosity SAE 80EP to Ford specification SQM-2C 9008-A	Duckhams Hypoid 80
5 Automatic transmission see text, Chapter 7		
Transmission number prefix E3RP	ATF to Ford specification SQM-2C 9010-A or ESP-M2C 138-CJ	Duckhams D-Matic
Transmission number prefix E6RP	ATF to Ford specification ESP-M2C 166-H	Duckhams Q-Matic

Fault diagnosis

Introduction

The vehicle owner who does his or her own maintenance according to the recommended schedules should not have to use this section of the manual very often. Modern component reliability is such that, provided those items subject to wear or deterioration are inspected or renewed at the specified intervals, sudden failure is comparatively rare. Faults do not usually just happen as a result of sudden failure, but develop over a period of time. Major mechanical failures in particular are usually preceded by characteristic symptoms over hundreds or even thousands of miles. Those components which do occasionally fail without warning are often small and easily carried in the vehicle.

With any fault finding, the first step is to decide where to begin investigations. Sometimes this is obvious, but on other occasions a little detective work will be necessary. The owner who makes half a dozen haphazard adjustments or replacements may be successful in curing a fault (or its symptoms), but he will be none the wiser if the fault recurs and he may well have spent more time and money than was necessary. A calm and logical approach will be found to be more satisfactory in the long run. Always take into account any warning signs or abnormalities that may have been noticed in the period preceding the fault – power loss, high or low gauge readings, unusual noises or smells, etc – and remember that failure of components such as fuses or spark plugs may only be pointers to some underlying fault.

The pages which follow here are intended to help in cases of failure to start or breakdown on the road. There is also a Fault Diagnosis Section at the end of each Chapter which should be consulted if the preliminary checks prove unfruitful. Whatever the fault, certain basic principles apply. These are as follows:

Verify the fault. This is simply a matter of being sure that you know what the symptoms are before starting work. This is particularly important if you are investigating a fault for someone else who may not have described it very accurately.

Don't overlook the obvious. For example, if the vehicle won't start, is there petrol in the tank? (Don't take anyone else's word on this particular point, and don't trust the fuel gauge either!) If an electrical fault is indicated, look for loose or broken wires before digging out the test gear.

Cure the disease, not the symptom. Substituting a flat battery with a fully charged one will get you off the hard shoulder, but if the underlying cause is not attended to, the new battery will go the same way. Similarly, changing oil-fouled spark plugs for a new set will get you moving again, but remember that the reason for the fouling (if it wasn't simply an incorrect grade of plug) will have to be established and corrected.

Don't take anything for granted. Particularly, don't forget that a 'new' component may itself be defective (especially if it's been rattling round in the boot for months), and don't leave components out of a fault diagnosis sequence just because they are new or recently fitted. When you do finally diagnose a difficult fault, you'll probably realise that all the evidence was there from the start.

Electrical faults

Electrical faults can be more puzzling than straightforward mechanical failures, but they are no less susceptible to logical analysis if the basic principles of operation are understood. Vehicle electrical wiring exists in extremely unfavourable conditions – heat, vibration and chemical attack – and the first things to look for are loose or corroded connections and broken or chafed wires, especially where the wires pass through holes in the bodywork or are subject to vibration.

All metal-bodied vehicles in current production have one pole of the battery 'earthed', ie connected to the vehicle bodywork, and in nearly all modern vehicles it is the negative (–) terminal. The various electrical components – motors, bulb holders etc – are also connected to earth, either by means of a lead or directly by their mountings. Electric current flows through the component and then back to the battery via the bodywork. If the component mounting is loose or corroded, or if a good path back to the battery is not available, the circuit will be incomplete and malfunction will result. The engine and/or gearbox are also earthed by means of flexible metal straps to the body or subframe; if these straps are loose or missing, starter motor, generator and ignition trouble may result.

Assuming the earth return to be satisfactory, electrical faults will be due either to component malfunction or to defects in the current supply. Individual components are dealt with in Chapter 12. If supply wires are broken or cracked internally this results in an open-circuit, and the easiest way to check for this is to bypass the suspect wire temporarily with a length of wire having a crocodile clip or suitable connector at each end. Alternatively, a 12V test lamp can be used to verify the presence of supply voltage at various points along the wire and the break can be thus isolated.

If a bare portion of a live wire touches the bodywork or other earthed metal part, the electricity will take the low-resistance path thus formed back to the battery: this is known as a short-circuit. Hopefully a short-circuit will blow a fuse, but otherwise it may cause burning of the insulation (and possibly further short-circuits) or even a fire. This is why it is inadvisable to bypass persistently blowing fuses with silver foil or wire.

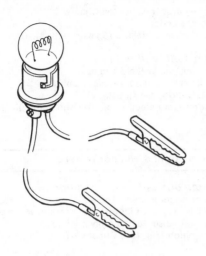

A simple test lamp is useful for tracing electrical faults

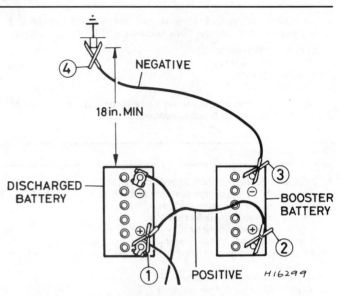

Jump start lead connections for negative earth vehicles – connect leads in order shown

Carrying a few spares can save you a long walk!

Spares and tool kit

Most vehicles are supplied only with sufficient tools for wheel changing; the *Maintenance and minor repair* tool kit detailed in *Tools and working facilities,* with the addition of a hammer, is probably sufficient for those repairs that most motorists would consider attempting at the roadside. In addition a few items which can be fitted without too much trouble in the event of a breakdown should be carried. Experience and available space will modify the list below, but the following may save having to call on professional assistance:

Spark plugs, clean and correctly gapped
HT lead and plug cap – long enough to reach the plug furthest from the distributor
Distributor rotor, condenser and contact breaker points (where applicable)
Drivebelt(s) – emergency type may suffice
Spare fuses
Set of principal light bulbs
Tin of radiator sealer and hose bandage

Exhaust bandage
Roll of insulating tape
Length of soft iron wire
Length of electrical flex
Torch or inspection lamp (can double as test lamp)
Battery jump leads
Tow-rope
Ignition water dispersing aerosol
Litre of engine oil
Sealed can of hydraulic fluid
Emergency windscreen
Wormdrive clips

If spare fuel is carried, a can designed for the purpose should be used to minimise risks of leakage and collision damage. A first aid kit and a warning triangle, whilst not at present compulsory in the UK, are obviously sensible items to carry in addition to the above.

When touring abroad it may be advisable to carry additional spares which, even if you cannot fit them yourself, could save having to wait while parts are obtained. The items below may be worth considering:

Clutch and throttle cables
Cylinder head gasket
Alternator brushes
Tyre valve core

One of the motoring organisations will be able to advise on availability of fuel etc in foreign countries.

Engine will not start

Engine fails to turn when starter operated
Flat battery (recharge, use jump leads, or push start)
Battery terminals loose or corroded
Battery earth to body defective
Engine earth strap loose or broken
Starter motor (or solenoid) wiring loose or broken
Automatic transmission selector in wrong position, or inhibitor switch faulty
Ignition/starter switch faulty
Major mechanical failure (seizure)
Starter or solenoid internal fault (see Chapter 12)

Starter motor turns engine slowly
Partially discharged battery (recharge, use jump leads, or push start)
Battery terminals loose or corroded
Battery earth to body defective
Engine earth strap loose
Starter motor (or solenoid) wiring loose
Starter motor internal fault (see Chapter 12)

Starter motor spins without turning engine
Flat battery
Starter motor pinion sticking on sleeve
Flywheel gear teeth damaged or worn
Starter motor mounting bolts loose

Engine turns normally but fails to start
Damp or dirty HT leads and distributor cap (crank engine and check for spark) – try moisture dispersant such as Holts Wet Start
Dirty or incorrectly gapped distributor points (if applicable)
No fuel in tank (check for delivery at carburettor)
Excessive choke (hot engine) or insufficient choke (cold engine)
Fouled or incorrectly gapped spark plugs (remove, clean and regap)
Other ignition system fault (see Chapter 4)

Other fuel system fault (see Chapter 3)
Poor compression
Major mechanical failure (eg camshaft drive)

Engine fires but will not run
Insufficient choke (cold engine)
Air leaks at carburettor or inlet manifold
Fuel starvation (see Chapter 3)
Ballast resistor defective, or other ignition fault (see Chapter 4)

Engine cuts out and will not restart

Engine cuts out suddenly – ignition fault
Loose or disconnected LT wires
Wet HT leads or distributor cap (after traversing water splash)
Coil or condenser failure (check for spark)
Other ignition fault (see Chapter 4)

Engine misfires before cutting out – fuel fault
Fuel tank empty
Fuel pump defective or filter blocked (check for delivery)
Fuel tank filler vent blocked (suction will be evident on releasing cap)
Carburettor needle valve sticking
Carburettor jets blocked (fuel contaminated)
Other fuel system fault (see Chapter 3)

Engine cuts out – other causes
Serious overheating
Major mechanical failure (eg camshaft drive)

Engine overheats

Ignition (no-charge) warning light illuminated
Slack or broken drivebelt – retension or renew (Chapter 12)

Ignition warning light not illuminated
Coolant loss due to internal or external leakage (see Chapter 2)
Thermostat defective
Low oil level
Brakes binding
Radiator clogged externally or internally
Electric cooling fan not operating correctly
Engine waterways clogged
Ignition timing incorrect or automatic advance malfunctioning
Mixture too weak

Note: *Do not add cold water to an overheated engine or damage may result*

Low engine oil pressure

Gauge reads low or warning light illuminated with engine running
Oil level low or incorrect grade
Defective gauge or sender unit
Wire to sender unit earthed
Engine overheating
Oil filter clogged or bypass valve defective
Oil pressure relief valve defective
Oil pick-up strainer clogged
Oil pump worn or mountings loose
Worn main or big-end bearings

Note: *Low oil pressure in a high-mileage engine at tickover is not necessarily a cause for concern. Sudden pressure loss at speed is far more significant. In any event, check the gauge or warning light sender before condemning the engine.*

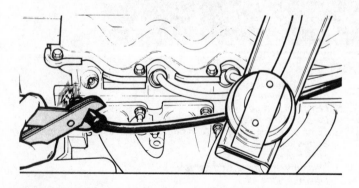

Insert a nail or similar item into plug cap, crank engine with ignition on and check for spark. Note use of insulated tool. End of nail must be within 5 mm (0.2 in) of block

Engine noises

Pre-ignition (pinking) on acceleration
Incorrect grade of fuel
Ignition timing incorrect
Distributor faulty or worn
Worn or maladjusted carburettor
Excessive carbon build-up in engine

Whistling or wheezing noises
Leaking vacuum hose
Leaking carburettor or manifold gasket
Blowing head gasket

Tapping or rattling
Incorrect valve clearances
Worn valve gear
Worn timing chain or belt
Broken piston ring (ticking noise)
Defective hydraulic tappets

Knocking or thumping
Unintentional mechanical contact (eg fan blades)
Worn drivebelt
Peripheral component fault (generator, water pump etc)
Worn big-end bearings (regular heavy knocking, perhaps less under load)
Worn main bearings (rumbling and knocking, perhaps worsening under load)
Piston slap (most noticeable when cold)

Chapter 1 Engine

For modifications, and information applicable to later models, see Supplement at end of manual

Contents

Specifications

Part A: OHV engines
General

Engine type	Four-cylinder, in-line overhead valve
Capacity:	
1.1 litre	1117 cc
1.3 litre	1297 cc
Bore	73.96 mm (2.91 in)
Stroke:	
1.1 litre	64.98 mm (2.56 in)
1.3 litre	75.48 mm (2.97 in)
Compression ratio:	
1.1 litre (pre-1986)	9.15:1
1.1 litre (1986 onwards)	9.5:1
1.3 litre	9.3:1
Firing order	1–2–4–3 (No 1 at timing cover end)

Cylinder block

Material	Cast iron
Number of main bearings:	
1.1 litre	3
1.3 litre	5
Cylinder bore (diameter):	
Standard (1)	73.940 to 73.950 mm (2.9110 to 2.9114 in)
Standard (2)	73.950 to 73.960 mm (2.9114 to 2.9118 in)
Standard (3)	73.960 to 73.970 mm (2.9118 to 2.9122 in)
Standard (4)	73.970 to 73.980 mm (2.9122 to 2.9126 in)
Oversize 0.5 mm	74.500 to 74.510 mm (2.9331 to 2.9335 in)
Oversize 1.0 mm	75.000 to 75.010 mm (2.9528 to 2.9531 in)

Main bearing shell inner diameter:
Standard	57.009 to 57.036 mm (2.2444 to 2.2455 in)
0.254 mm undersize	56.755 to 56.782 mm (2.2344 to 2.2355 in)
0.508 mm undersize	56.501 to 56.528 mm (2.2244 to 2.2255 in)
0.762 mm undersize	56.247 to 56.274 mm (2.2144 to 2.2155 in)
Camshaft bearing inner diameter	39.662 to 39.682 mm (1.5615 to 1.5623 in)

Crankshaft

Main bearing journal diameter:
Standard	56.990 to 57.000 mm (2.2437 to 2.441 in)
Standard with yellow dot (1.1 litre only)	56.980 to 56.990 mm (2.2433 to 2.2437 in)
0.254 mm undersize	56.726 to 56.746 mm (2.3330 to 2.2341 in)
0.508 mm undersize	56.472 to 56.492 mm (2.2233 to 2.2241 in)
0.762 mm undersize	56.218 to 56.238 mm (2.2133 to 2.2141 in)
Main bearing running clearance	0.009 to 0.046 mm (0.0004 to 0.0018 in)
Main bearing running clearance wear limit	0.056 mm (0.0022 in)

Crankpin (big-end) diameter:
Standard	42.99 to 43.01 mm (1.6925 to 1.6933 in)
0.254 mm undersize	42.74 to 42.76 mm (1.6827 to 1.6835 in)
0.508 mm undersize	42.49 to 42.51 mm (1.6728 to 1.6736 in)
0.762 mm undersize	42.24 to 42.26 mm (1.6630 to 1.6638 in)

Thrust washer thickness:
Standard	2.80 to 2.85 mm (0.1102 to 0.1122 in)
Oversize	2.99 to 3.04 mm (0.1177 to 0.1197 in)
Crankshaft endfloat	0.079 to 0.279 mm (0.0031 to 0.0110 in)
Maximum permissible journal and crankpin ovality and taper	0.0254 mm (0.001 in)

Camshaft

Number of bearings	3
Drive	Single chain
Thrust plate thickness	4.457 to 4.508 mm (0.175 to 0.177 in)

Inlet cam lift:
Pre-1986	5.985 mm (0.236 in)
1986 onwards	5.300 mm (0.209 in)

Exhaust cam lift:
Pre-1986	5.894 mm (0.232 in)
1986 onwards	5.300 mm (0.209 in)

Inlet cam length:
Pre-1986	33.198 to 33.274 mm (1.307 to 1.310 in)
1986 onwards	32.288 to 32.516 mm (1.272 to 1.281 in)

Exhaust cam length:
Pre-1986	33.442 to 33.518 mm (1.317 to 1.320 in)
1986 onwards	32.618 to 32.846 mm (1.285 to 1.294 in)
Camshaft bearing diameter	39.615 to 39.636 mm (1.560 to 1.561 in)
Camshaft bearing bush internal diameter	39.662 to 39.682 mm (1.562 to 1.563 in)
Camshaft endfloat	0.02 to 0.19 mm (0.0007 to 0.007 in)

Timing chain

Number of links	46
Length	438.15 mm (17.26 in)

Piston and piston rings

Diameter:
Standard (1)	73.910 to 73.920 mm (2.9098 to 2.9102 in)
Standard (2)	73.920 to 73.930 mm (2.9102 to 2.9106 in)
Standard (3)	73.930 to 73.940 mm (2.9106 to 2.9110 in)
Standard (4)	73.940 to 73.950 mm (2.9110 to 2.9114 in)
0.5 mm oversize	74.460 to 74.485 mm (2.9315 to 2.9325 in)
1.0 mm oversize	74.960 to 74.985 mm (2.9152 to 2.9522 in)
Piston-to-bore clearance	0.015 to 0.050 mm (0.006 to 0.0020 in)

Piston ring end gap:
Compression	0.25 to 0.45 mm (0.010 to 0.018 in)
Oil control	0.20 to 0.40 mm (0.008 to 0.016 in)

Gudgeon pin

Pin length	63.0 to 63.8 mm (2.48 to 2.51 in)

Pin diameter:
White	20.622 to 20.625 mm (0.8118 to 0.8120 in)
Red	20.625 to 20.628 mm (0.8120 to 0.8121 in)
Blue	20.628 to 20.631 mm (0.8121 to 0.8122 in)
Yellow	20.631 to 20.634 mm (0.8122 to 0.8124 in)
Interference fit in connecting rod at 21°C (70°F)	0.013 to 0.045 mm (0.0005 to 0.0017 in)
Clearance in piston at 21°C (70°F)	0.005 to 0.011 mm (0.0002 to 0.0004 in)

Cylinder head
Material	Cast iron
Maximum permissible cylinder head distortion measured over entire length	0.15 mm (0.006 in)
Minimum combustion chamber depth after skimming	9.07 mm (0.357 in)
Valve seat angle	45°
Valve seat width:	
Inlet	1.20 to 1.75 mm (0.047 to 0.068 in)
Exhaust	1.20 to 1.70 mm (0.047 to 0.067 in)
Seat cutter correction angle:	
Upper	30°
Lower	75°
Valve guide bore (standard)	7.907 to 7.938 mm (0.311 to 0.312 in)

Valves – general
Operation	Cam followers and pushrods
Valve timing – pre-1986:	
Inlet valve opens	21° BTDC
Inlet valve closes	55° ABDC
Exhaust valve opens	70° BBDC
Exhaust valve closes	22° ATDC
Valve timing – 1986 onwards:	
Inlet valve opens	14° BTDC
Inlet valve closes	46° ABDC
Exhaust valve opens	65° BBDC
Exhaust valve closes	11° ATDC
Valve clearance (cold):	
Inlet	0.22 mm (0.008 in)
Exhaust	0.59 mm (0.023 in)
Cam follower diameter	13.081 to 13.094 mm (0.515 to 0.516 in)
Cam follower clearance in bore	0.016 to 0.062 mm (0.0006 to 0.0024 in)
Valve spring type	Single
Number of coils	6
Valve spring free length:	
Pre-1986	42.0 mm (1.654 in)
1986 onwards:	
1.1 litre	41.2 mm (1.623 in)
1.3 litre	42.4 mm (1.670 in)

Inlet valve
Length	105.45 to 106.45 mm (4.154 to 4.194 in)
Head diameter:	
Pre-1986	38.02 to 38.28 mm (1.497 to 1.508 in)
1986 onwards:	
1.1 litre	32.89 to 33.15 mm (1.295 to 1.306 in)
1.3 litre	38.02 to 38.28 mm (1.497 to 1.508 in)
Stem diameter:	
Standard	7.866 to 7.868 mm (0.3097 to 0.3098 in)
0.076 mm oversize	7.944 to 7.962 mm (0.3128 to 0.3135 in)
0.38 mm oversize	8.249 to 8.267 mm (0.3248 to 0.3255 in)
Valve stem clearance in guide	0.021 to 0.070 mm (0.0008 to 0.0028 in)
Valve lift:	
Pre-1986	9.448 mm (0.372 in)
1986 onwards	8.367 mm (0.329 in)

Exhaust valve
Length:	
Pre-1986	105.15 to 106.15 mm (4.142 to 4.182 in)
1986 onwards	106.04 to 107.04 mm (4.177 to 4.217 in)
Head diameter	29.01 to 29.27 mm (1.142 to 1.153 in)
Stem diameter:	
Standard	7.846 to 7.864 mm (0.3089 to 0.3096 in)
0.076 mm oversize	7.922 to 7.940 mm (0.3119 to 0.3126 in)
0.38 mm oversize	8.227 to 8.245 mm (0.3239 to 0.3246 in)
Valve stem clearance in guide	0.043 to 0.092 mm (0.0017 to 0.0036 in)
Valve lift:	
Pre-1986	9.448 mm (0.372 in)
1986 onwards	8.367 mm (0.329 in)

Lubrication
Oil type/specification	Multigrade engine oil, viscosity SAE 10W/30 (or multigrade engine oil with a viscosity range suitable for the environmental temperature in which the vehicle is operated) – see viscosity chart (Duckhams QXR, Hypergrade, or 10W/40 Motor Oil)
Oil filter	Champion C104
Oil pump type	Rotor, external driven by gear on camshaft
Minimum oil pressure at 80°C (175°F):	
Engine speed 750 rpm	0.6 bar (8.5 lbf/in²)
Engine speed 2000 rpm	1.5 bar (21.3 lbf/in²)
Oil pressure warning lamp operates	0.32 to 0.53 bar (4.5 to 7.5 lbf/in²)

Relief valve opens	2.41 to 2.75 bar (34.3 to 39.1 lbf/in²)
Oil pump clearances:	
Outer rotor-to-body	0.14 to 0.26 mm (0.0055 to 0.0102 in)
Inner-to-outer rotor	0.051 to 0.127 mm (0.0020 to 0.0050 in)
Rotor endfloat	0.25 to 0.06 mm (0.0010 to 0.0024 in)

Torque wrench settings

	Nm	lbf ft
Main bearing cap bolts	88 to 102	65 to 75
Connecting rod bolts	29 to 36	21 to 27
Rear oil seal retainer bolts	16 to 20	12 to 15
Flywheel bolts	64 to 70	47 to 52
Timing chain tensioner	7 to 9	5 to 7
Camshaft thrust plate	4 to 5	3 to 4
Camshaft sprocket bolt	16 to 20	12 to 15
Timing cover bolts	7 to 10	5 to 8
Crankshaft pulley bolt	54 to 59	40 to 44
Oil pump to crankcase	16 to 20	12 to 15
Oil pump cover bolts	8 to 12	6 to 9
Sump bolts:		
Stage 1	6 to 8	4 to 6
Stage 2	8 to 11	6 to 8
Stage 3	8 to 11	6 to 8
Sump drain plug	21 to 28	15 to 21
Oil pressure switch	13 to 15	10 to 11
Rocker shaft pedestal bolts	40 to 46	30 to 34
Cylinder head bolts:		
Stage 1	10 to 15	8 to 11
Stage 2	40 to 50	30 to 37
Stage 3	80 to 90	59 to 66
Stage 4 (after 10 to 20 minutes)	100 to 110	74 to 81
Rocker cover	4 to 5	3 to 4
Engine to transmission	35 to 45	26 to 33
Right-hand engine mounting to body	41 to 58	30 to 43
Right-hand engine mounting bracket to engine	54 to 72	40 to 53
Right-hand engine mounting rubber insulator to brackets	70 to 95	52 to 70
Front transmission mounting bracket to transmission (pre-1986 models)	41 to 51	30 to 38
Front and rear transmission mounting bolts (pre-1986 models)	52 to 64	38 to 47
Transmission mountings to transmission (1986 models onwards)	80 to 100	59 to 74
Transmission support crossmember to body (1986 models onwards)	52	38

Part B: CVH engines
General

Engine type	Four-cylinder, in-line overhead camshaft
Capacity:	
1.1 litre	1117 cc
1.3 litre	1296 cc
1.4 litre	1392 cc
1.6 litre	1597 cc
Bore:	
1.1 litre	73.96 mm (2.91 in)
1.3 and 1.6 litre	79.96 mm (3.15 in)
1.4 litre	77.24 mm (3.04 in)
Stroke:	
1.1 litre	64.98 mm (2.56 in)
1.3 litre	64.52 mm (2.54 in)
1.4 litre	74.30 mm (2.92 in)
1.6 litre	79.52 mm (3.13 in)
Compression ratio:	
All except 1.6 litre Turbo	9.5:1
1.6 litre Turbo	8.3:1
Firing order	1–3–4–2 (No 1 at timing belt end)

Cylinder block

Material	Cast iron
Number of main bearings	5
Cylinder bore (diameter):	
1.1 litre:	
Standard (1)	73.94 to 73.95 mm (2.9110 to 2.9114 in)
Standard (2)	73.95 to 73.96 mm (2.9114 to 2.9118 in)
Standard (3)	73.96 to 73.97 mm (2.9118 to 2.9122 in)
Standard (4)	73.97 to 73.98 mm (2.9122 to 2.9126 in)
Oversize (A)	74.23 to 74.24 mm (2.9224 to 2.9228 in)
Oversize (B)	74.24 to 74.25 mm (2.9228 to 2.9232 in)
Oversize (C)	74.25 to 74.26 mm (2.9232 to 2.9236 in)

1.3 and 1.6 litre:
  Standard (1) .... 79.94 to 79.95 mm (3.1472 to 3.1476 in)
  Standard (2) .... 79.95 to 79.96 mm (3.1476 to 3.1480 in)
  Standard (3) .... 79.96 to 79.97 mm (3.1480 to 3.1484 in)
  Standard (4) .... 79.97 to 79.98 mm (3.1484 to 3.1488 in)
  Oversize (A) .... 80.23 to 80.24 mm (3.1587 to 3.1590 in)
  Oversize (B) .... 80.24 to 80.25 mm (3.1590 to 3.1594 in)
  Oversize (C) .... 80.25 to 80.26 mm (3.1594 to 3.1598 in)
1.4 litre:
  Standard (1) .... 77.22 to 77.23 mm (3.0424 to 3.0428 in)
  Standard (2) .... 77.23 to 77.24 mm (3.0428 to 3.0432 in)
  Standard (3) .... 77.24 to 77.25 mm (3.0432 to 3.0436 in)
  Standard (4) .... 77.25 to 77.26 mm (3.0436 to 3.0440 in)
  Oversize (A) .... 77.51 to 77.52 mm (3.0538 to 3.0542 in)
  Oversize (B) .... 77.52 to 77.53 mm (3.0542 to 3.0546 in)
  Oversize (C) .... 77.53 to 77.54 mm (3.0546 to 3.0550 in)
Main bearing shell inner diameter:
  Standard .... 58.011 to 58.038 mm (2.2839 to 2.2850 in)
  Undersize 0.25 mm .... 57.761 to 57.788 mm (2.2740 to 2.2751 in)
  Undersize 0.50 mm .... 57.511 to 57.538 mm (2.2642 to 2.2653 in)
  Undersize 0.75 mm .... 57.261 to 57.288 mm (2.2544 to 2.2554 in)

Crankshaft

Main bearing journal diameter:
  Standard .... 57.98 to 58.00 mm (2.2827 to 2.2835 in)
  Undersize 0.25 mm .... 57.73 to 57.75 mm (2.2728 to 2.2736 in)
  Undersize 0.50 mm .... 57.48 to 57.50 mm (2.630 to 2.2638 in)
  Undersize 0.75 mm .... 57.23 to 57.25 mm (2.2531 to 2.2539 in)
Main bearing running clearance .... 0.011 to 0.058 mm (0.0004 to 0.0023 in)
Thrust washer thickness:
  Standard .... 2.301 to 2.351 mm (0.0906 to 0.0926 in)
  Oversize .... 2.491 to 2.541 mm (0.0981 to 0.1000 in)
Crankshaft endfloat .... 0.09 to 0.30 mm (0.0035 to 0.0118 in)
Crankpin (big-end) diameter:
  1.1 engines:
    Standard .... 42.99 to 43.01 mm (1.6925 to 1.6933 in)
    Undersize 0.25 mm .... 42.74 to 42.76 mm (1.6827 to 1.6835 in)
    Undersize 0.50 mm .... 42.49 to 42.51 mm (1.6728 to 1.6736 in)
    Undersize 0.75 mm .... 42.24 to 42.26 mm (1.6630 to 1.6638 in)
    Undersize 1.00 mm .... 41.99 to 42.01 mm (1.6532 to 1.6539 in)
  1.3, 1.4 and 1.6 engines:
    Standard .... 47.89 to 47.91 mm (1.8854 to 1.8862 in)
    Undersize 0.25 mm .... 47.64 to 47.66 mm (1.8756 to 1.8764 in)
    Undersize 0.50 mm .... 47.39 to 47.41 mm (1.8657 to 1.8665 in)
    Undersize 0.75 mm .... 47.14 to 47.16 mm (1.8559 to 1.8567 in)
    Undersize 1.00 mm .... 46.89 to 46.91 mm (1.8461 to 1.8468 in)
Big-end bearing running clearance .... 0.006 to 0.060 mm (0.0002 to 0.0024 in)

Camshaft

Number of bearings 5
Drive .... Toothed belt
Camshaft thrust plate thickness .... 4.99 to 5.01 mm (0.1965 to 0.1972 in)
Cam lift:
  1.1, 1.3 and 1.4 litre .... 5.79 mm (0.2280 in)
  1.6 litre .... 6.09 mm (0.2398 in)
Inlet cam length:
  1.1, 1.3 and 1.4 litre .... 38.305 mm (1.5081 in)
  1.6 litre .... 38.606 mm (1.5200 in)
Exhaust cam length:
  1.1, 1.3 and 1.4 litre .... 37.289 mm (1.4681 in)
  1.6 litre .... 37.590 mm (1.4799 in)
Camshaft bearing diameter:
  1 .... 44.75 mm (1.7618 in)
  2 .... 45.00 mm (1.7717 in)
  3 .... 45.25 mm (1.7815 in)
  4 .... 45.50 mm (1.7913 in)
  5 .... 45.75 mm (1.8012 in)
Camshaft endfloat .... 0.05 to 0.15 mm (0.0020 to 0.0059 in)

Pistons and piston rings

Diameter – 1.1 litre:
  Standard 1 .... 73.910 to 73.920 mm (2.9098 to 2.9102 in)
  Standard 2 .... 73.920 to 73.930 mm (2.9102 to 2.9106 in)
  Standard 3 .... 73.930 to 73.940 mm (2.9106 to 2.9110 in)
  Standard 4 .... 73.940 to 73.950 mm (2.9110 to 2.9114 in)
  Standard service .... 73.930 to 73.955 mm (2.9106 to 2.9116 in)

Oversize 0.29 mm	74.210 to 74.235 mm (2.9217 to 2.9226 in)
Oversize 0.50 mm	74.460 to 74.485 mm (2.9315 to 2.9325 in)
Diameter – 1.3 and 1.6 litre:	
Standard 1	79.910 to 79.920 mm (3.1461 to 3.1465 in)
Standard 2	79.920 to 79.930 mm (3.1465 to 3.1468 in)
Standard 3	79.930 to 79.940 mm (3.1468 to 3.1472 in)
Standard 4	79.940 to 79.950 mm (3.1472 to 3.1476 in)
Standard service	79.930 to 79.955 mm (3.1468 to 3.1478 in)
Oversize 0.29 mm	80.210 to 80.235 mm (3.1579 to 3.1589 in)
Oversize 0.50 mm	80.430 to 80.455 mm (3.1665 to 3.1675 in)
Diameter – 1.4 litre:	
Standard 1	77.190 to 77.200 mm (3.0412 to 3.0416 in)
Standard 2	77.200 to 77.210 mm (3.0416 to 3.0420 in)
Standard 3	77.210 to 77.220 mm (3.0420 to 3.0424 in)
Standard 4	77.220 to 77.230 mm (3.0424 to 3.0428 in)
Standard service	77.210 to 77.235 mm (3.0420 to 3.0430 in)
Oversize 0.29 mm	77.490 to 77.515 mm (3.0531 to 3.0540 in)
Oversize 0.50 mm	77.710 to 77.735 mm (3.0617 to 3.0627 in)
Piston-to-bore clearance	0.010 to 0.045 mm (0.0004 to 0.0017 in)
Piston ring end gap:	
1.1 litre:	
Compression rings	0.25 to 0.45 mm (0.0098 to 0.0177 in)
Oil control ring	0.20 to 0.40 mm (0.0079 to 0.0158 in)
1.3, 1.4 and 1.6 litre:	
Compression rings	0.30 to 0.50 mm (0.0118 to 0.0197 in)
Oil control ring	0.40 to 1.40 mm (0.0158 to 0.0552 in)

Gudgeon pin

Pin length:	
1.1 litre	63.00 to 63.80 mm (2.480 to 2.512 in)
1.3, 1.4 and 1.6 litre	66.20 to 67.00 mm (2.606 to 2.638 in)
Pin diameter:	
White	20.622 to 20.625 mm (0.8119 to 0.8120 in)
Red	20.625 to 20.628 mm (0.8120 to 0.8121 in)
Blue	20.628 to 20.631 mm (0.8121 to 0.8122 in)
Yellow	20.631 to 20.634 mm (0.8122 to 0.8124 in)
Play in piston	0.005 to 0.011 mm (0.0002 to 0.0004 in)
Interference fit in piston	0.013 to 0.045 mm (0.0005 to 0.0018 in)

Connecting rod

Big-end bore diameter:	
1.1 litre	46.685 to 46.705 mm (1.8380 to 1.8388 in)
1.3, 1.4 and 1.6 litre	50.890 to 50.910 mm (2.0035 to 2.0043 in)
Small-end bore diameter	20.589 to 20.609 mm (0.8106 to 0.8114 in)
Big-end bearing shell inside diameter:	
1.1 litre:	
Standard	43.016 to 43.050 mm (1.6935 to 1.6949 in)
Undersize 0.25 mm	42.766 to 42.800 mm (1.6837 to 1.6850 in)
Undersize 0.50 mm	42.516 to 42.550 mm (1.6739 to 1.6752 in)
Undersize 0.75 mm	42.266 to 42.300 mm (1.6640 to 1.6654 in)
Undersize 1.00 mm	42.016 to 42.050 mm (1.6542 to 1.6555 in)
1.3, 1.4 and 1.6 litre:	
Standard	47.916 to 47.950 mm (1.8865 to 1.8878 in)
Undersize 0.25 mm	47.666 to 47.700 mm (1.8766 to 1.8779 in)
Undersize 0.50 mm	47.416 to 47.450 mm (1.8668 to 1.8681 in)
Undersize 0.75 mm	47.166 to 47.200 mm (1.8569 to 1.8582 in)
Undersize 1.00 mm	46.916 to 46.950 mm (1.8471 to 1.8484 in)
Big-end bearing running clearance	0.006 to 0.060 mm (0.0002 to 0.0024 in)

Cylinder head

Material	Light alloy
Maximum permissible cylinder head distortion measured over entire length	0.15 mm (0.006 in)
Minimum combustion chamber depth after skimming:	
1.1 litre	18.22 mm (0.717 in)
1.3 and 1.6 litre	19.60 mm (0.772 in)
1.4 litre	17.40 mm (0.685 in)
Valve seat angle	45°
Valve seat width	1.75 to 2.32 mm (0.689 to 0.0913 in)
Seat cutter:	
Upper correction angle	18°
Lower correction angle:	
1.1 litre	80° (inlet), 70° (exhaust)
1.3, 1.4 and 1.6 litre	75° (inlet), 70° (exhaust)

Valve guide bore:
    Standard .... 8.063 to 8.094 mm (0.3174 to 3187 in)
    Oversize 0.2 mm .... 8.263 to 8.294 mm (0.3253 to 0.3265 in)
    Oversize 0.4 mm .... 8.463 to 8.494 mm (0.3332 to 0.3340 in)
Camshaft bearing bore in head:
    1 .... 44.783 to 44.808 mm (1.7631 to 1.7639 in)
    2 .... 45.033 to 45.058 mm (1.7729 to 1.7739 in)
    3 .... 45.283 to 45.308 mm (1.7828 to 1.7838 in)
    4 .... 45.533 to 45.558 mm (1.7926 to 1.7936 in)
    5 .... 45.783 to 45.808 mm (1.8025 to 1.8034 in)
Valve lifter bore in head .... 22.235 to 22.265 mm (0.8754 to 0.8766 in)

Valves – general

Operation .... Rocker arms and hydraulic cam followers
Valve timing
    1.1 litre and 1.3 litre:
        Inlet valve opens .... 13° ATDC
        Inlet valve closes .... 28° ABDC
        Exhaust valve opens .... 30° BBDC
        Exhaust valve closes .... 15° BTDC
    1.4 litre:
        Inlet valve opens .... 15° ATDC
        Inlet valve closes .... 30° ABDC
        Exhaust valve opens .... 28° BBDC
        Exhaust valve closes .... 13° BTDC
    1.6 litre (except carburettor versions – 1986 onwards):
        Inlet valve opens .... 8° ATDC
        Inlet valve closes .... 36° ABDC
        Exhaust valve opens .... 34° BBDC
        Exhaust valve closes .... 6° BTDC
    1.6 litre (carburettor versions – 1986 onwards):
        Inlet valve opens .... 4° ATDC
        Inlet valve closes .... 32° ABDC
        Exhaust valve opens .... 38° BBDC
        Exhaust valve closes .... 10° BTDC
Valve lift:
    Inlet:
        1.1, 1.3 and 1.4 litre .... 9.56 mm (0.376 in)
        1.6 litre .... 10.09 mm (0.397 in)
    Exhaust:
        1.1, 1.3 and 1.4 litre .... 9.52 mm (0.374 in)
        1.6 litre .... 10.06 mm (0.396 in)
Valve spring free length .... 47.2 mm (1.859 in)

Inlet valve

Length:
    1.1 litre .... 135.74 to 136.20 mm (5.348 to 5.366 in)
    1.3 and 1.6 litre .... 134.54 to 135.0 mm (5.299 to 5.319 in)
    1.4 litre .... 136.29 to 136.75 mm (5.369 to 5.387 in)
Head diameter:
    1.1 litre .... 37.9 to 38.1 mm (1.493 to 1.501 in)
    1.3 and 1.6 litre .... 41.9 to 42.1 mm (1.650 to 1.658 in)
    1.4 litre .... 39.9 to 40.1 mm (1.572 to 1.579 in)
Stem diameter:
    Standard .... 8.025 to 8.043 mm (0.3161 to 0.3168 in)
    0.20 mm oversize .... 8.225 to 8.243 mm (0.3240 to 0.3247 in)
    0.40 mm oversize .... 8.425 to 8.443 mm (0.3319 to 0.3326 in)
Valve stem clearance in guide .... 0.020 to 0.063 mm (0.0007 to 0.0024 in)

Exhaust valve

Length:
    1.1 litre .... 132.62 to 133.08 mm (5.225 to 5.243 in)
    1.3 litre .... 131.17 to 131.63 mm (5.168 to 5.186 in)
    1.4 litre .... 132.97 to 133.43 mm (5.239 to 5.257 in)
    1.6 litre .... 131.57 to 132.03 mm (5.183 to 5.201 in)
Head diameter:
    1.1 litre .... 32.1 to 32.3 mm (1.264 to 1.272 in)
    1.3 litre .... 33.9 to 34.1 mm (1.335 to 1.343 in)
    1.4 litre .... 33.9 to 34.1 mm (1.335 to 1.343 in)
    1.6 litre .... 36.9 to 37.1 mm (1.453 to 1.461 in)
Valve stem diameter:
    Standard .... 7.999 to 8.017 mm (0.3151 to 0.3158 in)
    0.20 mm oversize .... 8.199 to 8.217 mm (0.3230 to 0.3237 in)
    0.40 mm oversize .... 8.399 to 8.417 mm (0.3309 to 0.3316 in)
Valve stem clearance in guide .... 0.046 to 0.089 mm (0.0018 to 0.0035 in)

Lubrication

Oil type/specification .... Multigrade engine oil, viscosity SAE 10W/30 (or multigrade engine oil with a viscosity range suitable for the environmental temperature in which the vehicle is operated) – see viscosity chart (Duckhams QXR, Hypergrade, or 10W/40 Motor Oil)

Oil filter – except Turbo models .... Champion C104
Oil filter – Turbo models .... Champion C102

Oil pump type:
    Pre-1986 .... Gear type driven by crankshaft
    1986 onwards .... Rotor type driven by crankshaft

Minimum oil pressure at 80°C (176°F):
    At 750 rpm .... 1.0 bar (14.5 lbf/in²)
    At 2000 rpm .... 2.8 bar (40.6 lbf/in²)
Oil pressure warning lamp operates .... 0.3 to 0.5 bar (4.3 to 7.2 lbf/in²)
Relief valve opens .... 4.0 bar (58 lbf/in²)
Oil pump clearances (rotor type pump only):
    Outer rotor to body .... 0.060 to 0.190 mm (0.002 to 0.0074 in)
    Inner to outer rotor .... 0.05 to 0.18 mm (0.0019 to 0.0070 in)
    Rotor endfloat .... 0.014 to 0.100 mm (0.0005 to 0.0039 in)

Torque wrench settings

	Nm	lbf ft
Main bearing caps	90 to 100	66 to 74
Connecting rod bolts	30 to 36	22 to 26
Oil pump to crankcase	8 to 11	6 to 8
Oil pump cover bolts	8 to 11	6 to 8
Oil pump pick-up tube to block	17 to 23	12 to 17
Oil pump pick-up tube to pump	8 to 11	6 to 8
Oil cooler threaded sleeve to block	55 to 60	40 to 44
Rear oil seal carrier bolts	8 to 11	6 to 8
Sump with multi-piece gasket:		
Stage 1	8 to 11	6 to 8
Stage 2	8 to 11	6 to 8
Sump with one-piece gasket:		
Stage 1	5 to 8	4 to 6
Stage 2	5 to 8	4 to 6
Flywheel to crankshaft	82 to 92	60 to 68
Torque converter drive plate to crankshaft	80 to 88	59 to 65
Crankshaft pulley bolt	100 to 115	74 to 85
Cylinder head bolts:		
Stage 1	25	18
Stage 2	55	40
Stage 3	Tighten by a further 90°	Tighten by a further 90°
Stage 4	Tighten by a further 90°	Tighten by a further 90°
Camshaft thrust plate	9 to 13	7 to 10
Camshaft sprocket bolt	54 to 59	40 to 43
Timing belt tensioner bolts	16 to 20	12 to 15
Rocker arm studs in head:		
Plain stud	10 to 15	7 to 11
Stud with nylon insert	18 to 23	13 to 17
Rocker arm nut	25 to 29	18 to 21
Rocker cover screws	6 to 8	4 to 6
Timing belt cover bolts	9 to 11	7 to 8
Sump drain plug	21 to 28	15 to 21
Engine to manual transmission	35 to 45	26 to 33
Engine to automatic transmission	30 to 50	22 to 37
Right-hand engine mounting to body	41 to 58	30 to 43
Right-hand engine mounting bracket to engine	76 to 104	56 to 77
Right-hand engine mounting rubber insulator to brackets	41 to 58	30 to 43
Front transmission mounting bracket to transmission (pre-1986 models)	41 to 51	30 to 38
Front and rear transmission mounting bolts (pre-1986 models)	52 to 64	38 to 47
Transmission mountings to transmission (1986 models onwards)	80 to 100	59 to 74
Transmission support crossmember to body (1986 models onwards)	52	38
Oil pressure switch	18 to 22	13 to 16

PART A: OHV ENGINES

1 General description

The 1.1 litre and 1.3 litre OHV engines are of four-cylinder, in-line overhead valve type (hence ohv), mounted transversely together with the transmission, at the front of the car.

The crankshaft on 1.1 litre engines is supported in three shell type main bearings, whereas the 1.3 litre unit features a five main bearing crankshaft. Apart from this difference and other minor alterations, the two engines are virtually the same in design and construction.

The connecting rods are attached to the crankshaft by horizontally split shell type big-end bearings and to the pistons by interference fit gudgeon pins. The aluminium alloy pistons are of the slipper type and are fitted with three piston rings; two compression and one oil control.

The camshaft is chain driven from the crankshaft and operates the valves via pushrods and rocker arms. The inlet and exhaust valves are each closed by a single valve spring and operate in guides integral with the cylinder head. The oil pump and distributor are driven by a skew gear on the camshaft while an eccentric cam operates the fuel pump lever.

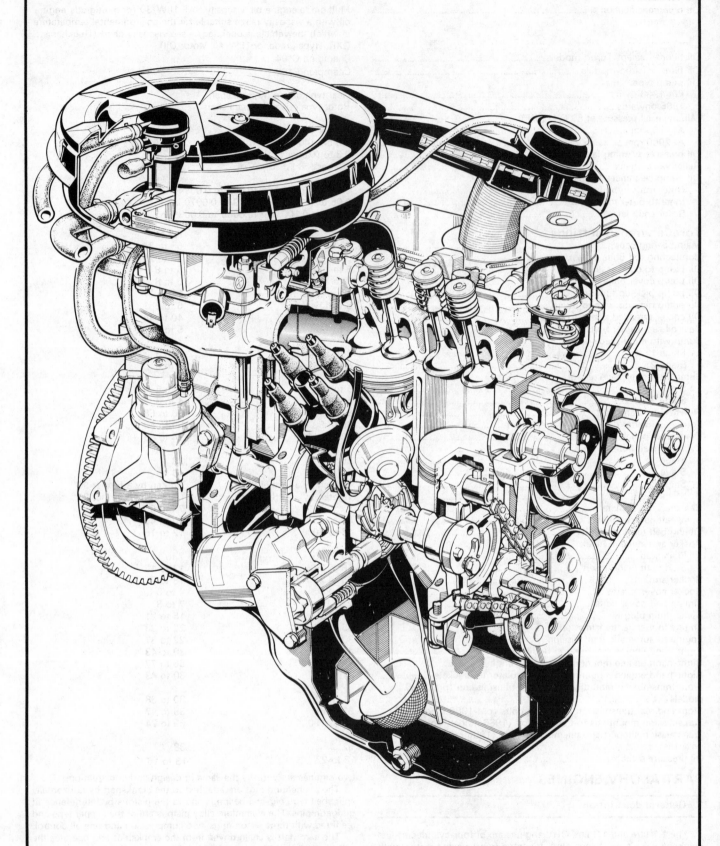

Fig. 1.1 Cutaway view of the 1.1 litre OHV engine (Sec 1)

The oil pump is mounted externally on the cylinder block just below the distributor, and the full flow type oil filter is screwed directly into the oil pump.

2 Maintenance and inspection

1   At the intervals given in *'Routine maintenance'* at the beginning of this manual carry out the following maintenance operations on the engine.

2   Visually inspect the engine joint faces, gaskets and seals for any sign of oil or water leaks. Pay particular attention to the areas around the rocker cover, cylinder head, timing cover and sump joint faces. Rectify any leaks by referring to the appropriate Sections of this Chapter.

3   Change the engine oil as described in the following paragraphs 4 to 10.

4   Apply the handbrake, jack up the front of the car and securely support it on stands.

5   Place a suitable container beneath the oil drain plug at the rear of the sump. Unscrew the plug using a spanner or socket and allow the oil to drain. Inspect the condition of the drain plug sealing washer and renew it, if necessary. Refit and tighten the plug after draining.

6   Move the bowl to the rear of the engine, under the oil filter.

7   Using a strap wrench, or filter removal tool, slacken the filter and then unscrew it from the engine and discard.

8   Wipe the mating face on the oil pump flange with a rag and then lubricate the seal of a new filter using clean engine oil.

9   Screw the filter into position and tighten it by hand only, do not use any tools.

10 Lower the car to the ground.

11 Refill the engine using the correct grade of oil, through the filler neck on the rocker cover. Fill until the level reaches the 'MAX' mark on the dipstick.

12 With the engine running, check for leaks around the filter seal.

13 Adjust the valve clearances using the procedure described in Section 6.

14 Carry out an inspection of the crankcase ventilation system as described in Chapter 3.

3 Major operations possible with the engine in the car

The following work can be carried out without having to remove the engine:

(a) *Cylinder head – removal and refitting*
(b) *Valve clearances – adjustment*
(c) *Sump – removal and refitting*
(d) *Rocker gear – overhaul*
(e) *Crankshaft front oil seal – renewal*
(f) *Pistons/connecting rods – removal and refitting*
(g) *Engine mountings – renewal*
(h) *Oil filter – removal and refitting*
(j) *Oil pump – removal and refitting*

4 Major operations requiring engine removal

The following work can only be carried out after removal of the engine from the car:

(a) *Crankshaft main bearings – renewal*
(b) *Crankshaft – removal and refitting*
(c) *Flywheel – removal and refitting*
(d) *Crankshaft rear oil seal – renewal*
(e) *Camshaft – removal and refitting*
(f) *Timing gears and chain – removal and refitting*

5 Cylinder head – removal and refitting

1   If the engine is in the car carry out the preliminary operations described in paragraphs 2 to 16.

2   Disconnect the battery negative terminal.

3   Refer to Chapter 3 and remove the air cleaner.

4   Refer to Chapter 2 and drain the cooling system.

5   Disconnect the hoses from the thermostat housing.

6   Disconnect the heater hose from the upper connection on the automatic choke housing, or inlet manifold as applicable.

7   Release the throttle cable from the carburettor operating lever by moving the spring clip and removing the bracket fixing bolt.

8   On manual choke models disconnect the choke cable from the linkage lever and support bracket.

9   Disconnect the fuel and vacuum pipes from the carburettor.

10 Disconnect the breather hose from the inlet manifold.

11 On vehicles with servo-assisted brakes, disconnect the vacuum hose from the inlet manifold.

12 Disconnect the HT leads from the spark plugs.

13 Disconnect the electrical leads from the temperature sender unit, the anti-run-on solenoid valve at the carburettor, and the radiator fan thermal switch.

14 Unbolt and remove the hot air box from the exhaust manifold.

15 Disconnect the exhaust downpipe from the manifold by unbolting the connecting flanges. Support the exhaust system at the front end.

16 Remove the oil filler cap with breather hose.

17 Extract the four screws and remove the rocker cover.

18 Unscrew and remove the four fixing bolts and lift away the rocker shaft assembly from the cylinder head.

19 Withdraw the pushrods, keeping them in their originally fitted

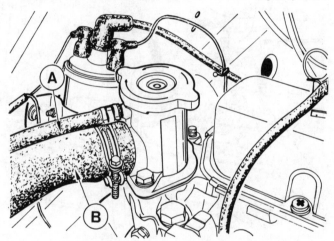

Fig. 1.2 Hose attachments at the thermostat housing on early models (Sec 5)

A   *Expansion tank hose*   B   *Radiator top hose*

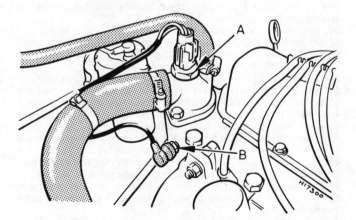

Fig. 1.3 Hose and electrical connections at the thermostat housing on later models (Sec 5)

A   *Radiator fan thermal switch*   B   *Temperature sender unit*

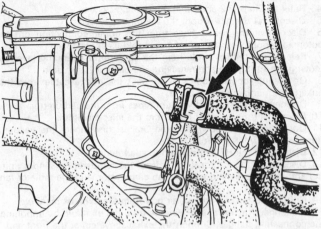

Fig. 1.4 Heater hose connection on choke housing (Sec 5)

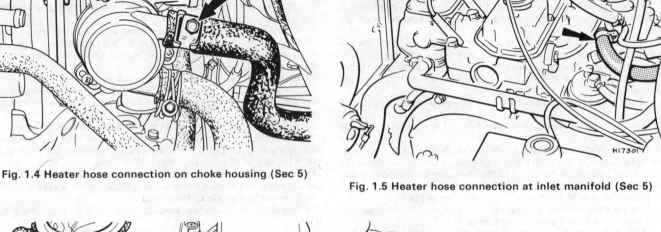

Fig. 1.5 Heater hose connection at inlet manifold (Sec 5)

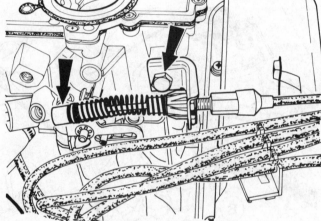

Fig. 1.6 Throttle cable disconnection points (Sec 5)

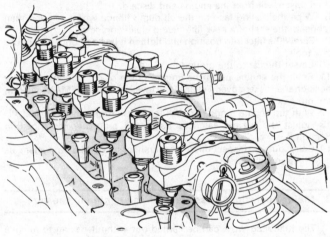

Fig. 1.7 Removing the rocker shaft assembly (Sec 5)

sequence. A simple way to do this is to punch holes in a piece of card and number them 1 to 8 from the thermostat housing end of the cylinder head.

20 Remove the spark plugs.

21 Unscrew the cylinder head bolts progressively in the reverse order to that given for tightening (see Fig. 1.8). Remove the cylinder head.

22 To dismantle the cylinder head, refer to Section 17.

23 Before refitting the cylinder head, remove every particle of carbon, old gasket and dirt from the mating surfaces of the cylinder head and block. Do not let the removed material drop into the cylinder bores or waterways, if it does, remove it. Normally, when a cylinder head is removed, the head is decarbonised and the valves ground in as described in Section 18 to remove all trace of carbon. Clean the threads of the cylinder head bolts and mop out oil from the bolt holes in the cylinder block. In extreme cases, screwing a bolt into an oil-filled hole can cause the block to fracture due to hydraulic pressure.

24 If there is any doubt about the condition of the inlet or exhaust gaskets, unbolt the manifolds and fit new ones to perfectly clean mating surfaces.

25 Locate a new cylinder head gasket on the cylinder block, making quite sure that the bolt holes, coolant passages and lubrication holes are correctly aligned.

26 Lower the cylinder head carefully into position on the block.

27 Screw in all the bolts finger tight and then tighten them in four stages and in the sequence shown in Fig. 1.8 to the specified torque.

28 Refit the pushrods in their original order.

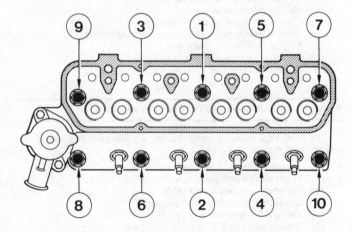

Fig. 1.8 Cylinder head bolt tightening sequence (Sec 5)

29 Lower the rocker shaft assembly into position, making sure that the rocker adjusting screws engage in the sockets at the ends of the pushrods.

30 Screw in the rocker pedestal bolts finger tight. At this stage, some of the rocker arms will be applying pressure to the ends of the valve stems and some of the rocker pedestals will not be in contact with the cylinder head. The pedestals will be pulled down however when the bolts are tightened to the specified torque, which should now be done.
31 Adjust the valve clearances as described in the next Section.
32 Refit the rocker cover. If the gasket is in anything but perfect condition, renew it.
33 Fit the oil filler cap and breather hose and the spark plugs. Tighten these to the specified torque. They are of tapered seat type, no sealing washers being used.
34 Connect the exhaust downpipe and fit the hot air box.
35 Reconnect all electrical leads, vacuum and coolant hoses.
36 Reconnect the throttle and choke cables as described in Chapter 3.
37 Refit the air cleaner as described in Chapter 3 and fill the cooling system as described in Chapter 2.
38 Reconnect the battery negative terminal.

6 Valve clearances – adjustment

1   This operation should be carried out with the engine cold and the air cleaner and rocker cover removed.
2   Using a ring spanner or socket on the crankshaft pulley bolt, turn the crankshaft in a clockwise direction until No 1 piston is at TDC on its compression stroke. This can be verified by checking that the pulley and timing cover marks are in alignment and that the valves of No 4 cylinder are rocking. When the valves are rocking, this means that the slightest rotation of the crankshaft pulley in either direction will cause one rocker arm to move up and the other to move down.
3   Numbering from the thermostat housing end of the cylinder head, the valves are identified as follows:

Valve No	Cylinder No
1 – Exhaust	1
2 – Inlet	1
3 – Exhaust	2
4 – Inlet	2
5 – Exhaust	3
6 – Inlet	3
7 – Exhaust	4
8 – Inlet	4

4   Adjust the valve clearances by following the sequence given in the following table. Turn the crankshaft pulley 180° (half a turn) after adjusting each pair:

Valves rocking	Valves to adjust
7 and 8	1 (Exhaust), 2 (Inlet)
5 and 6	3 (Exhaust), 4 (Inlet)
1 and 2	7 (Exhaust), 8 (Inlet)
3 and 4	5 (Exhaust), 6 (Inlet)

5   The clearances for the inlet and exhaust valves are different (see Specifications). Use a feeler gauge of the appropriate thickness to check each clearance between the end of the valve stem and the rocker arm. The gauge should be a stiff sliding fit. If it is not, turn the adjuster bolt with a ring spanner. These bolts are of stiff thread type and require no locking nut. Turn the bolt clockwise to reduce the clearance and anti-clockwise to increase it (photo).
6   Refit the air cleaner and rocker cover on completion of adjustment.

7 Sump – removal and refitting

1   Disconnect the battery negative lead and drain the engine oil (see Section 2).
2   Refer to Chapter 12 and remove the starter motor.
3   Unbolt and remove the clutch cover plate.
4   Extract the sump securing bolts and remove the sump. If it is stuck, prise it gently with a screwdriver but do not use excessive leverage. If it is very tight, cut round the gasket joint using a sharp knife.
5   Before refitting the sump, remove the front and rear sealing strips and gaskets. Clean the mating surfaces of the sump and cylinder block.
6   Stick new gaskets into position on the block using thick grease to

6.5 Valve clearance adjustment

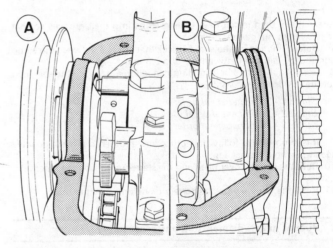

Fig. 1.9 Sump gasket fitting details at timing cover end (A) and flywheel end (B) (Sec 7)

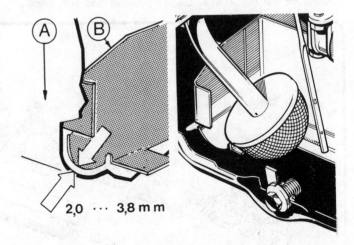

2,0 ··· 3,8 mm

Fig. 1.10 Sump and oil baffle clearance details (Sec 7)

A   Sump   B   Baffle

7.6 Fitting the sump gasket sealing strips to overlap the tabs on the gasket

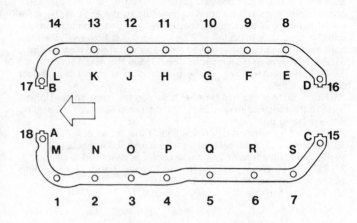

Fig. 1.11 Sump bolt tightening sequence (Sec 7)

retain them, then install new sealing strips into their grooves so that they overlap the gaskets (photo).

7   Before offering up the sump, check that the gap between the sump and the oil baffle is between 2.0 and 3.8 mm

8   Screw in the sump bolts and tighten in three stages to the specified torque in accordance with Fig. 1.11.

    Stage 1 – in alphabetical order
    Stage 2 – in numerical order
    Stage 3 – in alphabetical order

9   It is important to follow this procedure in order to provide positive sealing against oil leakage.

10 Refit the clutch cover plate and the starter motor and reconnect the battery.

11 Refill the engine with the correct grade and quantity of oil.

8   Rocker gear – dismantling and reassembly

1   With the rocker assembly removed as described in Section 5, extract the split pin from one end of the rocker shaft.

2   Take off the spring and plain washers from the end of the shaft.

3   Slide off the rocker arms, support pedestals and coil springs,

keeping them in their originally fitted order. Clean out the oil holes in the shaft.

4   Apply engine oil to the rocker shaft before reassembling and make sure that the flat on the end of the shaft is to the same side as the rocker arm adjuster screws. This is essential for proper lubrication of the components.

9   Crankshaft front oil seal – renewal

1   Disconnect the battery negative lead.

2   Slacken the alternator mounting and adjuster bolts and after pushing the alternator in towards the engine, slip off the drivebelt.

3   Unscrew and remove the crankshaft pulley bolt. To prevent the crankshaft turning while the bolt is being released, jam the teeth of the starter ring gear on the flywheel after removing the clutch cover plate or starter motor (Chapter 12) for access.

4   Remove the crankshaft pulley. This should come out using the hands but if it is tight, prise it carefully with two levers placed at opposite sides under the pulley flange.

5   Using a suitable claw tool, prise out the defective seal and wipe out the seat.

6   Install the new seal using a suitable distance piece, the pulley and its bolt to draw it into position. If it is tapped into position, the seal may be distorted or the timing cover fractured.

7   When the seal is fully seated, remove the pulley and bolt, apply grease to the seal rubbing surface of the pulley, install it and tighten the securing bolt to the specified torque.

8   Refit the clutch cover or starter motor.

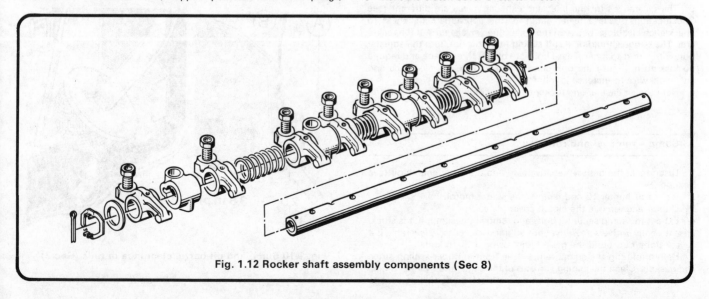

Fig. 1.12 Rocker shaft assembly components (Sec 8)

9 Fit and tension the drivebelt as described in Chapter 12 and reconnect the battery.

10 Piston/connecting rod assemblies – removal and refitting

1 Remove the cylinder head and the sump as described in Sections 5 and 7 respectively. Do not remove the oil pick-up filter or pipe, which is an interference fit.

2 Note the location numbers stamped on the connecting rod big-ends and caps, and to which side they face. No 1 assembly is nearest the timing cover and the assembly numbers are towards the camshaft side of the engine.

3 Turn the crankshaft by means of the pulley bolt until the big-end cap bolts for No 1 connecting rod are in their most accessible position. Unscrew and remove the bolts and the big-end cap complete with bearing shell. If the cap is difficult to remove, tap it off with a plastic-faced hammer.

4 If the bearing shells are to be used again (refer to Section 17), keep the shell taped to its cap.

5 Feel the top of the cylinder bore for a wear ridge. If one is detected, it should be scraped off before the piston/rod is pushed out of the top of the cylinder block. Take care when doing this not to score the cylinder bore surfaces.

6 Push the piston/connecting rod out of the block, retaining the bearing shell with the rod if it is to be used again.

7 Dismantling the piston/rod is covered in Section 17.

8 Repeat the operations on the remaining piston/rod assemblies.

9 To install a piston/rod assembly, have the piston ring gaps staggered as shown in the diagram (Fig. 1.14), oil the rings and apply a piston ring compressor. Compress the piston rings.

10 Oil the cylinder bores.

11 Wipe out the bearing shell seat in the connecting rod and insert the shell.

12 Lower the piston/rod assembly into the cylinder bore until the base of the piston ring compressor stands squarely on the top of the block (photo).

13 Check that the directional arrow on the piston crown faces towards the timing cover end of the engine (photo) and then apply the wooden handle of a hammer to the piston crown. Strike the head of the hammer sharply to drive the piston into the cylinder bore.

14 Oil the crankpin and draw the connecting rod down to engage with the crankshaft. Check that the bearing shell is still in position in the connecting rod.

15 Wipe the bearing shell seat in the big-end cap clean and insert the bearing shell (photo).

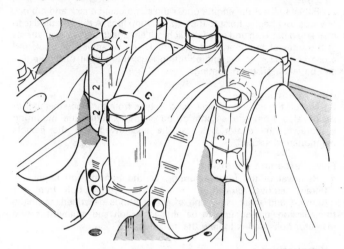

Fig. 1.13 Connecting rod and big-end cap identification numbers (Sec 10)

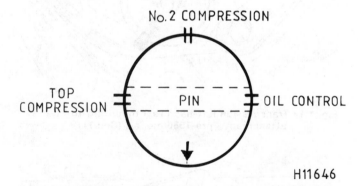

Fig. 1.14 Piston ring end gap positioning diagram (Sec 10)

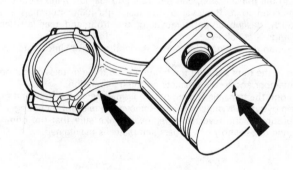

Fig. 1.15 Relative positions of piston directional arrow and oil squirt hole in connecting rod (Sec 10)

10.12 Fitting a piston/connecting rod assembly with ring compressor in position

10.13 Arrow on piston crown must face the timing cover when installed

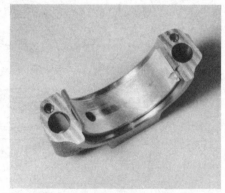

10.15 Fit the big-end bearing shell in the cap with the bearing tongue in the cap groove

16 Fit the cap, screw in the bolts and tighten to the specified torque.
17 Repeat the operations on the remaining pistons/connecting rods.
18 Refit the sump (Section 7) and the cylinder head (Section 5). Refill with oil and coolant.

11 Engine/transmission mountings – removal and refitting

Pre-1986 models

1 The engine mountings can be removed if the weight of the engine/transmission is first taken by one of the three following methods.

2 Either support the engine under the sump using a jack and a block of wood, or attach a hoist to the engine lifting lugs. A third method is to make up a bar with end pieces which will engage in the water channels at the sides of the bonnet lid aperture. Using an adjustable hook and chain connected to the engine lifting lugs, the weight of the engine can be taken off the mountings.

Rear mountings

3 Unbolt the mounting, according to type from the body member or panel, also from the engine or transmission. With the mounting withdrawn, the centre bolt can be unscrewed and the flexible component detached.

Front left-hand mounting

4 Removal of the front mounting on the transmission requires a different removal procedure. Remove the centre bolt from the mounting and then using one of the methods described, raise the transmission just enough to be able to unbolt and remove the two insulator bolts and withdraw the insulator.

All mountings

5 Refitting of all mountings is a reversal of removal. Make sure that the original sequence of assembly of washers and plates is maintained.

1986 models onwards

6 From 1986 onwards a longitudinal crossmember is mounted beneath the transmission, and the front and rear left-hand mountings are attached to it. Removal of the rear right-hand mounting is as previously described, but removal of the front and rear left-hand mountings is as follows.

7 Support the engine using one of the methods given in paragraphs 1 and 2.

8 Undo the nuts securing the mountings to the transmission support crossmember and to the brackets on the transmission.

9 Unbolt the transmission support crossmember at the front and rear and remove it from under the car. Remove the relevant mounting.

10 Refitting is the reversal of removal. Make sure that the original sequence of assembly of washers and plates is maintained.

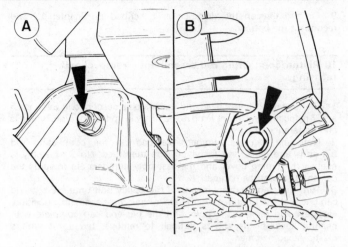

Fig. 1.16 Right-hand rear engine mounting attachments (Sec 11)

A   Mounting to side member   B   Mounting to inner wheel arch

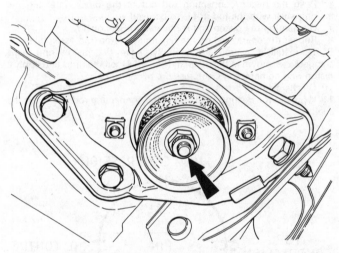

Fig. 1.17 Transmission left-hand rear mounting-to-bracket attachment – pre-1986 models (Sec 11)

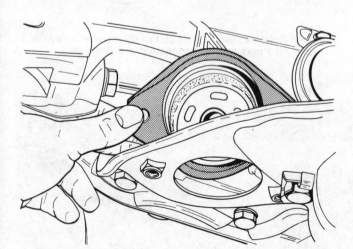

Fig. 1.18 Removing transmission left-hand rear mounting – pre-1986 models (Sec 11)

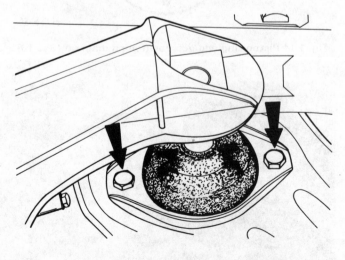

Fig. 1.19 Transmission left-hand front mounting attachments – pre-1986 models (Sec 11)

12 Oil pump – removal and refitting

1   The oil pump is externally mounted on the rear facing side of the crankcase.
2   Using a suitable removal tool (strap wrench or similar), unscrew and remove the oil filter cartridge and discard it.
3   Unscrew the three mounting bolts and withdraw the oil pump from the engine (photo).
4   Clean away the old gasket.
5   If a new pump is being fitted, it should be primed with engine oil before installation. Do this by turning its shaft while filling it with clean engine oil.
6   Locate a new gasket on the pump mounting flange, insert the pump shaft and bolt the pump into position.
7   Grease the rubber sealing ring of a new filter and screw it into position on the pump, using hand pressure only, not the removal tool.
8   Top up the engine oil to replenish any lost during the operations.

13 Lubrication system – description

1   Engine oil contained in the sump is drawn through a strainer and pick-up tube by an externally mounted oil pump of twin rotor design,.
2   The oil is then forced through a full-flow, throw-away type oil filter which is screwed onto the oil pump.
3   Oil pressure is regulated by a relief valve integral in the oil pump.
4   The pressurised oil is directed through the various galleries and passages to all bearing surfaces. A drilling in the big-end provides lubricaton for the gudgeon pins and cylinder bores. The timing chain and sprockets are lubricated by an oil ejection nozzle.

14 Engine – method of removal

The engine is removed complete with the transmission in a downward direction and then withdrawn from under the front of the car.

15 Engine/transmission – removal and separation

Removal
1   Disconnect the battery negative lead.
2   Place the transmission in fourth gear on four-speed versions, or reverse gear on the five-speed unit to aid adjustment of the gearchange linkage when refitting. On models produced from February 1987 onwards, place the transmission in second gear on four-speed versions, or fourth gear on five-speed versions.
3   Refer to Chapter 11 and remove the bonnet.
4   Refer to Chapter 3 and remove the air cleaner.
5   Refer to Chapter 2 and drain the cooling system.
6   Disconnect the radiator top and bottom hoses and the expansion tank hose at the thermostat housing.
7   Disconnect the heater hoses from the stub on the lateral coolant pipe, automatic choke housing or inlet manifold as applicable.
8   Disconnect the choke cable (where fitted) and the throttle cable from the carburettor throttle lever. Unbolt the cable support bracket and tie the cable assembly to one side of the engine compartment.
9   Disconnect the fuel pipe from the fuel pump and plug the pipe.
10 On vehicles equipped with power-assisted brakes, disconnect the vacuum pipe from the intake manifold.
11 Disconnect the leads from the following electrical components:

   (a) Alternator and electric fan temperature switch
   (b) Oil pressure sender
   (c) Coolant temperature sender
   (d) Reversing lamp switch
   (e) Anti-run on solenoid valve

12 Disconnect the HT and LT (distributor) wires from the coil terminals.
13 Unscrew the speedometer drive cable from the transmission and release the breather hose.
14 Disconnect the clutch cable from the release lever and from its transmission support.

12.3 Removing the oil pump

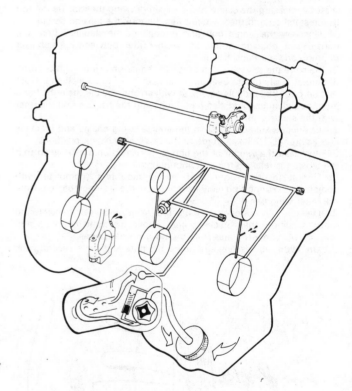

Fig. 1.20 Engine lubrication circuit (Sec 13)

15 Unbolt and remove the hot air box from the exhaust manifold.
16 Disconnect the exhaust downpipe from the manifold by extracting the two flange bolts. Support the exhaust pipe to avoid straining it.
17 The vehicle should now be jacked up and safety stands fitted to provide sufficient clearance beneath it to be able to remove the engine/transmission from below. A distance of 686 mm (27.0 in) is recommended between the floor and the bottom edge of the front panel.
18 Disconnect the exhaust system from its flexible mountings and remove the system complete.
19 Disconnect the starter motor leads and the engine earth strap.
20 Disconnect the gearchange rod from the transmission selector

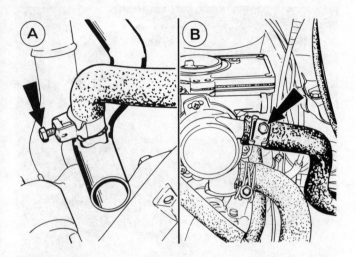

Fig. 1.21 Heater hose attachments at lateral coolant pipe
(A) and automatic choke housing (B) (Sec 15)

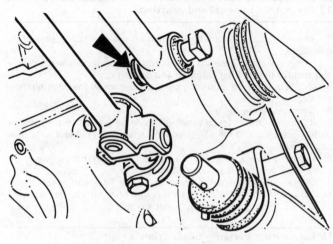

Fig. 1.22 Gearchange rod and stabiliser disconnection
points – washer fitted behind stabiliser arrowed (Sec 15)

shaft by releasing the clamp bolt and withdrawing the rod. Tie the rod
to the stabiliser and then where fitted, unhook the tension spring.

21 Unscrew the single bolt and disconnect the stabiliser from the
transmission housing, noting the washer fitted between the stabiliser
trunnion and the transmission.

22 Remove the driveshafts from the transmission using the procedure
described in Chapter 6, Section 6, paragraphs 17 to 23 inclusive. Note
that on pre-1986 models equipped with an anti-roll bar the right-hand
mounting clamp should also be undone and the bar lowered together
with the suspension arms.

23 Connect a suitable hoist to the engine using chains and brackets
and using Fig. 1.23 as a guide to the chain attachment positions.

24 Just take the weight of the engine/transmission assembly so that
the tension is relieved from the mountings.

25 Unbolt the rear right-hand engine mounting (complete with
coolant hose support on early models) from the side member and from
the inner wing panel.

26 On pre-1986 models unbolt the front and rear transmission
mountings from their brackets, and remove the front mounting and
anti-roll bar support plates from the body on both sides.

27 On 1986 models onwards undo the nuts and bolts securing the

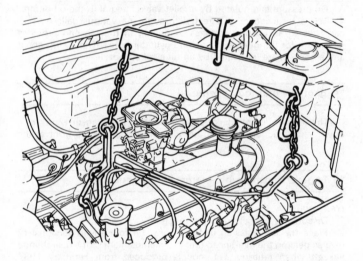

Fig. 1.23 Typical lifting gear connection to engine (Sec 15)

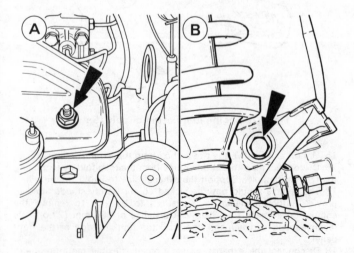

Fig. 1.24 Engine right-hand mounting attachment at side
member (A) and inner wing panel (B) (Sec 15)

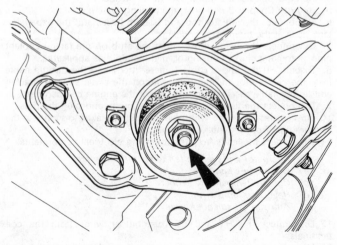

Fig. 1.25 Transmission rear mounting attachment (Sec 15)

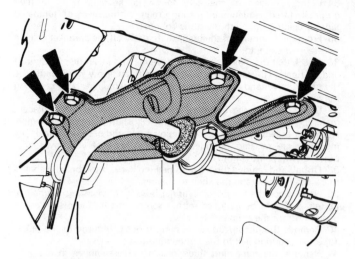

Fig. 1.26 Remove the anti-roll bar mounting plates on both sides – pre-1986 models (Sec 15)

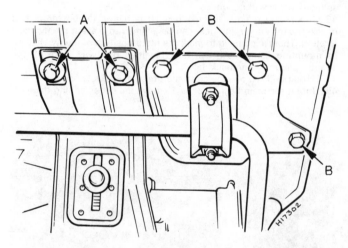

Fig. 1.27 Transmission support crossmember front mounting bolts (A) and anti-roll bar support plate bolts (B) – 1986 models onwards (Sec 15)

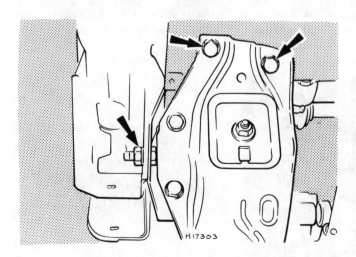

Fig. 1.28 Transmission support crossmember rear mounting bolts – 1986 models onwards (Sec 15)

transmission support crossmember to the body. The crossmember is removed with the engine/transmission assembly.

28 Carefully lower the engine/transmission and withdraw it from under the car. To ease the withdrawal operation, lower the engine/transmission onto a crawler board or a sheet of substantial chipboard placed on rollers or lengths of pipe.

Separation

29 Unscrew and remove the starter motor bolts and remove the starter.

30 Unbolt and remove the clutch cover plate from the lower part of the clutch bellhousing.

31 Unscrew and remove the bolts from the clutch bellhousing-to-engine mating flange.

32 Withdraw the transmission from the engine. Support its weight so that the clutch assembly is not distorted while the input shaft is still in engagement with the splined hub of the clutch driven plate.

16 Engine – complete dismantling

1 The need for dismantling will have been dictated by wear or noise in most cases. Although there is no reason why only partial dismantling cannot be carried out to renew such items as the timing chain or crankshaft rear oil seal, when the main bearings or big-end bearings have been knocking and especially if the vehicle has covered a high mileage, then it is recommended that a complete strip down is carried out and every engine component examined as described in Section 17.

2 Position the engine so that it is upright on a bench or other convenient working surface. If the exterior is very dirty it should be cleaned before dismantling using paraffin and a stiff brush or a water-soluble solvent.

3 Remove the coolant pipe from the side of the engine by disconnecting the hose clips and the securing bolt.

4 If not already done, drain the engine oil.

5 Remove the dipstick and unscrew and discard the oil filter.

6 Disconnect the HT leads from the spark plugs, release the distributor cap and lift it away complete with leads.

7 Unscrew and remove the spark plugs.

8 Disconnect the breather hose from the inlet manifold and remove it complete with the oil filler cap.

9 Disconnect the fuel and vacuum pipes from the carburettor and unbolt and remove the carburettor (refer to Chapter 3).

10 Unbolt the thermostat housing cover and remove it together with the thermostat (refer to Chapter 2).

11 Remove the rocker cover.

12 Remove the rocker shaft assembly (four bolts) (photo).

16.12 Removing the rocker shaft assembly

13 Withdraw the pushrods, keeping them in their originally fitted order (photo).
14 Remove the cylinder head complete with manifolds as described in Section 5.
15 Remove the distributor as described in Chapter 4.
16 Unbolt and remove the fuel pump.
17 Remove the oil pump (Section 12).
18 Pinch the two runs of the water pump drivebelt together at the pump pulley to prevent the pulley rotating and release the pulley bolts.
19 Release the alternator mounting and adjuster link bolts, push the alternator in towards the engine and remove the drivebelt.
20 Unbolt the alternator bracket and remove the alternator.
21 Unbolt and remove the water pump.
22 Unscrew the crankshaft pulley bolt. To do this, the flywheel starter ring gear will have to be jammed to prevent the crankshaft from turning.
23 Remove the crankshaft pulley. If this does not pull off by hand, carefully use two levers behind it placed at opposite points.
24 Place the engine on its side and remove the sump. Do not invert the engine at this stage, or sludge and swarf may enter the oilways.
25 Unbolt and remove the timing chain cover.
26 Take off the oil slinger from the front face of the crankshaft sprocket.
27 Slide the chain tensioner arm from its pivot pin on the front main bearing cap.
28 Unbolt and remove the chain tensioner (photo).
29 Bend back the lockplate tabs from the camshaft sprocket bolts and unscrew and remove the bolts.
30 Withdraw the sprocket complete with timing chain.
31 Unbolt and remove the camshaft thrust plate (photo).
32 Rotate the camshaft until each cam follower (tappet) has been pushed fully into its hole by its cam lobe.
33 Withdraw the camshaft, taking care not to damage the camshaft bearings (photo).

34 Withdraw each of the cam followers, keeping them in their originally fitted sequence by marking them with a piece of numbered tape or using a box with divisions (photo).
35 From the front end of the crankshaft, draw off the sprocket using a two-legged extractor.
36 Check that the main bearing caps are marked F (Front), C (Centre) and R (Rear). The caps are also marked with an arrow which indicates the timing cover end of the engine, a point to remember when refitting the caps.
37 Check that the big-end caps and connecting rods have adjacent matching numbers facing towards the camshaft side of the engine. Number 1 assembly is nearest the timing chain end of the engine. If any markings are missing or indistinct, make some of your own with quick-drying paint (photo).
38 Unbolt and remove the big-end bearing caps. If the bearing shell is to be used again, tape the shell to the cap.
39 Now check the top of the cylinder bore for a wear ring. If one can be felt, it should be removed with a scraper before the piston/rod is pushed out of the cylinder.
40 Remove the piston/rod by pushing it out of the top of the block. Tape the bearing shell to the connecting rod.
41 Remove the remaining three piston/rod assemblies in a similar way.
42 Unbolt the clutch pressure plate cover from the flywheel. Unscrew the bolts evenly and progressively until spring pressure is relieved, before removing the bolts. Be prepared to catch the clutch driven plate as the cover is withdrawn.
43 Unbolt and remove the flywheel. It is heavy, do not drop it. If necessary, the starter ring gear can be jammed to prevent the flywheel rotating. There is no need to mark the fitted position of the flywheel to its mounting flange as it can only be fitted one way. Take off the adaptor plate (engine backplate).
44 Unbolt and remove the crankshaft rear oil seal retainer.
45 Unbolt the main bearing caps. Remove the caps, tapping them off

16.13 Keep the pushrods in strict order after removal

16.28 Removing the timing chain tensioner

16.31 Camshaft thrust plate removal

16.33 Withdrawing the camshaft from the front of the engine

16.34 Using a valve grinding tool suction cup to withdraw the cam followers

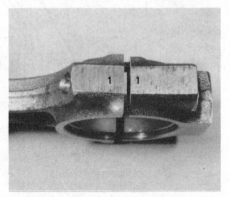

16.37 Connecting rod and big-end cap markings

if necessary with a plastic-faced hammer. Retain the bearing shells with their respective caps if the shells are to be used again, although unless the engine is of low mileage this is not recommended (see Section 17). To improve access to the No 2 main bearing bolt on 1.3 litre engines the oil pick-up tube can be removed by drifting it out. A new pick-up tube must be obtained for reassembly together with suitable adhesive to secure it in position.

46 Lift the crankshaft from the crankcase and lift out the upper bearing shells, noting the thrust washers either side of the centre bearing. Keep these shells with their respective caps, identifying them for refitting to the crankcase if they are to be used again.

47 With the engine now completely dismantled, each component should be examined as described in the following Section before reassembling.

17 Examination and renovation

1 Clean all components using paraffin and a stiff brush, except the crankshaft, which should be wiped clean and the oil passages cleaned out with a length of wire.

2 Never assume that a component is unworn simply because it looks all right. After all the effort which has gone into dismantling the engine, refitting worn components will make the overhaul a waste of time and money. Depending on the degree of wear, the overhauler's budget and the anticipated life of the vehicle, components which are only slightly worn may be refitted, but if in doubt it is always best to renew.

Crankshaft, main and big-end bearings

3 The need to renew the main bearing shells or to have the crankshaft reground will usually have been determined during the last few miles of operation when perhaps a heavy knocking has developed from within the crankcase or the oil pressure warning lamp has stayed on denoting a low oil pressure probably caused by excessive wear in the bearings.

4 Even without these symptoms, the journals and crankpins on a high mileage engine should be checked for out-of-round (ovality) and taper. For this a micrometer will be needed to check the diameter of the journals and crankpins at several different points around them. A motor factor or engineer can do this for you. If the average of the readings shows that either out-of-round or taper is outside permitted tolerance (see Specifications), then the crankshaft should be reground by your dealer or engine reconditioning company to accept the undersize main and big-end shell bearings which are available. Normally, the company doing the regrinding will supply the necessary undersize shells.

5 If the crankshaft is in good condition, it is wise to renew the bearing shells as it is almost certain that the original ones will have worn. This is often indicated by scoring of the bearing surface or by the top layer of the bearing metal having worn through to expose the metal underneath.

6 Each shell is marked on its back with the part number. Undersize shells will have the undersize stamped additionally on their backs.

7 Standard size crankshafts having main bearing journal diameters at the lower end of the tolerance range are marked with a yellow spot on the front balance weight. You will find that with this type of crankshaft, a standard shell is fitted to the seat in the crankcase but a yellow colour-coded shell to the main bearing cap.

8 If a green spot is seen on the crankshaft then this indicates that 0.25 mm (0.0098 in) undersize big-end bearings are used.

Cylinder bores, pistons, rings and connecting rods

9 Cylinder bore wear will usually have been evident from the smoke emitted from the exhaust during recent operation of the vehicle on the road, coupled with excessive oil consumption and fouling of spark plugs.

10 Engine life can be extended by fitting special oil control rings to the pistons. These are widely advertised and will give many more thousands of useful mileage without the need for a rebore, although this will be inevitable eventually. If this remedy is decided upon, remove the piston/connecting rods as described in Section 10 and fit the proprietary rings in accordance with the manufacturer's instructions.

11 Where a more permanent solution is decided upon, the cylinder block can be rebored by your dealer or engineering works, or by one of the mobile workshops which now undertake such work. The cylinder

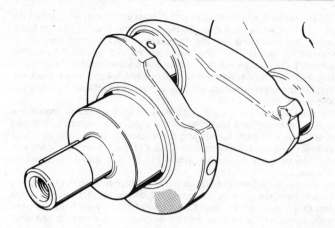

Fig. 1.29 Crankshaft main bearing journal size identification mark on balance web (Sec 17)

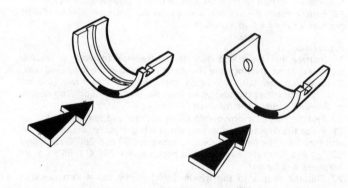

Fig. 1.30 Bearing shell colour identification markings (Sec 17)

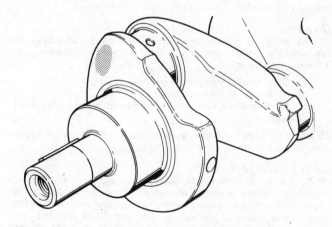

Fig. 1.31 Crankshaft big-end journal size identification mark on crank throw web (Sec 17)

bore will be measured both for out-of-round and for taper to decide how much the bores should be bored out. A set of matching pistons will be supplied in a suitable oversize to suit the new bores.

12 Due to the need for special heating and installing equipment for removal and refitting of the interference type gudgeon pin, the removal and refitting of pistons to the connecting rods is definitely a specialist job, preferably for your Ford dealer.

13 The removal and refitting of piston rings is however well within the scope of the home mechanic. Do this by sliding two or three old feeler blades round behind the top compression ring so that they are at equidistant points. The ring can now be slid up the blades and removed. Repeat the removal operations on the second compression ring and then the oil control ring. This method will not only prevent the rings dropping onto empty grooves as they are withdrawn, but it will also avoid ring breakage.

14 Even when new piston rings have been supplied to match the pistons, always check that they are not tight in their grooves and also check their end gaps by pushing them squarely down their particular cylinder bore and measuring with a feeler blade. Adjustment of the end gap can be made by careful grinding to bring it within the specified tolerance.

15 If new rings are being fitted to an old piston, always remove any carbon from the grooves beforehand. The best tool for this job is the end of a broken piston ring. Take care not to cut your fingers, piston rings are sharp. The cylinder bores should be roughened with fine glass paper to assist the bedding-in of the new rings.

Timing sprockets and chain

16 The teeth on the timing sprockets rarely wear, but check for broken or hooked teeth even so.

17 The timing chain should always be renewed at time of major engine overhaul. A worn chain is evident if when supported horizontally at both ends it takes on a deeply bowed appearance.

18 Finally check the rubber cushion on the tensioner spring leaf. If grooved or chewed up, renew it.

Flywheel

19 Inspect the starter ring gear on the flywheel for wear or broken teeth. If evident, the ring gear should be renewed in the following way. Drill the ring gear with two holes, approximately 7 or 8 mm (0.3 in) diameter and offset slightly. Make sure that you do not drill too deeply or you will damage the flywheel.

20 Tap the ring gear downward off its register and remove it.

21 Place the flywheel in the household refrigerator for about an hour and then heat the new ring gear to between 260 and 280°C (500 and 536°F) in a domestic oven. Do not heat it above 290°C (554°F) or its hardness will be lost.

22 Slip the ring onto the flywheel and gently tap it into position against its register. Allow it to cool without quenching.

23 The clutch friction surface on the flywheel should be checked for grooving or tiny hair cracks, the latter being caused by overheating. If these conditions are evident, it may be possible to surface grind the flywheel provided its balance is not upset. Otherwise, a new flywheel will have to be fitted – consult your dealer about this.

Oil pump

24 The oil pump should be checked for wear by unbolting and removing the cover plate and O-ring (photo) and checking the following tolerances:

    (a) Outer rotor to pump body gap
    (b) Inner rotor to outer rotor gap
    (c) Rotor endfloat (use a feeler blade and straight-edge across pump body)

25 Use feeler blades to check the tolerances and if they are outside the specified values, renew the pump (photo)

Oil seals and gaskets

26 Renew the oil seals on the timing cover and the crankshaft rear retainer as a matter of routine at time of major overhaul. Oil seals are cheap, oil is not! Use a piece of tubing as a removal and installing tool. Apply some grease to the oil seal lips and check that the small tensioner spring in the oil seal has not been displaced by the vibration caused during fitting of the seal.

27 Renew all the gaskets by purchasing the appropriate 'de-coke', short or full engine set. Oil seals may be included in the gasket sets.

Crankcase

28 Clean out the oilways with a length of wire or by using compressed air. Similarly clean the coolant passages. This is best done by flushing through with a cold water hose. Examine the crankcase and block for stripped threads in bolt holes; if evident, thread inserts can be fitted.

29 Renew any core plugs which appear to be leaking or which are excessively rusty.

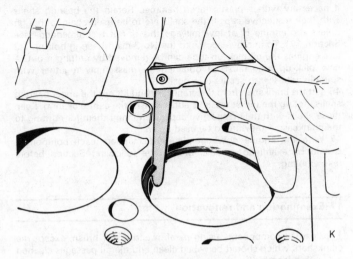

Fig. 1.32 Checking piston ring end gap (Sec 17)

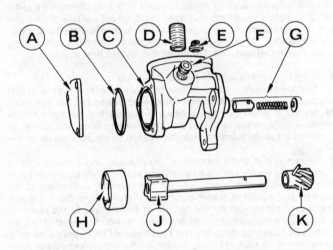

Fig. 1.33 Exploded view of the oil pump (Sec 17)

A Pump cover   F Blind plug
B O-ring   G Oil pressure relief valve
C Pump body   H Outer rotor
D Oil filter attachment stud J Inner rotor
E Filter relief valve   K Drive gear

30 Cracks in the casting may be rectified by specialist welding, or by one of the cold metal key interlocking processes available.

Camshaft and bearings

31 Examine the camshaft gear and lobes for damage or wear. If evident a new camshaft must be purchased, or one which has been 'built-up' such as are advertised by firms specialising in exchange components.

32 The bearing internal diameters should be checked against the Specifications if a suitable gauge is available; otherwise, check for movement between the camshaft journal and the bearing. Worn bearings should be renewed by your dealer.

33 Check the camshaft endfloat by temporarily refitting the camshaft and the thrust plate. If the endfloat exceeds the specified tolerance, renew the thrust plate.

Cam followers

34 It is seldom that the cam followers wear in their bores, but it is likely that after a high mileage, the cam lobe contact surface will show signs of a depression or grooving.

35 Where this condition is evident, renew the cam followers. Grinding out the wear marks will only reduce the thickness of the hardened metal of the cam follower and accelerate further wear.

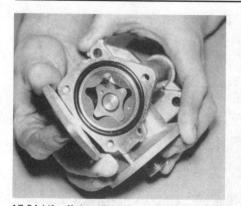

17.24 Lift off the oil pump cover and remove the O-ring (arrowed)

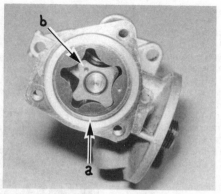

17.25 Check the oil pump rotor-to-body clearance (a) and the inner-to-outer rotor clearance (b)

17.38 Compress the valve spring to remove the collets

17.39 Remove the valve spring retainer and spring ...

17.40 ... followed by the valve

Cylinder head and rocker gear

36 The usual reason for dismantling the cylinder head is to de-carbonise and to grind in the valves. Reference should therefore be made to the next Section, in addition to the dismantling operations described here. First remove the manifolds.

37 Using a standard valve spring compressor, compress the spring on No 1 valve (valve nearest the timing cover). Do not overcompress the spring or the valve stem may bend. If it is found that when screwing down the compressor tool, the spring retainer does not release from the collets, remove the compressor and place a piece of tubing on the retainer so that it does not impinge on the collets and strike the end of the tubing a sharp blow with a hammer. Refit the compressor and compress the spring.

38 Extract the split collets and then gently release the compressor and remove it (photo).

39 Remove the valve spring retainer, the spring and the oil seal (photo).

40 Withdraw the valve (photo).

41 Repeat the removal operations on the remaining seven valves. Keep the valves in their originally fitted sequence by placing them in a piece of card which has holes punched in it and numbered 1 to 8 (from the timing cover end).

42 Place each valve in turn in its guide so that approximately one thrid of its length enters the guide. Rock the valve from side to side. If there is any more than an imperceptible movement, the guides will have to be reamed (working from the valve seat end) and oversize stemmed valves fitted. If you do not have the necessary reamer (tool No 21-242), leave this work to your Ford dealer.

43 Examine the valve seats. Normally, the seats do not deteriorate but the valve heads are more likely to burn away in which case, new valves can be ground in as described in the next Section. If the seats require re-cutting, use a standard cutter available from most accessory or tool stores or consult your motor engineering works.

44 Renewal of any valve seat which is cracked or beyond recutting is definitely a job for your dealer or motor engineering works.

45 If the cylinder head mating surface is suspected of being distorted due to persistent leakage of coolant at the gasket joint, then it can be checked and surface ground by your dealer or motor engineering works. Distortion is unlikely under normal circumstances with a cast iron head.

46 Check the rocker shaft and rocker arms pads which bear on the valve stem end faces for wear or scoring, also for any broken coil springs. Renew components as necessary after dismantling as described in Section 8. If the valve springs have been in use for 50 000 miles (80 000 km) or more, they should be renewed.

47 Reassemble the cylinder head by fitting new valve stem oil seals. Install No 1 valve (lubricated) into its guide and fit the valve spring with the closer coils to the cylinder head, followed by the spring retainer. Compress the spring and engage the split collets in the cutout in the valve stem. Hold them in position while the compressor is gently released and removed.

48 Repeat the operations on the remaining valves, making sure that each valve is returned to its original guide or if new valves have been fitted, into the seat into which it was ground.

49 On completion, support the ends of the cylinder head on two wooden blocks and strike the end of the valve stem with a plastic or copper-faced hammer, just a light blow to settle the components.

18 Cylinder head and pistons – decarbonising

1 With the cylinder head removed as described in Section 5, the carbon deposits should be removed from the combustion spaces using a scraper and a wire brush fitted into an electric drill. Take care not to damage the valve heads, otherwise no special precautions need be taken as the cylinder head is of cast iron construction.

2 Where a more thorough job is to be carried out, the cylinder head should be dismantled as described in the preceding Section so that the

valves may be ground in and the ports and combustion spaces cleaned, brushed and blown out after the manifolds have been removed.

3 Before grinding in a valve, remove the carbon and deposits completely from its head and stem. With an inlet valve, this is usually quite easy, simply scraping off the soft carbon with a blunt knife and finishing with a wire brush. With an exhaust valve the deposits are very much harder and those on the head may need a rub on coarse emery cloth to remove them. An old woodworking chisel is a useful tool to remove the worst of the head deposits.

4 Make sure that the valve heads are really clean, otherwise the rubber suction cup of the grinding tool will not stick during the grinding-in operations.

5 Before starting to grind in a valve, support the cylinder head so that there is sufficient clearance under for the valve stem to project fully without being obstructed.

6 Take the first valve and apply a little coarse grinding paste to the bevelled edge of the valve head. Insert the valve into its guide and apply the suction grinding tool to its head. Rotate the tool between the palms of the hands in a back-and-forth rotary movement until the gritty action of the grinding-in process disappears. Repeat the operation with fine paste and then wipe away all traces of grinding paste and examine the seat and bevelled edge of the valve. A matt silver mating band should be observed on both components, without any sign of black spots. If some spots do remain, repeat the grinding-in-process until they have disappeared. A drop or two of paraffin applied to the contact surfaces will increase the speed of grinding-in, but do not allow any paste to run down into the valve guide. On completion, wipe away every trace of grinding paste using a paraffin-moistened cloth.

7 Repeat the operations on the remaining valves, taking care not to mix up their originally fitted sequence.

8 The valves are refitted as described in Section 17.

9 An important part of the decarbonising operation is to remove the carbon deposits from the piston crowns. To do this, turn the crankshaft so that two pistons are at the top of their stroke and press some grease between these pistons and the cylinder walls. This will prevent carbon particles falling down into the piston ring grooves. Stuff rags into the other two bores.

10 Cover the oilways and coolant passages with masking tape and then using a blunt scraper remove all the carbon from the piston crowns. Take care not to score the soft alloy of the crown or the surface of the cylinder bore.

11 Rotate the crankshaft to bring the other two pistons to TDC and repeat the operations.

12 Wipe away the circle of grease and carbon from the cylinder bores.

13 Clean the top surface of the cylinder block by careful scraping.

19 Engine – reassembly

1 With everything clean, commence reassembly by oiling the bores for the cam followers and inserting them fully in their original sequence.

2 Lubricate the camshaft bearings and insert the camshaft from the timing cover end of the engine.

19.3 Secure the camshaft thrust plate bolts with the locktabs

3 Fit the thrust plate and tighten the fixing bolts to the specified torque. The endfloat will already have been checked as described in Section 17. Secure the bolts with the locktabs (photo).

4 Wipe clean the main bearing shell seats in the crankcase and fit the shells. Using a little grease, stick the semi-circular thrust washers on either side of the centre bearing so that the oil grooves are visible when the washers are installed (photo).

5 Check that the Woodruff key is in position on the front end of the crankshaft and tap the crankshaft sprocket into place using a piece of tubing.

6 Oil the bearing shells and lower the crankshaft into the crankcase (photo).

7 Wipe the seats in the main bearing caps and fit the bearing shells into them. Install the caps so that their markings are correctly positioned as explained at dismantling in Section 16.

8 Screw in the cap bolts and tighten evenly to the specified torque.

9 Now check the crankshaft endfloat. Ideally a dial gauge should be used, but feeler blades are an alternative if inserted between the face of the thrust washer and the machined surface of the crankshaft balance weight after having prised the crankshaft first in one direction and then the other (photo). Provided the thrust washers at the centre bearing have been renewed, the endfloat should be within the specified tolerance. If it is not, oversize thrust washers are available (see Specifications).

10 If the oil pick-up tube was previously removed on 1.3 litre engines a new tube should now be fitted. Apply a suitable adhesive (available from Ford dealers) to the area shown in Fig. 1.34 and fit the tube with the flat edge of the mounting flange parallel with the longitudinal axis of the engine.

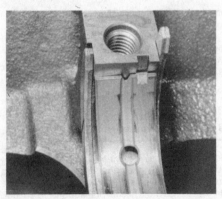
19.4 Fit the upper main bearing shell and thrust washers to the centre bearing

19.6 Lowering the crankshaft into its bearings

19.9 Using feeler blades to check crankshaft endfloat

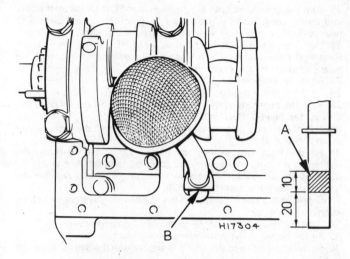

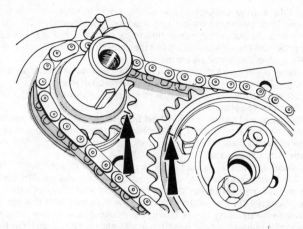

Fig. 1.34 Oil pick-up tube details – 1.3 litre engine (Sec 19)

A   *Area for application of adhesive*   B   *Edge must be parallel with engine longitudinal axis*

Fig. 1.35 Crankshaft and camshaft sprocket timing mark locations (Sec 19)

11 Rotate the crankshaft so that the timing mark on its sprocket is directly in line with the centre of the crankshaft sprocket mounting flange.

12 Engage the camshaft sprocket within the timing chain and then engage the chain around the teeth of the crankshaft sprocket. Push the camshaft sprocket onto its mounting flange. The camshaft sprocket bolt holes should now be in alignment with the tapped holes in the camshaft flange and both sprocket timing marks in alignment (Fig. 1.35). Turn the camshaft as necessary to achieve this, also withdraw the camshaft sprocket and reposition it within the loop of the chain. This is a 'trial and error' operation which must be continued until exact alignment of bolt holes and timing marks is achieved (photos).

13 Screw in the sprocket bolts to the specified torque and bend up the tabs of a new lockplate (photo).

14 Bolt the timing chain tensioner into position, retract the tensioner cam spring and then slide the tensioner arm onto its pivot pin. Release the cam tensioner so that it bears upon the arm (photo).

15 Fit the oil slinger to the front of the crankshaft sprocket so that its convex side is against the sprocket (photo).

19.12A Fit the timing chain and camshaft sprocket ...

19.12B ... with the sprocket timing marks aligned with the shaft centres

19.13 Secure the camshaft sprocket bolts with the locktabs

19.4 Refit the timing chain tensioner and arm

19.15 Fit the oil slinger with its convex side against the sprocket

16 Using a new gasket, fit the timing cover (photo), which will already have been fitted with a new oil seal (see Section 17). One fixing bolt should be left out at this stage as it also holds the water pump. Grease the oil seal lips and fit the crankshaft pulley. Tighten the pulley bolt to the specified torque.

17 Using a new gasket, bolt the crankshaft rear oil seal retainer into position. Tighten the bolts to the specified torque (photo).

18 Locate the engine adaptor (back) plate on its dowels and then fit the flywheel (photos).

19 Screw in and tighten the flywheel bolts to the specified torque. To prevent the flywheel turning, the starter ring gear can be jammed or a piece of wood placed between a crankshaft balance weight and the inside of the crankcase.

20 Install and centralise the clutch as described in Chapter 5.

21 The pistons/connecting rods should now be installed. Although new pistons may have been fitted to the rods by your dealer or supplier (see Section 17), it is worth checking to ensure that with the piston crown arrow pointing to the timing cover end of the engine, the oil hole in the connecting rod is on the left as shown (Fig. 1.15). Oil the cylinder bores.

22 Install the pistons/connecting rods as described in Section 10.

23 Fit the sump as described in Section 7.

24 Fit the oil pressure sender unit, if removed.

25 Turn the crankshaft until No 1 piston is at TDC (crankshaft pulley and timing cover marks aligned) and fit the oil pump complete with new gasket and a new oil filter as described in Section 12.

26 Using a new gasket, fit the fuel pump. If the insulating block became detached from the crankcase during removal, make sure that a new gasket is fitted to each side of the block.

27 Fit the water pump using a new gasket.

28 Fit the cylinder head as described in Section 5.

29 Refit the pushrods in their original sequence and the rocker shaft, also as described in Section 5.

30 Adjust the valve clearances (Section 6) and refit the rocker cover using a new gasket.

31 Fit the inlet and exhaust manifolds using new gaskets and tightening the nuts and bolts to the specified torque (Chapter 3).

32 Refit the carburettor using a new flange gasket and connect the fuel pipe from the pump (Chapter 3).

33 Screw in the spark plugs and the coolant temperature switch (if removed).

34 Refit the thermostat and the thermostat housing cover.

35 Fit the pulley to the water pump pulley flange.

36 Fit the alternator and the drivebelt and tension the belt as described in Chapter 12.

37 Refit the distributor as described in Chapter 4.

19.16 Fitting the timing cover

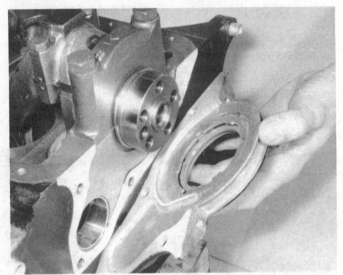

19.17 Fitting the crankshaft rear oil seal retainer

19.18A Locate the engine adaptor plate over the dowels ...

19.18B ... then refit and secure the flywheel

38 Refit the distributor cap and reconnect the spark plug HT leads.
39 Bolt on and connect the coolant pipe to the side of the cylinder block.
40 Fit the breather pipe from the oil filler cap to the inlet manifold and fit the cap.
41 Check the sump drain plug for tighteness. A new seal should be fitted at regular intervals to prevent leakage. Refit the dipstick.
42 Refilling with oil should be left until the engine is installed in the vehicle.

20 Engine/transmission – reconnection and installation

1 This is a direct reversal of removal and separation from the transmission. Take care not to damage the radiator or front wings during installation.

Reconnection
2 Reconnection of the engine and transmission is a reversal of separation, but if the clutch has been dismantled, check that the driven plate has been centralised as described in Chapter 5.

Installation
3 First check that the engine sump drain plug is tight and then, where applicable refit the selector shaft cap nut (removed to drain the transmission oil) together with its spring and interlock pin. Apply sealer to the cap nut threads when refitting (see Specifications – Chapter 6).
4 Manoeuvre the engine/transmission under the vehicle and attach the lifting hoist. Raise the engine/transmission carefully until the right-hand rear mounting can be engaged. Refit the mounting nut and bolt loosely only at this stage.
5 On pre-1986 models refit the front mounting and anti-roll bar

support plates, then refit the left-hand front and rear mountings loosely only.
6 On 1986 models onwards refit the transmission support crossmember.
7 Lower the hoist and let the power unit rest on its mountings. Ensure that none of the mountings are under strain, then tighten all the mounting nuts and bolts and remove the hoist.
8 The driveshafts and suspension arms should now be refitted using the procedure described in Chapter 6, Section 6, paragraphs 37 to 40.
9 Reconnect and adjust the gearchange linkage using the procedure described in Chapter 6, Section 3.
10 Fit the starter motor leads to their terminals.
11 Connect the engine earth leads.
12 Refit the exhaust system and bolt the downpipe to the manifold. Refit the hot air box which connects with the air cleaner.
13 Reconnect the clutch operating cable.
14 Reconnect the electrical leads, the fuel pipe, the brake vacuum hose and the speedometer cable.
15 Reconnect the throttle cable and the choke cable (where applicable) as described in Chapter 3.
16 Reconnect the radiator coolant hoses, and heater hoses.
17 Fill up with engine oil, transmission oil and coolant, then reconnect the battery (photo).
18 Refit the bonnet, bolting the hinges to their originally marked positions. Reconnect the screen washer pipe.
19 Fit the air cleaner and reconnect the hoses and the air cleaner intake spout.
20 Once the engine is running, check the dwell angle, timing, idle speed and mixture adjustment as applicable (refer to Chapters 3 and 4).
21 If a number of new internal components have been installed, run the vehicle at restricted speed for the first few hundred miles to allow time for the new components to bed in. It is also recommended that with a new or rebuilt engine, the engine oil and filter are changed at the end of the running-in period.

21 Fault diagnosis – ohv engine

Symptom	Reason(s)
Engine fails to turn over when starter operated	Discharged or defective battery Dirty or loose battery leads Defective starter solenoid or switch Engine earth strap disconnected Defective starter motor
Engine turns over but will not start	Ignition damp or wet Ignition leads to spark plugs loose Shorted or disconnected low tension leads Dirty, incorrectly set or pitted contact breaker points (where applicable) Faulty condenser Defective ignition switch Ignition LT leads connected wrong way round Faulty coil Contact breaker point spring earthed or broken (where applicable) No petrol in petrol tank Vapour lock in fuel line (in hot conditions or at high altitude) Blocked float chamber needle valve Fuel pump filter blocked Choked or blocked carburettor jets Faulty fuel pump
Engine stalls and will not start	Ignition failure – in severe rain or after traversing water splash No petrol in petrol tank Petrol tank breather choked Sudden obstruction in carburettor Water in fuel system
Engine misfires or idles unevenly	Ignition leads loose Battery leads loose on terminals Battery earth strap loose on body attachment point Engine earth lead loose Low tension lead to terminals on coil loose Low tension lead from distributor loose

Symptom	Reasons
Engine misfires or idles unevenly (continued)	Dirty, or incorrectly gapped spark plugs
	Dirty, incorrectly set or pitted contact breaker points (where applicable)
	Tracking across distributor cap (oily or cracked cap)
	Ignition too retarded
	Faulty coil
	Mixture too weak
	Sticking engine valve
	Incorrect valve clearance
	Air leak in carburettor
	Air leak at inlet manifold to cylinder head, or inlet manifold to carburettor
	Weak or broken valve springs
	Worn valve guides or stems
	Worn pistons and piston rings
Lack of power and poor compression	Burnt out exhaust valves
	Sticking or leaking valves
	Worn valve guides and stems
	Weak or broken valve springs
	Blown cylinder head gasket (accompanied by increase in noise)
	Worn pistons and piston rings
	Worn or scored cylinder bores
	Ignition timing wrongly set
	Contact breaker points incorrectly gapped (where applicable)
	Incorrect valve clearances
	Incorrectly set spark plugs
	Mixture too rich or too weak
	Dirty contact breaker points (where applicable)
	Fuel filters blocked causing top end fuel starvation
	Distributor automatic advance weights or vacuum advance and retard mechanism not functioning correctly
	Faulty fuel pump giving top end fuel starvation
Excessive oil consumption	Badly worn, perished or missing valve stem oil seals
	Excessively worn valve stems and valve guides
	Worn piston rings
	Worn pistons and cylinder bores
	Excessive piston ring gap allowing blow-by
	Piston oil return holes choked
Oil being lost due to leaks	Leaking oil filter gasket
	Leaking rocker cover gasket
	Leaking timing case gasket
	Leaking sump gasket
Unusual noises from engine	Worn valve gear (noisy tapping from top cover)
	Worn big-end bearings (regular heavy knocking)
	Worn main bearings (rumbling and vibration)
	Worn crankshaft (knocking, rumbling and vibration)

PART B: CVH ENGINES

22 General description

The 1.1 litre, 1.3 litre, 1.4 litre and 1.6 litre CVH (Compound Valve angle, Hemispherical combustion chambers) engines are of four-cylinder in-line overhead camshaft type, mounted transversely, together with the transmission, at the front of the car.

The crankshaft is supported in five main bearings within a cast iron crankcase.

The cylinder head is of light alloy construction, supporting the overhead camshaft in five bearings. Camshaft drive is by a toothed composite rubber belt, driven from a sprocket on the crankshaft.

The distributor is driven from the rear (flywheel) end of the camshaft by means of an offset dog.

The cam followers are of hydraulic type, which eliminates the need for valve clearance adjustment. The cam followers operate in the following way. When the valve is closed, pressurised engine oil passes through a port in the body of the cam followers and four grooves in the plunger and into the cylinder feed chamber. From this chamber, oil flows through a ball type non-return valve into the pressure chamber. The tension of the coil spring causes the plunger to press the rocker arm against the valve and to eliminate any free play.

As the cam lifts the cam follower, the oil pressure in the pressure chamber increases and causes the non-return valve to close the port feed chamber. As oil cannot be compressed, it forms a rigid link between the body of the cam follower, the cylinder and the plunger which then rise as one component to open the valve.

The clearance between the body of the cam follower and the cylinder is accurately designed to meter a specific quantity of oil as it escapes from the pressure chamber. Oil will only pass along the cylinder bore when pressure is high during the moment of valve opening. Once the valve has closed, the escape of oil will produce a small amount of free play and no pressure will exist in the pressure chamber. Oil from the feed chamber can then flow through the non-return valve into the pressure chamber so that the cam follower cylinder can be raised by the pressure of the coil spring, thus eliminating any play in the arrangement until the valve is operated again.

As wear occurs between rocker arm and valve stem, the quantity of oil which flows into the pressure chamber will be slightly more than

Fig. 1.36 Cutaway view of the CVH engine (Sec 22)

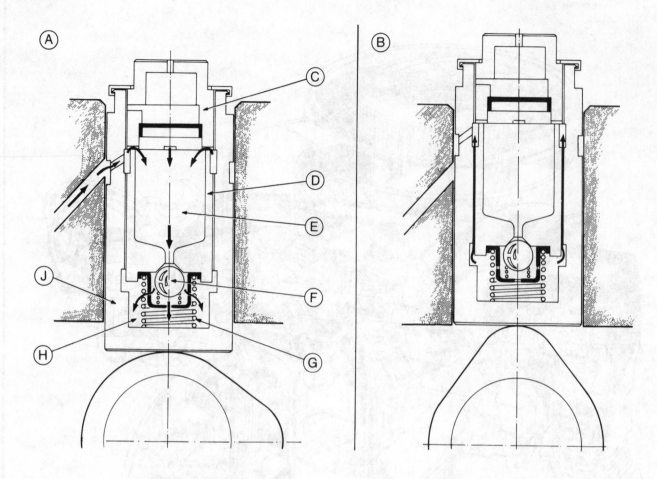

Fig. 1.37 Sectional views showing operation of hydraulic cam followers (Sec 22)

A	Valve closed	D	Cylinder	F	Non-return valve	H	Pressure chamber
B	Valve open	E	Feed chamber	G	Coil spring	J	Body
C	Plunger						

the quantity lost during the expansion cycle of the cam follower. Conversely, when the cam follower is compressed by the expansion of the valve, a slighly smaller quantity of oil will flow into the pressure chamber than was lost.

If the engine has been standing idle for a period of time, or after overhaul, when the engine is started up, valve clatter may be heard. This is a normal condition and will gradually disappear within a few minutes of starting up as the cam followers are pressurised with oil.

The water pump is mounted on the timing belt end of the cylinder block and is driven by the toothed belt.

A gear or rotor type oil pump is mounted on the timing belt end of the cylinder block and is driven by a gear on the front end of the crankshaft.

A full-flow oil filter of throw-away type is located on the side of the crankcase.

23 Maintenance and inspection

1   The maintenance procedures are the same as described in Part A: Section 2, but ignore any references to valve clearance adjustment. The sump drain plug and oil filter locations are as shown in the photos for this Section and are accessible from below the car.

2   Additionally at the specified interval the timing belt should be renewed as described in Section 26.

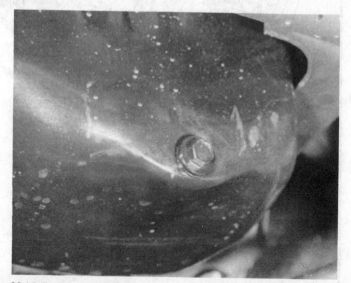

23.1A Engine oil drain plug ...

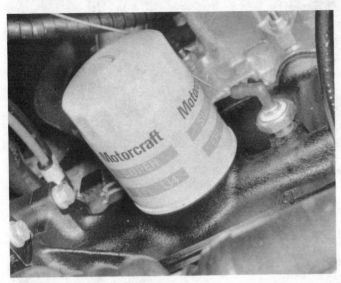

23.1B ... and oil filter locations

24 Major operations possible with the engine in the car

The following work can be carried out without having to remove the engine:

(a) Timing belt – renewal
(b) Camshaft oil seal – renewal
(c) Camshaft – removal and refitting
(d) Cylinder head – removal and refitting
(e) Crankshaft front oil seal – renewal
(f) Sump – removal and refitting
(g) Piston/connecting rod – removal and refitting
(h) Engine/transmission mountings – removal and refitting

25 Major operations requiring engine removal

The following work can only be carried out after removal of the engine from the car:

(a) Crankshaft main bearings – renewal
(b) Crankshaft – removal and refitting
(c) Flywheel – removal and refitting
(d) Crankshaft rear oil seal – renewal
(e) Oil pump – removal and refitting

26 Timing belt – removal, refitting and adjustment

Note: *Accurate adjustment of the timing belt entails the use of Ford special tools. An approximate setting can be achieved using the method described in this Section, but the tension should be checked by a dealer on completion.*

1 Disconnect the battery negative lead.
2 Release the alternator mounting and adjuster link bolts, push the alternator in towards the engine and slip the drivebelt off the pulleys.
3 Using a spanner on the crankshaft pulley bolt, turn the crankshaft until the notch on the pulley is aligned with the TDC (O) mark on the timing belt cover scale (photo). Now remove the distributor cap and check that the rotor arm is pointing towards the No 1 cylinder HT lead segment in the cap. If the rotor arm is pointing towards the No 4 cylinder segment, turn the crankshaft through another complete turn and realign the pulley notch with the TDC mark.
4 On early models unscrew the four bolts and remove the one-piece timing belt cover. On later models fitted with a two-piece cover,

unscrew the two upper bolts and remove the top half, then unscrew the two lower bolts. The lower half cannot be removed at this stage (photos).
5 Undo the bolts and remove the right-hand engine splash shield.
6 Using a ring spanner unscrew the crankshaft pulley retaining bolt. Remove the starter motor as described in Chapter 12 and lock the flywheel ring gear with a cold chisel or similar tool to prevent the crankshaft rotating (photo). Remove the pulley, followed by the timing belt cover lower half on later models.
7 Slacken the two bolts which secure the timing belt tensioner and, using a large screwdriver, prise the tensioner to one side to relieve the tautness of the belt. If the tensioner is spring-loaded, tighten one of the bolts to retain it in the slackened position.
8 If the original belt is to be refitted, mark it for direction of travel and also the exact tooth positions on all three sprockets.
9 Slip the timing belt off the camshaft, water pump and crankshaft sprockets.
10 Before refitting the belt, check that the crankshaft is still at TDC (the small projection on the belt sprocket front flange in line with the TDC mark on the oil pump housing – photo) and that the timing mark on the camshaft sprocket is opposite the TDC mark on the cylinder head – see Fig. 1.39 (photo). Adjust the position of the sprockets slightly, but avoid any excessive movement of the sprockets while the belt is off, as the piston crowns and valve heads may make contact.
11 Engage the timing belt with the teeth of the crankshaft sprocket and then pull the belt vertically upright on its right-hand run. Keep it taut and engage it with the teeth of the camshaft sprocket. Check that the positions of the sprockets have not altered (photo).
12 Wind the belt round the camshaft sprocket, around and under the tensioner and over the water pump sprocket (photo).
13 Refit the crankshaft pulley and tighten the bolt to the specified torque (photo), using the same procedure as used previously to stop the crankshaft turning. On later models make sure that the timing belt cover lower half is placed in positon before refitting the pulley.
14 To adjust the belt tension, slacken the tensioner and move it towards the front of the car to apply an initial tension to the belt. Secure the tensioner in this position.
15 Rotate the crankshaft through two complete revolutions, then return to the TDC position. Check that the camshaft sprocket is also at TDC as previously described.
16 Grasp the belt between thumb and forefinger at a point midway between the crankshaft and camshaft sprocket on the straight side of the belt. When the tension is correct it should just be possible to twist the belt through 90° at this point. Slacken the tensioner and using a large screwdriver as a lever, move it as necessary until the tension is correct. Tighten the tensioner bolts, rotate the camshaft to settle the belt, then recheck the tension. It will probably take two or three attempts to achieve success.

26.3 Crankshaft pulley notch (arrowed) aligned with TDC (O) mark on belt cover scale

26.4A Where a two-piece timing belt cover is fitted, undo the bolts ...

26.4B ... and remove the upper half

26.6 Using a stout bar to lock the flywheel ring gear

26.10A Crankshaft sprocket projection (arrowed) aligned with TDC mark on oil pump housing

26.10B ... and camshaft sprocket timing mark aligned with TDC mark on cylinder head

26.11 Place the timing belt in position ...

26.12 ... and wind the belt around the sprockets

26.13 Refitting the crankshaft pulley bolt

Fig. 1.38 Timing belt tensioner retaining bolts (Sec 26)

Fig. 1.39 Camshaft sprocket at TDC position (Sec 26)

17 It must be emphasised that this is an approximate setting only and should be rechecked by a Ford dealer at the earliest opportunity.
18 Refit the starter motor, engine splash shield, distributor cap and timing belt cover/s.
19 Refit the alternator drivebelt and adjust its tension as described in Chapter 12.
20 Reconnect the battery.

27 Camshaft oil seal – renewal

1 Disconnect the battery negative lead.
2 Release the timing belt from the camshaft sprocket, as described in the preceding Section.
3 Pass a bar through one of the holes in the camshaft sprocket to anchor the sprocket while the retaining bolt is unscrewed. Remove the sprocket.
4 Using a suitable tool, hooked at its end, prise out the oil seal.
5 Apply a little grease to the lips of the new seal and draw it into position using the sprocket bolt and a suitable distance piece.
6 Refit the sprocket, tightening the bolt to the specified torque wrench setting. Thread locking compound should be applied to the threads of the bolt.
7 Refit and tension the timing belt, as described in the preceding Section.
8 Reconnect the battery.

28 Camshaft – removal and refitting

1 Disconnect the battery negative lead.

Carburettor engine models
2 Refer to Chapter 3 and remove the air cleaner and the fuel pump.
3 Disconnect the throttle and where fitted the choke cable ends from the carburettor linkage, then undo the bolts and move the cable support bracket to one side.

Fuel-injection models
4 On XR3i and Cabriolet models disconnect the intake air hose between the fuel distributor and throttle housing and position it out of the way.
5 On RS Turbo models disconnect the intake air hose and the small connecting hose at the intake air duct, then undo the two bolts and remove the air duct from the rocker cover.

All models
6 Refer to Chapter 4 and remove the distributor.
7 Disconnect the crankcase ventilation hoses at the rocker cover,

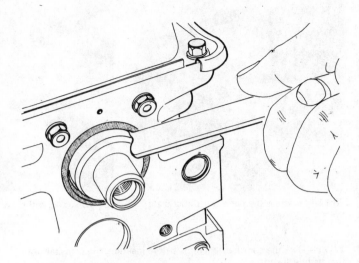

Fig. 1.40 Removing the camshaft oil seal (Sec 27)

undo and remove the bolts and washers and remove the rocker cover.
8 Unscrew the securing nuts and remove the rocker arms and guides. Keep the components in their originally installed sequence by marking them with a piece of numbered tape or by using a suitably sub-divided box.
9 Withdraw the hydraulic cam followers, again keeping them in their originally fitted sequence.
10 Slacken the alternator mounting and adjuster link bolts, push the alternator in towards the engine and slip the drivebelt from the pulleys.
11 Unbolt and remove the timing belt cover (top half only on later models with two-piece cover) and turn the crankshaft to align the timing mark on the camshaft sprocket with the one on the cylinder head.
12 Slacken the bolts on the timing belt tensioner, lever the tensioner against the tension of its coil spring (if fitted) and retighten the bolts. With the belt now slack, slip it from the camshaft sprocket.
13 Pass a rod or large screwdriver through one of the holes in the camshaft sprocket to lock it and unscrew the sprocket bolt. Remove the sprocket (photos).
14 Extract the two bolts and pull out the camshaft thrustplate (photos).
15 Carefully withdraw the camshaft from the distributor end of the cylinder head (photo).
16 Refitting the camshaft is a reversal of removal, but observe the following points.

28.13A Unscrewing the camshaft sprocket bolt

28.13B Removing the camshaft sprocket

28.14A Unscrew the camshaft thrust plate bolts ...

28.14B ... and withdraw the thrust plate

28.15 Withdrawing the camshaft

17 Lubricate the camshaft bearings before inserting the camshaft into the cylinder head.

18 It is recommended that a new oil seal is always fitted after the camshaft has been installed (see preceding Section). Apply thread locking compound to the sprocket bolt threads. Tighten the bolt to the specified torque.

19 Fit and tension the timing belt, as described in Section 26.

20 Oil the hydraulic cam followers with hypoid type transmission oil before inserting them into their original bores.

21 Refit the rocker arms and guides in their original sequence, use new nuts and tighten to the specified torque. It is essential that before each rocker arm is installed and its nut tightened, the respective cam follower is positioned at its lowest point (in contact with cam base circle). Turn the camshaft (by means of the crankshaft pulley bolt) as necessary to achieve this.

22 Use a new rocker cover gasket, and to ensure that a good seal is made, check that its location groove is clear of oil, grease and any portions of the old gasket. A length of sealant should be applied to the gasket recess where the cover engages under the timing belt cover. When in position tighten the cover retaining screws to the specified torque setting.

23 Refit the remainder of the components with reference to their relevant Chapters.

Fig. 1.41 Camshaft removal from flywheel end of cylinder head (Sec 28)

29 Cylinder head (carburettor engine models) – removal and refitting

Note: The cylinder head must only be removed when the engine is cold

1 Disconnect the battery earth lead.
2 Remove the air cleaner as described in Chapter 3.
3 Drain the cooling system as described in Chapter 2.
4 Disconnect the coolant hoses from the thermostat housing, automatic choke and inlet manifold as applicable (photo).

5 Disconnect the throttle and where fitted the choke cable ends from the carburettor linkage, then undo the bolts and move the cable support bracket to one side (photo).
6 Disconnect the fuel pipe from the fuel pump (photo).
7 Disconnect the vacuum servo hose (where fitted) from the inlet manifold (photo).
8 Where fitted, disconnect the fuel return pipe from the carburettor (photo).
9 Disconnect the remaining vacuum hoses at the carburettor and inlet manifold, noting their locations (photo).
10 Disconnect the leads from the temperature sender unit, ignition

29.4 Disconnecting the coolant hose from the thermostat housing

29.5 Disconnect the choke cable from the linkage clamp (arrowed)

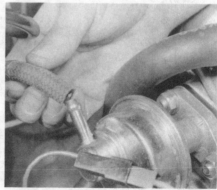

29.6 Disconnect the fuel feed pipe at the pump

29.7 Disconnecting the brake servo vacuum hose – arrowed (1.4 litre shown)

29.8 Fuel return pipe location (arrowed) on 1.4 litre engine

29.9 Vacuum hose attachments at the inlet manifold (1.4 litre shown)

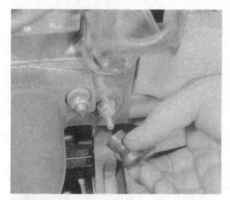

29.10A Disconnect the lead at the temperature sender ...

29.10B ... anti-run-on valve and back bleed solenoid where fitted (1.4 litre shown)

29.11 Unbolt the exhaust downpipe from the manifold

coil anti-run-on valve solenoid and where applicable, carburettor electric choke and back bleed solenoid (photos).

11 Unbolt the exhaust downpipe from the manifold by unscrewing the flange bolts. Support the exhaust pipe by tying it up with wire (photo).

12 Release the alternator mounting and adjuster link bolts, push the alternator in towards the engine and slip the drivebelt from the pulleys.

13 Unbolt and remove the timing belt cover (upper cover only on later models).

14 Slacken the belt tensioner bolts, lever the tensioner to one side against the pressure of the coil spring (if fitted) and retighten the bolts.

15 With the timing belt now slack, slip it from the camshaft sprocket.

16 Disconnect the leads from the spark plugs and unscrew and remove the spark plugs.

17 Remove the rocker cover (photo).

18 Unscrew the cylinder head bolts, progressively and in the sequence shown (photo). Discard the bolts, as new ones must be used at reassembly.

29.17 Rocker cover retaining bolt locations (arrowed)

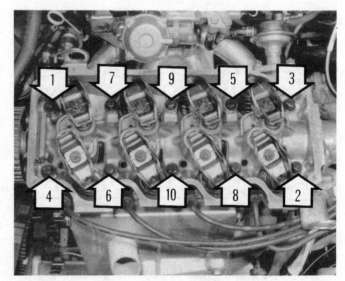

29.18 Cylinder head bolt removal sequence

19 Remove the cylinder head complete with manifolds. Use the manifolds if necessary as levers to rock the head from the block. Do not attempt to tap the head sideways off the block as it is located on dowels, and do not attempt to lever between the head and the block or damage will result.
20 Before installing the cylinder head, make sure that the mating surfaces of head and block are perfectly clean with the head locating dowels in position. Clean the bolt holes free from oil. In extreme cases it is possible for oil left in the holes to crack the block due to hydraulic pressure.
21 Turn the crankshaft to position No 1 piston about 20 mm (0.8 in) before it reaches TDC.
22 Place a new gasket on the cylinder block and then locate the cylinder head on its dowels. The upper surface of the gasket is marked OBEN-TOP (photos).
23 Install and tighten the **new** cylinder head bolts, tightening them in four stages (see Specifications). After the first two stages, the bolt heads should be marked with a spot of quick-drying paint so that the paint spots all face the same direction. Now tighten the bolts (Stage 3) through 90° (quarter turn) followed by a further 90° (Stage 4). Tighten the bolts at each stage only in the sequence shown in Fig. 1.42 before going on to the next stage. If all the bolts have been tightened equally, the paint spots should now all be pointing in the same direction (photo).
24 Fit the timing belt as described in Section 26.

25 Refitting and reconnection of all other components is a reversal of dismantling, with reference to the relevant Chapter.
26 On completion refill the cooling system as described in Chapter 2.

30 Cylinder head (fuel-injection models) – removal and refitting

Note: *The cylinder head must only be removed when the engine is cold*

XR3i and Cabriolet models
1 Disconnect the battery negative lead.
2 Disconnect the intake air hose at the throttle housing.
3 Drain the cooling system as described in Chapter 2.
4 Disconnect the crankcase ventilation hoses from the inlet manifold and rocker cover.
5 Disconnect the coolant hoses from the thermostat housing, inlet manifold and inlet manifold intermediate flange.
6 Disconnect the throttle cable from the throttle housing.
7 Relieve the fuel system pressure by *slowly* loosening the fuel feed pipe union at the warm-up regulator. Absorb fuel leakage in a cloth. Reference to the fuel-injection system layout in Chapter 3 will assist in identification of the relevant components where necessary.
8 Disconnect the vacuum servo hose from the inlet manifold.

29.22A Locate a new gasket on the cylinder block ...

29.22B ... with the markings (arrowed) uppermost

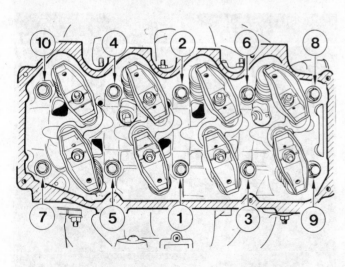
Fig. 1.42 Cylinder head bolt tightening sequence (Secs 29 and 30)

29.23 Tightening the cylinder head bolts

Fig. 1.43 Wiring connections on the fuel-injection system – XR3i and Cabriolet (Sec 30)

A Warm-up regulator   B Cold start valve   C Throttle valve stop earth   D Auxiliary air device
                                                     cable

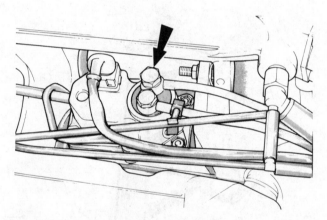

**Fig. 1.44 Fuel feed pipe union at the warm-up regulator –
XR3i and Cabriolet (Sec 30)**

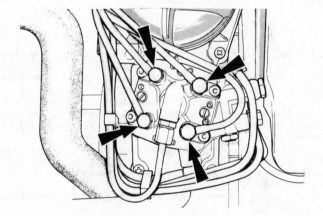

**Fig. 1.45 Injector pipe unions at the fuel distributor – XR3i
and Cabriolet (Sec 30)**

9   Disconnect the two fuel pipe unions at the warm-up regulator, the single pipe to the cold start valve and the four injector feed pipes at the fuel distributor. Recover the sealing washers located on each side of the banjo unions and seal all disconnected pipes and orifices to prevent dirt ingress.
10 Disconnect the vacuum hoses at the throttle housing after marking their locations to aid refitment.
11 Disconnect the wiring multi plugs at the cold start valve, warm-up regulator, and auxiliary air device, then disconnect the throttle valve stop earth cable.
12 Disconnect the leads from the spark plugs and remove the distributor cap. Disconnect the distributor multi plug.
13 The remainder of the removal and the refitting sequence is the same as described in Section 29, paragraphs 11 to 26 inclusive.

RS Turbo models
14 Disconnect the battery negative lead.
15 Drain the cooling system as described in Chapter 2.
16 Disconnect the intake air hose and the connecting hose at the intake air duct, then undo the two bolts and remove the air duct from the rocker cover. Disconnect the sensor multi plugs (photo).
17 Disconnect the coolant hoses from the thermostat housing, inlet manifold and inlet manifold intermediate flange.
18 Disconnect the crankcase ventilation hose at the rocker cover and the two vacuum hoses from the inlet manifold. Release the hoses from their clips.
19 Disconnect the brake servo vacuum hose at the inlet manifold.
20 Disconnect the throttle cable from the throttle housing.
21 Refer to Chapter 3 and remove the turbocharger.

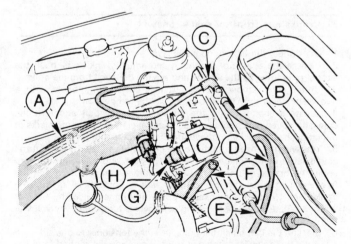

**Fig. 1.46 Wiring connections and hose attachments on the
fuel-injection system – RS Turbo (Sec 30)**

A Intake air duct
B Vacuum hose
C Crankcase ventilation valve
   hose
D Auxiliary air device hose
E Vacuum servo hose
F Mounting bracket
G Throttle position sensor
   multi-plug
H Charge air temperature
   sensor multi-plug

30.16 Air intake duct connecting hose clip (A) charge air temperature sensor multi-plug (B) and throttle position sensor multi-plug (C) on RS Turbo models

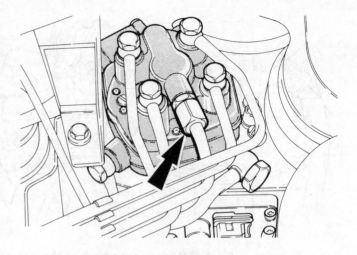

Fig. 1.47 Cold start valve union on fuel distributor – RS Turbo (Sec 30)

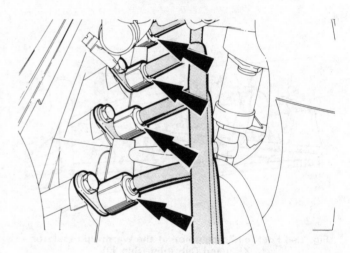

Fig. 1.48 Fuel pipe connections at the fuel injectors – RS Turbo (Sec 30)

22 Relieve the fuel system pressure by *slowly* loosening the cold start valve union on the top of the fuel distributor. Absorb fuel leakage in a cloth. Reference to the fuel-injection system layout in Chapter 3 will assist in identification of the relevant components where necessary.

23 Disconnect the fuel pipes at the fuel injectors and at the cold start valve. Recover the sealing washers located on each side of the banjo unions and seal all disconnected pipes and orifices to prevent dirt ingress. Move the fuel pipes clear of the cylinder head.

24 Disconnect the wiring multi plugs at the temperature gauge sender unit, ignition coil, throttle position sensor, solenoid control valve, coolant temperature sensor, thermo time switch, cold start valve and auxiliary air device.

25 Disconnect the leads from the spark plugs and remove the distributor cap.

26 The remainder of the removal and the refitting sequence is the same as described in Section 29, paragraphs 12 to 26 inclusive.

31 Crankshaft front oil seal – renewal

1 Disconnect the battery negative lead.

2 Release the alternator mounting and adjuster link bolts, push the alternator in towards the engine and slip the drivebelt from the pulleys.

3 Unbolt and remove the timing belt cover. On models with a two-piece cover only the upper half can be removed at this stage.

4 Locate a spanner onto the crankshaft pulley bolt and turn the crankshaft over in its normal direction of travel until the timing marks of the crankshaft sprocket and cylinder head are in alignment.

5 You will now need to remove the crankshaft pulley. To prevent the crankshaft turning, place the vehicle in gear and have an assistant apply the brakes or unbolt and remove the starter motor so that the flywheel ring gear can be jammed with a cold chisel or suitable implement. Unbolt the crankshaft pulley and remove it with its thrust washer. Where a two-piece timing belt cover is fitted, remove the lower half.

6 Slacken the belt tensioner bolts, lever the tensioner to one side and retighten the bolts. With the belt slack, it can now be slipped from the sprockets. Before removing the belt note its original position on the sprockets (mark the teeth with quick-drying paint), also its direction of travel.

7 Withdraw the crankshaft sprocket. If it is tight you will need to use a special extractor, but due to the confined space available you may need to lower the engine from its mounting on that side. Before resorting to this, try levering the sprocket free using screwdrivers. If the mounting is to be disconnected proceed as described in Part A: Section 11.

8 Remove the dished washer from the crankshaft, noting that the concave side is against the oil seal.

9 Using a suitably hooked tool, prise out the oil seal from the oil pump housing.

10 Grease the lips of the new seal and press it into position using the pulley bolt and suitable distance piece made from a piece of tubing.

11 Fit the thrust washer (concave side to oil seal), the belt sprocket and the pulley to the crankshaft. On models with a two-piece timing belt cover, place the lower half in position before refitting the pulley.

12 Fit and tension the timing belt by the method described in Section 26.

13 Fit the timing belt cover.

14 Refit and tension the alternator drivebelt (Chapter 12).

15 Remove the starter ring gear jamming device (if fitted), refit the starter motor and reconnect the battery.

32 Sump – removal and refitting

1 Disconnect the battery negative lead.

2 Drain the engine oil.

3 Remove the starter motor as described in Chapter 12.

4 Apply the handbrake, jack up the front of the car and support it on stands.

5 Unbolt and remove the cover plate from the clutch housing (photo).

32.5 Remove the clutch housing cover plate ...

32.6 ... and the right-hand engine splash shield

32.9A Fitting the sump sealing strips ...

32.9B ... followed by the side gaskets with their ends overlapped

32.10 Refitting the sump

6   Unbolt and remove the engine splash shield at the crankshaft pulley end (photo).

7   Unscrew the sump securing bolts progressively and remove them.

8   Remove the sump and peel away the gaskets and sealing strips.

9   Make sure that the mating surfaces of the sump and block are clean, then fit new end sealing strips into their grooves and stick new side gaskets into position using thick grease. The ends of the side gaskets should overlap the seals (photos). On later models a one-piece sump gasket is used. Before fitting, apply sealer to the joints of the cylinder block and rear oil seal carrier, and cylinder block and oil pump housing (four locations). Without applying any further sealer, locate the gasket into the grooves of the oil seal carrier and oil pump housing. To retain the gasket insert two or three studs into the cylinder block if necessary and remove them once the sump is in place.

10 Offer up the sump, taking care not to displace the gaskets and insert the securing bolts (photo). Tighten the bolts in two stages to the final torque given in the Specifications.

11 Refit the cover plate to the clutch housing and refit the engine splash shield.

12 Refit the starter motor.

13 Fill the engine with oil and reconnect the battery.

33 Pistons/connecting rods – removal and refitting

1   Remove the sump, as described in the preceding Section, and the cylinder head, as described in Section 29 or 30 as applicable.

2   Check that the connecting rod and cap have adjacent numbers at their big-end to indicate their position in the cylinder block (No 1 nearest timing cover end of engine) (photo).

3   Bring the first piston to the lowest point of its throw by turning the crankshaft pulley bolt and then check if there is a wear ring at the top of the bore. If there is, it should be removed using a scraper, but do not damage the cylinder bore.

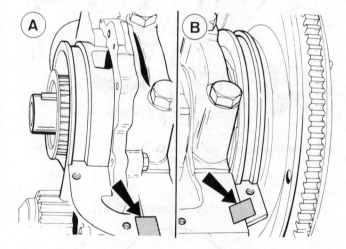

Fig. 1.49 Apply sealer to the areas shown when fitting a one piece sump gasket (Sec 32)

A   Oil pump housing-to-block joint
B   Rear oil seal carrier-to-block joint

4   Unscrew the big-end bolts and remove them.

5   Tap off the big-end cap. If the bearing shell is to be used again, make sure that it is retained with the cap. Note the two cap positioning roll pins.

6   Push the piston/rod out of the top of the block, again keeping the bearing shell with the rod if the shell is to be used again.

33.2 Connecting rod and big-end cap matching numbers

33.11 Fitting the bearing shell in the connecting rod

33.13 Installing a piston/connecting rod assembly

7 Repeat the removal operations on the remaining piston/rod assemblies.
8 Dismantling a piston/connecting rod is covered in Section 40.
9 To refit a piston/rod assembly, have the piston ring gaps staggered as shown in the diagram (Fig. 1.51). Oil the rings and apply a piston ring compressor. Compress the piston rings.
10 Oil the cylinder bores.
11 Wipe clean the bearing shell seat in the connecting rod and insert the shell (photo).

12 Insert the piston/rod assembly into the cylinder bore until the base of the piston ring compressor stands squarely on the top of the block.
13 Check that the directional arrow on the piston crown faces towards the timing cover end of the engine, then apply the wooden handle of a hammer to the piston crown. Strike the head of the hammer sharply to drive the piston into the cylinder bore and release the ring compressor (photo).
14 Oil the crankpin and draw the connecting rod down to engage with the crankshaft. Make sure the bearing shell is still in position.
15 Wipe the bearing shell seat in the big-end cap clean and insert the bearing shell (photo).
16 Lubricate the bearing shell with oil then fit the cap, aligning the numbers on the cap and the rod, screw in the bolts and tighten them to the specified torque setting (photos).
17 Repeat the operations on the remaining pistons/connecting rods.
18 Refit the sump (Section 32) and the cylinder head (Section 29 or 30). Refill the engine with oil and coolant.

34 Engine/transmission mountings – removal and refitting

Refer to Part A: Section 11.

35 Lubrication system – description

1 The oil pump draws oil from the sump through a pick-up pipe and then supplies pressurised oil through an oilway on the right-hand side

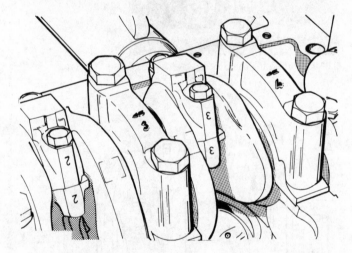

Fig. 1.50 Connecting rod and main bearing identification numbers (Sec 33)

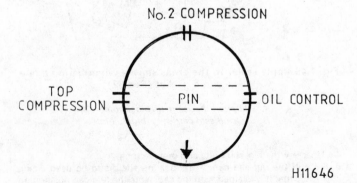

Fig. 1.51 Piston ring end gap positioning diagram (Sec 33)

NO. 2 COMPRESSION

TOP COMPRESSION

PIN

OIL CONTROL

H11646

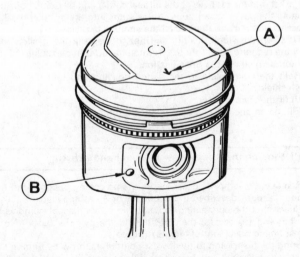

Fig. 1.52 Arrow (A) or cast nipple (B) must face the timing belt end of the engine when installed (Sec 33)

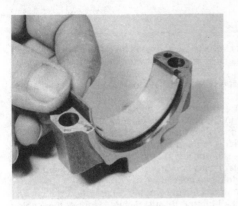

33.15 Fitting the bearing shell to the big-end cap

33.16A Fitting the big-end cap to the connecting rod

33.16B Tightening the big-end cap bolts to the specified torque

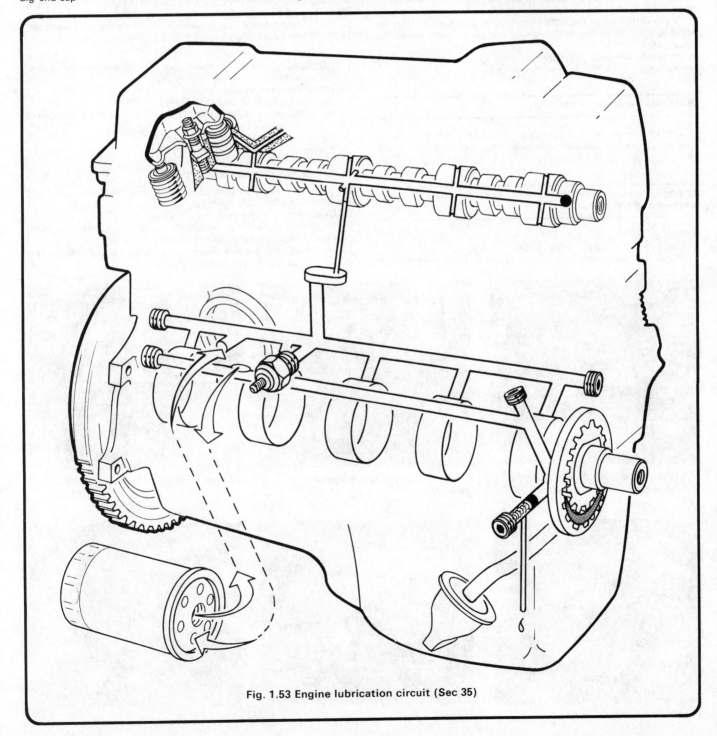

Fig. 1.53 Engine lubrication circuit (Sec 35)

of the engine into a full-flow oil filter. A pressure relief valve is incorporated inside the pump casing.

2 Filtered oil passes out of the filter casing through the central threaded mounting stud into the main oil gallery.

3 Oil from the main gallery lubricates the main bearings, and the big-end bearings are lubricated from oilways in the crankshaft.

4 The connecting rods have an oil hole in the big-end on the side towards the exhaust manifold. Oil is ejected from this hole onto the gudgeon pins and cylinder bores.

5 The oil pressure warning switch is located next to the oil filter and connected by an internal passage to the main oil gallery. Oil from this passage is supplied to the centre camshaft bearing.

6 Oil is provided to the other camshaft bearings by means of a longitudinal drilling within the camshaft.

7 The hydraulic cam followers (tappets) are supplied with oil through the grooves in the camshaft bearing journals and oilways in the cylinder head.

8 The contact face of the rocker arm is lubricated from ports in the tappet guides, while the end faces of the valve stems are splash lubricated.

9 An engine oil cooler is located under the oil filter on fuel-injection and automatic transmission models.

36 Engine – method of removal

The engine is removed complete with the transmission in a downward direction and then withdrawn from under the front of the car.

37 Engine/transmission (carburettor engine models) – removal and separation

Removal

1 Disconnect the battery negative lead.

2 Place the transmission in fourth gear on four-speed manual transmission models or reverse gear on the five-speed unit, to aid adjustment of the gearchange linkage when refitting. On models produced from February 1987 onwards, place the transmission in second gear on four-speed versions, or fourth gear on five-speed versions.

3 Refer to Chapter 11 and remove the bonnet.

4 Refer to Chapter 3 and remove the air cleaner.

5 Refer to Chapter 2 and drain the cooling system.

6 Disconnect the radiator top and bottom hoses and the expansion tank hose at the thermostat housing.

7 Disconnect the heater hoses from the automatic choke, thermostat housing and inlet manifold as applicable.

8 Disconnect the throttle cable (photo) and where fitted the choke cable ends from the carburettor throttle levers. Unbolt the cable support bracket and move the bracket and cable(s) to one side.

9 Disconnect the fuel feed pipe from the fuel pump and plug the pipe. Where fitted disconnect the fuel return hose at the carburettor.

10 Disconnect the brake servo vacuum hose from the inlet manifold.

11 Disconnect the leads from the following electrical components:

  (a) Alternator (photo)
  (b) Cooling fan temperature switch and temperature sender (photos)
  (c) Oil pressure sender (photo)
  (d) Reversing lamp switch (photo)
  (e) Anti-run-on valve solenoid (photo) and back bleed solenoid (where applicable)
  (f) Electric choke (where applicable)
  (g) Ignition coil
  (h) Distributor (photo)
  (i) Starter motor solenoid (photo)

12 Unscrew the speedometer drive cable from the transmission and release the breather hose (photo).

13 Disconnect the transmission earth strap.

14 On manual transmission models disconnect the clutch cable from the release lever and from the transmission support.

15 Disconnect the exhaust downpipe from the manifold flange and support the system to avoid undue strain.

37.8 Disconnecting the throttle cable end (1.3 litre engine)

37.11A Disconnecting the alternator multi-plug ...

37.11B ... cooling fan switch ...

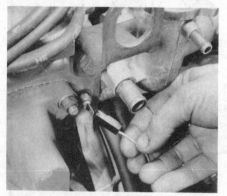
37.11C ... temperature sender ...

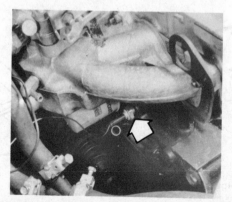
37.11D ... oil pressure switch ...

37.11E ... reversing lamp switch ...

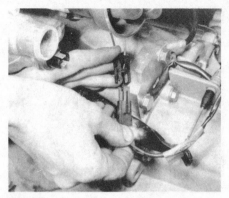

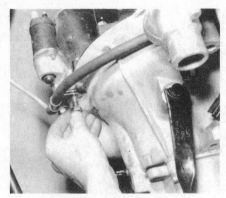

37.11F ... anti-run-on valve solenoid ...

37.11G ... distributor ...

37.11H ... and starter motor wiring connections on the 1.3 litre engine

37.12 Disconnect the speedometer cable (arrowed) at the transmission

37.18 Disconnect the gearchange rod at the selector shaft clamp

16 Apply the handbrake, jack up the front of the car and support it on stands to provide sufficient clearance beneath it to be able to remove the engine/transmission from below. A distance of 686 mm (27.0 in) is recommended between the floor and the bottom edge of the front panel.

17 Disconnect the exhaust system from its flexible mountings and remove the system complete.

18 On manual transmission models disconnect the gearchange rod from the transmission selector shaft by releasing the clamp bolt and withdrawing the rod (photo). Tie the rod to the stabiliser and then where fitted, unhook the tension spring. Unscrew the single bolt and disconnect the stabiliser from the transmission housing, noting the washer fitted between the stabiliser trunnion and the transmission.

19 On automatic transmission models refer to Chapter 7, Section 9 and disconnect the starter inhibitor switch wiring, the selector cable and the downshift linkage.

20 Remove the driveshafts from the transmission using the procedure described in Chapter 8, Section 5, paragraphs 6 to 12 for each driveshaft.

21 On pre-1986 models equipped with an anti-roll bar, undo the two bolts each side securing the anti-roll bar mounting clamps and remove the clamps.

22 On 1986 models onwards, undo the three bolts each side securing the anti-roll bar mounting plates to the body.

23 On automatic transmission models undo the transmission fluid cooler pipes and withdraw the pipes. Plug the unions to prevent dirt ingress.

24 Unbolt the right-hand and left-hand engine splash shields and remove them from under the car (photos).

25 On cars equipped with an Anti-lock Braking System (ABS) undo the hydraulic pipe mounting bracket bolt. Remove the modulator clamp bolt and pivot bolt each side and tie the modulator to the underbody (see Chapter 9).

26 Connect a suitable hoist to the engine using chains and the lifting brackets on the cylinder head.

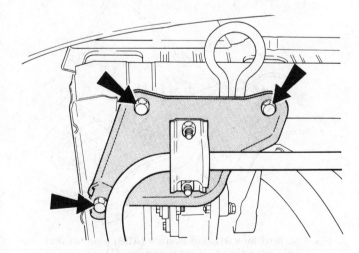

Fig. 1.54 Anti-roll bar mounting plate attachments – 1986 models onwards (Sec 37)

27 Just take the weight of the engine/transmission assembly so that the tension is relieved from the mountings.

28 Unbolt the rear right-hand engine mounting (complete with coolant hose support on early models) from the side member and from the inner wing panel (photos).

29 On pre-1986 models unbolt the front and rear transmission mountings from their brackets and remove the front mounting and anti-roll bar support plates from the body on both sides (photos).

30 On 1986 models onwards undo the nuts and bolts securing the

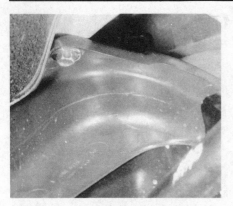

37.24A Remove the right-hand splash shield ...

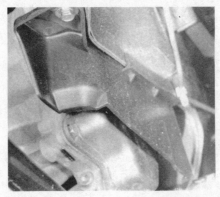

37.24B ... and left-hand splash shield

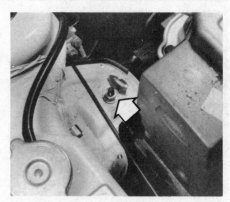

37.28A Right-hand engine mounting attachment (arrowed) at side member ...

37.28B ... and at the inner wing panel

37.29A Detach the left-hand front ...

37.29B ... and left-hand rear transmission mountings on pre-1986 models

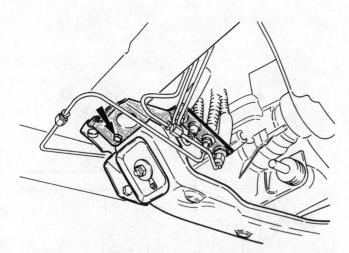

Fig. 1.55 Anti-lock Braking System (ABS) pipe bracket retaining bolt location (Sec 37)

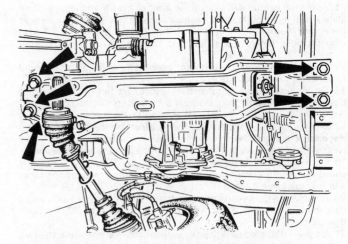

Fig. 1.56 Transmission support crossmember retaining bolt locations – 1986 models onwards (Sec 37)

transmission support crossmember to the body. The crossmember is removed with the engine/transmission assembly.

31 Carefully lower the engine/transmission and withdraw it from under the car. To ease the withdrawal operation, lower the engine/transmission onto a crawler board or a sheet of substantial chipboard placed on rollers or lengths of pipe (photo).

Separation (manual transmission models)

32 Unscrew and remove the starter motor bolts and remove the starter.
33 Unbolt and remove the clutch cover plate from the lower part of the clutch bellhousing.

34 Unscrew and remove the bolts from the clutch bellhousing-to-engine mating flange.
35 Withdraw the transmission from the engine. Support its weight so that the clutch assembly is not distorted while the input shaft is still in engagement with the splined hub of the clutch driven plate.

Separation (automatic transmission models)

36 Unscrew and remove the starter motor bolts and remove the starter motor.
37 Undo the two bolts and remove the torque converter cover plate.

37.31 Removing the engine/transmission assembly from under the car

38 Working through the cover plate aperture, unscrew and remove the four nuts securing the driveplate to the torque converter. For this to be accomplished it will be necessary to progressively turn the crankshaft for access to each nut in turn. Unscrew the nuts in a progressive manner, one turn at a time until removed.

39 Unscrew and remove the engine-to-transmission flange bolts and then separate the two units, but take care not to catch the torque converter studs on the driveplate. The torque converter is only loosely attached, so keep it in position in the transmission housing during and after removal of the transmission.

38 Engine/transmission (fuel-injection models) – removal and separation

Removal (XR3i and Cabriolet models)

1 Disconnect the battery negative lead.
2 Place the transmission in fourth gear on four-speed models or reverse gear on the five-speed unit to aid adjustment of the gearchange linkage when refitting. On models produced from February 1987 onwards, place the transmission in second gear on four-speed versions, or fourth gear on five-speed versions.
3 Refer to Chapter 11 and remove the bonnet.
4 Refer to Chapter 2 and drain the cooling system.
5 Remove the air intake hose between the fuel distributor and throttle housing.
6 Disconnect the radiator top and bottom hoses and the expansion tank hose at the thermostat housing.
7 Disconnect the heater hoses from the thermostat housing, and the three-way connection fitting on the oil cooler.
8 Disconnect the throttle cable end from the throttle lever and unbolt the cable bracket from the throttle housing.
9 Relieve the fuel system pressure by *slowly* loosening the fuel feed pipe union at the warm-up regulator. Absorb fuel leakage in a cloth. Reference to the fuel-injection system layout in Chapter 3 will assist in identification of the relevant components where necessary.
10 Disconnect the vacuum servo hose from the inlet manifold.
11 Disconnect the two fuel pipe unions at the warm-up regulator, the single pipe to the cold start valve and the four injector feed pipes at the fuel distributor. Recover the sealing washers located on each side of the banjo unions and seal all disconnected pipes and orifices to prevent dirt ingress.
12 Disconnect the leads from the following electrical components:

    (a) Alternator
    (b) Cooling fan temperature switch
    (c) Oil pressure sender
    (d) Reversing lamp switch

    (e) Ignition coil
    (f) Distributor
    (g) Starter motor solenoid
    (h) Cold start valve
    (j) Warm-up regulator
    (k) Auxiliary air device
    (l) Throttle valve stop earth cable

13 Unscrew the speedometer drive cable from the transmission and release the breather hose.
14 Disconnect the transmission earth strap.
15 Disconnect the clutch cable from the release lever and from the transmission support.
16 The remainder of the removal procedure is the same as described in Section 37, paragraphs 15 to 31 inclusive.

Removal (RS Turbo models)

17 Disconnect the battery negative lead.
18 Place the transmission in reverse gear to aid adjustment of the gearchange linkage when refitting. On models produced from February 1987 onwards, place the transmission in fourth gear.
19 Refer to Chapter 11 and remove the bonnet.
20 Refer to Chapter 2 and drain the cooling system.
21 Disconnect the air intake hose and connecting hose at the intake air duct. Disconnect the charge air temperature sensor multi plug, undo the two bolts securing the air duct to the rocker cover and remove the duct.
22 Undo the two bolts and remove the air cleaner assembly from the fuel distributor (photo).
23 Disconnect the radiator top and bottom hoses at the thermostat housing, radiator and turbocharger return pipe as applicable.
24 Disconnect the heater hoses from the thermostat housing, three-way connector piece and inlet manifold as applicable.
25 Refer to Chapter 3 and remove the turbocharger.
26 Disconnect the crankcase ventilation hose at the rocker cover and the two vacuum hoses from the top of the inlet manifold. Release the hoses from their clips.
27 Disconnect the vacuum servo hose from the inlet manifold.
28 Disconnect the hose at the solenoid control valve.
29 Disconnect the throttle cable at the throttle housing.
30 Relieve the fuel system pressure by *slowly* loosening the cold start valve union on the top of the fuel distributor. Absorb fuel leakage in a cloth.
31 Disconnect the fuel pipes at the fuel injectors and at the cold start valve. Recover the sealing washers located on each side of the banjo unions and seal all disconnected pipes and orifices to prevent dirt ingress. Move the fuel pipes clear of the engine.

38.22 Air cleaner retaining bolts (arrowed) on RS Turbo models

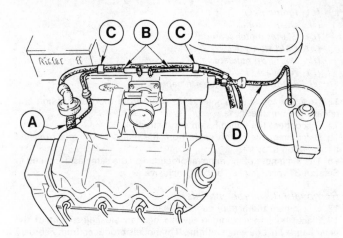

Fig. 1.57 Vacuum and breather hose connections – RS Turbo (Sec 38)

    A Crankcase ventilation hose
       at rocker cover
    B Vacuum hoses at inlet
       manifold
    C Retaining clips
    D Vacuum servo hose

32 Disconnect the wiring multi plugs at the temperature gauge sender unit, ignition coil, throttle position sensor, solenoid control valve, coolant temperature sensor, thermo-time switch, cold start valve, oil pressure switch and auxiliary air device (photo).

33 Disconnect the speedometer cable from the transmission and the fuel computer multi-plug (where fitted).

34 Disconnect the transmission earth strap.

35 Disconnect the clutch cable from the release lever and from the transmission support.

36 The remainder of the removal procedure is the same as described in Section 37, paragraphs 16 to 31 inclusive.

Separation (all models)

37 Separation from the manual or automatic transmission is as described in Section 37 paragraphs 32 to 35 or 36 to 39 as applicable.

39 Engine – complete dismantling

1 The need for dismantling will have been dictated by wear or noise in most cases. Although there is no reason why only partial dismantling cannot be carried out to renew such items as the oil pump or crankshaft

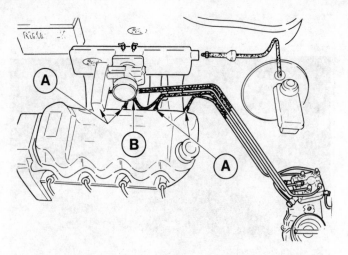

Fig. 1.58 Fuel pipe connections – RS Turbo (Sec 38)

    A Fuel injectors   *B Cold start valve*

rear oil seal, when the main bearings or big-end bearings have been knocking and especially if the vehicle has covered a high mileage, then it is recommended that a complete strip-down is carried out and every engine component examined as described in Section 40.

2 Position the engine so that it is upright and safely chocked on a bench or other convenient working surface. If the exterior of the engine is very dirty it should be cleaned before dismantling, using paraffin and a stiff brush or a water-soluble solvent.

3 Remove the alternator, the mounting bracket and exhaust heat shield, and the adjuster link (photos).

4 Disconnect the heater hose from the water pump.

5 Drain the engine oil and remove the filter and oil cooler where applicable.

6 Jam the flywheel starter ring gear to prevent the crankshaft turning and unscrew the crankshaft pulley bolt. Remove the pulley.

7 Unbolt and remove the timing belt cover (4 bolts). Note that the cover is in two halves on later models.

8 Slacken the two bolts on the timing belt tensioner, lever the tensioner against its spring pressure where applicable and tighten the bolts to lock it in position.

9 With the belt now slack, note its running direction and mark the mating belt and sprocket teeth with a spot of quick-drying paint. This is not necessary if the belt is being renewed.

10 Disconnect the spark plug leads and remove the distributor cap complete with HT leads (if not already done).

11 Unscrew and remove the spark plugs.

12 Disconnect the crankcase ventilation hose from its connector on the crankcase.

38.32 Coolant temperature sensor (A) thermo-time switch (B) and auxiliary air device (C) multi-plugs on RS Turbo models

39.3A Remove the alternator ...

39.3B ... and heat shield

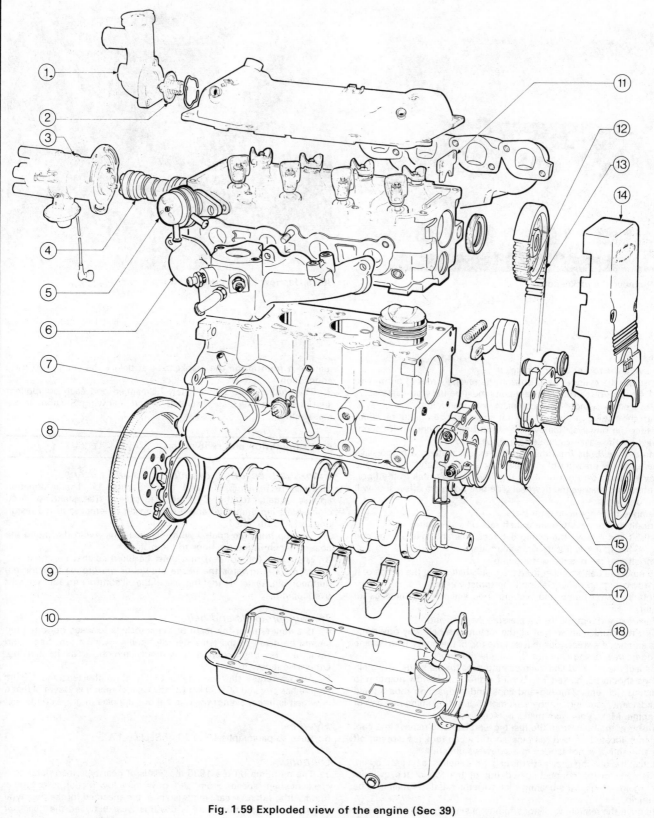

Fig. 1.59 Exploded view of the engine (Sec 39)

1	Thermostat housing	7	Oil pressure switch	11	Camshaft thrust plate	15	Water pump
2	Thermostat	8	Oil filter	12	Camshaft belt sprocket	16	Crankshaft belt sprocket
3	Distributor	9	Oil seal retainer	13	Timing belt	17	Timing belt tensioner
4	Camshaft	10	Oil pump pick-up tube and	14	Timing belt cover	18	Oil pump
5	Fuel pump		strainer		(one-piece type)		
6	Inlet manifold						

39.13 Remove the rocker cover

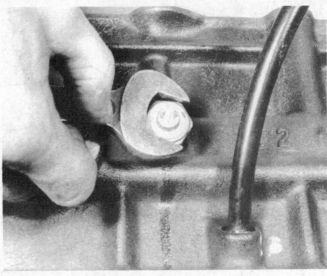
39.25 Unscrew the oil pressure switch

13 Remove the rocker cover (photo).
14 Unscrew the cylinder head bolts in the reverse order to tightening (Fig. 1.42) and discard them. New bolts must be used at reassembly.
15 Remove the cylinder head complete with manifolds.
16 Turn the engine on its side. Do not invert it as sludge in the sump may enter the oilways. Remove the sump bolts, withdraw the sump and peel off the gaskets and sealing strips.
17 Remove the bolts from the clutch pressure plate in a progressive manner until the pressure of the assembly is relieved and then remove the cover, taking care not to allow the driven plate to fall to the floor.
18 Unbolt and remove the flywheel. The bolt holes are offset so it will only fit one way.
19 Remove the engine adaptor plate.
20 Unbolt and remove the crankshaft rear oil seal retainer.
21 Unbolt and remove the timing belt tensioner and take out the coil spring. (This spring is not used on all models).
22 Unbolt and remove the water pump.
23 Remove the belt sprocket from the crankshaft using the hands or if tight, a two-legged puller. Take off the thrust washer.
24 Unbolt the oil pump and pick-up tube and remove them as an assembly.
25 Unscrew and remove the oil pressure switch (photo).
26 Turn the crankshaft so that all the pistons are half-way down the bores, and feel if a wear ridge exists at the top of the bores. If so, scrape the ridge away, taking care not to damage the bores.
27 Inspect the big-end and main bearing caps for markings. The main bearings should be marked 1 to 5 with a directional arrow pointing to the timing belt end. The big-end caps and connecting rods should have adjacent matching numbers. Number 1 is at the timing belt end of the engine. Make your own marks if necessary.
28 Unscrew the bolts from the first big-end cap and remove the cap. The cap is located on two roll pins, so if the cap requires tapping off make sure that it is not tapped in a sideways direction.
29 Retain the bearing shell with the cap if the shell is to be used again.
30 Push the piston/connecting rod out of the top of the cylinder block, again retaining the bearing shell with the rod if the shell is to be used again.
31 Remove the remaining pistons/rods in a similar way.
32 Remove the main bearing caps, keeping the shells with their respective caps if the shells are to be used again. Lift out the crankshaft.
33 Take out the bearing shells from the crankcase, noting the semi-circular thrust washers on either side of the centre bearing. Keep the shells identified as to position in the crankcase if they are to be used again.
34 Prise down the spring arms of the crankcase ventilation baffle and

remove it from inside the crankcase just below the ventilation hose connection.
35 The engine is now completely dismantled and each component should be examined as described in the following Section before reassembling.

40 Examination and renovation

Crankshaft, bearings, cylinder bores and pistons
1 Refer to paragraphs 1 and 15 of Section 17. The information applies equally to the CVH engine, except that standard sized crankshafts are unmarked and the following differences in the piston rings should be noted.
2 The top rings are coated with molybdenum. Avoid damaging the coating when fitting the rings to the pistons.
3 The lower (oil control) ring must be fitted so that the manufacturer's mark is towards the piston crown, or the groove towards the gudgeon pin. Take care that the rails of the oil control ring abut without overlapping.

Timing sprockets and belt
4 It is very rare for the teeth of the sprockets to wear, but attention should be given to the tensioner idler pulley. It must turn freely and smoothly, be ungrooved and without any shake in its bearing. Otherwise renew it.
5 Always renew the coil spring (if fitted) in the tensioner. If the engine has covered 60 000 km (36 000 miles) then it is essential that a new belt is fitted, even if the original one appears in good condition.

Flywheel
6 Refer to paragraphs 19 to 23 of Section 17.

Oil pump
7 The oil pump on pre-1986 models is of gear type incorporating a crescent shape spacer. From 1986 onwards a low friction rotor type is fitted. Although no wear limit tolerances are specified for the gear type pump, if on inspection there is obvious wear between the gears, or signs of scoring or wear ridges, the pump should be renewed. Similarly if a high mileage engine is being reconditioned it is recommended that a new pump is fitted. Inspection of the rotor type is covered in paragraphs 24 and 25 of Section 17.

Oil seals and gaskets
8 Renew the oil seals in the oil pump and in the crankshaft rear oil seal retainer as a matter of routine at time of major overhaul. It is

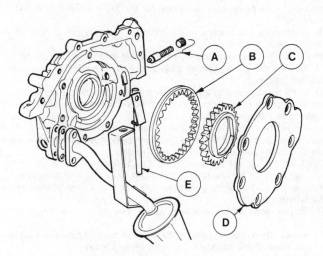

Fig. 1.60 Exploded view of the gear type oil pump (Sec 40)

A   Pressure relief valve   D   Oil pump cover
B   Driven gear   E   Return pipe
C   Driving gear

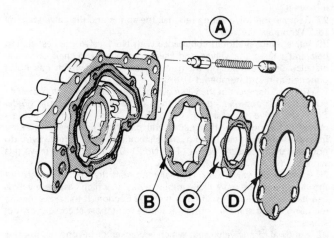

Fig. 1.61 Exploded view of the rotor type oil pump (Sec 40)

A   Pressure relief valve   C   Inner rotor
B   Outer rotor   D   Oil pump cover

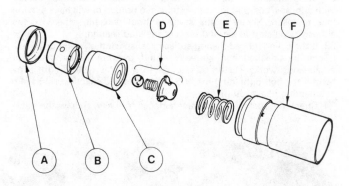

**Fig. 1.62 Exploded view of the hydraulic cam follower
(Sec 40)**

A   Circlip   D   Non-return valve
B   Plunger   E   Spring
C   Cylinder   F   Body

recommended that the new seals are drawn into these components using a nut and bolt and distance pieces, rather than tapping them into position, to avoid distortion of the light alloy castings.
9   Renew the camshaft oil seal after the camshaft has been installed.
10 Always smear the lips of a new oil seal with grease, and check that the small tensioner spring in the oil seal has not been displaced during installation.
11 Renew all gaskets by purchasing the appropriate engine set, which usually includes the necessary oil seals.

Crankcase
12 Refer to paragraphs 28 to 30 of Section 17.

Camshaft and bearings
13 Examine the camshaft gear and lobes for damage or wear. If evident, a new camshaft must be purchased, or one which has been built-up, such as are advertised by firms specialising in exchange components.
14 The bearing internal diameters in the cylinder head should be checked against the Specifications if a suitable gauge is available, otherwise check for movement between the camshaft journal and the bearing. If the bearings are proved to be worn, then a new cylinder head is the only answer as the bearings are machined directly in the cylinder head.
15 Check the camshaft endfloat by temporarily refitting the camshaft and thrust plate. If the endfloat exceeds the specified tolerance, renew the thrust plate.

Cam followers
16 It is seldom that the hydraulic type cam followers (tappets) wear in their cylinder head bores. If the bores are worn then a new cylinder head is called for.
17 If the cam lobe contact surface shows signs of a depression or grooving, grinding out the wear surface will not only remove the hardened surface of the follower but may also reduce its overall length to a point where the self-adjusting capability of the cam follower is exceeded and valve clearances are not taken up, with consequent noisy operation.
18 Cam followers cannot be dismantled so if they become worn after high mileage, they must be renewed. On refitting, it is only necessary to smear the outside surfaces with clean engine oil, as they are self priming and will fill with engine oil once the engine is running, although initial operation may be noisy until primed.

Cylinder head and rocker arms
19 The usual reason for dismantling the cylinder head is to decarbonise and to grind in the valves. Reference should therefore be

made to the next Section in addition to the dismantling operations described here.
20 Remove the intake and exhaust manifolds and their gaskets (Chapter 3) also the thermostat housing (Chapter 2).
21 Unscrew the nuts from the rocker arms and discard the nuts. New ones must be fitted at reassembly.
22 Remove the rocker arms and the hydraulic cam followers, keeping them in their originally fitted sequence. Keep the rocker guide and spacer plates in order.
23 The camshaft need not be withdrawn but if it is wished to do so, first remove the thrust plate and take the camshaft out from the rear of the cylinder head.
24 The valve springs should now be compressed. A standard type of compressor will normally do the job, but a forked tool (Part No 21-097) can be purchased or made up to engage on the rocker stud using a nut and distance piece to compress it.
25 Compress the valve spring and extract the split collets. Do not overcompress the spring, or the valve stem may bend. If it is found when screwing down the compressor tool that the spring retainer does not release from the collets, remove the compressor and place a piece of tubing on the retainer so that it does not impinge on the collets and place a small block of wood under the head of the valve. With the cylinder head resting flat down on the bench, strike the end of the tubing a sharp blow with a hammer. Refit the compressor and compress the spring.

26 Extract the split collets and then gently release the compressor and remove it.
27 Remove the valve spring retainer, the spring and the valve stem oil seal. Withdraw the valve.
28 Valve removal should commence with No 1 valve (nearest timing belt end). Keep the valves and their components in their originally installed order by placing them in a piece of card which has holes punched in it and numbered 1 to 8.
29 To check for wear in the valve guides, place each valve in turn in its guide so that approximately one third of its length enters the guide. Rock the valve from side to side. If any more than the slightest movement is possible, the guides will have to be reamed (working from the valve seat end) and oversize stemmed valves fitted. If you do not have the necessary reamer (Tool No 21-071 to 21-074), leave this work to your Ford dealer.
30 Examine the valve seats. Normally the seats do not deteriorate, but the valve heads are more likely to burn away, in which case new valves can be ground in as described in the next Section. If the seats require recutting, use a standard cutter, available from most accessory or tool stores.
31 Renewal of any valve seat which is cracked or beyond recutting is definitely a job for your dealer or motor engineering works.
32 If the rocker arm studs must be removed for any reason, a special procedure is necessary. Warm the upper ends of the studs with a blow-lamp flame (**not** a welder) before unscrewing them. Clean out the cylinder head threads with an M10 tap and clean the threads of oil or grease. Discard the old studs and fit new ones, which will be coated with adhesive compound on their threaded portion or will have a nylon locking insert. Screw in the studs without pausing, otherwise the adhesive will start to set and prevent the stud seating.
33 If the cylinder head mating surface is suspected of being distorted, it can be checked and surface ground by your dealer or motor engineering works. Distortion is possible with this type of light alloy head if the bolt tightening method is not followed exactly, or if severe overheating has taken place.
34 Check the rocker arm contact surfaces for wear. Renew the valve

springs if they have been in service for 80 000 km (50 000 miles) or more.
35 Commence reassembly of the cylinder head by fitting new valve stem oil seals (photos).
36 Oil No 1 valve stem and insert the valve into its guide (photo).
37 Fit the valve spring (closer coils to cylinder head), then the spring retainer (photos).
38 Compress the spring and engage the split collets in the cut-out in the valve stem. Hold them in position while the compressor is gently released and removed (photo).
39 Repeat the operations on the remaining valves, making sure that each valve is returned to its original guide or new valves have been fitted, into the seat into which it was ground.
40 Once all the valves have been fitted, support the ends of the cylinder head on two wooden blocks and strike the end of each valve stem with a plastic or copper-faced hammer, just a light blow to settle the components.
41 Fit the camshaft (if removed) and a new oil seal as described in Section 28.
42 Smear the hydraulic cam followers with hypoid type transmission oil and insert them into their original bores (photo).
43 Fit the rocker arms with their guides and spacer plates, use new nuts and tighten to the specified torque. It is important that each rocker arm is installed only when its particular cam follower is at its lowest point (in contact with the cam base circle) (photos).
44 Refit the exhaust and intake manifolds and the thermostat housing, using all new gaskets.

41 Cylinder head and pistons – decarbonising

1 With the cylinder head removed as described in Section 29 or 30 the carbon deposits should be removed from the combustion surfaces using a blunt scraper. Take great care as the head is of light alloy construction and avoid the use of a rotary (power-driven) wire brush.

40.35A Using a socket to install a valve stem oil seal

40.35B Valve stem oil seal installed

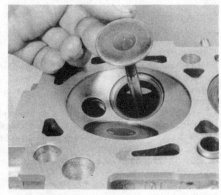
40.36 Inserting a valve into its guide

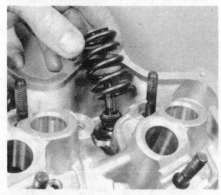
40.37A Fit the valve spring ...

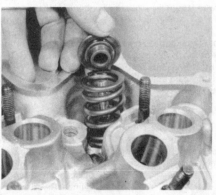
40.37B ... and spring retainer

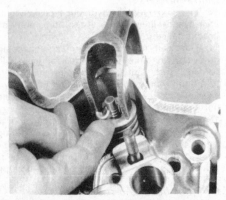
40.38 Compress the spring and fit the collets

40.42 Fitting a cam follower to its bore

40.43A Fit the rocker arm spacer plate ...

40.43B ... followed by the rocker arm and guide

2   Where a more thorough job is to be carried out, the cylinder head should be dismantled as described in the preceding Section so that the valves may be ground in, and the ports and combustion spaces cleaned and blown out after the manifolds have been removed.

3   Before grinding in a valve, remove the carbon and deposits completely from its head and stem. With an inlet valve this is usually quite easy, simply a case of scraping off the soft carbon with a blunt knife and finishing with a wire brush. With an exhaust valve, the deposits are very much harder and those on the valve head may need a rub on coarse emery cloth to remove them. An old woodworking chisel is a useful tool to remove the worst of the valve head deposits.

4   Make sure that the valve heads are really clean, otherwise the rubber suction cup grinding tool will not stick during the grinding-in operations.

5   Before starting to grind in a valve, support the cylinder head so that there is sufficient clearance under it for the valve stem to project fully without being obstructed, otherwise the valve will not seat properly during grinding.

6   Take the first valve and apply a little coarse grinding paste to the bevelled edge of the valve head. Insert the valve into its guide and apply the suction grinding tool to its head. Rotate the tool between the palms of the hands in a back-and-forth rotary movement until the gritty action of the grinding-in process disappears. Repeat the operation with fine paste and then wipe away all trace of grinding paste and examine the seat and bevelled edge of the valve. A matt silver mating band should be observed on both components, without any sign of black spots. If some spots do remain, repeat the grinding-in process until they have disappeared. A drop or two of paraffin applied to the contact surfaces will speed the grinding process, but do not allow any paste to run down into the valve guide. On completion, wipe away every trace of grinding paste using a paraffin-moistened cloth.

7   Repeat the operations on the remaining valves, taking care not to mix up their originally fitted sequence.

8   An important part of the decarbonising operation is to remove the carbon deposits from the piston crowns. To do this (engine in vehicle), turn the crankshaft so that two pistons are at the top of their stroke and press some grease between the pistons and the cylinder walls. This will prevent carbon particles falling down into the piston ring grooves. Plug the other two bores with rag.

9   Cover the oilways and coolant passages with masking tape and then using a blunt scraper, remove all the carbon from the piston crowns. Take great care not to score the soft alloy of the crown or the surface of the cylinder bore.

10   Rotate the crankshaft to bring the other two pistons to TDC and repeat the operations.

11   Wipe away the circles of grease and carbon from the cylinder bores.

12   Clean the top surfaces of the cylinder block by careful scraping.

42 Engine – reassembly

1   With everything clean and parts renewed where necessary, commence reassembly by inserting the ventilation baffle into the crankcase. Make sure that the spring arms engage securely (photo).

2   Insert the bearing half shells into their seats in the crankcase, making sure that the seats are perfectly clean (photo).

3   Stick the semi-circular thrust washers on either side of the centre bearing with thick grease. Make sure that the oil channels face outwards (photo).

4   Oil the bearing shells and carefully lower the crankshaft into position (photo).

5   Insert the bearings shells into the main bearing caps, making sure that their seats are perfectly clean. Oil the bearings and install the caps

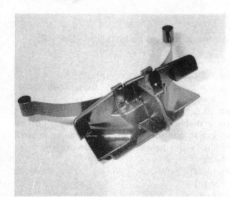

42.1 Crankcase ventilation baffle

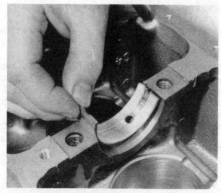

42.2 Inserting a main bearing shell into the crankcase

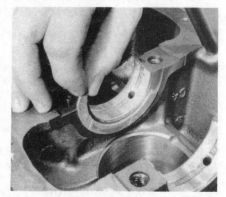

42.3 Locating the crankshaft thrust washers on the centre main bearing

42.4 Lowering the crankshaft onto its bearings

42.5A Fit the bearing shells to the main bearing caps ...

42.5B ... then fit the caps to their correct numbered locations ...

42.5C ... with the arrows on the caps pointing toward the timing belt end of the engine

42.7 Checking crankshaft endfloat with a feeler blade

in their correct numbered location and with the directional arrow pointing towards the timing belt end of the engine (photos).

6   Tighten the main bearing cap bolts to the specified torque.

7   Check the crankshaft endfloat. Ideally a dial gauge should be used, but feeler blades are an alternative if inserted between the face of the thrust washer and the machined surface of the crankshaft balance web, having first prised the crankshaft in one direction and then the other (photo). Provided the thrust washers at the centre bearing have been renewed, the endfloat should be within specified tolerance. If it is not, oversize thrust washers are available (see Specifications).

8   The pistons/connecting rods should now be installed. Although new pistons may have been fitted to the rods by your dealer or supplier due to the special tools needed, it is worth checking to ensure that with the piston crown arrow or cast nipple in the piston oil cut-out pointing towards the timing belt end of the engine, the F mark on the connecting rod or the oil ejection hole in the rod big-end is as shown (Fig. 1.63).

9   Oil the cylinder bores and install the pistons/connecting rods as described in Section 33.

10 Fit the oil pressure switch.

11 Before fitting the oil pump, action must be taken to prevent damage to the pump oil seal from the step on the front end of the crankshaft. First remove the Woodruff key and then build up the front end of the crankshaft using adhesive tape to form a smooth inclined surface to permit the pump seal to slide over the step without its lip turning back or the seal spring being displaced during installation (photo).

12 If the oil pump is new, pour some oil into it before installation in order to prime it and rotate its driving gear a few turns (photo).

13 Align the pump gear flats with those on the crankshaft and install the oil pump complete with new gasket. Tighten the bolts to the specified torque (photo).

14 Remove the adhesive tape and tap the Woodruff key into its groove (photo).

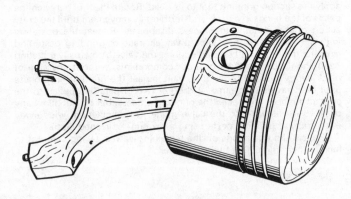

Fig. 1.63 Piston/connecting rod orientation (Sec 42)

15 Bolt the oil pump pick-up tube into position (photo).

16 To the front end of the crankshaft, fit the thrust washer (belt guide) so that its concave side is towards the pump (photo).

17 Fit the crankshaft belt sprocket. If it is tight, draw it into position using the pulley bolt and a distance piece. Make sure that the belt retaining flange on the sprocket is towards the front of the crankshaft and the nose of the shaft has been smeared with a little grease before fitting (photo).

18 Install the water pump using a new gasket and tightening the bolts to the specified torque (photo).

19 Fit the timing belt tensioner and its coil spring (where fitted). Lever the tensioner fully against spring pressure and temporarily tighten the bolts.

20 Using a new gasket, bolt on the rear oil seal retainer, which will

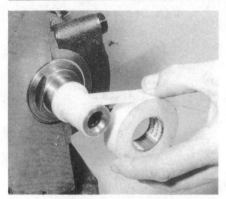

42.11 Using masking tape to eliminate the step on the crankshaft

42.12 Priming the oil pump prior to fitting

42.13 Oil pump installation

42.14 Crankshaft Woodruff key installation

42.15 Fitting the oil pump pick-up tube

42.16 Fit the timing belt guide with its concave side towards the pump

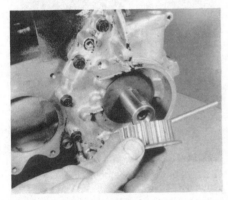

42.17 Fitting the crankshaft sprocket with the flange outward

42.18 Fitting the water pump

42.20 Crankshaft rear oil seal retainer with new seal prior to fitting

have been fitted with a new oil seal and the seal lips greased (photo).

21 Engage the engine adaptor plate on its locating dowels and then offer up the flywheel. It will only go on in one position as it has offset holes. Insert new bolts and tighten to the specified torque. The bolts should be pre-coated with thread sealant (photos).

22 Fit the clutch and centralise it (refer to Chapter 5).

23 With the engine resting on its side (not inverted unless you are quite sure that the pistons are not projecting from the block), fit the sump, gaskets and sealing strips as described in Section 32.

24 Fit the cylinder head as described in Section 29 or 30, using new bolts. Refit the manifolds (photo).

25 Install and tension the timing belt as described in Section 26.

26 Using a new gasket, fit the rocker cover.

27 Reconnect the crankcase ventilation hoses between the rocker cover and the crankcase (photos).

28 Screw in a new set of spark plugs, correctly gapped, and tighten to the specified torque – this is important. If the specified torque is exceeded, the plugs may be impossible to remove (see Chapter 4).

29 Fit the timing belt cover.

30 Fit the crankshaft pulley and tighten the bolt to the specified torque while the flywheel ring gear is locked to prevent it turning.

31 Smear the sealing ring of a new oil filter with a little grease, and screw it into position using hand pressure only. Where applicable, refit the oil cooler at the same time.

32 Install the engine mounting brackets, if removed (photo).

33 Refit the ancillaries. The alternator bracket and alternator (Chapter 12), the fuel pump (Chapter 3), the thermostat housing (Chapter 2), and the distributor (Chapter 4) (photo).

34 Fit the distributor cap and reconnect the HT leads.

35 Check the tightness of the oil drain plug and insert the dipstick.

42.21A Locate the adaptor plate on the dowels ...

42.21B ... fit the flywheel to the crankshaft ...

42.21C ... apply thread locking compound to the flywheel retaining bolts ...

42.21D ... and secure the flywheel

42.24A Fit the inlet manifold gasket ...

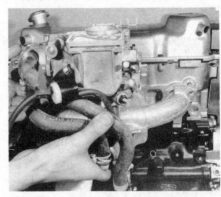

42.24B ... and manifold

42.24C Fit the exhaust manifold gasket ...

42.24D ... and the manifold

42.27A Connecting the crankcase rear ventilation hose ...

42.27B ... and the front hose

42.32 Fitting the right-hand engine mounting

42.33 Fitting the alternator mounting bracket

43 Engine/transmission – reconnection and installation

1 This is a direct reversal of removal and separation from the transmission. Take care not to damage the radiator or front wings during installation.

Reconnection

2 Make sure that the engine adaptor plate is correctly located on its dowels.

3 On manual transmission models check that the clutch driven plate has been centralised as described in Chapter 5. Smear the splines of the transmission input shaft with molybdenum disulphide grease and then, supporting the weight of the transmission, connect it to the engine by passing the input shaft through the splined hub of the clutch plate until the transmission locates on the dowels. Screw in the bolts and tighten to the specified torque. Refit the clutch cover plate and the starter motor (photo).

4 On automatic transmission models ensure that the torque converter is fully seated on the transmission, then locate the transmission on the engine dowels while at the same time guiding the torque converter studs through the holes in the driveplate. Screw in the engine-to-transmission bolts and tighten to the specified torque. Turn the crankshaft to provide access to each of the torque converter studs in turn, then fit and tighten the nuts. Refit the cover plate and the starter motor.

Installation

5 First check that the engine sump drain plug is tight and then, where applicable refit the selector shaft cap nut (removed to drain the manual transmission oil) together with its spring and interlock pin (photo). Apply sealer to the cap nut threads when refitting (see Specifications – Chapter 6).

6 Manoeuvre the engine/transmission under the vehicle and attach the lifting hoist. Raise the engine/transmission carefully until the right-hand rear mounting can be engaged. Refit the mounting nut and bolt but loosely only at this stage.

7 On pre-1986 models refit the front mounting and anti-roll bar support plates, then refit the left-hand front and rear mountings loosely only.

8 On 1986 models onwards, refit the transmission support crossmember.

9 Lower the hoist and let the power unit rest on its mountings. Ensure that none of the mountings are under strain, then tighten all the mounting nuts and bolts to the specified torque and remove the hoist.

10 The driveshafts and suspension arms should now be refitted using the procedure described in Chapter 8, Section 5, paragraphs 22 to 24 for each side.

11 Refit the anti-roll bar clamps and mounting plates as applicable.

12 On cars equipped with an Anti-lock Braking System (ABS), refit the modulators, drivebelts and the pipe mounting bracket, then adjust the modulator drivebelt tension as described in Chapter 9.

13 Refit the engine splash shields.

14 On automatic transmission models reconnect the fluid cooler pipes, then reconnect and adjust the selector cable and downshift linkage as described in Chapter 7.

15 On manual transmission models reconnect and adjust the gearchange linkage using the procedure described in Chapter 6, Section 3.

16 On RS Turbo models refer to Chapter 3 and refit the turbocharger.

17 Refit the exhaust system and bolt the downpipe to the manifold.

18 Check that everything has been reconnected underneath, then lower the car to the ground.

19 Where applicable reconnect the clutch operating cable.

20 Reconnect the transmission earth strap and speedometer cable.

21 Reconnect the coolant and heater hoses.

22 Reconnect the accelerator cable and where fitted the choke cable and adjust as described in Chapter 3.

23 Reconnect all fuel and vacuum hoses and pipes with reference to Chapter 3 where necessary. Use screw type hose clips to secure any hoses originally retained with crimped clips. On fuel-injection models use new sealing washers on each side of the banjo unions.

24 Reconnect all electrical wiring with reference to Chapters 2, 3, 4 and 12 and to any notes made during removal.

25 Fill up with engine oil, transmission oil or fluid and coolant, then reconnect the battery (photo).

26 Refit the bonnet and the air cleaner or on RS Turbo models the intake air duct.

27 Once the engine is running check the dwell angle, timing, idle speed and mixture as described in Chapters 3 and 4.

28 If a number of new internal components have been installed, run the vehicle at a restricted speed for the first few hundred miles to allow time for the new components to bed in. It is also recommended that with a new or rebuilt engine, the engine oil and filter are changed at the end of the running-in period.

44 Fault diagnosis – CVH engine

Refer to Part A: Section 21.

43.3 Connecting the engine and manual transmission

43.5 Fitting the selector shaft cap nut, spring and interlock pin

40.25 Filling the engine with oil

Chapter 2 Cooling system

For modifications, and information applicable to later models, see Supplement at end of manual

Contents

Specifications

System type .... Pressurised, pump-assisted thermo-syphon with front mounted radiator and electric cooling fan

Pressure cap rating
Up to 1986:
   1.1 litre OHV engine .... 0.9 bar (13.0 lbf/in²)
   1.3 and 1.6 litre CHV engine .... 0.85 to 1.1 bar (12.0 to 15.7 lbf/in²)
1986 onwards .... 0.98 to 1.2 bar (14.2 to 17.0 lbf/in²)

Thermostat
Type .... Wax
Start to open temperature .... 85° to 89°C (189° to 192°F)
Fully open temperature .... 102°C (223°F) (± 3°C/5°F for used thermostats)

Antifreeze
Type/specification .... Antifreeze to Ford specification SSM-97B 9103-A (Duckhams Universal Antifreeze and Summer Coolant)

Recommended concentration .... 45% by volume

Torque wrench settings

	Nm	lbf ft
Radiator mounting bolts:		
Pre-1986 models	6.8 to 9.5	5.0 to 7.0
1986 models onwards	20 to 27	14.8 to 20
Thermostat housing bolts:		
OHV engines	17 to 21	12.5 to 15.5
CVH engines	9 to 12	6.6 to 8.9
Water pump bolts:		
OHV engines	7 to 10	5.2 to 7.4
CVH engines	6.8 to 9.5	5 to 7
Water pump pulley (OHV engines)	8.5 to 10.6	6.3 to 7.8
Fan shroud to radiator:		
Pre-1986 models	6.8 to 9.5	5 to 7
1986 models onwards	3 to 5	2.2 to 3.7
Fan motor to shroud	8.6 to 12	6.3 to 8.8
Radiator drain plug	1.2 to 1.5	0.9 to 1.1

PART A: OHV ENGINES

1 General description

The cooling system is of the pressurised pump-assisted thermo-syphon type. The system consists of the radiator, water pump, thermostat, electric cooling fan, expansion tank and associated hoses.

The system functions as follows. When the coolant is cold the thermostat is shut and coolant flow is restricted to the cylinder block, cylinder head, inlet manifold and the vehicle interior heater matrix. As the temperature of the coolant rises, the thermostat opens allowing the coolant to pass into the radiator. The coolant now circulates through the radiator where it is cooled by the inrush of air when the car is in forward motion, supplemented by the operation of the radiator cooling fan. Coolant is then circulated from the base of the radiator, up through the water pump which is driven by a vee-belt from the crankshaft pulley, and into the cylinder block to complete the circuit.

When the engine is at normal operating temperature the coolant expands, and some of it is displaced into the expansion tank. The coolant collects in the tank and is returned to the radiator when the system cools. On 1.1 litre engines the system pressure cap is fitted to the thermostat housing and the expansion tank acts as a simple overflow bottle. On 1.3 litre engines the pressure cap is fitted to the expansion tank which is pressurised with the rest of the system.

The radiator cooling fan is mounted behind the radiator and controlled by a thermal switch located in the thermostat housing. When the coolant reaches a predetermined temperature the switch contacts close thus actuating the fan. On certain early models however, a thermal switch was not used and the cooling fan operated continuously whenever the ignition was switched on.

2 Maintenance and inspection

1   At the intervals specified in *'Routine maintenance'* at the beginning of this manual check the coolant level in the expansion tank when the engine is cold. The level should be between the 'MAX' and 'MIN' marks on the side of the tank

2   If the level is low, release the pressure cap on the thermostat housing by slowly turning it anti-clockwise until it reaches its stop. Wait until any pressure in the system has escaped, then press the cap downwards and turn it further in an anti-clockwise direction. Release the downward pressure slowly and remove the cap. Now lift up the filler cap on the expansion tank. Note that on later models a screw type pressure cap is fitted to the expansion tank and the cap on the thermostat housing is omitted. On these models slowly unscrew and then remove the expansion tank pressure cap.

3   Top up the expansion tank with a water and antifreeze mixture (see Section 4) until the level is up to the 'MAX' mark, then refit the caps. The system should only be topped up at the expansion tank, **not** at the thermostat housing.

4   With a sealed type cooling system topping-up should only be necessary at very infrequent intervals. If this is not the case, it is likely that there is a leak in the system. Check all hoses and joint faces for any staining or actual wetness, and rectify as necessary. If no leaks can be

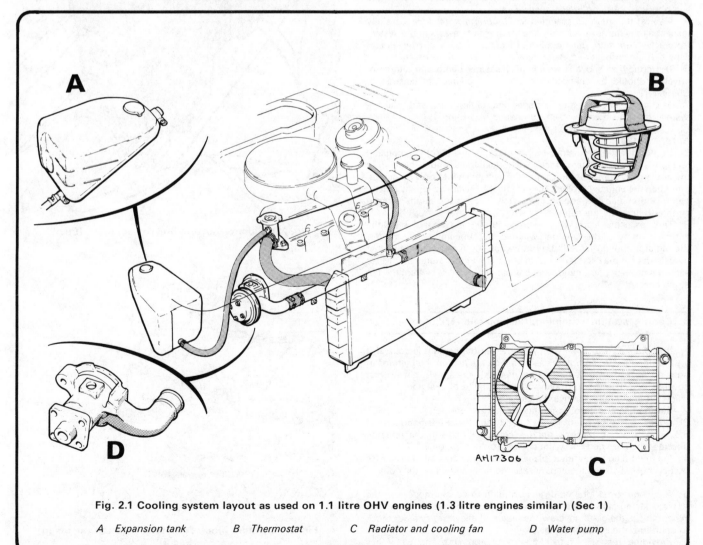

Fig. 2.1 Cooling system layout as used on 1.1 litre OHV engines (1.3 litre engines similar) (Sec 1)

A   Expansion tank   B   Thermostat   C   Radiator and cooling fan   D   Water pump

Fig. 2.2 Coolant level markings on expansion tank (Sec 2)

3.3 Radiator drain plug location (arrowed)

found it is advisable to have the system pressure tested, as the leak could possibly be internal. It is a good idea to keep a check on the engine oil level as a serious internal leak can often cause the level in the sump to rise, thus confirming suspicions.

5   Also, at the intervals specified in *'Routine maintenance'* carefully inspect all the hoses, hose clips, and visible joint gaskets of the system for cracks, corrosion, deterioration or leakage. Renew any hoses and clips that are suspect and also renew any gaskets, if necessary.

6   The condition and adjustment of the water pump and alternator drivebelt should be checked and these procedures are covered in Chapter 12.

7   At the less frequent intervals specified, drain, flush, and refill the system using fresh antifreeze, as described in Section 4.

Safety notes

8   Do not remove the thermostat housing pressure cap (or expansion tank pressure cap on later models) when the engine is hot. Checking of the coolant level and topping-up of the system should only be carried out when the engine is cold. If the cap must be removed for any reason before the engine has cooled completely, protect the hands using a cloth and unscrew the cap very slowly.

9   Take particular care when working under the bonnet with the engine running or the ignition switched on. On certain early models the radiator cooling fan will be running all the time, but on all other models the fan may suddenly cut in as engine temperature rises. Make sure that clothing, ties, hands and hair are kept well away from the fan at all times.

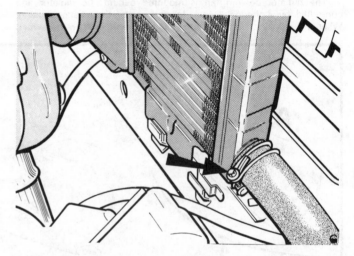

Fig. 2.3 Radiator bottom hose attachment (Sec 3)

3   Cooling system – draining, flushing and refilling

1   It is preferable to drain the system when the coolant is cold. If it must be drained when hot, release the pressure cap on the thermostat housing (or expansion tank on later models) very slowly, having first covered it with a cloth to avoid any possibility of scalding. Having relieved the pressure, remove the cap.

2   Set the heater control to the maximum heat position.

3   Check to see if a drain plug is fitted to the lower left-hand side of the radiator. If so, place a suitable container beneath the radiator, unscrew the plug and allow the coolant to drain (photo).

4   If a drain plug is not fitted, place the container beneath the radiator bottom hose. Slacken the clip, release the hose and allow the coolant to drain.

5   A cylinder block drain plug is also fitted to certain models on the forward facing side of the cylinder block, towards the flywheel end. Where this is the case, unscrew the plug and allow the cylinder block to drain into the container (Fig. 2.4).

6   Providing that the correct mixture of antifreeze and water has previously been maintained in the system, then no flushing should be

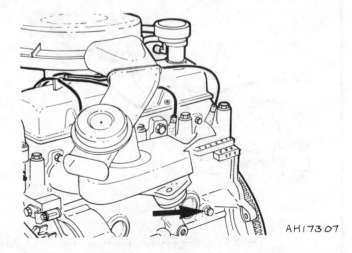

AH17307

Fig. 2.4 Cylinder block drain plug location (arrowed)
(Sec 3)

necessary and the system can be refilled immediately as described in the following paragraphs.

7   Where the system has been neglected however, and rust or sludge is evident at draining, then the system should be flushed through using a cold water hose inserted into the thermostat housing (thermostat removed – see Section 7). Continue flushing until the water flows clean from the disconnected bottom hose, radiator drain plug and cylinder block drain plug, as applicable. If, after a reasonable period the water still does not run clear, the radiator can be flushed with a good proprietary cleaning system such as Holts Radflush or Holts Speedflush.

8   If the radiator is suspected of being clogged, remove and reverse flush it as described in Section 6.

9   When the coolant is being changed, it is recommended that the overflow pipe is disconnected from the expansion tank and the coolant drained from the tank. If the interior of the tank is dirty, remove it and thoroughly clean it out.

10 After draining or flushing, reconnect all disconnected hoses and refit the drain plugs where applicable.

11 Using the correct antifreeze mixture (See Section 4) fill the system through the thermostat housing filler neck slowly until the coolant is nearly overflowing. Wait a few moments for trapped air to escape and add more coolant. Repeat until the level does not drop and refit the cap. Pour similar strength coolant into the expansion tank up to the 'MAX' mark and fit the cap.

12 On later models with a screw type pressure cap on the expansion tank, fill the system in the same way, but through the expansion tank rather than the thermostat housing.

13 On all models start the engine and run it to normal operating temperature then switch off. Once it has cooled, check and carry out any final topping-up to the expansion tank only.

4 Antifreeze mixture

1   Never operate the vehicle with plain water in the cooling system. Apart from the danger of freezing during winter conditions, an important secondary purpose of antifreeze is to inhibit the formation of rust and to reduce corrosion.

2   The coolant must be renewed at the intervals specified in *'Routine maintenance'* at the beginning of this manual. Although the antifreeze properties of the coolant will remain indefinitely, the effectiveness of the rust and corrosion inhibitors will gradually weaken.

3   It is recommended that Ford Super Plus antifreeze is used for filling and topping-up, as it has been specially formulated for use in Ford mixed metal engines (see *'Recommended lubricants and fluids'* at the beginning of this manual).

4   A solution of 45% antifreeze must be maintained in the system all year round which will provide adequate protection against frost, rust and corrosion.

5   After filling with antifreeze, a label should be attached to the radiator stating the type of antifreeze and the date installed. Any subsequent topping-up should be made with the same type and concentration of antifreeze.

6   Do not use engine antifreeze in the screen washer system, as it will cause damage to the vehicle paintwork. Screen wash antifreeze is available from most motor accessory shops.

5 Radiator fan – removal and refitting

1   Disconnect the battery negative terminal.

2   Disconnect the wiring plug at the fan motor and unclip the wiring from the shroud.

3   On pre-1986 models the fan shroud is secured to the radiator with four bolts. Unscrew the two upper bolts and slacken the two lower bolts.

4   For 1986 models onwards the shroud is retained by two bolts at the top and two clips at the bottom. Unscrew the two upper bolts.

5   On all models carefully lift the fan and shroud assembly upwards and out of the engine compartment, taking care not to damage the radiator.

6   Extract the retaining clip and remove the fan from the motor shaft.

7   Unscrew the three nuts and separate the motor from the shroud.

8   Reassembly and refitting are reversals of the removal and dismantling operations.

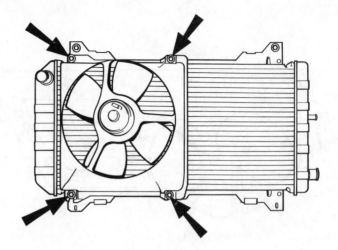

Fig. 2.5 Radiator fan shroud retaining bolts – pre-1986 models (Sec 5)

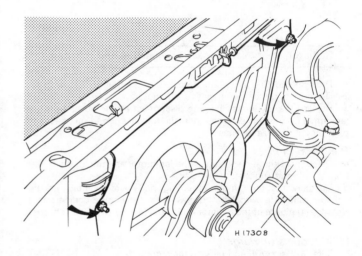

Fig. 2.6 Radiator fan shroud retaining bolts – 1986 models onwards (Sec 5)

Fig. 2.7 Fan motor retaining nuts – pre-1986 models (Sec 5)

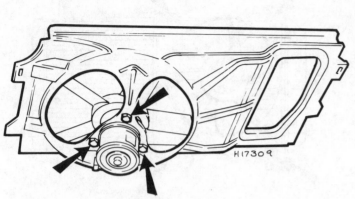

Fig. 2.8 Fan motor retaining nuts – 1986 models onwards (Sec 5)

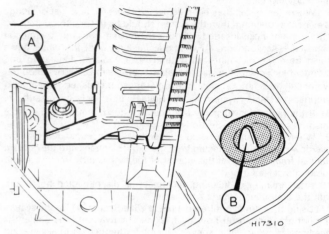

Fig. 2.9 Radiator lower retaining bolts (A) and upper lugs (B) – 1986 models onwards (Sec 6)

6 Radiator – removal, inspection, cleaning and refitting

1   Drain the cooling system as described in Section 3.
2   Disconnect the battery negative terminal.
3   Release the retaining clips and disconnect all the hoses from the radiator, and on vehicles with automatic transmission, disconnect and plug the oil cooler pipelines.

Pre-1986 models
4   Disconnect the wiring plug at the fan motor and unclip the wiring from the shroud (photo).
5   Unscrew the two upper mounting bolts and carefully lift the radiator, complete with fan and cowl from the engine compartment. Note that the base of the radiator is held in place by two lugs (photos).

1986 models onwards
6   Refer to Section 5 and remove the radiator fan.
7   To provide greater clearance for radiator removal, slacken the alternator mounting and adjustment arm bolts and push the alternator in towards the engine as far as it will go.
8   Unscrew the two radiator lower retaining bolts.
9   Move the bottom of the radiator in towards the engine, then lower it to disengage the two upper retaining lugs. Carefully lift the radiator from the engine compartment.

All models
10 If the purpose of removal was to thoroughly clean the radiator, first reverse flush it with a cold water hose. The normal coolant flow is from left to right (from the thermostat housing to the radiator) through the matrix and out of the opposite side.
11 If the radiator fins are clogged with flies or dirt, remove them with a soft brush or blow compressed air from the rear face of the radiator. It is recommended that the fan assembly is first removed as described in the preceding Section (if not already done). In the absence of a compressed air line, a strong jet from a water hose may provide an alternative method of cleaning.
12 If the radiator is leaking, it is recommended that a reconditioned or new one is obtained from specialists. In an emergency, minor leaks can be cured by using a radiator sealant such as Holts Radweld. If the radiator, due to neglect, requires the application of chemical cleaners, such as Holts Radflush or Holts Speedflush, then these are best used when the engine is hot and the radiator is in the vehicle. Follow the manufacturer's instructions precisely and appreciate that there is an element of risk in the use of most de-scaling products, especially in a system which incorporates alloy and plastic materials.
13 Refit the radiator by reversing the removal operations, but ensure that the rubber lug insulators are in position. Fill the cooling system as described in Section 3 and on later models adjust the alternator drivebelt as described in Chapter 12.

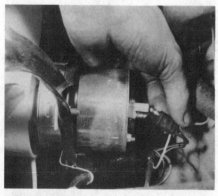

6.4 Disconnecting radiator fan wiring plug

6.5A Undo the radiator upper bolts ...

6.5B ... and lift out the unit complete with fan

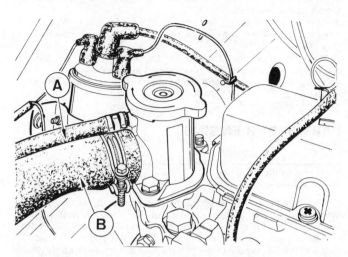

Fig. 2.10 Expansion tank hose (A) and radiator top hose (B) attachments at thermostat housing (Sec 7)

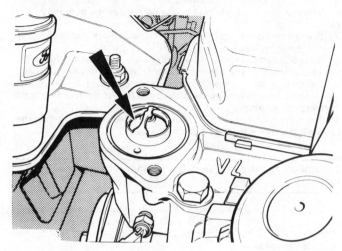

Fig. 2.11 Thermostat location in cylinder head (Sec 7)

7 Thermostat – removal, testing and refitting

1 Drain the cooling system as described in Section 3.
2 Slacken the clips and disconnect the hoses at the thermostat housing. Disconnect the radiator fan thermal switch wiring plug.
3 Unscrew the two bolts and remove the thermostat housing cover. If it is tight carefully tap it with a soft-faced mallet.
4 Extract the thermostat. If it is stuck tight in its seat, do not lever it out by its bridge piece, but cut round it with a very sharp knife.
5 To test the thermostat, first check that in a cold condition its valve plate is closed. Suspend it on a string in a pan of cold water together with a thermometer. Heat the water and check that the thermostat starts to open at the temperature given in the Specifications. It is difficult to check that the thermostat opens fully, as this occurs at a temperature above the boiling point of water.
6 Remove the thermostat from the water and check that the valve closes as the unit cools. If the thermostat does not operate as described, obtain a new thermostat.

7 Refitting is the reverse sequence to removal, but ensure that all traces of old gasket are removed from the housing mating faces and use a new gasket lightly smeared with jointing compound. Tighten the retaining bolts to the specified torque.
8 On completion, refill the cooling system as described in Section 3.

8 Water pump – removal and refitting

1 Drain the cooling system as described in Section 3.
2 Slacken the three water pump pulley retaining bolts. Any tendency for the pulley to turn as the bolts are undone can be restrained by depressing the top run of the drivebelt.
3 Release the alternator mounting and adjustment arm bolts, push the alternator in towards the engine and slip the drivebelt off the pulleys.
4 Unscrew the previously slackened pulley bolts and remove the pulley.

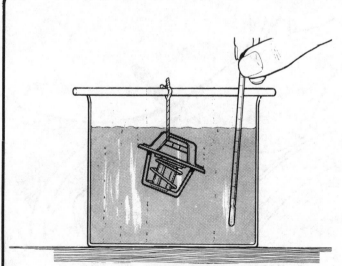

Fig. 2.12 Testing the thermostat (Sec 7)

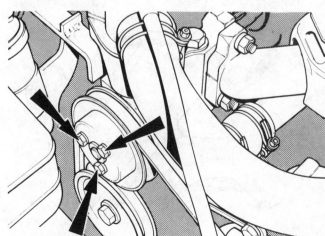

Fig. 2.13 Water pump pulley retaining bolts (Sec 8)

5　Release the clip and disconnect the hose at the pump outlet.

6　Unscrew the three retaining bolts and remove the pump from the cylinder block.

7　Peel away the old gasket from the cylinder block and thoroughly clean the mating face.

8　No provision is made for repair of the water pump and if the unit is leaking, noisy, or in any way unserviceable, renewal will be necessary.

9　Refitting is the reverse sequence to removal. Use a new gasket lightly smeared with jointing compound and tighten the retaining bolts to the specified torque.

10　Refill the cooling system as described in Section 3 and adjust the drivebelt tension as described in Chapter 12.

9 Radiator fan thermal switch – testing, removal and refitting

1　The thermal switch is located on the side of the thermostat housing on early models and in the thermostat housing cover on later versions. If the operation of the radiator fan is suspect, the thermal switch may be tested as follows.

2　Disconnect the wiring plug and bridge the two plug terminals with a length of wire or suitable metal object. The fan should now operate with the ignition switched on. If it does, the thermal switch is proved faulty and must be renewed. If the fan still does not operate, check the appropriate fuses, wiring and connections. If these are satisfactory it is likely that the fan motor itself is faulty.

3　To renew the thermal switch wait until the engine is cold, then remove the pressure cap on the thermostat housing or expansion tank as applicable.

4　Place a container beneath the thermostat housing to collect the small amount of coolant that will be released when the switch is removed.

5　Disconnect the wiring plug and unscrew the switch from its location.

6　Using a new sealing washer, refit and tighten the switch securely. Fit the wiring plug and top up the system as described in Section 3.

10 Temperature gauge sender unit – removal and refitting

1　With the engine cold unscrew the pressure cap on the thermostat housing or expansion tank as applicable, then refit it. This will release any residual pressure in the system and minimise coolant loss when the sender unit is removed.

2　Disconnect the wiring and unscrew the sender unit located on the forward facing side of the cylinder head, below the thermostat housing (Fig. 2.15).

3　To refit, smear the threads of the sender unit with jointing compound and screw it into the cylinder head securely.

4　Reconnect the wiring and top up the cooling system as described in Section 3.

PART B: CVH ENGINES

11 General description

The cooling system is of the pressurised pump-assisted thermo-syphon type. The system consists of the radiator, water pump, thermostat, electric cooling fan, expansion tank and associated hoses.

The system functions as follows. When the coolant is cold the thermostat is shut and and the coolant flow is restricted to the cylinder block, cylinder head, inlet manifold and the vehicle interior heater matrix. As the temperature of the coolant rises, the thermostat opens allowing the coolant to pass into the radiator. The coolant now circulates through the radiator where it is cooled by the inrush of air when the car is in forward motion, supplemented by the operation of the radiator cooling fan when necessary. Coolant is then circulated from the base of the radiator, up through the water pump which is driven by the engine timing belt, and into the cylinder block to complete the circuit.

When the engine is at normal operating temperature the coolant expands and some of it is displaced into the expansion tank. This coolant collects in the tank and is returned to the radiator when the system cools. On 1.1 litre engines the pressure cap is fitted to the thermostat housing and the expansion tank acts as a simple overflow bottle. On all other engines the pressure cap is fitted to the expansion tank which is pressurised with the rest of the system.

On all engines except 1.1 litre versions the radiator cooling fan is controlled by a thermal switch located in the thermostat housing. When the coolant reaches a predetermined temperature the switch contacts close thus actuating the fan. On 1.1 litre engines with standard equipment the cooling fan operates continuously whenever the ignition is switched on.

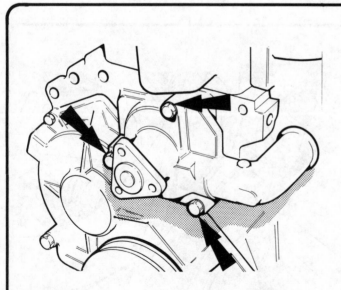

Fig. 2.14 Water pump retaining bolts (Sec 8)

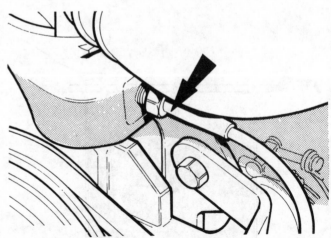

Fig. 2.15 Temperature gauge sender unit location in cylinder head (Sec 10)

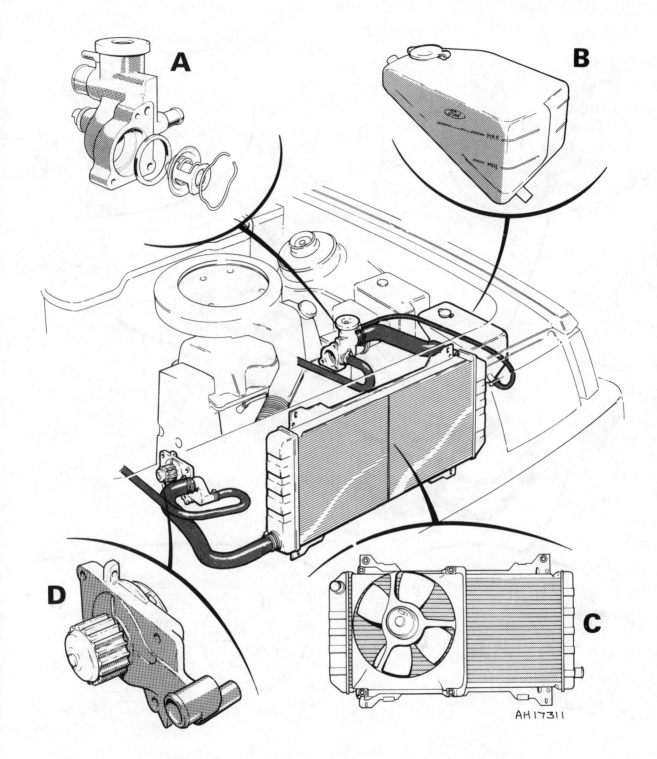

AH17311

Fig. 2.16 Cooling system layout as used on 1.1 litre CVH engines (Sec 11)

A   Thermostat and housing
B   Expansion tank
C   Radiator and cooling fan
D   Water pump

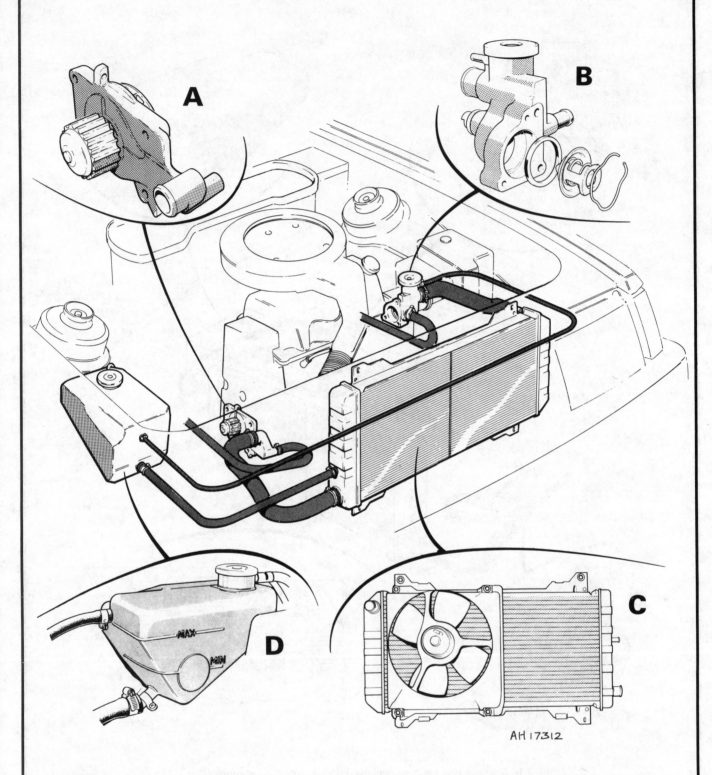

Fig. 2.17 Cooling system layout as used on pre-1986 1.3 and 1.6 litre CVH engines (later models similar) (Sec 11)

A   Water pump   B   Thermostat and housing   C   Radiator and cooling fan   D   Expansion tank

12 Maintenance and inspection

1   At the intervals specified in *'Routine maintenance'* at the beginning of this manual check the coolant level in the expansion tank when the engine is cold. The level should be between the 'MAX' and 'MIN' marks on the side of the tank (photo).

2   If the level is low, release the pressure cap (located on the thermostat housing on 1.1 litre engines and on the expansion tank on all other engines) by slowly turning it anti-clockwise until it reaches its stop. Wait until any pressure in the system has escaped, then press the cap downwards and turn it further in an anti-clockwise direction. Release the downward pressure slowly and remove the cap. Note that on later models a screw type pressure cap is fitted to the expansion tank and the cap on the thermostat housing is omitted. On these models slowly unscrew the cap a quarter of a turn, wait for the pressure in the system to escape, then remove the cap.

3   On 1.1 litre engines lift up the filler cap on the expansion tank.

4   Top up the expansion tank with a water and antifreeze mixture (see Part A: Section 4) until the level is up to the 'MAX' mark, then refit the caps. The system should be topped up at the expansion tank, *not* at the thermostat housing (photo).

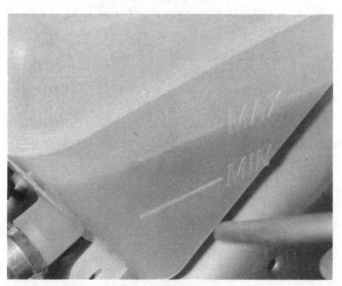

12.1 Coolant level markings on expansion tank

12.4 Top up the system at the expansion tank only

5   With a sealed type cooling system, topping up should only be necessary at very infrequent intervals. If this is not the case it is likely that there is a leak in the system. Check all hoses and joint faces for any staining or actual wetness and rectify as necessary. If no leaks can be found it is advisable to have the system pressure tested as the leak could possibly be internal. It is a good idea to keep a check on the engine oil level, as a serious internal leak can often cause the level in the sump to rise, thus confirming suspicions.

6   Also, at the intervals specified in *'Routine maintenance'* carefully inspect all the hoses, hose clips and visible joint gaskets of the system for cracks, corrosion, deterioration or leakage. Renew any hoses and clips that are suspect and also renew any gaskets, if necessary.

7   At the less frequent intervals specified, drain, flush and refill the system using fresh antifreeze, as described in Section 13.

Safety notes

8   Do not remove the thermostat housing or expansion tank pressure caps when the engine is hot. Checking of the coolant level and topping up of the system should only be carried out when the engine is cold. If the cap must be removed for any reason before the engine has cooled completely, protect the hands using a cloth and unscrew the cap very slowly. On pre-1986 1.3 and 1.6 litre engines never remove the thermostat housing cap prior to the expansion tank cap, and never interchange the two caps. The pressure cap is fitted to the expansion tank and the plain cap to the thermostat housing.

9   Take particular care when working under the bonnet with the engine running or the ignition switched on. On 1.1 litre engines the radiator cooling fan may be running all the time and on other engines the fan may cut in at any time as the engine temperature rises. Make sure that clothing, ties, hands and hair are kept well away from the fan at all times.

13 Cooling system – draining, flushing and refilling

1   The procedure is the same as that for OHV engines as described in Part A: Section 3, but before draining, release the pressure cap on the thermostat housing for 1.1 litre engines or at the expansion tank for all other engines, when the coolant is cold.

2   The location of the cylinder block drain plug (where fitted) is shown in Fig. 2.18.

3   If the radiator is suspected of being clogged, remove and reverse flush it as described in Section 17 or 18 according to model.

14 Antifreeze mixture

Refer to Part A: Section 4.

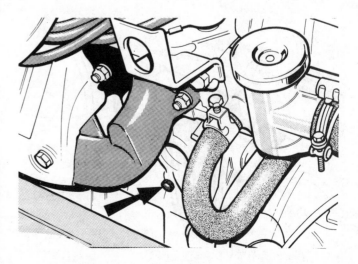

Fig. 2.18 Cylinder block drain plug location (arrowed)
(Sec 13)

15 Radiator fan (all models except RS Turbo) – removal and refitting

Refer to Part A: Section 5.

16 Radiator fan (RS Turbo models) – removal and refitting

1985 models

1   Disconnect the battery negative terminal.
2   Detach the transverse coolant hose from the two clips above the radiator.
3   Unscrew the three fan shroud retaining bolts.
4   Disconnect the upper and lower air hoses at the turbo intercooler mounted alongside the radiator.
5   Undo the two air cleaner retaining bolts and remove the air cleaner assembly.
6   Undo the single upper retaining screw and lift the intercooler to disengage the lower retaining peg. Remove the intercooler.
7   Undo the two upper radiator retaining bolts, disengage the lower guides and move the radiator towards the engine taking care not to stretch the hoses.
8   Disconnect the fan wiring multi-plug, release the cable tie and separate the fan wiring from the harness.
9   Carefully lift the fan up and out of its location. The fan, motor and shroud are serviced as an assembly on these models and further dismantling is not recommended.
10 Refitting is the reverse sequence to removal.

1986 models onwards

11 Disconnect the battery negative terminal.
12 Working through the aperture below the front bumper, release the wiring harness clips and unscrew the two shroud bracket retaining bolts – see Fig. 2.22 (photos).
13 Unhook the shroud from the top of the radiator, disconnect the wiring at the harness connector and remove the fan and shroud assembly from the front of the radiator.
14 Remove the fan guard from the shroud.
15 Extract the retaining circlip and washer, then withdraw the fan from the motor shaft.
16 Unscrew the three nuts, unclip the wiring and remove the motor from the shroud.
17 Reassembly and refitting are the reversals of the removal and dismantling operations.

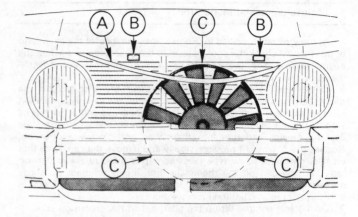

Fig. 2.19 Radiator fan removal details – 1985 RS Turbo (Sec 16)

A   Transverse cooling hose
B   Transverse cooling hose clips
C   Fan shroud retaining bolts

Fig. 2.20 Air cleaner retaining bolts (A) – 1985 RS Turbo (Sec 16)

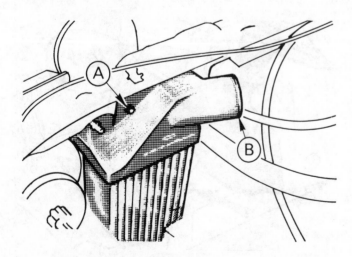

Fig. 2.21 Intercooler retaining bolt (A) and upper air hose connection (B) – 1985 RS Turbo (Sec 16)

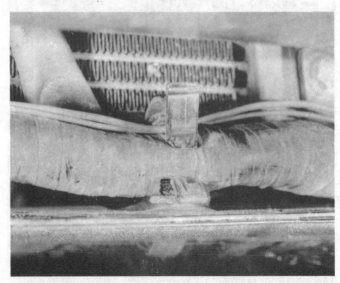

16.12A Release the wiring harness clips ...

16.12B ... to gain access to the fan shroud bolts on 1986 RS Turbo models

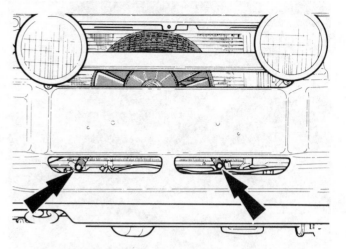

Fig. 2.22 Fan shroud bracket retaining bolts – RS Turbo from 1986 onwards (Sec 16)

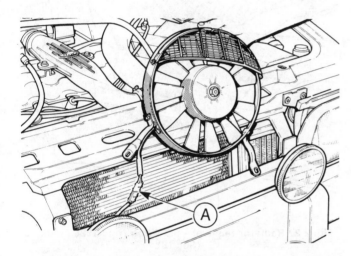

Fig. 2.23 Radiator fan removal – RS Turbo from 1986 onwards (Sec 16)

A   Wiring harness connector

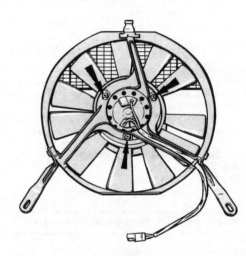

Fig. 2.24 Fan motor retaining nuts (arrowed) – RS Turbo from 1986 onwards (Sec 16)

17 Radiator (all models except RS Turbo) – removal, inspection, cleaning and refitting

Refer to Part A: Section 6.

18 Radiator (RS Turbo models) – removal, inspection, cleaning and refitting

1985 models

1   Drain the cooling system as described in Section 13.
2   Disconnect the battery negative terminal.
3   Release the retaining clips and disconnect all the coolant hoses from the radiator.
4   Refer to Section 16 and remove the radiator fan.
5   Lift the radiator up and out of the engine compartment.
6   For inspection and cleaning procedures refer to Part A: Section 6 paragraphs 10 to 12.
7   Refitting is the reverse sequence to removal. Fill the cooling system as described in Section 13.

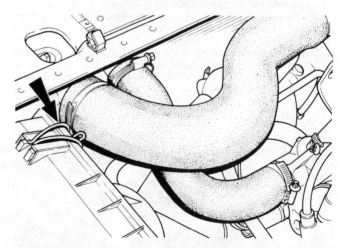

Fig. 2.25 Intercooler upper air hose attachment – RS Turbo from 1986 onwards (Sec 18)

1986 models onwards

8   Drain the cooling system as described in Section 13.
9   Disconnect the battery negative terminal.
10   Release the retaining clips and disconnect the coolant hoses at the radiator and the air hoses at the turbo intercooler (photo).

18.10 Turbo intercooler air hose attachment

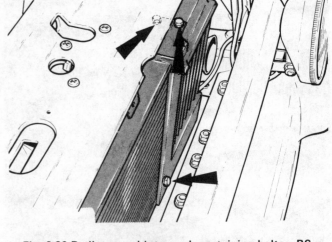

Fig. 2.26 Radiator and intercooler retaining bolts – RS Turbo from 1986 onwards (one lower bolt not shown) (Sec 18)

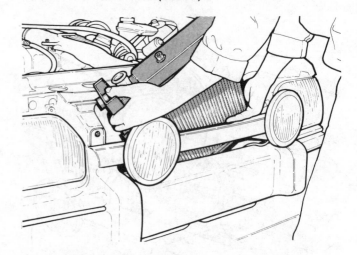

Fig. 2.27 Radiator removal – RS Turbo from 1986 onwards (Sec 18)

11 Refer to Section 16 and remove the radiator fan.
12 Undo the two radiator and intercooler lower retaining bolts.
13 Undo the four bolts securing the intercooler to the radiator and remove the intercooler from the front.
14 Manipulate the radiator up and out of its location from the front.
15 For inspection and cleaning procedures refer to Part A: Section 6, paragraphs 10 to 12.
16 Refitting is the reverse sequence to removal. Fill the cooling system as described in Section 13.

19 Thermostat – removal, testing and refitting

1   Drain the cooling system as described in Section 13.
2   Slacken the clips and disconnect the expansion tank hose, radiator hose and heater hose at the thermostat housing (photos).
3   Disconnect the radiator fan thermal switch wiring plug (photo).
4   Unscrew the three bolts and remove the thermostat housing from the cylinder head. If it is stuck, tap it off carefully with a soft-faced mallet.
5   Extract the retaining spring clip and withdraw the thermostat from the housing followed by the sealing ring (photos).
6   To test the thermostat refer to Part A: Section 7, paragraphs 5 and 6.
7   Before refitting, scrape away all traces of old gasket from the

cylinder head and thermostat housing and ensure that the mating faces are clean and dry.
8   Refitting is the reverse sequence to removal, but use a new sealing ring and a new gasket lightly smeared with jointing compound. Tighten the retaining bolts to the specified torque and on completion fill the cooling system as described in Section 13.

19.2A Disconnecting the radiator hose ...

19.2B ... and expansion tank hose at the thermostat housing

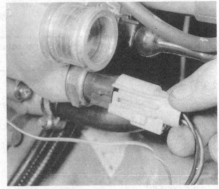

19.3 Disconnecting fan thermal switch wiring plug

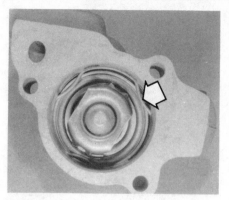

19.5A Extract the retaining spring clip (arrowed) ...

19.5B ... withdraw the thermostat ...

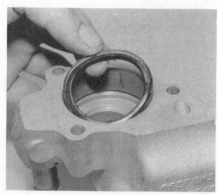

19.5C ... and remove the sealing ring

20 Water pump – removal and refitting

Note: *The following procedure entails the use of special tools to tension the timing belt after refitting the water pump. Read through the entire Section to familiarise yourself with the procedure and refer also to Chapter 1, Section 26.*

1 Drain the cooling system as described in Section 13.

2 On carburettor engines refer to Chapter 3 and remove the air cleaner to improve access.

3 Slacken the alternator mounting and adjustment arm bolts, push the alternator in towards the engine and slip the drivebelt off the pulleys.

4 Using a spanner on the crankshaft pulley bolt, turn the crankshaft until the notch on the pulley is aligned with TDC (O) mark on the timing belt cover scale (Fig. 2.28). Now remove the distributor cap and check that the rotor arm is pointing towards the No 1 cylinder HT lead segment in the cap. If the rotor arm is pointing towards No 4 cylinder segment, turn the crankshaft through another complete turn and realign the pulley notch with the TDC mark.

5 On early models unscrew the four bolts and remove the one-piece timing belt cover. On later models fitted with a two-piece cover, unscrew the two upper bolts and remove the top half, then unscrew the two lower bolts. The lower half cannot be removed at this stage.

6 Using a dab of quick drying paint, mark the teeth of the timing belt and their notches on the sprockets so that the belt can be engaged in its original position on reassembly.

7 Slacken the two timing belt tensioner retaining bolts and slide the tensioner sideways to relieve the tautness of the belt. If the tensioner is spring-loaded, tighten one of the bolts to retain it in the slackened position.

8 Slip the timing belt off the camshaft, tensioner and water pump sprockets (photo).

9 Remove the bolts and lift off the tensioner and, where fitted, the tensioning spring (photo).

10 Slacken the clips and disconnect the hoses at the water pump (photo).

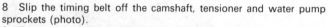

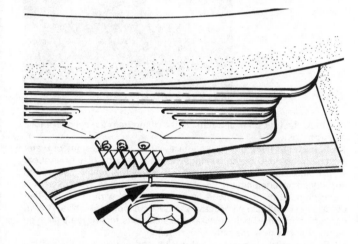

Fig. 2.28 Crankshaft pulley notch aligned with TDC (O) mark on timing belt cover scale (Sec 20)

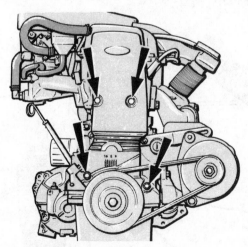

Fig. 2.29 Timing belt cover retaining bolts – early models with one-piece cover (Sec 20)

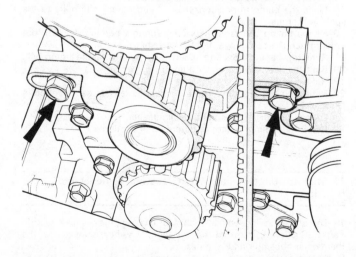

Fig. 2.30 Timing belt tensioner retaining bolts (Sec 20)

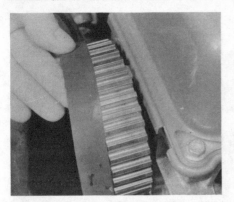

20.8 Removing the timing belt from the camshaft sprocket

20.9 Timing belt tensioner removal

20.10 Radiator hose attachment at water pump

20.11A Undo the four bolts ...

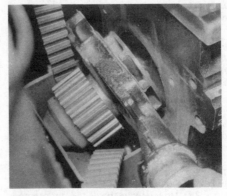

20.11B ... and remove the water pump

11 Undo the four bolts and remove the pump from the cylinder block face (photos).

12 Renewal of the pump will be necessary if there are signs of water leakage, roughness of the bearings, or excessive side play or endfloat at the sprocket. From 1983 onwards a revised water pump was introduced in conjunction with a two-piece timing belt cover. If a water pump is being renewed on an early model with one-piece belt cover, then it will also be necessary to obtain a replacement kit. This kit contains a modified belt cover and related parts to suit the later type pump which is now the only type supplied.

13 Scrape away all traces of old gasket and ensure that the mating faces are clean and dry.

14 Lightly smear jointing compound on both sides of a new gasket and locate the gasket on the cylinder block face.

15 Place the pump in position, then fit and tighten the bolts to the specified torque.

16 Fit the timing belt tensioners (and spring where applicable), but only tighten the bolts finger tight at this stage.

17 Refer to Chapter 1, Section 26 and refit and tension the timing belt.

18 Refit the hoses to the water pump.

19 Refit the timing belt cover(s).

20 Refit the alternator drivebelt and adjust its tension as described in Chapter 12.

21 On carburettor engines, refit the air cleaner.

22 Refill the cooling system as described in Section 13.

21 Radiator fan thermal switch – testing, removal and refitting

1 The procedure is identical to that for OHV engines as described in Part A: Section 9, but note that the thermal switch is located in the thermostat housing on all engines.

2 Before removing the switch, release the pressure cap on the thermostat housing for 1.1 litre engines or at the expansion tank for all other engines, when the coolant is cold.

22 Temperature gauge sender unit – removal and refitting

1 With the engine cold unscrew the pressure cap on the thermostat housing for 1.1 litre engines or at the expansion tank for all other engines, then refit it. This will release any residual pressure in the system and minimise coolant loss when the sender unit is removed.

2 Disconnect the wiring and unscrew the sender unit located on the forward facing side of the cylinder head, adjacent to the thermostat housing (Fig. 2.31).

3 To refit, smear the threads of the sender unit with jointing compound and screw it into the cylinder head securely.

4 Reconnect the wiring and top up the cooling system as described in Section 13.

Fig. 2.31 Temperature gauge sender unit location in cylinder head (Sec 22)

PART C: FAULT DIAGNOSIS

23 Fault diagnosis – cooling system

Symptom	Reason(s)
Overheating	Low coolant level (this may be the result of overheating for other reasons) Drivebelt slipping or broken (OHV engine only) Pressure cap faulty Thermostat defective Radiator blockage (internal or external), or grille restricted Ignition timing incorrect or distributor defective Faulty cooling fan thermal switch Faulty cooling fan Blown cylinder head gasket Water pump defective Faulty temperature gauge showing incorrect reading
Overcooling	Thermostat missing, defective or wrong heat range Faulty temperature gauge showing incorrect reading
Water loss – external	Loose hose clips Perished or cracked hoses Radiator core or side tank leaking Heater matrix leaking Pressure cap faulty Boiling due to overheating Leakage at component face on gasket Core plug leaking
Water loss – internal	Cylinder head gasket blown Cylinder head cracked or warped Crack or porosity in cylinder block, head or manifold
Corrosion	Infrequent draining and flushing Incorrect antifreeze mixture strength or incorrect type Combustion gasses contaminating coolant

Chapter 3
Fuel, exhaust and emission control systems

For modifications, and information applicable to later models, see Supplement at end of manual

Contents

Specifications

Carburettor engines

Air cleaner element

Application:

1.1 litre OHV engine	Champion W152
1.1 litre and 1.3 litre CVH engines	Champion W127
1.3 litre OHV engine	Champion W154
1.4 litre CVH engine:	
Up to October 1988	Champion W179
October 1988 on	Champion W226
1.6 litre CVH engine (except XR3 models):	
Up to 1986	Champion W169
1986 to October 1988	Champion W201
October 1988 on	Champion W226
1.6 litre CVH engine (XR3 models)	Champion W201

Fuel pump

Type	Mechanically-operated by eccentric on camshaft
Delivery pressure	0.24 to 0.38 bar (3.5 to 5.5 lbf/in²)

Carburettor
Type .... Ford variable venturi (VV) or Weber 2V
Application:
    1.1 litre OHV engine .... Ford VV
    1.1 litre CVH engine .... Ford VV
    1.3 litre OHV engine .... Ford VV
    1.3 litre CVH engine .... Ford VV
    1.4 litre CVH engine .... Weber 2V DFTM
    1.6 litre CVH engine (except XR3 models):
        Up to 1986 .... Ford VV
        1986 on .... Weber VV TLD
    1.6 litre CVH engine (XR3 models) .... Weber 2V DFT
Choke type:
    All models up to 1984 .... Automatic
    1.1 and 1.3 litre engines, 1984 on .... Manual
    1.4 and 1.6 litre engines, 1984 on .... Automatic

Ford carburettor specification
Idle speed (Cooling fan on):
    Manual transmission .... 750 to 850 rpm
    Automatic transmission .... 850 to 950 rpm
Idle mixture CO content .... 1.0 to 2.0%

Weber carburettor specification
Weber 2V DFTM:
    Idle speed (cooling fan on) .... 750 to 850 rpm
    Idle mixture CO content .... 1.25 to 1.75%
    Throttle kicker speed .... 1250 to 1350 rpm
    Fast idle speed .... 2600 to 2800 rpm
    Choke pull-down .... 2.7 to 3.2 mm (0.10 to 0.12 in)
    Float height .... 7.5 to 8.5 mm (0.30 to 0.33 in)

	Primary	Secondary
Venturi diameter	21 mm	23 mm
Air correction jet	200	165
Emulsion tube	F22	F60
Idle jet	42	60
Main jet	102	125

Weber 2V TLD:
    Idle speed (cooling fan on):
        Manual transmission .... 750 to 850 rpm
        Automatic transmission .... 850 to 950 rpm
    Idle mixture CO content .... 1.0 to 2.0%
    Throttle kicker speed .... 1050 to 1150 rpm
    Fast idle speed:
        Manual transmission .... 1850 to 1950 rpm
        Automatic transmission .... 1950 to 2050 rpm
    Choke pull-down:
        Manual transmission .... 4.0 to 5.0 mm (0.15 to 0.19 in)
        Automatic transmission .... 3.5 to 4.5 mm (0.13 to 0.17 in)
    Float height .... 28.5 to 29.5 mm (1.12 to 1.16 in)

	Primary	Secondary
Venturi diameter	21 mm	23 mm
Air correction jet	185	125
Emulsion tube	F105	F71
Main jet:		
Manual transmission	117	127
Automatic transmission	115	130

Weber 2V DFT:
    Idle speed (cooling fan on) .... 750 to 850 rpm
    Idle mixture CO content .... 1.0 to 1.5%
    Fast idle speed .... 2600 to 2800 rpm
    Choke pull-down .... 5.2 to 5.8 mm (0.20 to 0.22 in)
    Choke phasing .... 1.5 to 2.5 mm (0.06 to 0.09 in)
    Float height .... 34.5 to 35.5 mm (1.35 to 1.39 in)

	Primary	Secondary
Venturi diameter	24	25
Air correction jet	160	150
Emulsion tube	F30	F30
Idle jet	50	60
Main jet	115	125

Emission control system
Ported vacuum switch operating temperature:
    Two-port valve .... 52 to 55°C (125 to 131°F)
    Three-port valve .... 52 to 55°C (125 to 131°F)

Fuel requirement
Fuel octane rating .... 97 RON (four-star)

Torque wrench settings

	Nm	lbf ft
Carburettor to manifold	17 to 21	12 to 15
Fuel pump	16 to 20	11 to 14
Inlet manifold	16 to 20	11 to 14
Exhaust manifold	14 to 17	10 to 12
Exhaust downpipe to manifold	35 to 40	25 to 29
U-bolt clamps	35 to 40	25 to 29
Downpipe to front section connecting flange	35 to 47	25 to 34

Fuel-injected engines

General
System type .... Bosch K-Jetronic or KE-Jetronic continuous injection system
Application:
   XR3i and XR3i Cabriolet models .... Bosch K-Jetronic
   RS Turbo models .... Bosch KE-Jetronic
Fuel filter .... Champion L204

Air cleaner element
Champion U502

K-Jetronic system specification
Fuel pump type .... 12 volt electric roller cell type
Fuel pump delivery quantity (minimum) .... 0.7 litre (1.32 pints) in 30 seconds
Idle speed (cooling fan on) .... 750 to 850 rpm
Idle mixture CO content .... 1.0 to 1.5%
Main system pressure .... 4.7 to 5.5 bar (68 to 80 lbf/in²)
Control pressure (warm engine) .... 3.4 to 3.8 bar (39 to 45 lbf/in²)
Injector valve opening pressure .... 3.2 to 4.0 bar (46.4 to 51.5 lbf/in²)

KE-Jetronic system specification
Fuel pump type .... 12 volt electric roller cell type
Fuel pump delivery quantity (minimum):
   1985 models .... 1.1 litres (1.9 pints) in 60 seconds
   1986 models onwards .... 2.5 litres (4.4 pints) in 60 seconds
Idle speed (cooling fan on):
   1985 models .... 800 to 900 rpm
   1986 models onwards .... 920 to 960 rpm
Idle mixture CO content:
   1985 models .... 0.25 to 0.75%
   1986 models onwards .... 0.5 to 1.1%
Main system pressure .... 5.6 to 6.0 bar (82 to 87 lbf/in²)
Injector valve opening pressure .... 3.0 to 4.1 bar (43.5 to 59.5 lbf/in²)

Turbocharger
Type .... Garrett AiResearch T3
Maximum boost pressure .... 0.45 to 0.55 bar (6.5 to 7.9 lbf/in²)
Solenoid control valve operating range .... 2500 to 6000 rpm (approximately)

Fuel requirement
Fuel octane rating .... 97 RON (four-star)

Torque wrench settings
K-Jetronic

	Nm	lbf ft
Air cleaner retaining bolts	4.5 to 5	3.3 to 3.7
Fuel distributor-to-sensor plate screws	32 to 38	24 to 28
Sensor plate-to-air cleaner screws	8.5 to 10.5	6.3 to 7.7
Warm-up regulator bolts	3.5 to 5	2.6 to 3.7
Cold start valve bolts	3.5 to 5	2.6 to 3.7
Auxiliary air device bolts	3.5 to 5	2.6 to 3.7
Inlet manifold nuts	16 to 20	12 to 15
Throttle housing nuts	8.5 to 10.6	6.2 to 7.8
Exhaust manifold nuts	14 to 17	10 to 13
Exhaust downpipe to manifold	35 to 40	25 to 29
Banjo union bolts:		
Fuel distributor inlet and return	16 to 20	11 to 15
Fuel distributor injector pipes	5 to 8	3.7 to 6
Fuel distributor cold start valve feed pipe	5 to 8	3.7 to 6
Fuel distributor warm-up regulator feed and return pipes	5 to 8	3.7 to 6
Warm-up regulator inlet (M10)	11 to 15	8 to 11
Warm-up regulator outlet (M8)	5 to 8	3.7 to 6
Fuel pump, filter and accumulator	16 to 20	11 to 15

KE-Jetronic

	Nm	lbf ft
Air cleaner bolts	8.5 to 10.5	6.2 to 7.8
Fuel distributor-to-sensor plate screws	32 to 38	24 to 28
Cold start valve bolts	8.5 to 10.5	6.2 to 7.8

Torque wrench settings (continued)

	Nm	lbf ft
Auxiliary air device bolts	8.5 to 10.5	6.2 to 7.8
Inlet manifold nuts	16 to 20	11 to 15
Throttle housing nuts	8.5 to 10.6	6.2 to 7.8
Thermo-time switch	20 to 25	15 to 18
Charge air temperature sensor	20 to 25	15 to 18
Air intake duct to rocker cover	14 to 18	10 to 13
Cold start valve fuel supply pipe	5 to 8	3.7 to 6
Auxiliary air valve vacuum connection	4	3
Fuel pressure regulator unions	14 to 20	10 to 15
Fuel distributor unions	11 to 15	8 to 11
Fuel pump, filter and accumulator unions	16 to 20	11 to 15
Fuel injector pipe unions	10 to 12	7.3 to 8.8
Exhaust manifold to cylinder head	14 to 17	10 to 13
Turbocharger to exhaust manifold	21 to 26	15 to 19
Exhaust downpipe to turbocharger	35 to 40	25 to 29

PART A: CARBURETTOR AND ASSOCIATED FUEL SYSTEM COMPONENTS

1 General description

The fuel system on all models with carburettor induction is composed of a centrally mounted fuel tank, a fuel pump, a carburettor and an air cleaner.

The fuel tank is mounted under the floor pan beneath the rear seats. The tank is ventilated, has a simple filler pipe and a fuel gauge sender unit.

The fuel pump is a mechanical diaphragm type actuated by means of a pushrod bearing on an eccentric cam on the camshaft. The pump is a sealed unit and cannot be dismantled.

The carburettor may be either a Ford variable venturi (VV) type or one of three versions of the Weber 2V type, depending on model.

The air cleaner has a thermostatically or waxstat-controlled air intake, supplying either hot air from the exhaust manifold heat box or cold air from the front of the engine compartment. On the thermostatically-controlled type, a flap valve within the air cleaner unit regulates the air intake temperature according to operating conditions in conjunction with a vacuum diaphragm unit and a heat sensor unit. On the waxstat air cleaner, being progressively introduced from 1986 onwards the air cleaner operates in the same way as the thermostatically-controlled type, but the flap valve is controlled by a wax capsule. The capsule is mounted in the intake spout and operates the flap valve by expansion and contraction of the wax which varies according to temperature.

Warning: *Many of the procedures in this Chapter entail the removal of fuel pipes and connections which may result in some fuel spillage. Before carrying out any operation on the fuel system refer to the precautions given in Safety First! at the beginning of this manual and follow them implicitly. Petrol is a highly dangerous and volatile liquid and the precautions necessary when handling it cannot be overstressed.*

2 Maintenance and inspection

1 At the intervals specified in *'Routine maintenance'* at the beginning of this manual carry out the following checks and adjustments.
2 With the car over a pit, raised on a lift or securely supported on stands, carefully inspect the fuel pipes, hoses and unions for chafing, leaks and corrosion. Renew any pipes that are severely pitted with corrosion or in any way damaged. Renew any hoses that show signs of cracking or other deterioration.
3 Examine the fuel tank for leaks, particularly around the fuel gauge sender unit, and for signs of corrosion or damage.
4 From within the engine compartment, check the security of all fuel hose attachments and inspect the fuel hoses and vacuum hoses for kinks, chafing and deterioration.
5 Renew the air cleaner element as described in Section 4.
6 Check the operation of the throttle linkage and lubricate the linkage, cable and pedal pivot with a few drops of engine oil.
7 Check and if necessary adjust the carburettor idle speed and mixture settings as described in Section 14 or 21.

Caution: *Certain adjustment points in the fuel system are protected by 'tamperproof' caps, plugs or seals. In some EEC countries (though not yet in the UK) it is an offence to drive a vehicle with broken or missing tamperproof seals. Before disturbing a tamperproof seal, satisfy yourself that you will not be breaking any local or national laws by doing so, and fit a new seal after adjustment is complete where required by law. Do not break tamperproof seals on a vehicle which is still under warranty.*

3 Air cleaner filter element – renewal

1 To remove the air cleaner lid undo and remove the retaining screws or bolts on the top face of the lid (photos).
2 Where applicable release the lid retaining clips around the side of the air cleaner body (photo).

3.1A Removing the air cleaner retaining screws on 1.3 litre CVH engine ...

3.1B ... and air cleaner retaining screw locations on 1.4 litre CVH engine

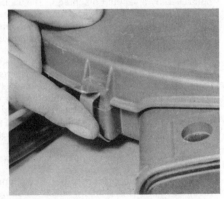
3.2 Release the air cleaner lid retaining clips where fitted

3.3 Removing the air cleaner element

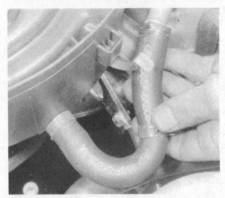

4.2 Disconnecting the crankcase ventilation hose at the air cleaner body

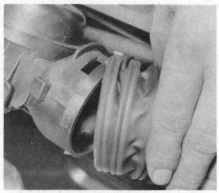

4.3 Cold air intake hose removal from air cleaner spout

3   Lift off the lid, remove and discard the paper element and wipe out the inside of the air cleaner body and lid (photo).
4   Place a new element in position and refit the lid.

4   Air cleaner assembly – removal and refitting

1   Disconnect the battery negative terminal.
2   Disconnect the crankcase ventilation hoses which are accessible from above, from the air cleaner body (photo).
3   Disconnect the cold air intake hose from the end of the air cleaner spout where applicable (photo).
4   Where fitted, on CVH engines, pull out the crankcase emission valve from the underside of the air cleaner body.
5   Undo the retaining screws or bolts on the air cleaner lid and lift the unit off the carburettor.
6   According to model, disconnect the vacuum hose and the remaining crankcase ventilation hose as applicable, then remove the air cleaner from the engine.
7   Refitting is a reversal of removal.

5   Air cleaner air temperature control – description and testing

Thermostatically-controlled air cleaner
1   On all pre-1986 models and certain models from 1986 onwards, the air cleaner is thermostatically-controlled by a vacuum operated system to provide air at the most suitable temperature for combustion with minimum emission levels.
2   This is accomplished by drawing in cold air from an intake at the front of the car, and hot air from a collector box on the exhaust manifold and blending them. The proportion of hot and cold air is varied by the position of a flap valve in the intake spout which itself is controlled by a vacuum diaphragm. The vacuum pressure is regulated by a heat sensor located within the air cleaner body to ensure that the appropriate degree of inlet manifold vacuum is applied to the flap valve, thus maintaining the air temperature within the preset limits.
3   To check the thermostatic control of the air cleaner the engine must be cold. First observe the position of the flap valve which should be fully closed prior to starting the engine. The flap valve can be observed using a mirror after disconnecting the intake hose.
4   Start the engine and check that the flap valve opens fully at idle speed to allow only hot air from the manifold to enter the air cleaner.
5   Should the flap valve remain in the closed position once the engine is started, then the diaphragm unit or the heat sensor is at fault and should be tested to isolate the defective unit.
6   Make sure that all vacuum lines are secure and free from leaks as a final check.
7   To check the operation of these components a vacuum pump is required. If one is available proceed as follows, if not, have the tests carried out by a dealer.
8   Detach the diaphragm-to-heat sensor vacuum line at the sensor end and connect a vacuum pump to the diaphragm unit. Apply a

vacuum up to 100 mm (4.0 in) of mercury and retain this whilst checking the flap valve.
9   If the flap valve is now open, then the heat sensor is faulty and must be renewed. If the valve remains shut, the diaphragm unit is faulty and

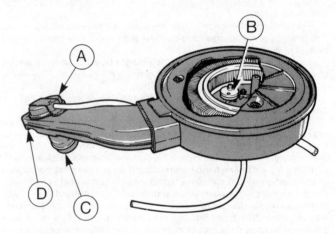

Fig. 3.1 Thermostatically controlled air cleaner components (Sec 5)

A   *Vacuum diaphragm*   C   *Hot air intake*
B   *Heat sensor*   D   *Cold air intake*

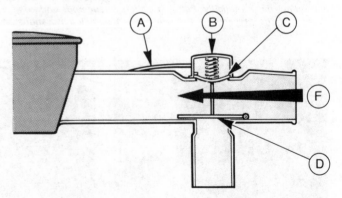

Fig. 3.2 Thermostatically controlled air cleaner operation under low vacuum conditions (Sec 5)

A   *Vacuum hose to heat sensor*   D   *Flap valve closed*
B   *Vacuum diaphragm*   F   *Cold air intake*
C   *Diaphragm*

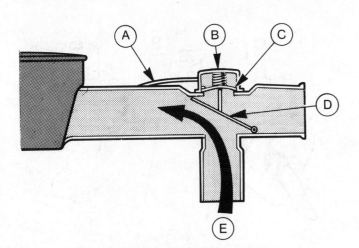

Fig. 3.3 Thermostatically-controlled air cleaner operation under high vacuum conditions (Sec 5)

A Vacuum hose to heat sensor	D Flap valve open
B Vacuum diaphragm	E Hot air intake
C Diaphragm	

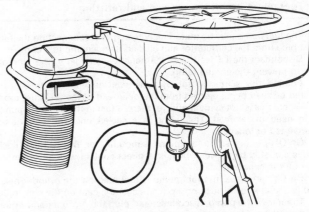

Fig. 3.4 Using a vacuum pump to test the operation of the thermostatically-controlled air cleaner (Sec 5)

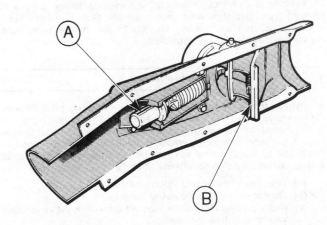

Fig. 3.5 Waxstat type air cleaner components in air cleaner spout (Sec 5)

A Wax capsule   B Flap valve

a new air cleaner will have to be obtained, as the diaphragm unit is not available separately.

10 After the checks, disconnect the vacuum pump and reconnect the vacuum line and intake hose.

Waxstat-controlled air cleaner

11 From 1986 onwards the waxstat type air cleaner is being progressively introduced to replace the thermostatically-controlled type used previously.

12 The waxstat air cleaner performs the same hot and cold air blending operation using a flap valve as described previously, but the flap valve is controlled by a wax capsule and is not dependent on manifold vacuum.

13 When the engine is cold the wax in the capsule contracts and the flap valve is pulled back to shut off the cold air intake. As engine ambient temperature rises the wax expands and the flap is opened to admit only cold air into the air cleaner.

14 To test the unit the engine must initially be cold.

15 Remove the manifold-to-air cleaner hot air hose and observe the position of the flap valve which should be open to allow only hot air to enter.

16 Refit the hose and warm up the engine to normal operating temperature.

17 Remove the hot air hose again and check the position of the flap valve. With the engine at normal operating temperature the flap should be closed to admit only cold air into the air cleaner.

18 If this is not the case the waxstat is defective and the air cleaner must be renewed as the waxstat is not available separately.

19 Refit the hot air hose on completion of the checks.

---

6 Fuel pump – cleaning

---

1 On certain early models the fuel pump has a detachable cover allowing access to the internal filter for cleaning. If this type of pump is fitted (identified by a raised cover secured with a screw) the filter can be cleaned as follows.

2 Place a piece of rag around the pump body to catch the fuel which will drain out when the cover is removed.

3 Unscrew and remove the single cover screw and lift off the cover.

4 Take out the rubber sealing ring and the filter screen from inside the cover.

5 Clean the screen by brushing it in clean fuel, then fit it into the cover, noting the projections on some screens which centralise it.

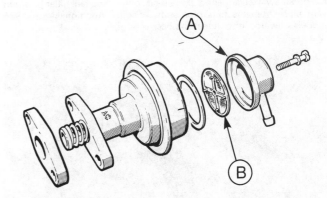

Fig. 3.6 CVH engine fuel pump filter components (Sec 6)

A Pump cover   B Filter

6 Fit the sealing ring. If it is not in good order, renew it.

7 Locate the cover on the pump body. On some pumps, the cover is correctly installed when the notch in the cover engages in the groove in the pump body.

8 Screw in the retaining screw, but do not overtighten it provided it is making a good seal.

7 Fuel pump – testing, removal and refitting

1   The fuel pump may be quite simply tested by disconnecting the fuel inlet pipe from the carburettor and placing its open end in a container.
2   Disconnect the LT lead from the negative terminal of the ignition coil to prevent the engine firing.
3   Actuate the starter motor. Regular well-defined spurts of fuel should be seen being ejected from the open end of the fuel inlet pipe.
4   Where this is not evident and yet there is fuel in the tank, the pump is in need of renewal. The pump is a sealed unit and cannot be dismantled or repaired.
5   On OHV engines, the fuel pump is mounted on the cylinder block and is actuated by a lever which is in direct contact with an eccentric cam on the camshaft.
6   On CVH engines, the fuel pump is mounted on the cylinder head and is actuated by a pushrod from an eccentric cam on the camshaft.
7   To remove the pump, disconnect and plug the fuel inlet and outlet hoses at the pump and then unbolt it from the engine (photo).
8   Retain any insulating spacers and remove and discard the flange gaskets.
9   On CVH engines, withdraw the push-rod (photo).
10 Refitting is a reversal of removal, but use new flange gaskets. If crimped type hose clips were used originally, these will have been destroyed when disconnecting the fuel hoses. Renew them with conventional nut and screw type clips.

8 Fuel tank – removal and refitting

1   The fuel tank will normally only need to be removed if it is severely contaminated with sediment or other substance, or requires repair.
2   As there is no drain plug incorporated in the tank, the best time to remove it is when it is nearly empty. If this is not possible, syphon as much fuel as possible from the tank into a container which can be sealed, but before doing so, observe the following precautions:

   (a) *Disconnect the battery, negative lead first*
   (b) *Do not smoke or bring naked lights near*
   (c) *Avoid placing the vehicle over an inspection pit as the fuel vapour is heavier than air*

3   With the rear of the vehicle raised and supported securely, disconnect the flexible hose connection between the sections of rigid fuel line at the front face of the tank (photo). On some models dual pipelines are used, the second one being a fuel return line which returns excess fuel from the carburettor.
4   Disconnect the electrical leads from the tank sender unit.
5   Brush away all adhering dirt and disconnect the tank filler pipe and vent pipes from the tank pipe stubs (photo). Additionally on 1986 models onwards, disconnect the filler vent pipe.

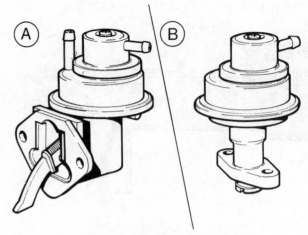

Fig. 3.7 Fuel pump assemblies (Sec 7)

   A   OHV engine fuel pump   *B   CVH engine fuel pump*

6   Support the tank and unscrew the bolts from the support straps (photo).
7   Lower the tank until the fuel hoses can be detached from the sender unit and from their retaining clips. On 1986 models onwards disconnect the small bore vent pipe located on the top face of the tank. Lower the tank fully and remove it from under the car.
8   If the tank is to be cleaned out, repaired or renewed, remove the sender unit. To do this, unscrew the unit in a clockwise direction using the special tool (23-014) or a suitable lever engaged behind the tabs.
9   If the tank contains sediment or water, clean it out by shaking vigorously using paraffin as a solvent. After several changes, rinse out finally with petrol.
10 If the tank is leaking, leave repair to a specialist company. Attempting to weld or solder the tank without it first having been steamed out for several hours is extremely dangerous.
11 Refit the sender unit using a new sealing ring.
12 Refit the tank into the vehicle by reversing the removal operations. Check all connections for leaks after the tank has been partly filled with fuel.

9 Throttle cable – adjustment

1   Disconnect the battery earth lead.
2   On manual transmission models remove the air cleaner unit, as given in Section 4.

7.7 CVH engine fuel pump removal

7.9 Removing the fuel pump push-rod

8.3 Fuel tank flexible hose connections at front of tank

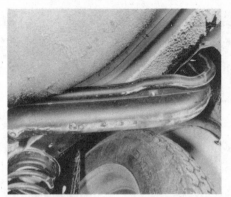

8.5 Fuel tank filler and vent pipe locations

8.6 Fuel tank support strap bolt

3   Get an assistant to sit in the driving seat and fully depress the accelerator pedal, then whilst it is depressed turn the cable adjuster at the carburettor or throttle cable mounting bracket connection to the point at which the linkage is just fully open.

4   Release the accelerator pedal then fully depress and release it again and check that when depressed the throttle is fully opened. Readjust if necessary.

5   On completion refit the air cleaner and reconnect the battery earth lead.

10 Throttle cable – removal and refitting

1   Disconnect the battery earth lead.

2   Working within the vehicle, remove the facia lower insulation panel.

3   Disconnect the cable from the upper end of the accelerator pedal arm. Do this by sliding off the spring clip to release the cable end from the ball-stud.

4   Working under the bonnet, release the cable from the bulkhead. This is probably more easily carried out if an assistant can punch the cable grommet out from inside the vehicle.

5   Remove the air cleaner (manual transmission models only).

6   The cable must now be detached from its bracket on the carburettor or, on automatic transmission models, from the throttle cable mounting bracket on the right-hand side of the engine. Prise out the clip then depress the four lugs on the retainer simultaneously so that the retainer can be slid out of its bracket (photos). Take care not to damage the outer cable.

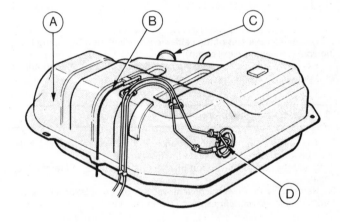

Fig. 3.8 Fuel tank assembly (Sec 8)

A   Fuel tank
B   Vent pipe
C   Fuel filler stub
D   Fuel gauge sender unit

Fig. 3.9 Throttle cable attachment at pedal end (Sec 10)

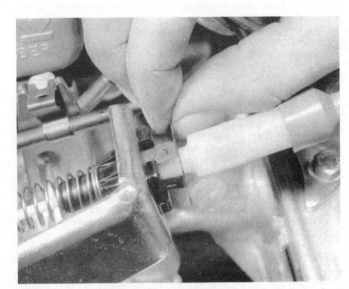

10.6A Prise out the throttle cable retaining clip ...

10.6B ... then release the cable retainer (arrowed)

10.7 Release the cable end fitting spring retaining clip

7 Disconnect the end of the cable from the ball-stud by sliding back the spring retaining clip (photo).
8 Fit the new cable by reversing the removal procedure, then adjust as described in Section 9.

11 Accelerator pedal – removal and refitting

1 The pedal can be removed once the throttle cable has been disconnected from it as described in Section 10.
2 Undo the two pedal support bracket retaining bolts and remove the pedal.
3 Refitting is the reversal of removal but on completion check the throttle cable adjustment as described in Section 9.

12 Choke control cable – removal, refitting and adjustment

Pre-1986 models

1 Disconnect the battery earth lead.
2 For improved access, remove the air cleaner unit (Section 4).
3 At the carburettor end of the cable, loosen the cable clamp bolt, detach the outer cable securing clip at the choke control bracket and disconnect the cable.
4 Working inside the car, remove the coin box from the lower facia panel (beneath the choke control knob).
5 Remove the clip retaining the cable control knob and withdraw the knob from the switch lever.
6 Remove the control switch bezel and then, reaching up underneath the facia withdraw the switch from the underside of the panel (through the coin box aperture).
7 The choke cable can now be pulled through the engine bulkhead and the switch removed.
8 Refitting is the reversal of removal, but in conjunction with the following adjustment procedure.
9 From either a flat strip of metal or preferably metal tubing make up a spacer as shown in Fig. 3.11.
10 Pull out the choke and locate the spacer behind the choke knob. Ensure that the spacer remains in position throughout the procedure.
11 At the carburettor end, mark the inner cable at a point 22 mm (0.86 in) from the end using pencil or tape. On some cables the cable may be kinked for reference at this point or a ferrule may be fitted.
12 Insert the cable in the cable clamp until the mark or ferrule is against the edge of the clamp. Tighten the clamp bolt.
13 Pull the outer cable so that the operating lever on the choke is against the 'full choke' stop on the housing. Secure the outer cable to its bracket, in this position, using the retaining clip.

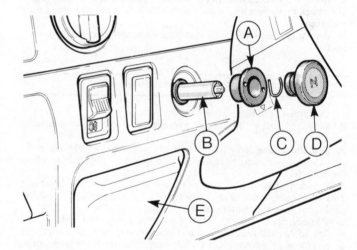

Fig. 3.10 Choke cable attachments at facia – pre-1986 models (Sec 12)

A   Bezel   D   Knob
B   Switch lever   E   Coin box
C   Knob retaining clip

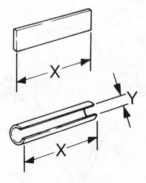

Fig. 3.11 Choke cable adjustment spacer dimensions – pre-1986 models (Sec 12)

X = 37.0 to 37.5 mm (1.45 to 1.47 in)
Y = 12.0 mm (0.47 in) minimum

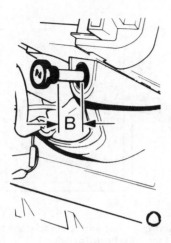

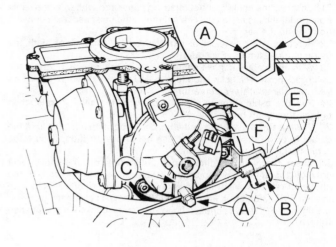

Fig. 3.12 Choke knob pulled out for adjustment with spacer (B) in position – pre-1986 models (Sec 12)

Fig. 3.13 Choke cable adjustment at carburettor – pre-1986 models (Sec 12)

A Cable clamp bolt	E Point 22.0 mm from cable
B Outer cable retaining clip	end
C Operating lever	F Full choke stop
D Cable clamp	

14 Remove the spacer and check that the operating lever contacts the 'choke off' stop and 'full choke' stop on the housing when the choke knob is pushed in and pulled out respectively. On completion of the adjustment ensure that there is a small clearance between the lever and the 'off stop' when the choke knob is pushed in.

1986 models onwards
15 Disconnect the battery earth lead.
16 Remove the air cleaner as described in Section 4.
17 At the carburettor end of the cable, loosen the cable clamp bolt, detach the outer cable securing clip at the choke control bracket and disconnect the cable (photo).
18 Working inside the car remove the steering column shrouds for access to the cable.
19 From behind the facia disconnect the warning light wire from the choke control assembly.
20 Using a small probe, depress the locking pin on the underside of the choke knob collar and remove the knob.

12.17 Releasing the choke cable clamp bolt (arrowed)

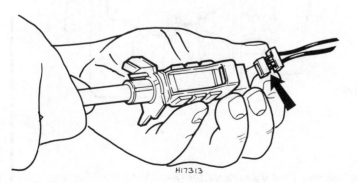

Fig. 3.14 Removing choke assembly warning light wire – 1986 models onwards (Sec 12)

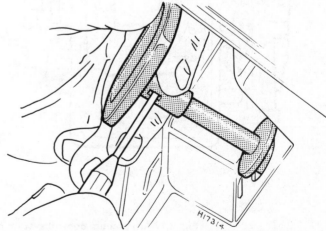

Fig. 3.15 Using a small probe to release choke knob locking pin – 1986 models onwards (Sec 12)

21 Unscrew the choke control retaining collar and withdraw the cable from under the facia. Pull the cable through the bulkhead and remove it from inside the car.

22 Refitting is the reversal of removal, but in conjunction with the following adjustment procedure.

23 With the cable in position in the facia and routed through the bulkhead, push the choke knob fully in and engage the inner cable end with the clamp at the carburettor.

24 Pull the cable through the clamp up to the cable ferrule, then tighten the clamp bolt.

25 Pull out the choke knob to the full choke position and also hold the choke lever on the carburettor in the full choke position. Secure the cable to the bracket with the clip.

26 Check that with the choke knob pulled fully out the choke lever contacts the full choke stop on the carburettor and returns fully to the choke off position when the knob is pushed in. On models fitted with the Ford VV carburettor, ensure that there is a small clearance between the choke lever and the choke off stop when the choke knob is pushed fully in.

13 Ford VV carburettor – general description

1 Due to the anti-pollution regulations being introduced in various countries, Ford developed a variable choke carburettor of their own design in order to comply with such regulations. The unit, known as the Ford VV (variable venturi) carburettor, provides improved fuel atomisation and air/fuel mixture ratio under normal operating conditions. It operates in the following manner.

2 Fuel is supplied to the carburettor via a needle valve which is actuated by the float. When the fuel level is low in the float chamber in the carburettor, the float drops and opens the needle valve. When the

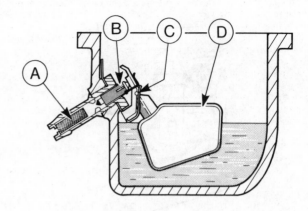

Fig. 3.16 Float chamber and fuel input system – Ford VV carburettor (Sec 13)

A Inlet filter	C Float pivot
B Needle valve	D Float

correct fuel level is reached the float will close the valve and shut off the fuel supply.

3 The float level on this type of carburettor is not adjustable since minor variations in the fuel level do not affect the performance of the carburettor. The valve needle is prevented from vibrating by means of a ball and light spring. To further ensure that the needle seals correctly it is coated in a rubber-like coating of Viton.

4 The float chamber is vented internally via the main jet body and

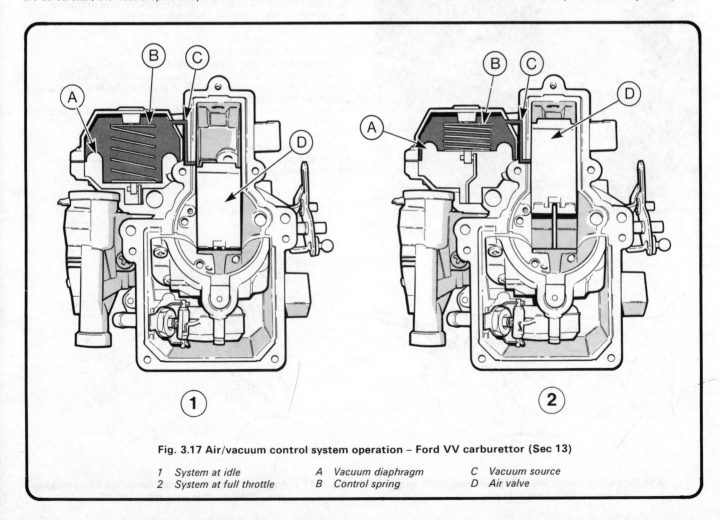

Fig. 3.17 Air/vacuum control system operation – Ford VV carburettor (Sec 13)

1 System at idle		A Vacuum diaphragm	C Vacuum source
2 System at full throttle		B Control spring	D Air valve

carburettor air inlet, thus avoiding the possibility of petrol vapour escaping into the atmosphere.

5 The air/fuel mixture intake is controlled by the air valve which is opened or closed according to the operating demands of the engine. The valve is actuated by a diaphragm which in turn opens or closes according to the vacuum supplied through the venturi between the air valve and the throttle butterfly. As the air valve and diaphragm are connected they open or close correspondingly.

6 When the engine is idling the air intake requirement is low and therefore the valve is closed, causing a high air speed over the main jet exit. However, as the throttle plate is opened, the control vacuum (depression within the venturi) increases and is diverted to the diaphragm which then releases the air valve to balance the control spring and control vacuum.

7 When the throttle is opened further this equality of balance is maintained as the air valve is progressivly opened to equalise the control spring and control vacuum forces throughout the speed range.

8 Fuel from the float chamber is drawn up the pick-up tube and then regulated through two jets and the tapered needle and into the engine. The vacuum within the venturi draws the fuel. At low engine speeds the needle taper enters the main jet to restrict the fuel demand. On acceleration and at higher engine speeds the needle is withdrawn through the main jet by the action of the air valve to which it is attached. As the needle is tapered, the amount by which it is moved regulates the amount of fuel passing through the main jet.

9 The sonic idle system as used on other Ford fixed jet carburettors is

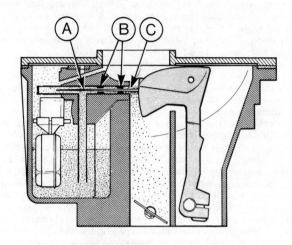

Fig. 3.18 Main jet system – Ford VV carburettor (Sec 13)

A   Tapered needle (metering rod)

B   Main and secondary jets
C   Main fuel outlet

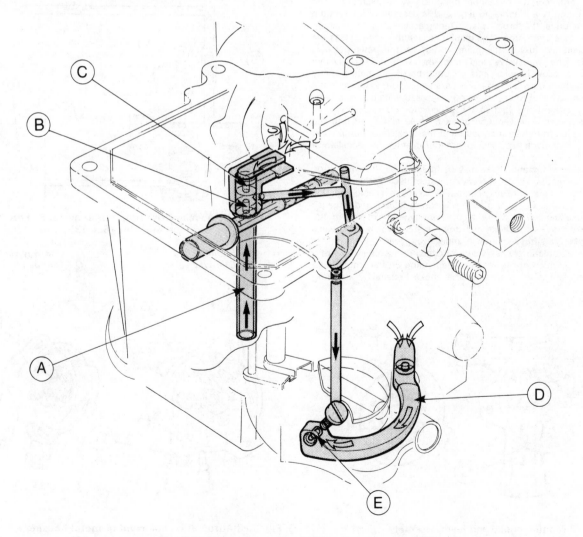

Fig. 3.19 Idle system – Ford VV carburettor (Sec 13)

A   Main pick-up tube
B   Idle jet

C   Idle air jet
D   Bypass gallery

E   Sonic discharge tube

also employed in the VV type, with 70% of the idle fuel mixture supplied via the sonic idle system and 30% from the main system. When idling, fuel is drawn through the main pick-up tube (Fig. 3.19) passes through the idle jet and then mixes with the air stream being supplied from the air bleed in the main jet body. The air/fuel mixture then passes on through the inner galleries to the mixture control screw which regulates the fuel supply at idle. This mixture then mixes with the air from the by-pass idle channel and finally enters the inlet manifold via the sonic discharge tube at an accelerated rate of flow.

10 Throttle actuation is via a progressive linkage which has a cam and roller mechanism. The advantage of this system is that a large initial throttle pressure allows only a small throttle plate opening. As the throttle is opened up and approaches its maximum travel the throttle plate movement accelerates accordingly. This system aids economy, and gives a good engine response through the operating range.

11 To counterbalance the drop in vacuum when initially accelerating, a restrictor is fitted into the air passage located between the control vacuum areas and the control diaphragm. This restrictor causes the valve to open slowly when an increase in air flow is made which in turn causes a higher vacuum for a brief moment in the main jet, caused by the increase in air velocity. This increase in vacuum causes the fuel flow to increase, thus preventing a 'flat spot'. The larger amounts of fuel required under heavy acceleration are supplied by the accelerator pump.

12 The accelerator pump injects fuel into the venturi direct when acceleration causes a drop in manifold pressure. This richening of the mixture prevents engine hesitation under heavy acceleration. The accelerator pump is a diaphragm type and is actuated from vacuum obtained from under the throttle plate. During acceleration the vacuum under the throttle plate drops, the diaphragm return spring closes the diaphragm and the fuel in the pump is fed via the inner galleries through the one-way valve and into the venturi. The system incorporates a back bleeder and vacuum break air hole. Briefly explained, the back bleed allows any excess fuel vapour to return to the float chamber when prolonged idling causes the carburettor temperature to rise and the fuel in the accelerator pump reservoir to become overheated. The vacuum break air hole allows air into the pump outlet pipe to reduce the vacuum at the accelerator pump jet at high speed. Too much fuel would otherwise enter the accelerator pump system.

13 A manual or automatic choke may be fitted to the VV carburettor, depending on model. Whilst the choke system itself is the same on both types, the manual choke is operated by means of a cable attached to the lever housing, the lever of which is spring-loaded and engages with the choke linkage. As with the automatic type choke system, the manual choke type has a choke pull-down system which deactivates the choke when it is not required; ie under heavy load.

14 The fully automatic choke system operates in accordance with a bi-metal spring which opens or closes depending on the temperature of engine coolant passing through the choke housing. The spring

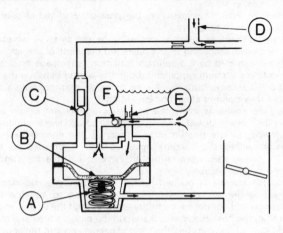

Fig. 3.20 Accelerator pump inlet system – Ford VV carburettor (Sec 13)

A   Return spring
B   Diaphragm
C   One-way valve
D   Vacuum break air hole
E   Back bleed
F   One-way valve

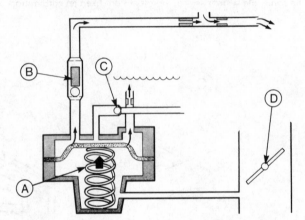

Fig. 3.21 Accelerator pump outlet system – Ford VV carburettor (Sec 13)

A   Return spring
B   One-way valve
C   One-way valve
D   Throttle plate

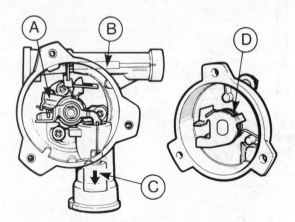

Fig. 3.22 Manual choke and lever assembly – Ford VV carburettor (Sec 13)

A   Choke linkage
B   Tapered needle (metering rod)
C   Pull-down piston
D   Spring-loaded lever

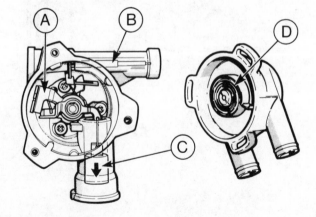

Fig. 3.23 Automatic choke and bi-metal housing – Ford VV carburettor (Sec 13)

A   Choke linkage
B   Tapered needle (metering rod)
C   Pull-down piston
D   Bi-metal coil

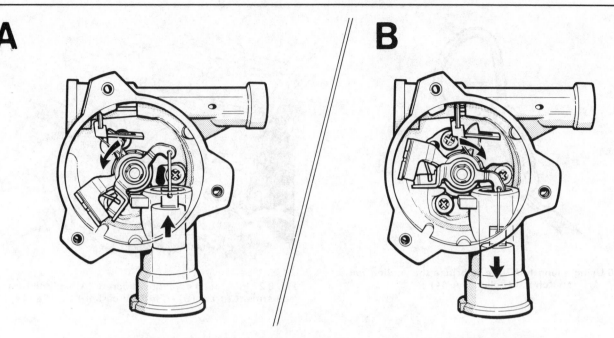

Fig. 3.24 Automatic choke operating conditions – Ford VV carburettor (Sec 13)

A   Choke fully on (cold engine)   *B   Choke off (warm engine)*

movement activates the choke mechanism, which consists of a variable needle jet and a variable supply of air. Fuel to the choke jet is fed from the main pick-up tube via the internal galleries within the main jet body. When the bi-metal spring is contracted (engine cold), it pulls the tapered needle from the jet to increase the fuel delivery rate. The spring expands as the engine warms up and the needle reduces the fuel supply as it re-enters the jet. The choke air supply is supplied via the venturi just above the throttle plate. The fuel mixes with the air in the choke air valve, whence it is delivered to the engine.

15 A choke pull-down system is employed whereby, if the engine is under choke, but is only cruising, ie not under heavy load, the choke is released. This is operated by the vacuum piston which is connected to the choke spindle by levers.

16 An anti-run-on valve is fitted, being visible on the outside of the body of the carburettor. This valve shuts off the fuel supply to the idle system when the engine is turned off and so prevents the engine running on or 'dieseling'. The solenoid valve is actuated electrically. When the ignition is turned off, it allows a plunger to enter and block the sonic discharge tube to stop the supply of fuel into the idle system. When the ignition is switched on the solenoid is actuated and the plunger is withdrawn from the tube.

17 A deceleration valve is fitted to the throttle butterfly (plate) valve and its purpose is to further regulate the air and fuel mixture supply to the intake manifold. The valve is normally held shut by a return spring, but during deceleration the higher manifold vacuum overrides the effect of the spring and opens the valve to allow an increase of air and fuel into the manifold. The valve is set during manufacture and **must not** be tampered with.

---

14 Ford VV carburettor – adjustment

Note: *Before carrying out any carburettor adjustment, ensure that the contact breaker points, ignition timing and spark plug gaps (as applicable) are set as specified and that the distributor is operating correctly. To carry out the adjustments an accurate tachometer will be required and the use of an exhaust gas analyser (CO meter) is also preferable. Refer to the caution at the end of Section 2 before proceeding.*

Idle speed

1   With the engine at normal operating temperature, connect a tachometer in accordance with the manufacturer's instructions.

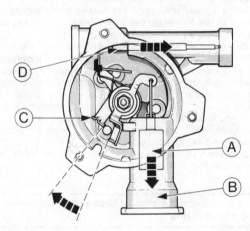

Fig. 3.25 Manual choke pull-down operation

– Ford VV carburettor (Sec 13)

A   Pull-down piston movement   *C   Choke lever fully*
B   High vacuum condition   *anti-clockwise*
                                                       D   Tapered needle closing

2   Disconnect the wiring multi-plug from the radiator cooling fan thermostatic switch in the thermostat housing and bridge the two contacts in the plug using a suitable length of wire. This is necessary so that the cooling fan runs continuously during adjustment.

3   On automatic transmission models slacken the adjuster screw on the throttle valve shaft lever to give clearance of 2 to 3 mm (0.079 to 0.118 in) – see Chapter 7, Section 4.

4   Ensure that the air cleaner is fitted and that its vacuum hoses are not in any way trapped or pinched, particularly between the air cleaner body and the top face of the carburettor.

5   Run the engine at 3000 rpm for 30 seconds, then allow it to idle and note the idle speed. If using an exhaust gas analyser it should be noted that initially the CO% reading will rise, but then fall and stabilise after a period of 5 to 25 seconds. The CO reading should then be as specified.

6   If necessary, adjust the idle speed adjustment screw to give the specified idle speed (Fig. 3.27).

Fig. 3.26 Using a length of wire to bridge the cooling fan switch multi-plug (Sec 14)

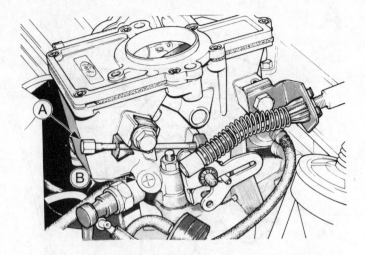

Fig. 3.27 Idle speed adjustment screw (A) and mixture adjustment screw (B) – Ford VV carburettor (Sec 14)

Idle mixture

7   Adjustment of the CO content (mixture) is not normally required during routine maintenance, but if the reading noted in paragraph 5 is not as given in the Specifications first remove the tamperproof plug, prising it free using a small screwdriver.

8   Run the engine at 3000 rpm for 30 seconds, then allow it to idle. Adjust the mixture screw (Fig. 3.27) within 10 to 30 seconds. If more time is required run the engine at 3000 rpm again for 30 seconds.

9   Adjust the idle speed if necessary and recheck the CO content.

10 Fit a new tamperproof plug to the mixture adjuster screw on completion. It should be noted that mixture adjustment without a CO analyser is not accurate and therefore not recommended.

11 On completion disconnect the instruments, remove the cooling fan bridging wire and reconnect the multi-plug.

12 On automatic transmission models adjust the downshift linkage as described in Chapter 7, Section 4.

15 Ford VV carburettor manual choke unit – removal, checking and refitting

1   Disconnect the battery negative lead.

2   Remove the air cleaner as described in Section 4.

3   Slacken the choke cable clamp bolt at the choke lever, detach the outer cable securing clip at the bracket and remove the cable from the carburettor.

4   Using a suitable Torx type key or socket bit, undo the three lever housing retaining screws and withdraw the lever housing, together with the choke cable bracket from the carburettor.

5   Carefully unscrew the three Torx screws which secure the main choke unit to the carburettor and withdraw the choke unit together with the gasket.

6   With the choke removed clean the unit inside by gently blowing out dust and any dirt with an air line or foot pump.

7   Using a small screwdriver or thin rod, raise the pull-down piston (Fig. 3.22) and allow it to drop under its own weight, checking that it falls smoothly to the lower limit of its travel.

8   Repeat this check but with the choke linkage lever held in various positions. If the piston binds in any position throughout its total travel, try cleaning the unit once more with an air line, nothing else, then repeat the checks. Under no circumstances attempt to ease a sticking piston with lubrication of any kind otherwise the calibration of the piston will be affected and its operating characteristics radically altered. Check also that the choke control spring leg is seated in its slot in the choke lever (Fig. 3.30). If not, carefully slip it back into place. Check the operation of the piston once more and if it still sticks, renew the choke unit and lever housing as an assembly.

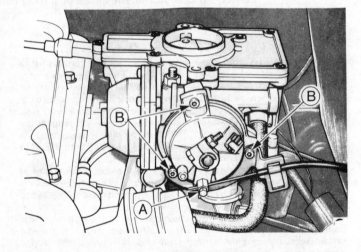

Fig. 3.28 Choke cable clamp bolt (A) and lever housing retaining screws (B) – Ford VV carburettor (Sec 15)

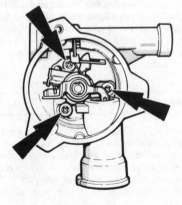

Fig. 3.29 Choke unit retaining screw locations – Ford VV carburettor (Sec 15)

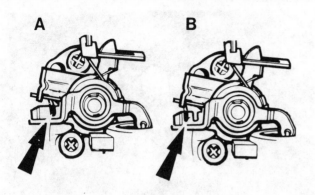

Fig. 3.30 Correct position of choke control spring leg – Ford VV carburettor (Sec 15)

A   *Correctly located*   B   *Incorrectly located*

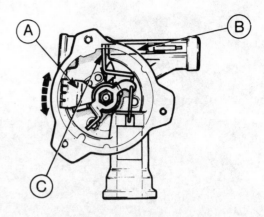

Fig. 3.31 Checking choke operation – Ford VV carburettor (Sec 15)

A   *Linkage lever*   C   *Needle bracket*
B   *Metering rod*

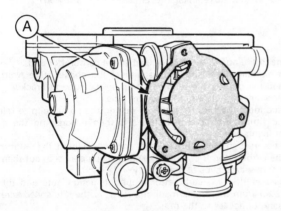

Fig. 3.32 Correct location of choke lever housing gasket with tab (A) positioned as shown – Ford VV carburettor (Sec 15)

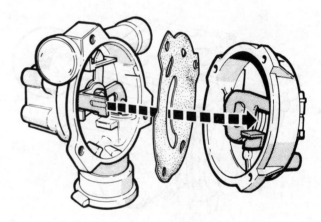

Fig. 3.33 Fitting lever housing to choke unit – Ford VV carburettor (Sec 15)

9   Check the choke metering rod by carefully moving the needle bracket (Fig. 3.31) through its full range of travel using a small screwdriver. As with the pull-down piston, the check should be made with the linkage lever held in various positions. Ensure that the rod does not bind in any position throughout its total travel. If binding does occur it may be lightly lubricated with 'Ballistol Spray' which should be available from main Ford dealers. Do not use any other lubricant otherwise a sludge build-up may occur, and do not allow overspray to contact the pull-down piston or linkage. If the metering rod is partially or completely seized, lubrication will not help and the choke unit and lever housing should be renewed as an assembly.
10   If both the metering rod and the pull-down piston are satisfactory but binding was noticed when moving the linkage lever, then the central shaft should be lightly lubricated from the rear of the choke unit using the 'Ballistol Spray'.
11   To refit the choke unit first position a new gasket onto the carburettor mating face, locate the choke unit and fit the retaining screws.
12   When refitting the lever housing, align the new gasket with the screw holes and with the tab of the gasket positioned as shown in Fig. 3.32. With the linkage lever at its mid travel position, fit the lever housing ensuring that the linkage lever engages with the spring-loaded arm in the lever housing (Fig. 3.33).
13   Secure the lever housing and choke cable bracket with the three retaining screws
14   Reconnect the choke cable and adjust it as described in Section 12.
15   Refit the air cleaner (Section 4), reconnect the battery, then adjust the idle speed and mixture settings (Section 14).

16 Ford VV carburettor automatic choke bi-metal housing – removal and refitting

1   Disconnect the battery negative lead.
2   Remove the air cleaner as described in Section 4.
3   Release any pressure in the cooling system by loosening the pressure cap (see Chapter 2), then detach the inlet and outlet hoses at the automatic choke unit. Clamp the hoses or position them with their ends facing upwards to minimise coolant leakage.
4   Mark the bi-metal housing-to-choke body joint with quick-drying paint to ensure correct realignment on reassembly.
5   Unscrew and remove the three bi-metal housing retaining screws and withdraw the housing and gasket (photo).
6   Refitting is a reversal of the removal procedure.
7   Use a new gasket between the main body and the bi-metal housing.
8   When fitting the bi-metal housing, engage the bi-metal coil with the linkage lever centre slot, then loosely fit the three retaining screws, starting with the lower one (photo).
9   Before tightening the retaining screws, align the paint mark on the bi-metal body with the choke body marking (Fig. 3.34).
10   Refit the air cleaner as described in Section 4 and top up the cooling system as described in Chapter 2.

16.5 Removing the automatic choke bi-metal housing

16.8 Automatic choke linkage lever centre slot (arrowed)

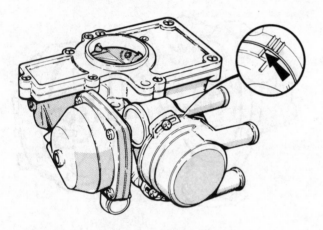
Fig. 3.34 Alignment marks on choke unit and bi-metal housing – Ford VV carburettor (Sec 16)

17 Ford VV carburettor automatic choke unit – removal, checking and refitting

1 Remove the bi-metal housing as described in Section 16, paragraph 1 to 5 inclusive.
2 Carefully remove the three screws within the choke housing body and withdraw the unit from the carburettor together with the gasket.
3 Carry out the checks described in Section 15 paragraphs 6 to 10.
4 If a new choke unit is to be fitted, it will first be necessary to tap out the securing screw holes for the bi-metal housing. The thread can be tapped out using the retaining screws which are of the thread-cutting type. **Do not** cut the threads with a standard tap.
5 Refit the choke housing body to the carburettor using a new gasket, then refit the bi-metal housing as described in Section 16.

18 Ford VV carburettor – removal and refitting

1 Disconnect the battery negative lead.
2 Remove the air cleaner as described in Section 4.
3 On automatic choke carburettors, if the engine is still hot, depressurise the cooling system by carefully releasing the pressure cap (see Chapter 2). Disconnect the coolant hoses from the automatic choke housing and clamp or plug them to prevent coolant loss.

4 Detach the anti-run-on valve lead at the carburettor end.
5 On manual choke models disconnect the choke cable from the lever and the outer cable from its clamp on the support bracket.
6 Disconnect the distributor vacuum pipe.
7 Disconnect the throttle cable by pulling the spring clip to release the end fitting from the ball-stud and then unscrewing the cable bracket fixing bolt.
8 Disconnect and plug the fuel inlet and, where fitted, the return hose from the carburettor. If crimped type hose clips are used, cut them off and fit screw type clips at reassembly.
9 Unscrew the two carburettor mounting flange nuts and lift the carburettor from the intake manifold. Remove the idle speed screw if necessary for access to the nuts.
10 Refitting is a reversal of removal, but make sure that a new flange gasket is used on perfectly clean mating surfaces.
11 On manual choke models readjust the choke cable on reconnection, as described in Section 12.
12 When reconnecting the vacuum pipe make sure that the fuel trap is correctly positioned.
13 When refitting the fuel inlet hose ensure that it is positioned in such a way that no part of the hose is closer than 11 mm (0.4 in) to the automatic choke coolant hoses. If this is not done fuel vaporization can occur under certain conditions.
14 On automatic choke models recheck the coolant level.
15 On completion restart the engine and check the idle speed and mixture adjustments, as given in Section 14.

19 Ford VV carburettor – overhaul

1 Complete overhaul of the carburettor is seldom required. It will usually be found sufficient to remove the top cover and mop out fuel, dirt and water from the fuel bowl and then blow through the accessible jets with air from a tyre pump or compressed air line. Do not direct air pressure into the accelerator pump air bleed or outlet, or the air valve vent, as diaphragm damage may occur. Refer to the caution at the end of Section 2 before proceeding.
2 To completely dismantle a carburettor, carry out the following operations, but remember that for a unit which has been in service for a high mileage it may be more economical to purchase a new or reconditioned one rather than to renew several individual components. Note that to dismantle the carburettor on later models a suitable set of Torx type keys or socket bits will be needed.
3 Remove the carburettor from the engine as described in Section 18 and clean away external dirt.

Fig. 3.35 Carburettor disconnection points for removal – Ford VV carburettor (Sec 18)

A   Fuel inlet hose
B   Choke cable connections
    (manual choke version)
C   Vacuum pipe
D   Throttle cable attachments
E   Idle speed adjustment screw
F   Anti-run-on valve load

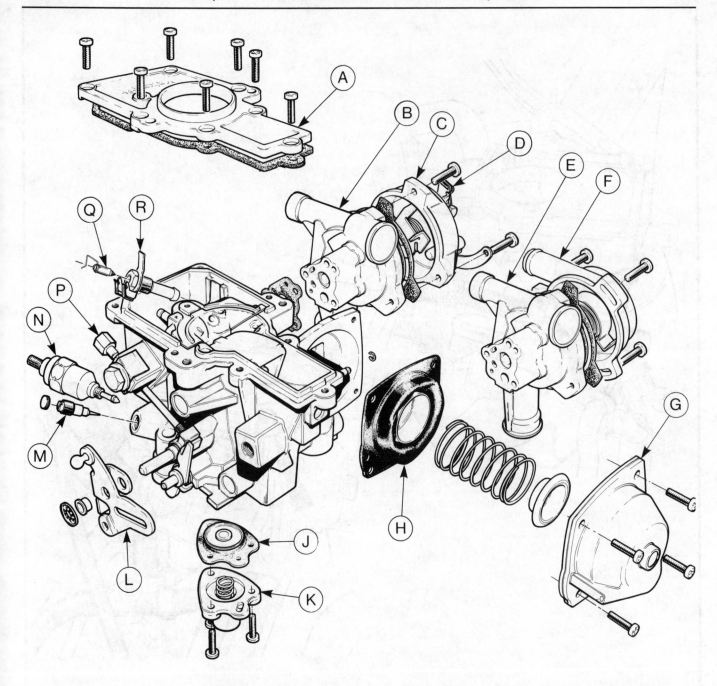

Fig. 3.36 Exploded view of the Ford VV carburettor (Sec 19)

A Top cover	E Automatic choke unit	H Air control diaphragm
B Manual choke unit	F Bi-metal housing	J Accelerator pump diaphragm
C Lever housing	G Air control vacuum	K Accelerator pump cover
D Choke cable bracket	diaphragm housing	L Throttle linkage

M Mixture adjustment screw
N Anti-run-on valve solenoid
P Idle speed adjustment screw
Q Fuel needle valve
R Float bracket

4   Extract the seven screws and lift off the top cover and gasket (photo).

5   Drain the fuel from the float bowl.

6   Using a thin-bladed screwdriver, prise out the metering rod tamperproof plug.

7   Unscrew and withdraw the main metering rod, making sure to keep the air valve closed during the process.

8   Extract the four screws and detach the main jet body and gasket (photo). Take out the accelerator pump outlet one-way valve ball and weight by inverting the carburettor and allowing the components to drop out.

9   On early versions lift out the float, float spindle and the fuel inlet needle valve. On versions where a spring clip is used to retain the float, unclip the float spindle and position the float clear of the needle valve. Using pointed nose pliers remove the needle valve.

10   Use a thin-bladed screwdriver and carefully prise free the mixture adjustment screw tamperproof plug, then unscrew and remove the mixture adjuster.

11   Extract the four screws and remove the air control vacuum diaphragm housing, the return spring and the spring seat. The diaphragm can be removed after the circlip is extracted (photos).

12   Invert the carburettor, remove the three screws and detach the

19.4 Removing carburettor top cover

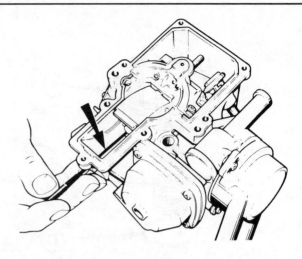

Fig. 3.37 Main metering rod removal (arrowed) – Ford VV carburettor (Sec 19)

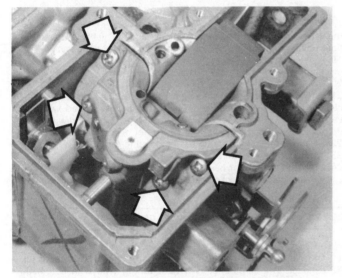

19.8 Main jet body retaining screw locations (arrowed)

19.11A Extract the retaining circlip (arrowed) ...

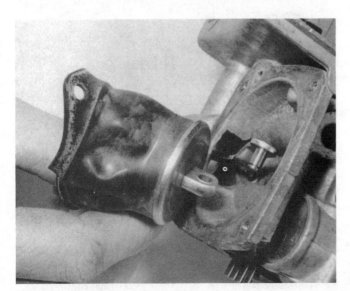

19.11B ... and remove the air control vacuum diaphragm

accelerator pump diaphragm, taking care not to lose the return spring, and where fitted the plate and spacer.

13 Clean out all drillings, jets and passages in the carburettor with compressed air – never by probing with wire. Examine all components for wear or damage and renew gaskets and diaphragms as a matter of course. If the air control vacuum diaphragm is black, this should be renewed with one of the later type which is more durable and is blue in colour. If the accelerator pump components do not include the metal plate and spacer as shown in Fig. 3.38, then a pump repair kit should be obtained which contains these additional parts.

14 Commence reassembly by making sure that the metering rod bias spring is correctly fitted to the air valve.

15 Fit the accelerator pump assembly, making sure that the gasket-faced side of the diaphragm is towards the cover.

16 Reconnect and refit the air valve control vacuum diaphragm housing, making sure that the vacuum hole in the diaphragm is in alignment with the gallery in the carburettor body and the housing (photo).

17 Relocate the mixture adjuster screw. Screw the adjuster in fully, then unscrew it by three full turns to provide the initial setting. Do not overtighten the screw when fitting.

18 Fit the fuel inlet needle valve, the float and the float pivot pin. The needle valve should be so installed that the spring-loaded plunger on

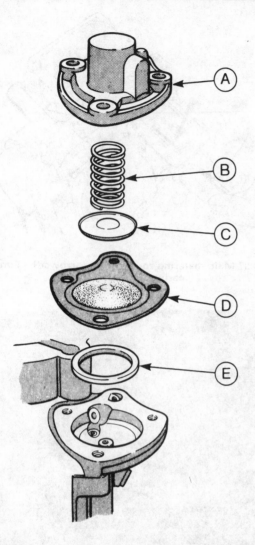

19.16 Diaphragm in position with holes correctly aligned

the valve will be in contact with the float once the fuel has entered the float bowl. Fit the spring clip on later versions where applicable.

19 Insert the accelerator pump ball and weight into the pump discharge passage (in that order).

20 Use a new gasket and fit the main jet body.

21 Very carefully slide the metering rod into position, hold the air valve closed and screw in the rod until its shoulder is aligned with the vertical face of the main jet body. If the rod binds when screwing it in, do not force it, but check the reason. Do not overtighten it.

22 Fit a new tamperproof plug to the metering rod hole.

23 Fit the top cover with a new gasket.

24 Once the carburettor has been fitted to the engine the idle speed and mixture must be checked and adjusted as described in Section 14.

20 Weber 2V carburettor – general description

Pre-1986 models

1   The Weber 2V unit is fitted to carburettor engine versions of the XR3 model. The carburettor is a dual venturi type with automatic electric choke, adjustable idle system and fixed size main jets.

Fig. 3.38 Modified accelerator pump components as fitted to later units – Ford VV carburettor (Sec 19)

A   Accelerator pump cover   D   Diaphragm
B   Return spring   E   Spacer
C   Metal plate

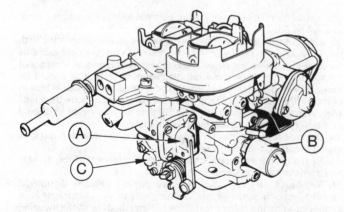

Fig. 3.39 Weber 2V DFT carburettor general view – XR3 models (Sec 20)

A   Accelerator pump housing   C   Power valve assembly
B   Anti-run-on valve solenoid

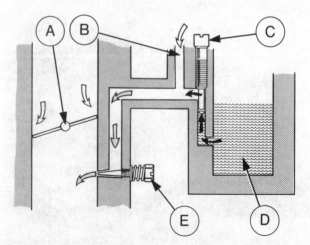

Fig. 3.40 Weber 2V carburettor idle system – XR3 models (Sec 20)

A   Throttle plate   D   Float chamber
B   Air bleed   E   Mixture screw
C   Idle jet

2 The unit is equipped with an accelerator pump to ensure smooth progression from the idle circuit to the main jet system and a vacuum-operated power valve to supply additional enrichment under high load conditions.

3 To prevent engine run-on when the ignition is switched off an anti-run-on valve is used to cut the fuel flow from the idle circuit.

4 The fully automatic electric choke system is energized by a small heater element fitted to the choke housing. Two pull-down systems and a fast idle system are also used to enrich the mixture under certain conditions and to hold the primary throttle plate open to increase idle speed when the engine is cold.

5 A more detailed description of the carburettor operation is as follows.

6 The idle system follows conventional practice and utilises an idle jet; air bleed and tamperproofed adjustable mixture screw. Fuel drawn from the float chamber is metered through the idle jet and partially atomized with air drawn from the air bleed. This mixture is fed down internal passages to the mixture screw where its volume can be adjusted before passing into the venturi.

7 When the ignition is switched off the plunger of the anti-run-on

valve moves out and blocks the idle mixture passage from idle jet to mixture screw. As the engine runs down after being switched off only air is drawn into the venturi and combustion cannot therefore continue.

8 For a fixed venturi carburettor to meet fuel consumption and exhaust emission requirements the main jets are calibrated to only suit the engine requirements in the one-quarter to three-quarters throttle range. To provide the necessary fuel enrichment at full throttle a power valve system is used.

9 The system comprises a vacuum-controlled, spring-loaded diaphragm valve and a fuel jet. Under normal running conditions inlet manifold vacuum is applied to the housing side of the diaphragm, drawing it back against spring pressure and closing the power valve. At the full throttle position very little vacuum is present and the spring pushes the diaphragm back which in turn opens the power valve. Additional fuel now passes through the carburettor passages and into the venturi; thus providing the additional enrichment for full throttle operation.

10 The fully automatic choke consists of an electrically-energized bi-metal coil, heat element, operating linkage, vacuum pull-down system and mechanical pull-down system. The bi-metal coil is heated by an element fitted to the choke housing and taking its power supply directly from the alternator rather than the battery. When the engine is not running the bi-metal coil will be fully wound up holding the choke plates closed. When the engine starts, power from the alternator heats the element which in turn causes the bi-metal coil to expand and begin to unwind. This action progressively opens the choke plates and continues until the engine reaches normal operating temperature, by which time the choke plates will be fully open.

11 When the engine is cold and running at light throttle openings the very rich mixture needed for starting is unnecessary. The vacuum pull-down system comes into operation under these conditions to pull the choke plates open against the action of the bi-metal coil. The system comprises a diaphragm, return spring, housing and connecting push-rod, which is attached to the choke plate linkage. During starting and acceleration the vacuum strength felt at the diaphragm is low and the operation of the choke is not affected. Under cruise conditions considerable manifold vacuum exists and is directed via a passage to the housing side of the diaphragm, thus pulling the diaphragm back against the pressure of the return spring. This movement is directed through the push-rod to open the choke plates and weaken the cold start mixture due to the increased volume of air now entering the venturi.

12 If a cold engine is driven at full throttle (which is to be avoided wherever possible) the amount of fuel passing through the engine will be far greater than required and could cause serious engine damage. To overcome this the mechanical pull-down system is used whereby a cam on the throttle linkage will open the choke plates mechanically against the action of the bi-metal coil and weaken the mixture.

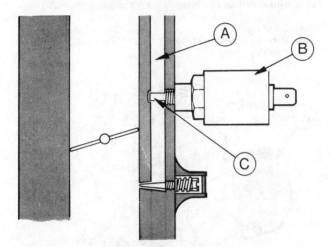

Fig. 3.41 Weber 2V carburettor idle mixture cut-off – XR3 models (Sec 20)

A Idle mixture passage
B Anti-run-on valve solenoid
C Anti-run-on valve plunger shutting off passage

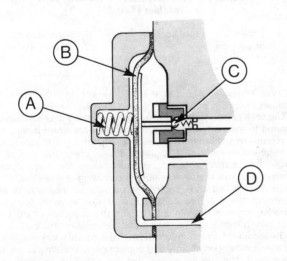

Fig. 3.42 Weber 2V carburettor power valve system under normal driving conditions – XR3 models (Sec 20)

A Return spring (compressed)
B Diaphragm (pulled back under vacuum)
C Power valve closed
D Vacuum supply passage (high vacuum)

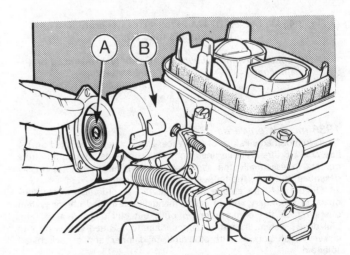

Fig. 3.43 Weber 2V carburettor automatic choke unit – XR3 models (Sec 20)

A Bi-metal coil   B Choke housing

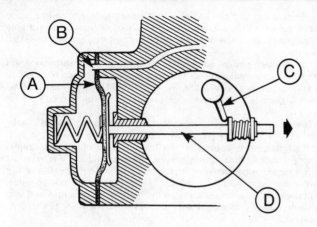

Fig. 3.44 Weber 2V carburettor vacuum pull-down system during starting and acceleration – XR3 models (Sec 20)

A Diaphragm
B Vacuum supply passage (low vacuum)
C Choke linkage
D Connecting push-rod

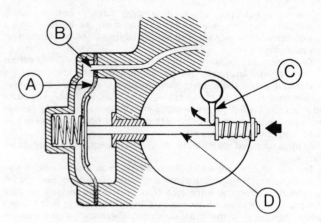

Fig. 3.45 Weber 2V carburettor vacuum pull-down system under cruise conditions – XR3 models (Sec 20)

A Diaphragm
B Vacuum supply passage (high vacuum)
C Choke linkage
D Connecting push-rod

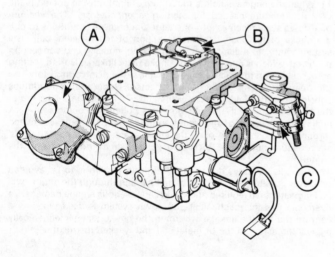

Fig. 3.46 Weber 2V DFTM carburettor general view – 1.4 litre models (Sec 20)

A Secondary venturi vacuum diaphragm
B Choke plate operating on primary venturi
C Throttle kicker

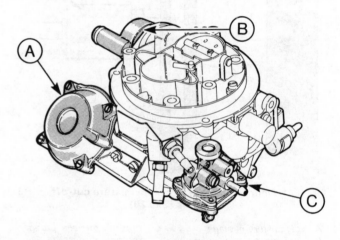

Fig. 3.47 Weber 2V TLD carburettor general view – 1.6 litre models (Sec 20)

A Secondary venturi vacuum diaphragm
B Automatic choke
C Throttle kicker

1986 models onwards

13 Two modified versions of the Weber 2V carburettor are used on 1.4 litre and 1.6 litre CVH engines from 1986 onwards. The carburettors operate in essentially the same way as the earlier unit previously described, but have the following additional features.
14 On the 1.4 litre engine the carburettor incorporates a vacuum-operated secondary venturi and a manually-controlled choke system operating on the primary venturi only, but still utilizing a vacuum pull-down system. In addition the carburettor is fitted with a throttle kicker, which acts as a throttle linkage damper, and a back bleed solenoid.
15 The throttle kicker is operated by manifold vacuum and delivered via a vacuum sustain valve. When the throttle is closed quickly the throttle kicker holds the throttle partially open allowing it to close progressively as the vacuum in the sustain valve decays. This results in

improved emission levels as the mixture entering the combustion chambers maintains combustion during deceleration.
16 The back bleed solenoid is used to control the amount of fuel being delivered to the venturi by the action of the accelerator pump. As the fuel requirements from the accelerator pump are considerably less on a hot engine than on a cold engine the back bleed solenoid plunger, energized by a thermal switch, partially blocks the pump discharge passage when the engine is at normal operating temperature.
17 On the 1.6 litre CVH engine the carburettor incorporates all the features of the 1.4 litre version except that a water temperature controlled automatic choke is fitted and the operation of the throttle kicker, which is only used on automatic transmission models is revised.
18 On automatic transmission models the throttle kicker is used to hold the throttle open slightly and prevent engine stalling when 'Drive' is engaged. The kicker is operated by manifold vacuum via an electrically-operated switch. With the transmission in 'neutral' or 'park' the switch is de-energized and blocks the vacuum supply to the kicker. In all other gear positions the switch is activated, vacuum is supplied to the kicker and the throttle is held slightly open. A throttle damper as used on previous automatic transmission models is also fitted to the throttle linkage to provide a progressive closing action.

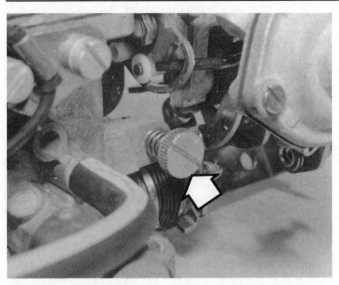

21.1A Weber 2V carburettor idle speed adjustment screw (arrowed) – 1.6 litre XR3 and 1.4 litre models

21.1B Weber 2V carburettor mixture adjustment screw tamperproof cap (arrowed) – 1.6 litre XR3 and 1.4 litre models

21 Weber 2V carburettor – adjustment

Idle speed and mixture adjustment

1 The procedure is the same as for the Ford VV carburettor as described in Section 14, but the adjusting screw locations are shown in photos 21.1A and 21.1B and in Figs. 3.48 and 3.49.

Fast idle speed (XR3 models)

2 Remove the air cleaner as described in Section 4.
3 Have the engine at normal operating temperature, with a tachometer connected in accordance with the manufacturer's instructions.
4 With the engine switched off, partially open the throttle by moving the cable at the carburettor. Close the choke plates with the fingers and hold them closed while the throttle is released. This has the effect of setting the choke mechanism in the high cam/fast idle position.
5 Release the choke valve plates and without touching the accelerator pedal, start the engine by just turning the key. Record the engine speed shown on the tachometer and compare the figure with that specified.

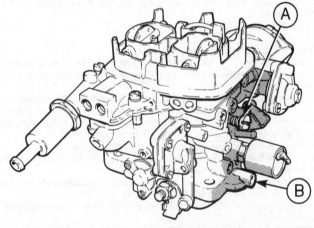

Fig. 3.48 Weber 2V carburettor idle speed adjustment screw (A) and mixture adjustment screw (B) – XR3 and 1.4 litre models (Sec 21)

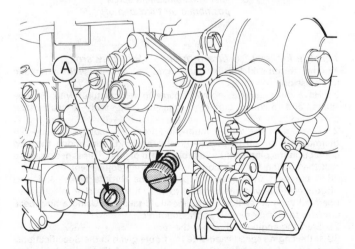

Fig. 3.49 Weber 2V carburettor mixture adjustment screw (A) and idle speed adjustment screw (B) – 1.6 litre models (Sec 21)

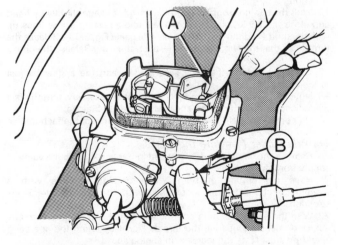

Fig. 3.50 Weber 2V carburettor choke linkage position for fast idle adjustment – XR3 models (Sec 21)

A   Choke plates held closed   B   Throttle held partially open

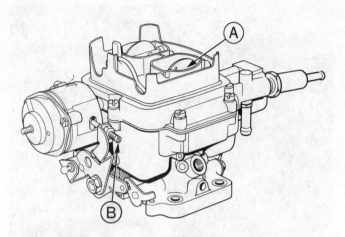

Fig. 3.51 Weber 2V carburettor fast idle adjustment – XR3 models (Sec 21)

A   *Choke plates in open position*   B   *Fast idle adjustment screw*

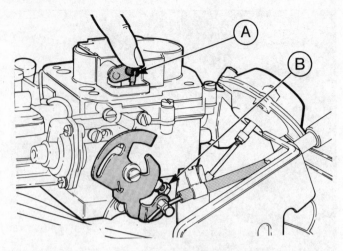

Fig. 3.52 Weber 2V carburettor fast idle adjustment – 1.4 litre models (Sec 21)

A   *Choke plates held open*   B   *Fast idle adjustment screw*

6   Where necessary turn the fast idle screw in or out to adjust the fast idle speed.
7   Refit the air cleaner.

Fast idle speed (1.4 litre models)
8   Adjust the engine idle speed and mixture settings as previously described, then switch off the engine. Leave the tachometer connected from the previous operation.
9   Undo the four bolts securing the air cleaner to the carburettor, disconnect the hot and cold air intake hoses and lift off the air cleaner. Position the air cleaner clear of the carburettor, but leave the crankcase breather hoses and the vacuum supply hose connected.
10   Pull the choke knob fully out and start the engine.
11   Using a finger on the linkage lever as shown in Fig. 3.52, hold the choke plate open and note the fast idle speed.
12   If adjustment is necessary turn the fast idle adjusting screw (Fig. 3.52) until the specified speed is obtained.
13   On completion refit the air cleaner and disconnect the tachometer.

Fast idle speed (1.6 litre models – 1986 onwards)
14   Remove the air cleaner as described in Section 4.
15   Have the engine at normal operating temperature with a tachometer connected in accordance with the manufacturer's instructions.
16   With the engine stopped, open the throttle linkage slightly by hand and close the choke plate until the fast idle adjusting screw lines up with the third (middle) step of the fast idle cam (Fig. 3.53). Release the throttle so that the fast idle screw rests on the cam. Release the choke plate.
17   Without touching the accelerator pedal, start the engine by just turning the key.
18   Note the fast idle speed and if adjustment is necessary, turn the fast idle adjusting screw until the specified speed is obtained.
19   On completion refit the air cleaner and disconnect the tachometer.

Throttle kicker (1.4 litre models)
20   Remove the air cleaner as described in Section 4. Plug the vacuum supply from the manifold.
21   Have the engine at normal operating temperature with a tachometer connected in accordance with the manufacturer's instructions.
22   With the engine running and the idle speed and mixture correctly adjusted, manually operate the throttle kicker by lifting the operating lever upwards. Note the increase in engine speed.
23   If the increased speed is outside the figure given in the Specifications, remove the tamperproof plug from the top of the kicker body and adjust the unit to give the specified speed.
24   Remove the tachometer and refit the air cleaner on completion.

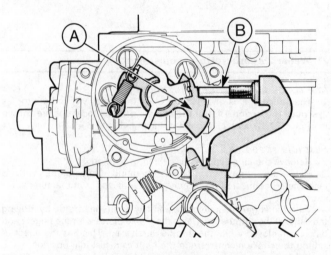

Fig. 3.53 Weber 2V carburettor fast idle adjustment – 1.6 litre models (Sec 21)

A   *Fast idle cam*
B   *Fast idle adjustment screw positioned on third step of cam*

Throttle kicker (1.6 litre models – 1986 onwards)
25   The throttle kicker is only fitted to models with automatic transmission.
26   Have the engine at normal operating temperature, with the idle speed and mixture correctly adjusted and with a tachometer connected.
27   Disconnect the wiring multi-plug from the radiator cooling fan thermostatic switch in the thermostat housing, and bridge the two contacts in the plug using a suitable length of wire. This is necessary so that the cooling fan runs continuously during adjustment.
28   Disconnect the vacuum supply at the throttle kicker and also disconnect the vacuum supply to the throttle kicker electrically-operated vacuum switch, at the manifold take-off. Using a new hose connect the kicker directly to the manifold.
29   Start the engine and record the rpm.
30   If the engine speed is outside the figure given in the Specifications, remove the tamperproof plug from the top of the kicker body and adjust the unit to give the specified speed.
31   On completion refit the vacuum connections in their original positions, reconnect the fan motor multi-plug and refit the air cleaner.

22 Weber 2V carburettor automatic choke unit – adjustment

XR3 models

1   Remove the air cleaner as described in Section 4.

2   Disconnect the electrical lead to the automatic choke.

3   Unscrew and remove the three screws which hold the automatic choke housing cover in position. Withdraw the cover and bi-metal coil, followed by the internal heat shield.

4   The choke plate vacuum pull-down should now be adjusted. To do this, fit a rubber band to the choke plate lever, open the throttle to allow the choke plates to close and then secure the band to keep the plates closed (Fig. 3.55).

5   Using a screwdriver, push the diaphragm open to its stop and measure the clearance between the lower edge of the primary choke plate and the air horn using a twist drill or other gauge rod. Where the clearance is outside that specified, remove the plug from the diaphragm housing and turn the screw, now exposed, in or out as necessary (Fig. 3.56).

6   Refit the plug and remove the rubber band.

7   The choke phasing must now be checked and adjusted. Hold the throttle partially open and set the fast idle cam so that the fast idle screw is located on the centre step of the cam. Release the throttle so that the cam is held in this position.

8   Push the choke plates downward until the step on the cam jams against the fast idle screw. Now measure the clearance between the lower edge of the primary choke plate and the air horn using a twist drill or gauge rod of suitable diameter.

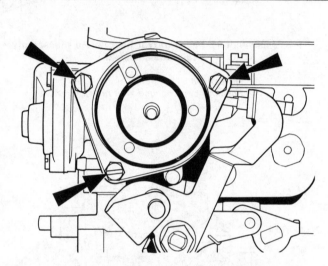

Fig. 3.54 Weber 2V carburettor automatic choke housing cover screw locations – XR3 models (Sec 22)

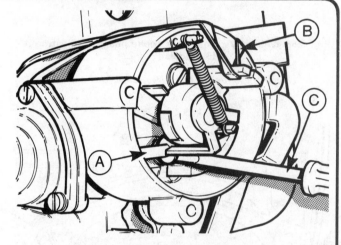

Fig. 3.55 Weber 2V carburettor vacuum pull-down check – XR3 models (Sec 22)

A   Diaphragm connecting push-rod
B   Rubber band holding choke plates closed
C   Screwdriver

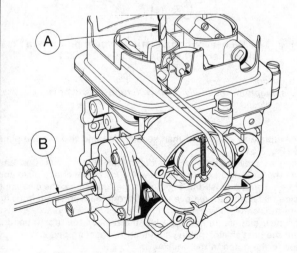

Fig. 3.56 Weber 2V carburettor vacuum pull-down adjustment – XR3 models (Sec 22)

A   Twist drill
B   Adjusting the pull-down setting

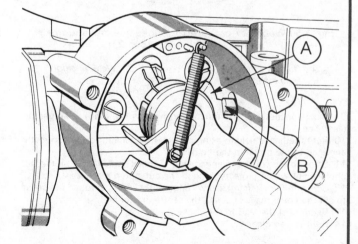

Fig. 3.57 Weber 2V carburettor choke phasing check – XR3 models (Sec 22)

A   Fast idle cam
B   Fast idle adjustment screw positioned on centre step of cam

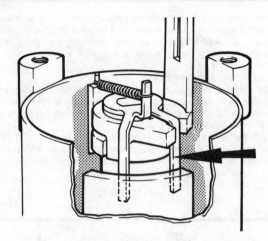

**Fig. 3.58 Weber 2V carburettor choke phasing adjustment –
XR3 models (Sec 22)**

Bend tag (arrowed) to achieve specified clearance

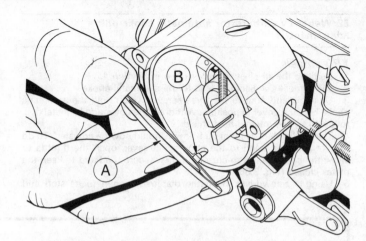

**Fig. 3.59 Weber 2V carburettor heat shield reassembly –
XR3 models (Sec 22)**

A   *Heat shield*
B   *Locating peg engaged with housing notch*

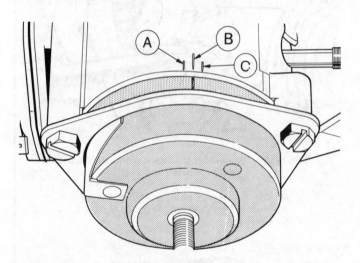

**Fig. 3.60 Weber 2V carburettor choke housing alignment
marks – XR3 models (Sec 22)**

A   *Rich position*   C   *Weak position*
B   *Index mark*

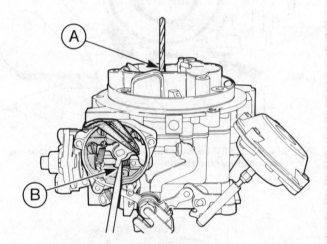

**Fig. 3.61 Weber 2V carburettor vacuum pull-down
adjustment – 1.6 litre models (Sec 22)**

A   *Twist drill*
B   *Diaphragm pushed fully open with rubber band holding choke
plate closed*

9   Where necessary, bend the tag (arrowed in Fig. 3.58) to adjust the clearance.
10 Refit the heat shield, making sure that the locating peg is correctly engaged in the notch in the housing.
11 Offer up the cover and engage the bi-metal coil with the slot in the choke lever which projects through the cut-out in the heat shield.
12 Screw in the retaining screws finger tight and then rotate the cover to set the cover mark opposite the centre index line.
13 Reconnect the lead to the choke.
14 Refit the air cleaner.

1.6 litre models – 1986 onwards
15 Remove the air cleaner as described in Section 4.
16 Release any pressure in the cooling system by loosening the pressure cap (see Chapter 2), then detach the water inlet and outlet hoses at the automatic choke unit. Clamp the hoses or position them with their ends facing upwards to minimise coolant leakage.
17 Undo the three screws and detach the choke bi-metal coil housing followed by the internal heat shield.
18 Fit a rubber band to the choke plate lever, open the throttle to allow

the choke plate to close, and then secure the band to keep the plate closed (Fig. 3.61).
19 Using a screwdriver, push the diaphragm open to its stop and measure the clearance between the lower edge of the choke plate and the air horn using a twist drill or other gauge rod. Where the clearance is outside that specified, remove the plug from the diaphragm housing and turn the screw, now exposed, in or out as necessary.
20 Fit a new diaphragm housing plug and remove the rubber band.
21 Refit the heat shield, making sure that the locating peg is correctly engaged in the notch in the housing.
22 Place the bi-metal coil housing in position with the coil engaged with the slot in the choke lever which projects through the cut-ou the heat shield.
23 Screw in the retaining screws finger tight and then rotate housing to set the mark opposite the dot punch mark on the cho body. Secure the housing.
24 Reconnect the hoses and refit the air cleaner.
25 Check and if necessary top up the cooling system as described in Chapter 2.

23 Weber 2V carburettor automatic choke unit – removal, checking and refitting

XR3 models

1 Remove the air cleaner as described in Section 4.
2 Disconnect the electrical lead to the automatic choke.
3 Undo the three choke housing cover retaining screws, withdraw the cover and bi-metal coil, followed by the internal heat shield.
4 Undo the six carburettor upper body retaining screws, hold the fast idle operating lever clear of the choke housing and lift off the upper body.
5 Undo the three screws securing the choke housing to the upper body, disconnect the link rod and remove the choke housing.
6 Undo the three screws and remove the vacuum pull-down housing cover, then withdraw the spring, diaphragm and operating rod assembly.
7 Extract the circlip on the end of the vacuum pull-down operating rod and slide off the rod components.
8 Make a note of the exact position of the choke mechanism return and tension springs then undo the shaft nut, withdraw the shaft from the choke housing and remove the linkages and cams.
9 Clean and inspect all the parts for wear, damage, cracking, or distortion. Pay particular attention to the condition of the pull-down diaphragm and the choke housing O-ring seal. Renew any parts as necessary.
10 Reassemble the choke mechanism shaft, linkages, cams and tension springs with reference to Figs. 3.63 and the notes made during removal. Secure the shaft with the retaining nut.
11 Assemble the components to the vacuum pull-down operating rod and secure with the circlip.

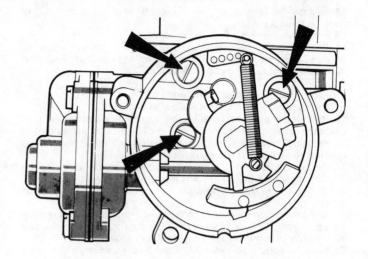

Fig. 3.62 Weber 2V carburettor choke housing retaining screw locations – XR3 models (Sec 23)

12 Locate the vacuum pull-down diaphragm and operating rod to the choke housing and with the diaphragm laying flat on the housing face, refit the cover and secure with the three screws.
13 Place the O-ring seal on the choke housing, then connect the housing to the link rod.

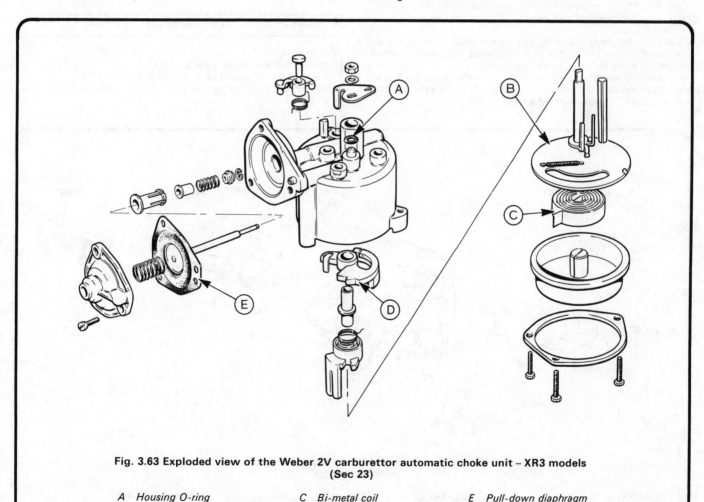

Fig. 3.63 Exploded view of the Weber 2V carburettor automatic choke unit – XR3 models (Sec 23)

A *Housing O-ring*	C *Bi-metal coil*	E *Pull-down diaphragm*
B *Heat shield*	D *Fast idle cam*	

14 Position the housing on the carburettor upper body and secure with the three screws.

15 Refit the upper body to the carburettor.

16 Before refitting the housing cover and bi-metal coil, refer to Section 22 and adjust the vacuum pull-down and choke phasing, then fit the cover and bi-metal coil as described.

1.6 litre models – 1986 onwards

17 Remove the air cleaner as described in Section 4.

18 Release any pressure in the cooling system by loosening the filler cap, then detach the water inlet and outlet hoses at the automatic choke unit. Clamp the hoses or position them with their ends facing upwards to minimise coolant leakage.

19 Disconnect the lead at the anti-run-on valve solenoid.

20 Disconnect the fuel supply and return hoses at the carburettor. If crimped type hose clips are used, cut them off and use screw type clips at reassembly.

21 Undo the six carburettor upper body retaining screws and remove the upper body. Note that four of the screws are of the Torx type and a suitable key or socket bit will be needed for removal.

22 With the upper body removed, undo the three screws and remove the choke bi-metal coil housing followed by the internal heat shield.

23 Undo the three screws securing the choke housing to the upper body, disconnect the link rod and remove the choke housing.

24 Undo the three screws and remove the vacuum pull-down housing cover, then withdraw the spring, diaphragm and operating rod assembly.

25 Make a note of the exact position of the choke mechanism return and tension springs, then undo the nut and remove the connecting rod, levers and link from the choke housing (Fig. 3.65).

26 Clean and inspect all the parts for wear, damage, cracking or distortion. Pay particular attention to the condition of the pull-down diaphragm and the choke housing O-ring seal. Renew any parts as necessary.

27 Reassemble the choke mechanism connecting rod, levers, link and springs with reference to Fig. 3.65 and the notes made during removal. Secure the assembly with the retaining nut.

28 Locate the vacuum pull-down diaphragm and operating rod in the choke housing and with the diaphragm laying flat on the housing face, refit the cover and secure with the three screws.

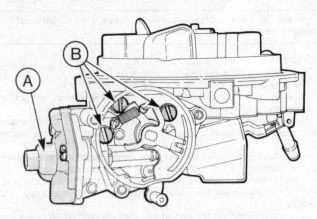

Fig. 3.64 Weber 2V carburettor pull-down housing cover (A) and choke housing retaining screws (B) – 1.6 litre models (Sec 23)

29 Locate the O-ring seal on the choke housing, then connect the housing to the link rod.

30 Position the housing on the carburettor upper body and secure with the three screws.

31 Refit the upper body to the carburettor.

32 Before refitting the bi-metal coil housing refer to Section 22 and adjust the vacuum pull-down, then fit the coil housing as described.

24 Weber 2V carburettor – removal and refitting

XR3 models

1 Disconnect the battery negative lead.

2 Remove the air cleaner as described in Section 4.

3 Disconnect the electrical leads at the electric choke and anti-run-on valve.

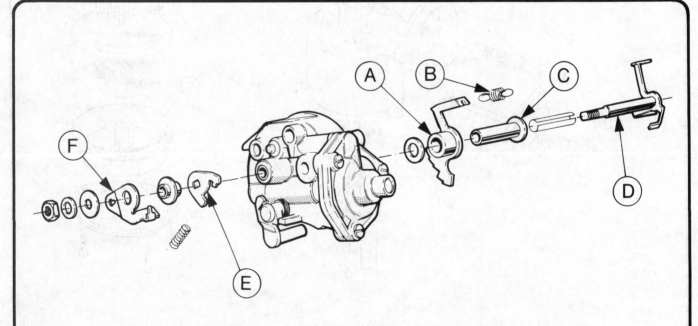

Fig. 3.65 Exploded view of the Weber 2V carburettor automatic choke unit – 1.6 litre models (Sec 23)

A　Upper choke operating link	C　Connecting rod sleeve	E　Pull-down link
B　Fast idle cam return spring	D　Connecting rod and lever	F　Actuating lever

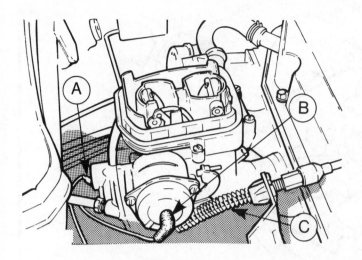

Fig. 3.66 Weber 2V carburettor disconnection points – XR3 models (Sec 24)

A   *Anti-run-on valve lead*   B   *Electric choke lead*
C   *Throttle cable*

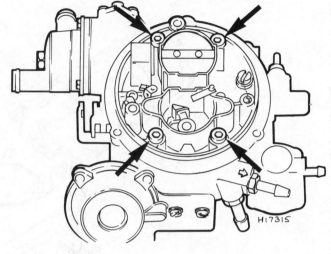

Fig. 3.67 Weber 2V carburettor mounting through-bolt locations – 1.6 litre models (Sec 24)

4   Disconnect the vacuum pipe at the carburettor outlet.
5   Disconnect the throttle cable by releasing the spring clip securing the end fitting to the ball-stud, then unscrewing the cable bracket fixing bolts.
6   Disconnect the fuel inlet and return hoses, noting their respective positions, and plug them after removal. If crimped type clips are used, cut them off and use screw type clips when refitting.
7   Undo the four mounting flange nuts and washers and withdraw the carburettor from the inlet manifold.
8   Refitting is the reverse sequence to removal, but use a new flange gasket and ensure that the mating surfaces are perfectly clean. Make sure that the vacuum pipe fuel trap is correctly positioned, and on completion check the idle speed and mixture settings as described in Section 21.

1.4 litre models
9   The procedure is identical to that just described for XR3 models except that a manual choke is fitted and the choke inner cable must be released by slackening the linkage clamp bolt.
10   Additionally when refitting, adjust the choke cable as described in Section 12.

1.6 litre models – 1986 onwards
11   Disconnect the battery negative lead.
12   Remove the air cleaner as described in Section 4.
13   If the engine is still hot, depressurise the cooling system by carefully releasing the pressure cap (see Chapter 2).
14   Disconnect the coolant inlet and outlet hoses at the automatic choke and clamp or plug their ends to prevent coolant loss.
15   Disconnect the throttle cable by releasing the spring clip securing the end fitting to the ball-stud, then unscrewing the cable bracket fixing bolts.
16   Disconnect the fuel inlet and return hoses, noting their respective positions, and plug them after removal. If crimped type clips are used, cut them off and use screw type clips when refitting.
17   Disconnect the distributor vacuum pipe and the throttle kicker vacuum pipe on automatic transmission models.
18   Disconnect the electrical lead at the anti-run-on valve solenoid.
19   Using a suitable Torx type key or socket bit, unscrew the four mounting through-bolts from the top of the carburettor and remove the unit from the manifold.
20   Refitting is the reverse sequence to removal, but use a new flange gasket and ensure that the mating faces are perfectly clean. On completion top up the cooling system as described in Chapter 2 and check the idle speed and mixture settings as described in Section 21.

25 Weber 2V carburettor – overhaul

XR3 models
1   Remove the carburettor from the engine as described in Section 24. Refer to the caution at the end of Section 2 before proceeding.
2   Unscrew the fuel filter at the inlet hose union.
3   Remove the carburettor upper body by unscrewing the six retaining screws, then lift the upper body off while holding the fast idle operating lever clear of the choke housing.
4   Mop out the fuel from the float chamber and extract the jets from the carburettor main body. Identify the jet locations before removal, with reference to Figs. 3.69.
5   Withdraw the accelerator pump discharge tube.
6   Undo the four screws, take off the accelerator pump cover and withdraw the diaphragm and spring.
7   Undo the three screws, take off the power valve cover and withdraw the diaphragm and spring.
8   Tap out the float retaining pin, remove the float and take out the needle valve. Remove the upper body gasket and unscrew the needle valve housing and washer.
9   This is the practical limit of dismantling on these carburettors. If wear is detected in the throttle spindle, plates or bearings it is recommended that a new carburettor is obtained.
10   Examine all the dismantled components for wear or damage and renew the gasket and diaphragms as a matter of routine. Clean all the jets, internal passages and galleries using air pressure – never probe with wire.
11   Commence reassembly by fitting the power valve diaphragm, spring and cover. Secure the cover with the three screws.
12   Refit the accelerator pump spring, diaphragm and cover and secure the cover with the four screws.
13   Refit the accelerator pump discharge tube and the jets to their original locations in the carburettor body.
14   Locate a new upper body gasket in position and refit the needle valve assembly and the float.
15   Refit the fuel filter and inlet hose union.
16   Check the float setting. To do this, hold the carburettor upper body vertically so that the float is hanging down and closing the needle valve. Measure the distance between the surface of the gasket and the base of the float. If adjustment is necessary to achieve the correct setting (see Specifications), bend the tag (A in Fig. 3.72).
17   Fit the upper body to the main body and secure with the six screws.
18   Once the carburettor has been fitted to the engine, the idle speed and mixture must be checked and adjusted as described in Section 21.

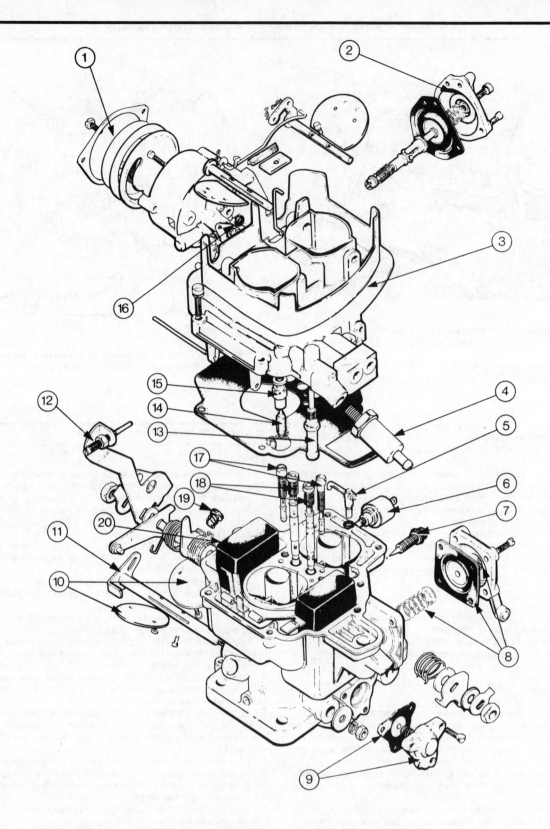

Fig. 3.68 Exploded view of the Weber 2V DFT carburettor – XR3 models (Sec 25)

1	Choke housing cover	6	Anti-run-on valve solenoid	12	Fast idle adjustment screw	17	Idle jets
2	Vacuum pull-down assembly	7	Mixture adjustment screw	13	Fuel return connection	18	Combined emulsion tube, air correction and main jets
3	Upper body	8	Accelerator pump assembly	14	Fuel inlet needle valve	19	Idle speed adustment screw
4	Fuel filter	9	Power valve assembly	15	Needle valve housing	20	Float
5	Accelerator pump discharge tube	10	Throttle valve plates	16	O-ring		
		11	Secondary throttle spindle				

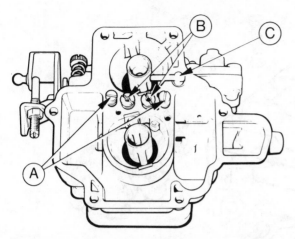

Fig. 3.69 Weber 2V carburettor jet locations – XR3 models (Sec 25)

A Idle jets
B Combined emulsion tube, air correction and main jets
C Accelerator pump discharge tube

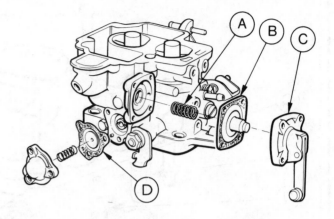

Fig. 3.70 Weber 2V carburettor accelerator pump and power valve component orientation – XR3 models (Sec 25)

A Return spring
B Accelerator pump diaphragm
C Accelerator pump cover
D Power valve diaphragm

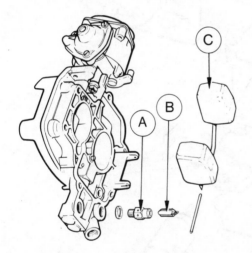

Fig. 3.71 Weber 2V carburettor float and needle valve components – XR3 models (Sec 25)

A Needle valve housing
B Needle valve
C Float

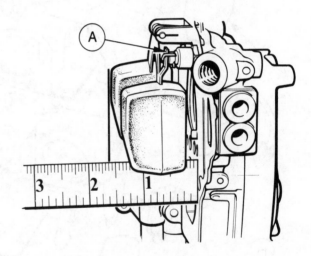

Fig. 3.72 Weber 2V carburettor float height adjustment – XR3 models (Sec 25)

A Adjustment tag

If by any chance the mixture screw was removed at overhaul, screw it in very gently until it seats and then unscrew it three full turns. This will provide a basic setting to get the engine started.

1.4 litre models

19 Remove the carburettor from the engine as described in Section 24.
20 Undo the two screws and nuts securing the throttle kicker to its mounting bracket and remove the kicker (photo).
21 Undo the screws and detach the throttle kicker (bracket) from the carburettor body. Note the anti-run-on valve solenoid lead located by one of the retaining screws.
22 Undo the four screws and lift off the throttle kicker cover, then take out the diaphragm and spring.
23 Undo the four screws and lift off the accelerator pump cover, then take out the diaphragm and spring.
24 Disconnect the secondary venturi vacuum unit operating rod by pushing the end of the rod downwards and twisting to release the ball socket end fitting (photo).
25 Undo the four screws and lift off the secondary venturi vacuum

unit cover (photo). Withdraw the spring and lift out the diaphragm.
26 Undo the three screws and lift off the power valve cover (photo), then take out the spring and diaphragm.
27 Using a sharp pointed instrument carefully prise out the idle mixture adjusting screw tamperproof plug (where fitted) and unscrew the mixture screw.
28 Undo the six screws (photo) and lift off the carburettor upper body (photo).
29 Undo the three screws (photo) and lift off the vacuum pull-down cover, then take out the spring and diaphragm (photo).
30 Undo the brass nut in the upper body, remove the washer and take out the fuel inlet filter (photos).
31 Extract the float retaining pin, unhook the float arm from the needle valve and remove the float assembly (photos).
32 Withdraw the needle valve and unscrew the needle valve housing (photo).
33 Mop out the fuel from the float chamber and extract the jets from the carburettor main body (photos). Identify the jet locations before removal with reference to Fig. 3.73.
34 If required separate the idle jets from their holders (photo) and the main jets from the emulsion tubes (photo).

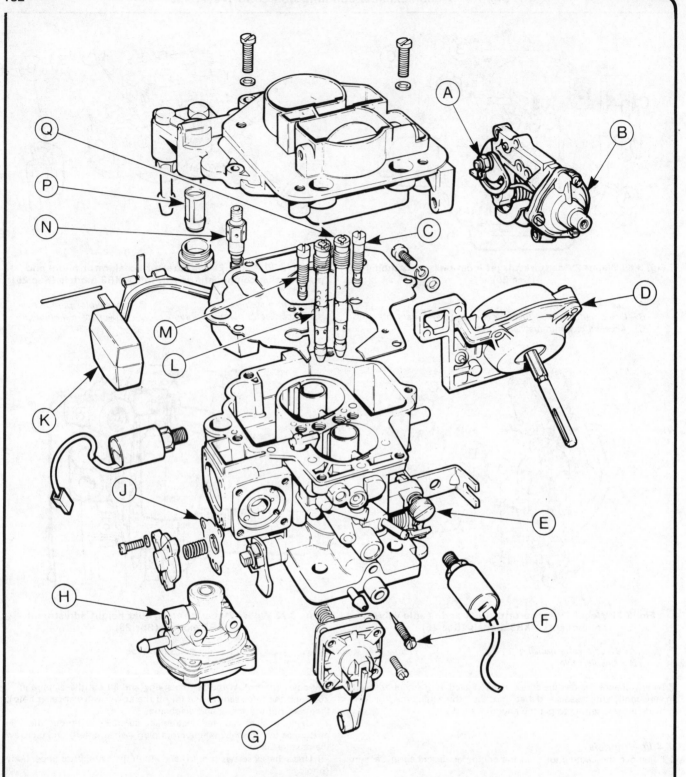

Fig. 3.73 Exploded view of the Weber 2V DFTM carburettor – 1.4 litre models (Sec 25)

A Manual choke assembly
B Vacuum pull-down unit
C Secondary idle jet

D Secondary venturi vacuum
   unit
E Idle speed adjustment screw
F Mixture adjustment screw

G Accelerator pump assembly
H Throttle kicker
J Power valve diaphragm
K Float

L Primary emulsion tube
M Primary idle jet
N Needle valve
P Fuel inlet filter
Q Secondary emulsion tube

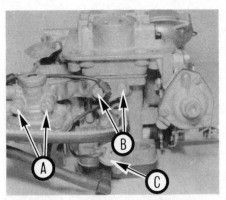

25.20 Throttle kicker-to-bracket screws (A), kicker bracket screws (B) and anti-run-on solenoid (C)

25.24 Disconnect the secondary venturi vacuum unit operating rod (arrowed)

25.25 Secondary venturi vacuum unit cover screws (arrowed)

25.26 Power valve location (arrowed)

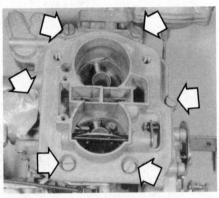

25.28A Upper body retaining screw locations (arrowed)

23.28B Removing the carburettor upper body

25.29A Vacuum pull-down cover screw locations (arrowed)

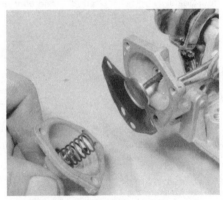

25.29B Removing the vacuum pull-down cover, spring and diaphragm

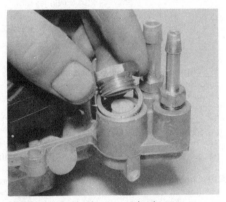

25.30A Undo the brass nut in the upper body ...

25.30B ... and remove the fuel inlet filter

25.31A Extract the float retaining pin ...

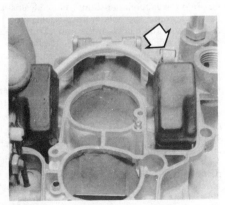

25.31B ... unhook the float arm from the needle valve (arrowed) and remove the float

25.32 Withdraw the needle valve

25.33A Removing the secondary idle jet ...

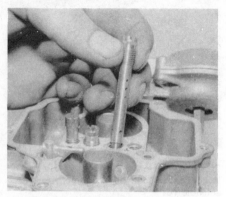

25.33B ... and secondary main jet with emulsion tube

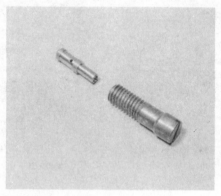

25.34A Idle jet removed from holder ...

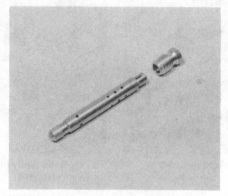

25.34B ... and emulsion tube removed from main jet

35 Withdraw the accelerator pump discharge tube and remove the carburettor gasket.

36 Carry out a careful inspection of the carburettor components with reference to paragraphs 9 and 10.

37 Commence reassembly by fitting the accelerator pump discharge tube and the jets to their main body locations.

38 Refit the float needle valve assembly, hook the float arm under the needle valve and secure the float with the retaining pin. Refit the fuel inlet filter and brass nut.

39 Check the float setting by holding the carburettor vertically so that the float is hanging down and closing the needle valve. Measure the distance between the upper body mating face and the upper surface of the float. If adjustment is necessary to achieve the correct setting (see Specifications) bend the float arm tag as necessary (Fig. 3.74).

40 Refit the vacuum pull-down assembly ensuring that the diaphragm lies flat and that the hole in the diaphragm and notch in the cover are aligned with the gallery in the upper body.

41 Move the choke mechanism to the fully closed position, then manually push the vacuum pull-down diaphragm operating rod up to its stop.

42 Using a twist drill shank or other gauge rod, measure the clearance between the lower edge of the choke plate and the air horn. Where the clearance is outside that specified, remove the tamperproof plug in the diaphragm cover and turn the adjustment screw as necessary. Fit a new plug on completion.

43 Position a new gasket on the carburettor body, refit the upper body and secure with the six screws.

44 Refit the power valve, secondary venturi vacuum unit, accelerator pump and throttle kicker assemblies using the reverse of the removal procedure, and with reference to the accompanying photos and illustrations.

45 Screw in the mixture adjusting screw until it lightly contacts its seat, then unscrew it three turns. This will provide an initial adjustment and allow the engine to be started.

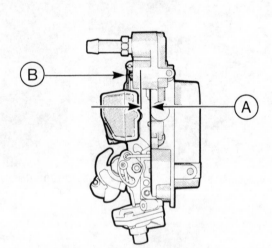

Fig. 3.74 Weber 2V carburettor float height adjustment – 1.4 litre models (Sec 25)

A Checking dimension   *B Float arm tag*

46 Once the carburettor has been refitted to the car, check and adjust the idle speed and mixture settings, the fast idle speed and the throttle kicker adjustment as described in Section 21.

1.6 litre models (1986 onwards)

47 Remove the carburettor from the engine as described in Section 24.

48 Undo the two screws, hold the throttle open and separate the carburettor upper body from the main body.

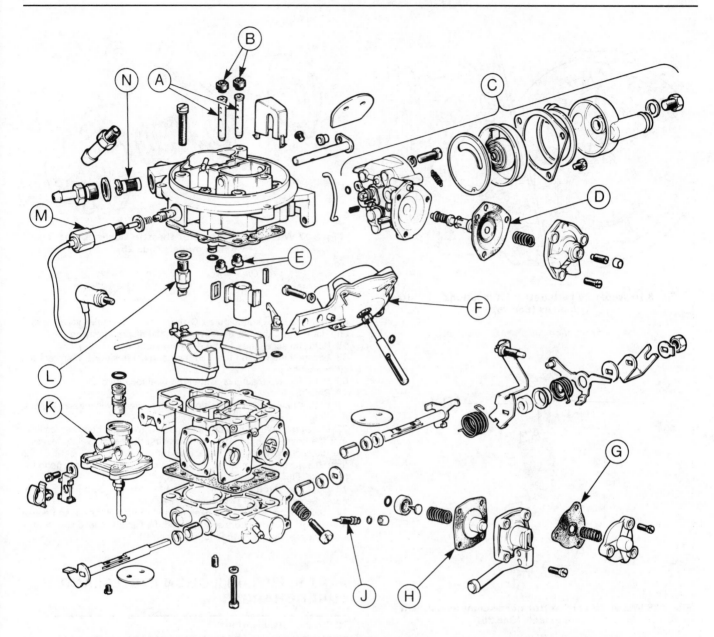

Fig. 3.75 Exploded view of the Weber 2V TLD carburettor – 1.6 litre models (Sec 25)

A Emulsion tubes
B Air correction jets
C Automatic choke assembly
D Vacuum pull-down
   diaphragm

E Main jets
F Secondary venturi vacuum
   unit
G Power valve diaphragm

H Accelerator pump diaphragm
J Mixture adjustment screw
K Throttle kicker (automatic
   transmission models)

L Needle valve
M Anti-run-on valve solenoid
N Fuel inlet filter

49 Tap out the float retaining pin, remove the float and lift out the needle valve. Remove the carburettor gasket.
50 Unscrew the needle valve housing and remove the washer.
51 Unscrew the fuel inlet in the upper body and remove the filter.
52 Unscrew the two air correction jets from the upper body. Identify the jet locations before removal with reference to Fig. 3.76. Now turn the upper body over and withdraw the emulsion tubes which are located beneath the air correction jets.
53 Unscrew the two main jets from the underside of the upper body, again noting their respective positions.
54 Mop out the fuel from the float chamber in the main body, then carefully prise out the accelerator pump discharge tube and O-ring seal.

55 Undo the four screws, lift off the accelerator pump cover and remove the diaphragm and spring. Ensure that the inlet valve, valve seat and O-ring have been withdrawn with the spring. If not, remove them from their locations in the main body.
56 On automatic transmission models undo the two throttle kicker retaining screws and withdraw the kicker. Disconnect the linkage and remove the unit. Undo the four screws, take off the throttle kicker cover and remove the diaphragm and spring.
57 Disconnect the secondary venturi vacuum unit operating rod by pushing the end of the rod downwards and twisting to release the ball socket end fitting.
58 Undo the four screws and lift off the secondary venturi vacuum unit cover. Withdraw the spring and lift out the diaphragm.

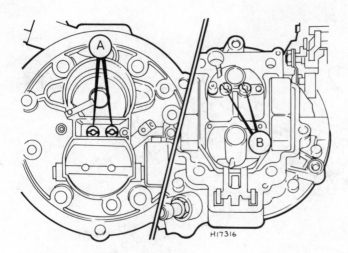

Fig. 3.76 Weber 2V carburettor jet locations – 1.6 litre models (Sec 25)

A   Air correction jets   B   Main jets

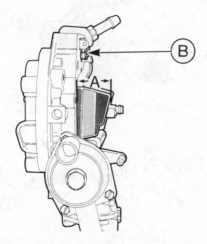

Fig. 3.78 Weber 2V carburettor float height adjustment – 1.6 litre models (Sec 25)

A   Checking dimension   B   Float tag

59 Using a sharp pointed instrument prise out the idle mixture adjusting screw tamperproof plug (if fitted) and unscrew the mixture screw.
60 Undo the three screws and lift off the power valve cover, then remove the spring and diaphragm.
61 Carry out a careful inspection of the carburettor components with reference to paragraphs 9 and 10.
62 Commence reassembly by screwing in the mixture adjusting screw until it lightly contacts its seat, then unscrew it three turns. This will provide an initial adjustment and allow the engine to be started.
63 Position the secondary venturi vacuum unit diaphragm on the housing. Ensure that the diaphragm lies flat and that the hole in the diaphragm and the notch in the cover are aligned with the vacuum gallery in the main body. Refit the spring and cover then connect the operating rod.
64 Refit the throttle kicker diaphragm, spring and cover as shown in Fig. 3.77. With the diaphragm lying flat, secure the cover with the four screws.
65 Refit the power valve diaphragm and spring, then fit the cover ensuring that the vacuum galleries are aligned and the diaphragm lies flat.

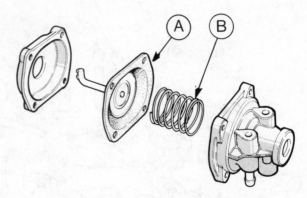

Fig. 3.77 Weber 2V carburettor throttle kicker components – 1.6 litre models (Sec 25)

A   Diaphragm   B   Return spring

66 Refit the accelerator pump O-ring, valve seat, inlet valve, spring and diaphragm, then fit the cover with the diaphragm lying flat.
67 Refit the accelerator pump discharge tube and O-ring.
68 Locate the emulsion tubes in their original positions, then refit the air correction jets.
69 Refit the two main jets to their original locations.
70 Refit the filter and fuel inlet.
71 With a new gasket in position refit the needle valve assembly and the float.
72 Check the float setting by holding the carburettor body vertically so that the float is hanging down and closing the needle valve. Measure the distance between the surface of the gasket and the base of the float. If adjustment is necessary to achieve the correct setting, bend the float tag (Fig. 3.78).
73 Hold the throttle partially open and refit the carburettor upper body. Secure with the two screws.
74 Once the carburettor has been refitted to the car, check and adjust the idle speed and mixture settings, and the fast idle speed and throttle kicker adjustment as described in Section 21.

PART B: FUEL-INJECTION SYSTEM AND TURBOCHARGER

26 General description

On fuel-injected models the fuel system comprises a centrally mounted fuel tank, electrically-operated fuel pump and Bosch K-Jetronic or KE-Jetronic continuous injection system according to model. The system is used in conjunction with a turbocharger on RS Turbo models.
A more detailed description of the various system components will be found later in this Chapter.

Warning: *Many of the procedures in this Chapter entail the removal of fuel pipes and connections which may result in some fuel spillage. Before carrying out any operation on the fuel system refer to the precautions given in Safety First! at the beginning of this manual and follow them implicitly. Petrol is a highly dangerous and volatile liquid and the precautions necessary when handling it cannot be overstressed.*

27 Maintenance and inspection

1   Refer to Part A: Section 2, but additionally the following should be carried out at the specified intervals.
2   Adjust the idle speed and mixture settings as described in Section 39.

3 Renew the air cleaner air filter element as described in Section 28.

4 Renew the fuel filter using the procedure described in Section 38.

28 Air cleaner and element – removal and refitting

K-Jetronic system

1 Disconnect the battery earth lead.

2 Unscrew and loosen off the air ducting-to-sensor plate unit securing band, then separate the two (photos).

3 Carefully pull free the shut-off valve hose from the air ducting connector. The hose is a press fit (photo).

4 Unscrew and remove the six air sensor plate-to-cleaner top cover retaining screws, but leave the plate unit in position for the moment.

5 Prise free and release the air cleaner cover retaining clips and detach the hose from the cover at the front (photo).

6 Carefully lift the sensor plate clear (photo), together with its gasket, and pivot it back out of the way. Withdraw the shut-off valve from the rear end of the cleaner case cover (photo) then lift out the cover (photo) and remove the element from the casing (photo).

7 If the air cleaner casing is to be removed you will need to detach the fuel filter from the side of the cleaner casing (leave the fuel lines attached to the filter) and the air intake hose from the front end of the case. Unscrew and remove the casing retaining nuts from the inner wing panel and lift out the casing.

8 Refitting is the reversal of the removal procedure. Wipe the casing clean before inserting the new element. When fitting the sensor plate unit into position on the top cover check that the gasket is in good condition and aligned correctly (photo).

9 Check that all connections are secure on completion.

28.2A Slacken the securing band screw ...

28.2B ... and lift the air duct away from the sensor plate unit

28.3 Detach the shut off valve hose

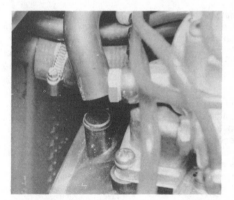
28.5 Detach the hose from the air cleaner casing cover at the front

28.6A Lift the sensor plate unit clear ...

28.6B ... detach the shut-off valve ...

28.6C ... lift out the cover ...

28.6D ... and withdraw the element

28.8 Locating the sensor unit gasket

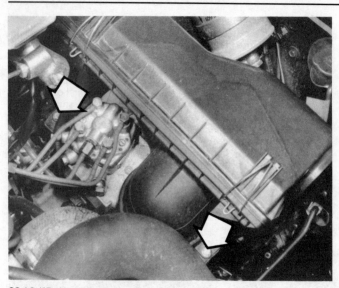

28.10 KE-Jetronic air cleaner retaining bolts (arrowed)

28.11 Lift off the air cleaner cover and remove the element

KE-Jetronic system

10 Undo the two bolts securing the air cleaner assembly to the air sensor plate unit (photo) and remove the air cleaner assembly.

11 Unclip the retaining clips and lift off the air cleaner top cover. Remove the filter element (photo).

12 Clean the inside of the air cleaner body and fit a new filter element. Place the top cover in position and secure with the clips.

13 Refit the unit to the air sensor plate and secure with the two bolts.

29 Fuel tank – removal and refitting

The procedures are the same as described in Part A: Section 8 but in addition disconnect the fuel tank-to-fuel pump hose from the rear face of the tank.

30 Throttle cable – adjustment

The procedure is the same as described in Part A: Section 9 except that the cable adjuster is situated in a bracket alongside the throttle housing.

31 Throttle cable – removal and refitting

The procedure is the same as described in Part A: Section 10 except that it is not necessary to remove the air cleaner and the location of the mounting bracket is alongside the throttle housing.

32 Accelerator pedal – removal and refitting

The procedure is the same as described in Part A: Section 11.

33 Bosch K-Jetronic fuel-injection system – description and operation

The Bosch K-Jetronic fuel-injection system is fitted to XR3i and XR3i Cabriolet models. The system is of the continuous injection type and supplies a precisely controlled quantity of atomized fuel to each cylinder under all operating conditions.

This system, when compared with conventional carburettor arrangements, achieves a more accurate control of the air/fuel mixture resulting in reduced emission levels and improved performance.

The main components of the fuel injection system fall into two groups:

A *Fuel tank*
   Fuel pump
   Fuel accumulator
   Fuel filter
   Fuel distributor/mixture control assembly
   Throttle valve (plate)
   Injector valves
   Air box (plenum chamber)
   Warm-up regulator
   Auxiliary air device
   Cold start valve
B *Thermo-time switch*
   Safety module
   Fuel shut-off valve
   Speed sensor module
   Wiring

The fuel tank is similar to the one described in Part A: Section 1 for carburettor type vehicles except that before removing it, the pipes to the fuel pump and accumulator and the pipe from the pressure regulator must be disconnected and plugged.

The fuel pump is of electrically-operated, roller cell type. A pressure relief valve is incorporated in the pump to prevent excessive pressure build-up in the event of a restriction in the pipelines.

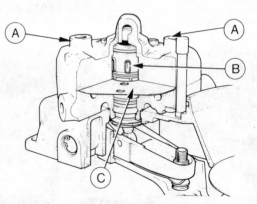

Fig. 3.79 Cutaway view of the K-Jetronic system fuel distributor (Sec 33)

A *Fuel outlet connections*   C *Diaphragm*
B *Control plunger and barrel*

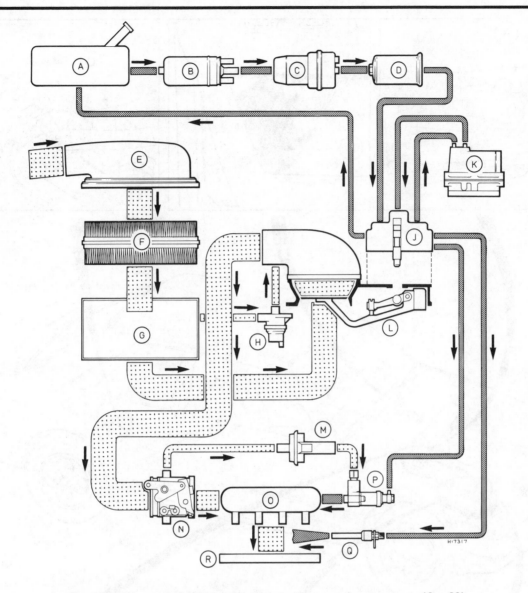

Fig. 3.80 K-Jetronic fuel-injection system layout and components (Sec 33)

A Fuel tank
B Pump
C Accumulator
D Filter
E Air intake

F Air filter
G Cleaner body
H Shut-off valve
J Fuel distributor

K Warm-up regulator
L Sensor plate
M Auxiliary air device
N Throttle housing

O Plenum chamber
P Cold start valve
Q Injectors
R Inlet manifold

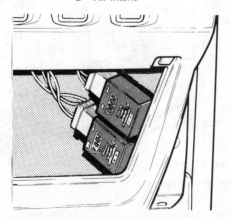

Fig. 3.81 K-Jetronic system speed sensing module and fuel pump safety module locations (Sec 33)

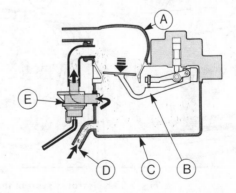

Fig. 3.82 K-Jetronic system fuel shut-off valve components (Sec 33)

A Air ducting
B Sensor plate
C Air cleaner body

D Air intake
E Shut-off valve (open)

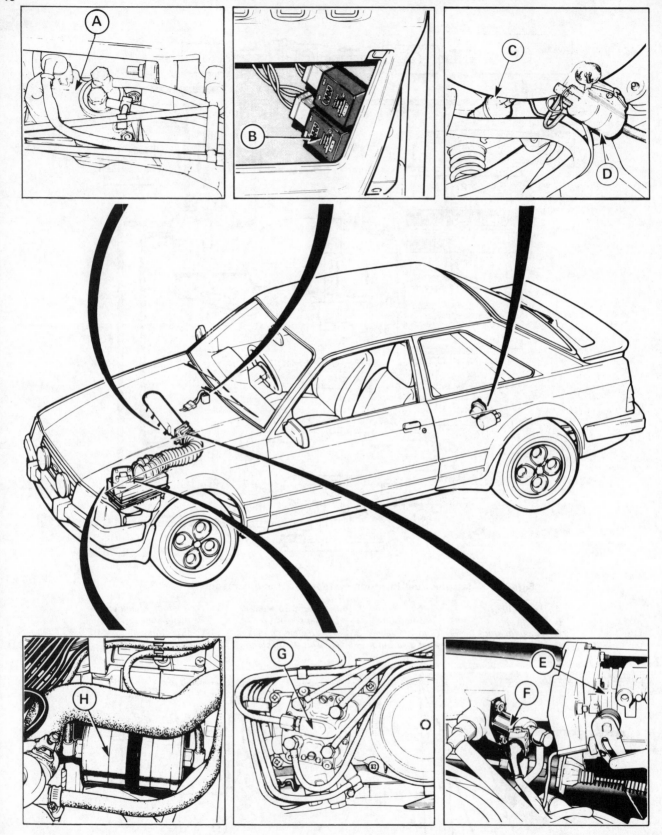

Fig. 3.83 K-Jetronic system main component locations (Sec 33)

A	Warm-up regulator	C	Fuel accumulator (early model location)	D	Fuel pump	F	Cold start valve
B	Speed sensing module			E	Throttle housing	G	Fuel distributor
						H	Fuel filter

The fuel accumulator has two functions, (i) to dampen the pulsation of the fuel flow, generated by the pump and (ii) to maintain fuel pressure after the engine has been switched off. This prevents a vapour lock developing with consequent hot starting problems.

The fuel filter incorporates two paper filter elements to ensure that the fuel reaching the injection system components is completely free from dirt.

The fuel distributor/mixture control assembly. The fuel distributor controls the quantity of fuel being delivered to the engine, ensuring that each cylinder receives the same amount. The mixture control assembly incorporates an air sensor plate and control plunger. The air sensor plate is located in the main airstream between the air cleaner and the throttle butterfly. During idling, the airflow lifts the sensor plate which in turn raises a control plunger which allows fuel to flow past the plunger and out of the metering slits to the injector valves. Increases in engine speed cause increased airflow which raises the control plunger and so admits more fuel.

It is important to note that each injection supply pipe connection in the distributor head has a screw adjacent to it. These four screws are **not** for adjustment and must not be removed or have their settings altered.

The throttle valve assembly is mounted in the main air intake between the mixture control assembly and the air box. The throttle valve plate is controlled by a cable connected to the accelerator pedal.

During manufacture the throttle plate is adjusted so that it is fractionally open, to avoid the possibility of it jamming shut, and it **must not** be repositioned. Idle speed adjustment is provided for by means of a screw which, according to its setting, restricts the airflow through the air bypass channel in the throttle housing.

The injector valves are located in the intake manifold and are designed to open at a fuel pressure of 3.5 bar (50.8 lbf/in²).

The air box is mounted on the top of the engine and functions as an auxiliary intake manifold directing air from the sensor plate to each individual cylinder.

The warm-up regulator is located on the intake manifold and incorporates two coil springs, a bi-metal strip and a control pressure valve. The regulator controls the fuel supplied to the control circuit which provides pressure variations to the fuel distributor control plunger. When the coil springs are pushing against the control pressure valve there is a high control pressure and this gives a weak mixture. The coil spring pressure application is controlled by the bi-metal strip which in turn is activated in accordance with engine temperature and an electrical heat coil.

The auxiliary air device is located on the intake manifold. It consists of a pivoted plate, bi-metal strip and heater coil. The purpose of this device is to supply an increased volume of fuel/air mixture during cold idling rather similar to the fast idle system on carburettor layouts.

The start valve system consists of an electrical injector and a **thermo-time switch**. Its purpose is to spray fuel into the air box to assist cold starting, the thermo-time switch regulating the amount of fuel injected.

The safety module is located under the facia panel on the driver's side and is coloured purple. Its purpose is to shut off the power supply to the fuel pump should the engine stall or the vehicle be involved in an accident. The module is basically a sensor which senses the ignition low tension circuit pulses. When the pulses stop the module is deactivated and power to the fuel pump is cut.

The fuel shut-off valve system is an economy device whereby air is drawn from within the air cleaner unit through the shut-off valve and directed into the ducting chamber above the air sensor plate causing a depression. This then causes the sensor plate to drop which, in turn, shuts off the fuel supply. The shut-off valve will only operate under the following circumstances:

(a) When the engine coolant temperature is at or above 35°C (95°F)
(b) When the throttle is closed and with the engine speed decelerating from speeds above 1600 rpm

The coolant temperature must be above that specified to ensure that the valve does not shut off the fuel supply during the initial engine warm-up period.

When the throttle is released to the closed position it contacts an electrical switch which will only operate once the specified coolant temperature is reached. This switch will activate the shut-off valve when the throttle is fully released and the engine speed is over 1600 rpm, but once the engine speed drops below 1400 rpm the switch and valve are deactivated. The engine speed is sensed by a **speed sensing module** which is coloured black and located beneath the facia panel on the driver's side.

34 Bosch KE-Jetronic fuel-injection system – description and operation

The Bosch KE-Jetronic fuel-injection system is fitted to Escort RS Turbo models and is a further development of the K-Jetronic system.

Apart from minor alterations the basic principles of the hydraulics and mechanics used on the K-Jetronic system are unchanged on the KE-Jetronic system. The main difference between the two types is that

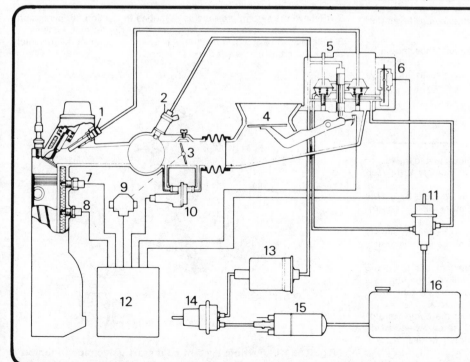

Fig. 3.84 KE-Jetronic fuel-injection system layout and components (Sec 34)

1 Injector
2 Cold start valve
3 Throttle plate
4 Sensor plate
5 Fuel distributor
6 Electro-magnetic pressure actuator
7 Thermo-time switch
8 Temperature sensor
9 Throttle position switch
10 Auxiliary air device
11 Pressure regulator
12 Control module
13 Fuel filter
14 Fuel accumulator
15 Fuel pump
16 Fuel tank

on the KE-Jetronic system all mixture corrections are controlled electronically by an electromagnetic pressure actuator incorporated in the fuel distributor. The pressure actuator is directly controlled by a variable electric current delivered by the fuel-injection control module. This module receiver inputs from the various engine sensors concerning engine temperature, engine load, throttle shift, throttle position and starter actuation. This information modifies a program stored in the module memory so that the electromagnetic pressure actuator, on receiving the signal from the module, can alter the mixture to suit all engine operating conditions. This renders the control pressure circuit and warm-up regulator of the K-Jetronic system unnecessary, and also undertakes the functions of the fuel shut-off valve, safety module and speed sensing module.

35 Fuel-injection system – precautions and general repair information

1   Due to the complexity of the fuel-injection system, and the need for special tools and test equipment, any work should be limited to the operations described in this Chapter. Other adjustments and system checks are beyond the scope of most readers and should be left to a Ford dealer.
2   Before disconnecting any fuel lines, unions or components thoroughly clean the component or connection and the adjacent area.
3   Place any removed components on a clean surface and cover them with plastic sheet or paper. Do not use fluffy rags for cleaning.
4   The system operates under pressure at all times and care must be taken when disconnecting fuel lines. Relieve the system pressure as described in the relevant Section before disconnecting any fuel lines under pressure. Refer to the warning note in Section 26 and always work with the battery negative lead disconnected and in a well ventilated area.
5   When working on the KE-Jetronic system the following additional precautions must be observed:

  (a) *Never start the engine when the battery is not firmly connected*
  (b) *Never disconnect the battery when the engine is running*
  (c) *If the battery is to be rapid charged from an external source it should be completely disconnected from the vehicle electrical system*
  (d) *The KE-Jetronic control unit must be removed from the car if temperatures are likely to exceed 80°C (176°F) as would be experienced, for example, in a paint spray oven, or if any electric welding is being carried out on the car*
  (e) *The ignition must be switched off when removing the control unit*

6   In the event of any malfunction in the system, reference should be made to the fault diagnosis section at the end of this Chapter, but first make a basic check of the system hoses, connections, fuses and relays for any obvious and immediately visible defects.

36 Fuel pump – removal and refitting

1   The fuel pump is bolted to the underside of the car just to the rear of the fuel tank. For access raise and support the car securely at the rear.
2   Disconnect the battery earth lead.
3   On the K-Jetronic system relieve the system pressure by slowly loosening the fuel feed pipe union at the warm-up regulator (photo). Absorb the fuel leakage in a cloth.
4   On the KE-Jetronic system relieve the system pressure by slowly loosening the cold start valve union on the top of the fuel distributor (Fig. 3.85). Absorb fuel leakage in a cloth.
5   Clamp the fuel inlet hose midway between the tank and the pump using a brake hose clamp, self-locking grips or similar. If the fuel level in the tank is low you may prefer to drain the fuel from the tank into a suitable container once the inlet hose is disconnected.
6   Disconnect the fuel inlet and outlet pipes from the pump (photo) catching fuel spillage in a suitable container. Once disconnected do not allow dirt to enter the pipes, temporarily plug or seal them if necessary.
7   Note the electrical connections to the pump and disconnect them.

8   Loosen the pump bracket retaining bolt and then withdraw the pump unit with rubber protector sleeve.
9   Refitting of the fuel pump is a reversal of the removal procedure. Renew the feed pipe from the tank if it is damaged or defective.
10 Check that the rubber protector sleeve is correctly positioned round the pump before tightening the clamp nut.
11 On completion, tighten the warm-up regulator or cold start valve fuel unions, reconnect the battery earth lead, start the engine and check for any fuel leaks.

37 Fuel accumulator – removal and refitting

Pre-1986 models
1   The fuel accumulator is mounted adjacent to the fuel pump, above the rear left-hand suspension arm.
2   Disconnect the battery negative lead.
3   Raise the rear of the car and support it on axle-stands.
4   Relieve the system pressure by slowly loosening the fuel feed pipe at the warm-up regulator. Absorb fuel leakage in a cloth.
5   Disconnect the fuel pipes from the fuel accumulator and catch the small quantity of fuel which will be released (photo).
6   Remove the clamp screw and remove the accumulator.
7   Refitting is a reversal of removal. Check for leaks on completion (with the engine restarted).

1986 models onwards
8   On later models with K-Jetronic and KE-Jetronic systems the fuel accumulator is located in the engine compartment behind the fuel distributor.
9   Disconnect the battery negative lead.
10 For access remove the air cleaner as described in Section 28.
11 Relieve the system pressure by slowly loosening the cold start valve union on the top of the fuel distributor (Fig. 3.85). Absorb fuel leakage in a cloth.
12 Disconnect the fuel pipes from the accumulator and catch the small quantity of fuel which will be released (photo).
13 Remove the clamp screw and remove the accumulator.
14 Refitting is a reversal of removal. Check for leaks on completion (with the engine restarted).

38 Fuel filter – removal and refitting

1   Disconnect the battery negative lead.
2   Relieve the system pressure as described in Section 36, paragraph 3, for K-Jetronic systems and paragraph 4 for KE-Jetronic systems.
3   Place absorbent rags beneath the filter and disconnect the fuel inlet and outlet connections (photo).

Fig. 3.85 KE-Jetronic system cold start valve pipe union on fuel distributor (Sec 36)

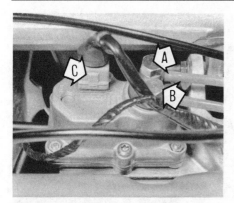

36.3 Warm-up regulator fuel feed pipe (A), outlet pipe (B) and wiring multi-plug (C)

36.6 Fuel pump outlet pipe (A), electrical connections (B) and pump bracket retaining bolt (C)

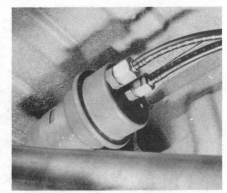

37.5 Fuel pipe connections at the underbody mounted fuel accumulator

37.12 Fuel inlet pipe (A) and outlet pipe (B) at the engine compartment mounted fuel accumulator

38.3 Fuel filter inlet pipe (A), outlet pipe (B) and clamp screw (C)

39.2 Idle speed adjustment screw (arrowed) on early K-Jetronic systems

4   Slacken the clamp bracket screw and withdraw the filter from the bracket.
5   Refitting is the reversal of removal, but ensure that the arrows on the filter body point in the direction of fuel flow; ie towards the outlet pipe union. On completion check for fuel leaks with the engine running.

39 Idle speed and mixture – adjustment

K-Jetronic system

1   The idle speed and fuel mixture adjustments will normally only be required after the installation of new components. Refer to the caution in Part A: Section 2 before proceeding.
2   On early models the idle speed adjustment screw is located on the rear of the throttle housing (photo), but access is severely limited unless the heater plenum chamber top cover is removed as described in Section 48.
3   On later models the idle speed adjustment screw is located on top of the throttle housing beneath a tamperproof plug (Fig. 3.86). Hook out the plug with a sharp pointed tool to gain access.
4   Before making any adjustments, warm the engine up to normal operating temperature and connect a tachometer in accordance with the manufacturer's instructions.
5   Increase the engine speed to 3000 rpm and hold it at this speed for 30 seconds, then allow the engine to idle, check the tachometer reading and if necessary turn the idle speed adjustment screw as required until the engine is idling at the specified speed.
6   To check the mixture adjustment an exhaust gas analyser is needed and should be connected in accordance with the manufacturer's instructions. A 3 mm Allen key will also be required to make any adjustments.
7   Before making any adjustments to the mixture, ensure that the idle speed is correct.

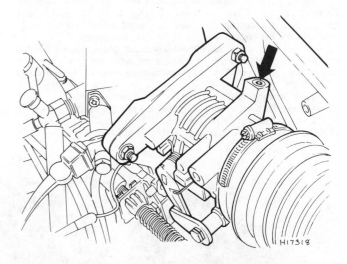

Fig. 3.86 K-Jetronic system idle speed adjustment screw location on later models (Sec 39)

8   Remove the tamperproof plug from the top of the mixture adjustment screw tube on top of the fuel distributor (photo).
9   Stabilise the exhaust gases as described in paragraph 5.
10 Insert the Allen key into the mixture screw tube and engage the adjusting screw. Turn the screw as necessary until the correct CO reading is obtained, then if required readjust the idling speed.
11 If the mixture adjustment cannot be finalised within 30 seconds

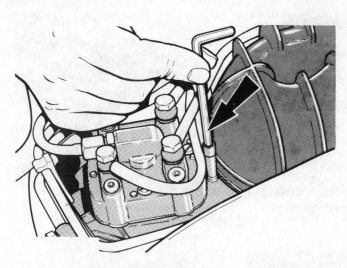

Fig. 3.87 Using an Allen key to adjust the K-Jetronic system mixture setting (Sec 39)

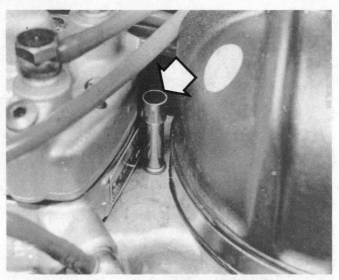

39.8 K-Jetronic system mixture adjustment screw location (arrowed)

from the moment of stabilising the exhaust gases, repeat the operations in paragraph 5 before continuing the adjustment procedure.
12 On completion fit a new tamperproof plug and disconnect the tachometer and exhaust gas analyser.

KE-Jetronic system

13 The idle speed and fuel mixture adjustments will normally only be required after the installation of new components.
14 The idle speed adjustment screw is located on the side of the throttle housing (photo).
15 Before making any adjustments, warm the engine up to normal operating temperature and connect a tachometer in accordance with the manufacturer's instructions.
16 Disconnect the wiring multi-plug at the pressure actuator on the side of the fuel distributor (photo).
17 Increase the engine speed to 3000 rpm and hold it at this speed for 30 seconds, then allow the engine to idle. Check the tachometer reading and if necessary turn the idle speed adjustment screw as required until the engine is idling at the specified speed.
18 To check the mixture adjustment an exhaust gas analyser is needed and should be connected in accordance with the manufacturer's instructions. A 3 mm Allen key will also be required to make any adjustments.
19 Before proceeding ensure that the idle speed is correct.
20 Unscrew the tamperproof plug from the mixture adjustment orifice on top of the fuel distributor (photo).
21 Stabilise the exhaust gases as described in paragraph 17.

22 Insert the Allen key into the mixture adjustment orifice and push down to engage the adjustment screw. Turn the adjustment screw clockwise to increase the CO reading and anti-clockwise to decrease it. Remove the Allen key, plug the orifice and check the CO reading.
23 If the mixture adjustment cannot be finalised within 30 seconds from the moment of stabilising the exhaust gases, repeat the operations in paragraph 17 before continuing the adjustment procedure. Make sure that the Allen key is removed before increasing the engine speed otherwise the fuel distributor will be damaged.
24 Continue adjustment until the correct CO reading is obtained, then if necessary readjust the idle speed.
25 Refit the tamperproof screw and reconnect the pressure actuator multi-plug. Disconnect the tachometer and exhaust gas analyser.

40 Fuel injectors and injector delivery pipes – removal and refitting

1 Disconnect the battery earth lead.
2 Detach the four supply pipes from the injectors, and use a rag to collect any spilled fuel.
3 Unscrew and remove the respective injector retaining bracket bolts, then withdraw the injectors and their O-ring seals (photo).
4 The injector fuel delivery pipes can be removed by unscrewing and removing the four banjo bolts at the distributor head. Note the respective pipe connections as they are detached and remove the pipes

39.14 Idle speed adjustment screw (arrowed) on KE-Jetronic systems

39.16 Pressure actuator wiring multi-plug (arrowed)

39.20 KE-Jetronic system mixture adjustment screw tamperproof plug (arrowed)

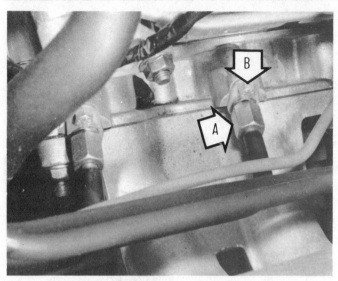

40.3 Injector fuel pipe union (A) and retaining bracket bolt (B)

complete with the plastic hoses and the injector harness. **Do not** separate the pipes or hoses from the injector harness.

5   Before reassembling the fuel delivery pipes, or the injectors, clean all pipe connections thoroughly and use new O-ring seals on the injectors. Use new seal washers on the banjo connections fitting two washers (one each side) per union. Do not overtighten the banjo bolts, or the washers may fracture.

6   Refitting of the injectors and the fuel delivery pipes is otherwise a reversal of the removal procedure. On completion check that the pipes and hoses are not distorted and when the engine is restarted check for any signs of leaks.

41 Cold start valve – removel and refitting

K-Jetronic system

1   Disconnect the battery earth lead.
2   Detach the electrical wiring multi-plug from the valve (photo).

3   Slowly unscrew and remove the fuel supply pipe banjo bolt. Take care on removal, as the system will be under pressure. Soak up fuel spillage with a cloth.
4   Unscrew and remove the two socket-head mounting bolts using an Allen key or Torx type key or socket bit on later models, and remove the valve.
5   Refitting is a reversal of the removal procedure. Do not overtighten the banjo bolt or the washers may fracture (use a new one each side of the union).
6   On completion restart the engine and check for signs of fuel leakage.

KE-Jetronic system

7   Disconnect the battery earth lead.
8   Disconnect the wiring multi-plug from the valve which is located underneath the throttle housing.
9   Slowly unscrew and remove the fuel supply pipe banjo union. Take care on removal, as the system will be under pressure. Soak up fuel spillage with a cloth.
10 Unscrew and remove the two Torx type mounting bolts using a Torx key or socket bit. Remove the valve from under the throttle housing.
11 Refitting is a reversal of removal. Do not overtighten the banjo bolt or the washers may fracture (use a new one each side of the union).
12 On completion restart the engine and check for leaks.

42 Auxiliary air device – removal and refitting

K-Jetronic system

1   Disconnect the battery earth lead.
2   Disconnect the wiring multi-plug and the two air hoses from the device which is located beneath the cold start valve.
3   Undo the two Torx type retaining bolts using a Torx key or socket bit and lift the unit away.
4   Refitting is a reversal of removal.

KE-Jetronic system

5   Apply the handbrake, jack up the front of the car and support it on stands.
6   Disconnect the battery negative lead.
7   Disconnect the auxiliary air device wiring multi-plug and the two air hoses.
8   Undo the two Torx type retaining bolts using a Torx key or socket bit and remove the unit from under the inlet manifold.
9   Refitting is a reversal of removal.

41.2 Disconnecting cold start valve wiring multi-plug

Fig. 3.88 KE-Jetronic system cold start valve location (Sec 41)

A   Fuel pipe union   B   Retaining bolts

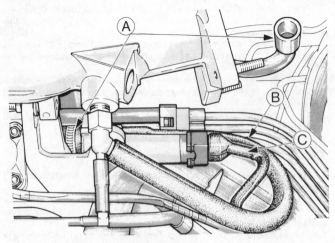

**Fig. 3.89 K-Jetronic system auxiliary air device connections
(Sec 42)**

A   Throttle housing hose   C   Wiring multi-plug
B   Cold start valve hose

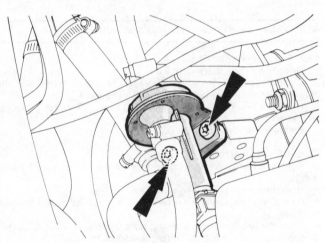

**Fig. 3.91 KE-Jetronic system auxiliary air device retaining
bolts (Sec 42)**

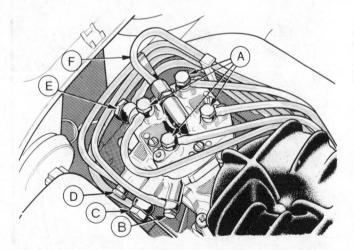

**Fig. 3.92 K-Jetronic fuel distributor pipe connections
(Sec 43)**

A   To injectors   D   From warm-up regulator
B   To cold start valve   E   Fuel inlet
C   Fuel return   F   To warm-up regulator

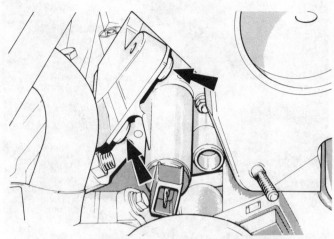

**Fig. 3.90 K-Jetronic system auxiliary air device retaining
bolt locations (Sec 42)**

43 Fuel distributor – removal and refitting

K-Jetronic system
1   Disconnect the battery negative lead.
2   Relieve the system pressure by slowly loosening the fuel feed pipe
union at the warm-up regulator (photo 36.3). Absorb the fuel leakage
in a cloth.
3   Disconnect the four injector feed pipes, the fuel inlet and return
pipes, and the warm-up regulator feed and return pipe banjo unions at
the fuel distributor. Note the sealing washers on each side of the banjo
unions which must be renewed on reconnection of the pipes. Take
care not to allow dirt to enter the pipes or their connection ports.
4   Unscrew the three retaining screws from the fuel distributor top
face and remove the unit from the car. Recover the sealing O-ring.
5   Refitting is a reversal of removal, but ensure perfectly clean mating
faces and use a new sealing O-ring and new washers for the banjo
unions. Check for any signs of leaks on completion and adjust the idle
speed and mixture settings as described in Section 39.
6   The main system fuel pressure should be checked and if necessary
adjusted by a Ford dealer to ensure satisfactory running of the system.

KE-Jetronic system
7   Disconnect the battery negative lead.
8   Relieve the system pressure by slowly loosening the cold start valve
union on the top of the fuel distributor (Fig. 3.85). Absorb fuel leakage
in a cloth.

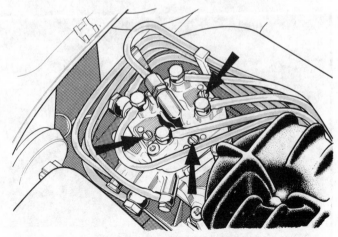

**Fig. 3.93 K-Jetronic system fuel distributor retaining
screws (Sec 43)**

43.11 KE-Jetronic fuel distributor retaining screws (arrowed)

44.9 Component attachments at the KE-Jetronic throttle housing

A Charge air temperature sensor multi-plug
B Throttle position sensor wiring multi-plug
C Throttle cable bracket
D Connecting hose retaining clip

9 Disconnect the four injector feed pipes, the cold start valve pipe and union adaptor, the fuel inlet pipe and pressure regulator return pipe from the fuel distributor. Note the sealing washers on each side of the banjo unions which must be renewed on reconnection of the pipes. Take care not to allow dirt to enter the pipes or their connection parts.
10 Disconnect the wiring multi-plug from the pressure actuator on the side of the fuel distributor.
11 Undo the two retaining screws and remove the fuel distributor. Recover the sealing O-ring (photo).
12 Refitting is a reversal of removal, but ensure perfectly clean mating faces and use a new sealing O-ring and new washers for the banjo unions. Check for any signs of leaks on completion and adjust the idle speed and mixture settings as described in Section 39.

44 Throttle housing – removal and refitting

K-Jetronic system
1 Disconnect the battery negative lead.
2 Slacken the retaining screw and detach the intake air hose from the throttle housing.
3 Disconnect the accelerator cable at the housing linkage as described in Section 31.
4 Disconnect the distributor vacuum hose and auxiliary air hose from the underside of the throttle housing.
5 Undo the four nuts and carefully withdraw the throttle housing from the manifold studs.
6 Refitting is a reversal of removal, but ensure that the mating faces are perfectly clean. Renew the gaskets, one on each side of the insulator block, if necessary.
7 On completion adjust the idle speed as described in Section 39.

KE-Jetronic system
8 Disconnect the battery negative terminal.
9 Disconnect the charge air temperature sensor and throttle position sensor wiring multi-plugs (photo).
10 Slacken the hose clip and detach the air intake hose from the intake duct.
11 Undo the two bolts securing the intake duct to the rocker cover slacken the throttle housing connecting hose clip and remove the intake duct (photo).
12 Extract the retaining clip and disconnect the throttle cable end from the linkage ball-stud.
13 Undo the two bolts and remove the throttle cable bracket from the throttle housing.

44.11 Air intake duct retaining bolts (arrowed)

14 Disconnect the auxiliary air hose, then undo the four nuts and remove the throttle housing.
15 Do not remove the throttle position sensor from the throttle housing unless absolutely necessary. If it must be removed, mark its position for refitting and then have it accurately adjusted by a Ford dealer on completion. This will also be necessary if the sensor or throttle housing are renewed.
16 Refitting is the reversal of removal, but use a new gasket and ensure clean mating faces. After refitting adjust the idle speed as described in Section 39.

45 Fuel pressure regulator – removal and refitting

1 The fuel pressure regulator is only used on KE-Jetronic systems and is located behind the fuel distributor (photo).

45.1 KE-Jetronic fuel pressure regulator location (arrowed) behind fuel distributor

2   Disconnect the battery negative lead.
3   Relieve the system pressure by slowly loosening the cold start valve union on the top of the fuel distributor (Fig. 3.85). Absorb fuel leakage in a cloth.
4   Place absorbent cloth beneath the regulator and undo the two fuel feed unions and the fuel return union.
5   Remove the securing tie and withdraw the regulator from its bracket.
6   Refitting is a reversal of removal. Ensure all unions are secure and on completion check for fuel leaks with the engine running.

46 Warm-up regulator – removal and refitting

1   The warm-up regulator is only used on K-Jetronic systems and is situated on the inlet manifold just to the rear of the rocker cover.

2   Disconnect the battery negative lead.
3   Relieve the system pressure by slowly loosening the fuel feed pipe union at the warm-up regulator (photo 36.3). Absorb the fuel leakage in a cloth.
4   After relieving the system pressure disconnect the fuel feed union completely, followed by the outlet union. Recover the sealing washers used on each side of the unions.
5   Disconnect the regulator wiring multi-plug.
6   Undo the two Torx type screws using a suitable Torx key or socket bit and remove the regulator from its location.
7   Refitting is a reversal of removal, but use new sealing washers on each side of the banjo unions and apply a thread-locking compound to the Torx retaining bolts. On completion check for leaks with the engine running.

47 Electro-magnetic pressure actuator – removal and refitting

1   The electro-magnetic pressure actuator is only used on KE-Jetronic systems and is located on the side of the fuel distributor (photo 39.16).
2   Disconnect the battery negative lead.
3   Remove the air cleaner as described in Section 28.
4   Relieve the system pressure by slowly loosening the cold start valve union on the top of the fuel distributor (Fig. 3.85). Absorb fuel leakage in a cloth.
5   Disconnect the wiring multi-plug, then undo the two screws securing the actuator to the fuel distributor. Remove the unit and the sealing O-rings.
6   Refitting is the reverse sequence to removal, but ensure both mating faces are clean. New O-rings must be used and care taken not to displace them when fitting. On completion check for fuel leaks with the engine running.

48 Fuel-injection control module – removal and refitting

1   The fuel-injection control module is only used on KE-Jetronic systems and is located in the engine compartment behind the heater plenum chamber and fan motor.
2   Disconnect the battery negative lead.
3   Remove the plenum chamber top cover rubber seal (photo).

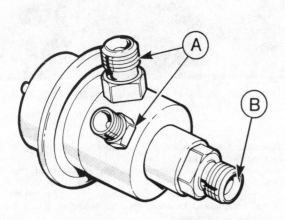

Fig. 3.94 KE-Jetronic fuel pressure regulator pipe connections (Sec 45)

A   Fuel feed   *B   Fuel return*

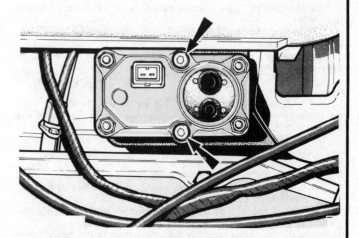

Fig. 3.95 K-Jetronic system warm-up regulator retaining screws (Sec 46)

48.3 Remove the plenum chamber rubber seal

48.4A Release the retaining clips ...

48.4B ... and lift off the plenum chamber top cover

48.5A Heater fan motor retaining nut

48.5B Removing the heater fan motor assembly ...

48.6 ... for access to the fuel-injection control module

4   Release the five retaining clips and lift off the plenum chamber top cover (photos).
5   Undo the two nuts securing the heater fan motor assembly to the bulkhead. Lift the unit off the studs and place it on the engine, but avoid straining the wiring (photos).
6   Disconnect the module wiring multi-plug, then undo the three screws and remove the unit from its location (photo).
7   Refitting is the reversal of removal. Take care not to trap the motor wiring when refitting the fan motor assembly and ensure that it is engaged in the slot provided in the housing (photo).

49 Charge air temperature sensor – removal and refitting

1   The charge air temperature sensor is only used on KE-Jetronic systems and is located in the air intake duct (photo).
2   Disconnect the battery negative lead.
3   Disconnect the wiring multi-plug and unscrew the sensor from its location.
4   Refitting is the reversal of removal.

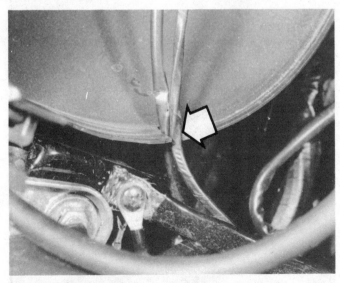

48.7 Fan motor wiring engaged in housing slot (arrowed)

49.1 Charge air temperature sensor location (arrowed)

50 Thermo-time switch – removal and refitting

1 Disconnect the battery negative lead.
2 Drain the cooling system as described in Chapter 2.
3 Raise the front of the car and support it on stands.
4 Disconnect the wiring multi-plug from the thermo-time switch located on the inlet manifold intermediate flange and accessible from under the car.
5 Unscrew the unit and remove it from its location.
6 Refitting is a reversal of removal. Refill the cooling system as described in Chapter 2.

51 Idle speed compensator – removal and refitting

1 The idle speed compensator is only fitted to K-Jetronic systems from 1986 onwards and is located in the centre of the engine compartment bulkhead.
2 Disconnect the battery negative lead.
3 Disconnect the electrical lead, undo the two screws and withdraw the unit. Detach the air hoses from each end and remove the compensator.
4 Refitting is a reversal of removal. The air hoses can be connected to either end and the arrows on the unit can be ignored.

52 Turbocharger – general description

1 Escort RS Turbo models are equipped with an exhaust driven turbocharger, which is a device designed to increase the engine's power output without increasing exhaust emissions or adversely affecting fuel economy. It does so by utilizing the heat energy present in the exhaust gases as they exit the engine.
2 Basically the turbocharger consists of two fans mounted on a common shaft. One fan is driven by the hot exhaust gases as they rush through the exhaust manifold and expand. The other draws in fresh air and compresses it before it enters the inlet manifold. By compressing the air, a larger charge can be let into each cylinder and greater power output is achieved.
3 The temperature of the intake air is reduced, thus increasing its density, by passing it through an intercooler, mounted alongside the radiator, prior to it entering the manifold.
4 The boost pressure generated by the turbocharger is controlled by a waste gate which when open allows a high proportion of the exhaust gases to bypass the turbocharger and directly enter the exhaust system. The turbocharger therefore loses speed and boost pressure is reduced.
5 The waste gate is opened and closed by the waste gate actuator through an actuator rod. The waste gate actuator is in turn controlled by the solenoid control valve which receives signals in the form of a pulsed voltage from the ignition system. Electronic Spark Control module (see Chapter 4). The Electronic Spark Control module receives data from various engine sensors, particularly the charge air temperature sensor in the intake air duct, which modify the module program to suit all operating conditions. The module then signals the solenoid control valve to open or close the waste gate via the waste gate actuator.
6 Lubrication oil for the turbocharger is taken from the engine lubricating circuit via a special branch line. The turbocharger shaft rotates in plain bearings through which a relatively large amount of oil is allowed to pass. Therefore when rotating, the shaft floats on a thick film of lubricating oil.
7 The turbocharger is a close tolerance, expensive component and servicing or repairs should be left to a dealer service department or specialist with turbocharger repair experience. Apart from the information in the following Sections, any other work on the turbocharger or its related components is beyond the scope of the average reader.

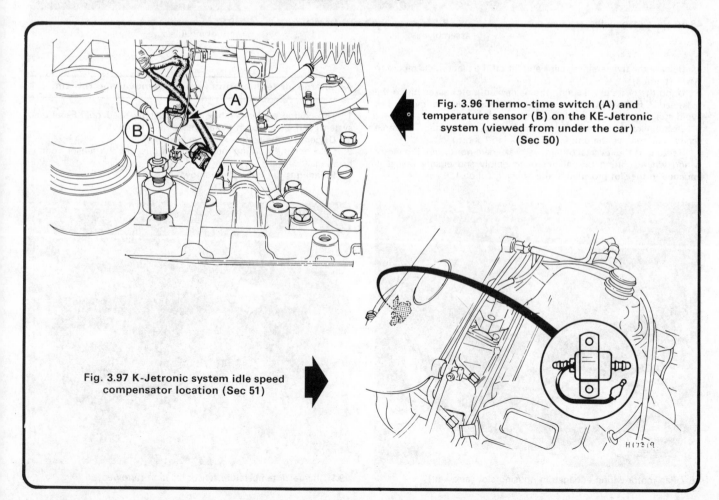

Fig. 3.96 Thermo-time switch (A) and temperature sensor (B) on the KE-Jetronic system (viewed from under the car) (Sec 50)

Fig. 3.97 K-Jetronic system idle speed compensator location (Sec 51)

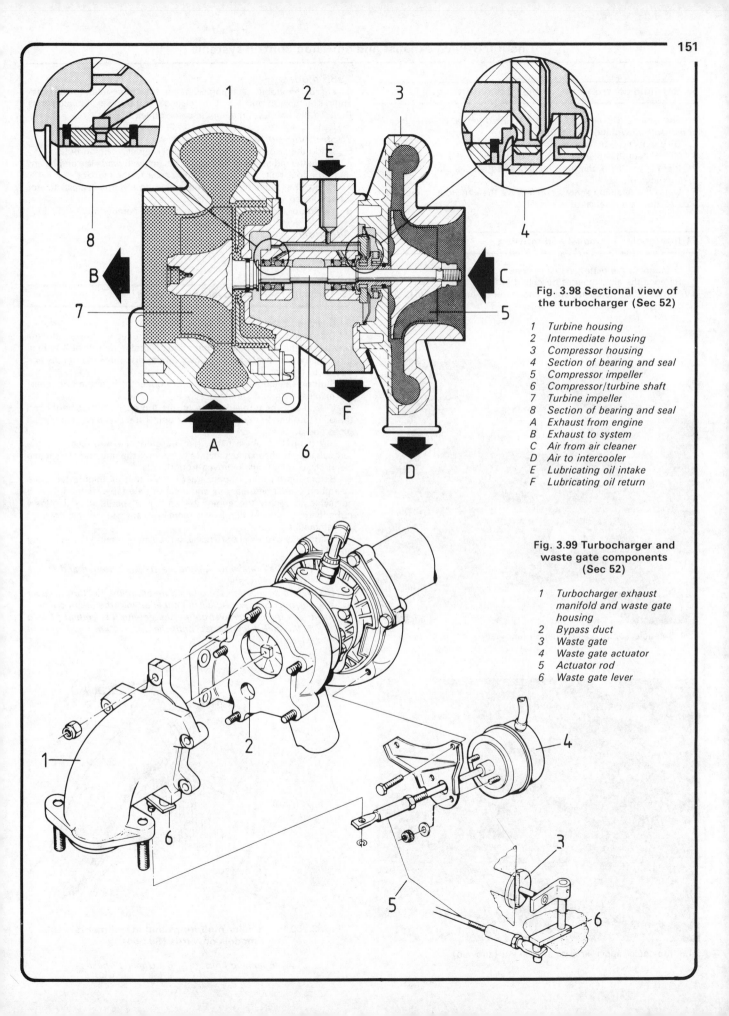

Fig. 3.98 Sectional view of the turbocharger (Sec 52)

1 Turbine housing
2 Intermediate housing
3 Compressor housing
4 Section of bearing and seal
5 Compressor impeller
6 Compressor/turbine shaft
7 Turbine impeller
8 Section of bearing and seal
A Exhaust from engine
B Exhaust to system
C Air from air cleaner
D Air to intercooler
E Lubricating oil intake
F Lubricating oil return

Fig. 3.99 Turbocharger and waste gate components (Sec 52)

1 Turbocharger exhaust manifold and waste gate housing
2 Bypass duct
3 Waste gate
4 Waste gate actuator
5 Actuator rod
6 Waste gate lever

53 Solenoid control valve – removal and refitting

1 The solenoid control valve is mounted on a bracket located underneath the ignition distributor (photo).
2 Disconnect the battery negative lead.
3 Disconnect the solenoid wiring multi-plug.
4 Identify and mark the hose locations at the solenoid connections, then remove the hoses.
5 Undo the retaining screws and remove the unit from its location.
6 Refitting is a reversal of removal.

54 Intercooler – removal and refitting

1 Disconnect the battery negative lead.
2 Remove the air cleaner as described in Section 28.
3 Remove the intercooler upper and lower air hoses (photo).

53.1 Solenoid control valve location (arrowed)

54.3 Intercooler upper air hose attachment (arrowed)

1985 models
4 Undo the upper retaining bolt, tilt the intercooler towards the engine at the top and lift up to disengage the lower retaining pins. Remove the unit from the engine compartment.

1986 models onwards
5 Undo the two radiator and intercooler lower retaining bolts.
6 Move the radiator and intercooler assembly towards the engine and undo the four bolts securing the intercooler to the radiator.
7 Undo the retaining bolt and move the horn nearest to the intercooler to one side.
8 Withdraw the intercooler from the engine compartment.

All models
9 Refitting is a reversal of removal.

55 Turbocharger – removal and refitting

1 Disconnect the battery negative lead.
2 Disconnect the turbocharger inlet and outlet air hoses and the hoses from the waste gate actuator and solenoid control valve at their turbocharger connections. Tape over all the disconnected unions and outlets to prevent dirt ingress.
3 Support the exhaust system and disconnect it from the turbocharger exhaust manifold (photo).
4 Disconnect the oil feed union on the top of the turbocharger and the oil return line from underneath the unit. Tape over all disconnected pipes and unions.
5 Blend up the tabwashers, then unscrew the nuts securing the turbocharger to the exhaust manifold. Remove the unit and store it in a clean plastic bag while removed from the car.
6 Before refitting the turbocharger ensure that all mating faces are clean and obtain new gaskets and a set of new tabwashers. It is also advisable to renew the engine oil and filter, particularly if a new turbocharger is being fitted or if there was any sign of previous oil contamination.
7 Refitting is a reversal of removal, but bearing in mind the following points:

(a) Tighten all retaining nuts to the specified torque and secure with the tabwashers
(b) Before connecting the oil feed union, prime the turbocharger bearings by injecting clean engine oil into the union orifice
(c) Crank the engine over on the starter with the ignition LT lead at the coil disconnected until the oil pressure warning light goes out

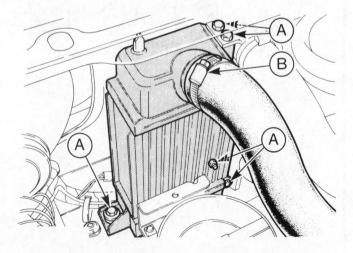

Fig. 3.100 Intercooler mountings and attachments – 1986 models onwards (Sec 54)

A Retaining bolts   B Upper air hose

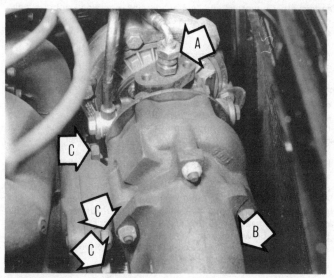

55.3 Turbocharger oil feed union (A), turbocharger exhaust manifold (B) and retaining nuts (C)

PART C: MANIFOLDS, EXHAUST AND EMISSION CONTROL SYSTEMS

56 General description

All models utilise a light alloy inlet manifold which on carburettor models is coolant heated to improve the atomisation of the fuel/air mixture.

The exhaust manifold is of cast iron construction and incorporates a heated air box as part of the air intake system on carburettor models.

The exhaust system fitted as original equipment is of single or two section type incorporating a silencer and expansion box and suspended on rubber mountings under the car.

A comprehensive description of the emission control system is given later in this Chapter.

57 Maintenance and inspection

1   At the intervals specified in 'Routine maintenance' at the beginning of this Chapter carry out the following operations.
2   With the vehicle raised on a hoist or supported on axle stands check the exhaust system for signs of leaks, corrosion or damage and check the rubber mountings for condition and security. Where damage or corrosion are evident renew the system complete or in sections as applicable using the procedures given in Section 61.
3   On RS Turbo models the tightness of the exhaust manifold and turbocharger retaining nuts should be checked at the intervals specified.
4   On OHV engines clean the oil filler cap and on CVH engines renew the crankcase ventilation filter as described in Section 63. Check the condition and security of all emission control components, hoses and unions.

58 Inlet manifold (carburettor models) – removal and refitting

1   Disconnect the battery negative lead.
2   Remove the air cleaner as described in Part A: Section 4.
3   Refer to Chapter 2 and drain the cooling system.
4   Remove the carburettor as described in Part A of this Chapter according to type.

5   Disconnect the manifold coolant hoses.
6   Make a careful note of all vacuum connections at the vacuum switches and solenoids and disconnect them.
7   Where applicable disconnect the switch wiring multi-plugs after noting their locations.
8   Undo the manifold retaining nuts and withdraw the manifold from the cylinder head studs. Recover the gasket.
9   Refitting is the reverse sequence to removal but use a new gasket and ensure that the mating faces are clean. On completion refill the cooling system as described in Chapter 2.

59 Inlet manifold (fuel-injection models) – removal and refitting

XR3i and XR3i Cabriolet
1   Disconnect the battery negative lead.
2   Remove the warm-up regulator, throttle housing, fuel injectors and cold start valve as described in Part B of this Chapter.
3   Refer to Chapter 2 and drain the cooling system.
4   Make a note of the vacuum hose, crankcase ventilation hose and wiring multi-plug locations as applicable and disconnect them.
5   Disconnect the coolant hoses at the manifold intermediate flange.
6   Check that all wiring and hoses have been disconnected from above and below the manifold, then undo the retaining nuts.
7   Withdraw the manifold and intermediate flange together with their gaskets.
8   Refitting is the reverse sequence to removal, but use a new gasket on each side of the intermediate flange. Refit the cold start valve, fuel injectors, throttle housing and warm-up regulator as described in Part B of this Chapter, and on completion refill the cooling system as described in Chapter 2.

RS Turbo (1985 to May 1986)
9   Disconnect the battery negative lead.
10 Remove the throttle housing, fuel injectors and cold start valve as described in Part B of this Chapter.
11 Refer to Chapter 2 and drain the cooling system.
12 Disconnect the crankcase ventilation hose and vacuum hose from the top of the plenum chamber.
13 Disconnect the vacuum servo hose from the side of the plenum chamber.
14 From below the inlet manifold remove the auxiliary air device as described in Part B of this Chapter, then disconnect the thermo-time switch and temperature sensor wiring multi-plugs after noting their locations.
15 Remove the oil cooler-to-inlet manifold connecting hose.
16 From above, undo the bolts and remove the plenum chamber support bracket.
17 Undo the nuts and remove the inlet manifold and plenum chamber from the cylinder head. Recover the gasket.
18 If required undo the nuts and separate the plenum chamber from the inlet manifold. Recover the gaskets.
19 Refitting is the reverse sequence to removal, but use new gaskets on all flange joints. Refit the auxiliary air device, cold start valve, fuel injectors and throttle housing as described in Part B of this Chapter, and on completion refill the cooling system as described in Chapter 2.

RS Turbo (May 1986 onwards)
20 Disconnect the battery negative lead.
21 Remove the throttle housing, fuel injectors, cold start valve and auxiliary air device as described in Part B of this Chapter.
22 Refer to Chapter 2 and drain the cooling system.
23 Disconnect the crankcase ventilation hose and vacuum hose from the top of the manifold and the vacuum servo hose from the side.
24 From beneath the manifold disconnect the thermo-time switch and temperature sensor wiring multi-plugs after noting their locations, and the coolant hoses from the intermediate flange.
25 Remove the oil cooler-to-manifold connecting hose.
26 Undo the retaining nuts and withdraw the manifold and intermediate flange together with their gaskets.
27 Refitting is the reverse sequence to removal, but use a new gasket on each side of the intermediate flange. Refit the auxiliary air device, cold start valve, fuel injectors and throttle housing as described in Part B of this Chapter and on completion refill the cooling system as described in Chapter 2.

60 Exhaust manifold – removal and refitting

1   Disconnect the battery negative lead.
2   On carburettor models remove the air cleaner as described in Part A: Section 4.
3   On RS Turbo models remove the turbocharger as described in Part B: Section 55.
4   Support the exhaust system on a jack or blocks, then disconnect the downpipe at the manifold.
5   Undo the nuts securing the manifold to the cylinder head and remove it from the engine. Recover the manifold gasket.
6   Refitting is the reverse sequence to removal. On RS Turbo models refit the turbocharger as described in Part B: Section 55.

61 Exhaust system – renewal

1   The layout of the exhaust system varies considerably according to model and engine. All except the RS Turbo versions can be renewed in sections as coupling sleeves are supplied enabling an old section to be cut out and a new one inserted without the need to renew the entire system all at once.
2   It is recommended when working on an exhaust system that the complete assembly be removed from under the vehicle by releasing the downpipe from the manifold and unhooking the flexible suspension hangers (photos).
3   Assemble the complete system, but do not fully tighten the joint clips until the system is back in the vehicle. Use a new exhaust manifold/flange gasket and check that the flexible mountings are in good order, also check the connecting flange joint.
4   Set the silencer and expansion box in their correct attitudes in relation to the rest of the system before finally tightening the joint clips.
5   Check that with reasonable deflection in either direction, the exhaust does not knock against any adjacent components.
6   Holts Flexiwrap and Holts Gun Gum exhaust repair systems can be used for effective repairs to exhaust pipes and silencer boxes, including ends and bends. Holts Flexiwrap is an MOT approved permanent exhaust repair.

62 Emission control systems – general description

1   Emission control consists of reducing the emission of noxious gases and vapours, which are by products of combustion, into the atmosphere. The system can be divided into three categories; fuel evaporative emission control, crankcase emission control and exhaust emission control. The components and system operation for Escort models operating in the United Kingdom are as follows.

Fuel evaporative emission control

2   Emission control regulations in the UK are far less strict than in certain other countries and fuel evaporative emission control simply consists of internal venting of the carburettor float chamber and closed circuit fuel tank ventilation.

Crankcase emission control

3   On OHV engines a closed circuit crankcase ventilation system is used ensuring that blow-by gases which pass the piston rings and collect in the crankcase, as well as oil vapour, are drawn into the combustion chambers to be burnt.
4   The system consists of a vented engine oil filler cap connected by one hose to the inlet manifold and by another to the air cleaner. The gas flow is controlled by a calibrated port in the oil filler cap and by manifold vacuum according to throttle position.
5   On CVH engines a closed circuit crankcase ventilation system is also used.
6   At light throttle openings, the emissions are drawn out of the rocker cover, through a control orifice in the crankcase ventilation filter (where fitted), and into the intake manifold. Under full throttle conditions the gas flow routing is still as just described, but in addition the gases are drawn through a filter and pass into the air cleaner.
7   This arrangement offsets any tendency for the fuel/air ratio to be adversely affected at full throttle.

Exhaust emission control

8   On carburettor engine models an exhaust emission control system is used of which the exact components fitted can vary according to model. In general the system operates as follows.
9   To improve driveability during warm-up conditions and to keep exhaust emission levels to a minimum, a vacuum-operated, temperature-sensitive emission control system is fitted to OHV and CVH engines covered by this manual. The system is designed to ensure that the rate of distributor vacuum advance is compatible with the change in fuel/air mixture flow under all throttle conditions, thus resulting in more complete combustion and reduced exhaust emissions.
10 Under part throttle cruising conditions, distributor vacuum advance is required to allow time for the fuel/air mixture in the cylinders to burn. When returning to a part throttle opening after accelerating or decelerating, the distributor vacuum increases before the fuel/air mixture has stabilised. On certain engines this can lead to short periods of incomplete combustion and increased exhaust emission. To reduce this condition a spark delay valve is incorporated in the vacuum line between the carburettor and distributor to reduce the rate at which the distributor advances. Under certain conditions, particularly during the period of engine warm-up, some models may suffer from a lack of throttle response. To overcome this problem a spark sustain valve may be fitted in the vacuum line either individually or in conjunction with the spark delay valve. This valve is used to maintain distributor vacuum under transient throttle conditions, thus stabilising the combustion process.
11 The operation of the valves is controlled by a ported vacuum

61.2A Exhaust silencer mounting ...

61.2B ... and expansion box mounting

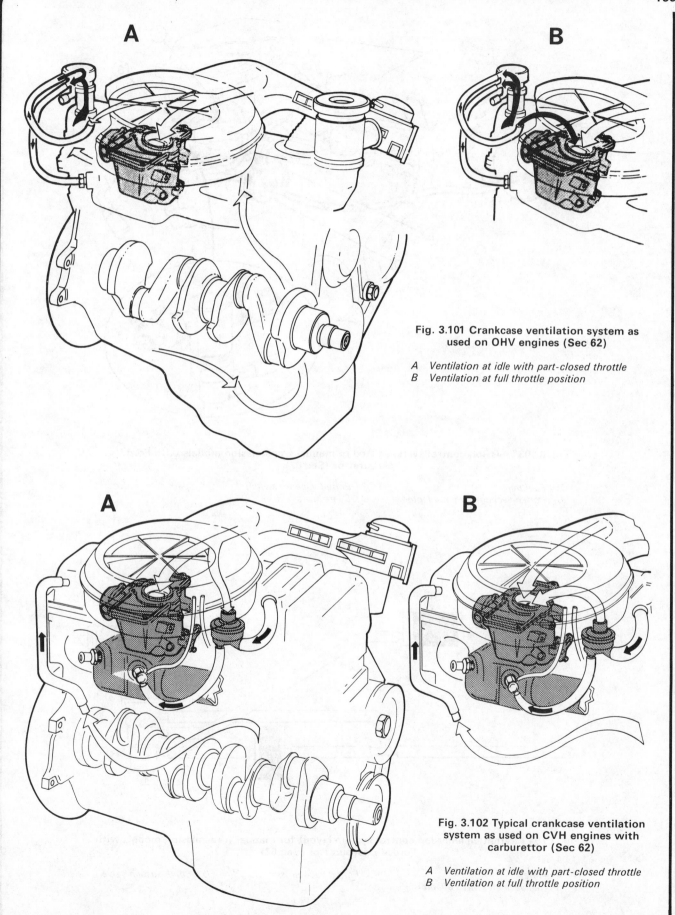

Fig. 3.101 Crankcase ventilation system as used on OHV engines (Sec 62)

A Ventilation at idle with part-closed throttle
B Ventilation at full throttle position

Fig. 3.102 Typical crankcase ventilation system as used on CVH engines with carburettor (Sec 62)

A Ventilation at idle with part-closed throttle
B Ventilation at full throttle position

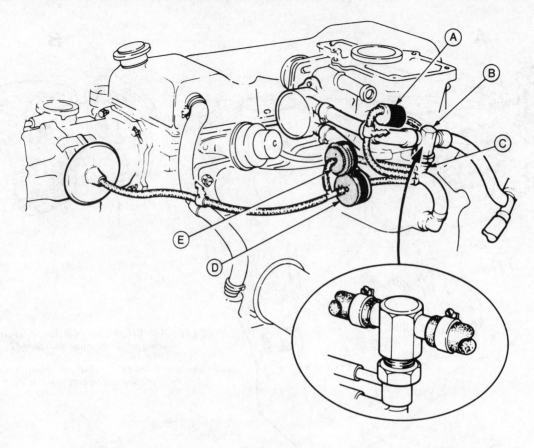

Fig. 3.103 Emission control system fitted to manual transmission models with Ford VV carburettor (Sec 62)

A   Fuel trap   C   Ported vacuum switch   E   Spark delay valve
B   Ported vacuum switch adaptor   D   Spark sustain valve

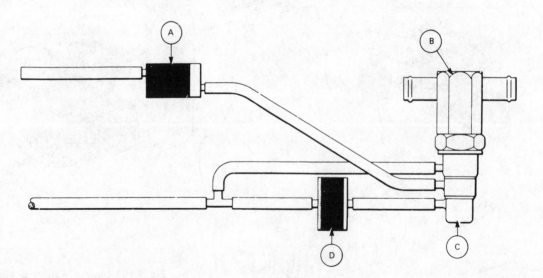

Fig. 3.104 Alternative emission control system layout for manual transmission models with Ford VV carburettor (Sec 62)

A   Fuel trap   C   Ported vacuum switch   D   Spark sustain valve
B   Ported vacuum switch adaptor

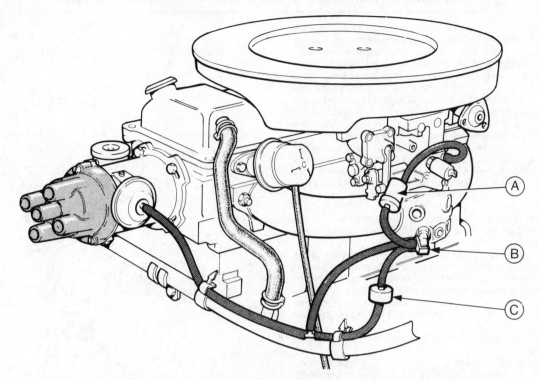

Fig. 3.105 Emission control system layout for manual transmission models with Weber 2V carburettor (Sec 62)

A Fuel trap   B Ported vacuum switch   C Spark sustain valve

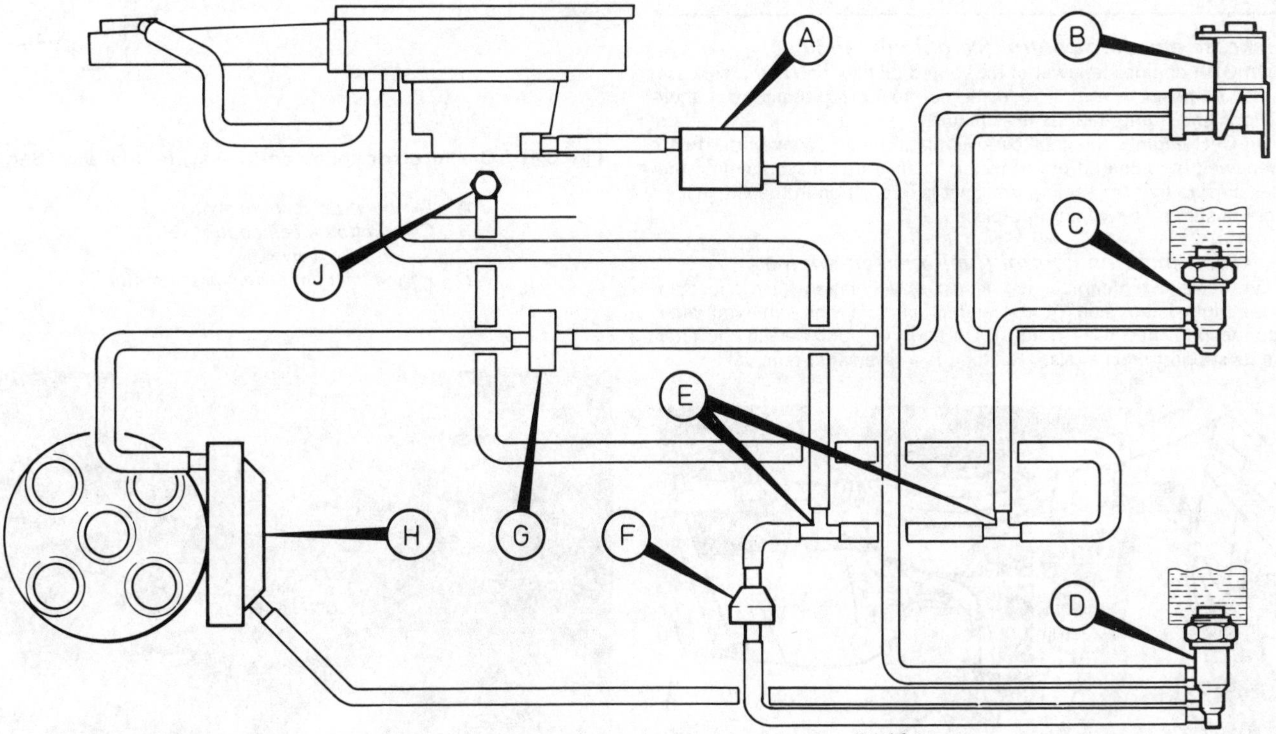

H17320

Fig. 3.106 Emission control system layout for automatic transmission models with Ford VV carburettor (Sec 62)

A Fuel trap   D Ported vacuum switch (green)   G Restrictor
B Two-way solenoid   E T-connectors   H Dual diaphragm distributor
C Ported vacuum switch (blue) F Check valve   J Inlet manifold connection

switch (PVS) which has the vacuum lines connected to it. The PVS operates in a similar manner to that of the thermostat in the cooling system. A wax filled sensor is attached to a plunger which operates a valve. The PVS is actuated by the engine cooling water and is sensitive to changes in engine operating temperature. When the engine is cold the sensor moves the plunger to open the upper and middle ports of the PVS. Therefore vacuum applied to the middle port is directed to the distributor via the upper port. As the engine warms up and coolant temperature increases, the wax expands and the plunger closes the upper port and opens the lower port. Vacuum applied to the centre port is now directed to the distributor via the lower port. In this way the spark sustain or delay valves can be activated or bypassed according to engine operation temperature. The vacuum applied to the middle port of the PVS is taken from a connection on the carburettor through a fuel trap. The fuel trap prevents fuel or fuel vapour from being drawn into the distributor vacuum unit.

12 The carburettor speed control system is an integral part of the emission control system on some UK models as well as for some overseas market models.

13 The system's function is to improve the air and fuel mixture when the engine is cold in low ambient temperatures. It achieves this by increasing the air volume into the intake manifold in order to weaken the mixture ratio which has been enriched by choke operation.

14 The carburettor speed control valve is fitted to a vacuum hose which is located between the air cleaner unit and the intake manifold on UK models.

15 The accompanying illustrations show adaptations of the system to suit various models.

16 Testing of the various components of the system is not within the scope of the home mechanic due to the need for a vacuum pump and gauge, but if a fault has been diagnosed by a garage having the necessary equipment, the renewal of a defective component can be carried out as described in the following Section.

---

63 Emission control system components – renewal

Crankcase emission control (carburettor engines)

1 On OHV engines renewal of the vented oil filler cap and crankcase ventilation hoses is simply a matter of removing them from their locations and fitting new parts as required.

2 On CVH engines the crankcase ventilation filter (where fitted) can be renewed by pulling it out of the air cleaner after disconnecting the hoses. Ensure that the sealing grommet is in position in the air cleaner before pushing a new filter into place.

Crankcase emission control (fuel-injected engines)

3 On fuel-injected engines the crankcase ventilation filter is located on the right-hand side of the engine and can be removed after disconnecting the hoses (photo). On early versions detach the filter from its support bracket also. Refitting is a reversal of removal.

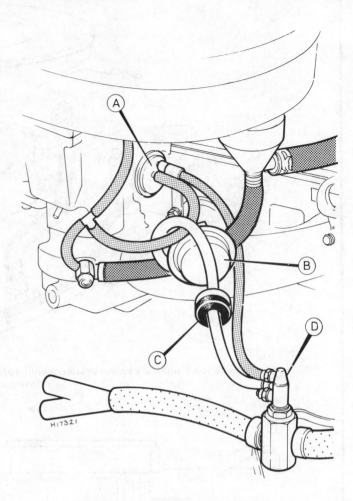

Fig. 3.107 Carburettor speed control system layout (Sec 62)

A   *Temperature vacuum switch*
B   *Carburettor speed control valve*
C   *Spark delay valve*
D   *Ported vacuum switch and adaptor*

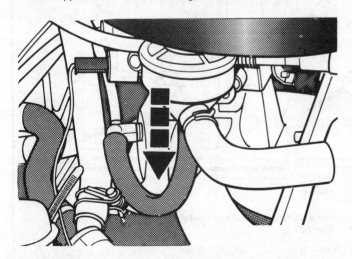

Fig. 3.108 Crankcase ventilation filter renewal on CVH engines with carburettor (Sec 63)

63.3 Crankcase ventilation filter location on KE-Jetronic fuel-injected engines

4   During the course of production modifications have been made to the crankcase ventilation system on K-Jetronic fuel-injected engines to eliminate stalling and rough idling caused by oil from the crankcase venting system contaminating the throttle housing.

5   Currently three versions of the system may be encountered on Escort fuel-injected models. If the stalling and rough idling problems are encountered on cars equipped with the Mk 1 or Mk 2 system, then they should be uprated to Mk 3 specification as described in the following paragraphs. It should be noted that even the latest (Mk 3) level system failed to cure the problem completely and at the beginning of 1986 a revised throttle housing was introduced. These can be identified by having their idle speed adjustment screw located on the top of the housing under a tamperproof cap, rather than underneath the housing as on early versions. The latest version of throttle housing can be fitted to early cars but the work should be carried out by a dealer, as numerous modifications are involved. The latest version of crankcase ventilation system should always be fitted first however, as follows.

6   As a preliminary operation, remove the idle speed adjustment screw and blow out the idle passage in the throttle housing using air pressure.

7   Refit the screw.

Fig. 3.109 Early (Mk 1) crankcase ventilation system on fuel-injection models (Sec 63)

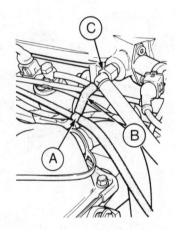

Fig. 3.110 Components of Mk 1 crankcase ventilation system – fuel-injection models (Sec 63)

A   T-connector
B   Short hose
C   Plenum chamber connector

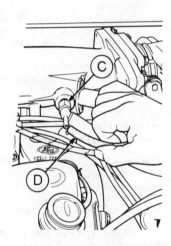

Fig. 3.111 Fuel shut-off valve hose (D) and plenum chamber connector (C) on Mk 1 type crankcase ventilation system – fuel-injection models (Sec 63)

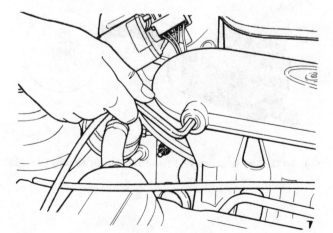

Fig. 3.112 Unscrewing the plenum chamber plug – fuel-injection models (Sec 63)

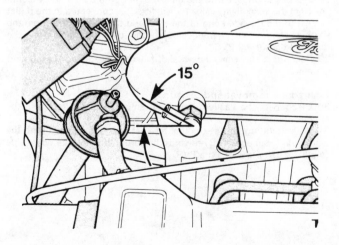

Fig. 3.113 Correct setting of plenum chamber angled connector – fuel-injection models (Sec 63)

Cars with earliest type (Mk 1) crankcase ventilation system

8   Remove and discard the crankcase ventilation filter vacuum hose.

9   Remove and discard the tee connector (A – Fig. 3.110) and also the short hose (B).

10 Fit the overrun fuel shut off valve hose (D – Fig. 3.111) to the plenum chamber connector (C).

11 Remove and discard the crankcase ventilation filter bracket.

12 Remove and discard the hose which runs between the ventilation filter and the rocker cover.

13 Turn the filter and its hose, which is connected to the air cleaner, so that the small spigot on the filter is uppermost.

14 Fit a new hose between the filter and rocker cover, secure it with the original hose clips.

15 Remove and discard the plug from the plenum chamber (Fig. 3.112) and in its place screw in the angled connectors. Set the connector as shown in Fig. 3.113.

16 Connect the ventilation filter to the angled connector using a new hose.

17 Seat the idle speed screw gently and then unscrew it two complete turns.

18 Bring the engine to normal working temperature and adjust the idle speed and mixture as described in Part B: Section 39.

Cars with Mk 2 crankcase ventilation system

19 Remove and discard the crankcase ventilation filter vacuum hose and fit a blanking cap to the hose connector on the throttle housing end of the plenum chamber.

20 Remove and discard the plug from the plenum chamber and substitute the new angled connector as described in paragraph 15.

21 Fit the new hose between the ventilation filter and the angled connector.

22 Repeat the operations described in paragraphs 17 and 18.

23 Later model cars have the crankcase ventilation filter hose connections as shown in Fig. 3.115.

Exhaust emission control

Spark delay/sustain valve – removal and refitting

24 Disconnect the vacuum lines at the valve and remove the valve from the engine.

25 When refitting a spark delay valve it must be positioned with the black side (marked CARB) towards the carburettor and the coloured side (marked DIST) towards the distributor. When refitting a spark sustain valve the side marked VAC must be towards the carburettor and the side marked DIST towards the distributor.

Ported vacuum switch – removal and refitting

26 Remove the filler cap from the expansion tank to reduce pressure in the cooling system. If the engine is hot, remove the cap slowly using a rag to prevent scalding.

27 Disconnect the vacuum lines and the water hoses, then unscrew the valve.

28 When refitting the valve, note that the vacuum line from the carburettor is connected to the middle outlet on the PVS, the vacuum line from the spark delay valve (where fitted) is connected to the outlet nearest to the threaded end of the PVS, and the vacuum line from the spark sustain valve is connected to the outlet furthest from the threaded end of the PVS.

29 Reconnect the water hoses and if necessary top up the cooling system.

Fuel trap – removal and refitting

30 Disconnect the vacuum lines and remove the fuel trap from the engine.

31 When refitting, make sure that the fuel trap is positioned with the black side (marked CARB) towards the carburettor and the white side (marked DIST) towards the PVS.

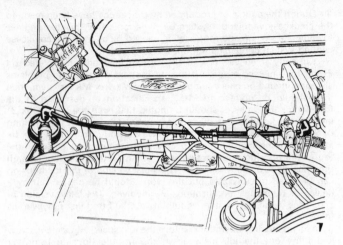

Fig. 3.114 Mk 2 crankcase ventilation system – fuel-injection models (Sec 63)

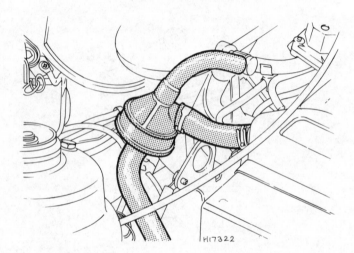

Fig. 3.115 (Mk 3) crankcase ventilation system – fuel-injection models (Sec 63)

Fig. 3.116 Fuel trap marked for direction of fitting (Sec 63)

PART D: FAULT DIAGNOSIS

64 Fault diagnosis – fuel system (carburettor models)

Note: *High fuel consumption and poor performance are not necessarily due to carburettor faults. Make sure that the ignition system is properly adjusted, that the brakes are not binding and that the engine is in good mechanical condition before tampering with the carburettor.*

Symptom	Reason(s)
Fuel consumption excessive	Air cleaner choked, giving rich mixture
	Leak from tank, pump or fuel lines
	Float chamber flooding due to incorrect level or worn needle valve
	Carburettor incorrectly adjusted
	Idle speed too high
	Choke faulty
	Excessively worn carburettor
Lack of power, stalling or difficult starting	Faulty fuel pump
	Leak on suction side of pump or in fuel line
	Intake manifold or carburettor flange gaskets leaking
	Carburettor incorrectly adjusted
	Faulty choke
	Emission control system defect
Poor or erratic idling	Weak mixture
	Leak in intake manifold
	Leak in distributor vacuum pipe
	Leak in crankcase extractor hose
	Leak in brake servo hose
	Emission control system defect

65 Fault diagnosis – fuel system (fuel-injection models)

Note: *The following fault diagnosis is mainly applicable to the K-Jetronic system. Although many of the items apply to the KE-Jetronic system, accurate fault diagnosis on these types should be left to a dealer with special dedicated test equipment. On all types refer to the special note at the beginning of the previous Section before proceeding.*

Symptom	Reason(s)
Engine will not start (cold)	Fuel pump faulty
	Auxiliary air device not opening
	Start valve not operating
	Start valve leak
	Sensor plate rest position incorrect
	Sensor plate and/or control plunger sticking
	Vacuum system leak
	Fuel system leak
	Thermo-time switch remains open
Engine will not start (hot)	Faulty fuel pump
	Warm control pressure low
	Sensor plate rest position incorrect
	Sensor plate and/or control plunger sticking
	Vacuum system leak
	Fuel system leak
	Leaky injector valve(s) or low opening pressure
	Incorrect mixture adjustment
	Damaged pressure regulator O-rings
Engine difficult to start (cold)	Cold control pressure incorrect
	Auxiliary air device not opening
	Faulty start valve
	Sensor plate rest position faulty
	Sensor plate and/or control plunger sticking
	Fuel system leak
	Thermo-time switch not closing
Engine difficult to start (hot)	Warm control pressure too high or too low
	Auxiliary air device faulty
	Sensor plate/control plunger faulty
	Fuel or vacuum leak in system
	Leaky injector valve(s) or low opening pressure
	Incorrect mixture adjustment

Symptom	Reason(s)
Rough idling (during warm-up period)	Incorrect cold control pressure Auxiliary air device not closing (or opening) Start valve leak Fuel or vacuum leak in system Leaky injector valve(s), or low opening pressure
Rough idling (engine warm)	Warm control pressure incorrect Auxiliary air device not closing Start valve leaking Sensor plate and/or control plunger sticking Fuel or vacuum leak in system Injector(s) leaking or low opening pressure Incorrect mixture adjustment
Engine backfiring into intake manifold	Warm control pressure high Vacuum system leak
Engine backfiring into exhaust manifold	Warm control pressure high Start valve leak Fuel system leak Incorrect mixture adjustment
Engine misfires (on road)	Fuel system leak
Engine 'runs on'	Sensor plate and or control plunger sticking Injector valve(s) leaking or low opening pressure
Excessive petrol consumption	Fuel system leak Mixture adjustment incorrect Low warm control pressure
High CO level at idle	Low warm control pressure Mixture adjustment incorrect Fuel system leak Sensor plate and/or control plunger sticking Start valve leak
Low CO level at idle	High warm control pressure Mixture adjustment incorrect Start valve leak Vacuum system leak
Idle speed adjustment difficult (too high)	Auxiliary air device not closing

Chapter 4 Ignition system

For modifications, and information applicable to later models, see Supplement at end of manual

Contents

Specifications

Part A: Contact breaker ignition system
General

System type	Mechanical contact breaker and coil ignition
Application	1.1 litre OHV and CVH engines up to 1986
Firing order:	
OHV engines	1–2–4–3
CVH engines	1–3–4–2
Location of No 1 cylinder	Crankshaft pulley end

Distributor

Type:	
OHV engines	Bosch
CVH engines	Bosch or Lucas
Direction of rotor arm rotation	Anti-clockwise viewed from cap
Contact breaker points gap:	
Bosch distributor	0.40 to 0.50 mm (0.016 to 0.020 in)
Lucas distributor	0.40 to 0.59 mm (0.016 to 0.023 in)
Dwell angle	48° to 52°

Ignition coil

Type	Low voltage for use with 1.5 ohm ballast resistance
Output:	
OHV engines	23.0 k volt (minimum)
CVH engines	25.0 k volt (minimum)
Primary resistance	1.2 to 1.4 ohms
Secondary resistance	5000 to 9000 ohms

HT leads

OHV engines	Champion CLS 8
CVH engines	Champion CLS 9

Ignition timing

OHV engines:	
Up to 1984	12° BTDC at 750 to 850 rpm
1984 onwards	6° BTDC at 750 to 850 rpm
CVH engines	12° BTDC at 750 to 850 rpm

Spark plugs
Type:

OHV engines	Champion RS9YCC or RS9YC
CVH engines	Champion RC7YCC or RC7YC

Electrode gap

RS9YCC and RC7YCC	0.8 mm (0.032 in)
RS9YC and RC7YC	0.7 mm (0.028 in)

Torque wrench settings

	Nm	lbf ft
Spark plugs:		
OHV engines	13 to 20	10 to 15
CVH engines	25 to 38	18 to 28
Distributor clamp pinch bolt (OHV engines)	4	3
Distributor clamp plate bolt (OHV engines)	10	7
Distributor mounting bolts (CVH engines)	7	5

Part B: Electronic ignition system

General
System type:

All models except RS Turbo	Inductive type electronic breakerless
RS Turbo models	Programmed electronic ignition with microprocessor control

Application:

Electronic breakerless ignition	All 1.3 and 1.6 litre engines; 1.1 litre and 1.4 litre from 1986 onwards
Programmed electronic ignition	All RS Turbo models

Firing order:

OHV engines	1–2–4–3
CVH engines	1–3–4–2
Location of No 1 cylinder	Crankshaft pulley end

Distributor
Type:

OHV engines	Bosch
CVH engines	Bosch or Lucas
Direction of rotor arm rotation	Anti-clockwise viewed from cap

Ignition coil

Type	Oil filled high output
Output	25.0 to 30.0 k volt according to application

Primary resistance:

All models except RS Turbo 1986 onwards	0.72 to 0.88 ohms
RS Turbo from 1986 onwards	1.0 to 1.2 ohms
Secondary resistance	4500 to 7000 ohms

HT leads

OHV engines	Champion CLS 8
CVH engines	Champion CLS 9

Ignition timing

OHV engines	6° BTDC at 750 to 850 rpm

CVH engines:

All models except RS Turbo:	
Manual transmission	12° BTDC at 750 to 850 rpm
Automatic transmission	12° BTDC at 850 to 950 rpm
RS Turbo models:	
1985	12° BTDC at 800 to 900 rpm
1986	12° BTDC at 920 to 960 rpm

Spark plugs
Type:

OHV engines	Champion RS9YCC or RS9YC
CVH carburettor engines	Champion RC7YCC or RC7YC
1.6 litre CVH fuel injection engine	Champion C6YCC RC6YC
Turbo engine	Champion C61YC

Electrode gap:

RS9YCC, RC7YCC, C6YCC spark plugs	0.8 mm (0.032 in)
RS9YC, RC7YC, RC6YC, C61YC	0.7 mm (0.028 in)

Torque wrench settings

	Nm	lbf ft
Spark plugs:		
OHV engines	13 to 20	10 to 15
CVH engines	25 to 38	18 to 28
Distributor clamp pinch bolt (OHV engines)	4	3
Distributor clamp plate bolt (OHV engines)	10	7
Distributor mounting bolts (CVH engines)	7	5

PART A: CONTACT BREAKER IGNITION SYSTEM

1 General description

A conventional contact breaker ignition system is used on 1.1 litre OHV and CVH engine models from the start of production up to the introduction of the revised model range in 1986.

The ignition system is divided into two circuits, low tension (primary) and high tension (secondary). The low tension circuit consists of the battery, ignition switch, primary coil windings and the contact breaker points and condenser. The high tension circuit consists of the secondary coil windings, the heavy ignition lead from the centre of the distributor cap to the coil, the rotor arm and the spark plug leads and spark plugs.

When the system is in operation, low tension voltage is changed in the coil into high tension voltage by the opening and closing of the contact breaker points in the low tension circuit. High tension voltage is then fed, via the carbon brush in the centre of the distributor cap, to the rotor arm of the distributor. The rotor arm revolves inside the distributor and each time it comes in line with one of the four metal segments in the distributor cap, which are connected to the spark plug leads, the opening and closing of the contact breaker points causes the high tension voltage to build up and jump the gap from the rotor arm to the appropriate metal segment. The voltage then passes via the spark plug lead to the spark plug, where it finally jumps the spark plug gap before going to earth.

The distributor used on the conventional ignition system may be of either Bosch or Lucas manufacture. The Bosch unit is identified by its brown cap retained by spring clips, whereas the Lucas distributor has a black cap retained by screws. The distributor is driven by a skew gear from the camshaft on the OHV engine and by an offset dog on the end of the camshaft on CVH engines.

The ignition advance is a function of the distributor and is controlled both mechanically and by a vacuum-operated system. The mechanical governor mechanism consists of two weights which move out from the distributor shaft as the engine speed rises due to centrifugal force. As they move outwards, they rotate the cam relative to the distributor shaft and so advance the spark. The weights are held in position by two light springs and it is the tension of the springs which is largely responsible for correct spark advancement.

The vacuum control consists of a diaphragm, one side of which is connected via a small bore hose to the carburettor, and the other side to the distributor. Depression in the inlet manifold and carburettor, which varies with engine speed and throttle position, causes the diaphragm to move, so moving the baseplate and advancing or retarding the spark. A fine degree of control is achieved by a spring in the diaphragm assembly. Additionally, on certain models one or more vacuum valves and temperature sensitive control valves may be incorporated in the vacuum line between inlet manifold or carburettor and the distributor. These control the duration of the vacuum felt at the distributor and are part of the vehicle emission control systems. Further details will be found in Chapter 3.

A ballast resistor is incorporated in the low tension circuit between the ignition switch and the coil primary windings. The ballast resistor consists of a grey coloured resistive wire running externally to the main loom between the ignition switch and coil. During starting this resistor is bypassed allowing full available battery voltage to be fed to the coil which is of a low voltage type. This ensures that during starting when there is a heavy drain on the battery, sufficient voltage is still available at the coil to produce a powerful spark. During normal running, battery voltage is directed through the ballast resistor to limit the voltage supplied to the coil to seven volts.

2 Maintenance and inspection

1 At the intervals supplied in *'Routine maintenance'* at the beginning of this manual, remove the distributor cap and thoroughly clean it inside and out with a dry lint-free cloth. Examine the four HT lead segments inside the cap. If the segments appear badly burnt or pitted, renew the cap. Make sure that the carbon brush in the centre of the cap is free to move and that it protrudes significantly from its holder.

2 Check the condition of the contact breaker points and renew them or adjust their gap as applicable using the procedures described in Sections 3 and 4.

3 Remove, clean, regap and test the spark plugs as described in Section 10. Renew the plugs in sets of four if any show signs of failure when tested, or if under visual inspection the end of the centre electrode is rounded off, or the earth electrode is eroded. The plugs must be renewed, regardless of visual appearance, if they have exceeded their recommended service life. Also check the spark plug HT leads for any signs of corrosion of the end fittings, which if evident should be carefully cleaned away. Wipe the leads clean (including the coil lead) over their entire length before refitting.

4 Check the condition and security of all leads and wiring associated with the ignition system. Make sure that no chafing is occurring on any of the wires and that all connections are secure, clean and free from corrosion.

3 Contact breaker points – adjustment

1 Spring back the retaining clips or undo the screws as appropriate and lift off the distributor cap.

2 Withdraw the rotor arm from the distributor shaft.

3 Using a screwdriver, gently prise the contact breaker points open to examine the condition of their faces. If they are rough, pitted or dirty they should be renewed as described in the next Section.

4 Assuming that the points are in a satisfactory condition or that they have just been renewed, the gap between the two faces should be checked and if necessary adjusted. This can be done using feeler gauges as described below, or preferably by using the more accurate dwell angle method as described from paragraph 8 onwards.

5 To adjust the points using feeler gauges, turn the crankshaft using a spanner on the crankshaft pulley bolt until the heel of the contact breaker arm is on the peak of one of the four cam lobes and the points are fully open. A feeler blade of thickness equal to the contact breaker points gap as given in the Specifications should now just slide between the point faces.

6 If adjustment is required, slacken the retaining screw slightly and move the fixed point as necessary to achieve the desired gap. The points can be easily moved by engaging a screwdriver in the slot on the end of the fixed point and levering against the corresponding slot or raised pips on the baseplate. After adjustment tighten the retaining screw and recheck the gap.

7 Refit the rotor arm and the distributor cap.

8 If a dwell meter is available adjust the contact breaker points by measuring and setting the dwell angle as follows.

9 The dwell angle is the number of degrees of distributor cam rotation during which the contact breaker points are closed; ie the period from when the points close after being opened by one cam lobe, until they are opened again by the next cam lobe. The advantages of

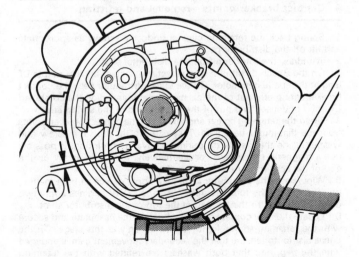

Fig. 4.1 Contact breaker points gap (A) – Bosch distributor (Sec 3)

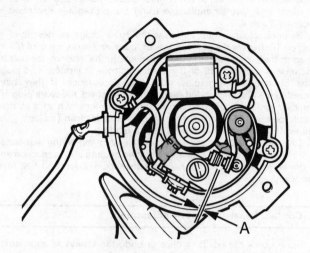

Fig. 4.2 Contact breaker points gap (A) – Lucas distributor (Sec 3)

setting the points by this method are that any wear of the distributor shaft or cam lobes is taken into account and the inaccuracies associated with using feeler gauges are eliminated. Also, on 1.1 litre CVH engines the static ignition timing is accurately set in production and adjustment of the ignition timing in service has been deleted from the maintenance schedule. Therefore dwell angle adjustment is far more critical on these engines.

10 In general a dwell meter should be used in accordance with the manufacturer's instructions. However, the use of one type of meter is outlined as follows.

11 Remove the distributor cap and rotor arm and connect one lead of the dwell meter to the '+' terminal on the coil and the other lead to the coil '–' terminal.

12 Whilst an assistant turns on the ignition and cranks the engine on the starter, observe the reading on the dwell meter scale. With the engine cranking the reading should be equal to the dwell angle given in the Specifications.

13 If the dwell angle is too small, the contact breaker points gap should be reduced and if the dwell angle is excessive the gap should be increased.

14 Adjust the points gap while the engine is cranking using the method described in paragraph 6. When the dwell angle is satisfactory, disconnect the meter, then refit the rotor arm and distributor cap.

4 Contact breaker points – removal and refitting

1 Spring back the retaining clips or undo the screws as appropriate and lift off the distributor cap.

2 Withdraw the rotor arm from the distributor shaft.

3 On the Bosch distributor disconnect the contact breaker points LT lead at the spade connector. On the Lucas distributor ease the contact breaker spring arm out of the plastic insulator and slide the combined LT and condenser lead out of the hooked end of the spring arm.

4 Undo the retaining screw and withdraw the contact breaker points from the distributor baseplate. Take care not to drop the screw and washer inside the distributor during removal and refitting. If possible use a magnetic screwdriver, or alternatively, retain the screw on the end of the screwdriver using a dab of grease.

5 Wipe clean the distributor cam, then apply a trace of high melting point grease to the four cam lobes. Also, on OHV engines apply two drops of light oil to the felt pad at the top of the distributor shaft.

6 Locate the new contact breaker points on the baseplate and secure with the retaining screw, lightly tightened only at this stage. On the Lucas distributor ensure that the secondary movement cam is engaged with the peg, and that both washers are refitted with the retaining screw.

7 Reconnect the LT lead, then refer to Section 3 and adjust the contact breaker points gap.

5 Condenser – removal and refitting

1 The purpose of the condenser is to prevent excessive arcing of the contact breaker points, and to ensure that a rapid collapse of the magnetic field, created in the coil, and necessary if a healthy spark is to be produced at the plugs, is allowed to occur.

2 The condenser is fitted in parallel with the contact breaker points. If it becomes faulty it will lead to ignition failure, as the points will be prevented from cleanly interrupting the low tension circuit.

3 If the engine becomes very difficult to start, or begins to miss after several miles of running, and the contact breaker points show signs of excessive burning, then the condition of the condenser must be suspect. A further test can be made by separating the contact breaker points by hand, with the ignition switched on. If this is accompanied by an excessively strong flash, it indicates that the condenser has failed.

4 Without special test equipment, the only reliable way to diagnose condenser trouble is to renew the suspect unit and note if there is any improvement in performance. To do this proceed as follows according to engine type.

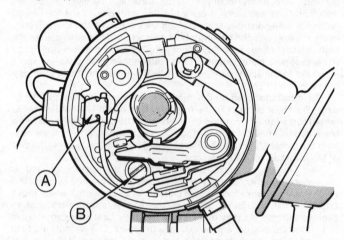

Fig. 4.3 Contact breaker points renewal – Bosch distributor (Sec 4)

A   LT lead connector   B   Contact breaker retaining screw

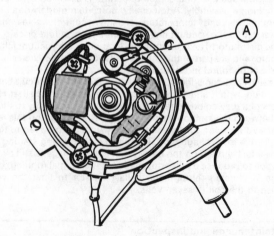

Fig. 4.4 Contact breaker points renewal – Lucas distributor (Sec 4)

A   Secondary movement cam and peg

B   Contact breaker retaining screw

OHV engines

5 Spring back the retaining clips and lift off the distributor cap. Withdraw the rotor arm from the distributor shaft.
6 Accurately mark the position of the distributor body in relation to the clamp plate, then slacken the clamp plate pinch bolt.
7 Turn the distributor body approximately 120° in a clockwise direction to expose the externally mounted condenser.
8 Disconnect the contact breaker points LT lead from the spade terminal, and the ignition LT lead at the coil.
9 Undo the retaining screw and withdraw the condenser from the side of the distributor body.
10 Place the new condenser in position and secure with the retaining screw.
11 Reconnect the LT leads, then turn the distributor back to its original position and align the marks made during removal. Tighten the clamp plate pinch bolt.
12 Refit the rotor arm and distributor cap. If in any doubt about the distributor position, check the ignition timing as described in Section 8.

CVH engines

13 Spring back the retaining clips or undo the screws as appropriate and lift off the distributor cap.
14 On the Bosch distributor disconnect the contact breaker points LT lead from the spade terminal, undo the retaining screw and withdraw the condenser from the side of the distributor body. Disconnect the ignition LT lead at the coil and remove the condenser.
15 On the Lucas distributor ease the contact breaker spring arm out of the plastic insulator and slide the combined LT and condenser lead out of the hooked end of the spring arm. Undo the condenser retaining screw and earth lead, disconnect the ignition LT lead at the coil, and withdraw the condenser and wiring from the distributor.
16 On all distributors refitting is the reverse sequence to removal.

---

6 Distributor – removal and refitting

OHV engines

1 Disconnect the leads from the spark plugs, spring back the retaining clips and lift off the distributor cap.
2 Disconnect the LT lead at the coil negative terminal and the vacuum hose at the distributor vacuum unit.
3 Remove No 1 spark plug (nearest the crankshaft pulley).
4 Place a finger over the plug hole and turn the crankshaft in the normal direction of rotation (clockwise viewed from the crankshaft pulley end) until pressure is felt in No 1 cylinder. This indicates that the piston is commencing its compression stroke. The crankshaft can be turned with a spanner on the pulley bolt.
5 Continue turning the crankshaft until the notch in the pulley is aligned with the 'O' mark on the timing scale just above the pulley. In this position No 1 piston is at Top Dead Centre (TDC) on compression.
6 Using a dab of quick drying paint, mark the position of the rotor arm on the rim of the distributor body. Make a further mark on the distributor body and a corresponding mark on the cylinder block.
7 Undo the bolt securing the distributor clamp plate to the cylinder block. Do not remove the distributor by releasing the clamp plate pinch bolt.
8 Withdraw the distributor from the cylinder block. As the distributor is removed, the rotor arm will move a few degrees clockwise. Note the new position of the rotor arm and make a second mark on the distributor body rim.
9 Before installing the distributor make sure that the crankshaft is still positioned at TDC as previously described. If a new distributor is being fitted, transfer the markings made during removal to the new unit.
10 Hold the distributor over its hole in the cylinder block with the mark made on the distributor body aligned with the mark on the cylinder block.
11 Position the rotor arm so that it points toward the mark made on the distributor rim after removal and push the distributor fully home. As the skew gears mesh the rotor arm will move anti-clockwise and should align with the first mark made on the distributor rim.
12 With all the marks aligned, refit and tighten the distributor clamp plate retaining bolt.
13 Reconnect the LT lead and vacuum hose, then refit the distributor cap, spark plug and plug leads.
14 Refer to Section 8 and adjust the ignition timing.

Fig. 4.5 Distributor turned through 120° for condenser renewal – Bosch distributor, OHV engines (Sec 5)

A   LT lead connector   B   Condenser retaining screw

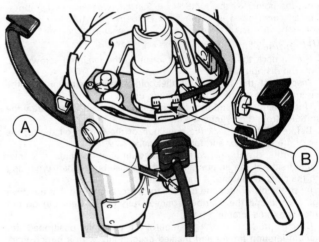

Fig. 4.6 Bosch distributor condenser renewal – CVH engines (Sec 5)

A   Condenser retaining screw   B   LT lead connector

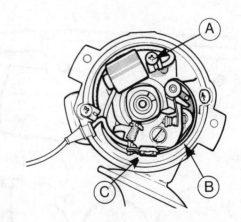

Fig. 4.7 Lucas distributor condenser renewal – CVH engines (Sec 5)

A   Condenser retaining screw   C   Hooked end of spring arm
B   Contact breaker spring arm

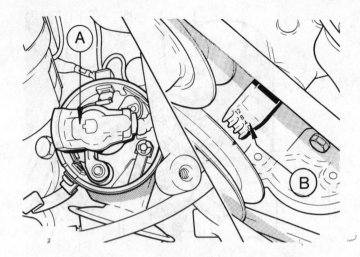

Fig. 4.8 Distributor removal – OHV engines (Sec 6)

A   Rotor arm facing distributor cap No 1 spark plug lead segment
B   Pulley notch aligned with TDC mark on timing scale

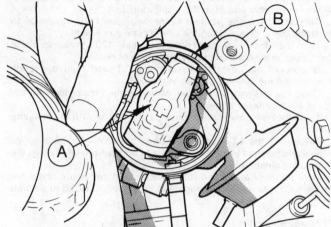

Fig. 4.9 Rotor arm position marked on distributor body after removal – OHV engines (Sec 6)

A   Rotor arm
B   Mark made on distributor body rim

CVH engines

15 Spring back the retaining clips, or undo the retaining screws and lift off the distributor cap.
16 Disconnect the LT lead at the coil negative terminal and the vacuum hose at the distributor vacuum unit.
17 Undo the three distributor flange retaining bolts and withdraw the distributor from the cylinder head.
18 Before refitting, check the condition of the O-ring oil seal at the base of the distributor and renew it if necessary.
19 Hold the distributor with the vacuum unit towards the inlet manifold side of the engine and align the distributor shaft drive dog with the slots in the end of the camshaft.
20 Insert the distributor and turn the rotor arm slightly so that the drive dogs engage and the distributor moves fully home. Refit but do not tighten the three retaining bolts.
21 During production the distributor is precisely positioned for optimum ignition timing and marked accordingly with a punch mark on the distributor mounting flange and the cylinder head (Fig. 4.12).
22 If the original distributor is being refitted, align the punch marks, tighten the distributor flange mounting bolts and refit the distributor cap, LT lead and vacuum hose.

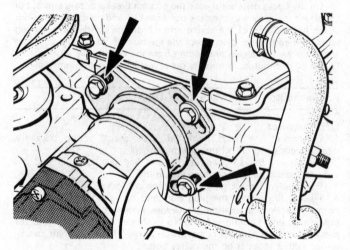

Fig. 4.10 Distributor flange retaining bolt locations – CVH engines (Sec 6)

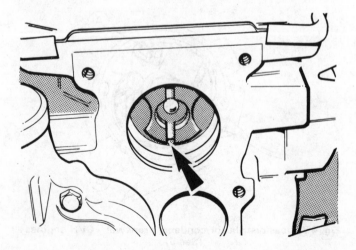

Fig. 4.11 Align distributor shaft drive dog with slots in camshaft – CVH engines (Sec 6)

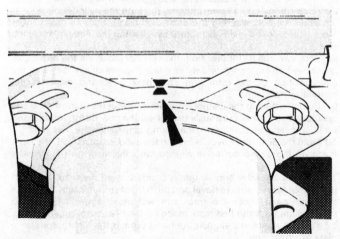

Fig. 4.12 Distributor mounting flange and cylinder head punch mark locations – CVH engines (Sec 6)

23 If a new distributor is being fitted, turn the distributor body so that the mounting bolts are positioned centrally in their elongated slots, then tighten the bolts just over finger tight. Refit the distributor cap, LT lead and vacuum hose, then adjust the ignition timing as described in Section 8.

7 Distributor – overhaul

Note: *Ensure that replacement parts are readily available before carrying out any overhaul or repair work on the distributor.*

OHV engines
1 Apart from renewal of the contact breaker points and condenser described previously, the only other repairs possible are renewal of distributor cap, rotor arm, vacuum unit and drive dog. Should the distributor be worn or unserviceable in any other respect, renewal of the complete unit will be necessary.
2 To renew the vacuum unit remove the distributor from the engine as described in Section 6.
3 Remove the rotor arm.
4 Extract the circlip securing the vacuum unit rod to the baseplate pivot post.

5 Undo the two vacuum unit retaining screws, tip the unit to release the rod from the baseplate pivot post, and withdraw it from the distributor body.
6 Reassembly and refitting are the reverse of the dismantling and removal procedures, but lubricate the baseplate pivot post with a high melting point grease.

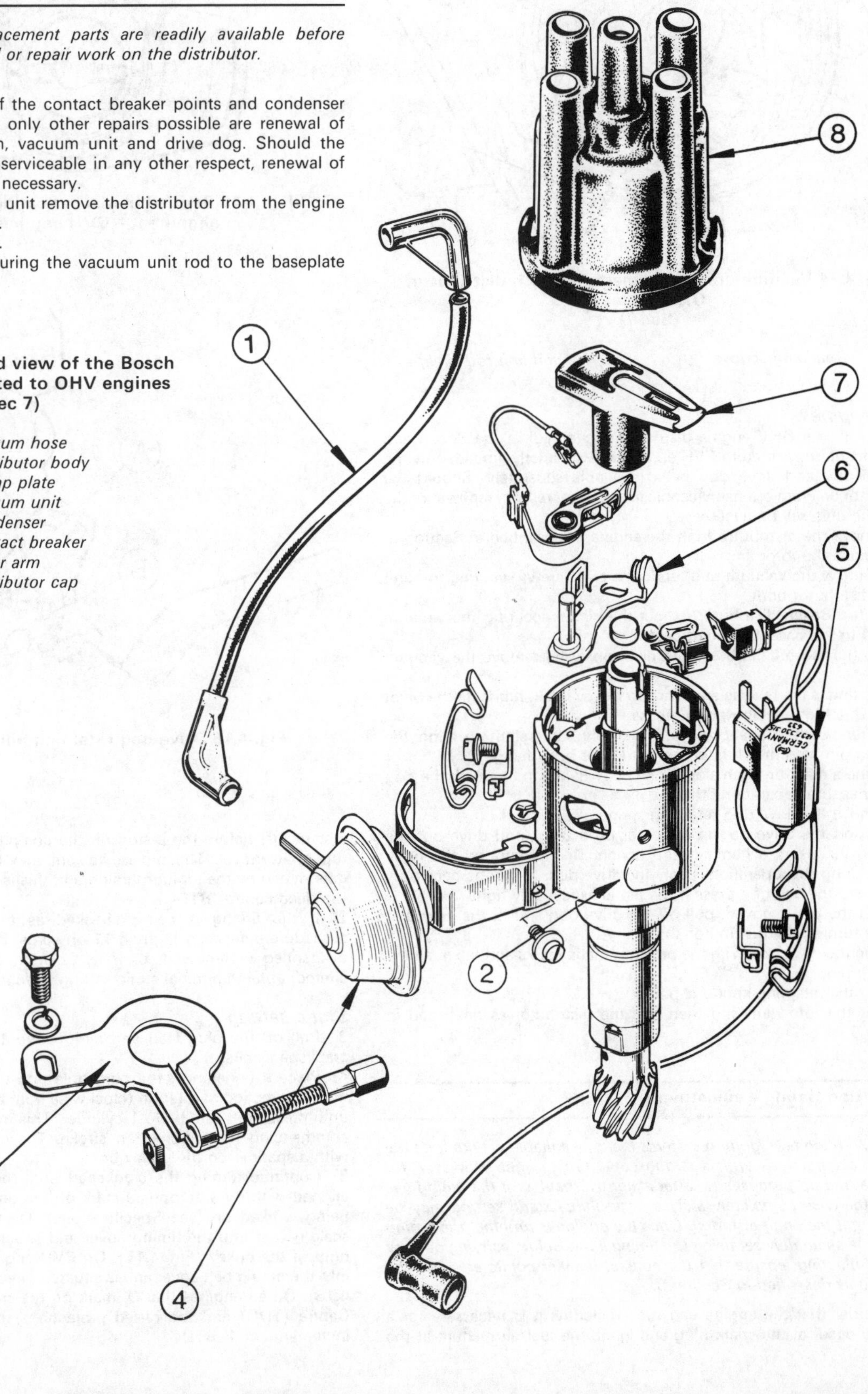

Fig. 4.13 Exploded view of the Bosch distributor as fitted to OHV engines (Sec 7)

1 Vacuum hose
2 Distributor body
3 Clamp plate
4 Vacuum unit
5 Condenser
6 Contact breaker
7 Rotor arm
8 Distributor cap

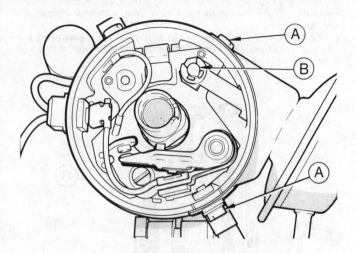

Fig. 4.14 Vacuum unit attachments – Bosch distributor,
OHV engines
(Sec 7)

A   Retaining screws   B   Vacuum unit rod circlip

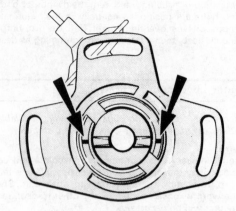

Fig. 4.15 Scribed marks indicating drive dog teeth
alignment – CVH engines (Sec 7)

CVH engines

7   As with the OHV engine distributors, overhaul of the Bosch and
Lucas distributors fitted to CVH engines is also strictly limited, only the
vacuum unit and drive dog being available separately. Should the
distributor be worn or unserviceable in any other respect renewal of the
complete unit will be necessary.
8   Remove the distributor from the engine as described in Section 6.
9   Remove the rotor arm.
10   To renew the vacuum unit, undo the two screws securing the unit
to the distributor body.
11   On the Bosch distributor extract the circlip securing the vacuum
unit rod to the baseplate pivot post.
12   Slip the rod off the baseplate pivot post and remove the vacuum
unit.
13   Refitting is the reverse sequence to removal, but lubricate the pivot
post with a high melting point grease.
14   To renew the drive dog, turn the distributor shaft to align the
retaining pin with the slots in the distributor body flange.
15   Scribe a mark on each side of the body flange in line with the dog
teeth to ensure accurate refitting.
16   Remove the drive dog retaining spring clip.
17   Support the drive dog in a vice or on a block and drive out the
retaining pin using a hammer and punch. Do not support the body
flange during this operation – only the drive dog. It may be necessary
to resort to the use of a press if the pin is excessively tight.
18   With the pin removed, pull off the drive dog and fit the new dog
without turning the distributor shaft.
19   Align the drive dog with the previous made marks and tap in a new
retaining pin.
20   Refit the retaining spring clip.
21   Refit the rotor arm and then refit the distributor as described in
Section 6.

8   Ignition timing – adjustment

Note: *With modern ignition systems the only suitable way to time the
ignition accurately is with a stroboscopic timing light. However, for
initial setting up purposes (ie after major overhaul, or if the timing has
been otherwise completely lost) a basic initial static setting may be
used to get the engine started. Once the engine is running, the timing
should be accurately set using the timing light. Before carrying out any
of the following, ensure that the contact breaker points are correctly
adjusted as described in Section 3.*

1   In order that the engine can run efficiently, it is necessary for a
spark to occur at the spark plug and ignite the fuel/air mixture at the

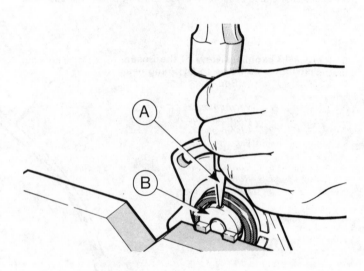

Fig. 4.16 Drive dog retaining pin removal (Sec 7)

A   Drift   B   Drive dog

instant just before the piston on the compression stroke reaches the
top of its travel. The precise instant at which the spark occurs is
determined by the ignition timing and this is quoted in degrees before
top dead centre (BTDC).
2   If the timing is being checked as a maintenance or service
procedure, refer to paragraph 11 onwards. If the distributor has been
dismantled or renewed, or if its position on the engine has been
altered, obtain an initial static setting as follows.

Static setting
3   Pull off the plug lead and remove No 1 spark plug (nearest the
crankshaft pulley).
4   Place a finger over the plug hole and turn the crankshaft in the
normal direction of rotation (clockwise from the crankshaft pulley end)
until pressure is felt in No 1 cylinder. This indicates that the piston is
commencing its compression stroke. The crankshaft can be turned
with a spanner on the pulley bolt.
5   Continue turning the crankshaft until the notch on the pulley is
aligned with the appropriate mark on the timing scale for the engine
being worked on (see Specifications). On OHV engines the timing
scale is cast into the timing cover and situated just above and to the
right of the pulley (Fig. 4.17). On CVH engines the scale is moulded
into the timing belt cover and is situated directly above the pulley (Fig.
4.18). On all engines the 'O' mark on the scale represents Top Dead
Centre (TDC) and the raised projections to the left of TDC are in
increments of 4° BTDC.

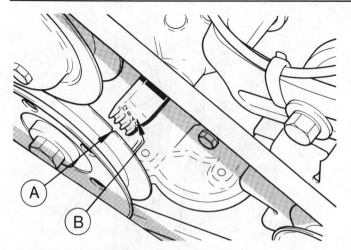

Fig. 4.17 Timing mark identification – OHV engines (Sec 8)

A   Notch on crankshaft pulley
B   Timing scale case into timing cover

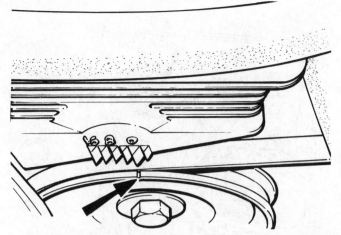

Fig. 4.18 Crankshaft pulley notch (arrowed) and timing scale – CVH engines (Sec 8)

6   Remove the distributor cap and check that the rotor arm is pointing towards the No 1 spark plug lead segment in the cap.
7   Slacken the distributor clamp pinch bolt (OHV engines) or the three distributor flange securing bolts (CVH engines).
8   Turn the distributor body anti-clockwise slightly until the contact breaker points are closed, then slowly turn the distributor body clockwise until the points just open. Hold the distributor body in this position and tighten the clamp pinch bolt or flange securing bolts as applicable.
9   Refit the distributor cap, No 1 spark plug and the plug lead.
10   It should now be possible to start and run the engine enabling the timing to be accurately checked with a timing light as follows.

Stroboscopic setting
11   Refer to the Specifications for the timing setting applicable to the engine being worked on and then highlight the appropriate mark on the timing scale and the notch in the pulley with a dab of white paint (see also paragraph 5).
12   Connect a timing light to the engine in accordance with the manufacturer's instructions (usually between No 1 spark plug and plug lead).
13   Disconnect the vacuum hose at the distributor vacuum unit and plug the hose.
14   Start the engine and allow it to idle.
15   Point the timing light at the timing marks. They should appear to be stationary with the crankshaft pulley notch in alignment with the appropriate notch on the scale.
16   If adjustment is necessary (ie the marks are not aligned) slacken the distributor clamp pinch bolt or flange securing bolts as applicable, and turn the distributor body as necessary to align the marks. Tighten the pinch bolt or flange bolts when the setting is correct.
17   A secondary use of the timing light is to check that the centrifugal and vacuum advance functions of the distributor are working.
18   The tests are not of course precise as would be the case if sophisticated equipment were used, but will at least indicate the serviceability of the unit.
19   With the engine idling, timing light connected and vacuum pipe disconnected and plugged as described in the preceding paragraphs, increase the engine speed to 2000 rpm and note the approximate distance which the pulley mark moves out of alignment with the mark on the scale.
20   Reconnect the vacuum pipe to the distributor and repeat the test when for the same increase in engine speed, the alignment differential of the timing marks should be greater than previously observed.
21   If the timing marks did not appear to move during the first test, a fault in the distributor centrifugal advance mechanism is indicated. No increased movement of the marks during the second test indicates a punctured diaphragm in the vacuum unit, or a leak in the vacuum line.
22   On completion of the adjustments and checks, switch off the engine and disconnect the timing light.

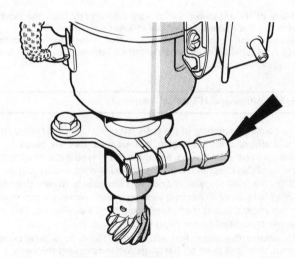

Fig. 4.19 Distributor clamp pinch bolt location – OHV engines (Sec 8)

9   Ignition coil – general

1   The ignition coil is mounted on the engine compartment right-hand inner valance on OHV engine models, and on the left-hand inner valance on CVH engine versions.
2   To remove the coil, disconnect the LT leads at the coil positive and negative terminals and the HT lead at the centre terminal.
3   Undo the mounting bracket retaining bolts and remove the coil.
4   Refitting is the reverse sequence to removal.
5   Accurate checking of the coil output requires the use of special test equipment and should be left to a dealer or suitably equipped automotive electrician. It is however possible to check the primary and secondary winding resistance using an ohmmeter as follows.
6   To check the primary resistance disconnect the LT and HT wiring at the coil and connect the ohmmeter across the coil positive and negative terminals. The resistance should be as given in the Specifications at the beginning of this Chapter.
7   To check the secondary resistance, connect one lead from the ohmmeter to the coil negative terminal, and the other lead to the centre HT terminal. Again the resistance should be as given in the Specifications.

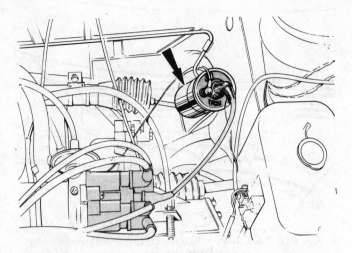

Fig. 4.20 Ignition coil location – CVH engines (Sec 9)

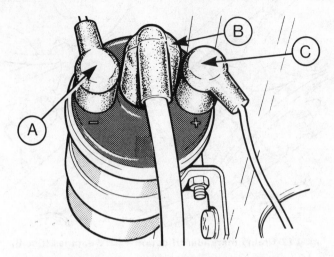

Fig. 4.21 Ignition coil terminal identification (Sec 9)

A   Negative LT terminal to distributor
B   HT terminal to distributor cap
C   Positive LT feed terminal

8   If any of the measured valves vary significantly from the figures given in the Specifications, the coil should be renewed.
9   If a new coil is to be fitted, ensure that it is of the correct low voltage type suitable for use in conventional ignition systems equipped with ballast resistance.

10 Spark plugs and HT leads – general

1   The correct functioning of the spark plugs is vital for the correct running and efficiency of the engine. It is essential that the plugs fitted are appropriate for the engine, and the suitable type is specified at the beginning of this chapter. If this type is used and the engine is in good condition, the spark plugs should not need attention between scheduled replacement intervals. Spark plug cleaning is rarely necessary and should not be attempted unless specialised equipment is available as damage can easily be caused to the firing ends.
2   To remove the plugs, first mark the HT leads to ensure correct refitment, then pull them off the plugs. When removing the leads, pull the terminal insulator at the end of the lead – not the lead itself.
3   Using a $^5/_8$ in AF (16 mm) spark plug spanner or suitable deep socket and extension bar, unscrew the plugs and remove them from the engine.
4   The condition of the spark plugs will also tell much about the overall condition of the engine.
5   If the insulator nose of the spark plug is clean and white, with no deposits, this is indicative of a weak mixture, or too hot a plug. (A hot plug transfers heat away from the electrode slowly – a cold plug transfers it away quickly).
6   If the tip and insulator nose are covered with hard black-looking deposits, then this is indicative that the mixture is too rich. Should the plug be black and oily, then it is likely that the engine is fairly worn, as well as the mixture being too rich.
7   If the insulator nose is covered with light tan to greyish brown deposits, then the mixture is correct and it is likely that the engine is in good condition.
8   The spark plug gap is of considerable importance, as if it is too large or too small, the size of the spark and its efficiency will be seriously impaired. The spark plug gap should be set to the figure given in the Specifications at the beginning of this Chapter.
9   To set it, measure the gap with a feeler gauge, and then bend open, or close, the *outer* plug electrode until the correct gap is achieved. The centre electrode should *never* be bent as this may crack the insulation and cause plug failure, if nothing worse.
10   Before fitting the plugs first ensure that the plug threads and the seating area in the cylinder head are clean, dry and free of carbon.
11   Screw the plugs in by hand initially and then fully tighten to the specified torque. If a torque wrench is not available, tighten the plugs

until initial resistance is felt, then tighten by a further $^1/_{16}$ of a turn for the taper seat plugs fitted to OHV engines, or $^1/_4$ of a turn for the gasket seat type fitted to CVH engines. Do not over-tighten the spark plugs, otherwise damage to the threads may occur and they will also be extremely difficult to remove in the future.
12   Refit the plug leads in the correct order ensuring that they are a secure fit over the plug ends. Periodically wipe the leads clean to reduce the risk of HT leakage by arcing and remove any traces of corrosion that may occur on the end fittings.

11 Fault diagnosis – contact breaker ignition system

By far the majority of breakdown and running troubles are caused by faults in the ignition system either in the low tension or high tension circuits.

There are two main symptoms indicating faults. Either the engine will not start or fire, or the engine is difficult to start and misfires. If it is a regular misfire (ie. the engine is running on only two or three cylinders), the fault is almost sure to be in the secondary or high tension circuit. If the misfiring is intermittent the fault could be in either the high or low tension circuits. If the car stops suddenly, or will not start at all, it is likely that the fault is in the low tension circuit. Loss of power and overheating, apart from faulty carburation settings, are normally due to faults in the distributor or to incorrect ignition timing.

Engine fails to start
1   If the engine fails to start and the car was running normally when it was last used, first check there is fuel in the petrol tank. If the engine turns over normally on the starter motor and the battery is evidently well charged, then the fault may be in either the high or low tension circuits. First check the HT circuit.
2   One of the commonest reasons for bad starting is wet or damp spark plug leads and distributor. Remove the distributor cap. If condensation is visible internally dry the cap with a rag and also wipe over the leads. Refit the cap. A moisture dispersant, such as Holts Wet Start, can be very effective in these situations. To prevent the problem recurring Holts Damp Start can be used to provide a sealing coat, so excluding any further moisture from the ignition system. In extreme difficulty, Holts Cold Start will help to start a car when only a very poor spark occurs.
3   If the engine still fails to start, check the voltage is reaching the plugs by disconnecting each plug lead in turn at the spark plug end, and holding the end of the cable about $^3/_{16}$ inch (5 mm) away from the cylinder block. Spin the engine on the starter motor.

4 Sparking between the end of the cable and the block should be fairly strong with a strong regular blue spark. (Hold the lead with rubber to avoid electric shocks). If voltage is reaching the plugs, then remove them and clean and regap them. The engine should now start.

5 If there is no spark at the plug leads, take off the HT lead from the centre of the distributor cap and hold it to the block as before. Spin the engine on the starter once more. A rapid succession of blue sparks between the end of the lead and the block indicate that the coil is in order and that the distributor cap is cracked, the rotor arm is faulty, or the carbon brush in the top of the distributor cap is not making good contact with the rotor arm.

6 If there are no sparks from the end of the lead from the coil, check the connections at the coil end of the lead. If it is in order start checking the low tension circuit.

7 Use a 12v voltmeter or a 12v bulb and two lengths of wire. With the ignition switched on and the points open, test between the low tension wire to the coil and earth. No reading indicates a break in the supply from the ignition switch. Check the connections at the switch to see if any are loose. Refit them and the engine should run.

8 With the points still open take a reading between the moving point and earth. No reading here indicates a break in the wire or poor connections between the coil ' − ' terminal and distributor, or a faulty coil. Take a further reading between the coil ' − ' terminal and earth. No reading confirms a faulty coil. For these tests it is sufficient to separate the points with a piece of dry paper while testing with the points open.

Engine misfires

9 If the engine misfires regularly, run it at a fast idling speed. Pull off each of the plug caps in turn and listen to the note of the engine. Hold the plug cap in a dry cloth or with a rubber glove as additional protection against a shock from HT supply.

10 No difference in engine running will be noticed when the lead from the defective circuit is removed. Removing the lead from one of the good cylinders will accentuate the misfire.

11 Remove it about $3/16$ inch (5 mm) away from the block. Re-start the engine. If the sparking is fairly strong and regular, the fault must lie in the spark plug.

12 The plug may be loose, the insulation may be cracked, or the points may have burnt away giving too wide a gap for the spark to jump. Worse still, one of the points may have broken off. Either renew the plug, or clean it, reset the gap and then test it.

13 If there is no spark at the end of the plug lead, or if it is weak and intermittent, check the ignition lead from the distributor to the plug. If the insulation is cracked or perished, renew the lead. Check the connections at the distributor cap.

14 If there is still no spark, examine the distributor cap carefully for tracking. This can be recognised by a very thin black line running between two or more electrodes, or between an electrode and some other part of the distributor. These lines are paths which now conduct electricity across the cap thus letting it run to earth. The only answer is a new distributor cap.

15 Apart from the ignition timing being incorrect, other causes of misfiring have already been dealt with under the Section dealing with the failure of the engine to start. To recap, these are that

  (a) The coil may be faulty giving an intermittent misfire;
  (b) There may be a damaged wire or loose connection in the low tension circuit;
  (c) The condenser may be faulty; or
  (d) There may be a mechnical fault in the distributor (broken driving spindle or contact breaker spring).

16 If the ignition timing is too far retarded, it should be noted that the engine will tend to overheat, and there will a quite noticeable drop in power. If the engine is overheating and the power is down, and the ignition timing is correct, then the carburettor should be checked, as it is likely that this is where the fault lies.

PART B: ELECTRONIC IGNITION SYSTEM

12 General description

A breakerless electronic ignition system is used on 1.3 litre and 1.6 litre engines from the start of production and on all engines from 1986 onwards. Two types of electronic ignition are used according to vehicle type. All models except RS Turbo versions are fitted with a breakerless distributor type system whereby the action of the contact breaker points are simulated electronically within the distributor, but control of ignition advance characteristics are still carried out in the conventional way using mechanical and vacuum systems. RS Turbo models are equipped with a fully electronic programmed ignition system utilizing a breakerless distributor in conjunction with micro-processor control of ignition advance characteristics for all engine operating conditions.

The operation of the two systems is as follows.

All models except RS Turbo

The ignition system is divided into two circuits, low tension (primary) and high tension (secondary). The low tension circuit consists of the battery, ignition switch, primary coil windings, electronic amplifier module and the signal generating system inside the distributor. The signal generating system comprises the trigger coil, trigger wheel, stator, permanent magnets and stator pick-up. The high tension circuit consists of the secondary coil windings, the heavy ignition lead from the centre of the distributor cap to the coil, the rotor arm and the spark plug leads and spark plugs.

When the system is in operation, low tension voltage is changed in the coil into high tension voltage by the action of the electronic amplifier module in conjunction with the signal generating system. As each of the trigger wheel teeth pass through the magnetic field created around the trigger coil in the distributor, a change in the magnetic field force (flux) is created which induces a voltage in the trigger coil. This voltage is passed to the electronic amplifier module which switches off the ignition coil primary circuit. This results in the collapse of the magnetic field in the coil which generates the high tension voltage. The high tension voltage is then fed via the carbon brush in the centre of the distributor cap to the rotor arm. The voltage passes across to the appropriate metal segment in the cap and via the spark plug lead to the spark plug where it finally jumps the spark plug gap to earth.

The distributor used on the electronic ignition system of OHV engines is of Bosch manufacture, whereas on CVH engines either a Bosch or Lucas unit may be used. Although the components of the signal generating system differ between the Bosch and Lucas distributors, the principles of operation of both are as just described. The distributor is driven by a skew gear from the camshaft on the OHV engine and by an offset dog on the end of the camshaft on CVH engines.

The ignition advance is a function of the distributor and is controlled both mechanically and by a vacuum operated system. The mechanical governor mechanism consists of two weights which move out from the distributor shaft as the engine speed rises due to centrifugal force. As they move outwards, they rotate the trigger wheel relative to the distributor shaft and so advance the spark. The weights are held in position by two light springs and it is the tension of the springs which is largely responsible for correct spark advancement.

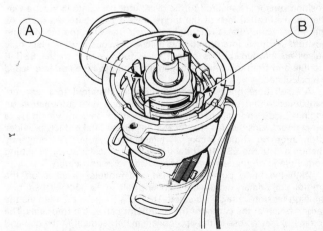

Fig. 4.22 Signal generating system – Bosch distributor (Sec 12)

A Trigger wheel   B Stator

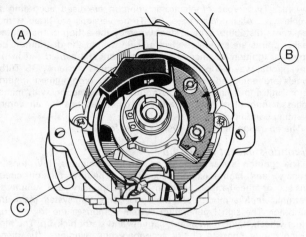

Fig. 4.23 Signal generating system – Lucas distributor
(Sec 12)

A   Trigger coil   C   Trigger wheel
B   Stator and permanent magnets

The vacuum control consists of a diaphragm, one side of which is connected via a small bore hose to the carburettor or throttle housing, and the other side to the distributor. Depression in the inlet manifold and/or carburettor, which varies with engine speed and throttle position, causes the diaphragm to move, so moving the baseplate and advancing or retarding the spark. A fine degree of control is achieved by a spring in the diaphragm assembly. Additionally, one or more vacuum valves and temperature sensitive control valves may be incorporated in the vacuum line between inlet manifold or carburettor and the distributor. These control the duration of the vacuum felt at the distributor and are part of the vehicle emission control systems. Further details will be found in Chapter 3.

RS Turbo models

RS Turbo models are equipped with a programmed electronic ignition system which utilizes computer technology and electro-magnetic circuitry to simulate all the functions of a conventional ignition distributor.

The two main components of the system are the electronic control module designated Electronic Spark Control II (ESC II), and a Hall effect electronic ignition distributor.

The distributor is mounted conventionally on the flywheel end of the cylinder head, and is driven directly off the camshaft by an offset dog coupling. Contained within the distributor is a trigger vane, permanent magnet and position sensor. The trigger vane is a cylindrical disc attached to the distributor shaft and having four slots on its vertical surface, one for each cylinder. The permanent magnet and position sensor are secured to the distributor baseplate in such a way that the vertical surface of the trigger vane passes between them. As the trigger vane rotates, the magnetic field between the magnet and position sensor is interrupted and a series of square wave electronic pulses are produced. This output wave form is sent to the ESC II module and from this, engine speed, ignition advance and idle speed are calculated.

A small bore hose connecting the inlet manifold to a vacuum transducer within the module supplies the unit with information on engine load, and a charge air temperature sensor, which is a temperature sensitive resistor located in the air intake duct, provides information on engine intake air temperature. From this constantly changing data the ESC II module selects a particular advance setting from a range of ignition characteristics stored in its memory.

With the firing point established, the module switches off the ignition coil primary circuit, the magnetic field in the coil collapses and the high tension voltage is created. This HT voltage is then fed via the carbon brush in the centre of the distributor cap to the rotor arm. The voltage passes across to the appropriate metal segment in the cap and via the spark plug lead to the spark plug where it finally jumps the spark plug gap to earth. At precisely the right instant the ESC II module switches the coil primary circuit back on and the cycle is repeated for each cylinder in turn.

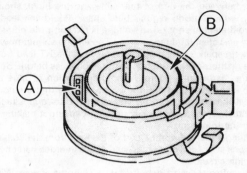

Fig. 4.24 Pulse generating components – RS Turbo models
(Sec 12)

A   Position sensor   B   Trigger vane

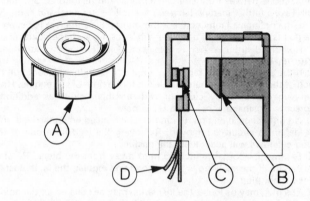

Fig. 4.25 Trigger vane and position sensor details – RS
Turbo models (Sec 12)

A   Trigger vane   C   Position sensor element
B   Permanent magnet   D   Sensor wiring

Additionally the ESC II module operates in conjunction with the fuel-injection and turbo systems to provide data on engine rpm to the fuel-injection control module, and to provide an overriding control of turbo boost pressure.

All models

Warning: *The voltages produced by the electronic ignition systems are considerably higher than those produced by a conventional system. Extreme care must be taken when working on the system with the ignition switched on, particularly by persons fitted with a cardiac pacemaker.*

13 Maintenance and inspection

Maintenance and inspection procedures for the electronic ignition system are the same as described in Part A: Section 2, but ignore all references to contact breaker points.

14 Distributor – removal and refitting

OHV engines

1   Disconnect the leads from the spark plugs, spring back the retaining clips and lift off the distributor cap.
2   Disconnect the distributor LT wiring multi-plug and the vacuum hose at the distributor vacuum unit.
3   Remove No 1 spark plug (nearest the crankshaft pulley).

4   Place a finger over the plug hole and turn the crankshaft in the normal direction of rotation (clockwise viewed from the crankshaft pulley end) until pressure is felt in No 1 cylinder. This indicates that the piston is commencing its compression stroke. The crankshaft can be turned with a spanner on the pulley bolt.

5   Refer to the Specifications and look up the ignition timing setting for the engine being worked on.

6   Continue turning the crankshaft until the notch in the pulley is aligned with the correct setting on the scale located just above and to the right of the pulley. The 'O' mark on the scale represents Top Dead Centre (TDC) and the raised projections to the left of TDC are in increments of 4° BTDC (Fig. 4.17).

7   Check that the rotor arm is pointing to the notch on the rim of the distributor body.

8   Make a mark on the distributor body and a corresponding mark on the cylinder block to aid refitting.

9   Undo the bolt securing the distributor clamp plate to the cylinder block, then withdraw the distributor from its location. As the distributor is removed, the rotor arm will move a few degrees clockwise. Note the new position of the rotor arm and make an alignment mark on the distributor body rim.

10 Before installing the distributor, make sure that the crankshaft is still positioned at TDC as previously described. If a new distributor is being fitted, transfer the markings made during removal to the new unit.

11 Hold the distributor over its hole in the cylinder block with the mark made on the distributor body aligned with the mark made on the cylinder block.

12 Position the rotor arm so that it points to the mark made on the distributor rim after removal, and push the distributor fully home. As the skew gears mesh, the rotor arm will move anti-clockwise and should align with the manufacturer's mark on the distributor rim.

13 With the distributor in place, turn the body slightly, if necessary so that the arms of the trigger wheel and stator are aligned, then refit and tighten the clamp plate bolt.

14 Reconnect the LT wiring multi-plug and vacuum hose, then refit the distributor cap, spark plug and plug leads.

15 Refer to Section 17 and adjust the ignition timing.

CVH engines

16 Spring back the retaining clips or undo the retaining screws and lift off the distributor cap.

17 Disconnect the LT wiring multi-plug and the vacuum hose(s) at the distributor vacuum unit (where applicable).

18 Undo the distributor flange retaining bolts and withdraw the distributor from the cylinder head (photo).

19 At the beginning of 1985 a modified distributor of either Bosch or Lucas manufacture was introduced for all CVH engines equipped with electronic ignition. The modified unit is identifiable from the earlier type by only having two retaining bolt flanges instead of the three used previously. If an early type distributor is being renewed, only the modified type will be supplied by Ford parts dealers and it will

therefore also be necessary to obtain an LT wire assembly (part No. 84AG-12045-BA) to adapt the existing wiring on the car to suit the modified distributor. It is also recommended by the manufacturers that a complete new set of HT leads to the latest Ford specification is

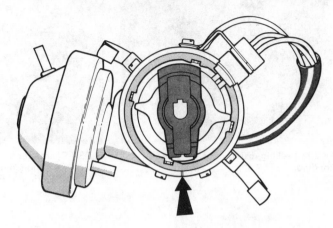

Fig. 4.26 Rotor arm aligned with manufacturers mark on distributor body rim – OHV engines (Sec 14)

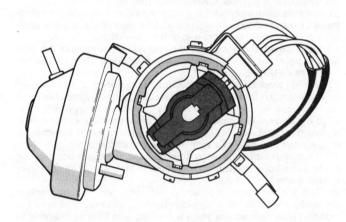

Fig. 4.27 Rotor arm position prior to refitting – OHV engines (Sec 14)

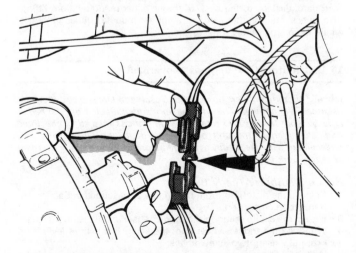

Fig. 4.28 Disconnecting distributor LT wiring multi plug – CVH engines (Sec 14)

14.18 Distributor flange upper retaining bolts (arrowed)

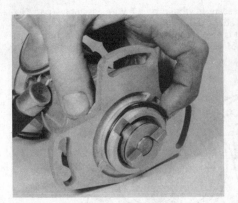

14.20 Checking distributor O-ring seal condition

14.23A Distributor mounting flange and cylinder head punch marks (arrowed) – early type distributor shown

14.23B Distributor mounting flange and cylinder head punch marks (arrowed) – later type distributor shown

obtained at the same time. Apart from connecting the new LT wire assembly which is described later in this Section, fitting the new distributor is the same as for earlier units, as follows.

20 Before refitting check the condition of the O-ring seal at the base of the distributor and renew it if necessary (photo).

21 Hold the distributor with the vacuum unit (where fitted) towards the inlet manifold side of the engine and align the distributor shaft drive dog with the slot in the end of the camshaft.

22 Insert the distributor and turn the rotor arm slightly so that the drive dogs engage and the distributor moves fully home. Refit but do not tighten the retaining bolts.

23 During production the distributor is precisely positioned for optimum ignition timing and marked accordingly with punch marks on the distributor mounting flange and the cylinder head (photos).

24 If the original distributor is being refitted, align the punch marks, tighten the distributor flange retaining bolts and refit the distributor cap, wiring multi-plug and vacuum hose(s) as applicable.

25 If a new distributor is being fitted, turn the distributor body so that the retaining bolts are positioned centrally in their elongated slots, then tighten the bolts just over finger tight.

26 Refit the distributor cap, wiring multi-plug and vacuum hose(s) (as applicable). If an early type distributor is being replaced with the modified type, connect the green wire of the new LT wire assembly to the coil negative terminal, the black wire to the positive terminal and the brown wire to a suitable earth. Join the existing coil wires to the stud terminals of the new wiring assembly, green to green and black to black (Fig. 4.29).

27 Adjust the ignition timing as described in Section 17.

15 Distributor (OHV engines) – overhaul

Note: *Ensure that replacement parts are readily available before carrying out any overhaul or repair work on the distributor*

1 Remove the distributor from the engine as described in Section 14.

2 Remove the rotor arm.

3 Extract the circlip securing the vacuum unit rod to the baseplate pivot post.

4 Undo the two vacuum unit retaining screws, tip the unit to release the rod from the baseplate pivot post and withdraw it from the distributor body.

5 Undo the two screws securing the electronic amplifier module to the distributor body and detach the module from the unit.

6 To remove the drive gear at the base of the distributor, support the gear in a vice or on a block and drive out the retaining pin using a hammer and punch. It may be necessary to resort to the use of a press if the pin is excessively tight. Withdraw the drive gear from the distributor shaft.

7 This is the limit of dismantling that can be undertaken on these distributors. Should the distributor be worn or unserviceable in any other respect, renewal of the complete unit will be necessary.

8 Reassembly and refitting is the reverse of the dismantling and

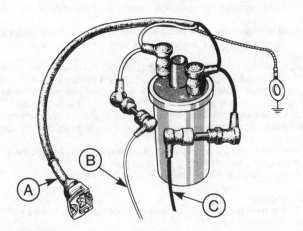

Fig. 4.29 LT wire assembly to suit modified distributor – CVH engines (Sec 14)

A	Wiring multi-plug to amplifier module	B	Green wire
		C	Black wire

removal procedures. Lubricate the baseplate pivot post with a high melting point grease and apply heat sink compound, available from Ford parts dealers, to the back of the amplifier module before fitting. Also check the condition of the amplifier module rubber grommet, where fitted, and renew if necessary.

16 Distributor (CVH engines) – overhaul

Note: *Two different versions of both Bosch and Lucas distributors are used on CVH engines. The later version is identifiable from the earlier type by only having two retaining bolt flanges instead of the three originally. Identify the unit being worked on and also ensure that replacement parts are readily available before carrying out any overhaul or repair work on the distributor.*

Bosch distributor (early type)

1 Remove the distributor from the engine as described in Section 14.

2 Remove the rotor arm.

3 Extract the circlip securing the trigger wheel to the distributor shaft.

4 Withdraw the trigger wheel from the shaft. If it is tight lever it up very carefully using two screwdrivers.

5 Undo the two screws securing the vacuum unit to the side of the distributor body. Tip the unit to release the rod from the baseplate pivot post and withdraw it from the distributor.

Are your plugs trying to tell you something?

Normal.
Grey-brown deposits, lightly coated core nose. Plugs ideally suited to engine, and engine in good condition.

Heavy Deposits.
A build up of crusty deposits, light-grey sandy colour in appearance.
Fault: Often caused by worn valve guides, excessive use of upper cylinder lubricant, or idling for long periods.

Lead Glazing.
Plug insulator firing tip appears yellow or green/yellow and shiny in appearance.
Fault: Often caused by incorrect carburation, excessive idling followed by sharp acceleration. Also check ignition timing.

Carbon fouling.
Dry, black, sooty deposits.
Fault: over-rich fuel mixture.
Check: carburettor mixture settings, float level, choke operation, air filter.

Oil fouling.
Wet, oily deposits. Fault: worn bores/piston rings or valve guides; sometimes occurs (temporarily) during running-in period.

Overheating.
Electrodes have glazed appearance, core nose very white – few deposits. Fault: plug overheating. Check: plug value, ignition timing, fuel octane rating (too low) and fuel mixture (too weak).

Electrode damage.
Electrodes burned away; core nose has burned, glazed appearance. Fault: pre-ignition. Check: for correct heat range and as for 'overheating'.

Split core nose.
(May appear initially as a crack). Fault: detonation or wrong gap-setting technique. Check: ignition timing, cooling system, fuel mixture (too weak).

WHY DOUBLE COPPER IS BETTER FOR YOUR ENGINE.

Unique Trapezoidal Copper Cored Earth Electrode — 50% Larger Spark Area — Copper Cored Centre Electrode

Champion Double Copper plugs are the first in the world to have copper core in both centre <u>and</u> earth electrode. This innovative design means that they run cooler by up to 100°C – giving greater efficiency and longer life. These double copper cores transfer heat away from the tip of the plug faster and more efficiently. Therefore, Double Copper runs at cooler temperatures than conventional plugs giving improved acceleration response and high speed performance with no fear of pre-ignition.

Champion Double Copper plugs also feature a unique trapezoidal earth electrode giving a 50% increase in spark area. This, together with the double copper cores, offers greatly reduced electrode wear, so the spark stays stronger for longer.

 FASTER COLD STARTING

 FOR UNLEADED OR LEADED FUEL

 ELECTRODES UP TO 100°C COOLER

 BETTER ACCELERATION RESPONSE

 LOWER EMISSIONS

 50% BIGGER SPARK AREA

 THE LONGER LIFE PLUG

Plug Tips/Hot and Cold.
Spark plugs must operate within well-defined temperature limits to avoid cold fouling at one extreme and overheating at the other.
Champion and the car manufacturers work out the best plugs for an engine to give optimum performance under all conditions, from freezing cold starts to sustained high speed motorway cruising.
Plugs are often referred to as hot or cold. With Champion, the higher the number on its body, the hotter the plug, and the lower the number the cooler the plug. For the correct plug for your car refer to the specifications at the beginning of this chapter.

Plug Cleaning
Modern plug design and materials mean that Champion no longer recommends periodic plug cleaning. Certainly don't clean your plugs with a wire brush as this can cause metal conductive paths across the nose of the insulator so impairing its performance and resulting in loss of acceleration and reduced m.p.g.
However, if plugs are removed, always carefully clean the area where the plug seats in the cylinder head as grit and dirt can sometimes cause gas leakage.
Also wipe any traces of oil or grease from plug leads as this may lead to arcing.

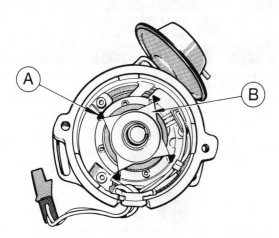

**Fig. 4.30 Trigger wheel and baseplate components – early
type Bosch distributor (Sec 16)**

A   *Stator*   B   *Trigger wheel*

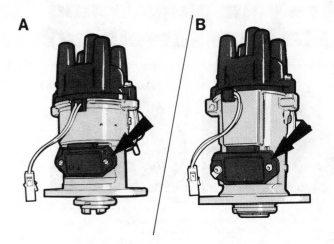

Fig. 4.31 Electronic amplifier module locations (Sec 16)

A   *Early type Bosch distributor*   B   *Early type Lucas distributor*

6   Undo the two screws securing the electronic amplifier module and
remove the module.
7   Extract the second circlip from the distributor shaft, then undo the
two baseplate retaining screws. Lift out the baseplate with stator and
trigger coil assembly.
8   To remove the drive dog, turn the distributor shaft to align the
retaining pin with the slots in the distributor body flange.
9   Scribe a mark on each side of the body flange in line with the dog
teeth, and also suitably mark the distributor shaft to ensure correct
orientation of both components when refitting.
10 Remove the drive dog retaining spring clip.
11 Support the drive dog in a vice or on a block and drive out the
retaining pin using a hammer and punch. **Do not** support the body
flange during this operation – only the drive dog. It may be necessary
to resort to the use of a press if the pin is excessively tight.
12 With the pin removed, withdraw the drive dog from the shaft.
13 This is the limit of dismantling that can be undertaken on these
distributors. Should the distributor be worn or unserviceable in any
other respect, renewal of the complete unit will be necessary.
14 Reassembly and refitting is the reverse of the dismantling and
removal procedure. Lubricate the baseplate pivot post with a high
melting point grease and apply heat sink compound, supplied with

new amplifier modules, to the back of the amplifier module before
fitting. When refitting the drive dog, align the marks made during
removal and secure the drive dog using a new retaining pin.

Bosch distributor (later type – except RS Turbo models)
15 Remove the distributor from the engine as described in Section 14.
16 Remove the rotor arm and the plastic shield (photos).
17 Undo the two screws securing the vacuum unit to the side of the
distributor body (photos). Tip the unit to release the rod from the
baseplate pivot post and withdraw it from the distributor.
18 Undo the two screws securing the electronic amplifier module and
remove the module (photos).
19 Extract the circlip securing the trigger wheel to the distributor shaft
(photo).
20 Withdraw the trigger wheel from the shaft by carefully levering it
up with two screwdrivers (photo). Recover the locating pin as the
trigger wheel is removed.
21 Extract the second circlip from the distributor shaft (photo), undo
the retaining screw on the side of the distributor body, and lift out the
baseplate with stator and trigger coil assembly (photo).
22 The remainder of the procedure is the same as for the early type
distributor as described in paragraphs 8 to 14 inclusive.

16.16A Removing the rotor arm ...

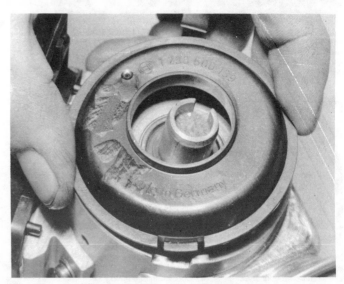

16.16B ... and plastic shield

16.17A Distributor left-hand vacuum unit retaining screw (arrowed) ...

16.17B ... and right-hand screw also securing distributor cap clip (arrowed)

16.18A Electronic amplifier retaining screw (arrowed)

16.18B Removing the amplifier

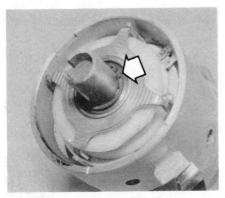

16.19 Trigger wheel retaining circlip (arrowed)

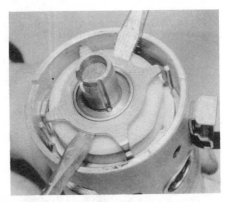

16.20 Using two screwdrivers to remove the trigger wheel

16.21A Distributor shaft second circlip (arrowed)

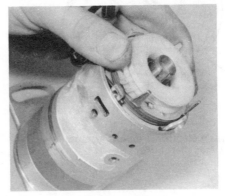

16.21B Removing the baseplate

Bosch distributor (RS Turbo models)

23 The distributor fitted to RS Turbo models is only serviced as a complete assembly, individual parts are not available separately. Should the unit be worn or unserviceable in any respect the distributor must be renewed.

Lucas distributor (early type)

24 Remove the distributor from the engine as described in Section 14.
25 Remove the rotor arm and the plastic shield.
26 Extract the trigger wheel retaining circlip and take off the washer and O-ring.
27 Withdraw the trigger wheel and the toothed collar.
28 Undo the screws securing the vacuum unit and condenser to the side of the distributor body. Lift off the condenser, release the vacuum unit rod from the baseplate and withdraw the vacuum unit.

29 Undo the two screws securing the electronic amplifier module and remove the module.
30 Undo the two baseplate retaining screws and lift out the baseplate with stator and trigger coil assembly. Do not disturb the two slotted nuts that secure the stator and magnet to the baseplate.
31 The remainder of the procedure is the same as for the Bosch distributor as described in paragraphs 8 to 14 inclusive.

Lucas distributor (later type)

32 Remove the distributor from the engine as described in Section 14.
33 Remove the rotor arm.
34 Undo the two screws securing the electronic amplifier module and remove the module.
35 Undo the three screws and separate the two halves of the distributor body.

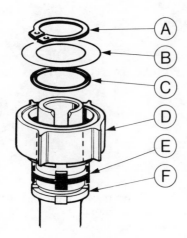

Fig. 4.32 Distributor shaft components – early type Lucas
distributor (Sec 16)

A   Circlip   D   Trigger wheel
B   Washer   E   Toothed collar
C   O-ring   F   Shaft slots

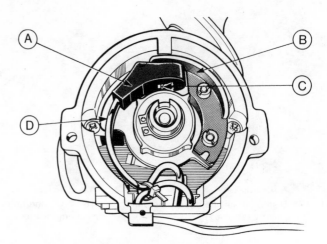

Fig. 4.33 Distributor baseplate components – early type
Lucas distributor (Sec 16)

A   Trigger coil   C   Stator pick-up
B   Stator   D   Module wiring

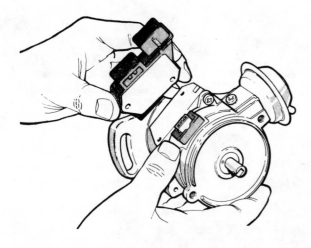

Fig. 4.34 Removing the electronic amplifier module – later
type Lucas distributor (Sec 16)

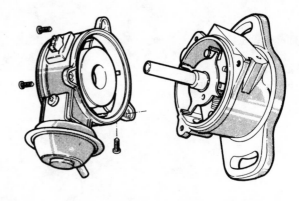

Fig. 4.35 Separating distributor body halves – later type
Lucas distributor (Sec 16)

36 Withdraw the plastic spacer ring from the body upper half.
37 Withdraw the rubber seal, then pull the connector off the trigger
coil terminals. Note the fitted direction of the connector to aid refitting.
38 Tip the trigger coil up and remove it from the body upper half.
39 Extract the stator retaining circlip and the upper shim.
40 Lift out the stator and the lower shim.
41 Slacken the vacuum unit retaining screw and remove the vacuum
unit.
42 This is the limit of dismantling that can be undertaken on these
distributors. Should the distributor be worn or unserviceable in any
other respect, renewal of the complete unit will be necessary.
43 Reassembly and refitting is the reverse of the dismantling and
removal procedures. Lubricate the vacuum unit peg with a high
melting point grease and apply heat sink compound, available from
Ford parts dealers, to the back of the amplifier module before refitting.

17 Ignition timing – adjustment

The procedure for adjusting the ignition timing on electronic
ignition systems is the same as the stroboscopic setting for contact
breaker systems, and reference should be made to Section 8,

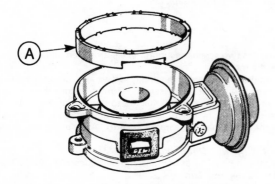

Fig. 4.36 Removing the plastic spacer ring – later type Lucas
distributor (Sec 16)

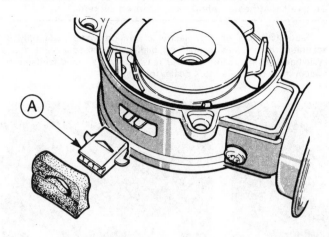

Fig. 4.37 Trigger coil terminal connector (A) and rubber seal – later type Lucas distributor (Sec 16)

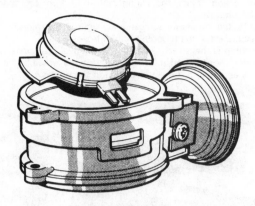

Fig. 4.38 Removing the trigger coil – later type Lucas distributor (Sec 16)

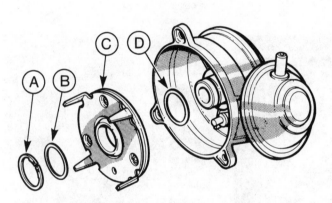

Fig. 4.39 Stator and shim details – later type Lucas distributor (Sec 16)

A Circlip	C Stator
B Upper shim	D Lower shim

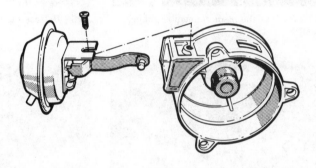

Fig. 4.40 Vacuum unit attachments – later type Lucas distributor (Sec 16)

paragraphs 11 to 22 inclusive. Note however that checking and adjustment should be carried out with the engine idling, vacuum hose(s) disconnected and the radiator cooling fan running.

18 Ignition coil – general

Refer to Part A: Section 9. Note that if the coil is to be renewed, ensure that it is of the type suitable for use in the electronic ignition system. The appropriate Ford coil is identified by its red label (photo).

19 Spark plugs and HT leads – general

Refer to Part A: Section 10.

20 Electronic Spark Control module (RS Turbo models) – removal and refitting

1 Disconnect the battery negative terminal.
2 Remove the heater plenum chamber top cover rubber seal (photo).

18.1 Ignition coil attachments and identification label

3 Release the five retaining clips and lift off the plenum chamber top cover (photos).
4 Undo the two nuts securing the heater fan motor assembly to the bulkhead. Lift the unit off the studs and place it on the engine. Avoid straining the wiring (photos).

5   Unclip and detach the wiring multi-plug from the spark control module (photo).

6   Undo the retaining screws and remove the module from the bulkhead. Detach the module vacuum hose.

7   Refitting is the reverse sequence to removal. Take care not to trap the motor wiring when refitting the fan motor assembly, and ensure that it is engaged in the slot provided in the housing.

21 Fault diagnosis – electronic ignition system

Fault diagnosis on the electronic ignition system can only be accurately carried out using Ford dedicated test equipment and a systematic test procedure. For this reason any suspected faults in the system must be referred to a dealer for diagnosis.

20.2 Remove the plenum chamber rubber seal

20.3A Release the retaining clips ...

20.3B ... and remove the plenum chamber top cover

20.4A Undo the fan motor retaining nuts (arrowed) ...

20.4B ... and remove the fan motor assembly

20.5 Spark control module wiring multi-plug (A) and vacuum hose (B)

Chapter 5 Clutch

For modifications, and information applicable to later models, see Supplement at end of manual

Contents

Specifications

Type .... Single dry plate operated by self-adjusting cable

Driven plate
Diameter:

1.1 litre Saloon	165 mm (6.5 in)
1.1 litre Estate and Van	190 mm (7.5 in)
1.3 and 1.4 litre (all models)	190 mm (7.5 in)
1.6 litre up to 1986:	
All models except RS Turbo	200 mm (7.9 in)
RS Turbo models	220 mm (8.7 in)
1.6 litre, 1986 onwards:	
All models	220 mm (8.7 in)
Lining thickness	3.23 mm (0.127 in) nominal

Pedal stroke .... 155 mm (6.1 in) nominal

Torque wrench settings

	Nm	lbf ft
Cover assembly to flywheel:		
165 mm (6.5 in) diameter clutch	9 to 11	7 to 8
190, 200 and 220 mm (7.5, 7.9 and 8.7 in) diameter clutches	16 to 20	12 to 15
Lever assembly-to-clutch fork bolt	31 to 38	23 to 28

1 General description

The clutch is of single dry plate diaphragm spring type, operated mechanically by a self-adjusting cable.

The clutch components comprise a steel cover assembly, clutch driven plate, release bearing and release mechanism. The cover assembly which is bolted and dowelled to the rear face of the flywheel contains the pressure plate and diaphragm spring.

The driven plate is free to slide along the transmission input shaft splines and is held in position between the flywheel and pressure plate by the pressure of the diaphragm spring.

Friction material is riveted to the driven plate which has a spring cushioned hub to absorb transmission shocks and to help ensure a smooth take-up of the drive.

Depressing the clutch pedal moves the release lever on the transmission by means of the cable. This movement is transmitted to the release bearing which moves inwards against the fingers of the diaphragm spring. The spring is sandwiched between two annular rings which act as fulcrum points. As the release bearing pushes the spring fingers in, the outer circumference pivots out, so moving the pressure plate away from the flywheel and releasing its grip on the driven plate.

When the pedal is released, the diaphragm spring forces the pressure plate into contact with the friction linings of the driven plate. The plate is now firmly sandwiched between the pressure plate and flywheel, thus transmitting engine power to the transmission.

The self-adjusting mechanism is incorporated in the clutch pedal and consists of a pawl, toothed segment and tension spring. When the pedal is released the tension spring pulls the quadrant through the teeth of the pawl until all free play of the clutch cable is taken up. When the pedal is depressed the pawl teeth engage with the quadrant teeth thus locking the quadrant. The particular tooth engagement position will gradually change as the components move to compensate for wear in the clutch driven plate and stretch in the cable.

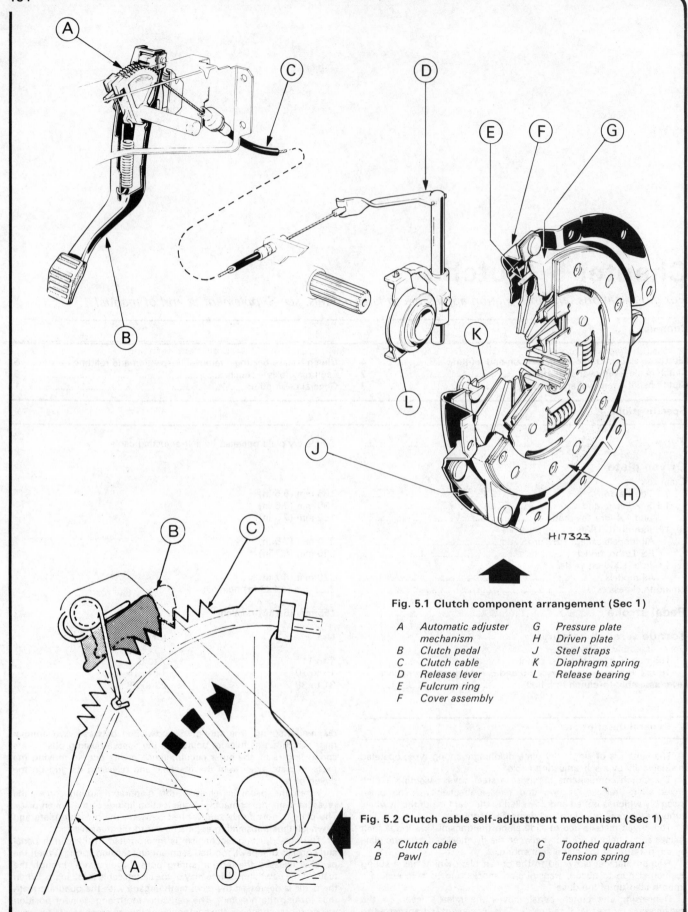

Fig. 5.1 Clutch component arrangement (Sec 1)

A	Automatic adjuster mechanism	G	Pressure plate
B	Clutch pedal	H	Driven plate
C	Clutch cable	J	Steel straps
D	Release lever	K	Diaphragm spring
E	Fulcrum ring	L	Release bearing
F	Cover assembly		

Fig. 5.2 Clutch cable self-adjustment mechanism (Sec 1)

A	Clutch cable	C	Toothed quadrant
B	Pawl	D	Tension spring

H17323

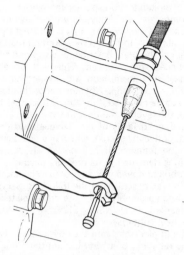

Fig. 5.3 Disconnecting clutch cable at transmission release lever (Sec 2)

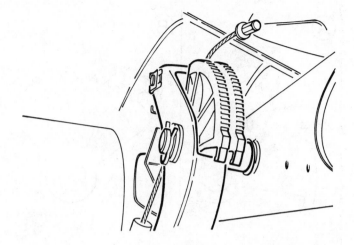

Fig. 5.4 Disconnecting clutch cable from self-adjusting quadrant at pedal (Sec 2)

2 Clutch cable – removal and refitting

1 Bend back the two tabs, release the two clips and remove the insulating panel below the facia on the driver's side.
2 Using pliers, pull the cable forward and sideways to disengage it from the release lever on the transmission.
3 Release the plastic clip securing the cable to the steering rack housing.
4 Release the cable from the clutch pedal quadrant, pull it through the bulkhead into the engine compartment and remove it from the car.
5 Refitting is the reverse sequence to removal but align the white band on the cable with the paint spot on the steering rack housing before fitting the cable securing clip.

3 Clutch pedal – removal and refitting

1 Bend back the two tabs, release the two clips and remove the insulating panel below the facia on the driver's side.
2 Using pliers, pull the cable forward and sideways to disengage it from the release lever on the transmission.
3 Extract the retaining clip securing the brake pedal to the master cylinder or servo linkage pushrod.
4 Detach the clutch cable from the pedal.
5 Remove the central retaining clip from the pedal cross-shaft. Note the position of the spacers and washers, then withdraw the cross-shaft towards the heater. Lift off the clutch and brake pedals.
6 The pedal can now be dismantled as necessary in order to renew the bushes, spring or adjustment mechanism.

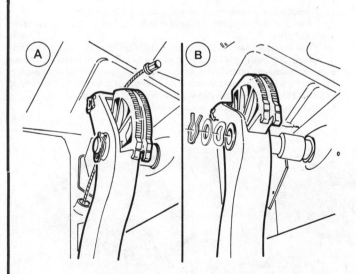

Fig. 5.5 Clutch pedal removal (Sec 3)

A   Removing cable from pedal quadrant
B   Removing pedal from pivot shaft

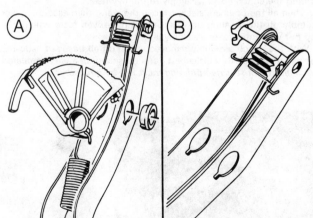

Fig. 5.6 Clutch pedal components (Sec 3)

A   Toothed quadrant, tension spring and pivot bushes
B   Pawl, pivot pin and clips

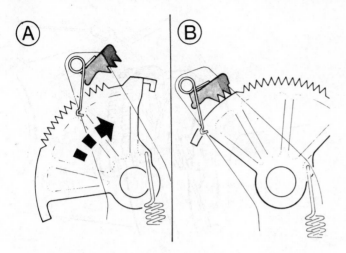

Fig. 5.7 Positioning of self-adjusting mechanism prior to
refitting pedal (Sec 3)

A   Lift pawl and turn quadrant
B   Pawl teeth resting on quadrant smooth face

7 To refit, first set the pawl with its spring so that the pawl is in
contact with the smooth part of the quadrant.
8 Position the pedals in the support bracket and refit the cross-shaft,
which should have been greased with molybdenum disulphide grease.
Ensure that the washers are refitted in the same position as noted
during removal then refit the central retaining clip to the cross-shaft.
9 Refit the master cylinder or servo linkage pushrod-to-brake pedal
retaining clip.
10 Connect the clutch cable to the pedal and, at the transmission end,
to the release lever.
11 Operate the clutch pedal two or three times and refit the facia lower
insulating panel.

4 Clutch assembly – removal, inspection and refitting

1 Remove the transmission as described in Chapter 6.
2 In a diagonal sequence, half a turn at a time, slacken the bolts
securing the clutch cover assembly to the flywheel.
3 When all the bolts are slack, remove them and then ease the cover
assembly off the locating dowels. Collect the driven plate which will
drop out when the cover assembly is removed.
4 With the clutch assembly removed, clean off all traces of asbestos
dust using a dry cloth. This is best done outside or in a well ventilated
area; *asbestos dust is harmful, and must not be inhaled.*

5 Examine the linings of the driven plate for wear and loose rivets,
distortion, cracks, broken torsion springs and worn splines. The surface
of the friction linings may be highly glazed, but, as long as the friction
material pattern can be clearly seen, this is satisfactory. If there is any
sign of oil contamination, indicated by a continuous, or patchy, shiny
black discolouration, the plate must be renewed and the source of the
contamination traced and rectified. This will be either a leaking
crankshaft oil seal or transmission input shaft oil seal – or both.
Renewal procedures are given in Chapter 1 and Chapter 6 respectively.
The plate must also be renewed if the lining thickness has worn down
to, or just above, the level of the rivet heads.
6 Check the machined faces of the flywheel and pressure plate. If
either is grooved, or heavily scored, renewal is necessary. The pressure
plate must also be renewed if any cracks are apparent, or if the
diaphragm spring is damaged or its pressure suspect.
7 With the gearbox removed it is advisable to check the condition of
the release bearing, as described in the following Section.
8 To refit the clutch assembly, place the driven plate in position with
the flat side marked FLYWHEEL SIDE or SHWUNGRADSEITE
towards the flywheel (photos)
9 Hold the plate in place and refit the cover assembly loosely on the
dowels. Refit the retaining bolts and tighten them finger tight so that
the driven plate is gripped, but can still be moved.
10 The clutch must now be centralised so that when the engine and
gearbox are mated, the gearbox input shaft splines will pass through
the splines in the centre of the hub.
11 Centralisation can be carried out quite easily by inserting a round
bar or long screwdriver through the hole in the centre of the driven
plate, so that the end of the bar rests in the hole in the centre of the
crankshaft. Moving the bar sideways or up and down will move the
plate in whichever direction is necessary to achieve centralisation.
With the bar removed, view the driven plate hub in relation to the hole
in the end of the crankshaft and the circle created by the ends of the
diaphragm spring fingers. When the hub appears exactly in the centre,
all is correct. Alternatively, if a clutch aligning tool can be obtained this
will eliminate all the guesswork obviating the need for visual
alignment.
12 Tighten the cover retaining bolts gradually, in a diagonal sequence
to the specified torque wrench setting (photo).
13 The transmission can now be refitted as described in Chapter 6.

5 Clutch release bearing – removal, inspection and refitting

1 Remove the transmission as described in Chapter 6.
2 Undo the bolt securing the release bearing fork to the release lever
shaft (photo).
3 Slide out the shaft and remove the bearing from the fork (photos).
4 Check the bearing for smoothness of operation and renew it if there
is any roughness or harshness as the bearing is spun. If this operation is
being carried out in conjunction with renewal of the clutch assembly, it
is advisable to renew the release bearing as a matter of course.
5 Refitting is the reverse sequence to removal.

4.8A Fit the driven plate with the flat side
towards the flywheel

4.8B Driven plate marking

4.12 Tightening the cover retaining bolts.
Note clutch aligning tool in position

5.2 Removing release bearing fork retaining bolt

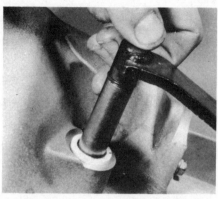

5.3A Slide out the release lever shaft ...

5.3B ... then separate the bearing from the fork. Fork locating roll pin arrowed

6 Fault diagnosis – clutch

Symptom	Reason(s)
Judder when taking up drive	Loose or worn engine/transmission mountings Driven plate friction linings worn or contaminated with oil Clutch cable sticking or defective Driven plate hub sticking on input shaft splines
Clutch fails to disengage	Clutch cable sticking or defective Excessive cable free play – self-adjusting mechanism inoperative Driven plate friction linings contaminated with oil Driven plate hub sticking on input shaft splines Release bearing fork retaining bolt sheared
Clutch slips	Clutch cable sticking or defective Self-adjusting mechanism inoperative Faulty pressure plate or weak or broken diaphragm spring Driven plate friction linings contaminated with oil
Noise when depressing clutch pedal	Worn release bearing Defective release mechanism Faulty pressure plate or diaphragm spring
Noise when releasing clutch pedal	Faulty pressure plate or diaphragm spring Broken driven plate torsion spring(s) Gearbox internal wear

Chapter 6 Manual transmission

For modifications, and information applicable to later models, see Supplement at end of manual

Contents

Specifications

Type .... Four or five forward speeds and reverse. Synchromesh on all forward speeds

Gear ratios

Four-speed transmission:
   1.1 litre OHV engine with 3 + E transmission:

1st	3.58 : 1
2nd	2.04 : 1
3rd	1.30 : 1
4th (E)	0.88 : 1
Reverse	3.77 : 1

   1.1 and 1.3 litre OHV, and 1.1, 1.3 and 1.4 litre CVH engines:

1st	3.58 : 1
2nd	2.04 : 1
3rd	1.35 : 1
4th	0.95 : 1
Reverse	3.77 : 1

   1.6 litre CVH engines:

1st	3.15 : 1
2nd	1.91 : 1
3rd	1.28 : 1
4th	0.95 : 1
Reverse	3.62 : 1

Five-speed transmission:
1.1 litre OHV, and 1.1, 1.3 and 1.4 litre CVH engines:
  1st .... 3.58 : 1
  2nd .... 2.04 : 1
  3rd .... 1.35 : 1
  4th .... 0.95 : 1
  5th .... 0.76 : 1
  Reverse .... 3.62 : 1
1.3 litre OHV, and 1.3 and 1.6 litre CVH engines:
  1st .... 3.15 : 1
  2nd .... 1.91 : 1
  3rd .... 1.28 : 1
  4th .... 0.95 : 1
  5th .... 0.76 : 1
  Reverse .... 3.62 : 1

Final drive ratios:

	Saloon and Estate	Van
Four-speed transmission:		
1.1 litre OHV engine with 3 + E transmission	3.58 : 1	3.58 : 1
1.1 litre OHV and CVH engines (up to 1986)	4.06 : 1	4.29 : 1
1.1 litre OHV engine (1986 onwards)	3.84 : 1	4.29 : 1
1.3 litre OHV, and 1.3 and 1.4 litre CVH engines	3.84 : 1	4.29 : 1
1.6 litre CVH engine (except XR3 models)	3.58 : 1	4.06 : 1
1.6 litre CVH engine (XR3 models)	3.84 : 1	–
Five-speed transmission:		
1.1 and 1.3 litre OHV engines, and 1.1, 1.3 and 1.4 litre CVH engines	3.84 : 1	–
1.6 litre CVH engine with carburettor (except XR3 models)	3.58 : 1	3.59 : 1
1.6 litre CVH engine with fuel injection	4.27 : 1	–
1.6 litre CVH engine (XR3 models)	3.84 : 1	–
1.6 litre CVH engine (XR3i models)	4.27 : 1	–
1.6 litre CVH engine (RS Turbo models)	3.82 : 1	–

General

Snap-ring thicknesses (mainshaft and input shaft bearings) ....
  1.86 to 1.89 mm (0.0732 to 0.0744 in)
  1.94 to 1.97 mm (0.0764 to 0.0776 in)
  2.01 to 2.04 mm (0.0791 to 0.0803 in)

Lubricant type/specification ....
  Hypoid gear oil, viscosity SAE 80EP to Ford specification SQM-2C 9008-A (Duckhams Hypoid 80)

Grease specification (assembly only – see text):
  Four-speed transmission ....
    To Ford specification SM1C-1020-B

  Five-speed transmission:
    Gears, contact and thrust faces, and synchroniser cones ....
      Molybdenum disulphide paste to Ford specification SM1C-4505-A
    5th gear on input shaft ....
      Ford grease type ESEA-M1C-1014-A
  Selector shaft locking assembly sealer ....
    Anaerobic retaining and sealing compound to Ford specification S-M4G-4645-AA or AB

Torque wrench settings

	Nm	lbf ft
Transmission assembly to engine	35 to 45	26 to 33
Clutch housing cover plate	35 to 45	26 to 33
Front transmission mounting bracket to transmission (pre-1986 models)	41 to 51	30 to 38
Front and rear transmission mounting bolts (pre-1986 models)	52 to 64	38 to 47
Transmission mountings to transmission (1986 models onwards)	80 to 100	59 to 74
Transmission support crossmember to body (1986 models onwards)	52	38
Lower arm mounting pivot bolt	51 to 64	38 to 47
Lower arm balljoint pinch-bolt	48 to 60	35 to 44
Starter motor bolts	35 to 45	26 to 33
Anti-roll bar clamp bolts	45 to 56	33 to 41
Gearchange rod clamp bolt	14 to 17	10 to 13
Gearchange stabiliser to transmission	50 to 60	37 to 44
Selector shaft locking mechanism cap nut	30	22
Oil filler plug	23 to 30	17 to 22
Gearchange housing to floor (pre-1984 models)	13 to 17	10 to 12
Gearchange housing to floor (1984 models onwards)	5 to 7	4 to 5
Transmission housing cover bolts (four-speed)	12 to 15	9 to 11
5th gear housing cover (five-speed)	8 to 11	6 to 8
Small housing-to-large housing bolts	21 to 27	15 to 20
5th gear selector pin clamp bolt (five-speed)	14 to 20	10 to 15
5th gear housing to main housing (five-speed)	12 to 15	9 to 11
Crownwheel to differential case:		
Saloon and Estate	98 to 128	72 to 94
RS Turbo	80 to 100	59 to 74
Van	75 to 90	55 to 66
Reversing light switch	23 to 30	17 to 22

1 General description

The manual transmission may be of four or five-speed type depending on model, year of manufacture and/or options fitted. Both transmission types are basically the same except that the five-speed version incorporates a modified selector mechanism, and an additional gear and synchro-hub contained in a housing attached to the side of the main transmission casing. Both transmission types use synchromesh gear engagement on all forward gears.

The mainshaft and input shaft carry the constant mesh gear cluster assemblies and are supported on ball and roller bearings. The short splined end of the input shaft eliminates the need for additional support from a crankshaft spigot bearing.

The synchromesh gear engagement is by sliding keys which act against baulk rings under the movement of the synchroniser sleeves. Gear selection is by means of a floor-mounted lever connected by a remote control housing and gearchange rod to the selector shaft in the gearbox. Selector shaft movement is transmitted to the selector forks via the guide shaft and guide levers.

The final drive (differential) unit is integral with the transmission and is located between the two transmission housings. On RS Turbo models a viscous coupling type limited slip differential is fitted as standard equipment.

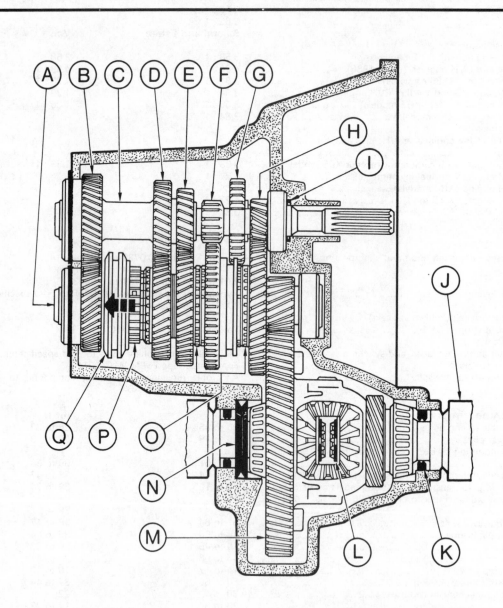

Fig. 6.1 Manual transmission and final drive gear arrangement – four-speed transmission (Sec 1)

A	Mainshaft	E	2nd gear	I	Input shaft oil seal	N	Diaphragm springs
B	4th gear	F	Reverse gear	J	Driveshaft joint	O	1st/2nd synchro
C	Input shaft	G	Reverse idler gear	K	Driveshaft oil seal	P	3rd/4th synchro
D	3rd gear	H	1st gear	L	Driveshaft snap-ring	Q	3rd/4th synchro ring
				M	Differential		(4th gear engaged)

Fig. 6.2 Sectional view of the five-speed transmission and early type gearchange mechanism (Sec 1)

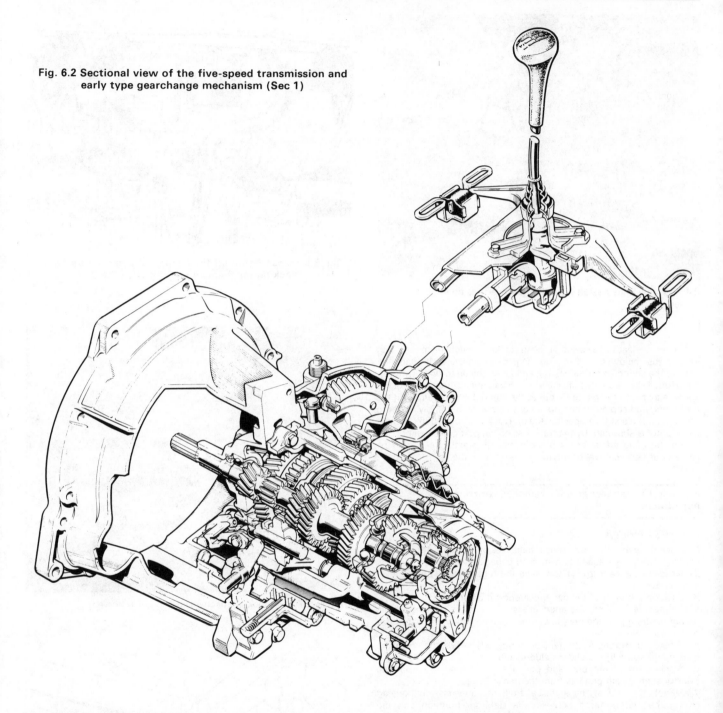

2 Maintenance and inspection

1 At the intervals given in Routine Maintenance at the beginning of this manual, carry out the following service operations on the transmission.

2 Carefully inspect the joint faces and oil seals for any sign of damage, deterioration or oil leakage.

3 At the same service interval check, and if necessary top up, the transmission oil using the following procedure.

4 With the car on level ground wipe the area around the filler plug (Fig. 6.3) then unscrew the plug using a socket spanner, or on later versions a suitable Torx type key or socket bit. Access can be gained from above or below the car (photo).

5 Locate the aluminium build code tag, which is secured to one of the transmission housing upper bolts, and note the transmission part number stamped on the tag. If the last letter of the part number suffix is

a D then the transmission was manufactured prior to August 1985. Transmissions manufactured from August 1985 have an E as the last letter of the part number suffix.

6 On the early type transmission (suffix letter D) the oil level must be maintained between 5 and 10 mm (0.2 and 0.4 in) below the lower edge of the filler plug hole.

7 If the transmission is of the later type (suffix letter E) the oil level must be maintained between 0 and 5 mm (0.2 in) below the lower edge of the filler plug hole.

8 To simplify the checking procedure a dipstick can be made from thin rod bent at right angles and having marks on one "leg" made with a file at 5 mm (0.2 in) intervals. Rest the unmarked leg on the lower edge of the filler plug hole with the marked leg immersed in the oil. Remove the dipstick, read off the level and top up if necessary using the specified grade of oil. Refit the filler plug on completion.

9 Renewal of the transmission oil is not a service requirement, but if draining is necessary prior to a repair or overhaul task place a suitable

2.4 Torx type transmission filler plug (arrowed) as fitted to later models

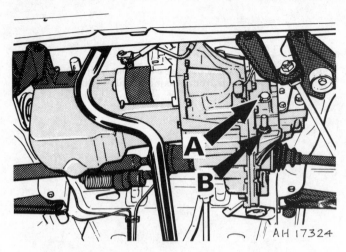

Fig. 6.3 Transmission oil filler plug (A) and selector shaft locking mechanism cap nut (B) (Sec 2)

container beneath the selector shaft locking mechanism cap nut located just below the filler plug (Fig. 6.3). Unscrew the cap nut, remove the spring and interlock pin and allow the oil to drain (photo). **Caution:** Take care when unscrewing the cap nut as the tension of the spring may cause the pin to fly out as the cap nut is released. Refit the pin, spring and cap nut when draining is complete, but apply sealer to the cap nut threads (see Specifications). Note that from 1986 onwards the cap nut is shrouded by the transmission support crossmember and cannot be removed *in situ*. On these models draining can only be carried out after removal of the transmission from the car.

3 Gearchange mechanism – removal, refitting and adjustment

Pre-1984 models

1   If working on the four-speed transmission engage 4th gear. If working on the five-speed transmission engage reverse gear.
2   Unscrew the gear lever knob, slide the rubber gaiter up the lever and remove it.
3   Jack up the front of the car and support it on stands.
4   To provide working clearance, release the exhaust system from its rubber mountings at the rear, lower the system slightly and support it on blocks.
5   Where fitted unhook the tension spring which runs between the gearchange rod and the chassis side-member.
6   Slacken the clamp bolt and pull the gearchange rod from the selector shaft which projects from the transmission.
7   Unbolt the end of the stabiliser from the transmission housing noting the washer fitted between the stabiliser trunnion and the transmission.
8   Undo the four nuts and recover the washers securing the gearchange housing to the floor. Withdraw the housing, gearchange rod and stabiliser assembly from under the car.
9   To refit, locate the housing over the four studs in the floorpan and loosely fit the nuts with their washers.
10 Reconnect the stabiliser ensuring that the washer is fitted between the stabiliser trunnion and the transmission.
11 Tighten the stabiliser retaining bolt to the specified torque then tighten the gearchange housing nuts, also to the specified torque. Refit the gaiter and gear lever knob.
12 Ensure that the selector shaft is free from grease and oil then engage the gearchange rod over the selector shaft end. Do not tighten the clamp bolt at this stage.
13 Where fitted reconnect the tension spring to the gearchange rod and chassis member.
14 Have an assistant move the gear lever into the 4th gear position

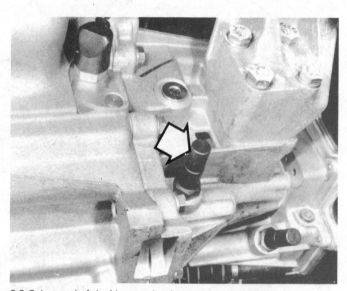

2.9 Selector shaft locking mechanism cap nut (arrowed)

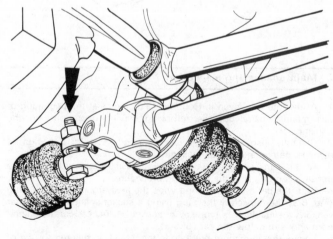

Fig. 6.4 Gearchange rod-to-selector shaft clamp bolt – arrowed (Sec 3)

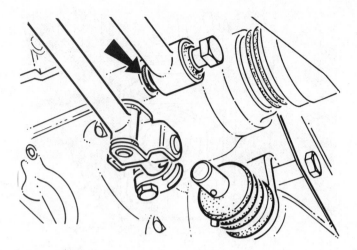

Fig. 6.5 Gearchange stabiliser-to-transmission attachment with spacing washer arrowed (Sec 3)

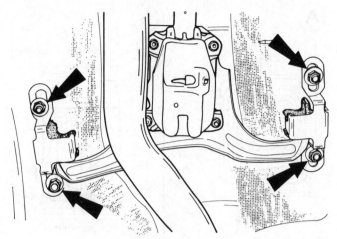

Fig. 6.6 Early type gearchange housing-to-floor attachments – arrowed (Sec 3)

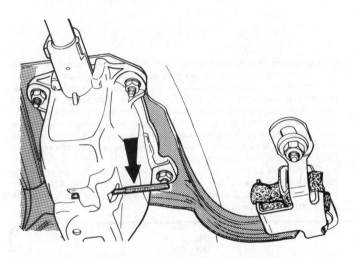

Fig. 6.7 Using a drift to lock the gear lever in the 4th gear position – four-speed transmission (Sec 3)

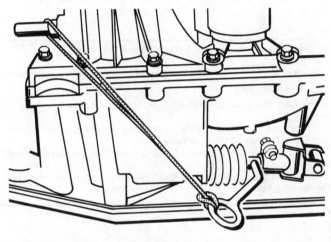

Fig. 6.8 Using an elastic band to take up selector shaft free play (Sec 3)

(four-speed transmission) or reverse gear position (five-speed transmission). From under the car lock the gear lever in place by inserting a 3.5 mm drift through the alignment hole in the gearchange housing (Fig. 6.7).

15 Ensure that the selector shaft is also in the corresponding 4th or reverse gear position as applicable by inserting a rod into the selector shaft hole, turning clockwise and pushing right in. Take up any play in the selector shaft by attaching an elastic band to the rod and transmission as shown in Fig. 6.8.

16 Tighten the gearchange rod clamp bolt then remove the drift and rod and check the action of the gearchange mechanism.

17 Reconnect the exhaust system and lower the car to the ground.

Models from 1984 to February 1987

18 If working on the four-speed transmission, engage 4th gear. If working on the five-speed transmission, engage reverse gear.

19 Unscrew the gear lever knob then disengage the outer rubber gaiter from the centre console. Slide the gaiter up and off the gear lever.

20 Release the inner rubber gaiter and slide it up and off the gear lever.

21 Jack up the front of the car and support it on stands.

22 Where fitted unhook the tension spring which runs between the gearchange rod and the chassis side-member.

23 Slacken the clamp bolt and pull the gearchange rod from the selector shaft which projects from the transmission.

24 Unbolt the end of the stabiliser from the transmission housing

noting the washer fitted between the stabiliser trunnion and the transmission.

25 From inside the car undo the four nuts securing the gearchange housing to the floor. Withdraw the housing, gearchange rod and stabiliser assembly from under the car.

26 To refit, locate the gearchange housing in position and loosely fit the retaining nuts from inside the car.

27 From below reconnect the stabiliser ensuring that the washer is fitted between the stabiliser trunnion and the transmission.

28 Tighten the stabiliser retaining bolt to the specified torque then tighten the gearchange housing nuts, also to the specified torque.

29 Refit the rubber gaiters and the gear lever knob.

30 Ensure that the selector shaft is free from grease and oil then engage the gearchange rod over the selector shaft end. Do not tighten the clamp bolt at this stage.

31 Where fitted reconnect the tension spring to the gearchange rod and chassis member.

32 Carry out the linkage adjustment procedure as described in paragraphs 14 to 16 inclusive then lower the car to the ground.

Models February 1987 onwards

33 The procedure is the same as that for 1984 to February 1987 models except that 2nd gear should be selected for four-speed transmissions, and 4th gear should be selected for five-speed transmissions.

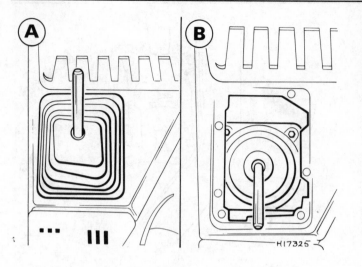

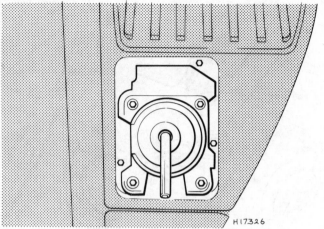

Fig. 6.9 Later type gearchange mechanism rubber gaiters (Sec 3)

A   Gear lever outer gaiter   B   Gear lever inner gaiter

Fig. 6.10 Later type gearchange housing-to-floor attachments (Sec 3)

4   Gearchange mechanism (four-speed transmission) – overhaul

Pre-1984 models

1   Remove the gearchange mechanism from the car as described in Section 3.
2   Undo the four nuts and bolts securing the housing cover and stabiliser assembly to housing body.
3   Withdraw the gear lever and housing cover from the stabiliser and housing body.
4   Unclip the upper guide shell and remove the gearchange rod from the housing body.

5   Extract the circlip from the gear lever then remove the rubber spring and spring carrier. Withdraw the gear lever from the housing cover.
6   Renew any worn components as necessary paying particular attention to the bush in the stabiliser trunnion. Any wear in this area can cause engine and transmission noise to be transmitted to the vehicle interior. Renew the bush if necessary by drawing it out using a long bolt and nut together with washers and a tube of suitable diameter. Fit the new bush in the same way ensuring that the voids are positioned in a horizontal plane.
7   Reassembly of the gearchange mechanism is the reverse sequence to dismantling. Ensure that the gear lever and housing cover is as shown in Fig. 6.11 and check that the gear lever end locates fully in the gearchange rod during assembly.

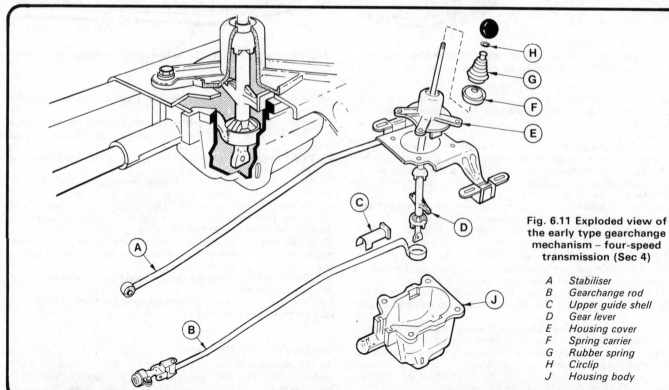

Fig. 6.11 Exploded view of the early type gearchange mechanism – four-speed transmission (Sec 4)

A   Stabiliser
B   Gearchange rod
C   Upper guide shell
D   Gear lever
E   Housing cover
F   Spring carrier
G   Rubber spring
H   Circlip
J   Housing body

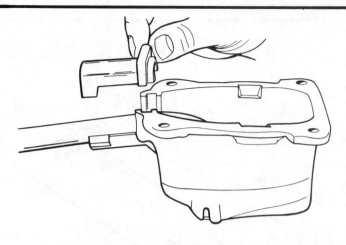

Fig. 6.12 Removing the early type mechanism guide shell – four-speed transmission (Sec 4)

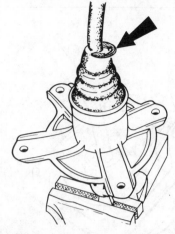

Fig. 6.13 Early type mechanism gear lever circlip (arrowed) – four-speed transmission (Sec 4)

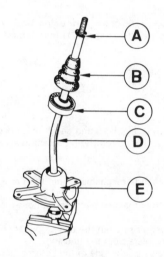

Fig. 6.14 Early type mechanism gear lever components – four-speed transmission (Sec 4)

A	Circlip	D	Gear lever
B	Rubber spring	E	Housing cover
C	Spring carrier		

Fig. 6.15 Exploded view of the later type gearchange mechanism – four-speed transmission (Sec 4)

A	Stabiliser	F	Spring carrier
B	Gearchange rod	G	Rubber spring
C	Upper guide shell	H	Circlip
D	Gear lever	J	Housing cover
E	Housing body		

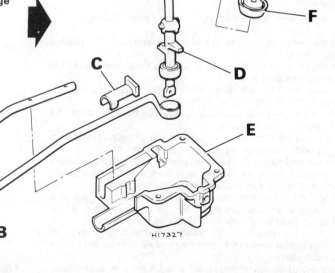

H17327

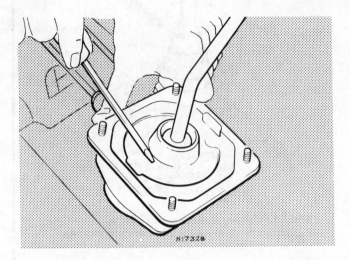

Fig. 6.16 Removing the later type gearchange mechanism damping plate – four-speed transmission (Sec 4)

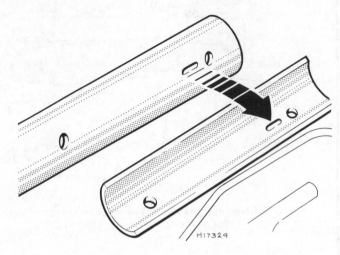

Fig. 6.17 Later type gearchange housing body projection and stabiliser slot – four-speed transmission (Sec 4)

1984 models onwards

8   Remove the gearchange mechanism from the car as described in Section 3.
9   Extract the circlip from the gear lever then remove the rubber spring and spring carrier.
10 Using a screwdriver, prise open the damping plate half shells then withdraw the damping plate from the housing.
11 Undo the four bolts and lift off the housing cover.
12 Remove the stabiliser from the housing body then unclip the upper guide shell and remove the gearchange rod.
13 Inspect the components for wear with reference to paragraph 6.
14 Reassembly is the reverse sequence to dismantling. When fitting the stabiliser ensure that the projection on the housing body engages with the corresponding slot in the stabiliser (Fig. 6.17).

---

5   Gearchange mechanism (five-speed transmission) – overhaul

---

Pre-1984 models

1   Remove the gearchange mechanism from the car as described in Section 3.
2   Undo the two screws on the side of the housing body and remove the tension springs.
3   Undo the screw at the base of the housing body and remove the tension spring and locking pin.
4   Undo the four nuts and bolts securing the housing cover and stabiliser assembly to the housing body.
5   Withdraw the gear lever and housing cover from the stabiliser and housing body.
6   Unclip the upper guide shell and remove the gearchange rod from the housing body then take out the two guide elements.
7   Extract the circlip from the gear lever then remove the rubber spring and spring carrier. Withdraw the gear lever from the housing cover.
8   Renew any worn components as necessary paying particular attention to the bush in the stabiliser trunnion. Any wear in this area can cause engine and transmission noise to be transmitted to the vehicle interior. Renew the bush if necessary by drawing it out using a long bolt and nut together with washers and a tube of suitable diameter. Fit the new bush in the same way and with the voids position in a horizontal plane.
9   Reassembly of the gearchange mechanism is the reverse sequence to dismantling. Ensure that the gear lever and housing cover

orientation is as shown in Fig. 6.19 and check that the gear lever end locates fully in the gearchange rod during assembly.

1984 models onwards

10 Remove the gearchange mechanism from the car as described in Section 3.
11 Extract the circlip from the gear lever then remove the rubber spring and spring carrier.
12 Using a screwdriver, prise open the damping plate half shells then withdraw the damping plate from the housing.
13 Undo the two screws on the side of the housing body and remove the tension springs.
14 Undo the screw at the base of the housing body and remove the tension spring and locking pin.
15 Undo the five bolts and nuts and lift off the housing cover.
16 Remove the stabiliser from the housing body then unclip the upper guide shell and remove the gearchange rod.
17 Inspect the components for wear with reference to paragraph 8.
18 Reassembly is the reverse sequence to dismantling. When fitting the stabiliser ensure that the projection on the housing body engages with the corresponding slot in the stabiliser (Fig. 6.22).

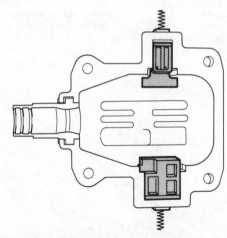

Fig. 6.18 Early type gearchange mechanism guide element locations – five-speed transmission (Sec 5)

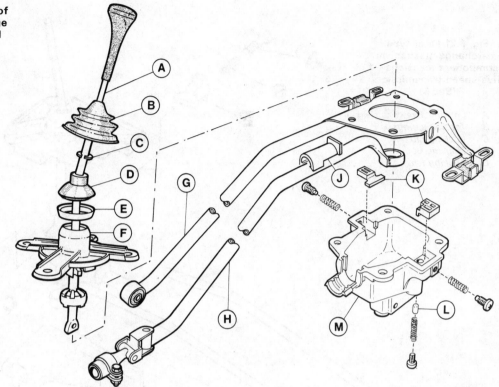

Fig. 6.19 Exploded view of the early type gearchange mechanism – five-speed transmission (Sec 5)

A Gear lever
B Rubber gaiter
C Circlip
D Rubber spring
E Spring carrier
F Housing cover
G Stabiliser
H Gearchange rod
J Upper guide shell
K Guide elements
L Locking pin
M Housing body

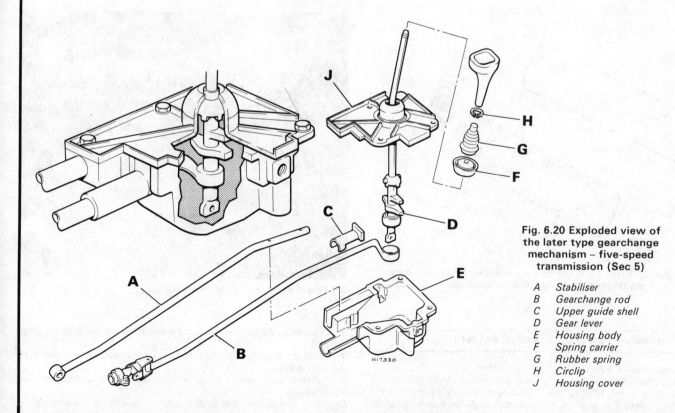

Fig. 6.20 Exploded view of the later type gearchange mechanism – five-speed transmission (Sec 5)

A Stabiliser
B Gearchange rod
C Upper guide shell
D Gear lever
E Housing body
F Spring carrier
G Rubber spring
H Circlip
J Housing cover

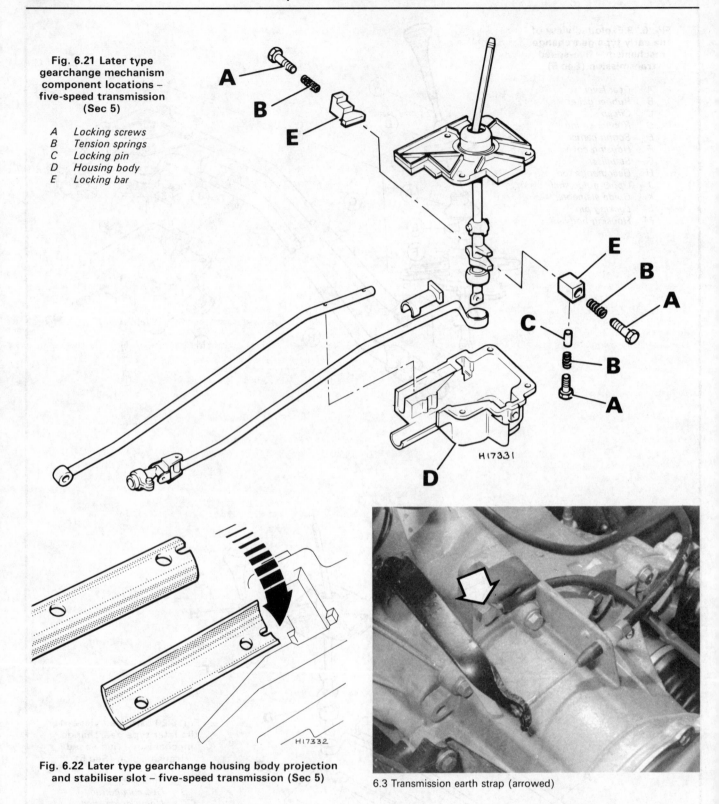

Fig. 6.21 Later type gearchange mechanism component locations – five-speed transmission (Sec 5)

A   *Locking screws*
B   *Tension springs*
C   *Locking pin*
D   *Housing body*
E   *Locking bar*

Fig. 6.22 Later type gearchange housing body projection and stabiliser slot – five-speed transmission (Sec 5)

6.3 Transmission earth strap (arrowed)

---

6   Transmission assembly – removal and refitting

1   Disconnect the battery negative terminal.
2   To ensure correct connection and adjustment of the gearchange mechanism when refitting the transmission on pre-February 1987 models, select 4th gear on four-speed models or reverse gear on five-speed models. On cars produced from February 1987 select 2nd gear on four-speed models or 4th gear on five-speed models.

3   Disconnect the earth strap from the top of the transmission housing (photo).
4   Undo the retaining nut and disconnect the speedometer cable at the transmission.
5   Pull the transmission breather hose out of the opening in the side-member.
6   Using pliers, pull the clutch cable forwards and sideways to disengage it from the release lever then withdraw it from the support bracket on the transmission.

6.13 Gearchange rod tension spring

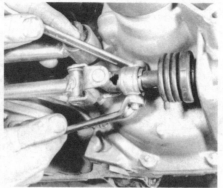

6.14 Removing the gearchange rod from the selector shaft

6.15 Removing the gearchange stabiliser

7 Where applicable tie the heater hose, which runs from the thermostat housing to the heater, to one side to provide greater access.

8 Jack up the front of the car and support it on axle stands.

9 Support the engine using a jack and suitable block of wood positioned under the sump.

10 Disconnect the wiring at the starter solenoid then undo the three nuts and·bolts and remove the starter motor.

11 Undo the two bolts and remove the cover plate from the lower face of the clutch housing.

12 Disconnect the reversing light switch wires.

13 Where fitted, unhook the tension spring which runs between the gearchange rod and the chassis side-member (photo).

14 Slacken the clamp bolt and pull the gearchange rod from the selector shaft which projects from the transmission (photo).

15 Unbolt the end of the gearchange stabiliser from the transmission housing and recover the spacer washer (photo).

16 On cars equipped with an anti-lock braking system refer to Chapter 9 and remove the modulator drive belt.

17 On pre-1986 models place a suitable container beneath the selector shaft locking mechanism cap nut (Fig. 6.3). Unscrew the cap nut, remove the spring and interlock pin and allow the transmission oil to drain. **Caution:** Take care when unscrewing the cap nut as the tension of the spring may cause the pin to fly out when the cap nut is released. Apply sealer to the cap nut threads when refitting (see Specifications). From 1986 onwards there is insufficient clearance to allow removal of the cap nut and the oil cannot be drained until the transmission has been removed.

18 Disconnect the right-hand front suspension lower arm balljoint from the hub carrier by removing the nut and pinch-bolt. Note that the pinch-bolt is of the socket-headed (Torx) type and a special key or socket bit, available from most accessory shops, will be required for removal.

19 Disconnect the lower suspension arm from the body at its inner end by removing the mounting pivot bolt.

20 Insert a lever between the inner constant velocity joint and the transmission. Firmly strike the lever while pulling outwards on the roadwheel to release the constant velocity joint from the differential. Withdraw the joint completely from the differential and suspend the driveshaft so that it does not hang down by more than 45°. If the transmission oil has not been drained be prepared for some spillage when the driveshaft is removed.

21 Repeat paragraphs 18, 19 and 20 for the left-hand driveshaft. After removal, retain the differential sun gears in alignment by inserting a dowel or similar, of suitable diameter into the differential so that it engages the sun gear on one side.

22 On pre-1986 models equipped with an anti-roll bar, undo the two bolts securing the left-hand mounting clamp and remove the clamp. Additionally, on 1985 RS Turbo models, disconnect the left-hand suspension tie-bar front mounting.

23 On 1986 models onwards undo the three bolts each side securing the anti-roll bar mounting plates to the body.

24 Where fitted remove the engine splash shields on the left and right-hand sides.

25 Support the transmission assembly using a suitable jack.

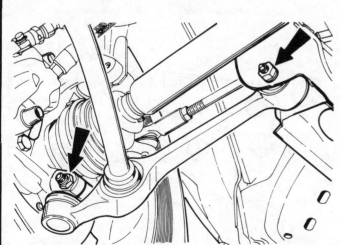

Fig. 6.23 Right-hand front suspension lower arm attachment at hub carrier and body – arrows (Sec 6)

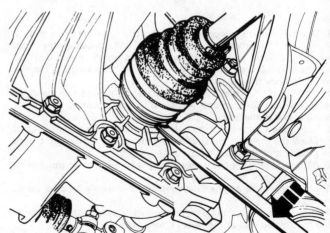

Fig. 6.24 Using a lever to release the constant velocity joint from the transmission (Sec 6)

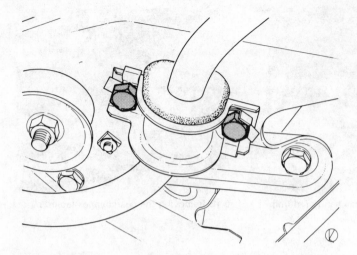

**Fig. 6.25 Anti-roll bar left-hand mounting clamp bolts –
pre-1986 models (Sec 6)**

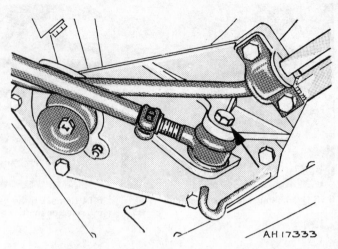

**Fig. 6.26 Suspension tie-bar left-hand front mounting
(arrowed) – 1985 RS Turbo models (Sec 6)**

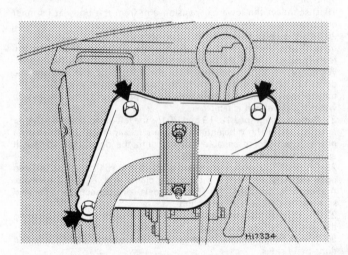

**Fig. 6.27 Anti-roll bar mounting plate attachments
(arrowed) – 1986 models onwards (Sec 6)**

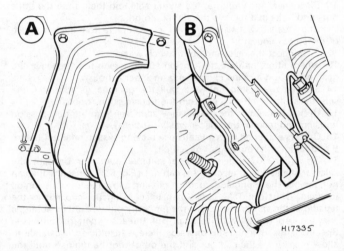

Fig. 6.28 Engine splash shield details (Sec 6)

A   *Right-hand side*   B   *Left-hand side*

26 Undo all the bolts securing the clutch housing flange to the engine.
27 On pre-1986 models undo the four bolts securing the front
mounting bracket to the transmission and the nut securing the
mounting to the body bracket. Also undo the bolts securing the rear
mounting body bracket to the body.
28 On 1986 models onwards, undo the two front bolts, two rear bolts
and additional side nut and bolt securing the transmission support
crossmember to the body.
29 Lower the engine and transmission assembly as far as possible and
withdraw the transmission squarely off the engine. Lower the unit to
the ground and withdraw it from under the car.
30 Before refitting, lightly smear the splined end of the input shaft
with molybdenum disulphide grease.
31 Check that the engine adaptor plate is correctly located on its
dowels.
32 Offer the transmission up to the engine and engage the input shaft
with the splined hub of the clutch driven plate.
33 Push the transmission into full engagement with the engine and
check that the unit sits on its locating dowels and that the adaptor
plate has not been displaced. Any reluctance for the transmission to
mate with the engine may be due to the splines of the input shaft and
clutch driven plate not engaging. Try swivelling the transmission

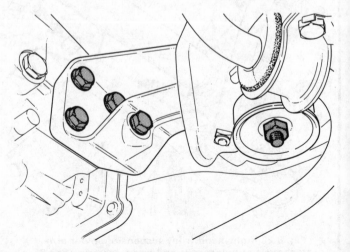

**Fig. 6.29 Transmission front mounting and bracket
attachments – pre 1986 models (Sec 6)**

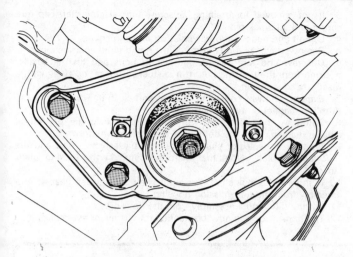

Fig. 6.30 Transmission rear mounting body bracket attachments – pre-1986 models (Sec 6)

slightly, or have an assistant rotate the crankshaft by applying a spanner to the crankshaft pulley bolt.

34 Once the transmission is fully engaged, screw in the two lower retaining bolts to hold it to the engine.

35 Refit the transmission mountings and/or support crossmember as applicable.

36 Refit all the clutch housing flange to engine retaining bolts then remove the engine and transmission support jacks.

37 Reconnect the anti-roll bar mountings and, on RS Turbo models the tie-bar mounting.

38 Fit a new snap-ring to the splines of the left-hand driveshaft constant velocity joint and, after removing the dowel used to maintain the sun gears in alignment, engage the joint with the differential. Firmly push the roadwheel inwards to force the joint home.

39 Reconnect the suspension lower arm to the body and hub carrier noting that the Torx bolt is positioned with its head to the rear. Tighten the mountings to the specified torque.

40 Repeat the foregoing operations on the right-hand driveshaft.

41 Reconnect the gearchange stabiliser to the transmission with the washer fitted between the stabiliser trunnion and the transmission housing.

42 Engage the gearchange rod with the selector shaft then adjust the mechanism as described in Section 3.

43 Where fitted reconnect the gearchange rod tension spring.

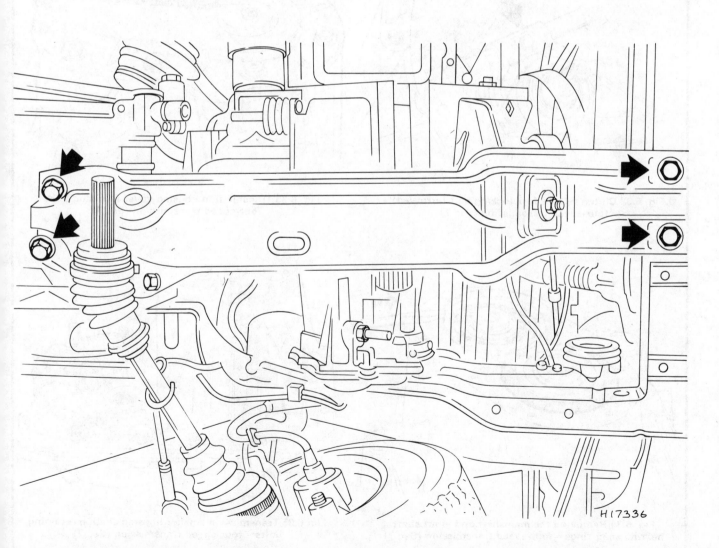

H17336

Fig. 6.31 Transmission support crossmember attachments (arrowed) – 1986 models onwards (Sec 6)

44 Refit the clutch housing cover plate, starter motor and reversing light wires.

45 Lower the car to the ground and reconnect the clutch cable and speedometer cable.

46 Reconnect the transmission earth strap and locate the breather hose in the side member opening.

47 Refill the transmission with the specified type and quantity of oil with reference to Section 2.

7 Four-speed transmission – dismantling

1 With the transmission removed from the vehicle, clean away external dirt and grease using paraffin and a stiff brush or a water-soluble solvent. Take care not to allow water to enter the transmission.

2 Unscrew the lockbolt which holds the clutch release fork to the shaft and remove the shaft, followed by the fork and release bearing.

3 If not removed for draining, unscrew the selector shaft cap nut, spring and interlock pin.

4 Unbolt and remove the transmission housing cover.

5 Remove the snap-rings from the main and input shaft bearings.

6 Unscrew and remove the connecting bolts and lift the smaller housing from the transmission. If it is stuck, tap it off carefully with a plastic-headed mallet.

7 Extract the swarf collecting magnet and clean it. Take care not to drop the magnet or it will shatter.

8 Withdraw the selector shaft, noting that the longer portion of smaller diameter is at the bottom as the shaft is withdrawn.

9 Remove the selector shaft coil spring, the selector forks and the shift locking plate. Note the roll pin located in the locking plate cut-out.

10 Withdraw the mainshaft, the input shaft and reverse gear as one assembly from the transmission housing.

11 Lift the differential assembly from the housing.

12 The transmission is now dismantled into its major assemblies.

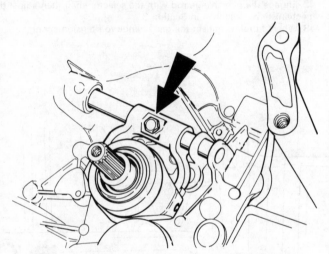

Fig. 6.32 Clutch release fork locking bolt (arrowed) – four-speed transmission (Sec 7)

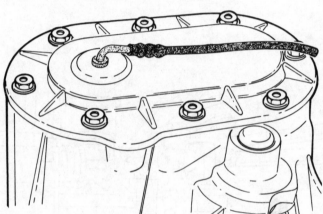

Fig. 6.33 Transmission housing cover retaining bolts – four-speed transmission (Sec 7)

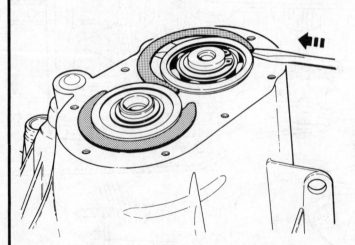

Fig. 6.34 Removing the mainshaft and input shaft bearing snap-rings – four-speed transmission (Sec 7)

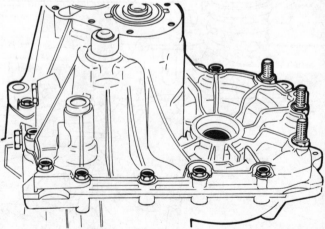

Fig. 6.35 Transmission smaller housing section retaining bolts – four-speed transmission (Sec 7)

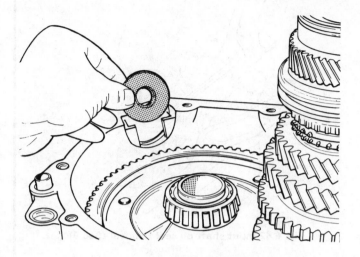

Fig. 6.36 Removing the swarf collecting magnet –
four-speed transmission (Sec 7)

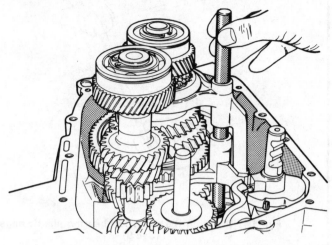

Fig. 6.37 Selector shaft removal – four-speed
transmission (Sec 7)

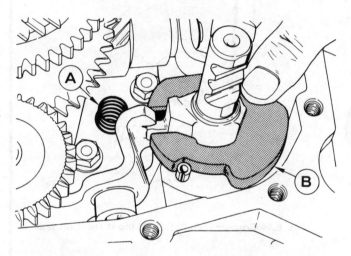

Fig. 6.38 Selector shaft coil spring (A) and shift locking
plate (B) – four-speed transmission (Sec 7)

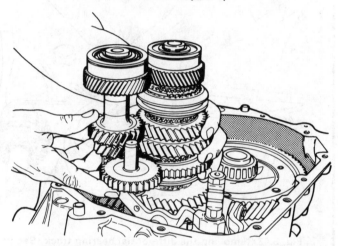

Fig. 6.39 Removing the mainshaft, input shaft and
reverse gear assemblies – four-speed transmission
(Sec 7)

8 Four-speed transmission – overhaul (general)

1 The need for further dismantling will depend upon the reasons for
removal of the transmission in the first place.
2 A common reason for dismantling will be to renew the synchro
units. Wear or malfunction in these components will have been
obvious when changing gear by the noise, or by the synchro being
easily beaten.
3 The renewal of oil seals may be required as evident by drips of oil
under the vehicle when stationary.
4 Jumping out of gear may mean renewal of the selector mechanism,
forks or synchro sleeves.
5 General noise during operation on the road may be due to worn
bearings, shafts or gears and when such general wear occurs, it will
probably be more economical to renew the transmission complete.
6 When dismantling the geartrains, always keep the components
strictly in their originally installed order.

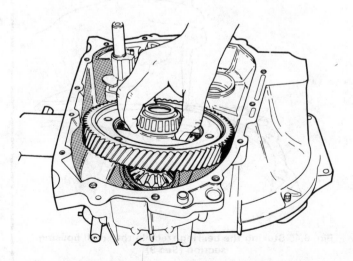

Fig. 6.40 Withdrawing the differential – four-speed
transmission (Sec 7)

9 Transmission housing and selector mechanism – overhaul

1 To remove the mainshaft bearing, break the plastic roller cage with
a screwdriver. Extract the rollers and the cage, the oil slinger and
retainers. Remove the bearing outer track.

Fig. 6.41 Breaking the mainshaft bearing plastic cage (Sec 9)

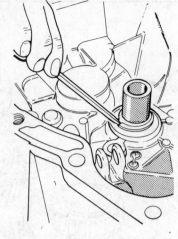

Fig. 6.42 Input shaft oil seal removal (Sec 9)

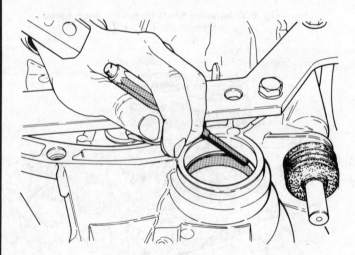

Fig. 6.43 Removing the differential bearing track (Sec 9)

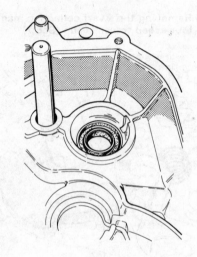

Fig. 6.44 Correct installation of input shaft oil seal (Sec 9)

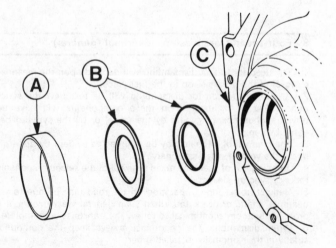

Fig. 6.45 Differential bearing diaphragm springs (Sec 9)

A   Bearing track   C   Small housing section
B   Diaphragm springs

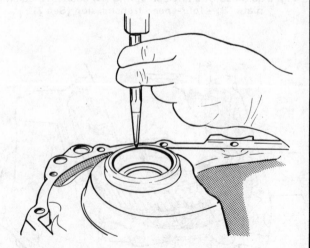

Fig. 6.46 Staking the bearing track in the small housing section (Sec 9)

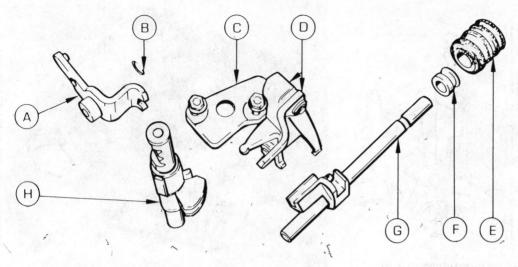

Fig. 6.47 Exploded view of the four-speed selector mechanism (Sec 9)

A   Reverse selector lever
B   Circlip
C   Guide, lever retaining plate
D   Guide levers
E   Gaiter
F   Oil seal
G   Selector shaft with dog
H   Guide shaft with dog

2 When fitting the new bearing, also renew the oil slinger.
3 When renewing the input shaft oil seal, drive the oil seal out by applying the drift inside the bellhousing.
4 The constant velocity joint (differential) oil seals should be renewed at time of major overhaul.
5 The differential bearing tracks can be removed, using a drift inserted from the large housing section.
6 The differential bearing outer track and the diaphragm adjustment springs can be driven out of the smaller housing section using a

suitable drift such as a piece of tubing.
7 Refit the input shaft oil seal so that its lips are as shown (Fig. 6.44). Apply grease to all the oil seal lips and check that the lip retaining spring has not been displaced during installation of the seal.
8 When installing the differential diaphragm springs and bearing track to the smaller housing section, note that the spring convex faces are towards each other. Stake the track with a light blow from a punch. This is only to hold the track during assembly of the remainder of the transmission.

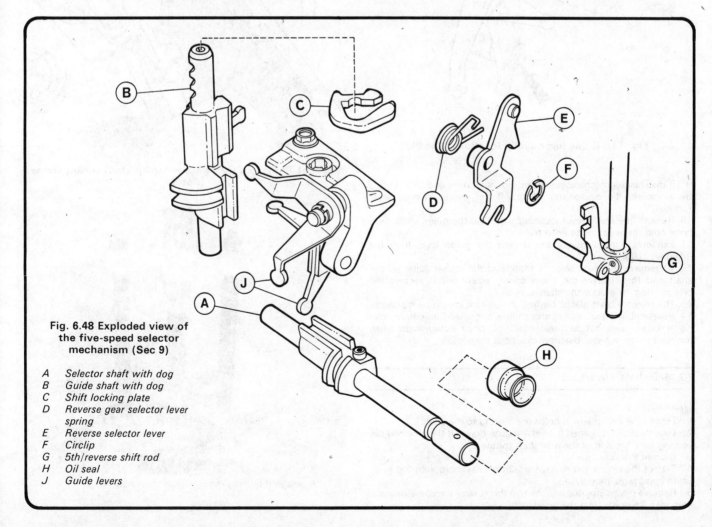

Fig. 6.48 Exploded view of the five-speed selector mechanism (Sec 9)

A   Selector shaft with dog
B   Guide shaft with dog
C   Shift locking plate
D   Reverse gear selector lever spring
E   Reverse selector lever
F   Circlip
G   5th/reverse shift rod
H   Oil seal
J   Guide levers

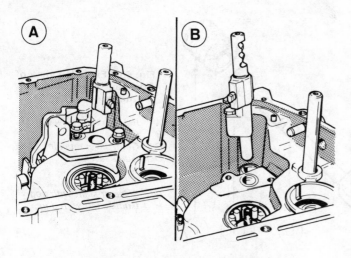

Fig. 6.49 Selector mechanism dismantling (Sec 9)

9.9 Reverse selector lever circlip (arrowed)

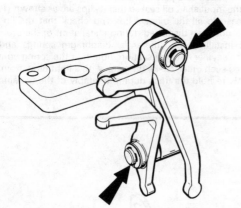

Fig. 6.50 Guide lever circlip locations (Sec 9)

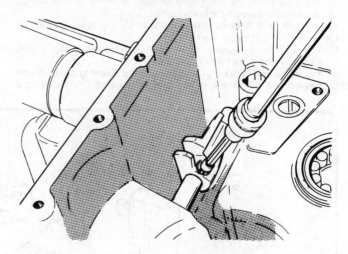

Fig. 6.51 Removing the selector dog-to-shaft socket screw (Sec 9)

9 If the selector mechanism is worn, sloppy or damaged, dismantle it by extracting the circlip and taking off the reverse selector lever (photo).

10 Remove the guide lever retaining plate and the guide shaft. Two bolts hold these components in place.

11 Extract the two circlips and detach the guide lever from the retaining plate.

12 To remove the main selector shaft, pull the rubber gaiter up the shaft and then extract the single socket screw which secures the selector dog. Withdraw the shaft.

13 The selector shaft plastic bushes and oil seal should be renewed.

14 Reassembly is a reversal of dismantling, but when fitting the rubber gaiter make sure that its drain tube will point downwards when installed in the vehicle. Use new circlips at reassembly.

10 Mainshaft – overhaul

Dismantling

1 Extract the circlip which holds the bearing to the shaft.

2 Using a puller, engaged behind 4th gear, draw off the gear and the bearing from the end of the mainshaft (photo).

3 Discard the bearing.

4 Extract the circlip and remove the 3rd/4th synchro with 3rd gear, using hand pressure only.

5 Remove the anchor ring and the two thrust semi-circular segments, then take 2nd gear from the mainshaft.

10.2 4th gear and bearing removal from mainshaft

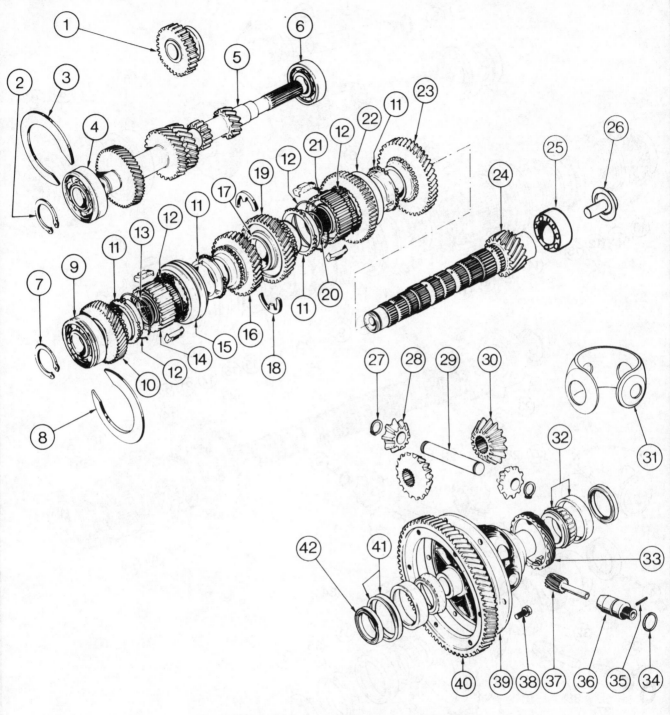

Fig. 6.52 Exploded view of the gear assemblies and associated components – four-speed transmission (Sec 10)

1	Reverse idler gear	12	Spring
2	Circlip	13	Circlip
3	Bearing snap-ring	14	3rd/4th synchro-hub
4	Bearing	15	Synchro sleeve
5	Input shaft	16	3rd gear
6	Bearing	17	Segment anchor ring
7	Circlip	18	Semi-circular thrust segment
8	Bearing snap-ring	19	2nd gear
9	Bearing	20	Circlip
10	4th gear	21	1st/2nd synchro-hub
11	Baulk ring	22	1st/2nd synchro sleeve with reverse gear

23	1st gear
24	Mainshaft
25	Bearing
26	Oil slinger
27	Circlip
28	Differential pinion
29	Differential shaft
30	Sun gear
31	Thrust cage

32	Tapered roller bearing
33	Speedometer drivegear
34	O-ring
35	Roll pin
36	Speedo drive pinion bearing
37	Speedo drive pinion
38	Crownwheel bolts
39	Differential case
40	Crownwheel
41	Diaphragm springs
42	Oil seal

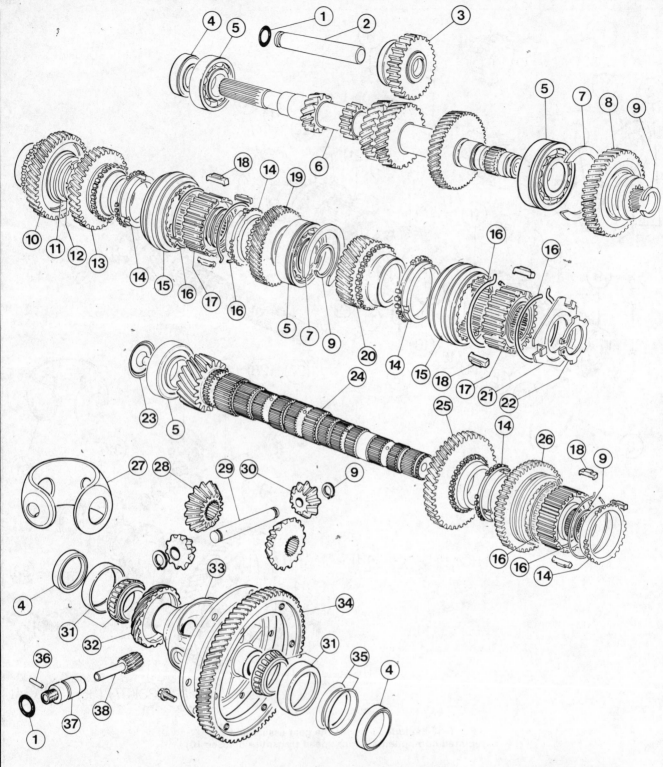

Fig. 6.53 Exploded view of the gear assemblies and associated components – five-speed transmission (Sec 10)

1	O-ring	11	Segment anchor ring	21	Retaining plate	30	Planet gear
2	Reverse idler gear shaft	12	Thrust segment	22	Circlip	31	Taper roller bearing
3	Reverse idler gear	13	3rd gear	23	Oil slinger	32	Speedometer drive worm
4	Radial oil seal	14	Baulk ring	24	Mainshaft	33	Differential housing
5	Bearing	15	Synchro sleeve	25	1st gear	34	Final drive gear
6	Input shaft	16	Retaining spring	26	1st/2nd synchro sleeve	35	Diaphragm springs
7	Snap-ring	17	Synchro hub		with reverse gear	36	Locking pin
8	5th gear	18	Sliding key	27	Thrust cage	37	Speedometer drive pinion
9	Circlip	19	4th gear	28	Sun gear		bearing
10	2nd gear	20	5th gear	29	Differential shaft	38	Speedometer drive pinion

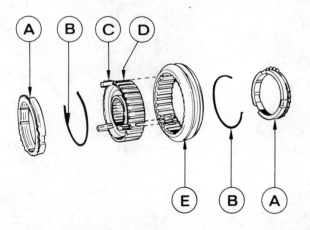

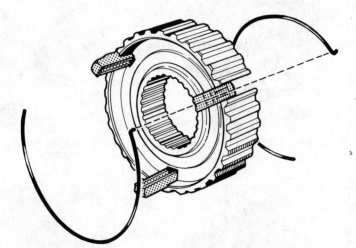

Fig. 6.54 Exploded view of the 3rd/4th synchro unit (Sec 10)

A Baulk ring
B Sliding key retaining spring
C Sliding key
D Hub
E Sleeve

Fig. 6.55 Fitted direction of sliding key retaining springs (Sec 10)

6 Extract the circlip and take off 1st/2nd synchro unit with 1st gear.
7 The mainshaft is now completely dismantled. Do not attempt to remove the drive pinion gear.

Synchronisers

8 The synchro units can be dismantled and new components fitted after extracting the circular retaining springs.
9 When reassembling the hub and sleeve, align them so that the cut-outs in the components are in alignment, ready to receive the sliding keys.
10 The two springs should have their hooked ends engaged in the same sliding key, but must run in opposing directions as shown in Fig. 6.55.
11 The baulk rings should be renewed iif they do not 'stick' when pressed and turned onto the gear covers, or if a clearance no longer exists between the baulk ring and the gear when pressed onto its cone.

Reassembly

12 With all worn or damaged components renewed, commence reassembly by oiling the shaft and then sliding 1st gear onto the shaft

so that the gear teeth are next to the pinion drivegear (photo).
13 Fit 1st/2nd synchro baulk ring (photo).
14 Fit 1st/2nd synchro so that reverse gear teeth on the unit are furthest from 1st gear (photo).
15 Fit the circlip to secure the synchro to the mainshaft (photo).
16 Slide on the synchro baulk ring (photo).
17 Slide on 2nd gear (photo).
18 Fit 2nd gear so that the cone is towards the baulk ring.
19 Fit the thrust semi-circular segments and their anchor ring (photos).
20 To the shaft fit 3rd gear so that its teeth are towards 2nd gear (photo).
21 Fit the baulk ring (photo).
22 Slide on 3rd/4th synchro so that its serrated edge is towards 3rd gear (photo).
23 Secure the synchro to the mainshaft with the circlip (photo).
24 Fit the baulk ring (photo).
25 Fit 4th gear (photo).
26 Fit the bearing so that its circlip groove is nearer the end of the shaft. Apply pressure only to the bearing centre track, using a press or a hammer and a piece of suitable diameter tubing (photos).
27 Fit the circlip to secure the bearing to the shaft. The mainshaft is now fully assembled (photos).

10.12 Fitting 1st gear to mainshaft

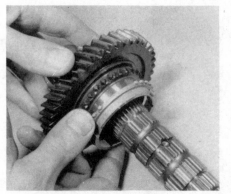

10.13 Fitting 1st/2nd baulk ring

10.14 Fitting 1st/2nd synchro unit

10.15 Fitting 1st/2nd synchro unit circlip (arrowed)

10.16 Engaging 1st/2nd synchro baulk ring with sliding keys

10.17 Fitting 2nd gear

10.19A Thrust segments in position ...

10.19B ... and retained by anchor ring

10.20 Fitting 3rd gear

10.21 Locating 3rd/4th synchro baulk ring on synchro unit cone face

10.22 3rd/4th synchro unit fitment with serrated edge towards 3rd gear

10.23 Securing 3rd/4th synchro unit with circlip

10.24 Engaging 3rd/4th synchro baulk ring with sliding keys

10.25 Fitting 4th gear

10.26A Mainshaft bearing fitment with circlip groove towards end of mainshaft

10.26B Using a tube to drive on mainshaft bearing

10.27A Fitting mainshaft bearing circlip

10.27B Mainshaft fully assembled

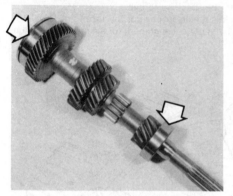

11.1 Input shaft bearings (arrowed)

11.2A Input shaft large bearing and retaining circlip (arrowed)

11.2B Input shaft smaller bearing

11 Input shaft – overhaul

1   The only components which can be renewed are the two ball bearing races (photo).
2   Remove the securing circlip from the larger one and extract both bearings with a two-legged extractor or a press (photos).
3   When fitting the new bearings, apply pressure to the centre track only, using a press or a piece of suitable diameter tubing and a hammer. When installing the larger bearing, make sure that the circlip groove is nearer the end of the shaft.

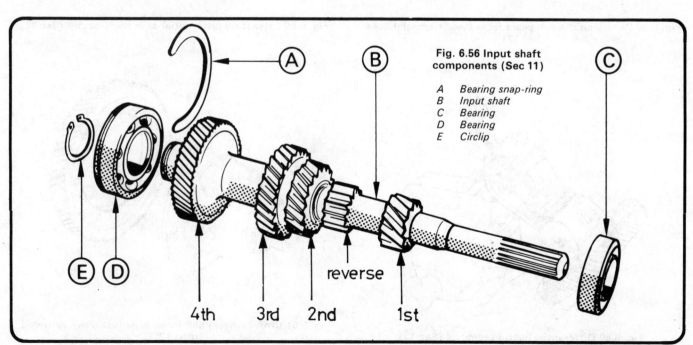

Fig. 6.56 Input shaft components (Sec 11)

A   Bearing snap-ring
B   Input shaft
C   Bearing
D   Bearing
E   Circlip

4th   3rd   2nd   reverse   1st

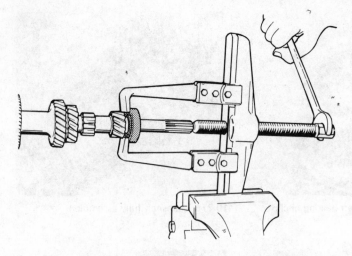

Fig. 6.57 Removing an input shaft bearing (Sec 11)

12 Differential – overhaul

All models except RS Turbo

1 With the differential removed from the transmission housing, twist both sun gears out of the differential case.

2 Extract one of the circlips from the end of the differential shaft, press the shaft out of the differential case and extract the planet gears and the cage.

3 The differential tapered roller bearings can be drawn off using a two-legged extractor.

4 The crownwheel can be separated from the differential case after removing the six securing bolts. Tap the components apart, using a plastic mallet.

5 If the crownwheel is to be renewed, then the gearbox mainshaft should be renewed at the same time, as the gear teeth are matched and renewal of only one component will give rise to an increase in noise during operation on the road.

6 Reassembly is a reversal of dismantling, but make sure that the deeply chamfered edge of the inside diameter is against the differential case. Tighten all bolts to the specified torque.

7 The sun gears should be held in position by inserting dowels or similar so that they will be in correct alignment for eventual installation of the driveshafts.

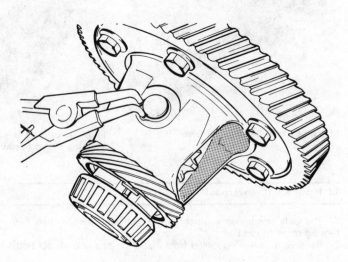

Fig. 6.58 Removing the sun gears from the differential case (Sec 12)

Fig. 6.59 Extracting differential case shaft circlip (Sec 12)

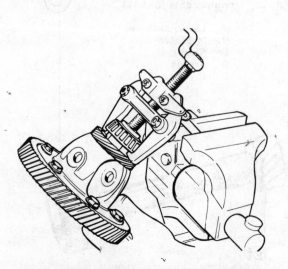

Fig. 6.60 Differential bearing removal (Sec 12)

Fig. 6.61 Crownwheel chamfered edge location – arrowed (Sec 12)

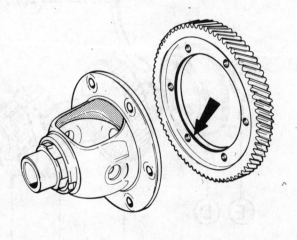

RS Turbo models

8 The limited slip differential fitted to RS Turbo models is a sealed unit and cannot be dismantled for overhaul. It is, however, possible to renew the crownwheel and the procedure for this operation is the same as described previously for conventional units.

13 Four-speed transmission – reassembly

1 With the larger housing section on the bench, lubricate the differential bearings with gear oil and insert the differential assembly into the housing (photo).
2 Slide reverse idler gear onto its shaft, at the same time engaging the selector lever in the groove of the gear which should be pointing downwards (photo).

3 In order to make installation of the mainshaft and input shaft easier, lift the reverse idler gear so that its selector lever is held by the reversing lamp switch spring-loaded ball (photo).
4 Mesh the gears of the mainshaft and the input shaft and install both geartrains into the transmission housing simultaneously (photo).
5 Lower the reverse idler gear and its selector lever.
6 Fit the shift locking plate (photo).
7 Engage 1st/2nd selector fork with the groove in the mainshaft synchro sleeve. This fork has the shorter actuating lever (photo).
8 Engage 3rd/4th selector fork with the groove in its synchro sleeve. Make sure that the end of this fork actuating lever is engaged with the shift locking plate (photo).
9 Insert the coil spring in the selector shaft hole and pass the shaft downwards through the holes in the forks, make sure that the longer section of the reduced diameter of the rod is pointing downwards (photos).

13.1 Inserting differential assembly into the housing

13.2 Engaging reverse idler gear with its shaft and selector lever

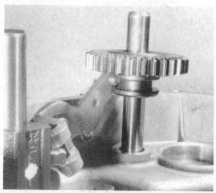
13.3 Reverse idler gear supported in raised position

13.4 Installing mainshaft and input shaft geartrains

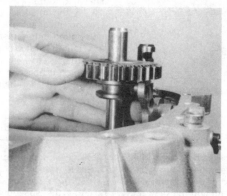
13.6 Fitting shift locking plate

13.7 Engaging 1st/2nd selector fork with synchro unit sleeve

13.8 Engaging 3rd/4th selector fork with synchro unit sleeve

13.9A Inserting selector shaft coil springs ...

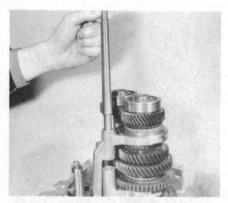
13.9B ... followed by the selector shaft

13.10 Using a screwdriver in selector shaft hole to engage 4th gear

11 Insert the magnetic swarf collector in its recess, taking care not to drop it (photo).
12 Locate a new gasket on the housing flange, install the smaller housing section and screw in and tighten the bolts to the specified torque (photos).
13 Fit the snap-rings to the ends of the main and input shafts. Cut-outs are provided in the casing so that the bearings can be levered upwards to expose the snap-ring grooves (photos). Snap-rings are available in three thicknesses and the thickest possible ring should be used which will fit into the groove. If any difficulty is experienced in levering up the bearing on the input shaft, push the end of the shaft from within the bellhousing.
14 Tap the snap-rings to rotate them so that they will locate correctly in the cut-outs in the cover gasket which should now be positioned on the end of the housing (photo). Fit a new gasket.
15 Fit the housing cover, screw in the bolts and tighten them to the specified torque (photo).
16 Fit the interlock pin, spring and cap nut for the selector shaft locking mechanism. The threads should be coated with jointing compound before installation.
17 Refit the clutch release shaft, lever and bearing into the bellhousing (photos).
18 The transmission is now ready for installation in the vehicle. Wait until it is installed before filling with oil.

14 Speedometer driven gear – removal and refitting

1   This work may be done without having to remove the transmission from the vehicle.
2   Using a pair of side cutting pliers, lever out the roll pin which secures the speedometer drive pinion bearing in the transmission housing.
3   Withdraw the pinion bearing, together with the speedometer drive cable. Separate the cable from the pinion by unscrewing the knurled ring or nut.

10 Actuate the appropriate selector fork to engage the correct gear: 4th on pre-February 1987 models or 2nd on later models. 4th gear is selected by inserting a rod in the hole in the end of the selector shaft which projects from the transmission casing and turning the shaft fully clockwise to its stop, then pushing the shaft inwards (photo). 2nd gear can be selected by turning the selector shaft fully clockwise (3rd/4th) and then gradually rotating it anti-clockwise until the shaft can be pushed inwards into 2nd gear.

13.11 Fitting the magnet

13.12A Locate a new gasket on the housing flange ...

13.12B ... and fit the smaller housing

13.13A Raising bearing for snap-ring installation

13.13B Fitting the bearing snap-ring

13.14 Bearing snap-rings and cover gasket in position

13.15 Fitting transmission housing cover

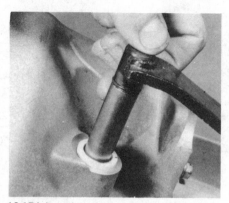

13.17A Inserting clutch release shaft ...

13.17B ... and securing release fork to the shaft

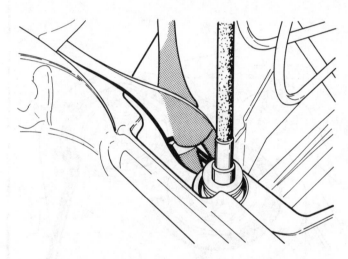

Fig. 6.62 Extracting speedometer pinion retaining roll pin (Sec 14)

4 Slide the pinion out of the bearing.
5 Always renew the O-ring on the pinion bearing before fitting.
6 Insert the pinion and bearing into the transmission housing using a back-and-forth twisting motion to mesh the pinion teeth with those of the drivegear. Secure with the roll pin.
7 Reconnect the speedometer cable.

15 Five-speed transmission – dismantling

1 With the gearbox removed from the vehicle, clean away external dirt and grease using paraffin and a stiff brush, or a water-soluble grease solvent. Take care not to allow water to enter the transmission.
2 Drain off any residual oil in the transmission through a driveshaft opening.
3 Unscrew the lockbolt which holds the clutch release fork to the shaft and remove the shaft, followed by the fork and release bearing (see Fig. 6.32).
4 If not removed for draining, unscrew the selector shaft cap nut, spring and interlock pin. Now remove the additional 5th gear selector shaft cap nut, spring and interlock pin.
5 Unbolt and remove the transmission housing cover.
6 Unscrew the clamp bolt and lift the 5th gear selector pin assembly off the shift rod.
7 Using circlip pliers, extract the 5th gear retaining snap-ring, then lift off the 5th gear, complete with synchro assembly and selector fork from the mainshaft.

8 Extract the circlip securing the 5th gear driving gear to the input shaft. Using a two-legged puller, draw the gear off the input shaft. *Do not re-use the old circlip when reassembling; a new one must be obtained.*
9 Unscrew the nine socket-headed bolts securing the 5th gear housing to the main housing and carefully lift it off.
10 Remove the snap-rings from the main and input shaft bearings.
11 Unscrew and remove the connecting bolts and gearbox mounting bolts, then lift the smaller housing from the transmission housing. If it is stuck, tap it off carefully with a plastic-headed mallet.
12 Extract the swarf-collecting magnet and clean it. Take care not to drop the magnet or it will shatter.
13 Release the circlips from the selector shaft guide sleeve and 1st/2nd gear selector fork. Carefully withdraw the guide sleeve.
14 Lift out the complete mainshaft assembly together with the input shaft, selector forks and reverse gear as a complete unit from the transmission housing.
15 Remove the selector shaft and the shift locking plate.
16 Finally lift the differential assembly from the housing.
17 The transmission is now dismantled into its major assemblies, which can be further dismantled if necessary, as described in Sections 9 to 12, but note the following differences when overhauling the mainshaft.
18 If overhauling the 5th gear synchronizer unit, note that the sliding keys are secured by means of a retaining plate. When assembling the unit proceed as described for the other synchro units (Section 10), but ensure that the retaining spring located between the hub and the retaining plate is pressing against the sliding keys (Fig. 6.72).
19 When reassembling the mainshaft, fit the 1st/2nd synchro so that

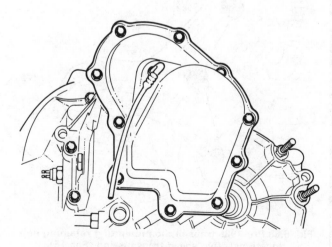

Fig. 6.63 Transmission housing cover retaining bolts – five-speed transmission (Sec 15)

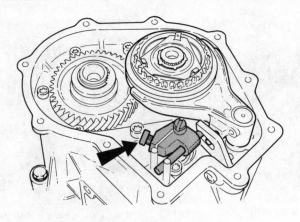

Fig. 6.64 5th gear selector pin clamp bolt (arrowed) – five-speed transmission (Sec 15)

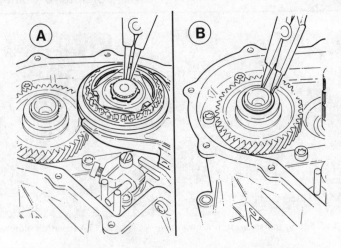

Fig. 6.65 Removing 5th gear retaining snap-ring (A) and input shaft circlip (B) – five-speed transmission (Sec 15)

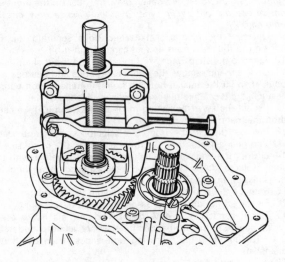

Fig. 6.66 Removing 5th gear from input shaft – five-speed transmission (Sec 15)

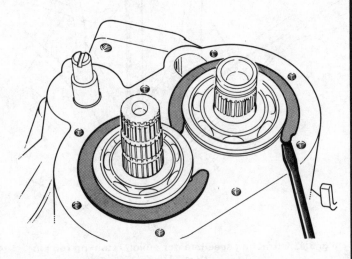

Fig. 6.67 Bearing snap-ring removal – five-speed transmission (Sec 15)

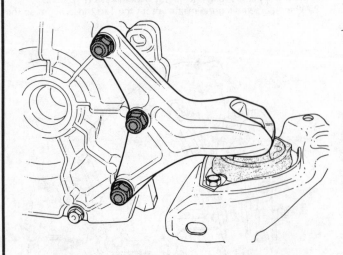

Fig. 6.68 Pre-1986 transmission mounting retaining bolt locations – five-speed transmission (Sec 15)

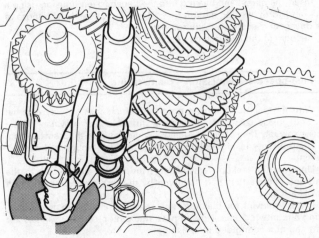

Fig. 6.69 Selector shaft guide sleeve and 1st/2nd gear selector fork circlip locations – five-speed transmission (Sec 15)

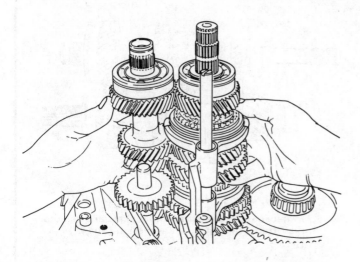

Fig. 6.70 Removing mainshaft, input shaft and reverse gear assemblies – five-speed transmission (Sec 15)

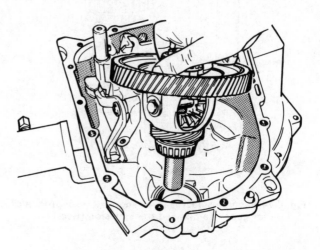

Fig. 6.71 Removing the differential – five-speed transmission (Sec 15)

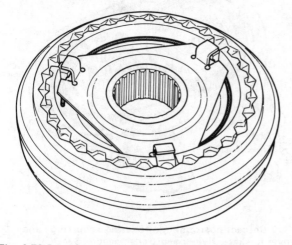

Fig. 6.72 5th gear synchro unit – five-speed transmission (Sec 15)

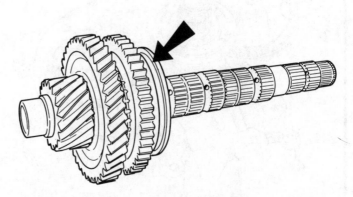

Fig. 6.73 Correct location of 1st/2nd synchro unit with selector groove positioned as shown (arrow) – five-speed transmission (Sec 15)

the reverse gear teeth on the unit are positioned towards 1st gear, with the selector groove facing 2nd gear (Fig. 6.73).
20 Should it be necessary to renew the input shaft or 5th gear, these components are now supplied as a matched pair in the form of a repair kit.

16 Five-speed transmission – overhaul (general)

1 As mentioned in the introduction of this Chapter, the five-speed transmission is virtually the same as the four-speed type, the main differences being the additional gear and synchro-hub, and a modified selector mechanism.
2 The overhaul procedures described previously for the four-speed transmission are therefore also applicable to the five-speed unit, but note the following.
3 It is important to note that during the assembly of the five-speed transmission the sub-assembly components should be lubricated with the special greases as shown in the Specifications.
4 On RS Turbo models the limited slip differential is a sealed assembly and cannot be dismantled for repair or overhaul. It is possible to renew the crownwheel using the procedure described in Section 12, but if any other repair is necessary a new unit must be obtained.
5 When referring to previous Sections for overhaul procedures, it should be noted that all photos, except where indicated, are of the

four-speed transmission. Due to the close resemblance of the two transmissions, the photos shown can also be used in most instances for pictorial guidance when working on the five-speed transmission.

17 Five-speed transmission – reassembly

1 With the larger housing section on the bench, lubricate the differential bearings with gear oil and insert the differential assembly into the housing.
2 Slide the reverse idler gear onto its shaft, at the same time engaging the selector lever in the groove of the gear which should be pointing downwards.
3 Refit the selector shaft and shift locking plate.
4 Refit the mainshaft and input shaft as an assembly complete with selector forms. Guide the selector forks past the shift locking plate, noting that the plate must be turned clockwise to bear against the dowel.
5 Install the selector shaft guide sleeve and secure the 1st/2nd gear selector fork on the guide sleeve using new circlips.
6 Refit the swarf-collecting magnet to its location in the housing.
7 Locate a new gasket on the housing flange and place the small housing section in position. Refit and tighten the retaining bolts to the specified torque. Refit the gearbox mounting bracket.
8 Fit the snap-rings to the ends of the main and input shafts. Cut-outs are provided in the casing so that the bearings can be levered upwards to expose the snap-ring grooves. Snap-rings are available in

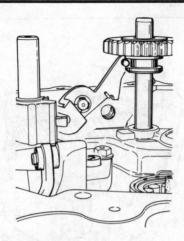

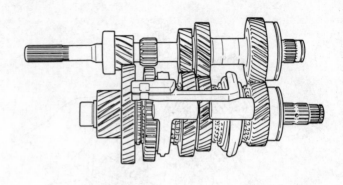

Fig. 6.74 Reverse selector lever engaged with groove of idler gear – five-speed transmission (Sec 17)

Fig. 6.75 Mainshaft meshed with input shaft and selector forks fitted – five-speed transmission (Sec 17)

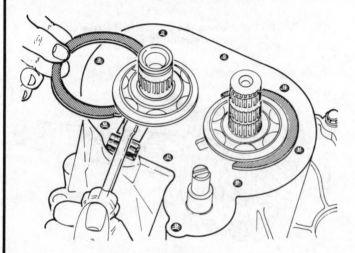

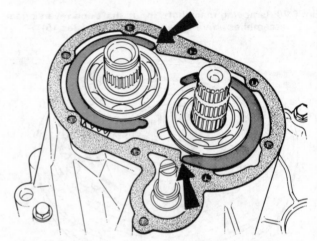

Fig. 6.76 Fitting mainshaft and input shaft bearing snap-rings – five-speed transmission (Sec 17)

Fig. 6.77 Correct positioning of bearing snap-rings and cover gasket – five-speed transmission (Sec 17)

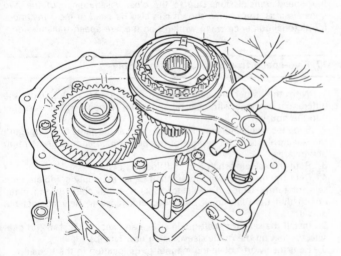

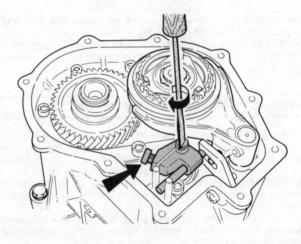

Fig. 6.78 Fitting 5th gear synchro unit and selector fork – five-speed transmission (Sec 17)

Fig. 6.79 Turning the shift rod clockwise with a screwdriver prior to tightening selector pin clamp bolt (arrowed) – five-speed transmission (Sec 17)

three thicknesses, and the thickest possible ring should be used which will fit into the groove. If any difficulty is experienced in levering up the bearing on the input shaft, push the end of the shaft from within the bellhousing.

9 Tap the snap-rings to rotate them so that they will locate correctly in the cut-outs in the 5th gear housing gasket, which should now be placed in position (Fig. 6.77).

10 Fit the 5th gear housing and tighten the retaining bolts to the specified torque.

11 Coat the splines of 5th gear and the input shaft with the special grease (see Specifications). Before fitting the 5th gear, check that the marks on the input shaft and gear web are the same colour.

12 Heat 5th gear to approximately 80°C (176°F), and then drift it into place on the input shaft. Fit a new circlip to the input shaft using a tube of suitable diameter as a drift.

13 Fit 5th gear, complete with synchro assembly and selector fork, onto the mainshaft and secure with the snap-ring.

14 Coat the threads of the 5th gear selector shaft locking mechanism cap nut with sealer (see Specifications). Fit the interlock pin, spring and cap nut, then tighten the nut to the specified torque.

15 Fit the 1st-4th and reverse gear selector shaft interlock pin, spring and cap nut after first coating the threads of the cap nut with sealer. Tighten the nut to the specified torque.

16 Refit the 5th gear selector pin assembly to the shift rod, but do not tighten the clamp bolt at this stage.

17 Engage 5th gear with the selector shaft by turning the shaft clockwise as far as it will go from the neutral position, and then pulling it fully out.

18 Slide the selector ring and selector fork onto 5th gear.

19 Rotate the shift rod clockwise viewed from the rear of the car as far as the stop, using a screwdriver, and retain it in this position. Smear the threads of the clamp bolt with thread locking compound, then fit it and tighten to the specified torque setting.

20 Place a new gasket in position and refit the housing cover, tightening the retaining bolts to the specified torque.

21 At this stage check the operation of the selector mechanism by engaging all the gears with the selector shaft.

22 Refit the clutch release shaft, lever and bearing into the bellhousing.

23 The transmission is now ready for installation in the vehicle. Wait until it is installed before filling with oil.

24 Use the selector shaft to engage an appropriate gear (for reconnection to the gearchange mechanism): reverse on pre-February 1987 models or 4th on later models. Reverse can be selected by turning the shaft fully clockwise and then pushing it inwards. 4th gear is selected by turning the shaft fully clockwise (5th/reverse) and then gradually rotating it anti-clockwise until it can be pushed inwards into 4th gear.

18 Fault diagnosis – manual transmission

Symptom	Reason(s)
Transmission noisy in neutral	Input shaft bearings worn
Transmission noisy only when moving (in all gears)	Mainshaft bearings worn Differential bearings worn Wear of differential crownwheel and mainshaft pinion teeth
Transmission noisy in only one gear	Worn, damaged or chipped gear teeth
Transmission jumps out of gear	Worn synchroniser units Worn selector shaft detent plungers or springs Worn selector forks
Ineffective synchromesh	Worn synchroniser units or baulk rings
Difficulty in engaging gears	Gear linkage adjustment incorrect Worn selector forks or selector mechanism Clutch fault (see Chapter 5)

Chapter 7 Automatic transmission

For modifications, and information applicable to later models, see Supplement at end of manual

Contents

Specifications

General

Transmission type	Ford ATX (automatic transaxle) with three forward speeds and reverse
Converter ratio	2.35 : 1
Transmission ratios:	
1st	2.79 : 1
2nd	1.61 : 1
3rd	1.00 : 1
Reverse	1.97 : 1
Final drive ratio	3.31 : 1
Oil cooler type	Twin tube in coolant radiator

Automatic transmission fluid type (see text – Section 3)

Early type transmission with identification number prefix E3RP-	Automatic transmission fluid to Ford specification SQM 2C 9010 A or ESP-M2C 138-CJ (Duckhams D-Matic)
Later type transmission with identification number prefix E6RP-	Automatic transmission fluid to Ford specification ESP-M2C 166-H (Duckhams Q-Matic)

Torque wrench settings

	Nm	lbf ft
Downshift/throttle valve shaft nut	13 to 15	10 to 11
Starter inhibitor switch	9 to 12	7 to 9
Oil cooler fluid pipes to transmission	22 to 24	16 to 18
Oil cooler fluid pipes to cooler	18 to 22	13 to 16
Transmission-to-engine retaining bolts	30 to 50	22 to 37
Torque converter-to-driveplate bolts	35 to 40	26 to 30
Driveplate to crankshaft	80 to 88	59 to 65
Torque converter cover plate bolts	7 to 10	5 to 7
Transmission mounting bolts	52 to 64	38 to 47
Selector cable bracket to engine	40 to 45	30 to 33
Throttle cable mounting bracket bolts	20 to 25	15 to 18
Downshift linkage control lever clamp bolt	5 to 7	4 to 5
Downshift linkage damper locknut	4.5 to 7.5	3 to 6
Gear selector housing bolts	8.5 to 9.5	6 to 7
Gear selector lever nut	20 to 23	15 to 17

1 General description

The automatic transmission used on Escort models is the Ford ATX (automatic transaxle) unit equipped with three forward speeds and reverse, and incorporating the final drive differential. The transmission is mounted transversely in line with the engine crankshaft.

The ATX transmission is a split torque type, whereby engine torque is transmitted to the geartrain by mechanical or hydraulic means in accordance with the gear selected and the roadspeed. This is achieved by using a torque converter with a bypass allowing the transmission a proportion of engine torque mechanically. This eliminates the hydraulic slip within the torque converter at high engine speeds resulting in greater efficiency and improved fuel economy.

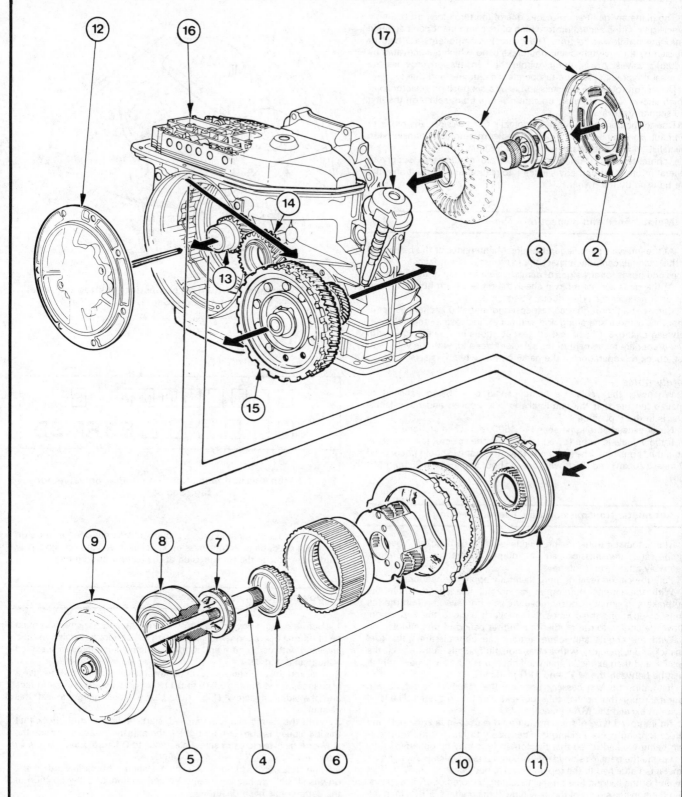

Fig. 7.1 Automatic transmission internal components (Sec 1)

1	Torque converter	5	2nd gear shaft
2	Damper	6	Planetary geartrain
3	Torque converter	7	One-way clutch
	mechanical bypass gear set	8	Top gear clutch
4	Turbine shaft	9	2nd gear clutch

10	Reverse gear clutch	15	Differential
11	Brake band	16	Valve block
12	Oil pump	17	Governor
13	Differential pinion		Arrows indicate course of power transmission
14	Intermediate gear		

The planetary geartrain provides one of the three forward or single reverse gear ratios according to which of its component parts are held stationary or allowed to turn. The geartrain components are held or released by three clutches and one brake band which are activated by hydraulic valves. An oil pump within the transmission provides the necessary hydraulic pressure to operate the clutches and brake.

Driver control of the transmission is by a six position selector lever which allows fully automatic operation with a hold facility on the first and second gear ratios.

Due to the complexity of the automatic transmission, any repair or overhaul work must be left to a Ford dealer or automatic transmission specialist with the necessary equipment for fault diagnosis and repair. The contents of this Chapter are therefore confined to supplying general information and any service information and instructions that can be used by the owner.

2 Maintenance and inspection

1   At the intervals specified in Routine Maintenance at the beginning of this manual, carefully inspect the transmission joint faces, oil seals, pipes and hoses for any signs of damage, deterioration or fluid leakage.
2   At the same service interval check the transmission fluid level and top up if necessary as described in Section 3.
3   Carry out a thorough road test ensuring that all gearchanges occur smoothly without snatching and without an increase in engine speed between changes. Check that all gear positions can be engaged with the appropriate movement of the selector lever and, with the vehicle at rest, check the operation of the parking pawl when P is selected.

Safety notes

4   Whenever the vehicle is being parked or is being serviced or repaired, ensure that the handbrake is fully applied and the selector lever is in the P position.
5   Never exceed an engine speed of 4500 rpm when stationary.
6   If the vehicle is to be towed at any time the selector lever must be set in the N position. The maximum towing distance should not exceed 12 miles (20 km) and the towing speed should not exceed 25 mph (40 kph).

3 Automatic transmission fluid – level checking

1   The automatic transmission fluid level must be checked when the engine and transmission are at normal operating temperature; preferably after a short journey.
2   Park the car on level ground, then fully apply the handbrake.
3   With the engine running at its normal idle speed, apply the footbrake and simultaneously move the selector lever through the full range of positions three times then move it back to the P position. Allow the engine to run at idle for a further period of one minute.
4   With the engine still idling, extract the transmission fluid level dipstick and wipe it dry, with a clean non-fluffy cloth. Fully reinsert the dipstick and then extract it again and check the fluid level mark, which must be between the MAX and MIN markings.
5   If topping-up is necessary, use only the specified fluid type and pour it through the dipstick tube, but take care not to overfill. The level must not exceed the MAX mark.
6   An improved type of transmission fluid is used in later models and before topping-up or refilling it is necessary to identify the transmission being worked on so that the correct fluid may be obtained.
7   Locate the transmission identification number which is stamped on a metal tag attached to the top of the valve body cover (Fig. 7.3). If, at the end of the second line on the metal tag, the prefix E3RP- appears, then the transmission is of the early type. If the prefix E6RP- then the unit is of the later type. Later transmissions can also be identified by having a black dipstick stating the fluid specification and type. Having determined whether the transmission is of the early or later type, refer to the Specifications for the fluid requirement. Under no circumstances may the later type fluid be used in the early type transmission, and *vice versa*.
8   If the fluid level was below the minimum mark when checked or is in constant need of topping-up, check around the transmission unit for any signs of excessive fluid leaks, and if present then they must be rectified without delay.

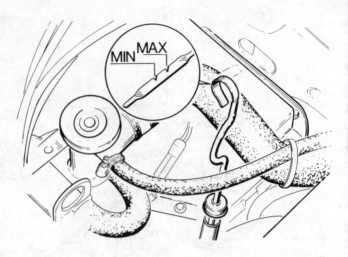

Fig. 7.2 Transmission fluid level dipstick location and level markings (Sec 3)

Fig. 7.3 Transmission identification number on valve body tag (Sec 3)

9   If the colour of the fluid is dark brown or black this denotes the sign of a worn brake band or transmission clutches in which case have your Ford dealer check the transmission at the earliest opportunity.

4 Downshift linkage – adjustment

1   Before making any adjustments the engine and transmission must be at normal operating temperature, with the correct transmission fluid level and with carburettor and ignition system adjustments as specified (Chapters 3 and 4).
2   Slacken the adjuster screw on the throttle valve shaft lever to give a clearance of 2 to 3 mm (0.079 to 0.118 in) between the stop end face and the adjuster screw (Fig. 7.5). Use a feeler gauge to set this clearance.
3   With the handbrake fully applied, start the engine and check that the idle speed is correct then tighten the adjuster screw to reduce the stop end face-to-adjuster screw clearance to 0.1 to 0.3 mm (0.004 to 0.012 in).
4   The following additional adjustment should be carried out if the downshift linkage has been removed and refitted, or if the position of the damper has been disturbed.
5   Slacken the locknut and screw in the damper to give a clearance of 1 mm (0.04 in) between the damper body and the bracket (Fig. 7.6). Use a feeler gauge or drill bit of suitable diameter to check this.
6   Slacken the linkage control lever clamp bolt, move the lever so that it just contacts the plastic cap of the damper rod and tighten the clamp bolt.
7   Make a reference mark on the damper body then turn the damper so that the damper body-to-bracket dimension is now 7 mm (0.28 in) (Fig. 7.7).
8   Hold the damper in this position and tighten the locknut.

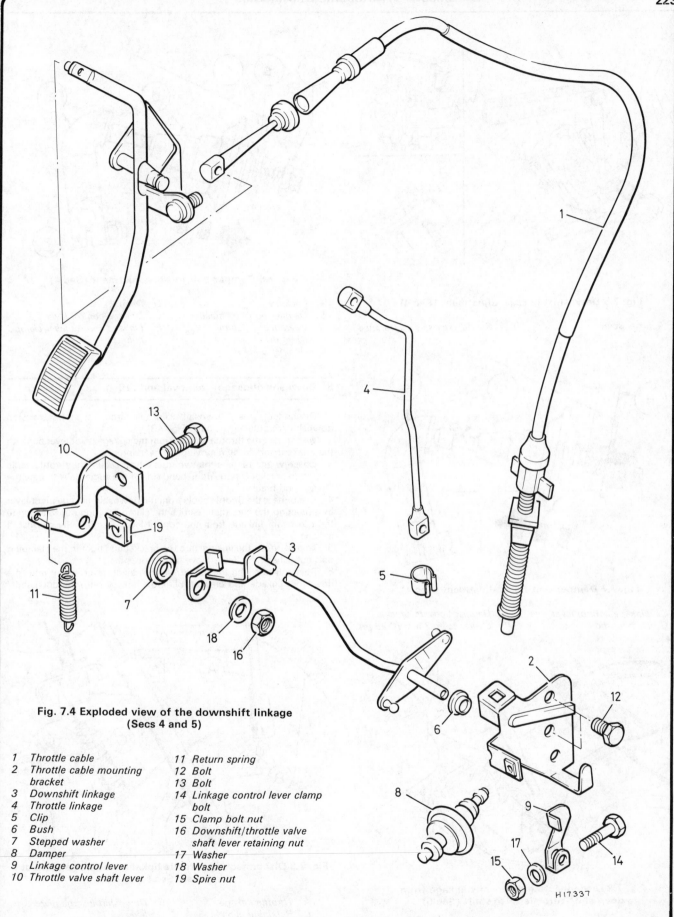

Fig. 7.4 Exploded view of the downshift linkage (Secs 4 and 5)

1 Throttle cable
2 Throttle cable mounting bracket
3 Downshift linkage
4 Throttle linkage
5 Clip
6 Bush
7 Stepped washer
8 Damper
9 Linkage control lever
10 Throttle valve shaft lever
11 Return spring
12 Bolt
13 Bolt
14 Linkage control lever clamp bolt
15 Clamp bolt nut
16 Downshift/throttle valve shaft lever retaining nut
17 Washer
18 Washer
19 Spire nut

H17337

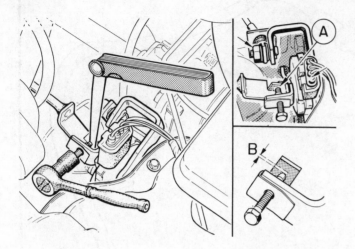

Fig. 7.5 Downshift linkage adjustment (Sec 4)

A   Adjuster screw   B   Adjuster screw clearance

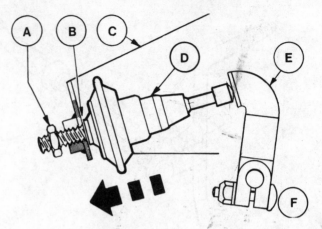

Fig. 7.6 Damper unit initial adjustment (Sec 4)

A   Locknut
B   Damper body-to-bracket
     clearance = 1 mm
     (0.04 in)
C   Damper bracket

D   Damper
E   Linkage control lever
F   Linkage control lever clamp
     bolt

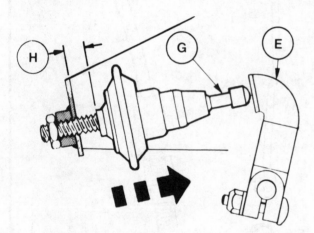

Fig. 7.7 Damper unit final adjustment (Sec 4)

E   Linkage control lever
G   Damper rod

H   Damper body-to-bracket
     clearance = 7 mm (0.28 in)

5   Downshift linkage – removal and refitting

1   Disconnect the downshift linkage from the transmission downshift/throttle valve shaft (Fig. 7.8).
2   Disconnect the throttle linkage from the linkage pivot lever beneath the intake manifold by removing the securing clip.
3   Unscrew and remove the two nuts which secure the throttle cable mounting bracket (on the right-hand side of the engine). Withdraw the linkage and bracket.
4   Disconnect the throttle cable from the downshift linkage pivot lever by extracting the clip, then remove the clamp bolt and nut to separate the downshift linkage from the control lever. Remove the downshift linkage.
5   To refit, insert the linkage into the bracket and tighten the clamping bolt nut. Check that lever movement is possible.
6   Reattach the throttle cable to the pivot lever, then refit the downshift linkage and bracket. Slide the linkage onto the downshift/

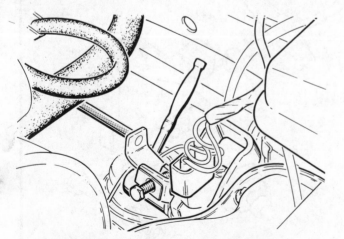

Fig. 7.8 Disconnecting downshift linkage from
downshift/throttle valve shaft (Sec 5)

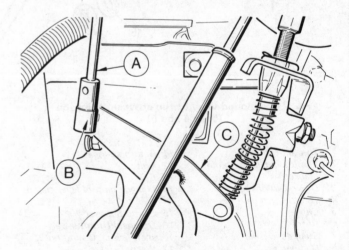

Fig. 7.9 Disconnecting throttle linkage from linkage pivot
lever (Sec 5)

A   Throttle linkage
B   Retaining clip

C   Downshift linkage pivot
     lever

throttle shaft of the transmission, fitting the stepped washer between the lever and linkage on the valve shaft. The bracket securing screws should be tightened to the specified torque setting.

7 Secure the throttle linkage to the downshift linkage pivot lever by refitting the retaining clip. Refit the downshift/throttle valve shaft nut.

8 Adjust the downshift linkage as described in Section 4.

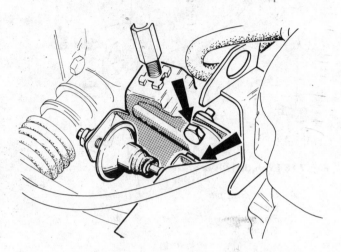

Fig. 7.10 Throttle cable mounting bracket retaining bolt locations – arrowed (Sec 5)

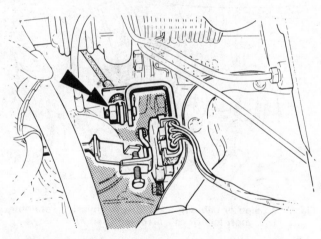

Fig. 7.11 Selector cable-to-selector shaft cable retaining nut – arrowed (Sec 6)

Fig. 7.13 Selector gate and stop plate retaining screw locations – arrowed (Sec 6)

6 Selector mechanism – removal and refitting

1 Move the selector lever to the D position.

2 At the transmission, slacken the nut securing the selector cable to the selector shaft lever (Fig. 7.8).

3 Unscrew and remove the gear selector lever knob, then carefully prise up and remove the selector gate cover from the console.

4 Remove the console unit which is secured in position by two screws at the rear and screws on each side at the front.

5 Remove the selector gate and stop plate which are secured by two screws, one on each corner at the front.

6 Disconnect the selector cable from the selector lever and housing by removing the securing clips, and, where applicable, the ball and socket joint.

7 Disconnect the escutcheon light holder from the lever housing, then unscrew and remove the four housing retaining screws. Lift the housing clear.

8 To dismantle the selector unit, unscrew the lever pivot pin retaining nut and remove the lever assembly from its housing, together with the bushes.

9 The lever can be removed from the guide by unhooking the spring, unscrewing the retaining pin nut and withdrawing the pin, washers and lever.

10 Reassembly of the selector unit is a reversal of the removal procedure. Tighten the selector lever nut to the specified torque

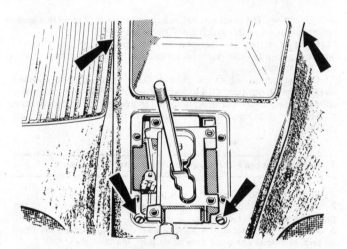

Fig. 7.12 Console unit retaining screw locations – arrowed (Sec 6)

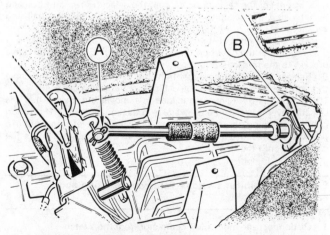

Fig. 7.14 Selector cable attachments (Sec 6)

A   Cable-to-selector lever securing clip (ball and socket joint on later models)

B   Cable-to-housing securing clip

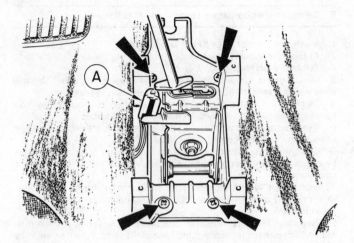

**Fig. 7.15 Selector lever housing retaining screw locations –
arrowed (Sec 6)**

A   Escutcheon light holder

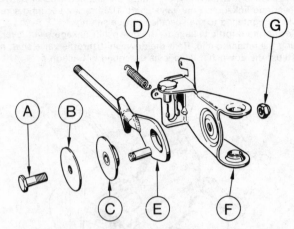

**Fig. 7.16 Exploded view of the selector lever components
(Sec 6)**

A   Lever pivot pin   E   Lever
B   Washer   F   Bush
C   Plastic spacer   G   Nut
D   Spring

wrench setting. The pivot pin nut must be tightened to provide a lever movement effort of 0.5 to 2.5 Nm (0.4 to 1.8 lbf ft).

11 Refitting of the gear selector unit is a reversal of the removal procedure. Tighten the retaining screws of the lever housing to the specified torque.

12 On completion, adjust the selector cable by moving the selector lever to the D position, check that the selector shaft lever is in the corresponding D position then retighten the cable nut. To prevent the threaded pin rotating as the nut is tightened, press the cable slot onto the thread.

7 Selector cable – removal, refitting and adjustment

1   Move the selector lever to the D position.
2   At the transmission, undo the nut securing the selector cable to the selector shaft lever (Fig. 7.11).
3   Unscrew and remove the selector lever knob, then carefully prise up and remove the selector gate cover from the console.
4   Remove the console unit which is secured in position by two screws at the rear and screws on each side at the front.
5   Remove the selector gate and stop plate which are secured by two screws, one at each front corner.
6   Disconnect the selector cable from the selector lever and housing by removing the securing clips and, where applicable, the ball and socket joint.
7   Jack up the front of the car and support it on axle stands.
8   From under the car undo the two bolts securing the selector cable bracket to the transmission.
9   Release the rubber grommet from the floorpan and pull the cable through the hole. Withdraw the cable from under the car.
10 Refitting is the reverse sequence to removal but ensure that the selector lever is in D and the linkage is in the corresponding D position before tightening the cable-to-selector shaft lever retaining nut. To prevent the threaded pin rotating as the nut is tightened, press the cable slot onto the thread.

8 Starter inhibitor switch – removal, refitting and adjustment

1   Disconnect the multi-plug connector from the switch.
2   Remove the retaining nut and disconnect the linkage from the throttle valve shaft lever on the transmission.
3   To remove the downshift linkage from the transmission, unscrew and remove the two securing screws to the location bracket on the right-hand side of the engine and pull the linkage free.

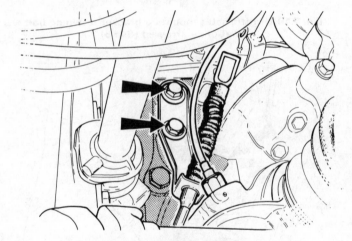

**Fig. 7.17 Selector cable bracket-to-transmission retaining
bolt locations – arrowed (Sec 7)**

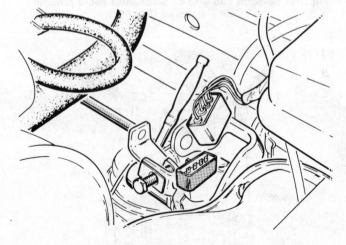

**Fig. 7.18 Disconnecting starter inhibitor switch multi-plug
and linkage retaining nut removal (Sec 8)**

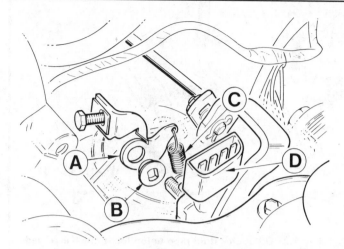

Fig. 7.19 Starter inhibitor switch removal (Sec 8)

A   Throttle valve shaft lever   C   Return spring
B   Stepped washer   D   Starter inhibitor switch

4   Remove the downshift/throttle valve shaft lever, together with the stepped washer and disconnect the return spring. Unscrew the two retaining screws and remove the starter inhibitor switch.
5   The switch must be renewed if it is known to be defective.
6   On refitting the starter inhibitor switch do not fully tighten the securing screws until it is adjusted for position. To do this first move the selector lever to the D position, then using a 2.3 mm (0.091 in) diameter drill shank as shown (Fig. 7.20) locate it into the hole in the switch body.
7   Move the switch whilst pushing on the drill so that the switch case aligns with the inner location hole in the switch and with the drill fully inserted so that the switch is immobilised, fully tighten the retaining screws to the specified torque.
8   With the switch in position, refitting of the downshift/throttle valve shaft lever and linkage is a reversal of the removal procedure, but readjust the downshift linkage as described in Section 4.

9   Automatic transmission – removal and refitting

1   Disconnect the battery negative terminal.
2   Refer to Chapter 3 and remove the air cleaner.
3   Disconnect the wiring multi-plug at the starter inhibitor switch.
4   Move the gear selector lever to position D then unscrew the nut securing the selector cable to the selector shaft lever. Press the cable slot onto the threaded pin to prevent the pin rotating as the nut is unscrewed (Fig. 7.11).
5   Slacken the downshift linkage adjuster screw then disconnect the downshift linkage from the downshift/throttle valve shaft by undoing the retaining nut (Fig. 7.8). To facilitate removal and subsequent refitting of the downshift linkage, undo the two throttle cable mounting bracket bolts on the right-hand side of the engine (Fig. 7.10).
6   Unscrew the two upper transmission-to-engine retaining bolts.
7   Jack up the front of the car and support it on axle stands. Ensure that the vehicle is high enough to allow removal of the transmission from below.
8   Support the engine under the sump using a jack and interposed block of wood. Alternatively support the engine from above using a crane or hoist.
9   Disconnect the speedometer drive cable and the reversing light switch leads.
10 Undo the two bolts and detach the selector cable bracket from the transmission assembly.
11 Refer to Chapter 12 and remove the starter motor.
12 Undo the two bolts and remove the torque converter cover plate.

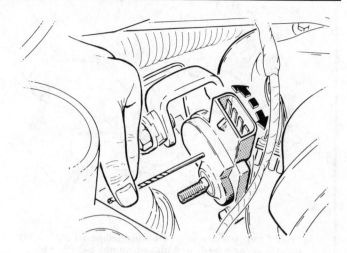

Fig. 7.20 Starter inhibitor switch adjustment (Sec 8)

13 Remove the driveshafts from the transmission as described in Chapter 8, Section 5. After removal of the driveshafts retain the differential sun gears in alignment by inserting a dowel of suitable diameter into the differential so that it engages the sun gear on one side.
14 Undo the nut securing the front transmission mounting to the support plate and the four bolts securing the support plate to the body.
15 Undo the transmission oil cooler fluid pipe union nuts at the transmission and withdraw the pipes. Plug the transmission and the pipe ends to prevent dirt ingress.
16 Undo the three bolts and remove the front mounting bracket from the transmission.
17 Undo the bolts and nuts and remove the rear mounting complete with bracket from the transmission and body.
18 Turn the flywheel as necessary to bring each of the torque converter retaining nuts in turn into an accessible position through the cover plate aperture. Undo and remove the nuts.
19 Support the transmission beneath the oil pan using a jack and interposed block of wood.
20 Undo the remaining transmission-to-engine retaining bolts and carefully withdraw and lower the transmission from the engine. As the unit is removed, hold the torque converter firmly against the transmission taking care not to allow the studs to catch on the driveplate.

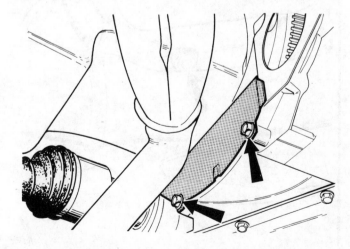

Fig. 7.21 Torque converter cover plate retaining bolt locations – arrowed (Sec 9)

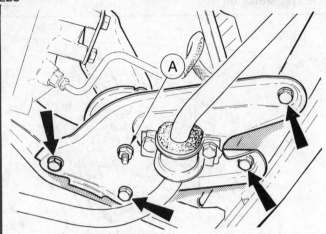

Fig. 7.22 Front transmission mounting support plate bolt locations (arrowed) and mounting nut (A) (Sec 9)

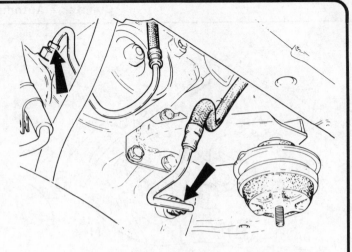

Fig. 7.23 Oil cooler fluid pipe union locations – arrowed (Sec 9)

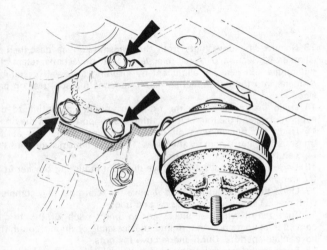

Fig. 7.24 Front mounting bracket bolt locations – arrowed (Sec 9)

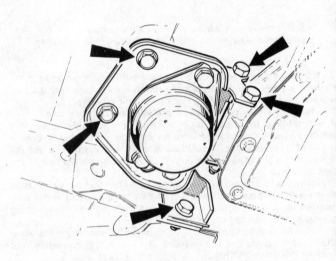

Fig. 7.25 Rear transmission mounting bracket and support plate bolt locations – arrowed (Sec 9)

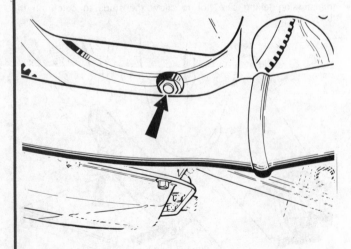

Fig. 7.26 Torque converter retaining nut accessible through the cover plate aperture – arrowed (Sec 9)

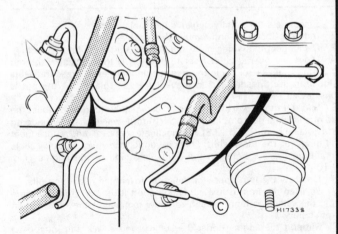

Fig. 7.27 Oil cooler fluid pipe positioning details (Sec 9)

A Dipstick/filler tube
B Pipe feed to oil cooler
C Pipe return from oil cooler

21 Refitting is the reverse sequence to removal bearing in mind the following points:

(a) *Tighten all nuts and bolts to the specified torque*
(b) *Connect the transmission oil cooler fluid pipes with reference to Fig. 7.27*
(c) *Refit the driveshafts with reference to Chapter 8, Section 5 and with new snap-rings on the end of the constant velocity joint splines*
(d) *Refit the downshift linkage and selector cable with reference to the adjustment procedures contained in Sections 4 and 7 respectively. Note that final adjustment of the downshift linkage can only be carried out after refitting and running the transmission to normal operating temperature*

(e) *Refill the transmission with the specified type and quantity of fluid (see Section 3 regarding fluid types)*

10 Fault diagnosis – automatic transmission

In the event of a fault occurring on the transmission, it is first necessary to determine whether it is of a mechanical or hydraulic nature and to do this the transmission must be in the car. Special test equipment is necessary for this purpose, together with a systematic test procedure, and the work should be entrusted to a suitably equipped Ford dealer or automatic transmission specialist.

Do not remove the transmission from the car for repair or overhaul until professional fault diagnosis has been carried out.

Chapter 8 Driveshafts

For modifications, and information applicable to later models, see Supplement at end of manual

Contents

Specifications

Type .... Unequal length solid (left-hand) or tubular (right-hand) shafts, splined to inner and outer constant velocity joints

Lubrication (overhaul only – see text)
Lubricant type .... Lithium based molybdenum disulphide grease to Ford specification S-MIC-75-A/SQM-1C-9004-A (Duckhams LBM 10)

Lubricant quantity .... 40g (1.4oz) per joint

Torque wrench settings

	Nm	lbf ft
Driveshaft retaining nut (threads lightly greased)	205 to 235	151 to 173
Lower arm mounting pivot bolt	51 to 64	38 to 47
Lower arm balljoint pinch-bolt	48 to 60	35 to 44
Brake caliper anchor bracket mounting bolts	50 to 66	37 to 49
Selector shaft locking mechanism cap nut	30	22
Roadwheel bolts	70 to 100	52 to 74

1 General description

Drive is transmitted from the differential to the front wheels by means of two unequal length driveshaft assemblies. The left-hand driveshaft is solid whereas the longer right-hand driveshaft is tubular and of larger diameter to reduce harmonic vibrations and resonance.

Both driveshafts are fitted with ball and cage type constant velocity joints at each end except for certain later models which are equipped with a tripod type inner constant velocity joint. On all models the inner joints are of the sliding type allowing lateral movement of the driveshaft to cater for suspension travel. Both constant velocity joints incorporate an externally splined stub shaft which engages with the differential sun gears (inner joint) or wheel hub (outer joint). The constant velocity joint inner members are internally splined to accept the driveshaft. Circlips, snap-rings and the driveshaft retaining nut are used to secure the assemblies.

The driveshaft lengths and weights vary slightly to suit the different engine/torque characteristics of the cars in the range and are therefore not interchangeable from model to model.

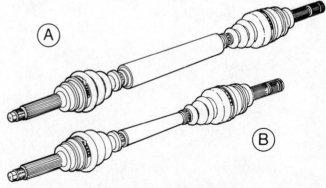

Fig. 8.1 Driveshaft assemblies (Sec 1)

A *Right-hand driveshaft*
B *Left-hand driveshaft*

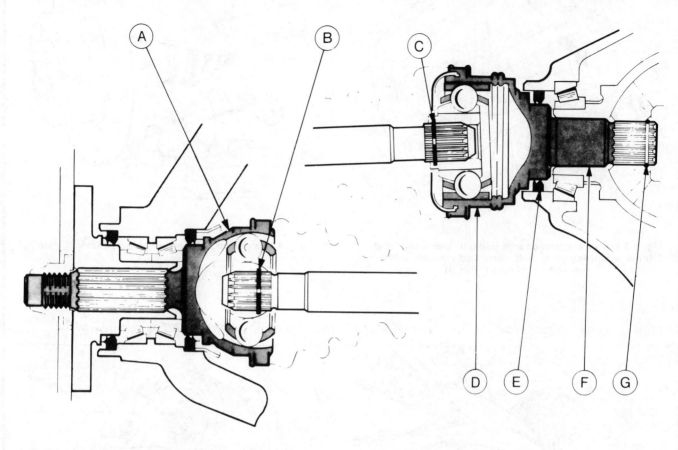

Fig. 8.2 Sectional view of ball and cage type constant velocity joints (Sec 1)

A   Outer constant velocity joint
B   Circlip
C   Circlip
D   Inner constant velocity joint

E   Oil seal
F   Inner joint stub shaft
G   Snap-ring

2   Maintenance and inspection

1   At the intervals given in Routine Maintenance at the beginning of this manual carry out a thorough inspection of the driveshafts and joints as follows.
2   Jack up the front of the car and support it securely on axle stands.
3   Slowly rotate the roadwheel and inspect the condition of the outer joint rubber bellows. Check for signs of cracking, splits or deterioration of the rubber which may allow the grease to escape and lead to water and grit entry into the joint. Also check the security and condition of the retaining clips. Repeat these checks on the inner constant velocity joints. If any damage or deterioration is found, the bellows should be renewed as described in Sections 3 or 4.
4   Continue rotating the roadwheel and check for any distortion or damage to the driveshaft. Check for any free play in the joints by first holding the driveshaft and attempting to rotate the wheel. Repeat this check by holding the inner joint and attempting to rotate the driveshaft. Any appreciable movement indicates wear in the joints, wear in the driveshaft splines or loose driveshaft retaining nut.
5   Road test the car and listen for a metallic clicking from the front as the car is driven slowly in a circle with the steering on full lock. If a clicking noise is heard this indicates wear in the outer constant velocity joint caused by excessive clearance between the balls in the joint and the recesses in which they operate. Remove and inspect the joint, as described in Section 6.
6   If vibration, consistent with road speed, is felt through the car when accelerating, there is a possibility of wear in the inner constant velocity joint. If so, renewal of the driveshaft inner joint will be necessary.

3   Inner constant velocity joint bellows – renewal

1   Jack up the front of the car, support it on axle stands and remove the roadwheel.
2   On cars equipped with an anti-lock braking system, refer to Chapter 9 and remove the modulator drivebelt cover.
3   Disconnect the front suspension lower arm balljoint from the hub carrier by removing the nut and pinch-bolt. Note that the pinch-bolt is of the socket-headed (Torx) type and a special key or socket bit (available from accessory shops) will be required for this purpose.
4   On models fitted with an anti-roll bar, disconnect the lower arm from the body at its inner end by removing the mounting pivot bolt.
5   Release both retaining clips from the bellows on the inner constant velocity joint and slide the bellows off the joint and along the shaft.
6   If the joint is of the ball and cage type, wipe away enough grease to expose the circlip which secures it to the driveshaft. Extract the circlip and pull the driveshaft out of the joint (Fig. 8.5).
7   If the joint is of the tripod type withdraw the driveshaft and spider from the joint outer member, extract the circlip and remove the spider from the driveshaft.
8   Slide the bellows off the end of the driveshaft.
9   Slide on the new bellows then connect the driveshaft to the constant velocity joint. On the ball and cage type joint, the circlip should be engaged in its groove in the joint and the shaft slid through it until it engages with the groove in the shaft.
10 Replenish the joint with grease of the specified type then pull the bellows over the joint.

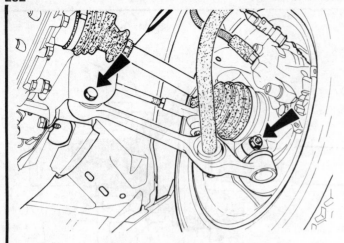

Fig. 8.3 Lower suspension arm balljoint pinch-bolt and inner mounting pivot bolt – arrowed (models with anti-roll bar shown) (Sec 3)

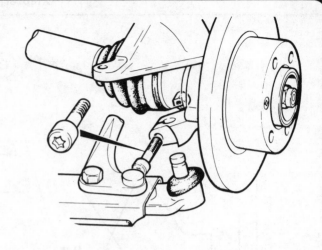

Fig. 8.4 Lower arm balljoint pinch bolt removal (Sec 3)

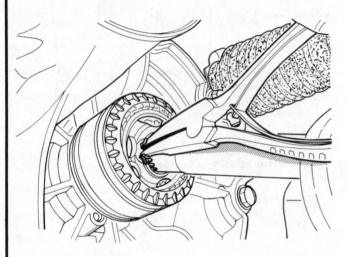

Fig. 8.5 Extracting driveshaft retaining circlip from ball and cage type inner joint (Sec 3)

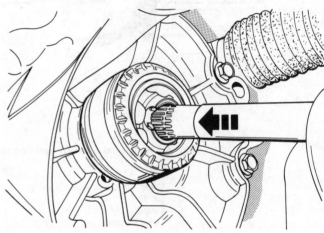

Fig. 8.6 Refitting driveshaft to ball and cage type inner joint with circlip in position (Sec 3)

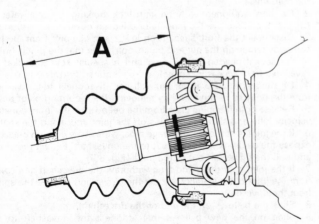

Fig. 8.7 Constant velocity joint bellows setting diagram (Secs 3 and 4)

A = setting dimension (see text)

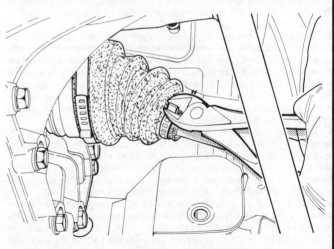

Fig. 8.8 Crimping bellows retaining clip to tighten (Secs 3 and 4)

11 Set the length of the bellows (dimension A in Fig. 8.7) according to model as follows:

Pre-1986 models:

1.1 litre	*127 mm (5.0 in)*
1.3 and 1.6 litre	*132 mm (5.20 in)*

1986 models onwards:

All models	*95 mm (3.74 in)*

12 Fit the new bellows retaining clips engaging the peg on the clip with the tightest possible hole. Now crimp the raised portion of the clip to tighten it securely.
13 Reconnect the suspension lower arm to the body (where applicable) and tighten the mounting pivot bolt to the specified torque.
14 Reconnect the lower arm balljoint to the hub carrier and insert the Torx bolt with its head to the rear. Refit the nut and tighten to the specified torque.
15 On cars equipped with an anti-lock braking system, refit the modulator drivebelt cover.
16 Refit the roadwheel and lower the car.

4 Outer constant velocity joint bellows – renewal

1 Unless the driveshaft is to be removed completely for other repair work to be carried out (see Section 5), the following method of bellows renewal is recommended to avoid having to disconnect the driveshaft from the hub carrier.
2 Remove the inner joint bellows as described in Section 3, paragraphs 1 to 8 inclusive.
3 Release both retaining clips from the bellows on the outer constant velocity joint and slide the bellows off the joint and along the driveshaft until it can be removed from the inner end.
4 Thoroughly clean the driveshaft then slide on the new bellows.
5 Replenish the outer joint with grease of the specified type then pull the bellows over the joint.
6 Set the length of the bellows (dimension A in Fig. 8.7) according to model as follows:

Pre-1986 models:

1.1 litre	*70 mm (2.76 in)*
1.3 and 1.6 litre	*82 mm (3.23 in)*

1986 models onwards:

All models	*95 mm (3.74 in)*

7 Fit the new bellows retaining clips engaging the peg on the clip with the tightest possible hole. Now crimp the raised portion of the

clip to tighten it securely. Make sure that the crimped part of the clip nearest the hub carrier does not foul the carrier when the driveshaft is rotated.
8 Refit the inner bellows as described in Section 3, paragraphs 9 to 16 inclusive.

5 Driveshaft assembly – removal and refitting

1 Remove the wheel trim and release the staking on the driveshaft retaining nut using a suitable punch.
2 Slacken the driveshaft retaining nut and the wheel bolts.
3 Jack up the front of the car, support it on stands and remove the roadwheel.
4 Undo the two bolts securing the brake caliper anchor bracket to the hub carrier.
5 Withdraw the anchor bracket and brake caliper, complete with disc pads, and suspend it from a convenient place under the wheel arch.
6 On cars equipped with an anti-lock braking system refer to Chapter 9 and remove the modulator drivebelt.
7 On pre-1986 manual transmission models, place a suitable container beneath the selector shaft locking mechanism cap nut (Fig. 8.10). Unscrew the cap nut, remove the spring and interlock pin and allow the transmission oil to drain. **Caution:** Take care when unscrewing the cap nut as the tension of the spring may cause the pin to fly out as the cap nut is released. Note that due to the revised transmission support crossmember shrouding the cap nut on 1986 models onward, and on all cars equipped with automatic transmission, the oil/fluid cannot be drained with the unit in the car. This will result in a quantity of transmission oil or fluid spillage when the driveshaft is removed. Be prepared for this with a container at the ready.
8 Disconnect the front suspension lower arm balljoint from the hub carrier by removing the nut and pinch-bolt. Note that the pinch-bolt is of the socket-headed (Torx) type and a special key or socket bit will be required for this purpose. These are readily available from most accessory shops.
9 On models fitted with an anti-roll bar, disconnect the lower arm from the body at its inner end by removing the mounting pivot bolt.
10 Insert a lever between the inner constant velocity joint and the transmission casing (Fig. 8.11). Firmly strike the lever to release the inner constant velocity joint from the differential. On automatic transmission models a groove is provided in the left-hand constant velocity joint for insertion of the lever, but on the right-hand side it will be necessary to use a small piece of wood to protect the oil pan when levering.

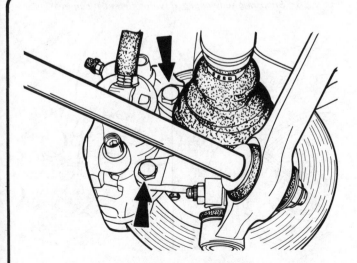

Fig. 8.9 Brake caliper retaining bolts – arrowed (Sec 5)

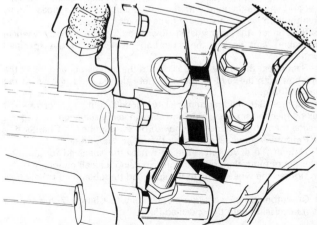

Fig. 8.10 Selector shaft locking mechanism cap nut location – arrowed (Sec 5)

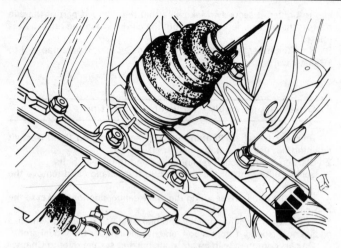

Fig. 8.11 Using a lever to release the inner constant velocity joint (Sec 5)

11 With the joint released, move the hub carrier outwards and pull the constant velocity joint out of the differential.

12 Suspend the driveshaft or support it in such a way as to avoid placing an angular strain on the constant velocity joints. The shaft must not hang down by more than 45° from the outer joint or 20° from the inner joint.

13 Remove the driveshaft retaining nut and washer.

14 Undo the retaining screw and withdraw the brake disc from the hub.

15 It should now be possible to pull the driveshaft out of the hub. If it is tight, use a two-legged puller to push it out (Fig. 8.12).

16 Withdraw the driveshaft assembly from under the car. If both driveshafts are to be removed at the same time retain the differential sun gears in alignment by inserting a dowel of suitable diameter into the differential so that it engages the sun gear on one side.

17 To refit the driveshaft, first lubricate the splines of the outer constant velocity joint, engage the joint with the hub splines and push the joint firmly into the hub.

18 Using the original driveshaft retaining nut and packing pieces, draw the constant velocity joint fully into the hub.

19 Remove the old nut and packing and fit the washer and a new nut, but only tighten the nut finger tight at this stage.

20 Refit the brake disc and caliper anchor bracket, tightening the anchor bracket bolts to the specified torque.

21 On cars equipped with an anti-lock braking system, refit the modulator drivebelt as described in Chapter 9.

22 Fit a new snap-ring to the splines of the inner constant velocity joint and engage the joint with the differential sun gear splines. Firmly push the hub carrier inwards to force the joint home.

23 Reconnect the suspension lower arm to the body (where applicable) and tighten the mounting pivot bolt to the specified torque.

24 Reconnect the lower arm balljoint to the hub carrier and insert the Torx bolt with its head to the rear. Refit the nut and tighten to the specified torque.

25 On pre-1986 manual transmission models, refit the selector shaft locking mechanism pin, spring and cap nut using sealer on the cap nut threads then fill the transmission with oil as described in Chapter 6.

26 Refit the roadwheel and lower the car to the ground.

27 Tighten the driveshaft retaining nut to the specified torque then stake the nut into the driveshaft groove using a small punch.

28 Tighten the wheel bolts to the specified torque and refit the wheel trim.

29 On automatic transmission models refer to Chapter 7 and top up the transmission with the specified fluid.

6 Driveshaft assembly – overhaul

1 Remove the driveshaft as described in Section 5.

2 Clean away external dirt and grease, release the bellows retaining clips and slide both bellows toward the centre of the driveshaft.

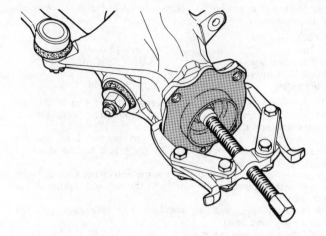

Fig. 8.12 Removing the driveshaft from the hub using a puller (Sec 5)

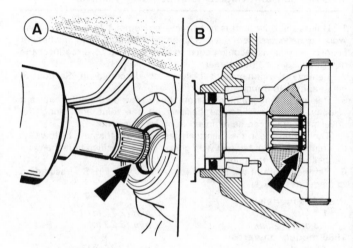

Fig. 8.13 Refitting driveshaft inner joint (Sec 5)

A Snap-ring in position on joint splines
B Snap-ring fully engaged with differential sun gear

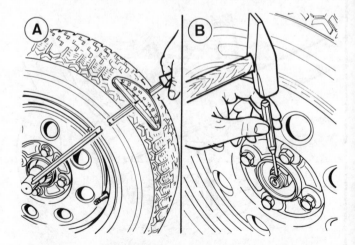

Fig. 8.14 Tighten driveshaft retaining nut to specified torque (A) and stake into driveshaft groove (B) (Sec 5)

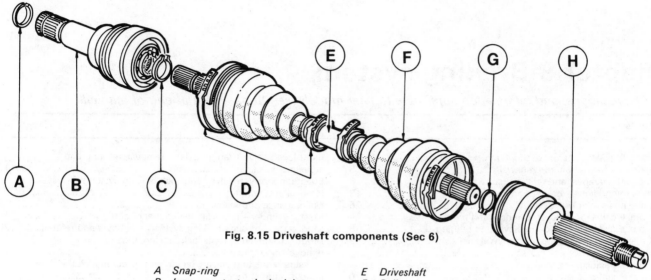

Fig. 8.15 Driveshaft components (Sec 6)

A Snap-ring
B Inner constant velocity joint
C Circlip
D Bellows retaining clips

E Driveshaft
F Bellows
G Circlip
H Outer constant velocity joint

3 To remove the outer constant velocity joint, wipe away enough grease to expose the retaining circlip. Using circlip pliers extract the circlip and withdraw the joint from the driveshaft. Remove the bellows.

4 If the inner constant velocity joint is of the ball and cage type remove it in the same way as for the outer joint.

5 If the inner constant velocity joint is of the tripod type (Fig. 8.16) withdraw the outer member then extract the circlip and withdraw the spider, complete with roller cups, from the driveshaft. Remove the bellows.

6 With the driveshaft dismantled, wipe away as much of the old grease as possible using rags only. Do not use any solvents.

7 On the ball and cage type joints move the internal parts of the joint around and check for signs of scoring, pitting and wear ridges on the balls, ball tracks and ball cage. If wear is evident or if the components move with very little resistance and rattle, then a new joint should be obtained.

8 On the tripod type joints check for signs of scoring, pitting and wear ridges on the roller cups and tracks of the outer member. Also check the roller cups for smooth operation and check the fit of the cups in the outer member. Renew the joint if wear is evident.

9 Check for wear of the constant velocity joint and driveshaft splines and check for side play with the joint temporarily assembled onto the driveshaft. Renew any parts as necessary.

10 Before reassembly obtain new rubber bellows and retaining clips for each dismantled joint along with the correct quantity of the specified grease.

11 Reassemble the driveshaft by reversing the dismantling operations. Use new circlips if necessary to retain the joints and pack the joints thoroughly with the specified grease. When refitting the bellows set

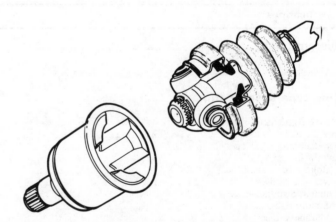

Fig. 8.16 Tripod type inner constant velocity joint (Sec 6)

their length and secure with the clips in accordance with the information contained in Section 3 or 4 depending on which joint (inner or outer) is being worked on.

12 Refit the driveshaft as described in Section 5. After fitting ensure that the crimped portion of the outer joint bellows clip does not foul the hub carrier as the driveshaft is rotated.

7 Fault diagnosis – driveshafts

Symptom	Reason(s)
Vibration and/or noise on turns	Lack of lubricant in constant velocity joint
	Worn outer constant velocity joint
Vibration when accelerating or on overrun	Worn inner constant velocity joint
	Bent or distorted driveshaft
Noise on taking up drive	Worn driveshaft or constant velocity joint splines
	Loose driveshaft retaining nut
	Worn constant velocity joints

See also Fault diagnosis – suspension and steering

Chapter 9 Braking system

For modifications, and information applicable to later models, see Supplement at end of manual

Contents

Specifications

System type	Diagonally split dual circuit, hydraulic with pressure regulating valve to rear brakes. Servo assistance and anti-lock braking system as standard or optional equipment according to model. Cable-operated handbrake on rear brakes
Fluid type/specification	Brake fluid to Ford specification SAM-6C 9103-A (Duckhams Universal Brake and Clutch Fluid)

Front brakes
Type	Solid or ventilated disc with single piston sliding calipers
Disc diameter	239.45 mm (9.43 in)
Disc thickness:	
Solid disc	10.0 mm (0.39 in)
Ventilated disc	24.0 mm (0.94 in)
Minimum disc thickness:	
Solid disc	8.7 mm (0.34 in)
Ventilated disc	22.7 mm (0.89 in)
Maximum disc run-out	0.15 mm (0.006 in)
Minimum disc pad thickness	1.5 mm (0.06 in)

Rear brakes
Type	Self-adjusting single leading shoe drum
Drum diameter:	
Standard hub/drum	180.0 mm (7.1 in)
Van, XR3i, RS Turbo and certain 1.6 litre models	203.2 mm (8.0 in)
Wheel cylinder diameter	17.78 mm, 19.05 mm or 22.2 mm (0.70 in, 0.75 in or 0.87 in) according to model – see text
Minimum brake shoe lining thickness	1.0 mm (0.4 in)

Torque wrench settings
	Nm	lbf ft
Caliper piston housing to anchor bracket	20 to 25	15 to 18
Caliper anchor bracket to hub carrier	50 to 66	37 to 49
Rear brake backplate bolts	45 to 55	33 to 40
Brake pressure regulating valve mounting bolts	20 to 25	15 to 18
Light laden valve to mounting bracket	20 to 25	15 to 18
Hydraulic unions	12 to 15	9 to 11
Master cylinder to servo	21 to 26	15 to 19
Modulator pivot bolt (ABS)	22 to 28	16 to 21
Modulator adjuster bolt (ABS)	22 to 28	16 to 21
Modulator drivebelt cover (ABS)	8 to 11	6 to 8
Load apportioning valve adjusting bracket nuts (ABS)	21 to 29	15 to 21
Load apportioning valve to mounting bracket (ABS)	21 to 29	15 to 21
Rear suspension arm inner mounting nuts	70 to 90	52 to 66
Front suspension lower arm balljoint pinch-bolt	48 to 60	35 to 44
Tie-rod balljoint nut	57 to 68	42 to 50

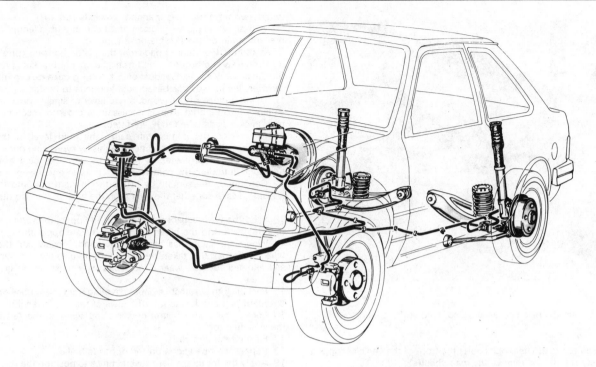

Fig. 9.1 General layout of the braking system as used on Saloon and Estate models (Sec 1)

1 General description

The braking system is of the dual circuit hydraulic type with disc brakes at the front and drum brakes at the rear. A diagonally split dual circuit hydraulic system is employed in which each circuit operates one front and one diagonally opposite rear brake from a tandem master cylinder. Under normal conditions both circuits operate in unison; however, in the event of hydraulic failure in one circuit, full braking force will still be available at two wheels. A pressure regulating valve on Saloon and Estate models, and a light laden valve on Van models is incorporated in the rear brake hydraulic circuit. The valve regulates the pressure applied to each rear brake and reduces the possibility of the rear wheels locking under heavy braking.

The front brakes utilize solid or ventilated discs according to model and are operated by single piston sliding type calipers. At the rear, leading and trailing shoes are operated by twin piston wheel cylinders and are self-adjusting by footbrake application. A cable-operated handbrake provides an independent mechanical means of rear brake operation.

From 1986 onwards an anti-lock braking system is available as standard or optional equipment according to model. Further information on this system will be found in later Sections of this Chapter.

2 Maintenance and inspection

1   At weekly intervals, check the fluid level in the translucent reservoir on the master cylinder. The fluid will drop very slowly indeed over a period of time to compensate for lining wear, but any sudden drop in level, or the need for frequent topping-up should be investigated immediately.

2   Always top up with hydraulic fluid which meets the specified standard and has been left in an airtight container. Hydraulic fluid is hygroscopic (absorbs moisture from the atmosphere) and must not be stored in an open container. Do not shake the tin prior to topping-up. Fluids of different makes can be intermixed provided they all meet the specification.

3   Inspect the thickness of the friction linings on the disc pads and brake shoes as described in the following Sections, at the intervals specified in Routine Maintenance.

4   The rigid and flexible hydraulic pipes and hoses should be inspected for leaks or damage regularly. Although the rigid lines are plastic-coated in order to preserve them against corrosion, check for damage which may have occurred through flying stones, careless jacking or the traversing of rough ground.

5   Bend the hydraulic flexible hoses sharply with the fingers and examine the surface of the hose for signs of cracking or perishing of the rubber. Renew if evident.

6   Renew the brake fluid at the specified intervals and examine all rubber components (including master cylinder and piston seals) with a critical eye, renewing where necessary.

3 Front disc pads – inspection and renewal

1   At the intervals specified in Routine Maintenance, place a mirror between the roadwheel and the caliper and check the thickness of the friction material of the disc pads. If the material has worn down to the specified minimum or less, the pads must be renewed as an axle set (four pads).

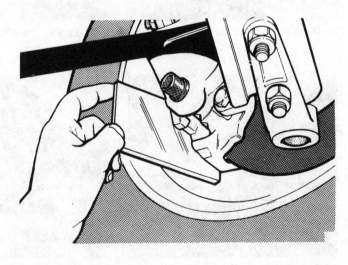

Fig. 9.2 Checking front disc pad wear using a mirror (Sec 3)

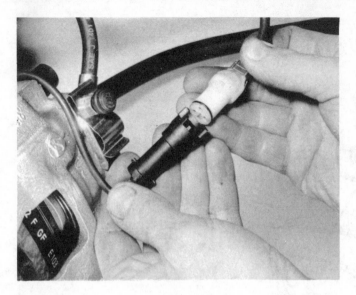

3.3 Disconnect the disc pad wear sensor lead at the connector

2   Slacken the roadwheel bolts, raise the front of the vehicle, support with safety stands and remove the roadwheel(s).
3   Where fitted, disengage the brake pad wear sensor from its retaining clip (beneath the bleed screw) and disconnect the lead connector (photo).
4   Using a screwdriver, prise free the retaining clip from the caliper (photo).
5   Using a 7 mm Allen key, unscrew the bolts until they can be

withdrawn from the caliper anchor brackets (photos).
6   Withdraw the piston housing and tie it up with a length of wire to prevent strain on the flexible hose (photo).
7   Withdraw the inboard pad from the piston housing (photo).
8   Withdraw the outboard pad from the anchor bracket (photo).
9   Clean away all residual dust or dirt, **taking care not to inhale the dust** as, being asbestos based, it is injurious to health.
10 Using a piece of flat wood, a tyre lever or similar, push the piston squarely into its bore. This is necessary in order to accommodate the new thicker pads when they are fitted.
11 Depressing the piston will cause the fluid level in the master cylinder reservoir to rise, so anticipate this by syphoning out some fluid using an old hydrometer or poultry baster. Take care not to drip hydraulic fluid onto the paintwork, it acts as an effective paint stripper.
12 Commence reassembly by fitting the inboard pad into the piston housing. Make sure that the spring on the back of the pad fits into the piston.
13 Feed the wear sensor wire through the opening in the caliper and then reattach it to the bleed screw clip (where applicable).
14 Where the cable has become unwound, loosely coil the surplus wire so that slack is taken out yet enough flexibility (25 mm/1 in) is still allowed for pad wear. The coiled wire must on no account be stretched.
15 Peel back the protective paper covering from the surface of the new outboard pad and locate it in the jaws of the caliper anchor bracket.
16 Locate the caliper piston housing and screw in the Allen bolts to the specified torque.
17 Fit the retaining clip.
18 Repeat the operations on the opposite brake.
19 Apply the footbrake hard several times to position the pads against the disc and then check and top up the fluid in the master cylinder reservoir.
20 Fit the roadwheel(s) and lower the vehicle.
21 Avoid heavy braking (if possible) for the first hundred miles or so when new pads have been fitted. This is to allow them to bed in and reach full efficiency.

3.4 Disc pad retaining clip

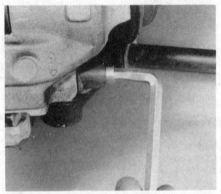

3.5A Unscrew the caliper bolt using an Allen key ...

3.5B ... and withdraw the bolt from the anchor bracket

3.6 Withdraw the caliper piston housing

3.7 Removing the inboard pad from the piston housing ...

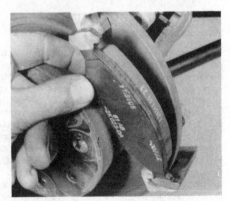

3.8 ... and the outboard pad from the anchor bracket

Fig. 9.3 Disc pad wear sensor connector (A) clipped to bleed screw (Sec 3)

4 Front brake caliper – removal, overhaul and refitting

1   Proceed as described in paragraphs 2 to 9 in the previous Section.

2   Disconnect the brake flexible hose from the caliper. This can be carried out in one of two ways. Either disconnect the flexible hose from the rigid hydraulic pipeline at the support bracket by unscrewing the union, or, once the caliper is detached, hold the end fitting of the hose in an open-ended spanner and unscrew the caliper from the hose. Do not allow the hose to twist, and plug its end after caliper removal.

3   Brush away all external dirt and pull off the piston dust-excluding cover.

4   Apply air pressure to the fluid inlet hole and eject the piston. Only low air pressure is needed for this, such as is produced by a foot-operated tyre pump.

5   Using a sharp pointed instrument, pick out the piston seal from the groove in the cylinder bore. Do not scratch the surface of the bore.

6   Examine the surfaces of the piston and the cylinder bore. If they are scored or show evidence of metal-to-metal rubbing, then a new piston housing will be required. Where the components are in good condition, discard the seal and obtain a repair kit.

7   Wash the internal components in clean brake hydraulic fluid or methylated spirit only, nothing else.

Fig. 9.4 Exploded view of the front brake caliper (Sec 4)

A   Piston housing-to-anchor bracket bolts
B   Anchor bracket
C   Retaining clip
D   Disc pad
E   Dust excluder
F   Piston seal
G   Piston
H   Piston housing
J   Disc pad

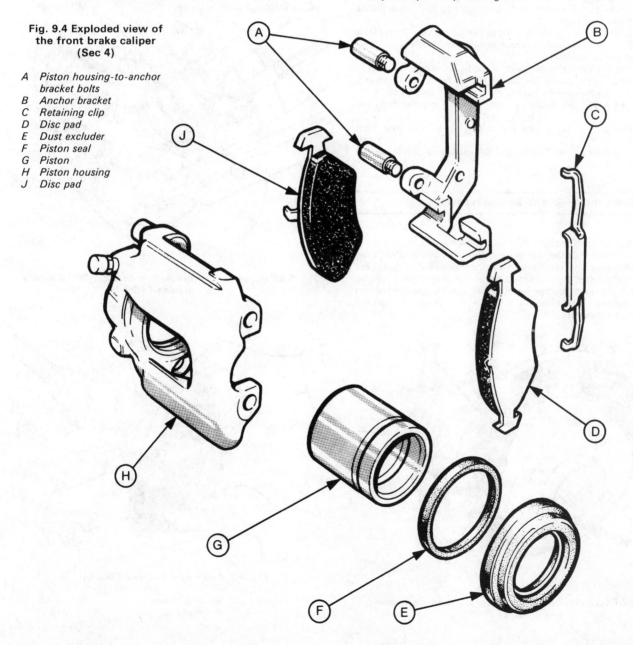

8   Using the fingers, manipulate the new seal into its groove in the cylinder bore.

9   Dip the piston in clean hydraulic fluid and insert it squarely into its bore.

10 Connect the rubber dust excluder between the piston and the piston housing, and then depress the piston fully.

11 Refit the caliper by reversing the removal operations, referring to paragraphs 12 to 17 in the previous Section.

12 Reconnect the brake hose to the caliper, taking care not to distort it. When secured it must not interfere with any of the adjacent steering or suspension components.

13 Bleed the brake hydraulic circuit as given in Section 12 or 24, as applicable, then refit the roadwheel(s) and lower the vehicle.

5   Front brake disc – inspection, removal and refitting

1   Fully apply the handbrake then loosen the front roadwheel bolts. Raise and support the front of the vehicle on safety stands and remove the roadwheel(s).

2   Examine the surface of the disc. If it is deeply grooved or scored or if any small cracks are evident, it must either be refinished or renewed. Any refinishing must not reduce the thickness of the disc to below a certain minimum (see Specifications). Light scoring on a brake disc is normal and should be ignored.

3   If disc distortion is suspected, the disc can be checked for run-out using a dial gauge or feeler blades located between its face and a fixed point as the disc is rotated.

4   Where the run-out exceeds the specified figure, renew the disc.

5   To remove a disc, unbolt the caliper anchor bracket, withdraw it and tie it up to the suspension strut to avoid strain on the flexible hose.

6   Extract the small disc retaining screw and pull the disc from the hub.

7   If a new disc is being installed, clean its surface free from preservative.

8   Refit the caliper anchor bracket and the roadwheel and lower the vehicle to the floor.

6   Rear brake shoes – inspection and renewal

Carburettor engine models except Van variants

1   Due to the fact that the rear brake drums are combined with the hubs, which makes removal of the drums more complicated than is the case with detachable drums, inspection of the shoe linings can be carried out at the specified intervals by prising out the small inspection plug from the brake backplate and observing the linings through the hole using a mirror (photo).

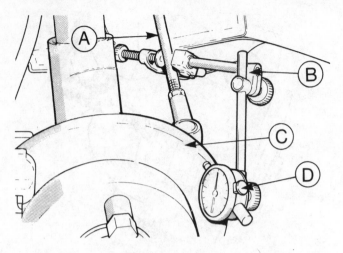

Fig. 9.5 Checking brake disc run-out (Sec 5)

A   Steering tie-rod   C   Brake disc
B   Dial gauge support fixture   D   Dial gauge

Fig. 9.6 Caliper anchor bracket-to-hub carrier retaining bolts – arrowed (Sec 5)

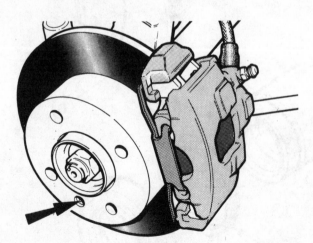

Fig. 9.7 Brake disc retaining screw location – arrowed (Sec 5)

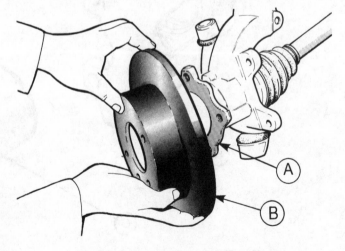

Fig. 9.8 Brake disc removal (Sec 5)

A   Hub carrier
B   Brake disc

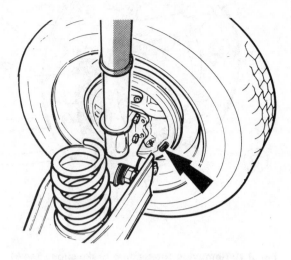

Fig. 9.9 Brake shoe viewing hole location in backplate – arrowed (Sec 6)

6.1 Checking rear brake lining wear with a mirror

2   A minimum thickness of friction material must always be observed on the shoes. If it is worn down to this level, renew the shoes.

3   Do not attempt to re-line shoes yourself but always obtain factory re-lined shoes.

4   Renew the shoes in an axle set (four shoes), even if only one is worn to the minimum.

5   Slacken the roadwheel bolts, raise the rear of the vehicle and support it securely. Remove the roadwheels.

6   Release the handbrake fully.

7   Tap off the hub dust cap, remove the split pin, nut retainer, nut and thrust washer (photos).

8   Pull the hub/drum towards you and then push it back enough to be able to take the outer bearing from the spindle (photo).

9   Remove the hub/drum and brush out any dust taking care not to inhale it (photo).

10 Remove the shoe hold-down spring from the leading shoe (photo). Do this by gripping the dished washer with a pair of pliers, depressing it and turning it through 90°. Remove the washer, spring

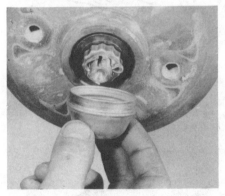

6.7A Remove the rear hub dust cap ...

6.7B ... extract the split pin and nut retainer ...

6.7C ... then unscrew the hub nut ...

6.7D ... and remove the thrust washer

6.8 Remove the hub outer bearing ...

6.9 ... followed by the hub/drum assembly

6.10 Removing the brake shoe hold-down washer and spring

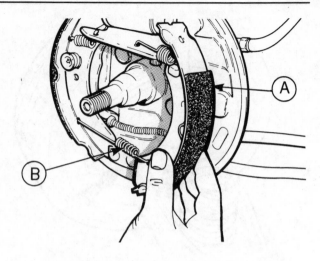

Fig. 9.10 Removing the leading brake shoe (Sec 6)

A   *Leading shoe*
B   *Lower spring*

and the hold-down post. Note the locations of the leading and trailing shoes and the cut-back of the linings at the leading ends.

11 Pull the leading shoe outwards and upwards away from the backplate.

12 Twist the shoe to disengage it from the return springs and adjuster strut. On models with the later type rear brake assembly (Fig. 9.14) it will be necessary to move the auto adjuster to maximum adjustment to disengage the shoe from the strut. Make a note of the return spring arrangement and hole locations if in any doubt.

13 Remove the trailing shoe in a similar way, at the same time withdrawing the adjuster strut.

14 Release the end of the handbrake cable from the lever on the shoe.

15 Disconnect the trailing shoe from the adjuster strut by pulling the shoe outwards and twisting the shoe spring.

16 Before reassembly, sparingly lubricate the brake shoe contact areas on the backplate, fixed abutment and wheel cylinder pistons with a high melting-point brake grease.

17 Commence reassembly by installing the trailing shoe. Do this by engaging the handbrake lever return spring to the shoe. Hook the strut onto the spring and lever it into position. Set the strut self-adjusting mechanism to its contracted position (early type) or maximum position (later type).

18 Locate the webs of the trailing shoe on the wheel cylinder and the fixed abutment, making sure that the lower end of the handbrake lever is correctly located on the face of the plastic plunger and not trapped behind it.

19 Fit the trailing shoe hold-down post and spring. Hold the leading shoe in position.

20 Connect the larger shoe return spring at the lower (abutment) position between both shoes.

21 Holding the leading shoe almost at right-angles to the backplate, connect the spring between it and the strut and then engage the bottom end of the shoe behind the abutment retainer plate.

22 Swivel the shoe towards the backplate so that the cut-out in its web passes over the quadrant lever. Fit the shoe hold-down post, spring and washer.

23 Centralise the shoes within the backplate by tapping them if necessary with the hand, then fit the hub/drum and slide the outer bearing onto the spindle.

24 Fit the thrust washer and hub nut finger tight only.

25 Tighten the hub nut to a torque of between 20 and 25 Nm (15 and 18 lbf ft), at the same time rotating the roadwheel in an anti-clockwise direction.

26 Unscrew the nut one half a turn and then tighten it only finger tight.

27 Fit the nut retainer so that two of its slots line up with the split pin hole. Insert a new split pin, bending the end **around** the nut, **not** over the end of the stub axle.

28 Tap the dust cap into position.

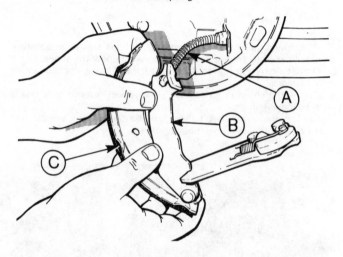

Fig. 9.11 Removing the handbrake cable from the trailing brake shoe (Sec 6)

A   *Handbrake cable*   B   *Lever*   C   *Trailing shoe*

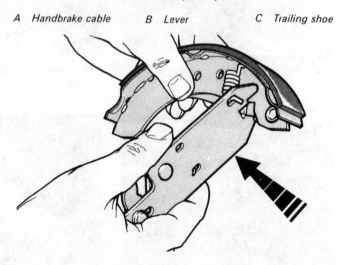

Fig. 9.12 Separating the trailing brake shoe from the adjuster strut (Sec 6)

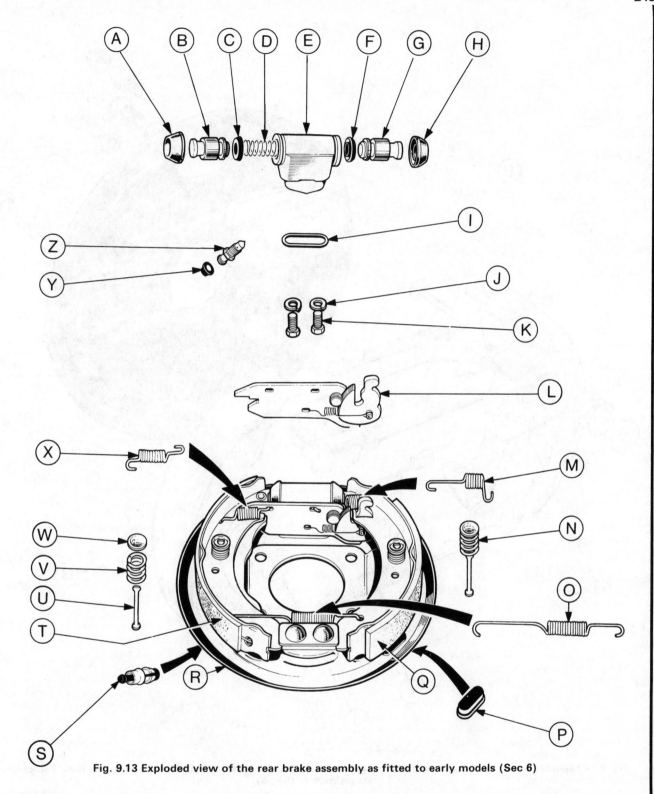

Fig. 9.13 Exploded view of the rear brake assembly as fitted to early models (Sec 6)

A Dust excluder	H Dust excluder	O Return spring	V Spring
B Piston	I Gasket	P Inspection hole plug	W Dished washer
C Seal	J Spring washer	Q Leading shoe	X Return spring
D Spring	K Mounting bolt	R Backplate	Y Dust cover
E Cylinder body	L Adjuster strut	S Handbrake lever plunger	Z Bleed screw
F Seal	M Return spring	T Trailing shoe	
G Piston	N Hold-down spring	U Hold-down post	

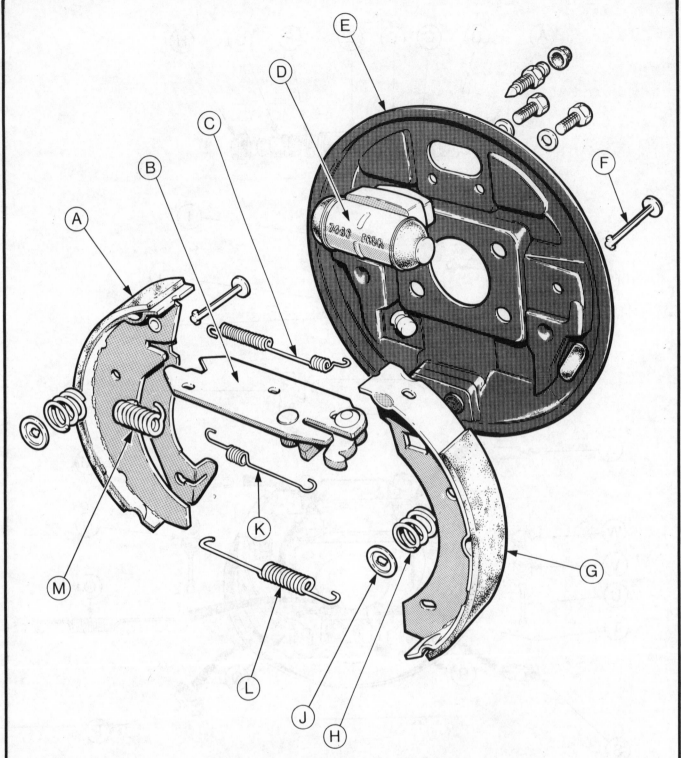

Fig. 9.14 Exploded view of the rear brake assembly as fitted to fuel-injected models, Van variants and later Saloon and Estate models (Sec 6)

A	Trailing shoe	E	Backplate	J	Dished washer
B	Adjuster strut	F	Hold-down post	K	Ratchet pawl spring
C	Spring	G	Leading shoe	L	Return spring
D	Wheel cylinder	H	Spring	M	Return spring

6.34 Removing the drum retaining screw on models with a separate brake drum

6.37A Brake shoe return spring and adjuster strut arrangement on Van, fuel-injected models and later Saloon and Estate models

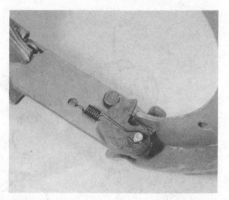

6.37B Automatic adjuster assembly on Van, fuel-injected models and later Saloon and Estate models

29 Refit the roadwheel and check that a small amount of hub bearing free play can be felt when the wheel is rocked at the top and bottom.
30 Depress the brake pedal fully several times to operate the self-adjusting mechanism then lower the car to the ground.
31 Recheck the tightness of the wheel bolts.

Fuel-injection engine models and Van variants
32 On these vehicles the brake drum is separate from the hub and can be removed without the need to remove the hub as well. The bearings will therefore not need to be readjusted during reassembly.
33 The brake shoe inspection and removal procedure is very similar to that described previously but note the following differences.
34 Before removing the drum unscrew the drum retaining screw (photo).
35 Disconnect the lower shoe return spring which bridges the shoes and then disconnect the handbrake cable from the lever.
36 Prise the shoes away from the lower pivot, twist them from the wheel cylinder and remove as an assembly.
37 With the shoes removed they can be separated from the strut. Note how the components are positioned before dismantling (photos).
38 Refitting is a reversal of the removal procedure.

7 Rear wheel cylinder – removal, overhaul and refitting

1   Remove the rear brake shoes, as described in the preceding Section.
2   Disconnect the fluid pipeline from the wheel cylinder and cap the end of the pipe to prevent loss of fluid. A bleed screw rubber dust cap is useful for this.
3   Unscrew the two bolts which hold the wheel cylinder to the brake backplate and remove the cylinder with sealing gasket.
4   Clean away external dirt and then pull off the dust-excluding covers.
5   The pistons and seals will probably shake out. If they do not, apply air pressure (from a tyre pump) at the inlet hole to eject them.
6   Examine the surfaces of the pistons and the cylinder bores for scoring or metal-to-metal rubbing areas. If evident, renew the complete cylinder assembly.
7   If the cylinder is to be renewed note that any one of three different sizes may be fitted according to model and year. The wheel cylinders are identified by a letter stamped on the rear face (Fig. 9.17) which corresponds to the following:

    Letter 'T' = 22.2 mm diameter cylinder
    Letter 'L' = 19.05 mm diameter cylinder
    Letter 'H' = 17.78 mm diameter cylinder

Ensure that the new cylinder obtained is the same as the one removed and more importantly, is the same as the cylinder on the other rear brake.
8   Where the components are in good condition, discard the rubber seals and dust excluders and obtain a repair kit.
9   Any cleaning should be done using hydraulic fluid or methylated spirit – nothing else.

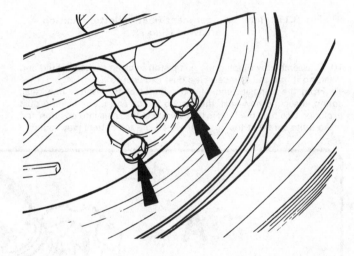

Fig. 9.15 Rear wheel cylinder retaining bolts – arrowed (Sec 7)

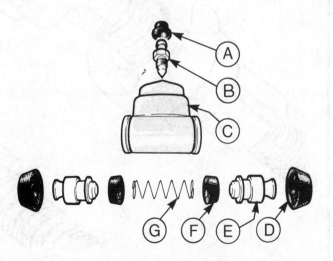

Fig. 9.16 Exploded view of the rear wheel cylinder (Sec 7)

A   Dust cap   E   Piston
B   Bleed screw   F   Piston seal
C   Wheel cylinder G   Spring
D   Dust excluder

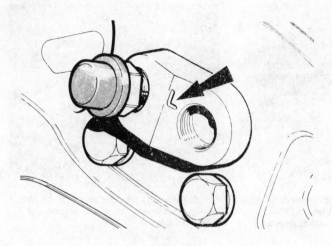

**Fig. 9.17 Wheel cylinder identification letter location –
arrowed (Sec 7)**

10 Reassemble by dipping the first piston in clean hydraulic fluid and inserting it into the cylinder. Fit a dust excluder to it.
11 From the opposite end of the cylinder body, insert a new seal, spring, a second new seal, the second piston and the remaining dust excluder. Use only the fingers to manipulate the seals into position and make quite sure that the lips of the seals are the correct way round.

12 Bolt the wheel cylinder to the backplate, reconnect the fluid line and refit the shoes (Section 6).
13 Refit the brake drum and roadwheel and lower the vehicle to the floor.
14 Bleed the brake hydraulic system as described in Section 12 or 24 as applicable.

8 Brake drum – inspection and renewal

1 Whenever a brake drum is removed, brush out dust from it, **taking care not to inhale it** as it contains asbestos and is injurious to health.
2 Examine the internal friction surface of the drum. If deeply scored, or so worn that the drum has become pocketed to the width of the shoes, then the drums must be renewed.
3 Regrinding is not recommended as the internal diameter will no longer be compatible with the shoe lining contact diameter.

9 Handbrake – adjustment

1 Adjustment of the handbrake is normally automatic by means of the self-adjusting mechanism working on the rear brake shoes.
2 However, due to cable stretch, occasional inspection of the handbrake adjusters is recommended. Adjustment must be carried out if the movement of the control lever becomes excessive.
3 Chock the front wheels then fully release the handbrake.
4 Raise and support the vehicle at the rear with safety stands.
5 Grip each adjustment plunger, one located on each rear brake backplate (photo), and move it in and out.

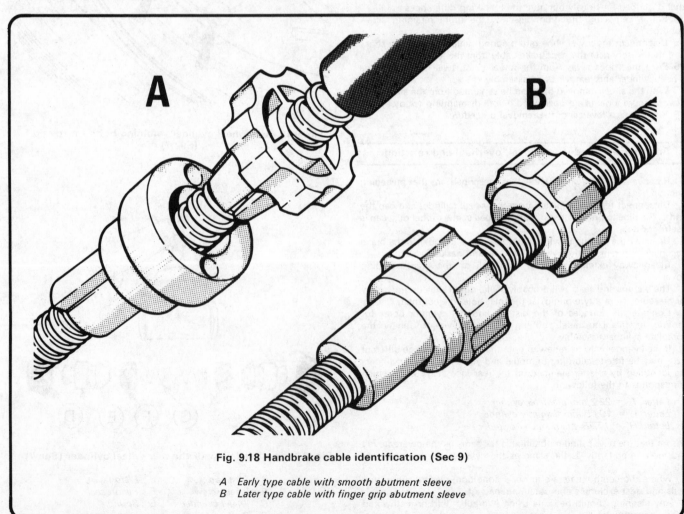

Fig. 9.18 Handbrake cable identification (Sec 9)

A Early type cable with smooth abutment sleeve
B Later type cable with finger grip abutment sleeve

9.5 Handbrake adjustment plunger location (arrowed) on backplate

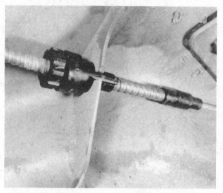

9.8A Early type handbrake cable adjuster with smooth abutment sleeve

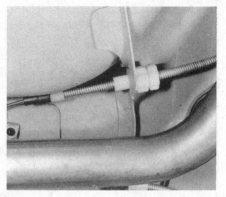

9.8B Later type handbrake cable adjuster with finger grip abutment sleeve

6   If the total movement of both plungers added together is between 0.5 and 2.0 mm (0.02 and 0.08 in) then adjustment of the handbrake is satisfactory. If the plunger movement is not as specified proceed as follows.

7   Two cable types are used on Escort models according to year of manufacture and it is necessary to identify the type being worked on before proceeding.

8   Locate the cable adjuster which is located just forward of the fuel tank. If the cable adjuster nut has finger grips but the abutment sleeve is smooth (photo), proceed as follows. If both the cable adjuster and abutment sleeve have finger grips, refer to paragraph 14 (Fig. 9.18) (photo).

9   Make sure that the abutment sleeve on the cable is fully engaged in its bracket slot. Unlock the adjusting nut by levering between the shoulders of the nut and the sleeve.

10 Now turn the adjuster nut to eliminate slackness from the cable so that it is just possible to rotate the adjustment plungers on the brake backplates.

11 Apply the handbrake fully to seat the adjusting nut against its sleeve.

12 If adjustment of the cable does not alter the plunger movement then the handbrake cable is likely to be binding or seized or the brake mechanism is at fault.

13 On completion lower the car to the ground.

14 If the cable adjuster and abutment sleeve both have finger grips check to see if a nylon locking pin is used to lock the adjusting nut in position (photo). If so remove the locking pin using pliers. Note that a

new pin will be needed after adjustment.

15 Slacken the adjusting nut then apply the footbrake hard several times to ensure full self-adjustment of the brake shoes.

16 Turn the abutment sleeve as necessary until the total movement of both adjustment plungers added together is between 0.5 and 2.0 mm (0.02 and 0.08 in).

17 Tighten the adjusting nut against the abutment sleeve as tight as possible by hand (2 clicks) then tighten it by a further 2 clicks (maximum) using a suitable wrench.

18 Where applicable fit a new locking pin and tap it into place.

19 On completion lower the car to the ground.

10 Handbrake cables – renewal

1   Chock the front wheels, then fully release the handbrake.

2   Raise and support the vehicle at the rear with axle stands.

Primary cable

3   Extract the spring clip and clevis pin and disconnect the primary cable from the equaliser (photo).

4   Working inside the vehicle, disconnect the cable from the hand-brake control lever, again by removal of clip and pin. Drift out the cable guide to the rear and withdraw the cable through the floorpan.

5   Refitting is a reversal of removal. Adjust the handbrake, if necessary, as described in Section 9.

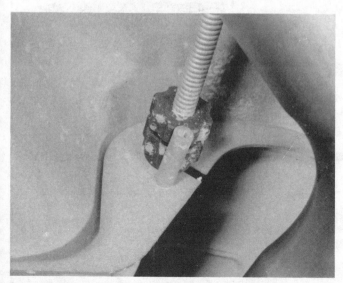

9.14 Handbrake cable adjuster nylon locking pin

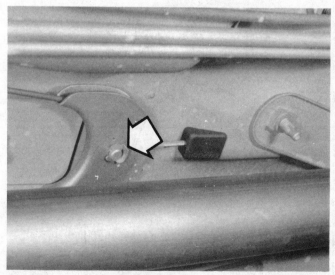

10.3 Primary cable-to-equaliser clevis pin and spring clip (arrowed)

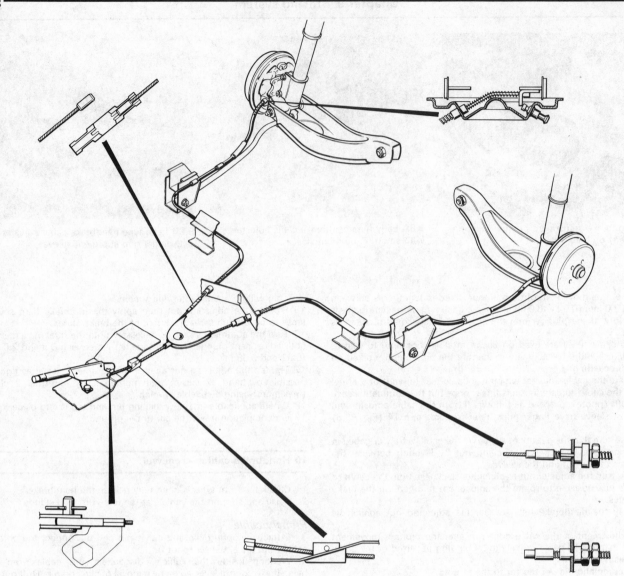

Fig. 9.19 Handbrake cable layout (Secs 10 and 11)

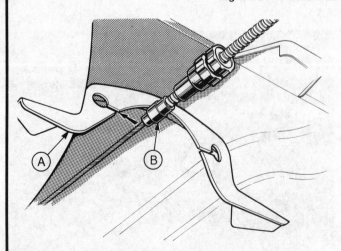

Fig. 9.20 Removing handbrake cable abutment sleeve from the body guide (Sec 10)

A *Body guide*   B *Secondary cable*

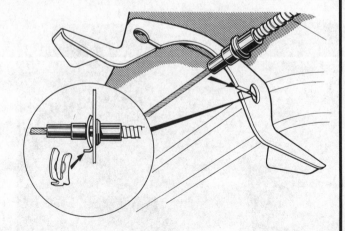

Fig. 9.21 Handbrake cable connector spring clip removal (Sec 10)

Secondary cable

6   Using the procedure described in Section 9, slacken the cable adjusting nut so that the abutment sleeve can be disengaged from its body guide.

7   Release the cable connector from its body guide by extracting the spring clip and passing the inner cable through the slit in the guide.

8   Now disconnect the cable from its body guide on the right-hand side of the vehicle.

9   Separate the cable assembly/equaliser from the primary cable by extracting the spring clip and clevis pin.

10 Release the cable from the body guides.

11 Remove the rear roadwheels and the brake drums.

12 Release the shoe hold-down spring so that the shoe can be swivelled and the handbrake lever unclipped from the relay lever.

13 Remove the cable ends through the brake backplate and withdraw the complete cable assembly from the vehicle.

14 Refitting is a reversal of removal. Grease the cable groove in the equaliser and adjust the handbrake, as described in Section 9.

11 Handbrake lever – removal and refitting

1   Chock the front wheels, raise and support the vehicle at the rear using stands then release the handbrake.

2   Working underneath, extract the spring clip and clevis pin and disconnect the primary cable from the equaliser.

3   From inside the car detach the handbrake warning switch.

4   Disconnect the cable from the handbrake lever by extracting the clip and pin.

5   Unscrew the lever securing bolts and remove the lever.

6   Refitting is the reverse sequence to removal. On completion adjust the handbrake cable, if necessary, as described in Section 9.

12 Hydraulic system – bleeding (conventional braking system)

Note: *On cars equipped with the Anti-lock Braking System, refer to Section 24*

1   This is not a routine operation but will be required after any component in the system has been removed and refitted or any part of the hydraulic system has been 'opened'. Where an operation has only affected one circuit of the hydraulic system, then bleeding will normally only be required to that circuit (front and rear diagonally opposite). If the master cylinder or the pressure regulating valve have been disconnected and reconnected, then the complete system must be bled.

2   When bleeding the brake hydraulic system on a Van, tie the light laden valve actuating lever to the right-hand rear roadspring so that it is in the fully open position. This will ensure full fluid flow during the bleeding operations.

3   One of three methods can be used to bleed the system.

Bleeding – two-man method

4   Gather together a clean jar and a length of rubber or plastic bleed tubing which will fit the bleed screw tightly. The help of an assistant will be required.

5   Take care not to spill fluid onto the paintwork as it will act as a paint stripper. If any is spilled, wash if off at once with cold water.

6   Clean around the bleed screw on the front right-hand caliper and attach the bleed tube to the screw.

7   Check that the master cylinder reservoir is topped up and then destroy the vacuum in the brake servo (where fitted) by giving several applications of the brake foot pedal.

8   Immerse the open end of the bleed tube in the jar, which should contain two or three inches of hydraulic fluid. The jar should be positioned about 300 mm (12.0 in) above the bleed nipple to prevent any possibility of air entering the system down the threads of the bleed screw when it is slackened.

9   Open the bleed screw half a turn and have your assistant depress the brake pedal slowly to the floor and then, after the bleed screw is retightened, quickly remove his foot to allow the pedal to return unimpeded. Repeat the procedure.

10 Observe the submerged end of the tube in the jar. When air bubbles cease to appear, tighten the bleed screw when the pedal is being held fully down by your assistant.

11 Top up the fluid reservoir. It must be kept topped up throughout the bleeding operations. If the connecting holes to the master cylinder are exposed at any time due to low fluid level, then air will be drawn into the system and work will have to start all over again.

12 Repeat the operations on the left-hand rear brake, the left-hand front and the right-hand rear brake in that order (assuming that the whole system is being bled).

13 On completion, remove the bleed tube. Discard the fluid which has been bled from the system unless it is required for bleed jar purposes, never use it for filling the system.

Bleeding – with one-way valve

14 There are a number of one-man brake bleeding kits currently available from motor accessory shops. It is recommended that one of

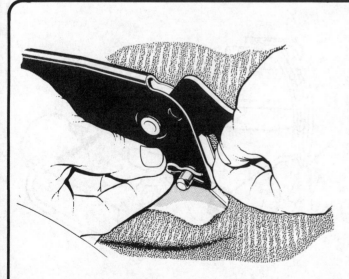

**Fig. 9.22 Removing handbrake lever clevis pin and clip
(Sec 11)**

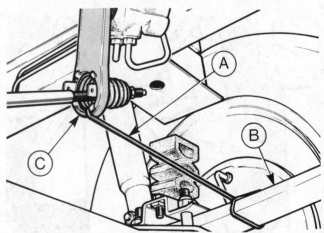

**Fig. 9.23 Light laden valve retained in open position –
Van models (Sec 12)**

A   Wire   C   Actuating lever
B   Roadspring

these kits should be used whenever possible as they greatly simplify the bleeding operation and also reduce the risk of expelled air or fluid being drawn back into the system.

15 Connect the outlet tube of the bleeder device to the bleed screw and then open the screw half a turn. Depress the brake pedal to the floor and slowly release it. The one-way valve in the device will prevent expelled air from returning to the system at the completion of each stroke. Repeat this operation until clean hydraulic fluid, free from air bubbles, can be seen coming through the tube. Tighten the bleed screw and remove the tube.

16 Repeat the procedure on the remaining bleed nipples in the order described in paragraph 12. Remember to keep the master cylinder reservoir full.

Bleeding – with pressure bleeding kit

17 These too are available from motor accessory shops and are usually operated by air pressure from the spare tyre.

18 By connecting a pressurised container to the master cylinder fluid reservoir, bleeding is then carried out by simply opening each bleed screw in turn and allowing the fluid to run out, rather like turning on a tap, until no air bubbles are visible in the fluid being expelled.

19 Using this system, the large reserve of fluid provides a safeguard against air being drawn into the master cylinder during the bleeding operations.

20 This method is particularly effective when bleeding 'difficult' systems or when bleeding the entire system at time of routine fluid renewal.

All systems

21 On completion of bleeding, top up the fluid level to the mark. Check the feel of the brake pedal, which should be firm and free from any 'sponginess' which would indicate air still being present in the system.

22 On Van models release the light laden valve actuating lever.

13 Master cylinder – removal, overhaul and refitting

1 Disconnect the leads from the level warning switch in the reservoir cap. Remove the cap.

2 Syphon out as much fluid as possible from the master cylinder reservoir using an old battery hydrometer or a poultry baster. Do not drip the fluid onto the paintwork as it will act as an effective paint stripper.

3 Disconnect the pipelines from the master cylinder by unscrewing the unions. Additionally on models equipped with the anti-lock braking system, release the clips and disconnect the two modulator fluid return pipes.

4 On non-servo models release the retaining clip securing the master cylinder pushrod to the brake pedal.

5 Unbolt the master cylinder unit from the servo unit or bulkhead, as applicable, and withdraw it.

6 Clean away external dirt and then detach the fluid reservoir by tilting it sideways and gently pulling. Remove the two rubber seals.

7 Secure the master cylinder carefully in a vice fitted with jaw protectors.

8 Unscrew and remove the piston stop bolt.

9 Pull the dust excluder back and, using circlip pliers, extract the circlip which is now exposed.

10 Remove the pushrod, dust excluder and washer.

11 Withdraw the primary piston assembly, which will already have been partially ejected.

12 Tap the end of the master cylinder on a block of wood and eject the secondary piston assembly.

13 Examine the piston and cylinder bore surface for scoring or signs of metal-to-metal rubbing. If evident, renew the cylinder complete.

14 Where the components are in good condition, dismantle the primary piston by unscrewing the screw and removing the sleeve. Remove the spring, retainer, seal and shim. Prise the second seal from the piston.

15 Dismantle the secondary piston in a similar way.

16 Discard all seals and obtain a repair kit.

17 Cleaning of components should be done in brake hydraulic fluid or methylated spirit – nothing else.

18 Using the new seals from the repair kit, assemble the pistons, making sure that the seal lips are the correct way round.

19 Dip the piston assemblies in clean hydraulic fluid and enter them into the cylinder bore.

20 Fit the pushrod complete with new dust excluder and secure with a new circlip.

21 Engage the dust excluder with the master cylinder.

22 Depress the pushrod and screw in the stop bolt.

23 Locate the two rubber seals and push the fluid reservoir into position.

24 It is recommended that a small quantity of fluid is now poured into the reservoir and the pushrod operated several times to prime the unit.

25 Refit the master cylinder by reversing the removal operations.

26 Bleed the complete hydraulic system on completion of work (see Section 12, or 24 as applicable).

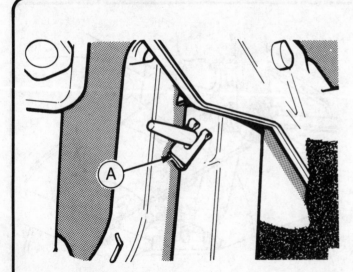

Fig. 9.24 Master cylinder push rod-to-pedal retaining clip (A) – non-servo models (Sec 13)

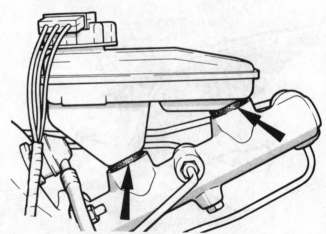

Fig. 9.25 Master cylinder reservoir rubber seals – arrowed (Sec 13)

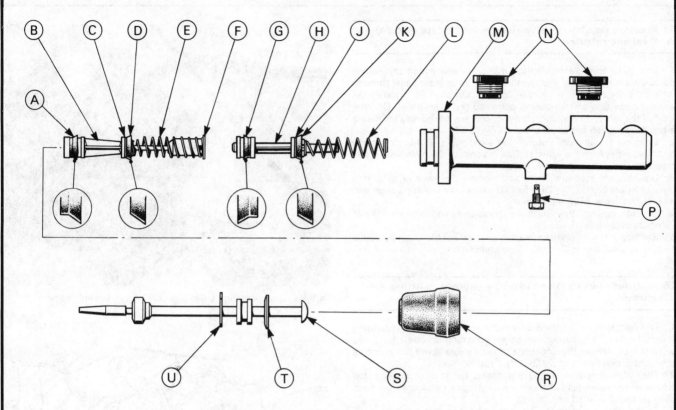

Fig. 9.26 Exploded view of the master cylinder (Sec 13)

A	Seal	F	Retainer
B	Primary piston	G	Seal
C	Shim	H	Secondary piston
D	Seal	J	Shim
E	Spring	K	Seal

L	Spring	S	Pushrod
M	Cylinder body	T	Washer
N	Reservoir seals	U	Circlip
P	Piston stop bolt		
R	Boot		

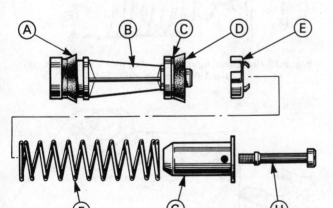

Fig. 9.27 Master cylinder primary piston components (Sec 13)

A	Seal	E	Retainer
B	Piston	F	Spring
C	Shim	G	Sleeve
D	Seal	H	Screw

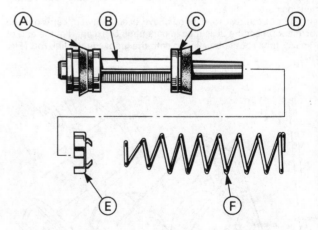

Fig. 9.28 Master cylinder secondary piston components (Sec 13)

A	Seal	D	Seal
B	Piston	E	Retainer
C	Shim	F	Spring

14 Pressure regulating valve (Saloon and Estate models) – removal and refitting

1   The brake pressure regulating valve is located within the engine compartment, just above the aperture in the wing inner panel through which the steering tie-rod passes (photo). On pre-1986 models the valves comprise a metal housing bolted to the inner panel. On later models the valves, one for each brake circuit, are individually located in a bracket attached to the inner panel (Fig. 9.30).
2   Unscrew the unions, noting their locations and disconnect the hydraulic pipes from the valve(s). Cap the ends of the pipes with bleed nipple dust caps to prevent fluid loss.
3   Unscrew the mounting bolts and remove the valve or mounting bracket as applicable. On later models extract the retaining clips and remove the valves from the bracket.
4   On both versions the valves are sealed units and only serviced as complete assemblies.
5   Refitting is the reverse sequence to removal but bleed the hydraulic system as described in Section 12 on completion.

15 Light laden valve (Van models) – removal, refitting and adjustment

1   The light laden valve used on Van models is a pressure regulating valve which reacts to suspension height according to vehicle load. The valve is mounted on the underside of the vehicle above the rear axle tube and is connected to the axle by a rod.
2   The valve should never be dismantled but it must be adjusted whenever the valve itself, the axle tube, spring or shock absorber have been removed, refitted or renewed.
3   Follow this adjustment procedure provided the original road-springs have been refitted, but when new valve linkage has been installed. Measure the dimension X (Fig. 9.33) and if necessary adjust the position of the nut to make the dimension between 10 and 12 mm (0.4 and 0.5 in). Rotate the spacer tube so that the dimension C (Fig. 9.34) is between 18.5 and 20.5 mm (0.73 and 0.81 in). Crimp the end of the spacer tube adjacent to the knurled section of the tube to prevent the tube from rotating.
4   If the original roadsprings have been refitted and also the original valve linkage, hold the threaded adjustment rod by means of its flats and turn the adjusting nut in either direction until the correct dimensions are obtained.
5   If one or both rear roadsprings have been renewed, carry out the adjustment procedure described in paragraph 3, except that the end of the spacer tube should be aligned with the groove in the link rod (Fig. 9.35).

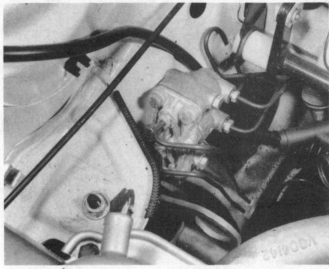

14.1 Pressure regulating valve location in engine compartment

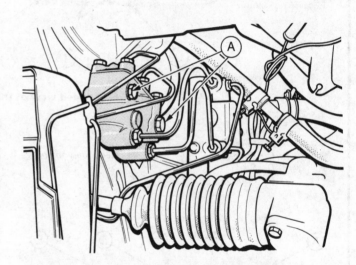

Fig. 9.29 Pressure regulating valve mounting bolts (A) – pre-1986 models (Sec 14)

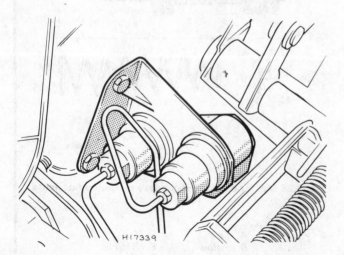

Fig. 9.30 Pressure regulating valves and mounting bracket – 1986 models onward (Sec 14)

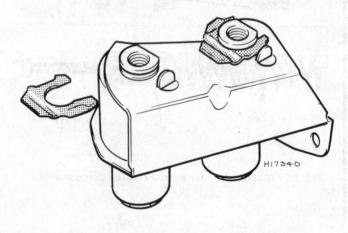

Fig. 9.31 Pressure regulating valve-to-bracket retaining clip – 1986 models onward (Sec 14)

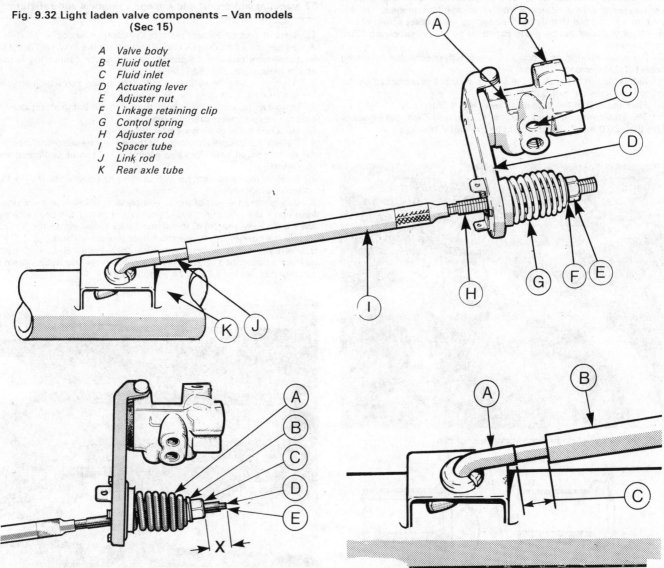

Fig. 9.32 Light laden valve components – Van models
(Sec 15)

A   Valve body
B   Fluid outlet
C   Fluid inlet
D   Actuating lever
E   Adjuster nut
F   Linkage retaining clip
G   Control spring
H   Adjuster rod
I   Spacer tube
J   Link rod
K   Rear axle tube

Fig. 9.33 Light laden valve adjustment diagram – Van
models (Sec 15)

A   Control spring   D   Threaded rod
B   Linkage retaining clip   E   Flats
C   Adjuster nut   X = 10 to 12 mm (0.4 to 0.5 in)

Fig. 9.34 Light laden valve linkage adjustment diagram with
original roadsprings – Van models (Sec 15)

A   Link rod   C = 18.5 to 20.5 mm (0.73 to 0.81 in)
B   Spacer tube

6   If the pressure regulating valve must be removed, first disconnect
the hydraulic pipelines from the valve and cap the pipes.
7   Unbolt the valve from its mounting bracket, lower the valve and
slide the spacer tube assembly off the link rod. Remove the link rod.
8   Refitting is a reversal of removal, but bleed the brakes (Section 12)
and adjust the valve as described above.

16 Hydraulic pipes and hoses – removal and refitting

1   Inspection has already been covered in Section 2 of this Chapter.
2   Always disconnect a flexible hose by prising out the spring anchor
clip from the support bracket (photo) and then, using two close-fitting
spanners, disconnect the rigid line from the flexible hose.
3   Once disconnected from the rigid pipe, the flexible hose may be
unscrewed from the caliper or wheel cylinder.
4   When reconnecting pipelines, or hose fittings, remember that all
union threads are to metric sizes. No copper washers are used at
unions and the seal is made at the swaged end of the pipe, so do not try
to wind a union in if it is tight yet still stands proud of the surface into
which it is screwed.

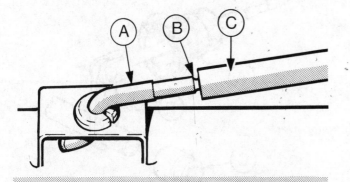

Fig. 9.35 Light laden valve linkage adjustment diagram with
new roadsprings – Van models (Sec 15)

A   Link rod   C   Spacer tube
B   Groove

5　A flexible hose must never be installed twisted, but a slight 'set' is permissible to give it clearance from an adjacent component. Do this by turning the hose slightly before inserting the bracket spring clip.
6　Rigid pipelines can be made to pattern by factors supplying brake components.
7　If you are making up a brake pipe yourself, observe the following essential requirements.
8　Before flaring the ends of the pipe, trim back the protective plastic coating by a distance of 5.0 mm (0.2 in).
9　Flare the end of the pipe as shown (Fig. 9.36).
10　The minimum pipe bend radius is 12.0 mm (0.5 in), but bends of less than 20.0 mm (0.8 in) should be avoided if possible.

16.2 Removing a flexible hose spring anchor clip

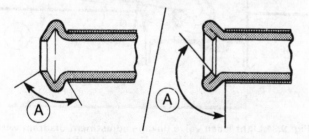

Fig. 9.36 Brake pipe flare (Sec 16)

A　Protective coating removed before flaring

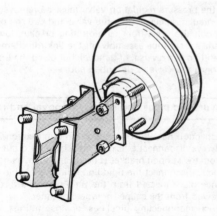

Fig. 9.37 Vacuum servo unit and mounting bracket (Sec 17)

17 Vacuum servo unit and linkage – removal and refitting

1　Refer to Section 13 and remove the master cylinder.
2　On fuel-injection models unclip and lift out the front section of the heater plenum chamber to provide access to the connecting linkage across the lower bulkhead (photo).
3　Working inside the vehicle, remove the spring clip which attaches the pushrod to the arm of the brake pedal.
4　Unscrew the nuts which hold the servo to its mounting bracket, also the servo support brace to the body.
5　Disconnect the valve hose from the servo.
6　Detach the linkage arm spring at the rear of the servo and then pull the servo forward until the servo operating rod can be unclipped from the linkage.
7　Remove the servo from the vehicle. It must be renewed if defective, no repair is possible.
8　If necessary, the rest of the servo operating linkage can be removed from under the instrument panel once the covering and cowl side trim have been removed from above the brake pedal inside the vehicle. Unbolt the connecting link bracket from the driver's side.
9　Refitting is the reverse sequence to removal. Refit the master cylinder as described in Section 13 and bleed the hydraulic system as described in Sections 12 or 24 as applicable.

17.2 Heater plenum chamber removal

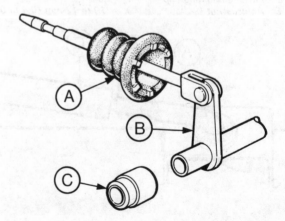

Fig. 9.38 Vacuum servo unit connecting linkage (Sec 17)

A　Grommet　　　　C　Bush
B　Connecting link

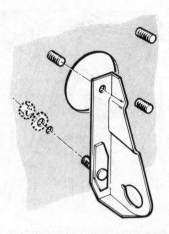

Fig. 9.39 Vacuum servo unit connecting link bracket on driver's side (Sec 17)

18 Brake pedal – removal and refitting

1   Working within the vehicle, remove the under-dash cover panel.
2   Extract the spring clip which connects the pushrod to the arm of the brake pedal.
3   Extract the circlip from the end of the pedal pivot shaft and withdraw the shaft with clutch pedal and the flat and wave washers.
4   Renew the bushes as necessary.
5   Reassembly and refitting are reversals of removal and dismantling. Apply a little grease to the bushes when installing.

Pedal travel – general

6   Although the braking system may be in satisfactory condition generally, it is possible that some drivers may feel that the brake pedal travel is excessive. The travel can be reduced in the following way if the upper surface of the pedal pad is less than 200.0 mm (7.9 in) above the metal surface of the floor.
7   Remove the brake pedal as described above.
8   Remove the white plastic bush (Fig. 9.41).
9   Fit a new bush which is red in colour and will increase the pedal height. Once this type of bush has been fitted it will not be possible to refit the anti-rattle retainer. This does not matter.
10 Adjust the stop-lamp switch as described in Section 19.

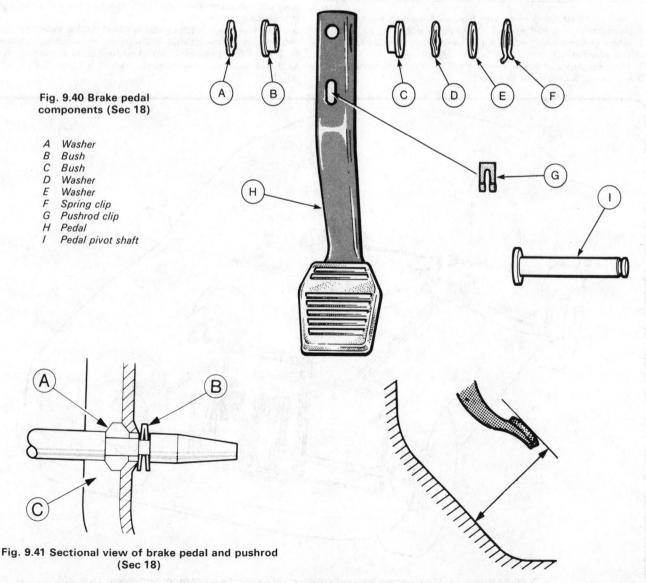

Fig. 9.40 Brake pedal components (Sec 18)

A   Washer
B   Bush
C   Bush
D   Washer
E   Washer
F   Spring clip
G   Pushrod clip
H   Pedal
I   Pedal pivot shaft

Fig. 9.41 Sectional view of brake pedal and pushrod (Sec 18)

A   White plastic bush   C   Pedal arm
B   Pushrod clip

Fig. 9.42 Brake pedal-to-floor height check – pedal released (Sec 18)

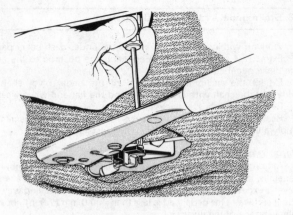

Fig. 9.43 Removing handbrake warning switch (Sec 19)

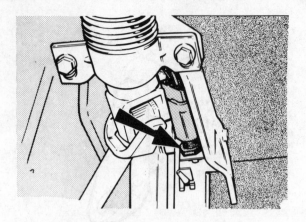

**Fig. 9.44 Brake stop-lamp switch locknut location –
arrowed (Sec 19)**

19 Braking warning lamps – description and renewal

1   All models are fitted with a low fluid level warning switch in the master cylinder reservoir cap and a brake pedal stop-lamp switch.
2   Some versions have front disc pad wear sensors and a handbrake 'ON' warning switch.
3   Warning indicator lamps are mounted on the instrument panel. Their renewal is covered in Chapter 12.

4   The handbrake 'ON' warning switch is attached to the handbrake lever and can be removed after disconnecting the wiring and undoing the retaining screw.
5   The stop-lamp switch can be removed by disconnecting the leads and unscrewing the locknut which holds the switch to its bracket.
6   When fitting the switch, adjust its position by screwing it in or out so that it does not actuate during the first 5.0 mm (0.2 in) of pedal travel.

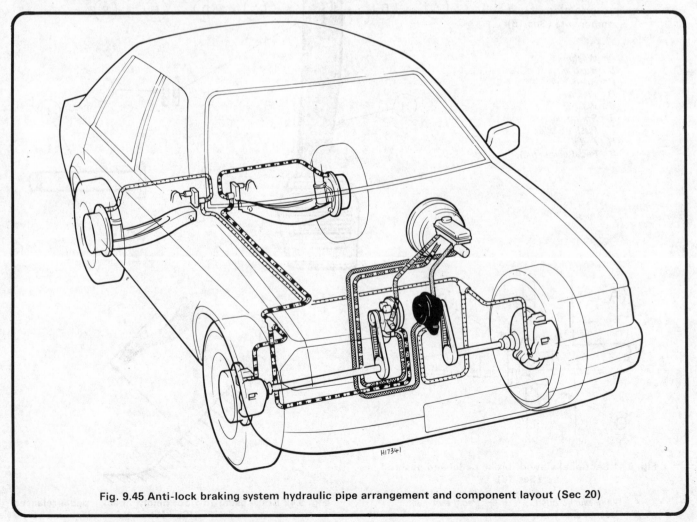

H17341

Fig. 9.45 Anti-lock braking system hydraulic pipe arrangement and component layout (Sec 20)

20 Anti-lock Braking System – description

From 1986 onward an anti-lock braking system is available as standard or optional equipment on certain Escort models.

The system comprises four main components: two modulators, one for each brake circuit, and two rear axle load apportioning valves, again, one for each brake circuit. Apart from the additional hydraulic piping the remainder of the braking system is the same as for conventional models.

The modulators are located in the engine compartment with one mounted on each side of the transmission, directly above the driveshaft inner constant velocity joints. Each modulator contains a shaft which actuates a flywheel by means of a ball and ramp clutch. A rubber toothed belt is used to drive the modulator shaft from the driveshaft inner constant velocity joint.

During driving and under normal braking the modulator shaft and the flywheel rotate together and at the same speed through the engagement of a ball and ramp clutch. In this condition hydraulic pressure fom the master cylinder passes to the modulators and then to each brake in the conventional way. In the event of a front wheel locking the modulator shaft rotation will be less than that of the flywheel and the flywheel will overrun the ball and ramp clutch. This causes the flywheel to slide on the modulator shaft, move inward and operate a lever which in turn opens a dump valve. Hydraulic pressure to the locked brake is released via a de-boost piston allowing the wheel to once again revolve. Fluid passed through the dump valve is returned to the master cylinder reservoir via the modulator return pipes. At the same time hydraulic pressure from the master cylinder causes a pump piston to contact an eccentric cam on the modulator shaft. The flywheel is then decelerated at a controlled rate by the flywheel friction clutch. When the speed of the modulator shaft and flywheel are once again equal the dump valve closes and the cycle repeats. This complete operation takes place many times a second until the vehicle stops or the brakes are released.

The load apportioning valves are mounted on the rear crossmember and connected to each rear suspension arm via a linkage. The valves regulate hydraulic pressure to the rear brakes in accordance with

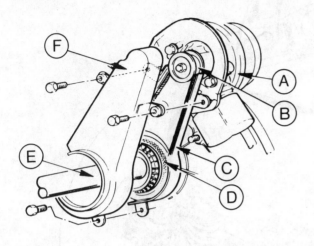

Fig. 9.46 Modulator and drivebelt details (Sec 20)

A Modulator
B Sprocket
C Drivebelt
D Constant velocity joint
E Driveshaft
F Drivebelt cover

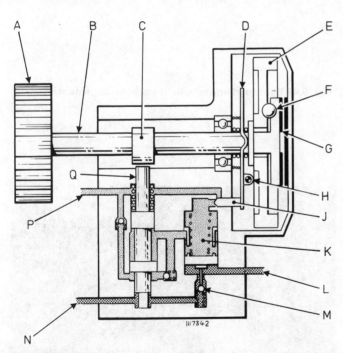

Fig. 9.47 Modulator operational diagram for normal braking (Sec 20)

A Sprocket
B Modulator shaft
C Eccentric cam
D Dump valve lever
E Flywheel
F Ball and ramp drive
G Clutch
H Pivot
J Dump valve
K De-boost piston
L Port to brakes
M Cut-off valve
N From master cylinder
P To master cylinder reservoir
Q Pump piston

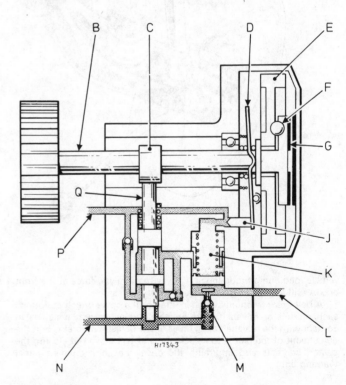

Fig. 9.48 Modulator operational diagram with brakes locked (Sec 20)

B Modulator shaft
C Eccentric cam
D Dump valve lever
E Flywheel
F Ball and ramp drive
G Clutch
J Dump valve
K De-boost piston
L Port to brakes
M Cut-off valve
N From master cylinder
P To master cylinder reservoir
Q Pump piston

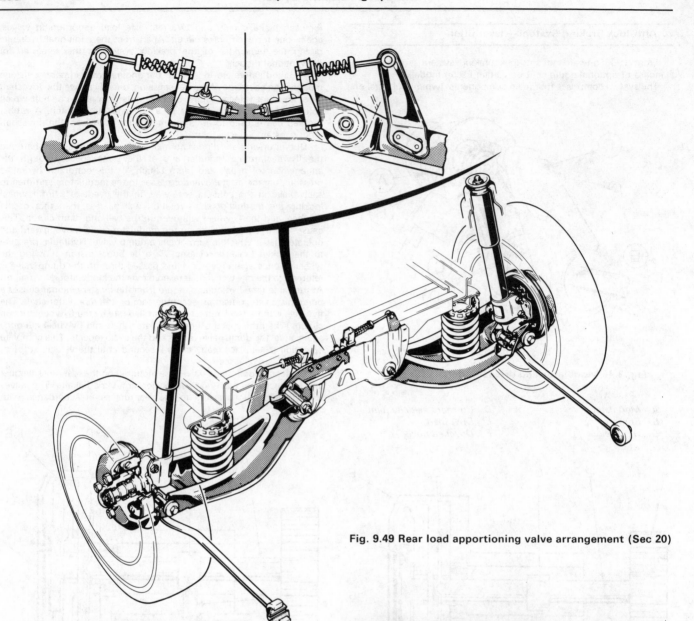

Fig. 9.49 Rear load apportioning valve arrangement (Sec 20)

vehicle load and attitude in such a way that braking force at the front brakes will always be greater than that at the rear.

A belt break warning switch is fitted to the cover which surrounds each modulator drivebelt. The switch contains an arm which is in contact with the drivebelt at all times. If the belt should break, or if the adjustment of the belt is too slack, the arm will move out closing the switch contacts and informing the driver via an instrument panel warning light.

21 Modulator drivebelt (anti-lock braking system) – removal and refitting

Right-hand side

1   Jack up the front of the car, support it on stands and remove the roadwheel.

2   Remove the belt break switch from the drivebelt cover by pushing it upward and carefully levering out the bottom edge. Pull the switch down, withdraw the switch arm from the opening in the cover and place the switch to one side (photo).

21.2 Removing the belt break switch from the modulator drivebelt cover

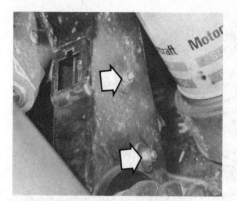

21.3 Drivebelt cover retaining nuts (arrowed)

21.4 Removing the drivebelt cover upwards to clear the oil filter

21.5 Modulator adjuster bolt (arrowed)

3   Undo the two drivebelt cover retaining nuts and washers (photo).
4   Withdraw the cover from the studs and remove it by moving it upwards to clear the oil filter (photo).
5   Slacken the modulator adjuster bolt (photo) move the modulator to relieve the tension on the drivebelt then slip the belt off the modulator sprocket.
6   Extract the split pin, undo the retaining nut and separate the tie-rod balljoint from the steering arm using a suitable balljoint separator tool.
7   Disconnect the front suspension lower arm balljoint from the hub carrier by removing the nut and pinch-bolt. Note that the pinch-bolt is of the socket-headed (Torx) type and a special key or socket bit will be required for this purpose. These are readily available from most accessory shops.
8   Place a suitable container beneath the driveshaft inner constant velocity joint.
9   Insert a lever between the inner constant velocity joint and the transmission housing. Firmly strike the lever to release the constant velocity joint from the differential.
10 Pull the driveshaft out of the transmission and slip the modulator drivebelt off the joint. Allow the transmission oil to drain into the container.
11 With the driveshaft disconnected, suspend it in such a way so as not to adopt an angle of more than 45° from the outer constant velocity joint.
12 Before refitting the drivebelt, renew the snap-ring fitted to the splines of the inner constant velocity joint.
13 Ensure that the modulator sprocket and constant velocity joint splines are clean and dry then slip the drivebelt over the joint.
14 Engage the joint splines with the differential and firmly push the hub carrier inwards to force the joint home.
15 Reconnect the lower arm balljoint to the hub carrier and insert the Torx bolt with its head to the rear. Refit the nut and tighten to the specified torque.
16 Reconnect the tie-rod balljoint to the steering arm, fit and tighten the nut to the specified torque and secure with a new split pin.
17 Slip the drivebelt over the modulator sprocket ensuring that it sits squarely in the sprocket teeth.
18 Move the modulator as necessary to tension the belt so that the belt deflection, under light finger pressure, is 5.0 mm (0.2 in). Check this using a ruler at a point midway between the two sprockets.
19 With the belt tensioned correctly, tighten the modulator adjuster bolt.
20 Refit the drivebelt cover and secure with the two nuts and washers.
21 Engage the belt break switch arm upwards through the opening in the drivebelt cover then locate the switch in position. Pull the switch downward to secure.
22 Refit the roadwheel and lower the car to the ground.
23 Top up the transmission oil as described in Chapter 6.

Left-hand side
24 The procedure is the same as for the right-hand side but note the following differences.
25 Remove the engine splash shield from the inner wheel arch.
26 When removing the drivebelt cover note that it is secured by three bolts, two at the top and one at the bottom.

27 To move the modulator for adjustment of the belt tension, use a suitable length of wood inserted through the steering tie-rod aperture in the inner wheel arch, to push on the modulator as necessary.

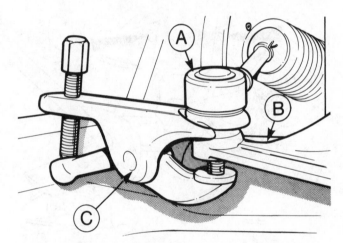

Fig. 9.50 Separating tie-rod balljoint from steering arm (Sec 21)

A   Balljoint   C   Balljoint separator tool
B   Steering arm

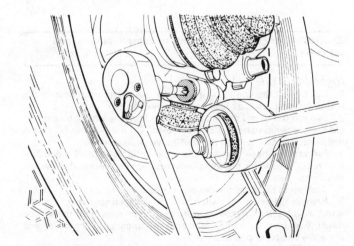

Fig. 9.51 Removing suspension lower arm balljoint pinch-bolt (Sec 21)

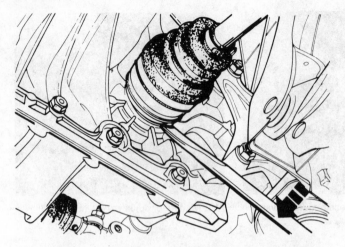

Fig. 9.52 Using a lever to release the driveshaft inner
constant velocity joint (Sec 21)

Conventional left-hand driveshaft shown for clarity

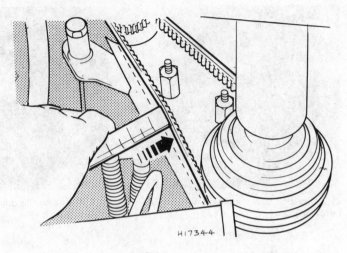

Fig. 9.53 Using a ruler to check right-hand drivebelt
adjustment (Sec 21)

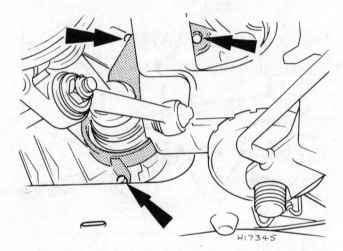

Fig. 9.54 Left-hand drivebelt cover retaining bolt locations –
arrowed (Sec 21)

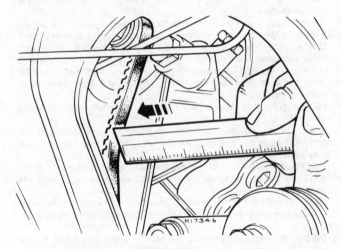

Fig. 9.55 Using a ruler to check left-hand drivebelt
adjustment (Sec 21)

22 Modulator (anti-lock braking system) – removal and refitting

Right-hand side

1   Disconnect the wiring plug from the level warning switch in the
master cylinder reservoir filler cap. Remove the cap.
2   Syphon out as much fluid as possible from the reservoir using an
old battery hydrometer or a poultry baster. Do not drip the fluid onto
the paintwork as it will act as an effective paint stripper.
3   Release the hose clip and disconnect the right-hand modulator
fluid return pipe at the master cylinder reservoir (nearest to the vacuum
servo unit – photo).
4   Jack up the front of the car and support it on stands.
5   Remove the belt break switch from the drivebelt cover by pushing it
upward and carefully levering out the bottom edge. Pull the switch
down, withdraw the switch arm from the opening in the cover and
place the switch to one side.
6   Undo the two drivebelt cover retaining nuts and washers.
7   Withdraw the cover from the studs and remove it by moving it
upwards to clear the oil filter.

8   Disconnect the two hydraulic pipes and hoses with the yellow
bands at the pipe bracket on the transmission support crossmember
(photo). Allow the remaining hydraulic fluid to drain into a suitable
container.
9   Slacken the modulator adjuster bolt, move the modulator to relieve
the tension on the drivebelt then slip the belt off the modulator
sprocket.
10 Undo and remove the adjuster bolt and the modulator pivot bolt
and withdraw the modulator from the engine compartment.
11 If required, disconnect the hydraulic hoses at the modulator after
removal. Plug or tape over all pipe ends and orifices to prevent dirt
ingress.
12 If a new unit is being fitted check that it has a yellow arrow marked
on its cover and a part number suffix 'A' indicating a right-hand side
modulator. Note that the units are not interchangeable from side to
side.
13 Reconnect the modulator hydraulic hoses if applicable.
14 Locate the modulator on its mounting bracket, fit the pivot bolt and
tighten it to the specified torque.
15 Slip the drivebelt over the modulator sprocket ensuring that it sits
squarely in the sprocket teeth.

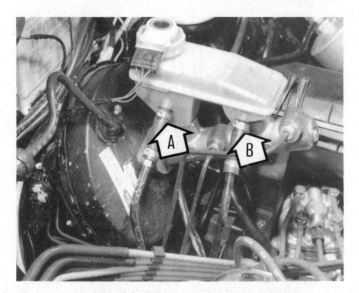

22.3 Modulator fluid return pipes at master cylinder reservoir

A To right-hand modulator

B To left-hand modulator

22.8 Hydraulic pipe and hose unions at the pipe bracket on the transmission support crossmember

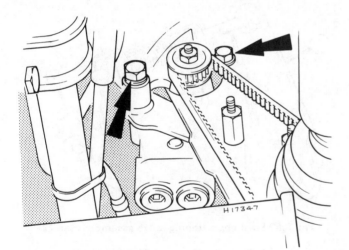
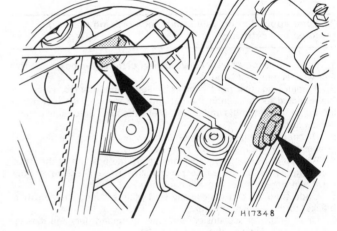

Fig. 9.56 Right-hand modulator adjuster and pivot bolts – arrowed (Sec 22)

Fig. 9.57 Left-hand modulator adjuster and pivot bolts – arrowed (Sec 22)

16 Move the modulator as necessary to tension the belt so that the belt deflection, under light finger pressure is 5.0 mm (0.2 in). Check this using a ruler at a point midway between the two sprockets.
17 With the belt tensioned correctly, tighten the modulator adjuster bolt.
18 Reconnect the two modulator hydraulic pipes and hoses.
19 Refit the drivebelt cover and secure with the two nuts and washers.
20 Engage the belt break switch arm upwards through the opening in the drivebelt cover then locate the switch in position. Pull the switch downwards to secure.
21 Lower the car to the ground.
22 Reconnect the modulator fluid return pipe to the master cylinder reservoir then fill the reservoir with fresh fluid of the specified type.
23 Bleed the hydraulic system as described in Section 24.

Left-hand side
24 Disconnect the wiring plug from the level warning switch in the master cylinder reservoir filler cap. Remove the cap.
25 Syphon out as much fluid as possible from the reservoir using an old battery hydrometer or a poultry baster. Do not drip the fluid onto the paintwork as it will act as an effective paint stripper.

26 Release the hose clip and disconnect the left-hand modulator fluid return pipe at the master cylinder reservoir (the one furthest away from the vacuum servo unit – photo 22.3).
27 Jack up the front of the car and support it on stands. Remove the left-hand roadwheel.
28 Remove the engine splash shield from the inner wheel arch.
29 Remove the belt break switch from the drivebelt cover by pushing it upwards and carefully levering out the bottom edge. Pull the switch down, withdraw the switch arm from the opening in the cover and place the switch to one side.
30 Undo the three bolts, two at the top and one at the bottom securing the drivebelt cover to the modulator bracket. Remove the cover.
31 Disconnect the two hydraulic pipes and hoses with the white bands at the pipe bracket on the transmission support crossmember (photo 22.8). Allow the remaining hydraulic fluid to drain into a suitable container.
32 Slacken the modulator adjuster bolt, move the modulator to relieve the tension on the drivebelt then slip the belt off the modulator sprocket.
33 Remove the distributor cap, rotor arm and shield. Disconnect the left-hand belt break switch wiring at the multi-plug.

34 Undo and remove the adjuster bolt and the modulator pivot bolt and withdraw the modulator upwards out of the engine compartment.
35 If required, disconnect the hydraulic hoses at the modulator after removal. Plug or tape over all pipe ends and orifices to prevent dirt ingress.
36 If a new unit is being fitted check that it has a white arrow marked on its cover and a part number suffix 'C' indicating a left-hand side modulator. Note that the units are not interchangeable from side to side.
37 Reconnect the modulator hydraulic pipes if applicable.
38 Locate the modulator on its mounting bracket, fit the pivot bolt and tighten it to the specified torque.
39 Slip the drivebelt over the modulator sprocket ensuring that it sits squarely in the sprocket teeth.
40 Adjust the drivebelt tension as described in paragraphs 16 and 17, but use a suitable length of wood inserted through the steering tie-rod aperture in the inner wheel arch, to push on the modulator as necessary.
41 Reconnect the two modulator hydraulic pipes and hoses.
42 Refit the drivebelt cover and secure with the three bolts.
43 Refit the belt break switch as described in paragraph 20.
44 Refit the engine splash shield.
45 Refit the roadwheel and lower the car to the ground.
46 Reconnect the belt break switch wiring multi-plug then refit the shield, rotor arm and distributor cap.
47 Reconnect the modulator fluid return pipe to the master cylinder reservoir then fill the reservoir with fresh fluid of the specified type.
48 Bleed the hydraulic system as described in Section 24.

23 Load apportioning valve (anti-lock braking system) – removal and refitting

1   Raise the car on a hoist or drive the rear of the car up on ramps. The rear wheels must not hang free.
2   If removing the right-hand side load apportioning valve on fuel-injected models, undo the nut and bolt securing the fuel pump mounting bracket to the underbody. Move the fuel pump aside to gain access to the valve.
3   Disconnect the hydraulic pipes at the valve then plug the pipes and orifices to prevent loss of fluid and dirt ingress.
4   As an aid to reassembly accurately mark the position of the valve adjusting bracket on the rear suspension arm. This will ensure that the valve adjustment is not lost when refitting.
5   Undo the nuts and remove the stud plate securing the adjusting bracket to the suspension arm.
6   Undo both rear suspension arm inner mounting nuts and remove the load apportioning valve mounting plate.
7   Undo the bolts securing the valve to the mounting plate and remove the valve and adjusting bracket from under the car.
8   If required separate the valve pushrod from the adjusting bracket by levering off the pushrod trunnion with a screwdriver. Lubricate the trunnion rubber bush to aid removal.
9   If a new valve is being fitted it will be supplied with nylon setting spacers and ties attached, to ensure correct adjustment of the valve. Leave these in position until the valve is installed.
10 Refit the pushrod trunnion to the adjusting bracket using a suitable socket and a vice.
11 Locate the valve on its mounting plate and secure with the retaining bolts.
12 Position the mounting plate over the suspension arm mounting bolts and secure with the nuts tightened to the specified torque.
13 Reconnect the hydraulic pipes to the valve.
14 Refit the stud plate and adjusting bracket to the suspension arm ensuring that the previously made marks are aligned if the original components are being refitted. Secure the adjusting bracket with the retaining nuts tightened to the specified torque.
15 If a new valve assembly is being fitted, remove the nylon setting spacers and ties.
16 Where applicable refit the fuel pump mounting bracket.
17 Lower the car to the ground.
18 It is recommended that the load apportioning valve adjustment be checked by a dealer if the original unit has been refitted. Special gauges are needed for this operation and it is not a DIY proposition.

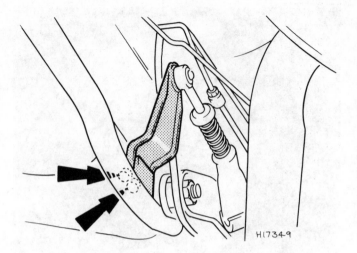

Fig. 9.58 Load apportioning valve adjusting bracket retaining bolt locations – arrowed (Sec 23)

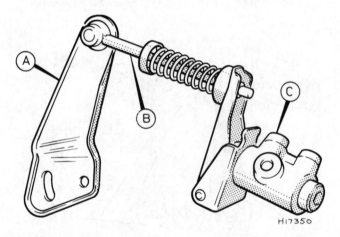

Fig. 9.59 Load apportioning valve assembly (Sec 23)

A   Adjusting bracket   C   Apportioning valve
B   Valve pushrod

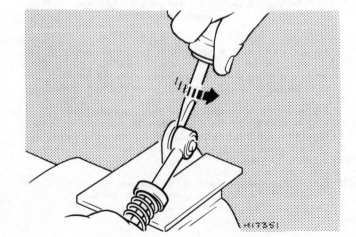

Fig. 9.60 Separating apportioning valve pushrod from adjusting bracket (Sec 23)

24 Hydraulic system – bleeding (anti-lock braking system)

1 On cars equipped with the anti-lock braking system there are two bleed procedures possible according to which part of the hydraulic system has been disconnected.

2 If any one of the following conditions are present, bleed procedure A should be adopted:

    (a) A modulator has been removed
    (b) A modulator-to-master cylinder return hose has been drained
    (c) The two modulator hydraulic hoses have been removed

3 If any one of the following conditions are present, bleed procedure B should be adopted:

    (a) Any condition where the master cylinder has been drained providing that the modulator fluid return pipe has not lost its head of fluid
    (b) Removal of any of the basic braking system components ie brake caliper, flexible hose or pipe, wheel cylinder, load apportioning valve

Bleed procedure A

4 Top up the master cylinder reservoir to the MAX mark using the specified type of fluid and keep it topped up throughout the bleed procedure.

5 Using a Torx type key or socket bit slacken the bypass valve on the relevant modulator by one to one and a half turns. The bypass valve is located between the two flexible hoses on the side of the modulator (Fig. 9.61).

6 Fully depress and hold depressed the auto bleed plunger on the modulator so that the plunger circlip contacts the modulator body (Fig. 9.62).

7 Have an assistant steadily pump the brake pedal at least twenty times while you observe the fluid returning to the master cylinder reservoir. Continue this operation until the returning fluid is free from air bubbles.

8 Release the auto bleed plunger ensuring that it has fully returned. Pull it out by hand if necessary.

9 Tighten the bypass valve on the modulator.

10 Now carry out bleed procedure B.

Bleed procedure B

11 This procedure is the same as for conventional braking systems and reference should be made to Section 12. Note, however, that all the weight of the car must be on the roadwheels, not suspended wheel free, otherwise the load apportioning valves will not bleed.

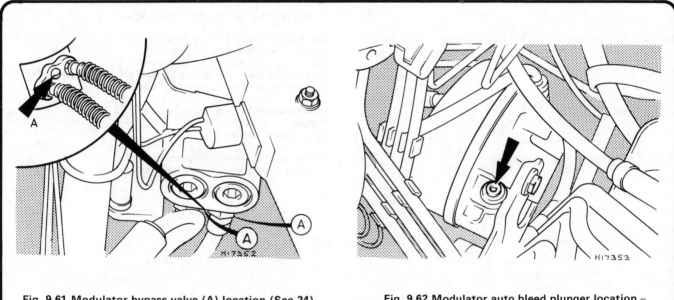

Fig. 9.61 Modulator bypass valve (A) location (Sec 24)

Fig. 9.62 Modulator auto bleed plunger location – arrowed (Sec 24)

Fault diagnosis overleaf

25 Fault diagnosis – braking system

Note: *Apart from checking the condition and adjustment of the modulator drivebelts, and all pipe and hose connections, any faults occuring on the Anti-lock Braking System should be referred to a Ford dealer for diagnosis*

Symptom	Reason(s)
Excessive pedal travel	Rear brake self-adjust mechanism inoperative Air in hydraulic system Faulty master cylinder
Brake pedal feels spongy	Air in hydraulic system Faulty master cylinder
Judder felt through brake pedal or steering wheel when braking	Excessive run-out or distortion of front discs or rear drums Disc pads or brake shoe linings worn Brake backplate or disc caliper loose Wear in suspension or steering components or mountings – see Chapter 10
Excessive pedal pressure required to stop car	Faulty servo unit, disconnected, damaged or insecure vacuum hose Wheel cylinder(s) or caliper piston seized Disc pads or brake shoe linings worn or contaminated Brake shoes incorrectly fitted Incorrect grade of pads or linings fitted Primary or secondary hydraulic circuit failure
Brakes pull to one side	Disc pads or linings worn or contaminated Wheel cylinder or caliper piston seized Seized rear brake self-adjust mechanism Disc pads or brake shoe linings renewed on one side only Tyre, steering or suspension defect – see Chapter 10
Brakes binding	Wheel cylinder or caliper piston seized Handbrake incorrectly adjusted Faulty master cylinder
Rear wheels locking under normal braking	Rear brake shoe linings contaminated Faulty pressure control or light laden valve as applicable

Chapter 10 Suspension and steering

For modifications, and information applicable to later models, see Supplement at end of manual

Contents

Specifications

Front suspension

Type	Independent by MacPherson struts with coil springs and integral telescopic shock absorbers. Anti-roll bar fitted to all models except pre-1983 1.1 litre versions

Rear suspension

Type:

Saloon and Estate models	Independent with coil springs, telescopic shock absorbers and tie-bars
Van models	Tubular axle located by semi-elliptic leaf springs and telescopic shock absorbers
Hub bearing grease	To Ford specification SAM-1C-9111A (Duckhams LB 10)

Steering

Type	Rack and pinion

Overhaul data:

Pre-May 1983 models:

Pinion turning torque	0.6 to 1.3 Nm (5 to 12 lbf in)
Tie-rod inner balljoint preload (articulation effort)	2.27 kgf (5.0 lbf)
Rack slipper shim thickness availability	0.127 mm (0.005 in), 0.19 mm (0.007 in), 0.25 mm (0.010 in), 0.38 mm (0.015 in), 0.50 mm (0.020 in)
Paper gasket thickness	0.14 mm (0.0055 in)

May 1983 models onward:

Pinion turning torque	0.3 to 1.3 Nm (2.7 to 12 lbf in)

Steering gear lubricant:

Oil	To Ford specification SQM-2C9003-AA
Semi-fluid grease	To Ford specification SAM1C-9106-AA

Front wheel alignment

Toe setting:
Pre-May 1983 models:
  Checking tolerance .... 1.5 mm (0.06 in) toe-in to 5.5 mm (0.22 in) toe-out
  Adjust to .... 1.0 mm (0.04 in) toe-in to 3.0 mm (0.12 in) toe-out
May 1983 models onward:
  Checking tolerance .... 0.5 mm (0.02 in) toe-in to 5.5 mm (0.22 in) toe-out
  Adjust to .... 1.5 mm (0.06 in) to 3.5 mm (0.14 in) toe-out
Camber and castor angles (nominal, for reference only)

	Camber	Castor
Pre-May 1983 models:		
Saloon:		
1.1 litre Base and L:		
Standard	1° 26′	2° 11′
Heavy duty	1° 55′	2° 10′
1.1 litre GL and Ghia:		
Standard	1° 11′	2° 09′
Heavy duty	1° 38′	2° 06′
1.3 and 1.6 litre Base and L:		
Standard	1° 47′	2° 33′
Heavy duty	1° 57′	2° 10′
1.3 and 1.6 litre GL and Ghia:		
Standard	1° 30′	2° 31′
Heavy duty	1° 42′	2° 09′
1.6 litre XR3	1° 22′	2° 39′
Estate:		
All models:		
Standard	1° 53′	2° 38′
Heavy duty	1° 53′	2° 16′
Van:		
All models	1° 17′	1° 24′
May 1983 to 1986:		
Saloon:		
1.1 and 1.3 litre 3-door:		
Standard	0° 13′	2° 15′
Heavy duty	0° 30′	2° 14′
1.3 litre 5-door:		
Standard	0° 10′	2° 24′
Heavy duty	0° 25′	2° 19′
1.6 litre 3-door:		
Standard	0° 06′	2° 20′
Heavy duty	0° 30′	2° 14′
1.6 litre 5-door:		
Standard	0° 03′	2° 22′
Heavy duty	0° 25′	2° 19′
1.6 litre automatic transmission:		
Standard	1° 14′	2° 19′
Heavy duty	0° 30′	2° 14′
1.6 litre XR3i	−0° 51′	2° 47′
1985 RS Turbo	0° to −2° 0′	3° 0′
Estate:		
1.1 and 1.3 litre:		
Standard	0° 29′	2° 39′
Heavy duty	0° 29′	2° 18′
1.6 litre:		
Standard	0° 33′	2° 40′
Heavy duty	0° 33′	2° 18′
Van:		
35	−0° 17′	1° 39′
55	−0° 17′	1° 19′
1986 models onward:		
Saloon:		
All 3-door models except XR3i and RS Turbo:		
Standard	0° 10′	2° 4′
Heavy duty	0° 25′	2° 4′
All 5-door models:		
Standard	0° 6′	2° 11′
Heavy duty	0° 25′	2° 4′
XR3i and RS Turbo:		
Standard	−0° 53′	2° 36′
Heavy duty	0° 25′	2° 4′
Estate:		
All models except 1.6 litre with automatic transmission:		
Standard	0° 27′	2° 26′
Heavy duty	0° 27′	2° 4′

	Camber	Castor
1.6 litre with automatic transmission:		
Standard	0° 31'	2° 26'
Heavy duty	− 0° 57'	2° 6'
Van:		
35	− 0° 18'	1° 7'
55	0° 20'	1° 26'
Tolerance range (all models):		
Camber	± 1° 0'	
Castor	± 1° 0'	
Maximum allowable side-to-side variation (all models):		
Camber	± 1° 15'	
Castor	± 1° 0'	

Roadwheels

Wheel size:
    Steel wheels 13x4.50, 13x5, 14x6
    Alloy wheels 14x5.50, 14x6, 15x6

Tyres

Tyre size:
    Saloon and Estate models .... 145 SR 13, 155 SR/TR 13, 175/70 SR/HR 13, 175/65 HR 14, 185/60 HR 13, 185/60 HR 14, 195/50 VR 15
    Van models .... 155 SR 13, 165 RR 13

Tyre pressures – cold in bar (lbf/in²):	Front	Rear
Saloon and Estate models:		
145 SR 13 (pre-1986 models):		
Up to 3 occupants	1.8 (26)	1.8 (26)
Fully laden	2.0 (29)	2.3 (33)
145 SR 13 (1986 models onward):		
Up to 3 occupants	1.6 (23)	2.0 (29)
Fully laden	2.0 (29)	2.3 (33)
155 SR/TR 13 (manual transmission models):		
Up to 3 occupants	1.6 (23)	2.0 (29)
Fully laden	2.0 (29)	2.3 (33)
155 SR/TR 13 (automatic transmission models):		
Up to 3 occupants	1.8 (26)	2.0 (29)
Fully laden	2.0 (29)	2.3 (33)
175/70 SR/HR 13:		
Up to 3 occupants	1.8 (26)	1.8 (26)
Fully laden	2.0 (29)	2.3 (33)
175/65 HR 14:		
Up to 3 occupants	1.6 (23)	2.0 (29)
Fully laden	2.0 (29)	2,3 (33)
185/60 HR 13:		
Up to 3 occupants	1.8 (26)	1.8 (26)
Fully laden	2.0 (29)	2.3 (33)
185/60 HR 14:		
Up to 3 occupants	1.6 (23)	2.0 (29)
Fully laden	2.0 (29)	2.3 (33)
195/50 VR 15:		
Up to 3 occupants	1.8 (26)	1.8 (26)
Fully laden	1.8 (26)	2.0 (29)
Van models:		
155 SR 13:		
Up to 3 occupants	1.8 (26)	1.8 (26)
Fully laden	1.8 (26)	2.6 (38)
165 RR 13:		
Up to 3 occupants	1.8 (26)	1.8 (26)
Fully laden	1.8 (26)	3.0 (44)

Increase the above pressures by 0.1 bar (1.5 lbf/in²) for every 6 mph (10 kph) above 100 mph (160 kph) for sustained high speed use

Torque wrench settings

	Nm	lbf ft
Front suspension		
Driveshaft retaining nut (threads lightly greased)	205 to 235	151 to 173
Lower arm mounting pivot bolt	51 to 64	38 to 47
Lower arm balljoint pinch-bolt	48 to 60	35 to 44
Brake caliper anchor bracket mounting bolts	50 to 66	37 to 49
Suspension strut to hub carrier	80 to 90	59 to 66
Tie-bar to lower arm (pre-1983 1.1 litre models)	75 to 90	55 to 66
Tie-bar to mounting bracket (pre-1983 1.1 litre models)	44 to 55	32 to 41
Anti-roll bar to lower arm	90 to 110	66 to 81
Anti-roll bar clamp nuts and bolts	45 to 56	33 to 41
Tie-bar to lower arm (1985 RS Turbo models)	90 to 110	66 to 81
Tie-bar-to-anti-roll bar clamp (1985 RS Turbo models)	22 to 26	16 to 19
Tie-bar front pivot nut (1985 RS Turbo models)	70 to 90	52 to 66
Suspension strut top mounting to body (pre-May 1983 models)	20 to 24	15 to 18
Suspension strut-to-body retaining nut (May 1983 models onward)	40 to 52	30 to 38

	Nm	lbf ft
Suspension strut top mounting piston rod nut	52 to 65	38 to 48
Rear suspension (Saloon and Estate models)		
Lower arm inboard pivot bolt	70 to 90	52 to 66
Lower arm-to-stub axle carrier through-bolt	60 to 70	44 to 52
Shock absorber top mounting nut	42 to 52	31 to 38
Shock absorber to stub axle carrier	70 to 90	52 to 66
Tie-bar front mounting pivot bolt	70 to 90	52 to 66
Tie-bar-to-stub axle carrier nut	70 to 90	52 to 66
Brake backplate to stub axle carrier	45 to 55	33 to 41
Rear suspension (Van models)		
Roadspring U-bolt nuts	36 to 45	27 to 33
Roadspring shackle nuts	40 to 50	30 to 37
Roadspring eye bolt nuts	70 to 90	52 to 66
Shock absorber top mounting bracket to body	20 to 25	15 to 18
Shock absorber to top mounting bracket	40 to 50	30 to 37
Brake backplate to stub axle	45 to 55	33 to 41
Steering		
Steering gear to bulkhead bolts	45 to 50	33 to 37
Tie-rod outer balljoint to steering arm	25 to 30	18 to 22
Tie-rod outer balljoint-to-tie-rod locknut	57 to 68	42 to 50
Steering column shaft coupling pinch-bolt	45 to 56	33 to 41
Steering wheel nut	27 to 34	20 to 25
Rack slipper cover plate bolts (pre-May 1983 models)	6.2 to 9.0	4.6 to 6.6
Pinion bearing cover plate bolts (pre-May 1983 models)	17 to 24	13 to 18
Rack slipper plug (post-May 1983 models)	4 to 5	3 to 4
Tie-rod inner balljoint to rack	68 to 90	50 to 66
Roadwheels		
Roadwheel bolts (all models)	70 to 100	52 to 74

1 General description

The independent front suspension is of the MacPherson strut type, incorporating coil springs and integral telescopic shock absorbers. Lateral location of each strut assembly is by a forged or pressed steel lower suspension arm containing rubber inner mounting bushes and incorporating a balljoint at their outer ends. On pre-May 1983 1.1 litre models, fore and aft location of the pressed steel lower suspension arms is by a tie-bar. On post May 1983 1.1 litre models and all other variants the forged steel lower arms are interconnected by an anti-roll bar which also provides fore and aft location of both suspension arms. Additional location is provided by an adjustable tie-bar on 1985 RS Turbo models. The hub carriers which contain the hub bearings, brake calipers and the hub/disc assemblies are bolted to the MacPherson struts and connected to the lower arms via the balljoints.

On Saloon and Estate models the rear suspension is also fully independent by means of pressed steel lower suspension arms, coil springs and separate telescopic shock absorbers. The suspension arms are attached to the underbody at their inner ends through rubber bushes and to the stub axle carrier at their outer ends, again through rubber bushes. The shock absorbers are bolted to the stub axle carriers at their lower ends which also carry the rear brake backplate as well as the rear hub/drum assemblies. Fore and aft location of the lower arms is by a tie-bar and an anti-roll bar is also fitted to models with fuel-injection.

The rear suspension on Van variants consists of a transverse beam axle located and supported by a single leaf spring on each side, and utilizing telescopic shock absorbers to control vertical movement. A stub axle is welded to each end of the axle and these carry the rear brake backplates and the hub/drum assemblies.

The steering gear is of the conventional rack and pinion type located behind the front wheels. Movement of the steering wheel is transmitted to the steering gear by means of a steering shaft containing two universal joints. The front wheels are connected to the steering gears by tie-rods each having an inner and outer balljoint.

2 Maintenance and inspection

1 At regular intervals (see Routine Maintenance) a thorough inspection of all suspension and steering components should be carried out using the following procedure as a guide.

Front suspension and steering
2 Apply the handbrake, jack up the front of the car and support it securely on axle stands.
3 Visually inspect the lower balljoint dust covers and the steering rack and pinion bellows for splits, chafing, or deterioration. Renew the bellows or the balljoint assembly, as described in Sections 21, 4 and 5 respectively, if any damage is apparent.
4 Grasp the roadwheel at the 12 o'clock and 6 o'clock positions and try to rock it. Very slight free play may be felt, but if the movement is appreciable, further investigation is necessary to determine the source. Continue rocking the wheel while an assistant depresses the footbrake. If the movement is now eliminated or significantly reduced, it is likely that the hub bearings are at fault. If the free play is still evident with the footbrake depressed, then there is wear in the suspension joints or mountings. Pay close attention to the lower balljoint and lower arm mounting bushes. Renew any worn components, as described in the appropriate Sections of this Chapter.
5 Now grasp the wheel at the 9 o'clock and 3 o'clock positions and try to rock it as before. Any movement felt now may again be caused by wear in the hub bearings or the steering tie-rod inner or outer balljoints. If the outer balljoint is worn the visual movement will be obvious. If the inner joint is suspect it can be felt by placing a hand over the rack and pinion bellows and gripping the tie-rod. If the wheel is now rocked, movement will be felt at the inner joint if wear has taken place. Repair procedures are described in Section 22 and 28 respectively.
6 Using a large screwdriver or flat bar check for wear in the anti-roll bar mountings (where fitted) and lower arm mountings by carefully levering against these components. Some movement is to be expected, as the mountings are made of rubber, but excessive wear should be obvious. Renew any bushes that are worn.
7 With the car standing on its wheels, have an assistant turn the steering wheel back and forth about one eighth of a turn each way. There should be no lost movement whatever between the steering wheel and roadwheels. If this is not the case, closely observe the joints and mountings previously described, but in addition check the steering shaft universal joints for wear and also the rack and pinion steering gear itself. Any wear should be visually apparent and must be rectified, as described in the appropriate Sections of this Chapter.

Rear suspension
8 Chock the front wheels, jack up the rear of the car and support it securely on axle stands.

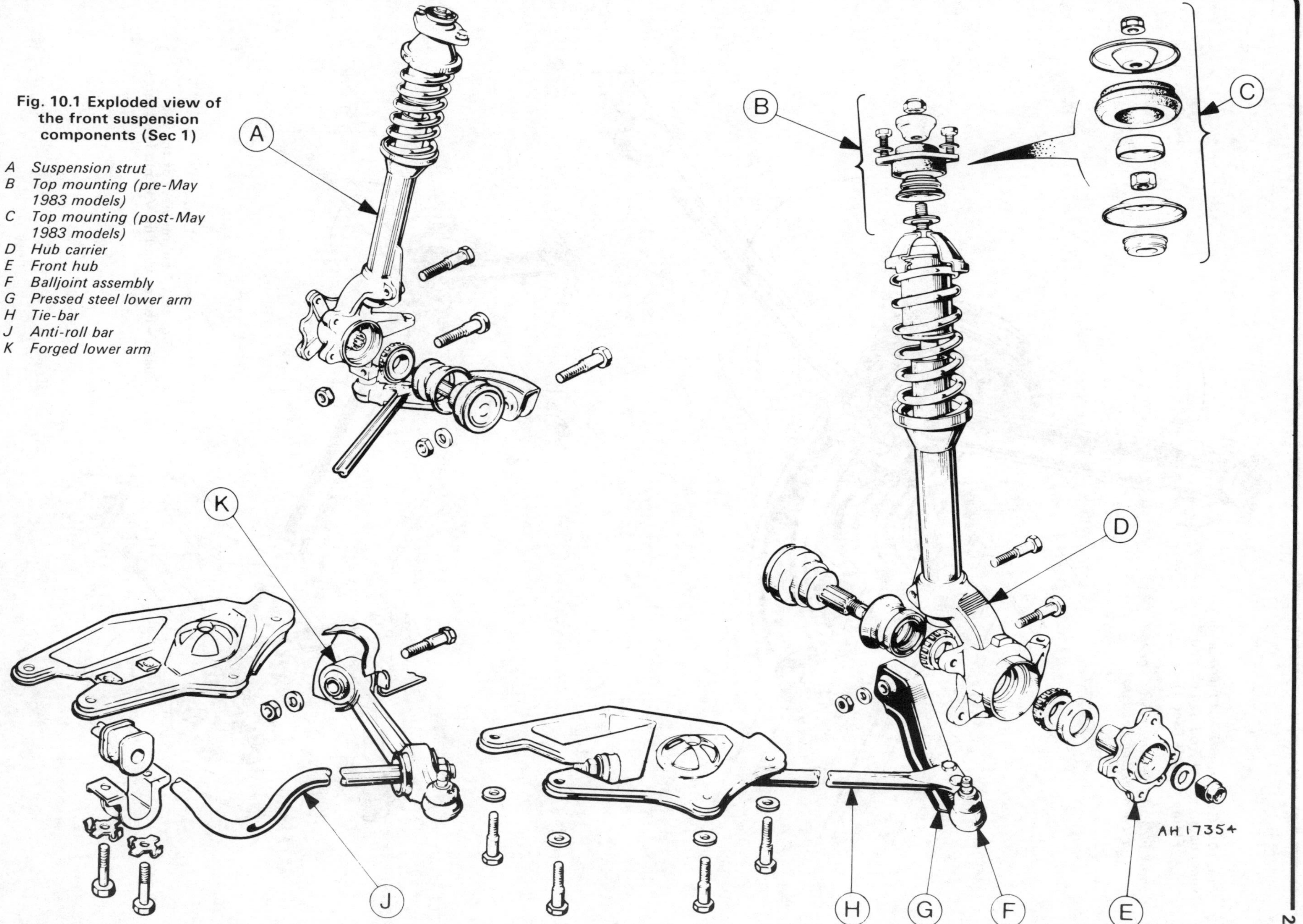

Fig. 10.1 Exploded view of
the front suspension
components (Sec 1)

A   Suspension strut
B   Top mounting (pre-May
    1983 models)
C   Top mounting (post-May
    1983 models)
D   Hub carrier
E   Front hub
F   Balljoint assembly
G   Pressed steel lower arm
H   Tie-bar
J   Anti-roll bar
K   Forged lower arm

AH 1735+

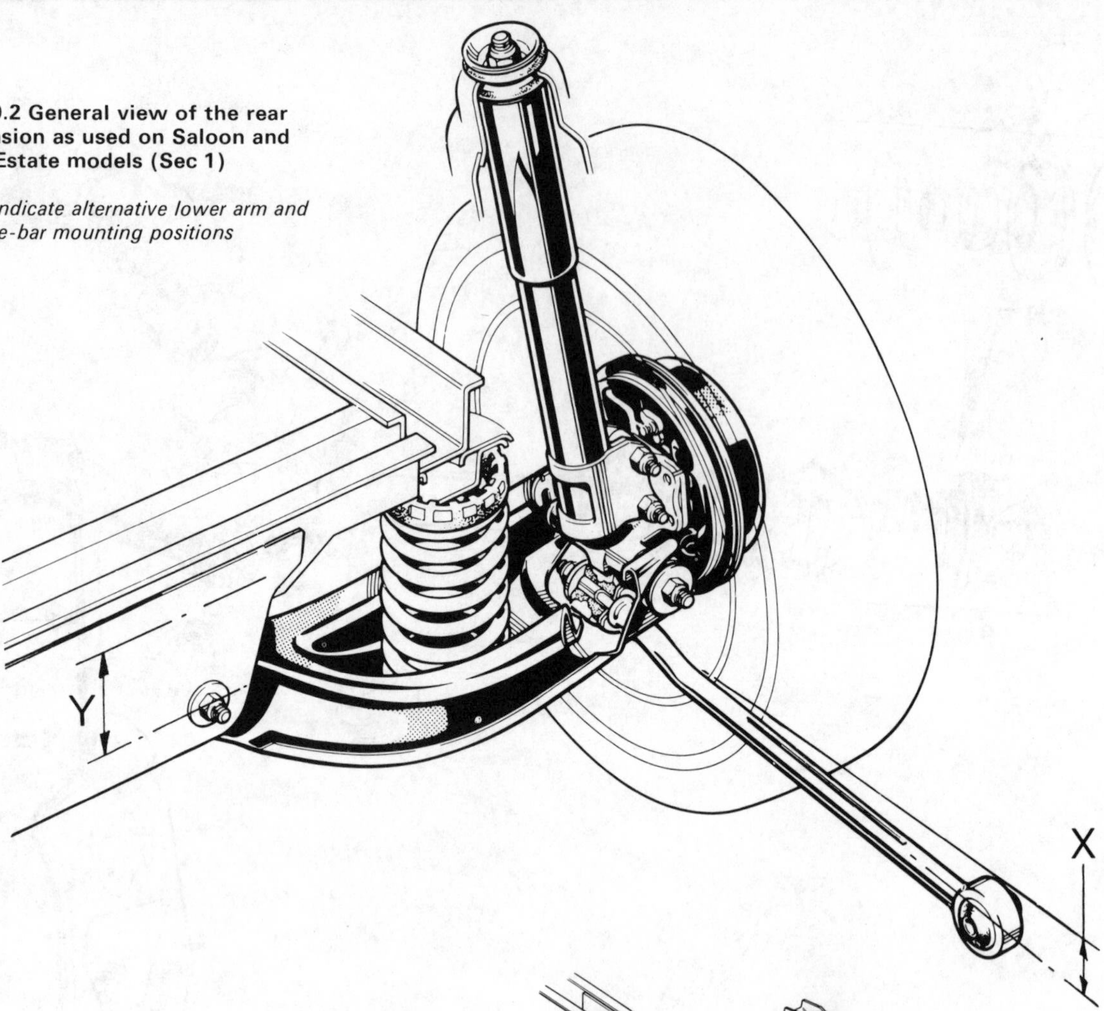

Fig. 10.2 General view of the rear suspension as used on Saloon and Estate models (Sec 1)

X and Y indicate alternative lower arm and tie-bar mounting positions

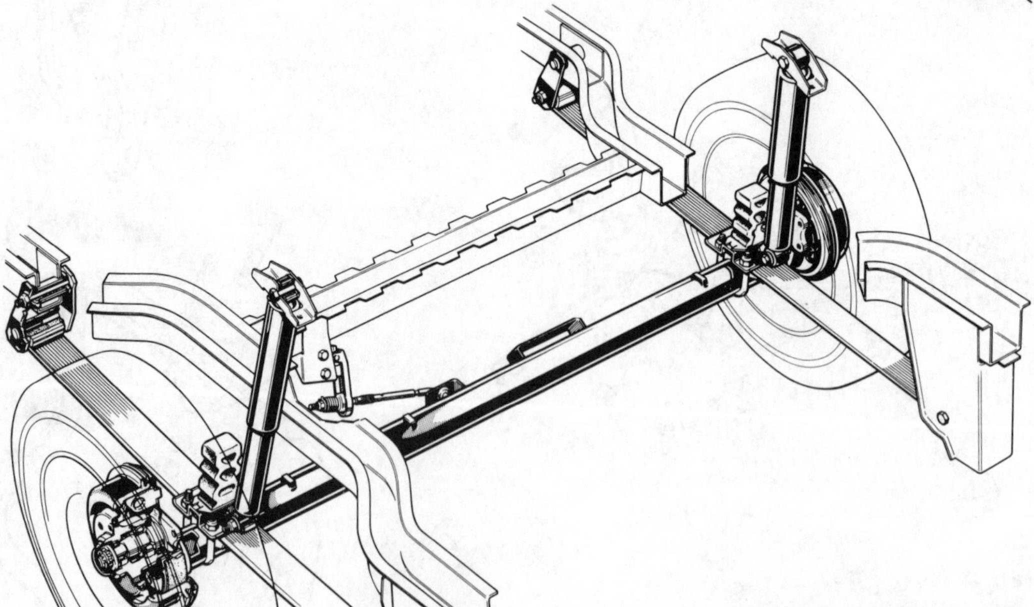

Y

X

Fig. 10.3 General view of the rear suspension as used on Van models (Sec 1)

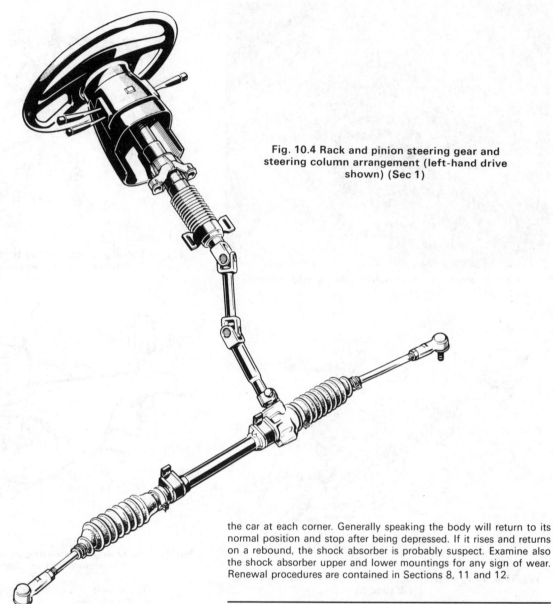

Fig. 10.4 Rack and pinion steering gear and steering column arrangement (left-hand drive shown) (Sec 1)

the car at each corner. Generally speaking the body will return to its normal position and stop after being depressed. If it rises and returns on a rebound, the shock absorber is probably suspect. Examine also the shock absorber upper and lower mountings for any sign of wear. Renewal procedures are contained in Sections 8, 11 and 12.

3 Front hub bearings – removal and refitting

1   Remove the wheel trim and release the staking on the driveshaft retaining nut using a suitable punch (photo).
2   Slacken the driveshaft retaining nut and the wheel bolts.
3   Jack up the front of the car, support it on stands and remove the roadwheel.
4   Undo the two bolts securing the brake caliper anchor bracket to the hub carrier.
5   Withdraw the anchor bracket and brake caliper complete with disc pads and suspend it from a convenient place under the wheel arch.
6   Remove the driveshaft retaining nut and washer.
7   Undo the retaining screw and withdraw the brake disc from the hub.
8   Using a two-legged puller draw off the hub.
9   Extract the split pin and unscrew the castellated nut from the steering tie-rod balljoint.
10 Release the balljoint from the steering arm using a balljoint separator tool.
11 Disconnect the lower arm balljoint from the hub carrier by removing the nut and pinch-bolt. Note that the pinch-bolt is of the socket-headed (Torx) type and a special key or socket bit (available from accessory shops) will be required for this purpose.
12 Undo the bolt which secures the hub carrier to the base of the suspension strut.

9   Visually inspect the rear suspension components, attachments and linkages for any visible signs of wear or damage.
10 Grasp the roadwheel at the 12 o'clock and 6 o'clock positions and try to rock it. Any excess movement here indicates wear or incorrect adjustment of the hub bearings which may also be accompanied by a rumbling sound when the wheel is spun. Repair procedures are described in Sections 9 and 10.

Wheels and tyres
11 Carefully inspect each tyre, including the spare, for signs of uneven wear, lumps, bulges or damage to the sidewalls or tread face. Refer to Section 30 for further details.
12 Check the condition of the wheel rims for distortion, damage and excessive run-out. Also make sure that the balance weights are secure with no obvious signs that any are missing. Check the torque of the wheel bolts and check the tyre pressures.

Shock absorbers
13 Check for any signs of fluid leakage around the shock absorber body. Should any fluid be noticed the shock absorber is defective internally and renewal is necessary.
14 The efficiency of the shock absorber may be checked by bouncing

3.1 Release the staking on the driveshaft retaining nut (arrowed) using a punch

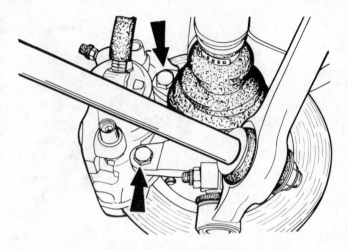

Fig. 10.5 Brake caliper anchor bracket-to-hub carrier retaining bolts – arrowed (Sec 3)

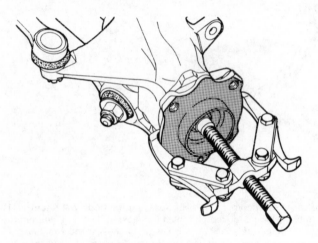

Fig. 10.6 Using a two-legged puller to draw off the wheel hub (Sec 3)

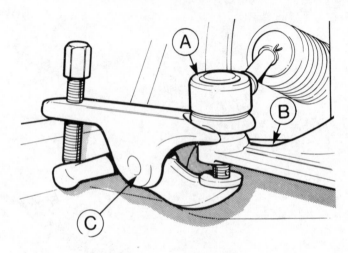

Fig. 10.7 Releasing the steering tie-rod balljoint using a separator tool (Sec 3)

A   Balljoint   C   Balljoint separator tool
B   Steering arm

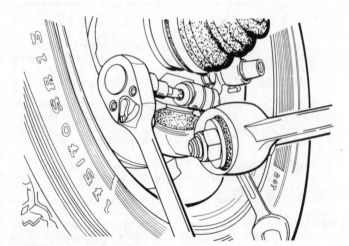

Fig. 10.8 Removing the lower arm balljoint Torx type pinch-bolt (Sec 3)

13 Using a suitable lever, separate the carrier from the strut by prising open the clamp jaws.
14 Support the driveshaft so that it does not hang down by more than 20° from the horizontal then withdraw the hub carrier.
15 Support the hub carrier in a vice fitted with protected jaws.
16 Using pliers, pull out the dust shield from the groove in the hub carrier.
17 Prise out the inner and outer oil seals.
18 Lift out the bearings.
19 With a suitable drift, drive out the bearing tracks. Take care not to damage the bearing track carrier surface during removal since any burrs on the surface could prevent the new tracks seating correctly during assembly.
20 Clean away all old grease from the hub carrier.
21 Drive the new bearing tracks squarely into their seats using a piece of suitable diameter tubing.
22 Liberally pack a high quality lithium based grease into the bearings, making sure to work plenty into the spaces between the rollers. Note that the cavity between the inner and outer bearings in the carrier **must not** be packed with grease since this could cause a pressure build-up and result in the seals leaking.
23 Install the bearing to one side of the carrier, then fill the lips of the new oil seal with grease and tap it squarely into position.

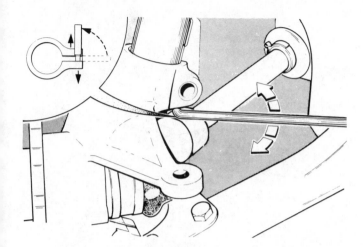

Fig. 10.9 Using a lever to spread the hub carrier clamp jaws (Sec 3)

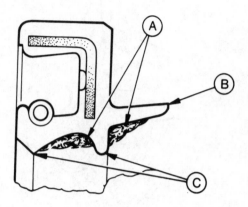

Fig. 10.10 Sectional view of the hub bearing oil seal (Sec 3)

A Grease applied to cavity between oil seal lips
B Axial sealing lip
C Radial sealing lips

Fig. 10.11 Hub carrier (B) and dust shield (A) (Sec 3)

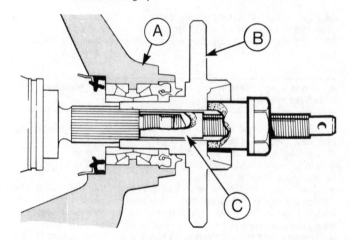

Fig. 10.12 Using special tool 14-022 to fit the front hub and driveshaft (Sec 3)

A Hub carrier
B Hub
C Tool 14-022

24 Fit the bearing and its seal to the opposite side in a similar way.
25 Fit the dust shield by tapping it into position using a block of wood.
26 Smear the driveshaft splines with grease, then install the carrier over the end of the driveshaft.
27 Connect the carrier to the suspension strut and tighten the bolt to the specified torque.
28 Reconnect the suspension lower arm balljoint to the carrier and secure by passing the pinch-bolt through the groove in the balljoint stud. The head of the pinch-bolt should be to the rear.
29 Reconnect the tie-rod to the steering arm, tighten the castellated nut to the specified torque and secure with a new split pin.
30 Install the hub/disc and push it on to the driveshaft as far as it will go using hand pressure only.
31 The threaded end of the driveshaft joint should be protruding far enough through the hub to enable it to be drawn fully home using the old driveshaft nut and packing washers. If this is not the case it will be necessary to use Ford special tool 14-022 or a suitable alternative (Fig. 10.12).
32 With the hub in place fit a new driveshaft retaining nut and the washer but only tighten the nut hand tight at this stage.
33 Refit the brake disc and caliper anchor bracket, tightening the anchor bracket bolts to the specified torque.
34 Refit the roadwheel and lower the car to the ground.

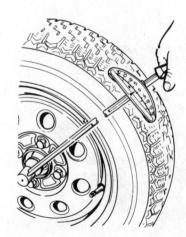

Fig. 10.13 Tightening the driveshaft retaining nut (Sec 3)

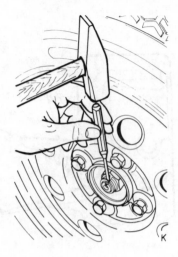

Fig. 10.14 Staking the driveshaft retaining nut (Sec 3)

35 Tighten the driveshaft retaining nut to the specified torque then stake the nut into the driveshaft groove using a small punch.
36 Tighten the wheel bolts to the specified torque and refit the wheel trim.

4 Front suspension lower arm (forged type) – removal, overhaul and refitting

1 The forged type suspension arm is fitted to all models except pre-May 1983 1.1 litre versions.
2 Jack up the front of the car and support it on stands.
3 Undo the nut and remove the pivot bolt securing the lower arm at its inboard end (photo).
4 Disconnect the lower arm balljoint from the hub carrier by removing the nut and pinch-bolt. Note that the pinch-bolt is of the socket-headed (Torx) type and a special key or socket bit (available from accessory shops) will be required for this purpose (photos).
5 Unscrew and remove the nut, washer and bush from the end of the anti-roll bar (or tie-bar on 1985 RS Turbo models). Withdraw the arm from under the car.
6 Renewal of the pivot bush at the inboard end of the arm is possible using a vice and small tubes of suitable diameter. Lubricate the new bush thoroughly with rubber grease to ease installation.
7 If the balljoint is worn it will be necessary to renew the arm complete as the balljoint cannot be removed separately.

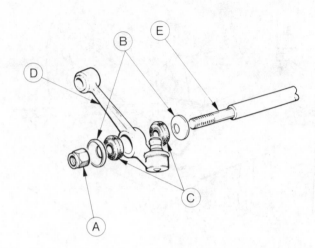

Fig. 10.15 Anti-roll bar-to-lower arm mounting (Sec 4)

A   Nut   D   Lower arm
B   Dished washer   E   Anti-roll bar
C   Bushes

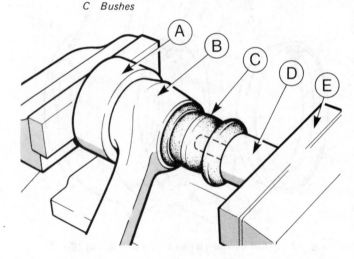

Fig. 10.16 Method of fitting lower arm inboard pivot bush (Sec 4)

A   Tubular spacer   D   Tube or socket
B   Lower arm   E   Vice
C   Bush

4.3 Suspension lower arm disconnected at inboard end

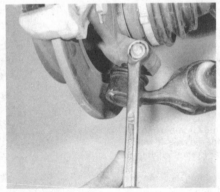

4.4A Removing the lower arm balljoint pinch-bolt nut

4.4B Separating the balljoint from the hub carrier

8 Refitting is the reverse sequence to removal. Tighten all nuts and bolts to the specified torque with the weight of the car on its roadwheels. When refitting the Torx pinch-bolt note that the head of the bolt must face the rear of the car.

5 Front suspension lower arm (pressed steel type) – removal, overhaul and refitting

1 The pressed steel type suspension is only fitted to pre-May 1983 1.1 litre models.
2 Jack up the front of the car and support it on stands.
3 Undo the nut and remove the pivot bolt securing the lower arm at its inboard end.
4 Undo the two nuts which secure the tie-bar and lower arm balljoint to the lower arm. Separate the arm from the tie-bar and remove it from under the car.
5 Renewal of the pivot bush is carried out in the same way as described in Section 4, paragraph 6.

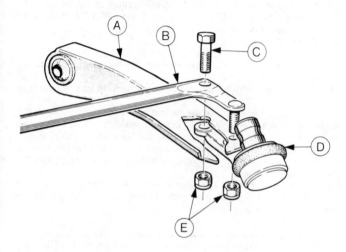

Fig. 10.17 Pressed steel type lower arm components (Sec 5)

A   Lower arm   D   Balljoint
B   Tie-bar   E   Retaining nuts
C   Retaining bolt

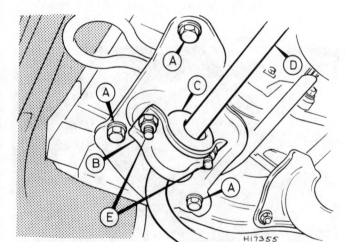

Fig. 10.19 Anti-roll bar front mounting clamp details – post-1986 models (Sec 6)

A   Body bracket bolts   D   Anti-roll bar
B   Clamp   E   Retaining nuts
C   Bush

6 If the balljoint is worn it can be renewed after removing it from the hub carrier as described in Section 4, paragraph 4.
7 Refitting is the reverse sequence to removal. Tighten all nuts and bolts to the specified torque with the weight of the car on its roadwheels. If the balljoint has been removed, refit the Torx pinch-bolt with its head towards the rear of the car.

6 Front anti-roll bar – removal and refitting

1 The anti-roll bar is used in conjunction with the forged type suspension lower arm.
2 Jack up the front of the car and support it on stands.
3 Where fitted flatten the lockplate tabs and unscrew the two bolts or two nuts each side securing the anti-roll bar clamps to the underbody.
4 Disconnect the ends of the anti-roll bar by unscrewing the nuts and removing the washers and the bushes (photo). Note that the nut on the right-hand side of the anti-roll bar has a **left-hand thread** and is unscrewed by turning it clockwise.
5 On 1985 RS Turbo models separate the ends of the anti-roll bar from the tie-bars by releasing the clamp nuts and bolts (Fig. 10.21).
6 On all models except 1985 RS Turbo undo the nut and remove the pivot bolt securing one of the suspension lower arms at its inboard end.

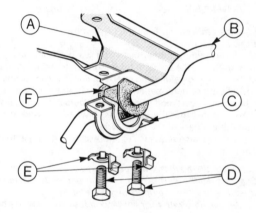

Fig. 10.18 Anti-roll bar front mounting clamp details – pre-1986 models (Sec 6)

A   Body bracket   D   Retaining bolts
B   Anti-roll bar   E   Lockplates
C   Clamp   F   Bush

6.4 Anti-roll to lower arm retaining nut (arrowed)

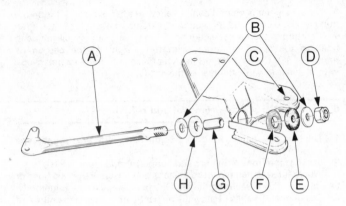

Fig. 10.20 Front tie-bar mountings – pre-May 1983 1.1 litre models (Sec 7)

A	Tie-bar	E	Front insulator
B	Flat washers	F	Bush
C	Mounting bracket	G	Steel sleeve
D	Retaining nut	H	Rear insulator

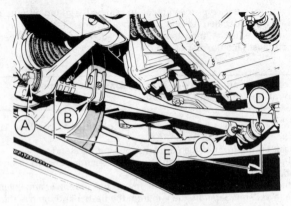

Fig. 10.21 Front tie-bar mountings – 1985 RS Turbo models (Sec 7)

A	Retaining nut	E	Basic setting length = 565
B	Anti-roll bar clamp		± 1.5 mm (22.24 ± 0.06
C	Adjustment clamp		in)
D	Front mounting bolt		

7 Withdraw the anti-roll bar from the lower arms and remove it from under the car.

8 Remove the remaining rubber bush and washer from each end of the anti-roll bar. Smear the bar with rubber grease to aid bush removal.

9 Inspect the bushes carefully and renew them if they show any signs of cracking, splitting or deformation. Bushes of different material have been introduced on Escort models during the course of production and it is therefore essential that the bushes are always renewed in sets of four to ensure that all are of the same type.

10 Refitting is the reverse sequence to removal but bearing in mind the following points:

   (a) Lubricate the bushes with rubber grease to aid refitting
   (b) Ensure that the end of the anti-roll bar with the left-hand thread is fitted to the right-hand side of the car
   (c) Fit the washers with their concave sides facing away from the bushes
   (d) Tighten all nuts and bolts with the weight of the car on its roadwheels
   (e) Where lockplates are used bend up the tabs to lock the bolts after tightening.

10 Undo the nut and bolt and remove the tie-bar-to-anti-roll bar clamp.

11 Undo the tie-bar front nut and pivot bolt and remove the bar from under the car.

12 Do not alter the length of the tie-rod otherwise the steering castor angle will have to be reset. If the length has been altered or if a new tie-bar is being fitted, set the length to the basic setting as shown in Fig. 10.21. The length can be adjusted by slackening the forward clamp bolt and turning the threaded portion as necessary. Tighten the clamp after adjustment.

13 Refitting is the reverse sequence to removal but tighten all nuts and bolts to the specified torque with the weight of the car on its roadwheels.

8 Front suspension strut – removal, overhaul and refitting

1 Slacken the roadwheel bolts, raise the front of the vehicle and support it securely on stands, then remove the roadwheel.

2 Support the underside of the driveshaft on blocks or by tying it up to the rack-and-pinion steering housing.

3 Where fitted, detach the brake hose and location grommet from the strut location bracket (photo), then unscrew and remove the

7 Front tie-bar – removal and refitting

Pre-May 1983 1.1 litre models

1 Jack up the front of the vehicle and support securely on stands.

2 Unscrew and remove the nut which holds the tie-bar to the large pressed steel mounting bracket. Take off the dished washer and the rubber insulator.

3 Disconnect the lower arm balljoint from the hub carrier by removing the nut and pinch-bolt. Note that the pinch-bolt is of the socket-headed (Torx) type and a special key or socket bit (available from accessory shops) will be required for this purpose.

4 Unbolt the opposite end of the tie-bar from the suspension arm.

5 Withdraw the tie-bar from its pressed steel bracket and take off the remaining washer, insulator and steel sleeve.

6 Where necessary the bush in the pressed steel mounting bracket can be renewed if the old bush is drawn out using a bolt, nut and suitable distance pieces.

7 Refitting the tie-bar is a reversal of removal. Finally tighten all nuts and bolts to the specified torque only when the weight of the vehicle is again on its roadwheels. When refitting the Torx pinch-bolt note that the head of the bolt must face the rear of the car.

1985 RS Turbo models

8 Jack up the front of the vehicle and support it on stands.

9 Undo the nut and remove the washer and bush securing the end of the tie-bar to the suspension arm.

8.3 Brake hose and grommet location in strut (A) and strut-to-hub carrier pinch-bolt (B)

8.4A Suspension strut-to-turret mounting bolts on pre-1983 models

8.4B Removing the nut cover ...

8.4C ... and strut retaining nut on post-1983 models

Note Allen key to prevent piston rod turning

pinch-bolt which holds the base of the suspension strut to the hub carrier. Using a suitable tool, lever the sides of the slot in the carrier apart until it is free from the strut.

4   On pre-May 1983 models undo the two bolts securing the strut to the inner wing turret (photo). On post-May 1983 models lift off the cover then unscrew the strut retaining nut. Prevent the piston rod from turning using a 6 mm Allen key (photos).

5   Withdraw the complete strut assembly from under the front wing.

6   Clean away external dirt and mud.

7   If the strut has been removed due to oil leakage or to lack of damping, then it should be renewed with a new or factory reconditioned unit. Dismantling of the original strut is not recommended and internal components are not generally available.

8   Before the strut is exchanged, the coil spring will have to be removed. To do this, a spring compressor or compressors will be needed. These are generally available from tool hire centres or they can be purchased at most motor accessory shops.

9   Engage the compressor over four coils of the spring and compress the spring sufficiently to release spring tension from the top mounting.

10   Once the spring is compressed, unscrew and remove the nut from the end of the piston rod which retains the top mounting. As there will be a tendency for the piston rod to turn while the nut is unscrewed, insert a 6 mm Allen key to hold the rod still.

11   Remove the top mounting and lift off the spring and compressor.

12   The compressor need not be released if the spring is to be fitted immediately to a new strut. If the compressor is to be released from the spring, make sure that you do it slowly and progressively.

13   The top mounting can be dismantled by sliding off the thrust bearing and withdrawing the spring upper seat, gaiter spring and, where fitted, insulator. Also, if fitted, slide the bump stop from the piston rod.

14   Renew any worn or damaged components. If the front strut and/or coil spring is to be removed then it is advisable also to renew the equivalent assembly on the other side.

15   Fit the spring to the strut, making sure that the ends of the coils locate correctly in the shaped parts of the spring seats.

16   Fit the top mounting components, being very careful to maintain the correct order of assembly of the individual components.

17   Gently release and remove the spring compressor.

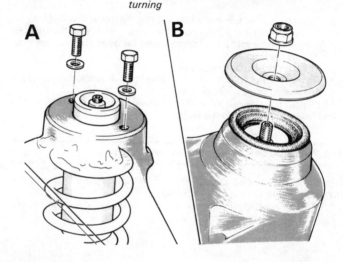

Fig. 10.22 Front suspension strut upper mounting removal (Sec 8)

A   Pre-May 1983 models   *B   Post-May 1983 models*

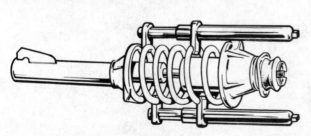

Fig. 10.23 Coil spring retained with spring compressors (Sec 8)

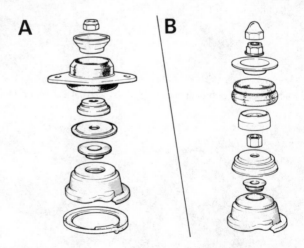

Fig. 10.24 Exploded view of the suspension strut upper mounting components (Sec 8)

A   Pre-May 1983 models   *B   Post-May 1983 models*

18 With the spring compressor removed, check that the ends of the spring are fully located in the shaped sections of the spring seatings, then refit the strut using the reverse of the removal procedure. Lower the vehicle so that it is standing on its roadwheels before tightening the top mounting bolts or nut to the specified torque.

9 Rear hub bearings – adjustment

1 Raise and support the rear of the vehicle on stands. Release the handbrake.
2 This adjustment will normally only be required if, when the top and bottom of the roadwheel are gripped and 'rocked', excessive movement can be detected in the bearings. Slight movement is essential.
3 Remove the roadwheel. Using a hammer and cold chisel, tap off the dust cap from the end of the hub.
4 Extract the split pin and take off the nut retainer.
5 Tighten the hub nut to a torque of between 20 and 25 Nm (15 and 18 lbf ft), at the same time rotating the brake drum in an anti-clockwise direction.
6 Unscrew the nut one half a turn and then tighten it only finger tight.
7 Fit the nut retainer so that two of its slots line up with the split pin hole. Insert a new split pin, bending the end **around** the nut, **not** over the end of the stub axle.
8 Tap the dust cap into position.
9 Recheck the play as described in paragraph 2. A fractional amount of wheel movement **must** be present.
10 Repeat the operations on the opposite hub, refit the roadwheels and lower the vehicle to the floor.

10 Rear hub bearings – removal and refitting

1 Raise and support the rear of the vehicle on stands. Remove the roadwheel and release the handbrake.
2 On fuel-injected models and Van versions undo the retaining screw

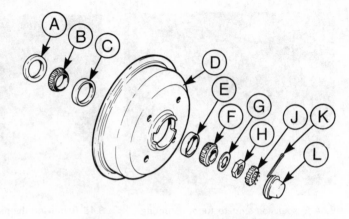

Fig. 10.25 Exploded view of the rear hub bearings (Sec 10)

A Oil seal
B Inboard bearing
C Bearing outer track
D Hub and drum
E Bearing outer track
F Outboard bearing

G Thrust washer
H Retaining nut
J Nut retainer
K Split pin
L Dust cap

and withdraw the brake drum from the hub.
3 Tap off the dust cap from the end of the hub (photo).
4 Extract the split pin and remove the nut retainer (photo).
5 Unscrew and remove the nut and take off the thrust washer (photos).
6 Pull the hub/drum off the stub axle slightly then push it back. This will now leave the outboard bearing ready to be taken off the stub axle (photo).
7 Withdraw the hub/drum (photo).

10.3 Removing rear hub dust cap

10.4 Extracting rear hub split pin

10.5A Unscrewing rear hub retaining nut ...

10.5B ... and removing the thrust washer

10.6 Rear hub outboard bearing removal

10.7 Removal of rear hub/drum assembly

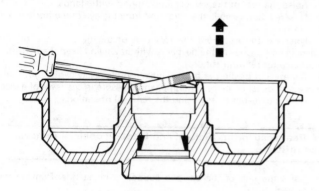

Fig. 10.26 Removing the hub bearing oil seal (Sec 10)

11.3 Rear shock absorber top mounting

8   Prise the oil seal from the hub and take out the inboard taper roller bearing.

9   Using a suitable punch, drive out the bearing outer tracks, taking care not to burr the bearing seats.

10 If new bearings are being fitted to both hubs, do not mix up the bearing components but keep them in their individual packs until required.

11 Drive the new bearing tracks squarely into their hub recesses.

12 Pack both bearings with the specified grease, working plenty into the rollers. Be generous, but there is no need to fill the cavity between the inner and outer bearings.

13 Locate the inboard bearing and then grease the lips of a new oil seal and tap it into position.

14 Fit the hub onto the stub axle, taking care not to catch the oil seal lips.

15 Fit the outboard bearing and the thrust washer and screw on the nut.

16 Adjust the bearings as described in Section 9.

17 On fuel-injected models and Van versions refit the brake drum and secure with the retaining screw.

18 Refit the roadwheel and lower the car to the ground.

Fig. 10.27 Removing the shock absorber top mounting nut – Saloon and Estate models (Sec 11)

11 Rear shock absorber (Saloon and Estate models) – removal, testing and refitting

1   Slacken the roadwheel bolts, raise the rear of the vehicle, support it on stands and remove the roadwheel.

2   Support the suspension lower arm with a jack.

3   Open the tailgate and lift the parcel tray to expose the shock absorber top mounting (photo).

4   Remove the cap and then unscrew the nut from the shock absorber spindle. To prevent the spindle turning, use an Allen key in the socket provided.

5   Take off the cap and insulator.

6   Separate the brake hydraulic hose from the shock absorber by slackening the centre locking nut and easing the hose and pipe down and out of the slot in the bracket. On the right-hand side there is very little clearance for a spanner and it may be easier if the roadspring is removed as described in Section 14.

7   Undo the two bolts securing the shock absorber to the stub axle carrier and withdraw the unit, together with cup and bump rubber, from under the wheel arch.

8   To test the shock absorber, grip its lower mounting in a vice so that the unit is vertical.

9   Fully extend and retract the shock absorber ten or twelve times. Any lack of resistance in either direction will indicate the need for renewal, as will evidence of leakage of fluid.

10 Refitting is a reversal of removal, but if a new unit is being installed, prime it first in a similar way to that described for testing.

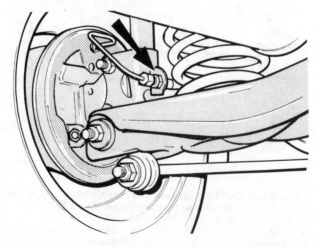

Fig. 10.28 Brake hydraulic hose-to-shock absorber attachment (arrowed) – Saloon and Estate models (Sec 11)

12 Rear shock absorbers (Van models) – removal, testing and refitting

1   Raise and support the rear of the vehicle on stands. Place a jack beneath the rear axle tube and just raise it slightly.
2   Disconnect the shock absorber lower mounting by unscrewing the nut and pivot bolt.
3   Unbolt the top mounting bracket from the body and withdraw the unit.
4   Undo the nut and pivot bolt to separate the mounting bracket from the shock absorber.
5   Test the unit as described in the preceding Section and refit by reversing the removal operations.

13 Rear tie-bar (Saloon and Estate models) – removal and refitting

1   Before attempting to remove a tie-bar, note the location of all washers and bushes. These control the rear wheel alignment and they must be returned to their original locations.

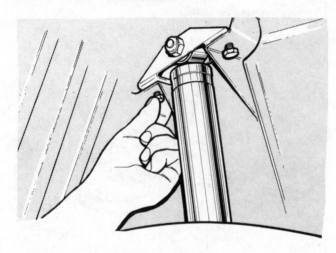

Fig. 10.29 Removing the rear shock absorber top mounting bracket – Van models (Sec 12)

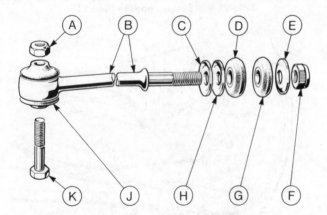

Fig. 10.31 Exploded view of the rear tie-bar mountings – Saloon and Estate models (Sec 13)

A   Nut
B   Tie-bar
C   Washer (additional washers
    may be fitted)
D   Bush
E   Washer
F   Nut
G   Bush
H   Washer (additional washers
    may be fitted)
J   Bush
K   Pivot bolt

2   Raise the rear of the vehicle and support with stands.
3   Unscrew and remove the pivot bolt from the eye at the front end of the tie-bar.
4   Unscrew the nut from the rear end of the tie-bar, take off the washers and bushes as the tie-bar is withdrawn and keep them in strict sequence for refitting (photo).
5   Renewal of the tie-bar flexible bush is quite easily carried out using sockets or distance pieces and applying pressure in the jaws of a vice.
6   Refit the tie-bar by reversing the removal operations.

14 Rear roadspring (Saloon and Estate models) – removal and refitting

1   Raise the rear of the car and support it on stands. Remove the roadwheel.
2   Support the suspension lower arm by placing a jack beneath the spring seating.
3   On models equipped with a rear anti-roll bar disconnect the bar from the shackles by levering them apart with a screwdriver.
4   Undo the nut and remove the lower arm inboard pivot bolt.
5   Slowly lower the jack beneath the arm and remove the spring and insulator pad.
6   Refitting is the reverse sequence to removal. If applicable the plastic sleeved end of the coil spring must be at the upper end when

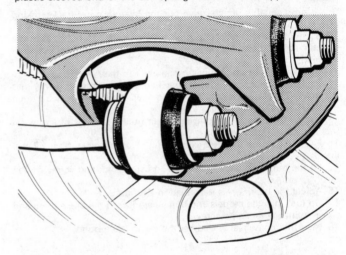

Fig. 10.30 Rear tie-bar-to-stub axle carrier attachment – Saloon and Estate models (Sec 13)

13.4 Tie-bar-to-stub axle carrier retaining nut (arrowed)

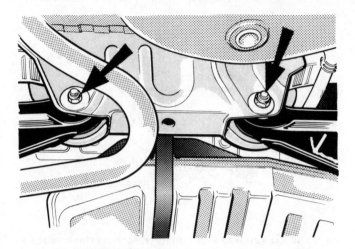

Fig. 10.32 Lower arm inboard pivot nuts and bolts (arrowed) – Saloon and Estate models (Secs 14 and 16)

Fig. 10.33 Rear roadspring and insulator pad – Saloon and Estate models (Sec 14)

fitted. Tighten all nuts and bolts to the specified torque with the car standing on its roadwheels.

15 Rear roadspring (Van models) – removal and refitting

1 To remove the single leaf type rear roadspring from the van, raise the rear of the vehicle and support it securely under the body members. Support the axle tube using a jack or stands.
2 Unscrew the spring U-bolt nuts and withdraw the bump rubber plate complete with shock absorber lower attachment.
3 Disconnect the shackle from the rear end of the roadspring and pull the spring downward.
4 Unscrew and remove the spring front eye bolt and nut.
5 Remove the spring from under the vehicle.
6 Refit by reversing the removal operations, but do not tighten the nuts to the specified torque until the weight of the vehicle has been lowered onto the wheels.
7 On completion adjust the braking system light laden valve as described in Chapter 9.

16 Rear suspension lower arm (Saloon and Estate models) – removal and refitting

1 Raise the rear of the car and support it on stands.
2 On cars equipped with the anti-lock braking system, refer to Chapter 9 and remove the load apportioning valve adjusting bracket from the lower arm.
3 If an anti-roll bar is fitted, disconnect the shackles from the lower arm by levering them apart with a screwdriver.
4 Support the lower arm using a jack located beneath the roadspring.
5 Undo the nut and remove the arm inboard pivot bolt.
6 Undo the nut, remove the outboard pivot through-bolt then lower the jack and remove the spring and insulator pad.
7 Withdraw the lower arm from the car.
8 Refitting is the reverse sequence to removal. If applicable the plastic sleeved end of the coil spring must be at the upper end when fitted. Tighten all nuts and bolts to the specified torque with the car standing on its roadwheels. On cars equipped with the anti-lock braking system, refit the load apportioning valve adjusting bracket as described in Chapter 9.

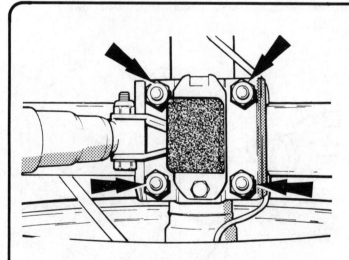

Fig. 10.34 Rear roadspring U-bolt nuts (arrowed) – Van models (Sec 15)

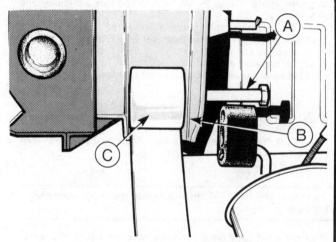

Fig. 10.35 Rear roadspring front eye bolt – Van models (Sec 15)

A Pivot bolt
B Mounting bracket
C Spring eye

17 Rear stub axle carrier (Saloon and Estate models) – removal and refitting

1   Raise and support the rear of the car on stands. Remove the roadwheel.
2   Remove the rear hub as described in Section 10.
3   Remove the rear brake shoe assembly, as described in Chapter 9. You will also need to disconnect the brake fluid pipe at its connection to the wheel cylinder. Plug the pipe and cylinder connections to prevent fluid loss and the ingress of dirt.
4   Extract the handbrake cable through the backplate, then unscrew the four backplate retaining bolts and withdraw the backplate.
5   Position a jack under the lower arm and support it.
6   Undo the two nuts and remove the bolts securing the shock absorber to the stub axle carrier.
7   Undo the nut and remove the lower arm outboard pivot through-bolt.
8   Accurately record the location and number of washers at the tie-bar attachment then undo the nut and withdraw the stub axle carrier.
9   If the stub axle is damaged or worn excessively then it must be renewed.
10 Refitting is a reversal of the removal procedure, but note the following:

   (a) *When reassembling the tie-bar to the stub axle ensure that the spacers, washers and bushes are correctly located (as noted during removal)*
   (b) *Do not fully tighten the suspension retaining nuts and bolts to their specified torque settings until the vehicle is lowered and standing on its roadwheels*
   (c) *Refit and connect the brake assembly components, as given in Chapter 9. Leave bleeding the hydraulic circuit until after the hub and brake drum are refitted*
   (d) *Adjust the hub bearings, as detailed in Section 9*

18 Rear axle tube (Van models) – removal and refitting

1   Raise the rear of the vehicle and support it on stands. Remove the rear roadwheels.
2   Support the axle tube on a jack preferably of trolley type.
3   Remove the rear hub as described in Section 10.
4   Disconnect the brake hydraulic pipes and hoses at the axle tube bracket. Plug the pipe and hose ends after removal.
5   Disconnect the brake pipe unions at the rear wheel cylinders then undo the four bolts each side and remove both rear brake backplates.
6   Undo the axle-to-roadspring retaining U-bolt nuts and remove the U-bolts.
7   Lower the axle tube to the ground while at the same time sliding the light laden valve link rod from its spacer tube. Remove the link rod and bush from the axle tube.
8   Withdraw the axle from under the vehicle.
9   Refitting is the reverse sequence to removal bearing in mind the following:

   (a) *Adjust the hub bearings as described in Section 9*
   (b) *Tighten the U-bolt nuts to the specified torque with the weight of the vehicle on its roadwheels*
   (c) *Bleed the brake hydraulic system and adjust the light laden valve as described in Chapter 9*

19 Rear anti-roll bar (Saloon and Estate models) – removal and refitting

1   Slacken the left-hand roadwheel bolts, raise and support the rear of the car on stands. Remove the roadwheel.
2   Lever the shackles from the right- and left-hand suspension lower arms (photo).
3   Unbolt the anti-roll bar from the underbody, carefully noting the relative fixing locations.
4   Release the fuel lines from their securing clips. Support the fuel tank and remove the three tank mounting bolts. Carefully lower the tank on its support.

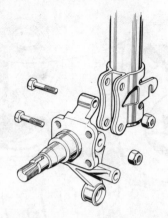

Fig. 10.36 Rear stub axle and shock absorber attachment – Saloon and Estate models (Sec 17)

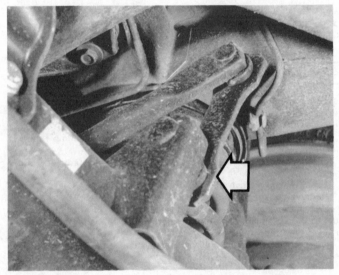

19.2 Anti-roll bar-to-lower arm shackle attachment (arrowed)

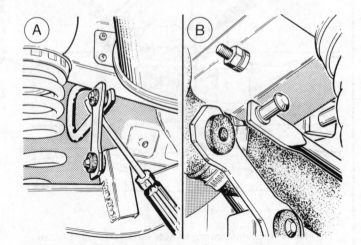

Fig. 10.37 Disconnecting the rear anti-roll bar shackles – Saloon and Estate models (Sec 19)

A   Left-hand side   B   Right-hand side

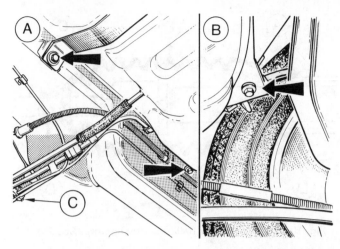

Fig. 10.38 Fuel tank attachment details (Sec 19)

A   *Mounting bolts (arrowed)*
B   *Mounting bolt (arrowed)*
C   *Fuel line clips*

5   Withdraw the anti-roll bar from the left-hand side of the vehicle.
6   To remove the rubber bushes from the anti-roll bar simply prise open the bush retainers with a screwdriver. Press the retainers together so that the fixing holes are in line when refitting.
7   Refitting is a reversal of removal. The fuel tank must be bolted in position before securing the anti-roll bar. Ensure the underbody fixings are refitted in their original locations.
8   Lubricate the shackle bushes with soap solution before reconnecting them to the lower arms.

20 Rear suspension angles – general

1   The rear wheel toe and camber angles are set in production and do not require checking under normal service conditions. Of the two, only the toe setting can be adjusted, camber angle being fixed by production sizes and tolerances.
2   The only time that angles will need to be checked will be after an accident in which the rear of the car has suffered damage or where a rear end skid has caused a side impact on a rear roadwheel.
3   Severely worn components of the rear suspension can also cause the angles to be misaligned, in which case renewal of the defective components should rectify the suspension angles and alignment.

4   The actual settings have been revised a number of times as a result of component changes during the course of production and also to improve directional stability. The settings also vary according to model year, engine size and optional equipment, and to list all the settings would be beyond the scope of this manual. If in any doubt about the rear suspension angles, or if the rear tyre wear appears excessive it is recommended that the car be taken to a Ford dealer for accurate checking on optical alignment equipment.

21 Steering gear bellows – renewal

1   At the first indication of a split or grease leakage from the bellows, renew them.
2   Loosen off the roadwheel bolts, raise the front of the vehicle and support on stands. Remove the roadwheels.
3   Measure and take note of the amount of thread on the tie-rod which is exposed (photo). This will ensure correct toe-setting on reassembly.
4   Loosen off the tie-rod outer ball-joint locknut.
5   Extract the split pin and remove the nut from the balljoint taper pin.
6   Using a suitable balljoint extractor, separate the balljoint taper pin from the eye of the steering arm (photo).
7   Unscrew the balljoint from the end of the tie-rod, also the locknut. As a double check for correct repositioning of the tie-rod balljoint when reassembling, note the number of turns required to remove it.
8   Release the clip from the end of the damaged bellow and slide it from the rack and the tie-rod (photo).
9   When ordering the new bellows and retaining clips also specify the diameter of the tie-rod which will vary according to manufacture and can be checked with a ruler or calipers. This is important since if the wrong size bellows are fitted they will not seal or possibly be damaged on fitting.
10 If a damaged bellow has caused steering lubricant loss it will be necessary to drain any remaining lubricant and renew it. To do this turn the steering wheel gently to expel as much lubricant as possible from the rack housing. If the opposing bellow is not being renewed it is recommended that it is released from the rack housing to allow the old lubricant to be removed from that end, too.
11 Smear the narrow neck of the new bellows with grease and slide into position over the tie-rod, ensuring that the bellows are correctly located in the tie-rod groove on the outer bellow end (where applicable).
12 If new bellows are being fitted to the pinion end of the rack, leave the bellows unclamped at this stage.
13 If the bellows are being fitted to the rack support bush end of the rack housing, clamp the inner end of the bellows.
14 Always use new screw-type clamps, never re-use the old factory-fitted wire type when securing the bellows.
15 Screw the locknut into position on the tie-rod, followed by the outer tie-rod balljoint. Screw the joint the exact number of turns noted during removal.
16 Connect the balljoint to the steering arm, tighten the nut to the specified torque and insert a new split pin to secure.

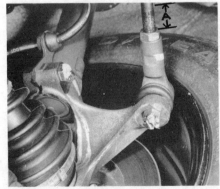

21.3 Steering tie-rod outer balljoint showing exposed threads (A) on tie-rod

21.6 Releasing tie-rod balljoint using separator tool

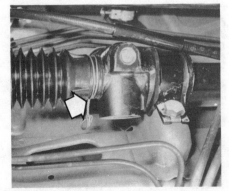

21.8 Bellows-to-rack and pinion housing wire type retaining clip (arrowed)

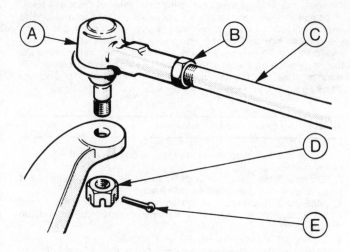

Fig. 10.39 Steering tie-rod outer balljoint details
(Secs 21 and 22)

A   Balljoint   D   Castellated retaining nut
B   Locknut   E   Split pin
C   Tie-rod

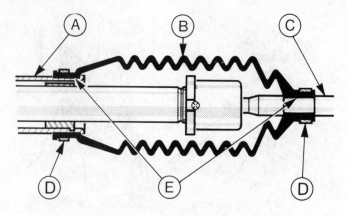

Fig. 10.40 Steering gear bellows attachments (Sec 21)

A   Rack housing   D   Retaining clips
B   Bellows   E   Apply a smear of grease
C   Steering tie-rod   when fitting

17 If applicable, renew the steering gear lubricant, as described in
Section 28.
18 Tighten the bellow retaining clamp(s).
19 Refit the roadwheels and lower the vehicle to the ground. Settle
the suspension by bouncing the front end.
20 Tighten the balljoint locknut and check the amount of tie-rod
thread exposed. It should be as noted when dismantling and therefore
provide the correct toe-setting, but in any case the alignment should
really be checked at the earliest opportunity, as described in Section 20
or by your Ford dealer.

22 Steering tie-rod outer balljoint – renewal

1   If as the result of inspection the tie-rod outer balljoints are found to
be worn, remove them as described in the preceding Section.
2   When the balljoint nuts are unscrewed, it is sometimes found that
the balljoint taper pin turns in the eye of the steering arm to prevent the
nut from unscrewing. Should this happen, apply pressure to the top of
the balljoint using a length of wood as a lever to seat the taper pin
while the nut is unscrewed. When this condition is met with, a balljoint

extractor is unlikely to be required to free the taper pin from the
steering arm.
3   With the tie-rod removed, wire brush the threads of the tie-rod and
apply grease to them.
4   Screw on the new balljoint to take up a position similar to the
original. Due to manufacturing differences, the fitting of a new
component will almost certainly mean that the front wheel alignment
will require some adjustment. Check this as described in Section 29.
5   Connect the balljoint to the steering arm, as described in Section
21.

23 Steering wheel – removal and refitting

1   According to model, either pull off the steering wheel trim, prise out
the insert which carries the Ford motif at the centre, or carefully prise
up and lift off the horn push followed by the contact plate (photos).
2   Insert the ignition key and turn it to position I.
3   Hold the steering wheel from turning and have the front
roadwheels in the straight-ahead attitude. Unscrew the steering wheel
retaining nut using a socket and extension (photo).
4   Withdraw the steering wheel from the shaft.
5   Where applicable note the steering shaft direction indicator cam
which has its peg uppermost.
6   Refitting is the reverse sequence to removal. Check that the
roadwheels are still in the straight-ahead position and locate the
steering wheel with the larger section between the spokes uppermost.
Tighten the steering wheel retaining nut to the specified torque.

23.1A Steering wheel trim removal

23.1B Prising up the steering wheel horn
push ...

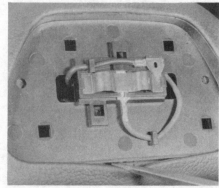

23.1C ... followed by the contact plate

23.3 Steering wheel retaining nut

24 Steering wheel – alignment

1 Owing to the fact that the steering wheel is located on a hexagon shaped steering shaft, it may be difficult to obtain perfect steering wheel alignment due to lack of fine adjustment.
2 It is therefore acceptable to adjust the tie-rods to give unequal lengths.
3 Check that the front roadwheels are in the straight-ahead position and that the toe setting is as specified.
4 If the steering wheel is more than 30° out of alignment, remove it and centralise it as much as possible on its shaft.
5 To adjust the steering wheel through a small angle, carry out the following operations.
6 Release the tie-rod balljoint locknuts.
7 Turn one tie-rod clockwise and the opposite one anti-clockwise by the identical amount. For every 1° of steering wheel angular error, turn each tie-rod through 30°.

8 Once the steering wheel has been centralised (front wheels in straight-ahead position), retighten the tie-rod balljoint locknuts.
9 Although the toe setting should not have altered, check the front wheel alignment as described in Section 29.

25 Steering column lock – removal and refitting

Note: *For ignition switch removal see Chapter 12, Section 17.*

1 To remove the ignition switch/column lock, the shear-head bolt must be drilled out.
2 Access for drilling can only be obtained if the steering column is lowered. To do this, remove the shrouds from the upper end of the column by extracting the fixing screws. Disconnect the battery earth lead.
3 Unscrew the bonnet release lever mounting screw and position the lever to one side.
4 Disconnect the steering column clamps. The lower one is of bolt and nut type, while the upper one is of stud and nut design.
5 Lower the shaft/column carefully until the steering wheel rests on the seat cushion.
6 Centre-punch the end of the shear-bolt which secures the steering column lock and then drill it out. Remove the ignition switch/column lock.
7 When fitting the new lock, check for correct operation and then tighten the securing bolt until its head breaks off.
8 Raise the steering column and reconnect the clamps.
9 Refit the bonnet release lever and the column shrouds.
10 Reconnect the battery.

26 Steering column – removal, overhaul and refitting

1 Disconnect the battery negative terminal.
2 Turn the ignition key and rotate the steering wheel to bring the front roadwheels to the straight-ahead position.
3 Working within the engine compartment, unscrew and remove the pinch-bolt which holds the steering shaft to the splined pinion shaft of the rack-and-pinion steering gear.
4 Remove the steering wheel, as described in Section 23.
5 Remove the direction indicator cam from the top end of the steering shaft (where fitted).

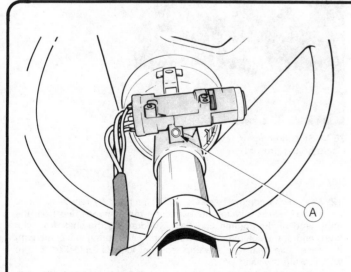

Fig. 10.41 Steering column lock assembly shear bolt (A) (Sec 25)

Pre-1986 version shown

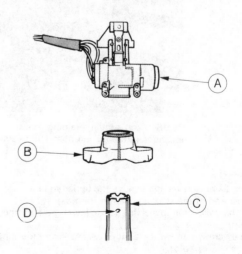

Fig. 10.42 Steering column lock components – pre-1986 models (Sec 25)

A   Lock housing
B   Upper clamp
C   Column tube
D   Shear bolt indentation

26.6A Removing the steering column upper...

26.6B ... and lower shrouds on a pre-1986 model ...

26.6C ... and on a post-1986 version

26.7 Removing the facia lower panel

26.8 Bonnet release lever removal

26.9A Steering column switch removal on a pre-1986 model ...

26.9B ... and switch retaining screw locations (arrowed) on post-1986 versions

26.11 Steering column lower mounting clamp bolts (arrowed)

6 Extract the fixing screws and remove the upper and lower shrouds from the upper end of the steering column (photos).

7 Remove the insulation panel from the lower part of the facia (photo).

8 Extract the screw, remove the bonnet release lever mounting and place it to one side (photo).

9 Take out the fixing screws and remove the switches from the steering column (photos).

10 Disconnect the wiring harness multi-plug at the side of the column.

11 Unbolt the upper and lower clamps from the steering column and then withdraw the column/shaft into the vehicle. If any difficulty is experienced in separating the lower shaft from the pinion gear, prise the coupling open very slightly with a screwdriver (photo).

12 Wear in the column bearings can be rectified by renewing them. Access to them is obtained by extracting the tolerance ring from the upper end of the column and then withdrawing the shaft from the lower end of the column. The lower bearing and spring will come with it. Make sure that the steering column lock is unlocked before withdrawing the shaft.

13 If the upper bearing is to be renewed, first remove the lock assembly by drilling out the shear-head bolt. The upper bearing may now be levered out of its seat.

14 Commence reassembly by tapping the new upper bearing into its seat in the lock housing. Refit the column upper clamp and bush.

15 Locate the column lock on the column tube and screw in a new shear-head bolt until its head breaks off.

16 Insert the conical spring into the column tube so that the larger

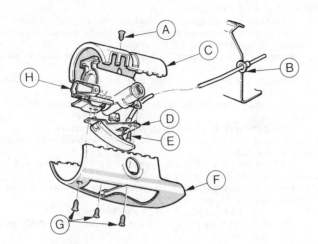

Fig. 10.43 Steering column shroud details – pre 1986 models
(Sec 26)

A	Shroud screw
B	Bonnet release cable
C	Upper shroud
D	Bonnet release lever
E	Release lever mounting
	screw
F	Lower shroud
G	Shroud screws
H	Lock housing

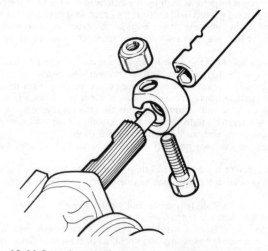

Fig. 10.44 Steering shaft-to-pinion shaft clamp and
pinch-bolt (Sec 26)

diameter end of the spring is against the lowest convolution of the collapsible section of the column tube.

17 Slide the lower bearing onto the shaft so that its chamfered edge will mate with the corresponding one in the column lower bearing seat when the shaft is installed.

18 Insert the shaft into the lower end of the steering column. Make sure that the lock is unbolted and pass the shaft up carefully through the upper bearing.

19 Fit the bearing tolerance ring and waved washer.

20 Fit the direction indicator cancelling cam to the top of the shaft, making sure that the peg will be uppermost when the column is in the in-car attitude (where fitted).

21 Fit the steering wheel to the shaft, screwing on the nut sufficiently tightly to be able to pull the lower bearing into the column tube with the bearing slots correctly aligned with the pegs on the tube.

22 Refit the column, making sure to engage the coupling at its lower end with the splined pinion shaft.

23 Bolt up the column upper and lower clamps.

24 Reconnect the wiring harness multi-plug.

25 Refit the combination switches to the steering column.

26 Reconnect the bonnet release lever.

27 Fit the column shrouds.

28 Check that the steering wheel is correctly aligned (wheels in the straight-ahead position). If not, remove the steering wheel and realign it (see also Section 24).

29 Tighten the steering wheel nut to the specified torque and then insert the motif or horn push into the centre of the steering wheel.

30 Refit the insulation panel to the lower facia.

31 Tighten the coupling pinch-bolt at the base of the steering shaft.

32 Reconnect the battery negative terminal.

27 Steering gear – removal and refitting

1 Set the front roadwheels in the straight-ahead position.

2 Raise the front of the vehicle and fit stands. Remove the front roadwheels.

3 Working under the bonnet, remove the pinch-bolt from the coupling at the base of the steering column shaft.

4 Extract the split pins from the tie-rod balljoint taper pin nuts, unscrew the nuts and remove them.

5 Separate the balljoints from the steering arms using a suitable separator tool.

6 Flatten the locktabs on the steering gear securing bolts and unscrew and remove the bolts (photo). Withdraw the steering gear

27.6 Steering gear-to-bulkhead mounting showing retaining bolt and locktab (arrowed)

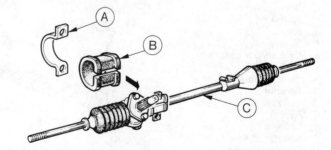

Fig. 10.45 Steering gear mounting details (Sec 27)

A Clamp	C Steering gear
B Bush	

downwards to separate the coupling from the steering shaft and then take it out from under the front wing.

7 Refitting is a reversal of removal. If a new rack-and-pinion assembly is being installed, the tie-rods balljoints will have to be removed from the original unit and screwed onto the new tie-rods to

approximately the same setting. If a note was not made of the position of the original tie-rod balljoints on their rods, inspection of the threads will probably indicate their original location. In any event it is important that the new balljoints are screwed on an equal amount at this stage.

8   Make sure that the steering gear is centred. Do this by turning the pinion shaft to full lock in one direction and then count the number of turns required to rotate it to the opposite lock. Now turn the splined pinion shaft through half the number of turns just counted.

9   Check that the roadwheels and the steering wheel are in the straight-ahead attitude, offer up the steering gear and connect the shaft coupling without inserting the pinch-bolt.

10 Bolt up the gear housing and lock the bolts with their lockplate tabs.

11 Reconnect the tie-rod balljoints to the steering arms. Tighten the securing nuts to the specified torque setting and fit new split pins to secure.

12 Tighten the coupling pinch-bolt to the specified torque. Refit the roadwheels and lower the vehicle to the floor.

13 If the tie-rods were disturbed or if a new assembly was installed, check and adjust the wheel alignment, as described in Section 29.

28 Steering gear – overhaul

Note: *The following procedures should only be carried out by persons having a reasonable level of automotive experience and access to certain special tools or suitable alternatives*

Pre-May 1983 models

1   If the steering gear has given good service over a high mileage then it is strongly recommended that a new or factory reconditioned unit is installed, rather than overhaul the original assembly.

2   Remove the steering gear from the vehicle as described in Section 27.

3   Remove the tie-rod balljoints and the bellows as described in Section 21.

4   Drain the lubricant by turning the splined pinion shaft from lock-to-lock.

5   Mount the gear in a vice fitted with jaw protectors.

6   Centre-punch the pins which secure the balljoint housings at the ends of the rack.

7   Drill out the pins using a 4.0 mm (0.16 in) diameter drill. Do not drill deeper than 9.5 mm (0.4 in).

8   Using a C-spanner and an open-ended spanner, release the balljoint housings from their locknuts.

9   Withdraw the housings, tie-rods and ball seats.

10 Unbolt and remove the rack slipper cover plate, shim pack, gasket, spring and slipper.

11 Unbolt and remove the pinion bearing cover plate and remove the gasket and the pinion oil seal.

12 Withdraw the pinion/bearing assembly.

13 Withdraw the rack from the housing.

14 With the steering gear dismantled, clean and inspect all components. Renew the pinion shaft seal as a matter of routine, also the cover plate gaskets.

15 If the pinion upper bearing is worn it can only be renewed as an assembly with the pinion. The pinion lower bearing, which is of needle roller type, can be renewed independently.

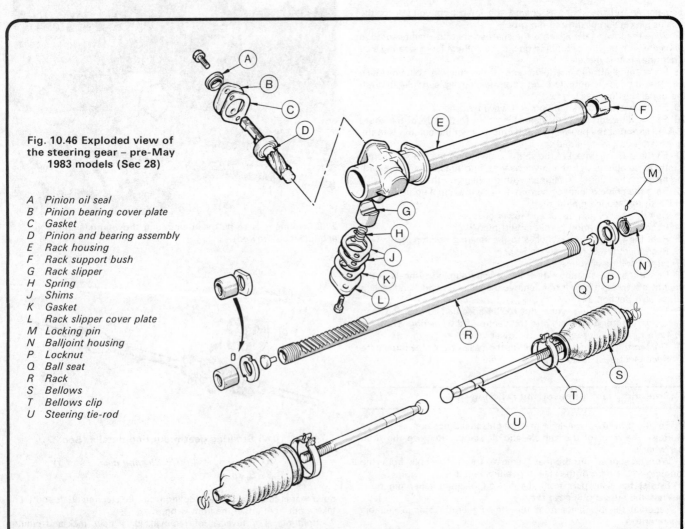

Fig. 10.46 Exploded view of the steering gear – pre-May 1983 models (Sec 28)

A   Pinion oil seal
B   Pinion bearing cover plate
C   Gasket
D   Pinion and bearing assembly
E   Rack housing
F   Rack support bush
G   Rack slipper
H   Spring
J   Shims
K   Gasket
L   Rack slipper cover plate
M   Locking pin
N   Balljoint housing
P   Locknut
Q   Ball seat
R   Rack
S   Bellows
T   Bellows clip
U   Steering tie-rod

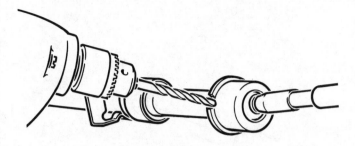

Fig. 10.47 Drilling out the balljoint housing locking pins –
pre-May 1983 steering gear (Sec 28)

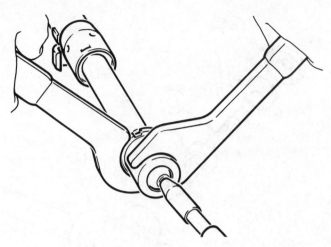

Fig. 10.48 Unscrewing the balljoint housings from their
locknuts – pre-May 1983 steering gear (Sec 28)

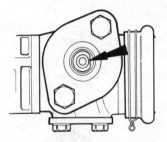

Fig. 10.49 Steering gear pinion alignment – pre-May 1983
steering gear (Sec 28)

Flat on pinion shaft arrowed

16 The rack support bush is also renewable separately.

17 Commence reassembly by inserting the rack into the housing.

18 Insert the pinion/bearing into the housing. Do this with the rack held central in the housing. Once installed, check that the flat on the end of the pinion shaft is at 90° to the centre-line of the rack and facing the correct way (Fig. 10.49).

19 Locate a new gasket in position and fit the pinion bearing cover plate and the oil seal. Apply some jointing compound to the bolt threads before screwing them in. Tighten the bolts to the specified torque.

20 Fit the rack slipper to the housing.

21 Ideally, a dial gauge should be used to record the rack slipper height deflection as the rack is moved from lock-to-lock by turning the pinion.

22 Using a micrometer, make up a shim pack greater in thickness by 0.015 to 0.150 mm (0.0006 to 0.0060 in) than the dial gauge deflection. The shim pack thickness must include the gasket.

23 Refit the spring, shims gasket and cover plate then tighten the bolts to the specified torque.

24 Now check the turning torque of the splined pinion. The correct torque is given in the Specifications. If a suitable torque wrench with splined connector is not available, wind a length of cord round the splined pinion shaft, attach it to a spring balance and take a reading just as the balance is pulled to start the pinion turning.

25 Where a dial gauge is not available, then remove one shim at a time and check the turning torque with the cord as just described until sufficient shims have been removed to bring the torque within the specified range. With a factory-assembled rack, it is unlikely that stiff steering will be encountered, requiring the addition of shims.

26 Assemble the tie-rod balljoints to their seats at the ends of the rack. Make sure that the ball seats are lubricated with the specified grease.

27 The preload (articulation effort) of the tie-rod balljoints, must now be measured and adjusted. Do this by tightening the ball housing until the force required to move the tie-rod from the mid-point of its arc of travel is as given in the Specifications. To measure this, attach a spring balance to the threaded part of the tie-rod about 6.0 mm (0.25 in) from the end of the rod.

28 Adjust the ball housing as necessary to achieve the specified setting and then using a C-spanner, tighten the locking ring nut without moving the position of the ball housing. Recheck the setting.

29 The ball housings/locknuts must now be pinned. Do this by centre-punching the joint between the housing and the lockring and drilling carefully down the joint faces. The hole must be 4.0 mm (0.16 in) in diameter and with a maximum depth of 9.5 mm (0.4 in). These new holes must be drilled even if it was found that the original holes came into alignment when the ball preload was finally adjusted.

30 Insert new pins into the holes and retain them by peening over the edges of their holes.

31 Fit one set of bellows and secure with clamps at both ends. Make sure that the bellows are not twisted and if wire was used to secure them originally, discard it in favour of proper clips.

32 Add 95 cc (0.17 pt) of the specified lubricant. Move the rack from lock-to-lock to assist the entry of the lubricant into the steering gear.

33 Fit the second set of bellows and their clamps.

34 Re-check the pinion turning torque. Readjust the thickness of the shim pack if necessary.

Post-May 1983 models

35 If the steering gear has given good service over a high mileage then it is strongly recommended that a new or factory reconditioned unit is installed, rather than overhaul the original assembly.

36 Remove the steering gear from the vehicle, as described in Section 27.

37 Remove the tie-rod balljoints and the bellows, as described in Section 21.

38 Drain the lubricant by turning the splined pinion shaft from lock-to-lock.

39 The steering rack must now be fully traversed in one direction (left or right) so that the rack teeth are fully exposed. Fit the rack into position in a vice fitted with protector jaws. Locate as shown in Fig. 10.51 and then unscrew the tie-rod inner balljoints from the steering rack.

40 Having removed the first tie-rod, mark it left or right, as applicable, to ensure that it is correctly refitted on reassembly.

41 Remove the opposite tie-rod in a similar manner.

42 Unscrew and remove the rack slipper plug using Ford special tool 13-009A, if available. Extract the spring and slipper.

43 Unscrew and remove the pinion retaining nut. The reverse end of Ford special tool 13-009A is designed for this purpose since it fits into the slots in the head of the nut. If this tool is not available, carefully drift the nut loose. Remove the nut seal.

44 The pinion and bearing assembly can now be withdrawn from the housing.

45 Withdraw the rack from the housing using a twisting action, then remove the rack support bush.

46 With the steering gear dismantled, clean and inspect all components. Check for excessive wear or damage of the various components and renew as necessary. Renewal of the pinion nut seal and the track support bush should be undertaken as a matter of course.

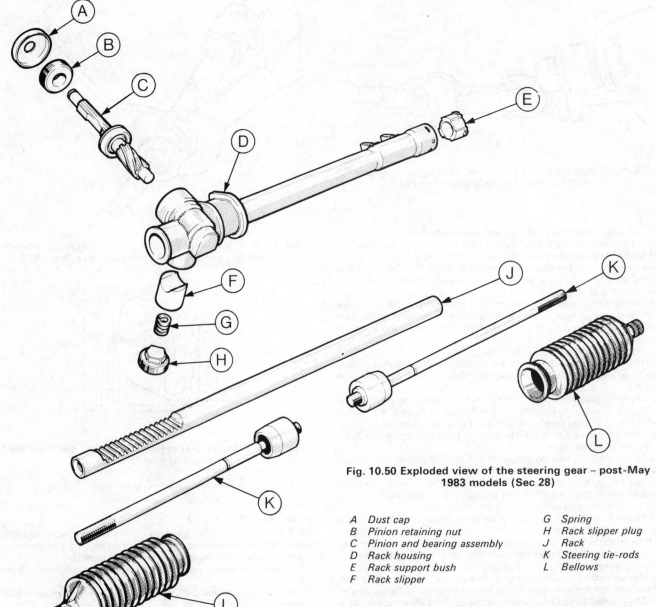

Fig. 10.50 Exploded view of the steering gear – post-May 1983 models (Sec 28)

A   Dust cap
B   Pinion retaining nut
C   Pinion and bearing assembly
D   Rack housing
E   Rack support bush
F   Rack slipper
G   Spring
H   Rack slipper plug
J   Rack
K   Steering tie-rods
L   Bellows

47 Commence reassembly by inserting the new rack support bush into position in the rack tube.

48 Smear the rack lightly with specified semi-fluid grease and then fit the rack tube over the rack and position it so that the rack is centralised.

49 Smear the pinion teeth with the semi-fluid grease and locate the pinion and bearing unit into position in the rack housing. When fitted the pinion flat must be at 90° to the slipper plug (facing the housing pinion end).

50 Before fitting the pinion nut smear its threads with sealant and then tighten it. If Ford special tool 13-009A is not available you will need to fabricate a castellated socket to locate into the slots of the nut to achieve this. When tightened, peen the edges of the nut into position with the steering rack housing.

51 Check that the steering rack is still centralised, then fit rack slipper and spring into position. Before fitting the retaining plug, coat its thread with a suitable thread sealant.

52 Tighten the slipper plug to the specified torque setting and then unscrew it 60° to 70°.

53 The pinion turning torque must now be set and for this you will

need Ford special tool 13-004 which is a pinion socket and also tool 15-041 which is a preload gauge. If these tools are not available, have the pinion turning torque checked and set by a Ford dealer.

54 Assuming the specials tools are available, fit the socket and gauge into position on the pinion and turn the pinion through 180° anti-clockwise, then clockwise through 360° whilst noting the torque reading. Rotate the pinion back (anti-clockwise) 180°.

55 The pinion turning torque should be as given in the Specifications, but if adjustment is necessary, rotate the slipper plug in the direction required to increase or decrease the reading to that specified.

56 With the correct adjustment made, stake punch around the edge of the plug and housing surfaces to secure the plug in position.

57 Move the rack fully to the right or left and clamp the rack in a vice fitted with soft jaw protectors. Refit the appropriate tie-rod to the rack. If fitting the original tie-rods tighten them so that the stake marks align with the steering rack grooves when fully fitted. Service replacement tie-rods must be fitted and tightened to the specified torque setting using a suitable open-ended torque wrench adaptor. Service replacement tie-rods have flat sections on them for this purpose. When tightened, stake punch the tie-rod balljoints to the rack groove.

58 Smear the inner surface of the rack bellows where they contact the rack housing and tie-rod with grease and fit the bellows, ensuring correct location with the tie-rod groove.

59 Add 120 cc of the specified oil to the tube and 70 cc of semi-fluid

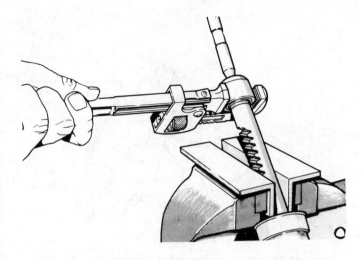

Fig. 10.51 Tie-rod removal and refitting method – post-May 1983 steering gear (Sec 28)

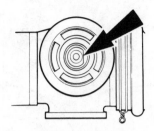

Fig. 10.52 Steering gear pinion alignment – post-May 1983 steering gear (Sec 28)

Flat on pinion shaft arrowed

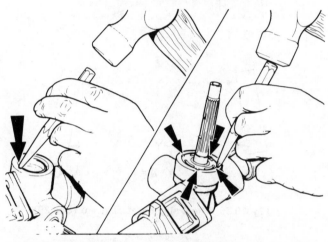

Fig. 10.54 Secure pinion cover and slipper plug in position by stake punching at points indicated – post-May 1983 steering gear (Sec 28)

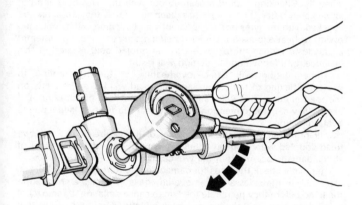

Fig. 10.53 Pinion turning torque check method using Ford special tools – post-May 1983 steering gear (Sec 28)

grease to the gear housing end. If new bellows are being fitted ensure that the correct replacement types are fitted – refer to Section 21 for details.

60 Secure the bellows with new screw-type clamp clips (do not re-use the original wire type clips).

61 The pinion cover must now be filled with grease and fitted to complete reassembly.

62 Refit the tie-rod balljoints, as described in Section 21.

29 Steering angles and wheel alignment

1   Accurate front wheel alignment is essential to good steering and for even tyre wear. Before considering the steering angles, check that the tyres are correctly inflated, that the roadwheels are not buckled, the hub bearings are not worn or incorrectly adjusted and that the steering linkage is in good order.

2   Wheel alignment consists of four factors:

Camber is the angle at which the road wheels are set from the vertical when viewed from the front or rear of the vehicle. Positive camber is the angle (in degrees) that the wheels are tilted outwards at the top from the vertical.

Castor is the angle between the steering axis and a vertical line when viewed from each side of the vehicle. Positive castor is indicated

when the steering axis is inclined towards the rear of the vehicle at its upper end.

Steering axis inclination is the angle, when viewed from the front or rear of the vehicle, between the vertical and an imaginary line drawn between the upper and lower suspension swivel balljoints or upper and lower strut mountings.

Toe is the amount by which the distance between the front inside edges of the roadwheel rims differs from that between the rear inside edges. If the distance at the front is less than that at the rear, the wheels are said to toe-in. If the distance at the front inside edges is greater than that at the rear, the wheels toe-out.

3   Due to the need for precision gauges to measure the small angles of the steering and suspension settings, it is preferable to leave this work to your dealer. Camber and castor angles are set in production and are not adjustable. If these angles are ever checked and found to be outside specification then either the suspension components are damaged or distorted, or wear has occurred in the bushes at the attachment points.

4   If you wish to check the toe setting yourself, first make sure that the lengths of both tie-rods are equal when the steering is in the straight-ahead position. This can be measured reasonably accurately by counting the number of exposed threads on the tie-rod adjacent to the balljoint assembly (refer also to Section 24).

5   Adjust, if necessary, by releasing the locknut from the balljoint assembly and the clamp at the small end of the bellows.

6   Obtain a tracking gauge. These are available in various forms from accessory stores, or one can be fabricated from a length of steel tubing, suitably cranked to clear the sump and bellhousing, and having a setscrew and locknut at one end.

7   With the gauge, measure the distance between the two inner rims of

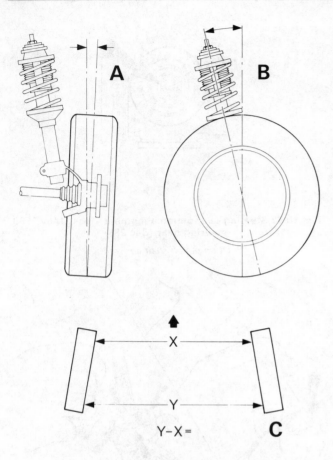

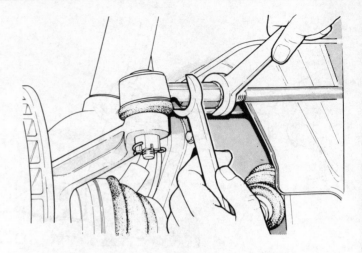

Fig. 10.56 Slackening tie-rod balljoint locknut for toe setting adjustment (Sec 29)

Fig. 10.55 Wheel alignment diagram (Sec 29)

A Camber
B Castor
C Toe setting

the roadwheels (at hub height) at the rear of the wheel. Push the vehicle forward to rotate the wheel through 180° (half a turn) and measure the distance between the wheel inner rims, again at hub height, at the front of the wheel. This last measurement should differ from the first one by the specified toe-in/toe-out (see Specifications).
8   Where the toe setting is found to be incorrect, release the tie-rod balljoint locknuts and turn the tie-rods by an equal amount. Only turn them through a quarter turn at a time before re-checking the alignment. Do not grip the threaded part of the tie-rod during adjustment and make sure that the bellows outboard clip is released, otherwise the bellows will twist as the tie-rod is rotated. When each tie-rod is viewed from the rack housing, turning the rods clockwise will increase the toe-out. Always turn the tie-rods in the same direction when viewed from the centre of the vehicle, otherwise they will become unequal in length. This would cause the steering wheel spoke alignment to alter and also cause problems on turning with tyre scrubbing.
9   On completion of adjustment, tighten the tie-rod balljoint locknuts without altering the setting of the tie-rods. Hold the balljoint assembly at the mid-point of its arc of travel (flats are provided on it for a spanner) while the locknuts are tightened.
10 Finally, tighten the bellows clamps.
11 For rear wheel alignment refer to Section 20.

30 Wheels and tyres – general care and maintenance

Wheels and tyres should give no real problems in use provided that a close eye is kept on them with regard to excessive wear or damage. To this end, the following points should be noted.
Ensure that tyre pressures are checked regularly and maintained

correctly. Checking should be carried out with the tyres cold and not immediately after the vehicle has been in use. If the pressures are checked with the tyres hot, an apparently high reading will be obtained owing to heat expansion. Under no circumstances should an attempt be made to reduce the pressures to the quoted cold reading in this instance, or effective underinflation will result.
Underinflation will cause overheating of the tyre owing to excessive flexing of the casing, and the tread will not sit correctly on the road surface. This will cause a consequent loss of adhesion and excessive wear, not to mention the danger of sudden tyre failure due to heat build-up.
Overinflation will cause rapid wear of the centre part of the tyre tread coupled with reduced adhesion, harsher ride, and the danger of shock damage occurring in the tyre casing.
Regularly check the tyres for damage in the form of cuts or bulges, especially in the sidewalls. Remove any nails or stones embedded in the tread before they penetrate the tyre to cause deflation. If removal of a nail does reveal that the tyre has been punctured, refit the nail so that its point of penetration is marked. Then immediately change the wheel and have the tyre repaired by a tyre dealer. Do not drive on a tyre in such a condition. In many cases a puncture can be simply repaired by the use of an inner tube of the correct size and type. If in any doubt as to the possible consequences of any damage found, consult your local tyre dealer for advice.
Periodically remove the wheels and clean any dirt or mud from the inside and outside surfaces. Examine the wheel rims for signs of rusting, corrosion or other damage. Light alloy wheels are easily damaged by 'kerbing' whilst parking, and similarly steel wheels may become dented or buckled. Renewal of the wheel is very often the only course of remedial action possible.
The balance of each wheel and tyre assembly should be maintained to avoid excessive wear, not only to the tyres but also to the steering and suspension components. Wheel imbalance is normally signified by vibration through the vehicle's bodyshell, although in many cases it is particularly noticeable through the steering wheel. Conversely, it should be noted that wear or damage in suspension or steering components may cause excessive tyre wear. Out-of-round or out-of-true tyres, damaged wheels and wheel bearing wear/maladjustment also fall into this category. Balancing will not usually cure vibration caused by such wear.
Wheel balancing may be carried out with the wheel either on or off the vehicle. If balanced on the vehicle, ensure that the wheel-to-hub relationship is marked in some way prior to subsequent wheel removal so that it may be refitted in its original position.
General tyre wear is influenced to a large degree by driving style – harsh braking and acceleration or fast cornering will all produce more rapid tyre wear. Interchanging of tyres may result in more even wear, but this should only be carried out where there is no mix of tyre types on the vehicle. However, it is worth bearing in mind that if this is

completely effective, the added expense of replacing a complete set of tyres simultaneously is incurred, which may prove financially restrictive for many owners.

Front tyres may wear unevenly as a result of wheel misalignment. The front wheels should always be correctly aligned according to the settings specified by the vehicle manufacturer.

Legal restrictions apply to the mixing of tyre types on a vehicle. Basically this means that a vehicle must not have tyres of differing construction on the same axle. Although it is not recommended to mix tyre types between front axle and rear axle, the only legally permissible combination is crossply at the front and radial at the rear. When mixing radial ply tyres, textile braced radials must always go on the front axle, with steel braced radials at the rear. An obvious disadvantage of such mixing is the necessity to carry two spare tyres to avoid contravening the law in the event of a puncture.

In the UK, the Motor Vehicles Construction and Use Regulations apply to many aspects of tyre fitting and usage. It is suggested that a copy of these regulations is obtained from your local police if in doubt as to the current legal requirements with regard to tyre condition, minimum tread depth, etc.

31 Fault diagnosis – suspension and steering

Note: *Before diagnosing steering or suspension faults, be sure that the trouble is not due to incorrect tyre pressures, mixtures of tyre types or binding brakes*

Symptom	Reason(s)
Vehicle pulls to one side	Incorrect wheel alignment Wear in front suspension or steering components Accident damage to steering on suspension components
Steering stiff or heavy	Lack of steering gear lubricant Seized balljoint Wheel alignment incorrect Steering rack or column bent or damaged
Excessive play in steering	Worn steering or suspension joints Wear in steering shaft universal joints Worn rack and pinion assembly
Wheel wobble and vibration	Roadwheels out of balance Roadwheels buckled or distorted Faulty or damaged tyre Worn steering or suspension joints Wheel bolts loose Worn rack and pinion assembly
Tyre wear uneven	Wheel alignment incorrect Worn steering or suspension components Wheels out of balance Accident damage

Chapter 11 Bodywork

For modifications, and information applicable to later models, see Supplement at end of manual

Contents

Specifications

Torque wrench setting	Nm	lbf ft
All seat belt anchor bolts	29 to 41	21 to 30

1 General description

The body is of welded steel construction available in 3 or 5-door Hatchback, 3 or 5-door Estate, soft-top Cabriolet, or Van configurations.

The body is of monocoque construction and is of energy-absorbing design.

Rust and corrosion protection is applied to all new vehicles and includes zinc phosphate dipping and wax injection of box sections and door interiors.

All body panels are welded, including the front wings, so it is recommended that major body damage repairs are left to your dealer.

2 Maintenance – bodywork and underframe

1 The general condition of a vehicle's bodywork is the one thing that significantly affects its value. Maintenance is easy but needs to be regular. Neglect, particularly after minor damage, can lead quickly to further deterioration and costly repair bills. It is important also to keep watch on those parts of the vehicle not immediately visible, for instance the underside, inside all the wheel arches and the lower part of the engine compartment.

2 The basic maintenance routine for the bodywork is washing – preferably with a lot of water, from a hose. This will remove all the loose solids which may have stuck to the vehicle. It is important to flush these off in such a way as to prevent grit from scratching the finish. The wheel arches and underframe need washing in the same way to remove any accumulated mud which will retain moisture and tend to encourage rust. Paradoxically enough, the best time to clean the underframe and wheel arches is in wet weather when the mud is thoroughly wet and soft. In very wet weather the underframe is usually cleaned of large accumulations automatically and this is a good time for inspection.

3 Periodically, except on vehicles with a wax-based underbody protective coating, it is a good idea to have the whole of the underframe of the vehicle steam cleaned, engine compartment included, so that a thorough inspection can be carried out to see what minor repairs and renovations are necessary. Steam cleaning is available at many garages and is necessary for removal of the accumulation of oily grime which sometimes is allowed to become thick in certain areas. If steam cleaning facilities are not available, there are one or two excellent grease solvents available such as Holts Engine Cleaner or Holts Foambrite which can be brush applied. The dirt can

then be simply hosed off. Note that these methods should not be used on vehicles with wax-based underbody protective coating or the coating will be removed. Such vehicles should be inspected annually, preferably just prior to winter, when the underbody should be washed down and any damage to the wax coating repaired using Holts Undershield. Ideally, a completely fresh coat should be applied. It would also be worth considering the use of such wax-based protection for injection into door panels, sills, box sections, etc, as an additional safeguard against rust damage where such protection is not provided by the vehicle manufacturer.

4   After washing paintwork, wipe off with a chamois leather to give an unspotted clear finish. A coat of clear protective wax polish, like the many excellent Turtle Wax polishes, will give added protection against chemical pollutants in the air. If the paintwork sheen has dulled or oxidised, use a cleaner/polisher combination such as Turtle Extra to restore the brilliance of the shine. This requires a little effort, but such dulling is usually caused because regular washing has been neglected. Care needs to be taken with metallic paintwork, as special non-abrasive cleaner/polisher is required to avoid damage to the finish. Always check that the door and ventilator opening drain holes and pipes are completely clear so that water can be drained out (photos). Bright work should be treated in the same way as paint work. Windscreens and windows can be kept clear of the smeary film which often appears, by the use of a proprietary glass cleaner like Holts Mixra. Never use any form of wax or other body or chromium polish on glass.

3   Maintenance – upholstery and carpets

Mats and carpets should be brushed or vacuum cleaned regularly to keep them free of grit. If they are badly stained remove them from the vehicle for scrubbing or sponging and make quite sure they are dry before refitting. Seats and interior trim panels can be kept clean by wiping with a damp cloth and Turtle Wax Carisma. If they do become stained (which can be more apparent on light coloured upholstery) use a little liquid detergent and a soft nail brush to scour the grime out of the grain of the material. Do not forget to keep the headlining clean in the same way as the upholstery. When using liquid cleaners inside the vehicle do not over-wet the surfaces being cleaned. Excessive damp could get into the seams and padded interior causing stains, offensive odours or even rot. If the inside of the vehicle gets wet accidentally it is worthwhile taking some trouble to dry it out properly, particularly where carpets are involved. *Do not leave oil or electric heaters inside the vehicle for this purpose.*

4   Minor body damage – repair

The photographic sequences on pages 298 and 299 illustrate the operations detailed in the following sub-sections.
Note: *For more detailed information about bodywork repair, the Haynes Publishing Group publish a book by Lindsay Porter called The Car Bodywork Repair Manual. This incorporates information on such aspects as rust treatment, painting and glass fibre repairs, as well as details on more ambitious repairs involving welding and panel beating.*

Repair of minor scratches in bodywork

If the scratch is very superficial, and does not penetrate to the metal of the bodywork, repair is very simple. Lightly rub the area of the scratch with a paintwork renovator like Turtle Wax New Color Back, or a very fine cutting paste like Holts Body + Plus Rubbing Compound, to remove loose paint from the scratch and to clear the surrounding bodywork of wax polish. Rinse the area with clean water.

Apply touch-up paint, such as Holts Dupli-Color Color Touch or a paint film like Holts Autofilm, to the scratch using a fine paint brush; continue to apply fine layers of paint until the surface of the paint in the scratch is level with the surrounding paintwork. Allow the new paint at least two weeks to harden: then blend it into the surrounding paintwork by rubbing the scratch area with a paintwork renovator or a very fine cutting paste, such as Holts Body + Plus Rubbing Compound or Turtle Wax New Color Back. Finally, apply wax polish from one of the Turtle Wax range of wax polishes.

Where the scratch has penetrated right through to the metal of the bodywork, causing the metal to rust, a different repair technique is required. Remove any loose rust from the bottom of the scratch with a

penknife, then apply rust inhibiting paint, such as Turtle Wax Rust Master, to prevent the formation of rust in the future. Using a rubber or nylon applicator fill the scratch with bodystopper paste like Holts Body + Plus Knifing Putty. If required, this paste can be mixed with cellulose thinners, such as Holts Body + Plus Cellulose Thinners, to provide a very thin paste which is ideal for filling narrow scratches. Before the stopper-paste in the scratch hardens, wrap a piece of smooth cotton rag around the top of a finger. Dip the finger in cellulose thinners, such as Holts Body + Plus Cellulose Thinners, and then quickly sweep it across the surface of the stopper-paste in the scratch; this will ensure that the surface of the stopper-paste is slightly hollowed. The scratch can now be painted over as described earlier in this Section.

Repair of dents in bodywork

When deep denting of the vehicle's bodywork has taken place, the first task is to pull the dent out, until the affected bodywork almost attains its original shape. There is little point in trying to restore the original shape completely, as the metal in the damaged area will have stretched on impact and cannot be reshaped fully to its original contour. It is better to bring the level of the dent up to a point which is about ⅛ in (3 mm) below the level of the surrounding bodywork. In cases where the dent is very shallow anyway, it is not worth trying to pull it out at all. If the underside of the dent is accessible, it can be hammered out gently from behind, using a mallet with a wooden or plastic head. Whilst doing this, hold a suitable block of wood firmly against the outside of the panel to absorb the impact from the hammer blows and thus prevent a large area of the bodywork from being 'belled-out'.

Should the dent be in a section of the bodywork which has a double skin or some other factor making it inaccessible from behind, a different technique is called for. Drill several small holes through the metal inside the area – particularly in the deeper section. Then screw long self-tapping screws into the holes just sufficiently for them to gain a good purchase in the metal. Now the dent can be pulled out by pulling on the protruding heads of the screws with a pair of pliers.

The next stage of the repair is the removal of the paint from the damaged area, and from an inch or so of the surrounding 'sound' bodywork. This is accomplished most easily by using a wire brush or abrasive pad on a power drill, although it can be done just as effectively by hand using sheets of abrasive paper. To complete the preparation for filling, score the surface of the bare metal with a screwdriver or the tang of a file, or alternatively, drill small holes in the affected area. This will provide a really good 'key' for the filler paste.

To complete the repair see the Section on filling and re-spraying.

Repair of rust holes or gashes in bodywork

Remove all paint from the affected area and from an inch or so of the surrounding 'sound' bodywork, using an abrasive pad or a wire brush on a power drill. If these are not available a few sheets of abrasive paper will do the job just as effectively. With the paint removed you will be able to gauge the severity of the corrosion and therefore decide whether to renew the whole panel (if this is possible) or to repair the affected area. New body panels are not as expensive as most people think and it is often quicker and more satisfactory to fit a new panel than to attempt to repair large areas of corrosion.

Remove all fittings from the affected area except those which will act as a guide to the original shape of the damaged bodywork (eg headlamp shells etc). Then, using tin snips or a hacksaw blade, remove all loose metal and any other metal badly affected by corrosion. Hammer the edges of the hole inwards in order to create a slight depression for the filler paste.

Wire brush the affected area to remove the powdery rust from the surface of the remaining metal. Paint the affected area with rust inhibiting paint like Turtle Wax Rust Master; if the back of the rusted area is accessible treat this also.

Before filling can take place it will be necessary to block the hole in some way. This can be achieved by the use of aluminium or plastic mesh, or aluminium tape.

Aluminium or plastic mesh or glass fibre matting, such as the Holts Body + Plus Glass Fibre Matting, is probably the best material to use for a large hole. Cut a piece to the approximate size and shape of the hole to be filled, then position it in the hole so that its edges are below the level of the surrounding bodywork. It can be retained in position by several blobs of filler paste around its periphery.

Aluminium tape should be used for small or very narrow holes. Pull a piece off the roll and trim it to the approximate size and shape required, then pull off the backing paper (if used) and stick the tape over the hole; it can be overlapped if the thickness of one piece is insufficient. Burnish down the edges of the tape with the handle of a screwdriver or similar, to ensure that the tape is securely attached to the metal underneath.

Bodywork repairs – filling and re-spraying

Before using this Section, see the Sections on dent, deep scratch, rust holes and gash repairs.

Many types of bodyfiller are available, but generally speaking those proprietary kits which contain a tin of filler paste and a tube of resin hardener are best for this type of repair, like Holts Body + Plus or Holts No Mix which can be used directly from the tube. A wide, flexible plastic or nylon applicator will be found invaluable for imparting a smooth and well contoured finish to the surface of the filler.

Mix up a little filler on a clean piece of card or board – measure the hardener carefully (follow the maker's instructions on the pack) otherwise the filler will set too rapidly or too slowly. Alternatively, Holts No Mix can be used straight from the tube without mixing, but daylight is required to cure it. Using the applicator apply the filler paste to the prepared area; draw the applicator across the surface of the filler to achieve the correct contour and to level the filler surface. As soon as a contour that approximates to the correct one is achieved, stop working the paste – if you carry on too long the paste will become sticky and begin to 'pick up' on the applicator. Continue to add thin layers of filler paste at twenty-minute intervals until the level of the filler is just proud of the surrounding bodywork.

Once the filler has hardened, excess can be removed using a metal plane or file. From then on, progressively finer grades of abrasive paper should be used, starting with a 40 grade production paper and finishing with 400 grade wet-and-dry paper. Always wrap the abrasive paper around a flat rubber, cork, or wooden block – otherwise the surface of the filler will not be completely flat. During the smoothing of the filler surface the wet-and-dry paper should be periodically rinsed in water. This will ensure that a very smooth finish is imparted to the filler at the final stage.

At this stage the 'dent' should be surrounded by a ring of bare metal, which in turn should be encircled by the finely 'feathered' edge of the good paintwork. Rinse the repair area with clean water, until all of the dust produced by the rubbing-down operation has gone.

Spray the whole repair area with a light coat of primer, either Holts Body + Plus Grey or Red Oxide Primer – this will show up any imperfections in the surface of the filler. Repair these imperfections with fresh filler paste or bodystopper, and once more smooth the surface with abrasive paper. If bodystopper is used, it can be mixed with cellulose thinners to form a really thin paste which is ideal for filling small holes. Repeat this spray and repair procedure until you are satisfied that the surface of the filler, and the feathered edge of the paintwork are perfect. Clean the repair area with clean water and allow to dry fully.

The repair area is now ready for final spraying. Paint spraying must be carried out in a warm, dry, windless and dust free atmosphere. This condition can be created artificially if you have access to a large indoor working area, but if you are forced to work in the open, you will have to pick your day very carefully. If you are working indoors, dousing the floor in the work area with water will help to settle the dust which would otherwise be in the atmosphere. If the repair area is confined to one body panel, mask off the surrounding panels; this will help to minimise the effects of a slight mis-match in paint colours. Bodywork fittings (eg chrome strips, door handles etc) will also need to be masked off. Use genuine masking tape and several thicknesses of newspaper for the masking operations.

Before commencing to spray, agitate the aerosol can thoroughly, then spray a test area (an old tin, or similar) until the technique is mastered. Cover the repair area with a thick coat of primer; the thickness should be built up using several thin layers of paint rather than one thick one. Using 400 grade wet-and-dry paper, rub down the surface of the primer until it is really smooth. While doing this, the work area should be thoroughly doused with water, and the wet-and-dry paper periodically rinsed in water. Allow to dry before spraying on more paint.

Spray on the top coat using Holts Dupli-Color Autospray, again building up the thickness by using several thin layers of paint. Start spraying in the centre of the repair area and then work outwards, with a side-to-side motion, until the whole repair area and about 2 inches of the surrounding original paintwork is covered. Remove all masking material 10 to 15 minutes after spraying on the final coat of paint.

Allow the new paint at least two weeks to harden, then, using a paintwork renovator or a very fine cutting paste such as Turtle Wax New Color Back or Holts Body + Plus Rubbing Compound, blend the edges of the paint into the existing paintwork. Finally, apply wax polish.

Plastic components

With the use of more and more plastic body components by the vehicle manufacturers (eg bumpers, spoilers, and in some cases major body panels), rectification of more serious damage to such items has become a matter of either entrusting repair work to a specialist in this field, or renewing complete components. Repair of such damage by the DIY owner is not really feasible owing to the cost of the equipment and materials required for effecting such repairs. The basic technique involves making a groove along the line of the crack in the plastic using a rotary burr in a power drill. The damaged part is then welded back together by using a hot air gun to heat up and fuse a plastic filler rod into the groove. Any excess plastic is then removed and the area rubbed down to a smooth finish. It is important that a filler rod of the correct plastic is used, as body components can be made of a variety of different types (eg polycarbonate, ABS, polypropylene).

Damage of a less serious nature (abrasions, minor cracks etc) can be repaired by the DIY owner using a two-part epoxy filler repair material, like Holts Body + Plus or Holts No Mix which can be used directly from the tube. Once mixed in equal proportions (or applied direct from the tube in the case of Holts No Mix), this is used in similar fashion to the bodywork filler used on metal panels. The filler is usually cured in twenty to thirty minutes, ready for sanding and painting.

If the owner is renewing a complete component himself, or if he has repaired it with epoxy filler, he will be left with the problem of finding a suitable paint for finishing which is compatible with the type of plastic used. At one time the use of a universal paint was not possible owing to the complex range of plastics encountered in body component applications. Standard paints, generally speaking, will not bond to plastic or rubber satisfactorily, but Holts Professional Spraymatch paints to match any plastic or rubber finish can be obtained from dealers. However, it is now possible to obtain a plastic body parts finishing kit which consists of a pre-primer treatment, a primer and coloured top coat. Full instructions are normally supplied with a kit, but basically the method of use is to first apply the pre-primer to the component concerned and allow it to dry for up to 30 minutes. Then the primer is applied and left to dry for about an hour before finally applying the special coloured top coat. The result is a correctly coloured component where the paint will flex with the plastic or rubber, a property that standard paint does not normally possess.

5 Major body damage – repair

Where serious damage has occured or large areas need renewal due to neglect, it means that completely new sections or panels will need welding in, and this is best left to professionals. If the damage is due to impact, it will also be necessary to completely check the alignment of the bodyshell structure. Due to the principle of construction, the strength and shape of the whole car can be affected by damage to one part. In such instances the service of a dealer with specialist checking jigs are essential. If a body is left misaligned, it is first of all dangerous, as the car will not handle properly, and secondly uneven stresses will be imposed on the steering, engine and transmission, causing abnormal wear or complete failure. Tyre wear may also be excessive.

6 Bonnet – removal and refitting

1 Open the bonnet and support it on its stay.
2 Disconnect the screen washer pipe on the underside of the bonnet lid (photo).
3 Mark round the hinge plates on the underside of the bonnet lid as an aid to refitting.
4 With an assistant supporting one side of the bonnet lid, unbolt the hinges and lift the lid from the vehicle.
5 Refit by reversing the removal operations. If a new bonnet is being installed, position it so that an equal gap is provided at each side when it is being closed.
6 The bonnet should close smoothly and positively without excessive pressure. If it does not, carry out the following adjustment.
7 Screw in the bump stops which are located on the front upper cross

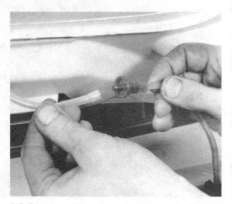

6.2 Disconnecting the windscreen washer fluid pipe

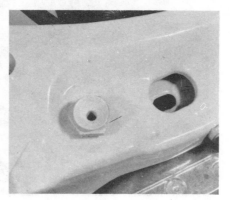

6.7 Bonnet bump stop

6.8 Bonnet striker and safety catch

rail (photo). Close the bonnet and then readjust the bump stops until the bonnet is flush with the wing upper surfaces.

8   Adjust the striker centrally in relation to the latch. Release it by unscrewing its pressed steel locknut (photo).

9   Screw the striker in or out until the bonnet fully closes under its own weight when allowed to drop from a point 300 mm (12 in) above its released position.

7 Bonnet release cable – removal and refitting

1   Working inside the vehicle, extract the three screws and remove the steering column shroud. Open the bonnet. If the cable is broken, the release latch must be operated using a suitably shaped bar through the grille aperture.

2   Extract the single screw and remove the cable bracket from the steering column.

3   Working within the engine compartment, pull the cable grommet from the bonnet latch bracket and then disengage the cable end fitting from the latch (photo).

4   Unclip the cable from the side of the engine compartment.

5   Withdraw the cable through the engine compartment rear bulkhead into the vehicle interior.

6   Refitting is a reversal of removal.

8 Bonnet lock – removal and refitting

1   Extract the three securing screws from the lock and lower it until the cable can be disconnected.

2   Withdraw the lock from below the top rail.

3   Refit by reversing the removal operations.

9 Radiator grille – removal and refitting

1   The grille is held in position by four spring clips (photo).

2   Once these clips are released, the grille can be removed from the body panel.

3   Refit by reattaching the spring clips.

10 Body adhesive emblems and mouldings – removal and refitting

1   The radiator grille emblem, the front wing motif, the tailgate emblems and the body side mouldings are all of the self-adhesive type.

2   To remove these devices, it is recommended that a length of nylon cord is used to separate them from their mounting surfaces.

7.3 Bonnet cable attachment at latch and bracket

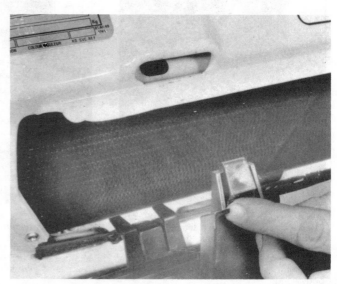

9.1 Radiator grille spring clip

1

This photographic sequence shows the steps taken to repair the dent and paintwork damage shown above. In general, the procedure for repairing a hole will be similar; where there are substantial differences, the procedure is clearly described and shown in a separate photograph.

2

First remove any trim around the dent, then hammer out the dent where access is possible. This will minimise filling. Here, after the large dent has been hammered out, the damaged area is being made slightly concave.

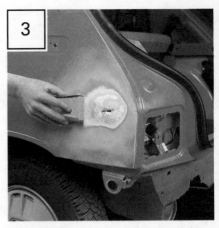

3

Next, remove all paint from the damaged area by rubbing with coarse abrasive paper or using a power drill fitted with a wire brush or abrasive pad. 'Feather' the edge of the boundary with good paintwork using a finer grade of abrasive paper.

4

Where there are holes or other damage, the sheet metal should be cut away before proceeding further. The damaged area and any signs of rust should be treated with Turtle Wax Hi-Tech Rust Eater, which will also inhibit further rust formation.

5

For a large dent or hole mix Holts Body Plus Resin and Hardener according to the manufacturer's instructions and apply around the edge of the repair. Press Glass Fibre Matting over the repair area and leave for 20-30 minutes to harden. Then ...

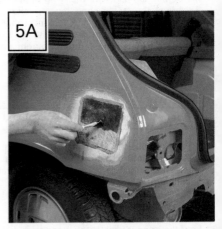

5A

... brush more Holts Body Plus Resin and Hardener onto the matting and leave to harden. Repeat the sequence with two or three layers of matting, checking that the final layer is lower than the surrounding area. Apply Holts Body Plus Filler Paste as shown in Step 5B.

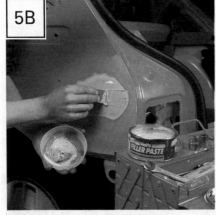

5B

For a medium dent, mix Holts Body Plus Filler Paste and Hardener according to the manufacturer's instructions and apply it with a flexible applicator. Apply thin layers of filler at 20-minute intervals, until the filler surface is slightly proud of the surrounding bodywork.

5C

For small dents and scratches use Holts No Mix Filler Paste straight from the tube. Apply it according to the instructions in thin layers, using the spatula provided. It will harden in minutes if applied outdoors and may then be used as its own knifing putty.

6

Use a plane or file for initial shaping. Then, using progressively finer grades of wet-and-dry paper, wrapped round a sanding block, and copious amounts of clean water, rub down the filler until glass smooth. 'Feather' the edges of adjoining paintwork.

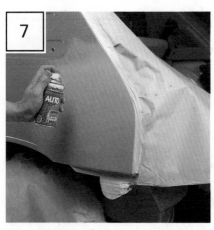

Protect adjoining areas before spraying the whole repair area and at least one inch of the surrounding sound paintwork with Holts Dupli-Color primer.

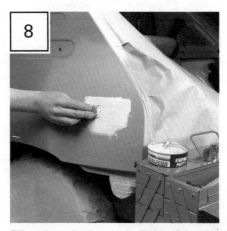

Fill any imperfections in the filler surface with a small amount of Holts Body Plus Knifing Putty. Using plenty of clean water, rub down the surface with a fine grade wet-and-dry paper – 400 grade is recommended – until it is really smooth.

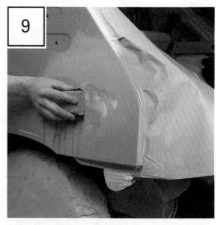

Carefully fill any remaining imperfections with knifing putty before applying the last coat of primer. Then rub down the surface with Holts Body Plus Rubbing Compound to ensure a really smooth surface.

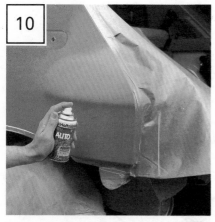

Protect surrounding areas from overspray before applying the topcoat in several thin layers. Agitate Holts Dupli-Color aerosol thoroughly. Start at the repair centre, spraying outwards with a side-to-side motion.

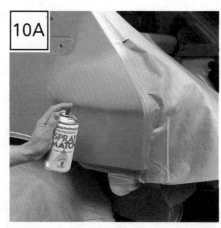

If the exact colour is not available off the shelf, local Holts Professional Spraymatch Centres will custom fill an aerosol to match perfectly.

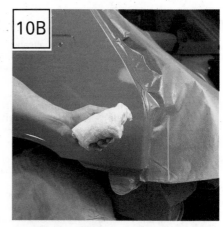

To identify whether a lacquer finish is required, rub a painted unrepaired part of the body with wax and a clean cloth.

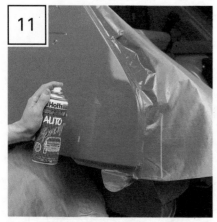

If *no* traces of paint appear on the cloth, spray Holts Dupli-Color clear lacquer over the repaired area to achieve the correct gloss level.

The paint will take about two weeks to harden fully. After this time it can be 'cut' with a mild cutting compound such as Turtle Wax Minute Cut prior to polishing with a final coating of Turtle Wax Extra.

When carrying out bodywork repairs, remember that the quality of the finished job is proportional to the time and effort expended.

Fig. 11.1 Removing tailgate adhesive badge (Sec 10)

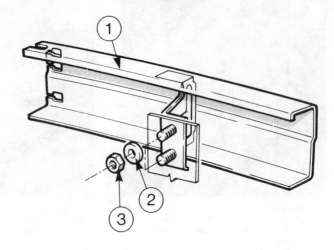

Fig. 11.2 Front bumper attachments – pre-1986 models (Sec 11)

1	Bumper bar	3	Retaining nut
2	Washer		

3 New emblems have adhesive already applied and a protective backing. Before sticking them into position, clean off all the old adhesive from the mounting surface of the vehicle.

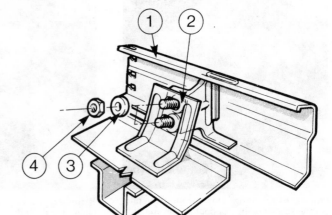

Fig. 11.3 Rear bumper attachments – pre-1986 models (Sec 11)

1	Bumper bar	3	Washer
2	Mounting bracket	4	Fixing nut

11 Bumper moulding and bumper sections (pre-1986 Saloon and Estate models) – removal and refitting

Moulding

1 Where so equipped, remove the overriders (Section 14).
2 Release the moulding from the bumper by compressing the jaws of the retaining clips inside the bumper.
3 Slide the moulding from the end retainers, noting that the front bumper moulding is in two parts.
4 To refit, push the moulding into position and fully engage the clips.

Sections

5 To remove the bumper complete, open the bonnet or tailgate according to whether the front or rear bumper is being removed and unscrew the bumper, securing nuts from each end of the bumper.
6 Withdraw the bumper from the vehicle. With the rear bumper, the number plate wiring plugs will have to be disconnected.
7 Release the locking tangs using pliers as shown (Fig. 11.4) and pull or tap the quarter section free using a piece of soft wood to prevent damage. If required the quarter section end retaining clips can be removed from the body by twisting through 90° and pulling free.
8 Reassembly and refitting are reversals of the removal and dismantling.

12 Bumper assembly (Saloon and Estate models, 1986 onwards) – removal and refitting

Front bumper

1 Undo the single screw each side securing the bumper to the edge of the wheel arch.
2 From under the wheel arch undo the single bumper retaining nut on each side.
3 From within the engine compartment undo the single nut each side securing the bumper to the front body panel.
4 Carefully withdraw the bumper from the front of the car.
5 Refitting is the reversal of removal.

Rear bumper

6 Undo the three screws each side securing the bumper to the edge of the wheel arch.
7 From inside the luggage compartment undo the two bumper retaining nuts each side.

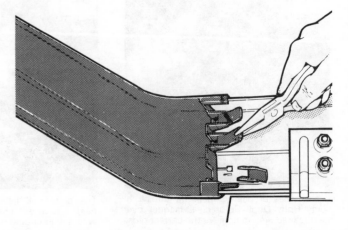

Fig. 11.4 Removing rear quarter bumper retaining tangs – pre-1986 models (Sec 11)

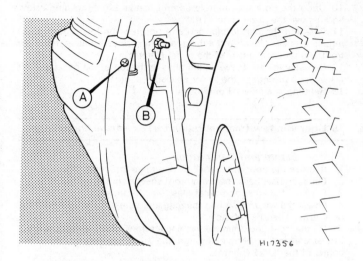

Fig. 11.5 Front bumper-to-arch screw (A) and retaining nut (B) – 1986 models onwards (Sec 12)

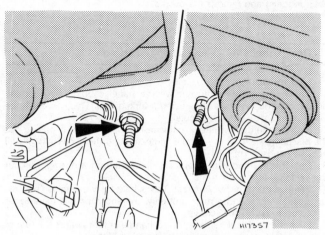

Fig. 11.6 Front bumper retaining nuts in engine compartment – 1986 models onwards (Sec 12)

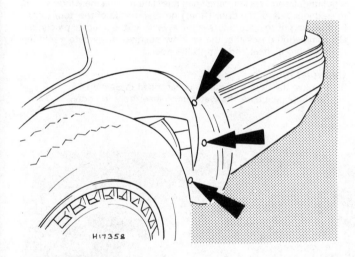

Fig. 11.7 Rear bumper-to-wheel arch screws – 1986 models onwards (Sec 12)

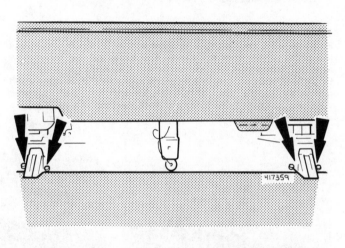

Fig. 11.8 Rear bumper attachments in luggage compartment – 1986 models onwards (Sec 12)

8 Disconnect the number plate lamp wiring, ease the sides of the bumper outward and withdraw it from the car.
9 Refitting is a reversal of removal.

13 Bumper components (Van models) – removal and refitting

1 Removal and refitting of the front bumpers is as described in the preceding Sections. To remove either rear quarter bumper, prise out the number plate lamp, disconnect the bulbholder and extract the two Torx screws. Refitting is a reversal of removal.

14 Bumper overriders – removal and refitting

1 On pre-1986 models the overrider is held to the bumper by a clamp screw. Find this screw on the underside of the bumper and release it – the overrider can then be withdrawn. If headlamp washers are fitted, disconnect the fluid hose as the overrider is withdrawn.
2 On 1986 models onwards the bumper assembly must be removed

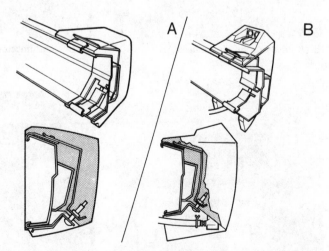

Fig. 11.9 Bumper overrider details – pre-1986 models (Sec 14)

A Without headlamp washer
B With headlamp washer

for access. Once this is done undo the two nuts (or single screw on XR3i models) and remove the overrider.
3 In all cases refitting is a reversal of removal.

15 Door trim panel – removal and refitting

Pre-1986 models
1 On Ghia versions only, remove the panel capping by carefully prising out the retaining clips using a forked tool. This can easily be made from a piece of scrap metal.
2 Remove the door window regulator handle. Do this by prising out the plastic insert from the handle and extracting the screw which will now be exposed (photos).
3 On vehicles fitted with electrically operated front windows, pull out the switches and remove the door pocket finisher.
4 Remove the door pull/armrest. This is held by two screws (photo). On Base models with a door pull only, the end caps will have to be prised up to reveal the screws.
5 Push the door lock remote control handle bezel towards the rear of the vehicle to release it from its retaining lugs (photo).
6 Again using the forked tool, pass it round the edge of the panel between the panel and the door and release each of the panel clips in turn. Lift the panel from the door (photo).
7 Refitting is a reversal of removal.

1986 models onwards
8 Remove the door window regulator handle. Do this by prising out the plastic insert from the handle and extracting the screw now exposed. Remove the washer from behind the handle (photos).
9 Prise off the door pull handle capping, undo the three screws and remove the handle (photos). On vehicles with electrically operated windows, pull out the switches and disconnect the wiring.

10 Undo the door lock remote control handle bezel retaining screw and remove the bezel (photos).
11 Prise out the plastic trim cap and unscrew the lower front panel retaining screw. Unscrew the three remaining screws, one at the upper front and two at the rear of the panel (photos).
12 Carefully release the retaining clips at the top of the panel and lift upwards to disengage the lower brackets (photo).
13 Refitting is a reversal of removal.

16 Door window (manual regulator) – removal and refitting

Saloon, Estate and Van models
1 Remove the door trim panel, as described in Section 15.
2 Carefully peel back the waterproof sheet from the door.
3 Prise off the inner and outer glass weatherstrips.
4 Lower the window so that the regulator connector is level with the door lower aperture.
5 On the front door, remove the single screw which retains the glass run extension (accessible through the small aperture at the lower corner of the door) (photo).
6 On the rear door, remove the upper and lower screws which secure the divisional channel and quarter window in position. Remove the door quarter window.
7 On front and rear doors, detach the window channel from the regulator ball and socket joints then raise and remove the window from the exterior side of the door (front) or interior side of the door (rear).
8 Refitting of the door glass is the reversal of the removal procedure. On completion check that the window operates freely before refitting the waterproof sheet and trim to the door.

Cabriolet models
9 Remove the door trim panel as described in Section 15.
10 Carefully peel back the waterproof sheet from the door.

15.2A Prise out the plastic insert ...

15.2B ... and unscrew the regulator handle

15.4 Unscrew the armrest

15.5 Removing the remote control handle bezel

15.6 Door trim panel removal

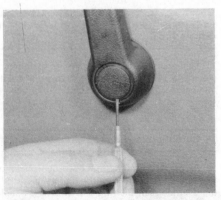
15.8A On 1986 models onwards prise out the insert ...

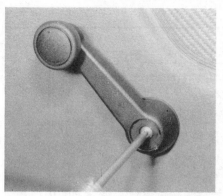

15.8B ... unscrew and remove the regulator handle ...

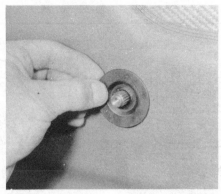

15.8C ... and washer

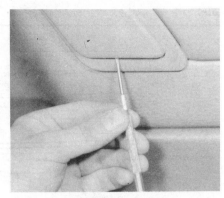

15.9A Prise out the door pull handle capping ...

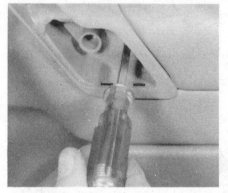

15.9B ... undo the screws ...

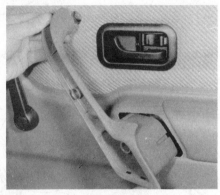

15.9C ... and remove the handle

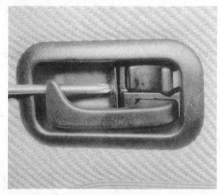

15.10A Undo the remote control handle bezel retaining screw ...

15.10B ... and remove the bezel

15.11A Release the trim cap and undo the screw ...

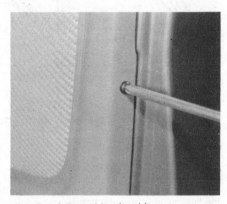

15.11B ... followed by the side screws

15.12 Lift the trim panel upwards to disengage the lower brackets

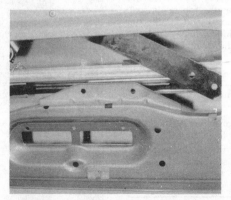

16.4 Regulator to window attachment accessible through door aperture

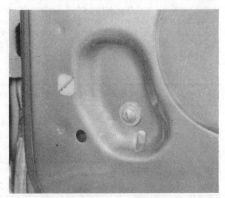

16.5 Glass run extension retaining screw

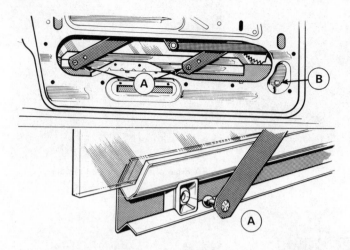

Fig. 11.10 Window channel to regulator attachments (A) and glass run extension securing screw (B) (Sec 16)

Fig. 11.11 Removing the door window glass (Sec 16)

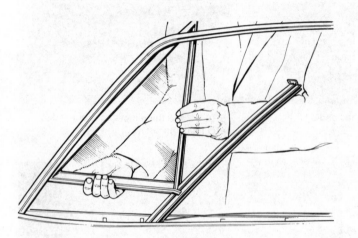

Fig. 11.12 Removing the rear door quarter window (Sec 16)

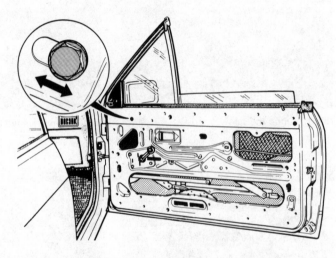

Fig. 11.13 Window stop adjustment bolt – Cabriolet models (Sec 16)

11 Remove the door weatherstrip and rubber end block.
12 Lower the window and, working through the aperture, disconnect the linkage arms from the bottom rail.
13 Lift the glass upwards from the door.
14 Refitting is a reversal of removal, but adjust the window stop as follows. Loosen the adjustment bolt (Fig. 11.13) then raise the window until the top edge of the glass touches the top guide seal. Now position the stop on the regulator mechanism and tighten the bolt. Check that, with the door shut and the window fully raised, the top front corner of the glass is under the lip of the weatherstrip. Make any final adjustments as necessary.

17 Door window (electric regulator) – removal and refitting

1 Refer to Chapter 12, Section 46, paragraphs 4 to 9 inclusive. Remove the glass as described in Section 16 of this Chapter.

18 Door window regulator (mechanical) – removal and refitting

1 Remove the door trim panel, as described in Section 15.
2 Carefully peel back the waterproof sheet from the door (photo).

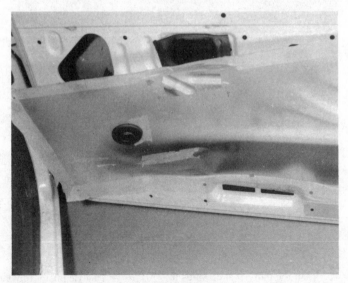

18.2 Peeling back the door waterproof sheet

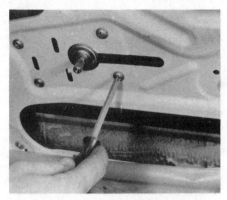
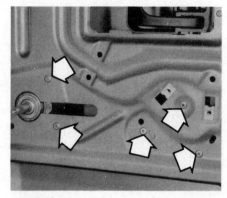
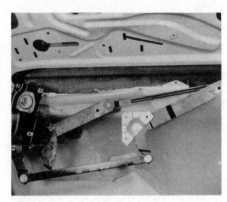

18.4A Removing the regulator retaining screws

18.4B Regulator retaining rivet location (arrowed)

18.5 Withdrawing the window regulator

3   Lower the glass so that the channel and regulator attachments are accessible through the door aperture. Detach the ball and socket joints (two for the front door, one for the rear door).
4   Lower the glass to the base of the door, then undo the seven screws, or drill out the seven rivets on later models, which secure the regulator in position. Note that on some models only five retaining rivets may be used (photos).
5   With the screws or rivets removed, the regulator unit can be withdrawn from the aperture in the door (photo).
6   Refitting is a reversal of the removal procedure. Align the regulator with the respective holes before screwing or pop riveting it to secure. The ball and socket joints are a push-fit to the glass channel, but support the channel when pushing on the joint.
7   Since the screw fixing regulator is no longer being manufactured, replacing the regulator on early models with the later type regulator necessitates drilling out the retaining holes to 7 mm (0.276 in). Special J-nuts must then be fitted to the regulator positioned in line with each of the seven securing holes. The regulator can then be attached to the door shell using seven M6 x 10 mm screws. Do not use any other screw type.

19 Door window regulator (electrical) – removal and refitting

1   Refer to Chapter 12, Section 46 for details of the removal and refitting of the electrically operated window regulator.

20 Rear door quarter window – removal and refitting

1   Proceed as described in Section 16, paragraphs 1 to 4 inclusive, also paragraph 6.
2   Refit in reverse order of removal. On completion check that the adjustable window can be freely regulated before refitting the waterproof sheet and door trim.

21 Fixed rear quarter window – removal and refitting

1   The glass is removed complete with weatherstrip by pushing it out from inside the vehicle.
2   The lip of the weatherstrip must be released from the top and sides of the window aperture using a suitable tool before exerting pressure to remove the assembly.
3   Refit using a cord as described in Section 30.

22 Rear quarter window glass and regulator (Cabriolet models) – removal and refitting

1   Fully lower the roof and remove the weatherstrip and window channel from the centre pillar.

2   Extract the clip and pull back the trim to expose the upper seat belt anchorage. Unscrew the bolt and place the seat belt to one side.
3   Lower the window and remove the regulator handle.
4   Fold the rear seat cushion forwards.
5   Remove the inner and outer window weatherstrips and the quarter panel rubber end block.
6   Remove the front quarter trim panel.
7   Remove the roof lever knob and bezel, then remove the trim panel (3 screws) with the lever in the locked position and disconnect the speaker wires.
8   Peel off the waterproof sheet then, working through the aperture, unbolt the window rail from the regulator.
9   Move the window rearwards from the regulator then lift it from the car.
10 To remove the regulator, extract the six screws and withdraw it through the aperture.
11 Refitting is a reversal of removal, but adjust the glass so that the upper and rear edges touch the weatherstrip using the screws shown in Fig. 11.14.

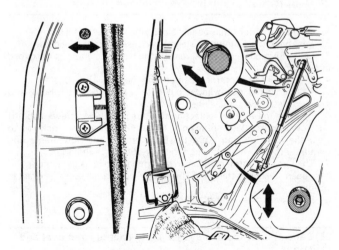

Fig. 11.14 Rear quarter window adjustments – Cabriolet models (Sec 22)

23 Door exterior handle – removal and refitting

1   Remove the door trim panel as described in Section 15.
2   Peel back the waterproof sheet as necessary to gain access (photo).
3   Undo the two screws and withdraw the handle from the door (photo).
4   Disconnect the control rod and remove the handle.
5   Refitting is a reversal of removal.

23.2 Peel back the waterproof sheet for access to the door handle

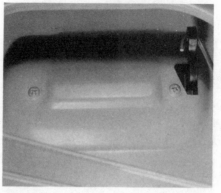

23.3 Door exterior handle retaining screws

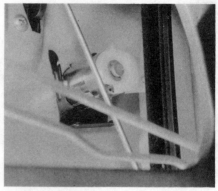

24.5 Door lock cylinder, retaining clip and control rods

24.6 Door lock retaining screws

24.7 Remote control handle retaining screw

24 Door lock and cylinder – removal and refitting

1   Remove the door trim panel as described in Section 15.
2   Peel back the waterproof sheet as necessary to gain access.
3   On 1986 models onwards, remove the exterior handle as described in Section 23.
4   Disconnect the control rods from the lock.
5   To remove the lock cylinder, pull out the retaining clip (photo) and seal and withdraw the cylinder.
6   Remove the lock by extracting the three securing screws (photo) and lowering the lock sufficiently to permit the cylinder lock rod to clear the lock housing. Turn the latch around the door frame and withdraw the assembly through the rear cut-out in the door.
7   The remote control handle can be removed once its connecting rod has been disconnected and the single securing screw extracted (photo).
8   Refitting is a reversal of removal.

25 Central door locking system components – removal and refitting

1   Refer to Chapter 12, Sections 43 and 44 for a description of the system and component removal and refitting procedures.

26 Doors – removal and refitting

Front door (pre-1986 models)

1   Open the door fully and support its lower edge on a jack or blocks covered with a pad of cloth to prevent scratching.
2   Unscrew the two bolts which hold the check arm bracket to the body and disconnect the arm.

3   Remove the scuff plate from the sill at the bottom of the door aperture.
4   Unclip the lower cowl side trim panel, and where fitted remove the radio speaker (Chapter 12).
5   Remove the heater duct.
6   On cars with electrically operated windows, mirrors or central locking, disconnect the wiring multi-plug from inside the passenger compartment and feed the wires through the aperture in the pillar.
7   Unbolt the door lower hinge from the body pillar (photo).
8   Unbolt the upper hinge from the body pillar, then lift the door from the vehicle.

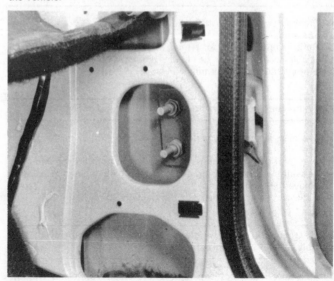

26.7 Front door lower hinge attachment

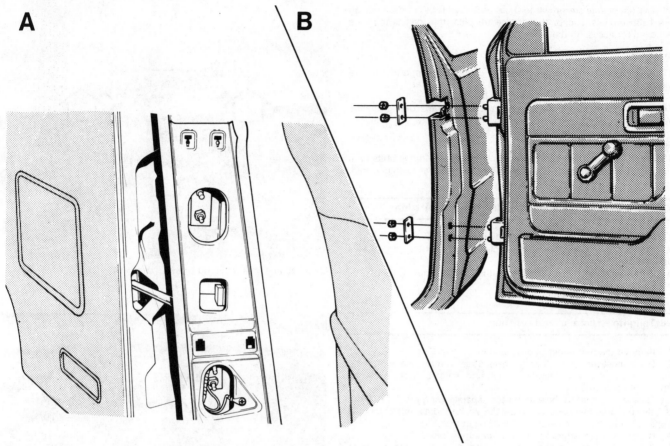

Fig. 11.15 Door hinge assemblies – pre-1986 models (Sec 26)

A   Rear door   B   Front door

26.10 Front door upper hinge pin (arrowed) on 1986 models
onwards

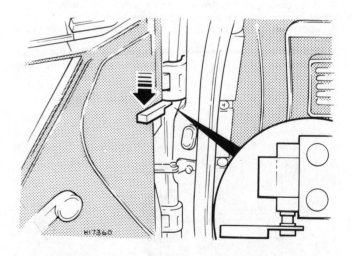

**Fig. 11.16 Front door upper hinge pin removal using special
tool – 1986 models onwards (Sec 26)**

Front door (1986 models onwards)

9   On these models it is necessary to extract the pin from the upper
hinge rather than unbolting the hinge from the pillar.
10   To do this, ideally special tool 41-018 is needed, but a suitable

alternative can be made from a piece of metal with a U-shaped cut-out
which will engage under the head of the pin (photo). Strike the tool
downward to remove the pin. When refitting, tap the pin upwards into
place. Apart from this the procedure is the same as for pre-1986
models.

Rear door (Saloon models)

11 The operations are similar to those described for the front door on pre-1986 models, except that the centre pillar trim panels must be removed for access to the hinge bolts.

Rear doors (Van models)

12 Begin by opening the door to its full extent and supporting it on a jack or blocks, with a pad of cloth used to prevent scratching.
13 Disconnect the check strap from its lower edge.
14 Unbolt the hinges from the door and remove the door from the vehicle.

All doors

15 When refitting the doors, do not fully tighten the hinge bolts until the alignment of the door within the body aperture has been checked.

27 Tailgate lock and cylinder – removal and refitting

1 Remove the trim panel as described in Section 33.
2 Extract the lock cylinder retaining clip, disconnect the control rods and remove the cylinder.
3 Undo the three screws and detach the lock assembly (photo).
4 Refitting is a reversal of removal.

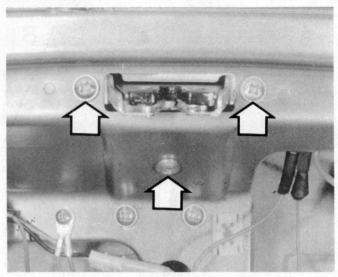

27.3 Tailgate lock retaining screws (arrowed)

28 Tailgate – removal and refitting

1 Remove the trim panel as described in Section 33.
2 Disconnect the wiring from the heated rear window element, radio aerial, wiper motor tailgate speakers and tailgate lock motor as applicable (photo).
3 Tie a strong cord to the end of each separate wiring loom. Pull out the flexible grommets and withdraw the wiring looms until the cords appear. Untie the looms, leaving the cords in the tailgate.
4 Repeat this procedure for the washer supply pipe.
5 With an assistant supporting the tailgate, prise off the stout clips or release the pegs and disconnect the support struts from the tailgate (photo).
6 From the top edge of the tailgate aperture, remove the weatherstrip. Release the headlining clips from the flange.
7 Undo the screws and remove the pillar trim on each side, then pull the headlining down for access to the hinge bolts.
8 With the tailgate supported, undo the nuts from the hinge bolts and remove the tailgate.
9 Refitting is a reversal of removal. Adjust the position of the tailgate in the aperture at the hinge bolts and the closing action at the striker plate (photo).

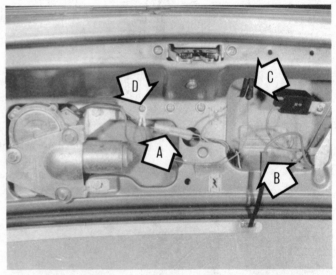

28.2 Electrical connections at the tailgate (1986 model shown)

A *Wiper motor*   C *Feed and relay connectors*
B *Radio aerial connection*   D *Earthing point*

28.5 Releasing tailgate strut retaining clip

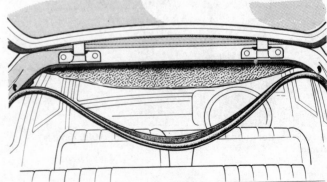

Fig. 11.17 Releasing the weatherstrip prior to tailgate removal (Sec 28)

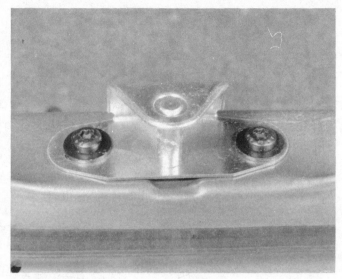

28.9 Tailgate striker

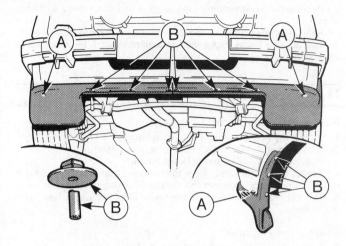

Fig. 11.18 Front spoiler attachments – XR3 models (Sec 29)

A Retaining screws   B Retaining pegs

29 Spoilers and wheel arch deflectors – removal and refitting

1   The spoilers and wheel arch deflectors fitted to XR3, XR3i, Cabriolet and RS Turbo models are secured by screws, rivets and clips, or a combination of all three.
2   The screw and rivet fasteners are concealed under blanking plugs which are prised out to gain access to the screw or rivet as applicable. These can then be drilled out or unscrewed and the spoiler or wheel arch deflector withdrawn.
3   Refitting is a reversal of removal.

30 Windscreen – removal and refitting

The average DIY mechanic is advised to leave windscreen removal and refitting to an expert. For the owner who insists on doing it himself, the following paragraphs are given.
1   All models are fitted with a laminated glass screen and in consequence even if cracked, it will probably be removed as one piece.
2   Cover the bonnet in front of the windscreen with an old blanket to protect against scratching.
3   Remove the wiper arms and blades (see Chapter 12).
4   Working inside the vehicle, push the lip of the screen weatherseal under the top and the sides of the body aperture flange.
5   With an assistant standing outside the car to restrain the screen, push the glass complete with weatherseal out of the bodyframe.
6   Where fitted, extract the bright moulding from the groove in the weatherstrip and then pull the weatherstrip off the glass.
7   Unless the weatherstrip is in good condition, it should be renewed.
8   Although sealant it not normally used with these screens, check that the glass groove in the weatherstrip is free from sealant or glass chippings.
9   Commence refitting by fitting the weatherstrip to the glass. Locate a length of nylon or terylene cord in the body flange groove of the weatherstrip so that the ends of the cord emerge at the bottom centre and cross over by a length of about 150 mm (6.0 in).
10 Offer the screen to the body and engage the lower lip of the weatherstrip on its flange. With an assistant applying gentle, even pressure on the glass from the outside, pull the ends of the cord simultaneously at right-angles to the glass. This will pull the lip of the weatherstrip over the body flange. Continue until the cord is released from the centre top and the screen is fully fitted.
11 If a bright moulding was removed, refit it now. This can be one of the most difficult jobs to do without a special tool. The moulding should be pressed into its groove just after the groove lips have been

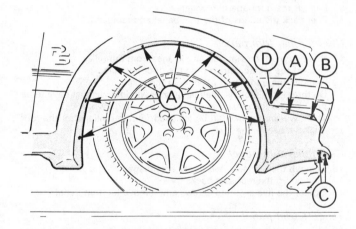

Fig. 11.19 Front wheel arch extension attachments – RS Turbo models (Sec 29)

A and B Rivets   D Screw cap
C Screws

prised open to receive it. Take care not to cut the weatherstrip if improvising with a made-up tool.

31 Tailgate glass – removal and refitting

1   The operations are very similar to those described for windscreen renewal in the preceding Section.
2   Disconnect the leads from the heated rear window/radio aerial and the wiper motor (where fitted).
3   The tailgate glass is of toughened type, not laminated, so if it has shattered, remove all granular glass with a small vacuum cleaner.

32 Rear window glass (Cabriolet models) – removal and refitting

1   Disconnect the heated rear window wiring and pull the wiring from the weatherstrip.
2   Have an assistant support the window frame from outside then push out the glass from the inside.

3 Remove the weatherstrip from the glass and clean away all traces of sealant.
4 Refit in reverse order to removal using the method described in Section 30, and finally apply suitable sealant beneath the outer lip of the weatherstrip.

33 Interior trim panels – removal and refitting

Rear quarter trim panel

1 Unbolt the seat belt from its floor mounting.
2 Pass the belt buckle slide through the panel aperture.
3 Pull the seat cushion and backrest forward.
4 Extract the single screw from the quarter panel and then using a suitable forked tool, lever out the clips and remove the panel.
5 The clips and ashtray are detachable after the panel has been withdrawn.

Cowl side trim panel

6 Extract the two screws from the scuff plate (photo).
7 Remove the two clips and detach the panel by pulling it from its two locating pegs (photo).

Windscreen pillar trim panel

8 The windscreen will have to be removed as described in Section 30.
9 Pull off the door aperture weatherstrip.
10 Peel back the edges of the trim panel and remove it.

Centre pillar trim panels

11 Remove the two seat belt anchorages from the pillar.
12 Pull off the weatherstrips from the door apertures.
13 Remove the upper trim panel from the pillar.
14 On three-door models, the rear quarter window will first have to be removed before the pillar trim panel can be withdrawn.
15 The lower trim panel can be removed from the pillar after the four screws have been extracted.

Rear pillar trim panel

16 Remove the rear seat belt upper anchorage.
17 Fold down the rear seat back.
18 Extract the five securing screws and remove the trim panel.

Tailgate trim panel

19 This comprises a flat panel secured with push-in type clips. If a rear wiper is fitted, this will have a moulded cover over the wiper motor secured by quarter-turn fasteners.
20 To remove the moulded cover, turn the heads of the fasteners through 90° to release them (photo).

Rear wheelhouse covers

21 These are fitted to certain Base and L models and are of moulded type. On Ghia versions the covers are cloth covered while on 5-door versions, the covers have an upper finisher held by two screws.

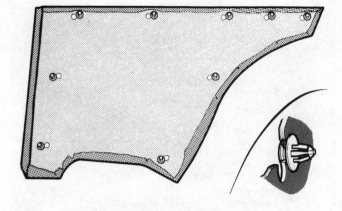

Fig. 11.20 Rear quarter trim panel (Sec 33)

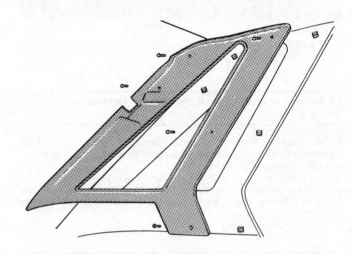

Fig. 11.21 Rear pillar trim panel (Sec 33)

Load space trim panel

22 These take the form of moulded panels on 'high series' trim models and flat panels on Base and L versions. The panels are held in position by external clips.

Door trim panels

23 Refer to Section 15 of this Chapter.

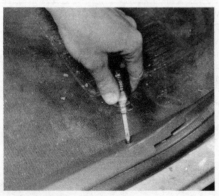

33.6 Removing the sill scuff plate

33.7 Removing cowl side trim

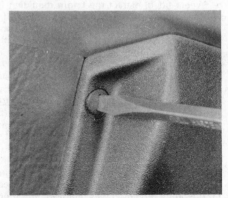

33.20 Releasing the tailgate moulded cover fasteners

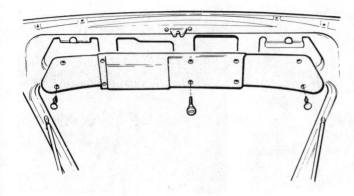

Fig. 11.22 Tailgate trim panel (Sec 33)

34 Rear parcel shelf – removal and refitting

1   Open the tailgate fully and disengage the parcel shelf lifting strap loops from the tailgate retaining knobs.
2   Lift out the parcel shelf pivot pins from their notches in the support brackets and withdraw the shelf.
3   Pull each strap loop through its hole in the rear edge of the shelf by disengaging the upper and lower retaining collars.
4   The shelf brackets are secured with pop rivets which must be drilled out if the brackets are to be removed.
5   Refitting is a reversal of removal.

35 Glove compartment – removal and refitting

Pre-1986 models

1   Open the glovebox lid and extract the screws which hold the glovebox to the facia.
2   Remove the latch (two screws).
3   Remove the single screw inside the top of the glove compartment which holds it to the moulded bracket. Withdraw the glove compartment.
4   Refitting is a reversal of removal.

1986 models onwards

5   Undo the two screws and remove the glove compartment lid.
6   Remove the latch (two screws) and disconnect the lamp wiring (where fitted).
7   Undo the three screws and remove the glove compartment.
8   Refitting is a reversal of removal.

36 Passenger grab handles – removal and refitting

1   These handles are secured to the roof by screws concealed by small cover plates.
2   To expose the screws, prise out the cover plates. Remove the screws and handle.
3   Refit by reversing the removal operations.

37 Interior mirror – removal and refitting

1   The interior mirror is bonded to the windscreen glass. If it must be removed, grip the mirror firmly and push it forward to break the adhesive bond.
2   When refitting the mirror, the following preliminary work must first be carried out.
3   Remove existing adhesive from the windscreen glass using a suitable solvent. Allow the solvent to evaporate. The location of the mirror base is marked on the glass with a black patch, so that there should not be any chance of an error when fitting.
4   If the original mirror is being refitted, clean away all the old adhesive from the mirror mounting base, and apply a new adhesive patch to it.
5   If a new windscreen is being installed, peel off the protective layer from the black patch, which is pre-coated with adhesive.
6   Peel off the protective layer from the mirror adhesive patch and locate the mirror precisely onto the black patch on the screen. Hold it in position for at least two minutes.
7   For best results, the fitting of a bonded type mirror should be carried out in an ambient temperature of 70°C (158°F). The careful use of a blower heater on both the glass and mirror should achieve this temperature level.

38 Exterior mirror – removal and refitting

Without remote control

1   Using a screwdriver, prise off the triangular trim panel from inside the mirror mounting position.
2   Unscrew the three screws and withdraw the mirror.

With remote control

3   Two types of remote control mirror are used on Escort models. On the original version, a special wrench is needed to unscrew the mirror actuator bezel, although a C-spanner may serve as a substitute. Once the bezel is removed the mirror is removed as for the non-remote control type.
4   On later versions extract the retaining circlip and pull off the remote control handle (photos).
5   Extract the trim cover, undo the screw and remove the triangular trim panel (photos).
6   Undo the three screws and remove the mirror (photo).

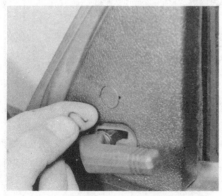

38.4A Remote control mirror handle circlip

38.4B Removing the remote control handle

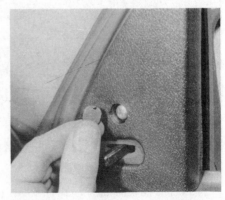

38.5A Extract the trim cover and undo the screw ...

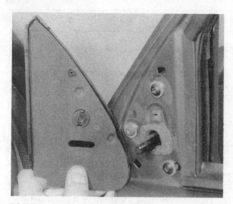

38.5B ... then remove the trim panel

38.6 Removing the door mirror retaining screws

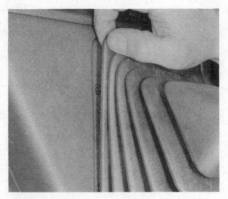

39.2 Releasing the rubber gaiter at the centre console

7   On the electrically operated mirror, remove the door trim panel as described in Section 15 and disconnect the wiring multi-plug. The mirror is then removed in the same way as the non-remote control type.

All mirrors

8   Refitting is a reversal of removal.

39 Centre console – removal and refitting

1   Remove the gear lever knob.
2   Pull the rubber gaiter up the lever and remove it (photo).
3   Undo the four screws and remove the console (photo).
4   Refitting is a reversal of removal.

40 Sunroof – adjustment

1   The sunroof panel can be adjusted within its aperture and for flush fitting with the roof panel in the following way.
2   To correct the panel-to-aperture gap, bend the weatherstrip flange as necessary.

3   To adjust the panel height at its front edge, release the corner screws, raise or lower the panel as necessary and then tighten the screws.
4   To adjust the panel height at its rear edge, release the two screws at each side on the link assemblies and push the links up or down within the limits of the elongated screw holes. Retighten the screws when alignment is correct.

41 Sunroof panel – removal and refitting

1   To remove this type of glass panel, pull the sun blind into the open position and have the sliding roof closed.
2   Wind the sliding roof handle in an anti-clockwise direction for one complete turn.
3   Remove the three screws and clips which connect the lower frame and glass.
4   Turn the handle to close the sliding roof and remove the three screws from each side which hold the glass to the sliding gear.
5   Remove the glass panel by lifting it from the outside of the vehicle.
6   To refit the panel, have the roof closed, locate the glass and secure with the three screws on each side. Once the screws are secure give the handle one complete turn in a clockwise direction.

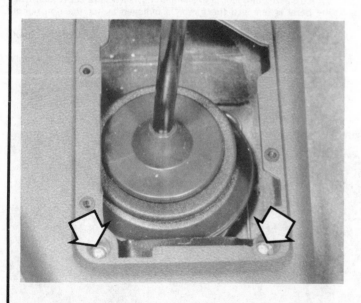

39.3 Centre console lower retaining screws (arrowed)

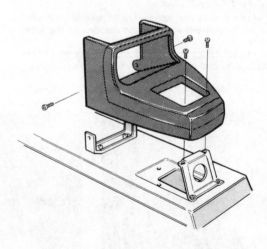

Fig. 11.23 Centre console attachments (Sec 39)

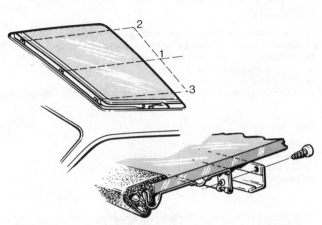

Fig. 11.24 Fixing sequence for sunroof panel retaining screws (Sec 41)

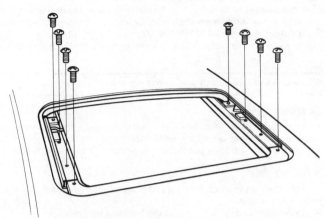

Fig. 11.25 Sunroof sliding gear to roof screws (Sec 42)

7   Set the glass to align with the roof panel and locate the lower frame to glass brackets. Insert the clips through the brackets.
8   Insert the retaining screws in the sequence shown in Fig. 11.24.

42 Sunroof sliding gear – removal and refitting

1   Remove the glass panel as described in the preceding Section.
2   Turn the sliding roof regulator handle clockwise to the fully closed position. Extract the three screws and remove the regulator handle and the handle cup.
3   Extract the four screws from each side which hold the sliding gear to the roof. Lift up the front of the gear and withdraw it from the front of the sliding roof aperture.
4   Refitting is a reversal of removal.
5   Adjust if necessary as described in Section 40.

43 Folding roof (Cabriolet models) – removal and refitting

1   Remove the rear side, wheel arch and roof stowage compartment trim panels.
2   Disconnect the heated rear window wiring and pull it from the weatherstrip.
3   Release the roof front locking catches.
4   Unscrew the nuts and remove the rear window frame guides.
5   Remove the screws shown in Fig. 11.26 from each side.
6   Unscrew the nuts at both tensioning cable blocks.
7   Pull the roof and cable from the rail and release the cable.
8   With the roof frame upright, unbolt the strap retaining brackets.
9   Remove the headlining wire screw and unhook the wire.
10 Disconnect the gas struts.
11 Lower the front of the roof then unscrew the three mounting bolts on each side.
12 Lift the complete folding roof from the car.
13 Refitting is a reversal of removal, but do not tighten the mounting bolts or tensioning block nuts until the front of the roof is locked and the rear beading is in the rail. It may be necessary to use a tamping tool to ensure the tensioning cable is fully inserted in the rail. A little sealant should be applied at the points where the cable passes through the covering.

44 Front seat and slide – removal and refitting

1   Slide the seat as far forward as it will go.
2   Unscrew and remove the bolts which retain the rear of the seat slides to the floor pan.
3   Slide the seat as far to the rear as it will go and remove the bolts which secure the front ends of the slides to the floor.

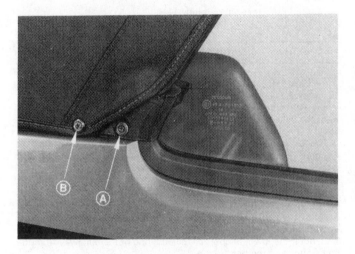

Fig. 11.26 Protection cover screw (A) and tensioning screw (B) – Cabriolet models (Sec 43)

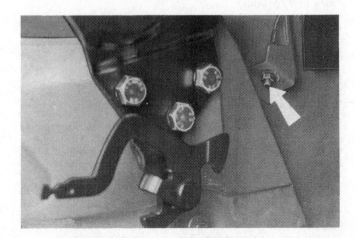

Fig. 11.27 Cable tensioning block nut (arrowed) – Cabriolet models (Sec 43)

4 Remove the seat from the vehicle interior.
5 If the seat slides must be detached from the seat, invert the seat and remove the two bolts from each side. Detach the cross-rod and clips.
6 Refitting is a reversal of removal. Tighten the front bolts before the rear ones to ensure that the seat is located evenly on the floorpan.

45 Rear seat – removal and refitting

Cushion

1 Unscrew and remove the Torx (socket-headed) screws from the seat cushion hinges which are located on each side.
2 Lift the cushion from the floor and remove it from the vehicle.

Backrest

3 Fold the seat cushion forward and then fold the seat back down to expose the hinges.
4 Extract the screws which hold the backrest to the hinges.
5 Remove the backrest from the vehicle.

Both parts

6 Refitting is a reversal of removal.

46 Seat belts – maintenance, removal and refitting

Maintenance

1 Periodically check the belts for fraying or other damage. If evident, renew the belt.
2 If the belts become dirty, wipe them with a damp cloth using a little liquid detergent only.
3 Check the tightness of the anchor bolts and if they are ever disconnected, make quite sure that the original sequence of fitting of washers, bushes and anchor plate is retained.
4 Never modify the belt or alter its attachment point to the body.

Front belt (3-door)

5 Slide the belt stalk cover upwards to expose the anchor bolt.
6 Unbolt the stalk.
7 Unbolt the lower anchor rail, pull the end of the rail away from the panel and slide the belt from it.
8 Prise the moulded cap from the centre pillar anchorage and remove the bolt.
9 Prise the belt guide runner from the rear quarter trim panel and slide the runner from the belt.
10 Remove the rear quarter trim panel (Section 33).
11 Unbolt the reel/belt assembly from the inner rear quarter body panel.

Front belt (5-door)

12 Refer to paragraph 5 and remove the stalk.
13 Refer to paragraph 8 and remove the anchor bolt.
14 Unbolt the inertia reel and the anchor plate from the centre pillar. Remove the pillar lower trim panel (Section 33).

Front belt (Cabriolet)

15 Unbolt the centre stalk.
16 Remove the clip and pull back the trim to expose the upper anchor. Unscrew the anchor bolt.
17 Unbolt and pull out the lower mounting rail. Slide the belt from the rail.
18 Remove the rear quarter trim panel then pull the belt through the slot in the panel and through the pillar guide.
19 Unbolt the inertia reel unit.

Rear belt (Saloon)

20 Raise the rear seat cushion and remove the anchor bolt from the floor pan.
21 Unclip the elasticated strap from the lower belt buckle.
22 Unbolt the inertia reel anchor plate from the floor.
23 Unbolt the belt from the body pillar upper section.
24 Prise out the belt guide runner from the rear package tray support panel and slide the runner from the belt.

25 Raise the inertia reel cover, unscrew the reel mounting bolt and withdraw reel and spacer.

Rear belt (Estate)

26 Repeat the operations described in paragraphs 20 to 22.
27 Raise the moulded cap from the support strap mounting, slide the mounting plate to one side until the large hole passes over the bolt head and the strap can be removed.
28 Unscrew the cap and bolt.
29 Raise the cover on the inertia reel to expose the bolt and unbolt the reel.

Rear belt (Cabriolet)

30 Raise the rear seat cushion.
31 Release the buckles from the elasticated straps.
32 Unbolt the seat belts from their floor mountings.
33 Refitting is a reversal of removal.

All belts

34 Refitting of all belts is a reversal of removal. Ensure that spacers, plates and washers are in correct sequence and tighten all bolts to the specified torque wrench settings.

47 Facia – removal and refitting

Pre-1986 models

1 Disconnect the battery negative lead.
2 Remove the under-dash cover panels.
3 Refer to Chapter 10 and remove the steering column assembly.
4 Refer to Chapter 12 and remove the instrument panel.
5 Where applicable, refer to Chapter 12 and remove the warning indicator control unit of the auxiliary warning system, and where fitted, the fuel computer.
6 Detach the heater controls, switches and wiring multi-plugs, with reference to Chapter 12 and Section 50 of this Chapter.
7 Remove the ashtray and cigar lighter mounting panel.
8 Remove the radio and its mounting bracket (Chapter 12).
9 Disconnect the wire from the loudspeaker and remove the speaker (four screws).
10 Remove the glovebox (Section 35).
11 Where fitted, remove the choke cable (Chapter 3).
12 Detach the vent ducts and demister hoses from the heater.
13 Extract the securing screws and clips (Figs, 11.28 and 11.29) and remove the facia panel complete with crash pad.
14 The crash padding can be detached by removing the glove compartment mounting bracket and lock bracket, withdrawing the side and centre face level vents and extracting all the securing clips.
15 Refitting is a reversal of removal.

1986 models onwards

16 Disconnect the battery negative lead.
17 Refer to Chapter 10 and remove the steering column assembly.
18 Refer to Chapter 12 and remove the instrument panel.
19 Where applicable, refer to Chapter 12 and remove the warning indicator control unit of the auxiliary warning system and where fitted, the fuel computer.
20 Remove the choke cable, where fitted, as described in Chapter 3.
21 Remove the heater control knobs.
22 Undo the two heater control facia panel screws, pull panel out and disconnect the wiring multi-plug. Remove the panel.
23 Remove the ashtray.
24 Refer to Chapter 12 and remove the radio or radio/cassette player.
25 Undo the radio/ashtray facia panel screws, withdraw the panel and disconnect the cigar lighter wiring, if fitted. Remove the panel.
26 Remove the glovebox as described in Section 35.
27 Undo the nine screws and one nut securing the facia, then remove the unit from the car.
28 The crash padding can be removed after undoing the screws from behind the facia.
29 Refitting is a reversal of removal.

315

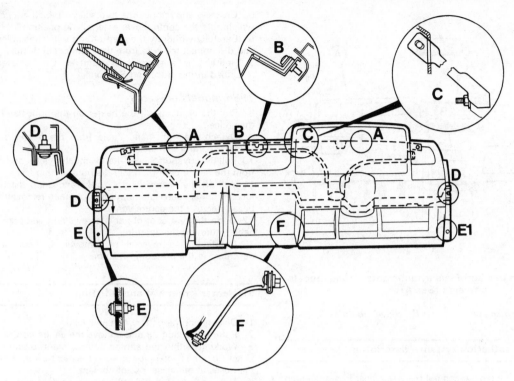

Fig. 11.28 Crash pad and facia attachments – pre-1986 Base and L models (Sec 47)

A   Clip   D   Screw   F   Screw
B   Screw   E   Screw
C   Nut   E1 Screw (L models only)

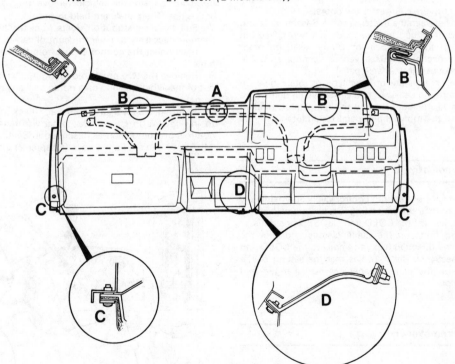

Fig. 11.29 Crash pad and facia attachments – pre-1986 GL and Ghia models (Sec 47)

A   Screw   C   Screw
B   Clip   D   Screw

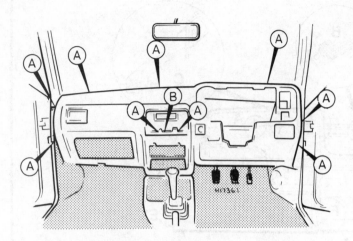

Fig. 11.30 Crash pad and facia attachments – 1986 models onwards (Sec 47)

A   Retaining screws   *B   Retaining nuts*

48 Heating and ventilation system – description

The heater is of the type which utilises waste heat from the engine coolant. The coolant is pumped through the matrix in the heater casing where air, force-fed by a duplex radial fan, disperses the heat into the vehicle interior.

Fresh air enters the heater or the ventilator ducts through the grille at the rear of the bonnet lid. Air is extracted from the interior of the vehicle through outlets at the rear edges of the doors.

There are differences between the heater used on Base models and other versions in the Escort range. On Base models, a two-speed fan switch is used instead of the three-position switch used on other versions. On all models except the Base version, central and side window vents are incorporated in the facia panel.

The heater/ventilator controls are of lever type or rotary type on later models, operating through cables to flap valves which deflect the air flowing through the heater both to vary the temperature and to distribute the air between the footwell and demister outlets.

49 Heater controls – adjustment

1   On heaters with lever control, set both control levers approximately 2.0 mm (0.08 in) up from their lowest setting, On heaters with rotary controls set the controls just off the COLD and CLOSED positions.
2   Release the securing bolts on the cable clamps and pull the temperature control and air direction flap valve arms to the COLD and CLOSED positions respectively. Check to see that the setting of the levers or rotary knobs on the control panel has not changed and retighten the cable clamps.

50 Heater controls – removal and refitting

Pre-1986 models

1   Working inside the vehicle, remove the dash lower trim panel from the right-hand side. The panel is secured by two metal tags and two clips.
2   Detach the air ducts from the right-hand side of the heater casing and swivel them to clear the control cables.
3   Disconnect the control cables from the heater casing.
4   Giving a sharp jerk, pull the knobs from the control levers on the facia panel, then press the control indicator plate downwards and remove it.

5   Unscrew and remove the two screws which are now exposed and which hold the control lever assembly in position.
6   Carefully withdraw the control unit with the cables from the facia and disconnect the wire from the illumination lamp.
7   Refitting is a reversal of removal. On completion, adjust as described in the preceding Section.

1986 models onwards

8   Pull the air ducts off the heater on the right-hand side and move them clear.
9   Detach the right-hand cable from the heater casing and temperature control flap lever.
10 Pull the cover off the left-hand actuating lever and detach the cable from the heater casing and air distribution flap lever.
11 Pull off the heater control knobs and undo the two screws, one located under each outer control knob, then remove the control panel bezel. Remove the centre vents.
12 Undo the two control panel screws and withdraw the panel with cables, through the aperture.
13 Refitting is a reversal of removal. On completion adjust as described in the preceding Section.

51 Heater – removal and refitting

1   Disconnect the battery negative lead.
2   Refer to Section 39 and remove the centre console.
3   Working within the engine compartment, disconnect the coolant hoses from the heater pipe stubs at the rear bulkhead. Raise the ends of the hoses to minimise loss of coolant.
4   The heater matrix will still contain coolant and should be drained by blowing into the upper heater pipe stub and catching the coolant which will be ejected from the lower one.
5   Remove the cover plate and gasket from around the heater pipe stubs. This is held to the bulkhead by two self-tapping screws.
6   Working inside the vehicle, remove the dash lower trim panels from both sides. The panels are held in position by clips and tags.
7   Pull the air distribution ducts from the heater casing and swivel them as necessary to clear the control cables.
8   Disconnect the control cables from the heater casing and the flap arms.
9   Remove the two heater mounting nuts and lift the heater assembly out of the vehicle, taking care not to spill any remaining coolant on the carpet.
10 Refitting is a reversal of removal. Check that the heater casing seal to the cowl is in good order, otherwise renew it. Adjust the heater controls on completion as described in Section 49.
11 Top up the cooling system (Chapter 2) and reconnect the battery.

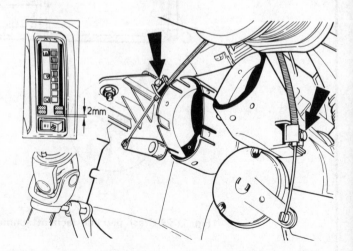

Fig. 11.31 Heater control cable connections (arrowed) – pre-1986 models (Sec 49)

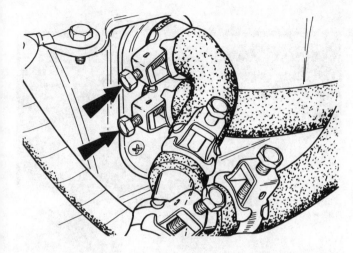

Fig. 11.32 Coolant hose connections at heater pipe stubs
(Sec 51)

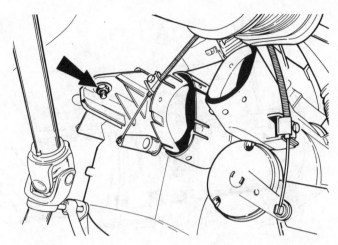

Fig. 11.33 Heater mounting nut location – left-hand side
(Sec 51)

52 Heater casing – dismantling and reassembly

1   With the heater removed from the vehicle as previously described, extract the two securing screws and slide the matrix out of the heater casing.
2   If further dismantling is necessary, cut the casing seal at the casing joint, prise off any securing clips and separate the two halves of the casing.
3   Remove the air flap valves. It should be noted that the lever for the air distribution valve can only be removed when the mark on the lever is in alignment with the one on the gearwheel.
4   If the heater matrix is leaking, it is best to obtain a new or reconditioned unit. Home repairs are seldom successful. A blocked matrix can sometimes be cleared using a cold water hose and reverse flushing, but avoid the use of searching chemical cleaners.
5   Reassembly is a reversal of removal. Take care not to damage the fins or tubes of the matrix when inserting it into the casing.

53 Heater motor/fan – removal and refitting

1   Open the bonnet, disconnect the battery and pull off the rubber seal which seals the air intake duct to the bonnet lid when the lid is closed.
2   Prise off the five spring clips from the plenum chamber cover and detach the cover at the front.
3   Disconnect the wiring harness multi-plug, and the earth lead at its body connection adjacent to the heater pipe stub cover plate on the engine compartment bulkhead.
4   Unscrew and remove the fan housing mounting nuts and lift the housing from the engine compartment (photo).
5   Insert the blade of a screwdriver and prise off the securing clips so that the fan covers can be removed.
6   Remove the resistor and lift out the motor/fan assembly.
7   Reassembly and refitting are reversals of dismantling and removal.

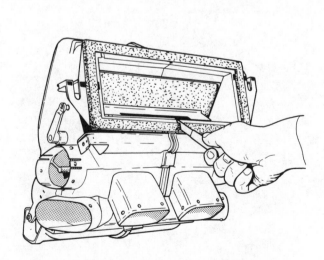

Fig. 11.34 Cutting heater casing seal (Sec 52)

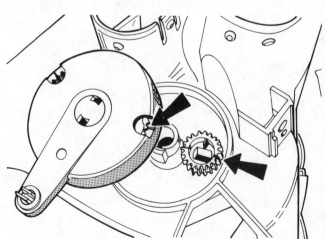

Fig. 11.35 Air distribution valve lever and gear marks
(Sec 52)

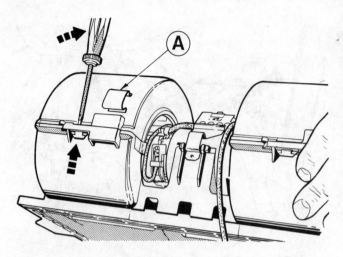

Fig. 11.36 Removing the heater fan cover and clip (A)
(Sec 53)

53.4 Heater motor/fan (cover removed)

Chapter 12 Electrical system

For modifications, and information applicable to later models, see Supplement at end of manual

Contents

Specifications

System type .... 12 volt, negative earth

Battery
Type .... 12 volt lead-acid, 35 to 52 Ah depending on model
Charge condition:
   Poor .... 12.4 volts or less
   Normal .... 12.6 volts
   Good .... 12.7 volts or over

Alternator
Rated output (13.5 V at 6000 rpm engine speed) ....

	Bosch	Lucas	Motorola	Mitsubishi
	28A (G1-28A)	28A (A115/28)	28A (265 00)	–
	35A (K1-35A)	36A (A115/36)	35A (2652 F)	–
	45A (K1-45A)	45A (A133/45)	45A (2627 G)	–
	55A (K1-55A)	55A (A133/55)	–	55A (A00 5T)
	70A (K1-70A)	55A (A127/55)	–	–
	–	70A (A127/70)	–	–
Minimum brush length	5.0 mm (0.20 in)	5.0 mm (0.20 in)	4.0 mm (0.16 in)	5.0 mm 0.20 in)
Regulator voltage at 4000 rpm with 3 to 7A load (all models)	13.7 to 14.6 volts			

Starter motor

Type	Pre-engaged
Make:	
Bosch	0.8 kW, 0.85 kW, 0.9 kW, 0.95 kW
Lucas	8M 90, 9M 90, M 79
Nippondenso	0.6 kW, 0.9 kW
Number of brushes:	
All starters except Nippondenso 0.6 kW	4
Nippondenso 0.6 kW	2
Minimum brush length:	
Bosch	10.0 mm (0.39 in)
Lucas	8.0 mm (0.31 in)
Nippondenso 0.6 kW	10.0 mm (0.39 in)
Nippondenso 0.9 kW	9.0 mm (0.35 in)
Armature endfloat:	
Bosch	0.30 mm (0.012 in)
Lucas	0.25 mm (0.010 in)
Nippondenso	0.60 mm (0.024 in)

Bulbs

Headlamp:	
Halogen	60/55
Tungsten	50/45W
Front sidelamp	4W
Front indicator lamp	21W
Stop/tail lamp	21/5W
Reversing lamp	21W
Rear foglamp	21W
Rear indicator lamp	21W
Rear number plate lamp	5W
Auxiliary lamp (Halogen)	55W
Foglamp (Halogen)	55w
Instrument cluster warning lamps	1.3W
Panel illumination	2.6W
Cigar lighter illumination	1.4W
Glove compartment lamp	2W
Luggage compartment lamp	10W
Interior lamp	10W

Windscreen wiper blades
Champion C-4501

Torque wrench settings

	Nm	lbf ft
Horn to body	25 to 35	18 to 26
Windscreen wiper arm to pivot mounting	15 to 18	11 to 13
Rear wiper arm to pivot mounting	12 to 15	9 to 11
Reversing lamp switch to transmission	16 to 20	12 to 15
Door window motor mounting bolts	4 to 5	3 to 4
Window regulator bolts	4 to 5	3 to 4

1 General description

The electrical system is of the 12 volt negative earth type, and consists of a 12 volt battery, alternator, starter motor and related electrical accessories, components and wiring. The battery is of the low maintenance or maintenance-free, 'sealed for life' type and is charged by an alternator which is belt-driven from the crankshaft pulley. The starter motor is of the pre-engaged type incorporating an integral solenoid. On starting, the solenoid moves the drive pinion into engagement with the flywheel ring gear before the starter motor is energised. Once the engine has started, a one-way clutch prevents the motor armature being driven by the engine until the pinion disengages from the flywheel.

Further details of the major electrical systems are given in the relevant Sections of this Chapter.

Caution: *Before carrying out any work on the vehicle electrical system, read through the precautions given in Safety First! at the beginning of this manual and in Section 2 of this Chapter.*

2 Electrical system – precautions

It is necessary to take extra care when working on the electrical system to avoid damage to semi-conductor devices (diodes and transistors), and to avoid the risk of personal injury. In addition to the precautions given in Safety First! at the beginning of this manual, observe the following items when working on the system.

1 *Always remove rings, watches, etc before working on the electrical system.* Even with the battery disconnected, capacitive discharge could occur if a component live terminal is earthed through a metal object. This could cause a shock or nasty burn.

2 *Do not reverse the battery connections.* Components such as the alternator or any other having semi-conductor circuitry could be irreparably damaged.

3 If the engine is being started using jump leads and a slave battery, connect the batteries *positive to positive* and *negative to negative.* This also applies when connecting a battery charger.

4 Never disconnect the battery terminals, or alternator multi-plug connector, when the engine is running.

5 The battery leads and alternator multi-plug must be disconnected before carrying out any electric welding on the car.

6 Never use an ohmmeter of the type incorporating a hand cranked generator for circuit or continuity testing.

3 Maintenance and inspection

1 At regular intervals (see Routine Maintenance) carry out the following maintenance and inspection operations on the electrical system components.

2 Check the operation of all the electrical equipment, ie wipers, washers, lights, direction indicators, horn etc. Refer to the appropriate Sections of this Chapter if any components are found to be inoperative.

3 Visually check all accessible wiring connectors, harnesses and

retaining clips for security, or any signs of chafing or damage. Rectify any problems encountered.

4   Check the alternator drivebelt for cracks, fraying or damage. Renew the belt if worn or, if satisfactory, check and adjust the belt tension. These procedures are covered in Section 7.

5   Check the condition of the wiper blades and if they are cracked or show signs of deterioration, renew them, as described in Section 34. Check the operation of the windscreen and tailgate washers. Adjust the nozzles using a pin, if necessary.

6   Check the battery terminals, and if there is any sign of corrosion disconnect and clean them thoroughly. Smear the terminals and battery posts with petroleum jelly before refitting the plastic covers. If there is any corrosion on the battery tray, remove the battery, clean the deposits away and treat the affected metal with an anti-rust preparation. Repaint the tray in the original colour after treatment.

7   From 1982 Ford models have progressively been fitted with a maintenance-free battery during production. The maintenance-free battery is of 'sealed for life' cell design and does not require routine topping-up with distilled water. The only maintenance requirement with this battery type is to inspect the battery lead terminals for security and any sign of corrosion.

8   On early models equipped with a low maintenance type battery, or on later models where the battery has been replaced by one of this type from another source, the electrolyte level should be maintained just above the tops of the cells, or up to the mark on the battery case where applicable. If topping-up is necessary, add distilled water to each cell as necessary after unscrewing the cell caps or lifting up the top cover.

9   Top up the windscreen and rear window washer reservoirs and check the security of the pump wires and water pipes.

10 It is advisable to have the headlight aim adjusted using optical beam setting equipment.

11 While carrying out a road test check the operation of all the instruments and warning lights, and the operation of the direction indicator self-cancelling mechanism.

4   Battery – testing and charging

Standard and low maintenance battery – testing

1   If the car covers a small annual mileage it is worthwhile checking the specific gravity of the electrolyte every three months to determine the state of charge of the battery. Use a hydrometer to make the check and compare the results with the following table.

	Ambient temperature above 25°C (77°F)	Ambient temperature below 25°C (77°F)
Fully charged	1.210 to 1.230	1.270 to 1.290
70% charged	1.170 to 1.190	1.230 to 1.250
Fully discharged	1.050 to 1.070	1.110 to 1.130

Note that the specific gravity readings assume an electrolyte temperature of 15°C (60°F); for every 10°C (18°F) below 15°C (60°F) subtract 0.007. For every 10°C (18°F) above 15°C (60°F) add 0.007.

2   If the battery condition is suspect first check the specific gravity of electrolyte in each cell. A variation of 0.040 or more between any cells indicates loss of electrolyte or deterioration of the internal plates.

3   If the specific gravity variation is 0.040 or more, the battery should be renewed. If the cell variation is satisfactory but the battery is discharged, it should be charged as described later in this Section.

Maintenance-free battery – testing

4   In cases where a 'sealed for life' maintenance-free battery is fitted, topping-up and testing of the electrolyte in each cell is not possible. The condition of the battery type can therefore only be tested using a battery condition indicator or a voltmeter.

5   If testing the battery using a voltmeter, connect it across the battery and compare the result with those given in the Specifications under 'charge condition'. The test is only accurate if the battery has not been subject to any kind of charge for the previous six hours. If this is not the case switch on the headlights for 30 seconds then wait four to five minutes before testing the battery after switching off the headlights. All other electrical components must be switched off, so check that the doors and tailgate are fully shut when making the test.

6   If the voltage reading is less than the 12.2 volts then the battery is discharged, whilst a reading of 12.2 to 12.4 volts indicates a partially discharged condition.

7   If the battery is to be charged, remove it from the vehicle (Section 5) and charge it as described later in this Section.

Standard and low maintenance battery – charging

8   Charge the battery at a rate of 3.5 to 4 amps and continue to charge the battery at this rate until no further rise in specific gravity is noted over a four hour period.

9   Alternatively, a trickle charger charging at the rate of 1.5 amps can be safely used overnight.

10 Specially rapid 'boost' charges which are claimed to restore the power of the battery in 1 to 2 hours are not recommended as they can cause serious damage to the battery plates through overheating.

11 While charging the battery note that the temperature of the electrolyte should never exceed 37.8°C (100°F).

Maintenance-free battery – charging

12 This battery type takes considerably longer to fully recharge than the standard type, the time taken being dependent on the extent of discharge, but it can take anything up to three days.

13 A constant voltage type charger is required, to be set, when connected, to 13.9 to 14.9 volts with a charger current below 25 amps. Using this method the battery should be useable within three hours, giving a voltage reading of 12.5 volts, but this is for a partially discharged battery and, as mentioned, full charging can take considerably longer.

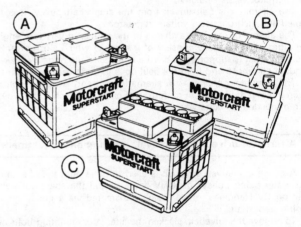

Fig. 12.1 Battery types (Sec 3 and 4)

A   Maintenance-free sealed cell type
B   Maintenance-free removable cell top type
C   Low maintenance type

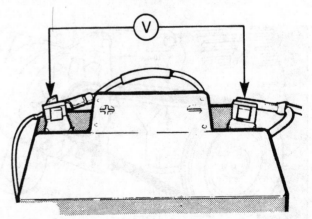

Fig. 12.2 Battery test method using voltmeter (Sec 4)

14 If the battery is to be charged from a fully discharged state (condition reading less than 12.2 volts) have it recharged by your Ford dealer or local automotive electrician as the charge rate is higher and constant supervision during charging is necessary.

5 Battery – removal and refitting

1 The battery is located on the left-hand side of the engine compartment on a bulkhead platform (photo).
2 Disconnect the leads at the negative (earth) terminal by undoing the retaining nut and removing the bolt. Disconnect the positive terminal leads in the same way.
3 Undo the bolts securing the two battery clamps and remove the clamps.
4 Lift the battery from its location, keeping it in an upright position to avoid spilling electrolyte on the paintwork.
5 Refitting is the reverse sequence to removal. Smear petroleum jelly on the terminals when refitting and always connect the positive lead first and the negative lead last.

6 Alternator – description

1 One of a number of different makes of alternator may be fitted, dependent upon model and engine capacity. The maximum output of the alternator varies similarly.
2 The alternator is belt-driven from the crankshaft pulley, it is fan cooled and incorporates a voltage regulator.
3 The alternator provides a charge to the battery at very low engine revolutions and basically consists of a stator in which a rotor rotates. The rotor shaft is supported in ball-bearings, and slip rings are used to conduct current to and from the field coils through carbon brushes.
4 The alternator generates ac (alternating current) which is rectified by an internal diode system to dc (direct current) which is the type of current needed for battery storage.

7 Alternator drivebelt – removal, refitting and adjustment

1 A conventional vee drivebelt is used to drive both the alternators and water pump pulleys on OHV engines, and the alternator pulley only on CVH engines, power being transmitted via a pulley on the engine crankshaft.
2 To remove the drivebelt, slacken the alternator mounting bolts and the bolts on the adjuster link and push the alternator in towards the engine as far as possible.
3 Withdraw the belt from the pulleys. In some instances it may also be necessary to remove the adjuster link-to-alternator bolt to avoid straining the drivebelt.

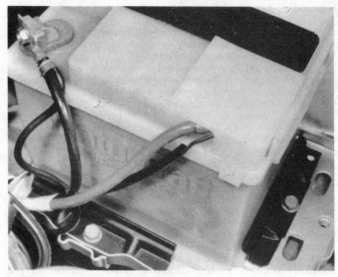

5.1 Battery lead connections and clamps

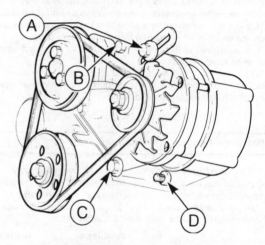

Fig. 12.3 Alternator mounting and adjuster link bolts (Sec 7)

A   Adjuster link-to-alternator bolt
B   Adjuster link-to-engine bolt
C   and D   Alternator mounting bolts

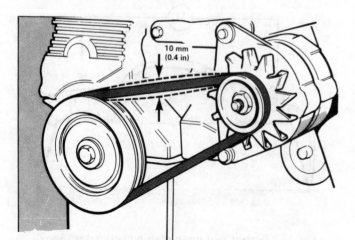

Fig. 12.4 Drivebelt tension checking point – CVH engines (Sec 7)

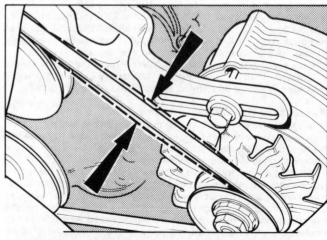

Fig. 12.5 Drivebelt tension checking point – OHV engines (Sec 7)

4 Fit the belt by slipping it over the pulley rims. If necessary remove the adjuster link-to-alternator bolt, if not already done, to avoid straining the belt. Never be tempted to remove or refit the drivebelt by prising it over a pulley rim otherwise the pulley or the drivebelt internal webbing will be damaged.

5 To tension the belt pull the alternator away from the engine until the belt is fairly taut, and tighten the adjuster link-to-alternator bolt. Check that the total deflection of the belt, using finger pressure at a point midway between the alternator and crankshaft or water pump pulleys is 10 mm (0.4 in). A little trial and error may be necessary to obtain the correct tension. If the belt is too slack, it will slip in the pulleys and soon become glazed or burnt. This is often indicated by a screeching noise as the engine is accelerated, particularly when the headlights or other electrical accessories are switched on. If the belt is too tight the bearings in the water pump and/or alternator will soon be damaged.

6 Once the tension is correct, tighten the remaining adjuster link bolt, front mounting bolt and rear mounting bolt in that order.

7 If a new belt has been fitted the tension should be rechecked and adjusted again if necessary after the engine has run for approximately ten minutes.

8 Alternator – removal and refitting

1 The operations are similar for all makes of alternator.

2 Disconnect the battery negative terminal then disconnect the multi-plug or leads from the rear of the alternator.

3 Release the mounting and adjuster link bolts (photo), push the alternator in towards the engine and remove the drivebelt. It may be necessary to remove the adjuster link-to-alternator bolt to facilitate removal of the drivebelt.

4 Undo and remove the mounting nuts and bolts and adjuster link bolt, if not already removed, and withdraw the alternator from the engine.

5 Refitting is the reverse sequence to removal but ensure that the mounting bolts and washers are assembled as shown in Fig. 12.6. Adjust the drivebelt tension as described in Section 7.

9 Alternator – fault tracing and rectification

Due to the specialist knowledge and equipment required to test or repair an alternator, it is recommended that, if the output is suspect, the car be taken to an automobile electrician who will have the facilities for such work. Because of this recommendation, information in the following Section is limited to the inspection and renewal of the brushes and regulator. Should the alternator not charge, or the system be suspect, the following points should be checked before seeking further assistance.

(a) Check the drivebelt condition and tension
(b) Ensure that the battery is fully charged
(c) Check the ignition warning light bulb and renew it if blown

10 Alternator brushes and regulator – renewal

1 With the alternator removed from the engine, clean the external surfaces free from dirt.

Bosch

2 Extract the regulator screws from the rear cover and withdraw the regulator. Check the brush length and, if less than the specified minimum, renew them.

3 Unsolder the brush wiring connectors and remove the brushes and the springs.

4 Refit by reversing the removal operations.

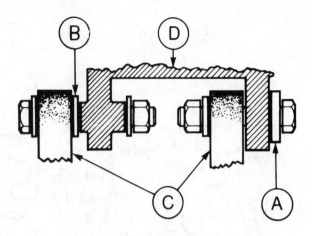

Fig. 12.6 Correct fitting of alternator mounting components – early models (Sec 8)

A Large washer
B Small washer (pre-1985 CVH engines only)
C Mounting bracket
D Alternator

8.3 Alternator mounting bolt arrangement – later models

Lucas

5 Remove the alternator rear cover.

6 Extract the brush box retaining screws and withdraw the brush assemblies from the brush box.

7 If the length of the brushes is less than the specified minimum, renew them. Refit by reversing the removal operations.

8 To remove the regulator, disconnect the wires from the unit and unscrew the retaining screw (A115 and A133 units only – three screws on A127 type).

9 Refit by reversing the removal operations, but check that the small plastic spacer and the connecting link are correctly located.

Motorola

10 Extract the two regulator securing screws, disconnect the two regulator leads and withdraw the unit.

11 Extract the brush box retaining screw and pull and tilt the brush box from its location, taking care not to damage the brushes during the process.

12 If necessary, unsolder the brush connections.

13 Fit the new brushes by reversing the removal operations.

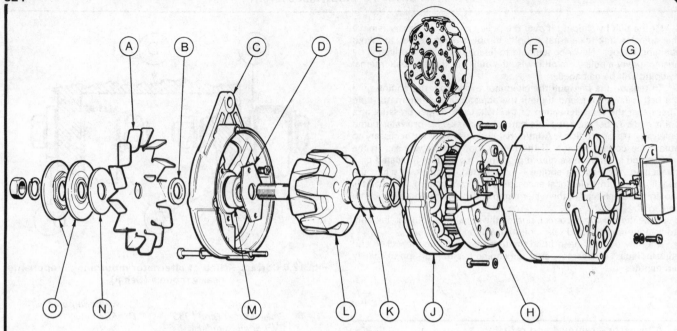

Fig. 12.7 Exploded view of the Bosch G1 and K1 series alternators (Sec 10)

A   Fan
B   Spacer
C   Drive end housing
D   Drive end bearing retaining
    plate
E   Slip ring end bearing
F   Slip ring end housing
G   Brush box and regulator
H   Rectifier diode pack
J   Stator
K   Slip rings
L   Rotor
M   Drive end bearing
N   Spacer
O   Pulley

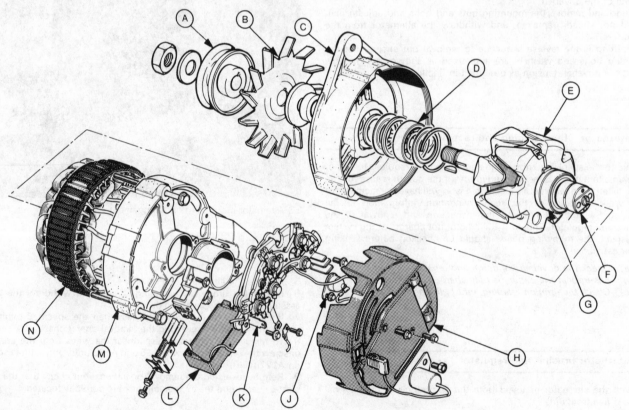

Fig. 12.8 Exploded view of the Lucas A115 and A133 alternator (Sec 10)

A   Pulley
B   Fan
C   Drive end housing
D   Drive end bearing
E   Rotor
F   Slip ring
G   Slip ring end bearing
H   End cover
J   Anti-surge diode
K   Diode plate
L   Voltage regulator
M   Slip ring end housing
N   Stator

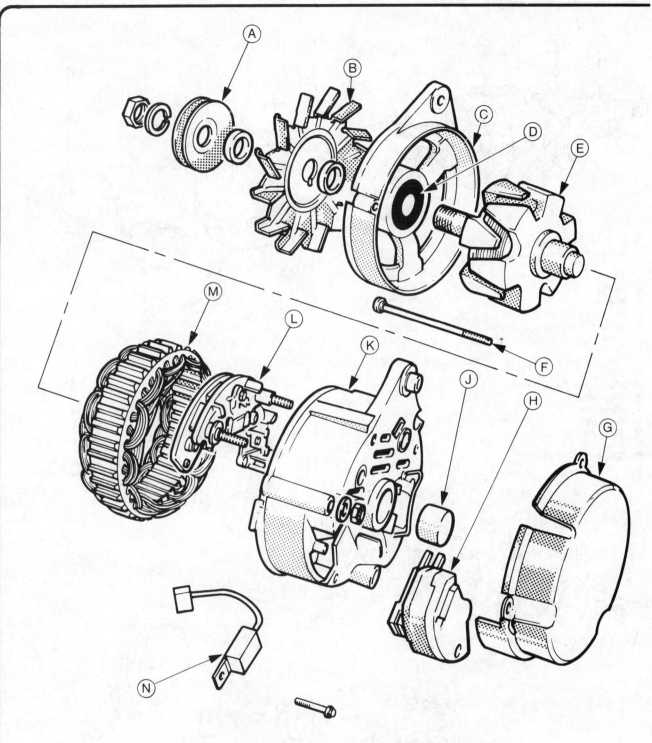

Fig. 12.9 Exploded view of the Lucas A127 alternator (Sec 10)

A Pulley
B Fan
C Drive end housing
D Drive end bearing
E Rotor
F Through-bolt
G End cover
H Brush box and regulator
J Slip ring end bearing
K Slip ring end housing
L Rectifier pack
M Stator
N Suppressor

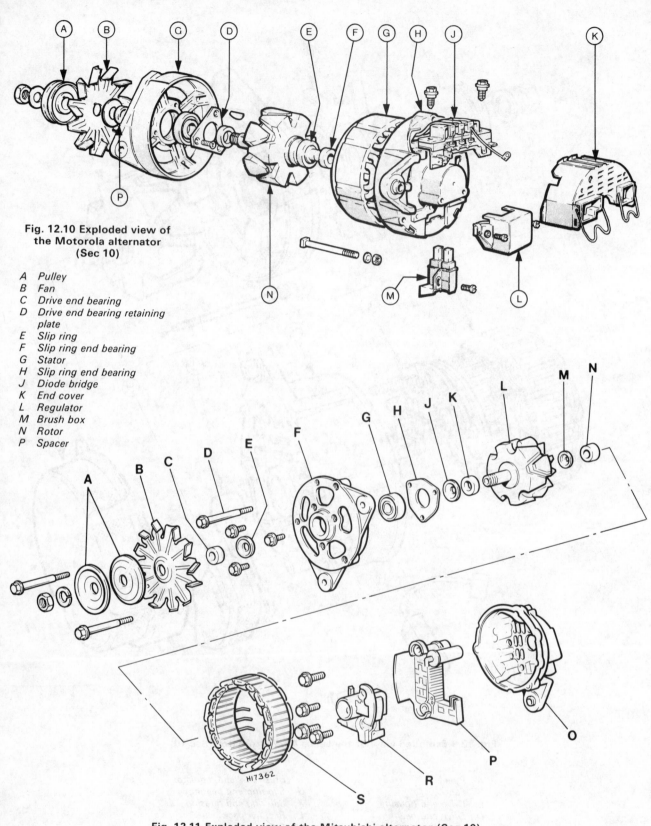

Fig. 12.10 Exploded view of the Motorola alternator (Sec 10)

A Pulley
B Fan
C Drive end bearing
D Drive end bearing retaining plate
E Slip ring
F Slip ring end bearing
G Stator
H Slip ring end bearing
J Diode bridge
K End cover
L Regulator
M Brush box
N Rotor
P Spacer

Fig. 12.11 Exploded view of the Mitsubishi alternator (Sec 10)

A Pulley
B Fan
C Large spacer
D Through-bolt
E Dust cap
F Drive end housing
G Drive end bearing
H Bearing retainer
J Dust seal
K Small spacer
L Rotor
M Seal
N Bearing
O Slip ring end housing
P Diode pack
R Brush box
S Stator

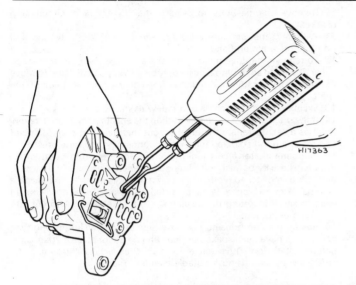

Fig. 12.12 Using a soldering iron to heat the slip ring end housing – Mitsubishi alternator (Sec 10)

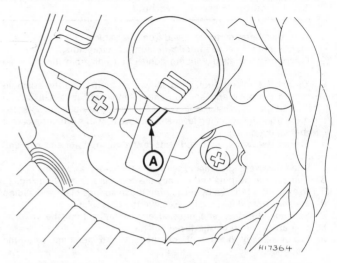

Fig. 12.13 Using a length of wire (A) to hold bushes in the retracted position – Mitsubishi alternator (Sec 10)

Mitsubishi

14 Undo the three housing through-bolts and remove the slip ring end housing. It may be necessary to apply heat from a high-power (200 watt) soldering iron to the centre of the end housing for a few minutes (Fig. 12.12) if the housing refuses to free from the rotor.
15 Undo the four bolts and remove the stator and rectifier assembly from the slip ring end housing.
16 Unsolder the brush box-to-rectifier pack terminal and remove the brush box.
17 Renew the brush box and brushes if they are worn below the specified minimum.
18 Fit the new brushes by reversing the removal operations. Insert a suitable piece of wire through the access hole in the housing to keep the brushes retracted as the housing is fitted. After fitting the housing release the brushes by removing the wire.

11 Starter motor – testing in the car

1 If the starter motor fails to operate, first check the condition of the battery by switching on the headlamps. If they glow brightly then gradually dim after a few seconds, the battery is in an uncharged condition.

2 If the battery is satisfactory, check the starter motor main terminal and the engine earth cable for security. Check the terminal connections on the starter solenoid – located on top of the starter motor.
3 If the starter fails to turn, use a voltmeter, or 12 volt test lamp and leads, to ensure that there is battery voltage at the solenoid main terminal (containing the cable from the battery positive terminal).
4 With the ignition switched on and the ignition key in position III, check that voltage is reaching the solenoid terminal with the connector, and also the starter main terminal.
5 If there is no voltage reaching the connector there is a wiring or ignition switch fault. If voltage is available, but the starter does not operate, then the starter or solenoid is likely to be at fault.

12 Starter motor – removal and refitting

1 Disconnect the battery.
2 Working from under the vehicle, disconnect the main starter motor cable and the two wires from the starter solenoid (photo).
3 Unbolt the starter motor and withdraw it from its location (photo).
4 Refit by reversing the removal operations.

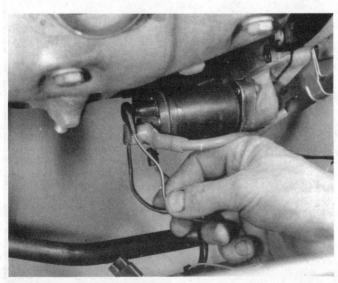

12.2 Starter solenoid connections

12.3 Starter motor lower retaining bolts

13 Starter motor (Bosch) – overhaul

1   With the starter motor removed from the vehicle and cleaned, grip the starter motor in a vice fitted with soft jaw protectors.
2   Disconnect the field winding connecting link from the solenoid stud.
3   Extract the solenoid retaining screws and withdraw the solenoid yoke from the drive end housing and solenoid armature. On certain versions of the Bosch starter it is now possible to unhook the solenoid armature from the actuating lever and remove it. If this is not the case it can be removed later.
4   Extract the two screws and remove the commutator end cap and rubber seal.
5   Wipe away any grease and withdraw the C-clip and shims.
6   Remove the tie-nuts and remove the commutator end housing.
7   Remove the brushes by prising the brush springs clear and sliding the brushes from their holders. Remove the brushplate.
8   Separate the drive end housing and armature from the yoke by tapping apart with a plastic-faced hammer.
9   If not already done, unhook the solenoid armature from the actuating lever.

10 Remove the tie-bolts to release the drive pinion clutch stop bracket.
11 Withdraw the armature assembly and unhook the actuating arm from the drive pinion flange.
12 To remove the drive pinion from the armature shaft, drive the stop collar down the shaft with a piece of tubing to expose the clip. Remove the clip from its groove and slide the stop collar and drive pinion off the shaft.
13 Examine the components and renew as necessary.
14 If the brushes have worn to less than the specified minimum, renew them as a set. To renew the brushes, cut their leads at their midpoint and make a good soldered joint when connecting the new brushes.
15 The commutator face should be clean and free from burnt spots. Where necessary burnish with fine glass paper (**not** emery) and wipe with a fuel-moistened cloth. If the commutator is in really bad shape it can be skimmed on a lathe provided its diameter is not reduced excessively. If recutting the insulation slots, take care not to cut into the commutator metal.
16 Renew the end housing bushes which are of self-lubricating type and should have been soaked in clean engine oil for at least 20 minutes before installation. Drive out the old brushes, whilst supporting the endplate/housing, using a suitable mandrel or drift.

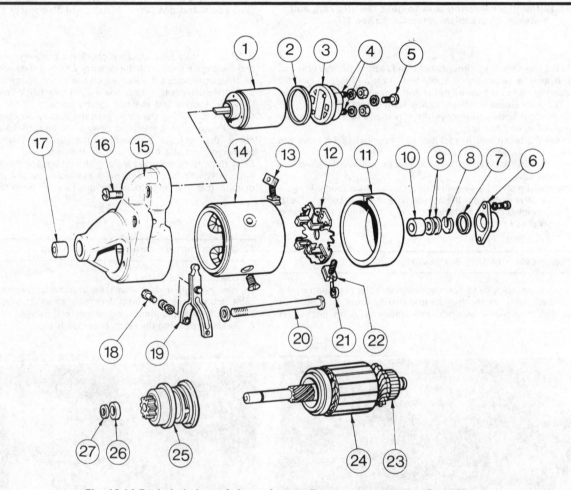

Fig. 12.14 Exploded view of the early type Bosch starter motor (Sec 13)

1	Solenoid yoke	8	C-clip	15	Drive end housing	22 Brush
2	Gasket	9	Shim	16	Solenoid fixing screw	23 Commutator
3	Contact switch assembly	10	Bearing	17	Bearing	24 Armature
4	Main terminals	11	Commutator end housing	18	Pivot screw	25 Drive pinion/roller clutch
5	Retaining screws	12	Brush box	19	Actuating lever	26 Stop collar
6	End cover	13	Link connector	20	Tie-bolt	27 Clip
7	Seal	14	Main casing (yoke)	21	Brush spring	

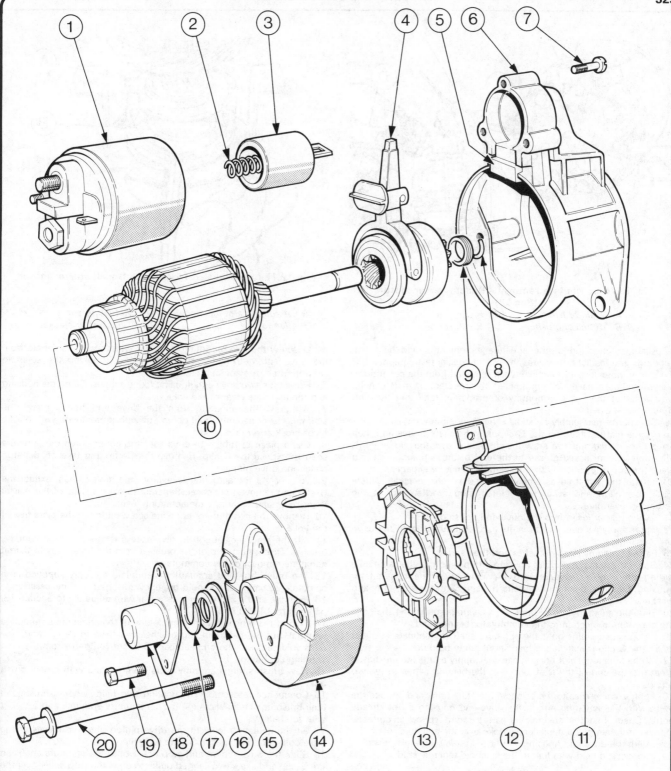

Fig. 12.15 Exploded view of the later type Bosch starter motor (Sec 13)

1 Solenoid yoke	6 Drive end housing	11 Main casing (yoke)	16 Spacer
2 Solenoid spring	7 Solenoid bolt	12 Pole shoe	17 C-clip
3 Solenoid armature	8 C-clip	13 Brushplate	18 End cap
4 Actuating lever	9 Stop collar	14 Commutator end housing	19 End cap screw
5 Rubber block	10 Armature	15 Sealing ring	20 Tie-bolt

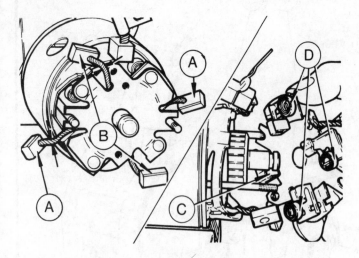

Fig. 12.16 Brushplate removal – Bosch starter motor
(Sec 13)

A Field brushes   C Brushplate
B Terminal brushes   D Brush springs

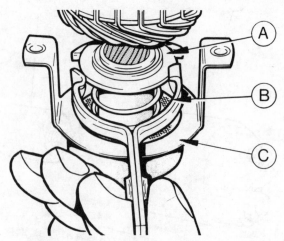

Fig. 12.17 Actuating arm location – Bosch starter motor
(Sec 13)

A Actuating arm locating   B Actuating arm
   flange   C Clutch stop bracket

17 Accurate checking of the armature, commutator and field coil windings and insulation requires the use of special test equipment. If the starter motor was inoperative when removed from the car and the previous checks have not highlighted the problem, then it can be assumed that there is a continuity or insulation fault and the unit should be renewed.
18 Commence reassembly by sliding the drive pinion and stop collar onto the armature shaft. Fit the C-clip into the shaft groove and then use a two-legged puller to draw the stop collar over the clip.
19 Apply lithium based grease to the end of the actuating arm and place the arm in position with the solenoid armature engaged,.
20 Locate the armature assembly in the drive end bracket. Where applicable align and secure the clutch stop bracket and fit the actuating lever pivot.
21 Fit the rubber insert into the drive end housing.
22 Guide the yoke over the armature and tap housing onto the drive end housing.
23 Fit the brush plate, the brushes and their springs.
24 Guide the commutator end housing into position, at the same time sliding the rubber insulator into the cut-out in the commutator housing. Secure the commutator end housing with the stud nuts and washers.
25 Slide the armature into position in its bearings so that the shaft has the maximum projection at the commutator bearing end.
26 Fit sufficient shims onto the armature shaft to eliminate endfloat when the C-clip is installed, which should now be done.
27 Fit the armature shaft bearing cap seal, apply a little lithium-based grease to the end of the shaft and refit the bearing cap with its two screws.
28 Apply some grease to the solenoid armature hook and engage the hook with the actuating arm in the drive end housing if not already done. Check that the solenoid armature return spring is correctly located and then guide the solenoid yoke over the armature. Align the yoke with the drive end housing and fit the three securing screws.
29 Connect the field wire link to the solenoid terminal stud.

14 Starter motor (Lucas) – overhaul

8M 90 and 9M 90 type

1 With the starter removed from the vehicle and cleaned, grip it in a vice fitted with soft jaw protectors.
2 Remove the plastic cap from the commutator endplate.
3 Using a very small cold chisel, remove the star clip from the end of the armature shaft. Do this by distorting the prongs of the clip until it can be removed.
4 Disconnect the main feed link from the solenoid terminal.

5 Unscrew the two mounting nuts and withdraw the solenoid from the drive end housing, at the same time unhooking the solenoid armature from the actuating lever.
6 Extract the two drive end housing fixing screws. Guide the housing and the armature clear of the yoke.
7 Withdraw the armature from the drive end housing and the actuating lever assembly will come out with it, complete with plastic pivot block and rubber pad.
8 Use a piece of tubing to drive the stop collar down the armature shaft to expose the C-clip. Remove the C-clip and take off the stop collar and drive pinion.
9 To separate the actuating lever from the drive pinion, extract the C-clip and remove the spacer. Separate the two halves of the plastic drive collar and withdraw the actuating lever.
10 Remove the commutator endplate screws and tap the plate free of the yoke.
11 Lift the plate far enough to give access to the two field winding brushes. Disconnect two of the brushes from the brush box to permit complete removal of the commutator endplate.
12 The brush box and commutator endplate are only supplied as a complete assembly and should be renewed together, if necessary.
13 Examine all the components for wear with reference to Section 13, paragraphs 14 to 17.
14 Two of the brushes come complete with the commutator endplate terminal, but the field winding brushes will have to be cut and new ones soldered. Cut the original leads 6.0 mm (0.24 in) from the field winding conductor.
15 New brush springs are only supplied complete with a new brush box.
16 Commence reassembly by locating two field winding brushes in their brush box channels. Align the commutator endplate and secure it with four screws.
17 Fit the actuating lever to the drive pinion, the two halves of the drive collar and the spacer. Secure with the C-clip.
18 Slide the drive pinion and stop collar onto the armature shaft. Fit the C-clip and use a two-legged puller to draw the stop collar over the clip.
19 Hook the plastic pivot block over the actuating arm, position the rubber pad and insert into the solenoid mounting housing.
20 Guide the armature into the drive end housing.
21 Guide the armature and drive end housing through the yoke and align the armature shaft with the endplate bush. Secure the yoke and housing with two fixing screws.
22 Fit a new star clip to the end of the armature shaft, making sure that it is firmly fixed to eliminate shaft endfloat. Fit the plastic cap.
23 Locate the solenoid armature onto the actuating arm, guide the solenoid yoke over the armature and secure with studs and nuts.
24 Refit the connecting link between the solenoid and the main feed terminal.

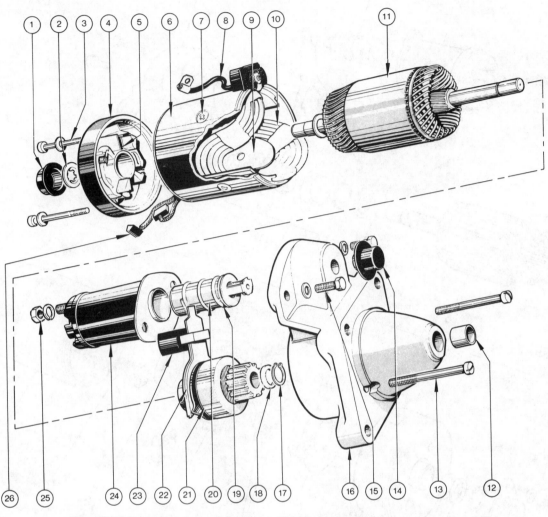

Fig. 12.18 Exploded view of the Lucas 8M 90 and 9M 90 starter motor (Sec 14)

1 Dust cap	8 Link connector	15 Solenoid fixing screw	21 Drive assembly
2 Star clip	9 Pole plate	16 Drive end housing	22 Actuating lever
3 Endplate bolt	10 Field coils	17 C-clip	23 Pivot
4 Endplate	11 Armature	18 Stop collar	24 Solenoid body
5 Brush housing	12 Bearing	19 Return spring	25 Terminal nut and washer
6 Main casing (yoke)	13 Housing screws	20 Solenoid armature	26 Brushes
7 Pole screw	14 Dust cover		

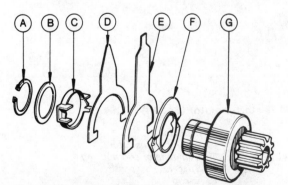

**Fig. 12.19 Drive pinion and actuating lever components –
Lucas 8M 90 and 9M 90 starter motor (Sec 14)**

A   C-clip
B   Spacer
C and F   Drive collar
D and E   Actuating lever
G   Drive pinion

M 79 type

25 With the starter motor removed from the vehicle and cleaned, grip it in a vice fitted with soft jaw protectors.

26 Disconnect the connecting link from the solenoid terminal.

27 Undo the two endplate cap screws and remove the cap.

28 Extract the C-clip and remove the spacers from the end of thhe armature shaft.

29 Undo the two commutator end housing screws and withdraw the end housing.

30 Undo the solenoid yoke screws and slide the yoke off the drive end housing and armature.

31 Disconnect the solenoid armature from the actuating lever and remove the armature.

32 Undo the two drive end housing screws and withdraw the housing from the yoke and armature.

33 Slide the armature out of the yoke taking care not to damage the brushes. The actuating lever, plastic support block and rubber pad will be removed with the armature.

34 Use a piece of tubing to drive the stop collar down the armature shaft to expose the C-clip. Remove the C-clip and take off the stop collar and drive pinion.

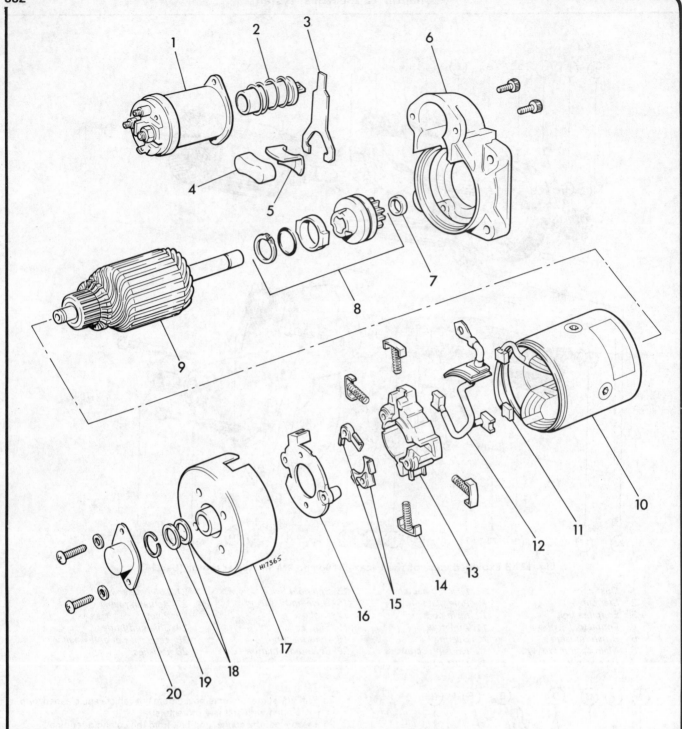

Fig. 12.20 Exploded view of the Lucas M 79 starter motor (Sec 14)

1	Solenoid yoke	8 Pinion assembly	15 Insulator
2	Solenoid armature	9 Armature	16 Brush box insulator
3	Actuating lever	10 Main casing (yoke)	17 Commutator end housing
4	Rubber block	11 Field bushes	18 Spacers
5	Plastic support block	12 Brush link	19 C-clip
6	Drive end housing	13 Brush box	20 End plate cap
7	Stop collar	14 Retaining spring	

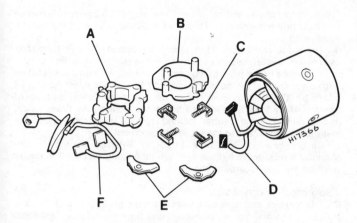

Fig. 12.21 Brush box components – Lucas M 79 starter motor (Sec 14)

A Brush box	D Field brushes
B Brush box insulator	E Insulators
C Retaining springs	F Brush link

35 To remove the actuating lever remove the circlip and slide the lever and pivot assembly off the pinion.

36 Remove the retaining springs and remove the brushes from the brush box.

37 Examine all the components for wear with reference to Section 13, paragraphs 14 to 17.

38 Two of the brushes come complete with the brush link wire but the field winding brushes will have to be cut and new ones soldered in place.

39 Commence reassembly by fitting the actuating lever to the pinion and securing with the circlip.

40 Slide the drive pinion and stop collar onto the armature shaft. Fit the C-clip and use a two-legged puller to draw the stop collar over the clip.

41 Fit the armature to the yoke and locate the actuating lever plastic support and rubber block in the drive end housing.

42 Engage the solenoid armature with the actuating lever then refit and secure the solenoid yoke.

43 Refit the drive end housing retaining screws.

44 Locate the brush box over the commutator, fit the brushes in their locations and fit the nylon cover over the brushes. Retain the brushes with the springs and clips.

45 Refit the commutator end housing and secure with the two screws.

46 Refit the armature spacers and C-clip followed by the end cap.

47 Re-attach the connecting link to the solenoid terminal.

15 Starter motor (Nippondenso) – overhaul

1 With the starter motor removed from the engine and cleaned, secure it in a vice fitted with soft jaw protectors.

2 Disconnect the field winding connector from the solenoid terminal.

3 Remove the solenoid retaining nuts.

4 Withdraw the solenoid and unhook the armature hook from the actuating lever.

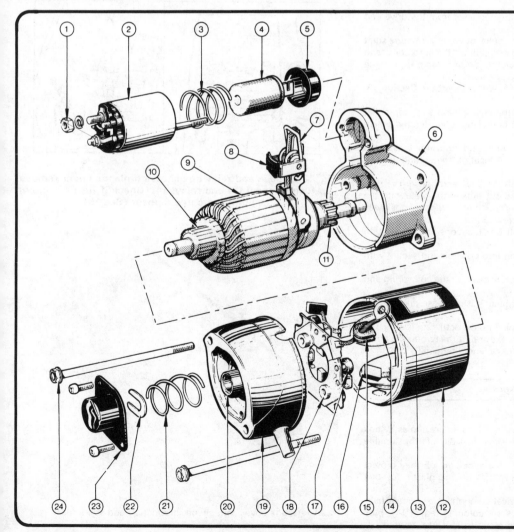

Fig. 12.22 Exploded view of the Nippondenso starter motor (Sec 15)

1 Solenoid terminal nut
2 Solenoid yoke
3 Return spring
4 Solenoid armature
5 Seal
6 Drive end housing
7 Actuating lever
8 Pivot
9 Armature
10 Commutator
11 Drive pinion/roller clutch
12 Main casing
13 Link connector
14 Pole shoe
15 Seal
16 Brush
17 Brush spring
18 Brush plate
19 Commutator end housing
20 Bush
21 Spring
22 C-clip
23 End cover
24 Tie-bolt

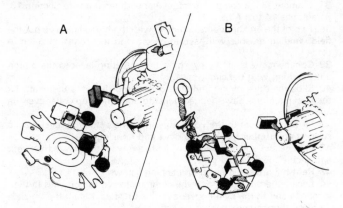

Fig. 12.23 Brushes and brushplate – Nippondenso starter motor (Sec 15)

A 0.6 kw starter   *B 0.9 kw starter*

5   Remove the bearing cap (two screws).
6   Slide the C-washer from its groove in the armature shaft and take off the coil spring.
7   Unbolt and remove the rear housing cover.
8   Withdraw two field brushes and remove the brush gear mounting plate.
9   Withdraw the armature and drive end housing from the main housing.
10 Withdraw the armature and the actuating lever from the drive end housing. Remove the actuating lever.
11 Use a piece of tubing to tap the stop collar down the armature shaft to expose the C-clip. Remove the clip and pull off the stop collar and drive pinion. To avoid damaging the clutch, do not clamp it in a vice when driving the stop collar down the armature.
12 Examine all the components for wear with reference to Section 13, paragraphs 14 to 17.
13 Commence reassembly by sliding the drive pinion and stop collar onto the armature shaft. Fit the C-clip and using a two-legged puller, draw the stop collar over the clip.
14 Align the actuating lever in the drive end housing. Guide the armature into position, at the same time locating the actuating lever onto the drive pinion flange.
15 Tap the yoke into engagement with the drive end housing.
16 Locate the brush plate, aligning the cut-outs in the plate with the loops in the field winding. The brush assembly will be positively located when the fixing screws are screwed in.
17 Position the brushes in their brush box locations and retain with their springs.
18 Guide the commutator end housing into position and secure with the fixing nuts.
19 To the commutator end of the armature shaft, fit the coil spring and the C-clip.
20 Smear the end of the shaft with lithium based grease and then fit the cap (two screws).
21 Connect the solenoid armature hook onto the actuating lever in the drive end housing. Align the solenoid yoke and fit the two fixing bolts.
22 Re-attach the connecting link to the solenoid terminal.

16 Fuses, relays and circuit breakers

Pre-1986 models

1   The fuses and most of the relays are located in a plastic box attached to the bulkhead on the driver's side of the engine compartment.
2   The fuses are numbered to identify the circuit which they protect and the circuits are represented by symbols on the plastic fusebox cover (photos).
3   When an accessory or other electrical component or system fails, always check the fuse first. The fuses are coloured red (10A), blue (15A), yellow (20A), clear (25A) and green (30A). Always renew a

fuse with one of an identical rating. Never renew a fuse more than once without finding the source of the trouble. Spare fuses are carried in the fusebox lid.
4   The radio, and where fitted, electrically operated aerial, have their own in-line circuit fuses, or are fused in the rear of the radio casing.
5   Relays are of the plug-in type and will be found within the fusebox with a symbol on the cover designating the relay circuit. Additional relays for the headlamp washers, fuel injection system and speed sensor (where fitted) are located below the facia on the driver's side, and a relay for the central locking system is located under the instrument panel next to the glove compartment.
6   Circuit breakers are only fitted to vehicles equipped with electrically operated windows or a central locking system. The circuit breakers are also located in the fusebox.

1986 models onwards

7   The fusebox and its location are the same on later models but the fuse positions and circuits protected have been rearranged. Additional fuses are still used and located as for early models.
8   Relays located in the fusebox have their circuits designated by a symbol for identification. Up to six additional relays are located under the instrument panel on the driver's side. These are used in conjunction with the speed sensor, diode assembly, fuel-injection system, heated windscreen, and dim-dip lighting system. On certain RS Turbo models, a relay to prevent radio interference by the ignition system is fitted adjacent to the fuel-injection module behind the plenum chamber in the engine compartment.
9   The direction indicator/hazard flasher relay is located at the rear of the direction indicator multi-function switch on the steering column.

H16318

Fig. 12.24 Fuse and relay box showing plastic cover removal (2), fuse removal (3) and relays (4). Check if fuse has blown at point indicated in inset (Sec 16)

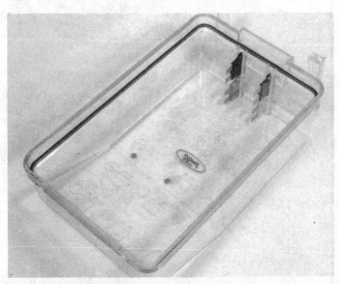

16.2A Fusebox cover with circuit information and spare fuses

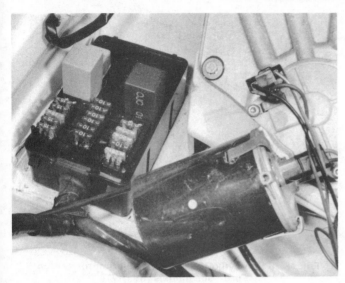

16.2B Fusebox location on engine compartment bulkhead (cover removed to show fuses and relays)

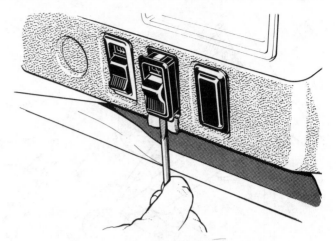

Fig. 12.25 Rear window wash/wipe switch removal – pre-1986 models (Sec 17)

17 Switches – removal and refitting

General
1   Disconnect the battery negative terminal before removing any switches.

Pre-1986 models
Wiper delay switch
2   Remove the switch knob and the bezel nut.
3   Withdraw the switch through the parcel tray and disconnect it from the wiring harness.
Rear foglamp, heated rear window, rear window wash/wipe switches
4   Using a screwdriver carefully prise the switch from the facia panel.
5   Disconnect the wiring multi-plug and remove the switch.
Steering column multi-function switches
6   Undo the screws and remove the upper and lower steering column shrouds.
7   Undo the switch retaining screws, disconnect the wiring multi-plug and remove the switch.
Load space lamp switch
8   Open the tailgate and release the four trim panel fasteners.
9   Disconnect the lead from the switch and remove the switch retaining screw.
Local space lamp switch (Cabriolet)
10 Open the boot lid and undo the switch retaining screw.
11 Withdraw the switch and disconnect the lead. Tape the lead to the rear panel to prevent it dropping in the hole.
Courtesy lamp switch
12 Extract the screw securing the switch to the door pillar.
13 Withdraw the switch from its rubber shroud and disconnect the lead. Tape the lead to the pillar to prevent it dropping in the hole (photo).
Ignition switch
14 Undo the screws and remove the steering column lower shoud.
15 Insert the ignition key into the lock and turn it to position I.
16 Using a flat-bladed screwdriver, depress the switch retaining clip, at the same time pulling out the switch using the ignition key.
Reversing lamp switch
17 On manual transmission models the switch is located on the forward facing side of the transmission housing beneath the clutch release lever.
18 Working in the engine compartment disconnect the switch wiring and unscrew the switch.
19 On automatic transmission models the reversing lamp switch is combined with the starter inhibitor switch, and reference should be made to Chapter 7.

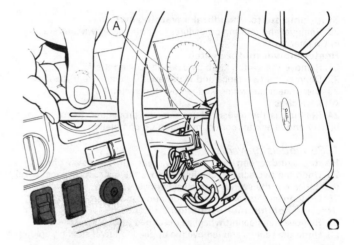

Fig. 12.26 Steering column multi-function switch removal – pre-1986 models (Sec 17)

A   Switch retaining screws

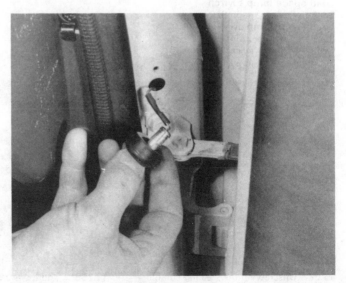

17.13 Courtesy lamp switch removal from door pillar

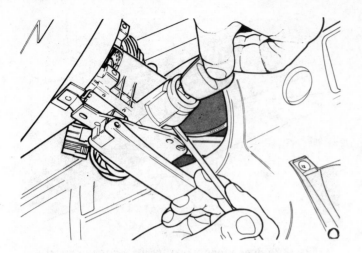

Fig. 12.27 Ignition switch removal using a screwdriver to depress the switch retaining clip – pre-1986 models (Sec 17)

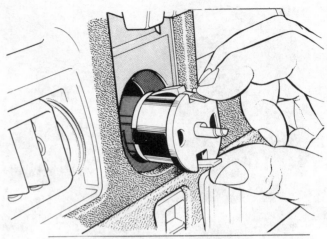

Fig. 12.28 Removing the heater blower motor switch – pre-1986 models (Sec 17)

Stop-lamp switch/handbrake warning switch
20 Removal and refitting procedures for both these switches are given in Chapter 9.

Heater blower motor switch
21 Remove the switch knob by carefully pulling it off.
22 Depress the two tangs and withdraw the switch from the facia.
23 Disconnect the wiring and remove the switch.

All switches
24 Refitting is the reverse of the removal procedure. Reconnect the battery and check for correct operation on completion.

1986 models onwards
Heated windscreen/rear window, rear foglamp switches
25 Undo the two screws, carefully remove the instrument panel bezel then prise out the switch with a screwdriver (photo).
26 Disconnect the wiring multi-plug and remove the switch.

Steering column multi-function switches
27 Remove the steering wheel as described in Chapter 10.
28 Undo the screws and remove the upper and lower steering column shroud (photos).
29 Undo the retaining screws and remove the switch from the steering column (photo).
30 Disconnect the switch wiring multi-plug.
31 If removing the direction indicator multi-function switch, remove the hazard flasher switch and relay if required.

Load space lamp switch
32 Refer to paragraph 8.

Load space lamp switch (Cabriolet)
33 Refer to paragraph 10.

Courtesy lamp switch
34 Refer to paragraph 12.

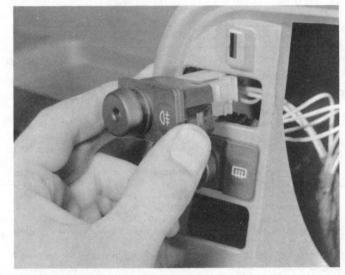

17.25 Rear foglamp switch removal

Ignition switch
35 Undo the screws and remove the steering column lower shroud.
36 Insert the ignition key into the switch and turn it to position I.
37 Using a thin pointed tool, depress the lock spring through the access hole in the lock housing. Pull on the key while holding the lock

17.28A Unscrewing the steering column shroud upper ...

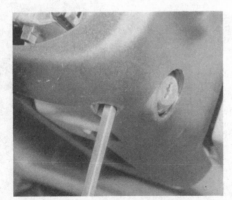

17.28B ... and lower retaining screws

17.29 Steering column multi-function switch removal

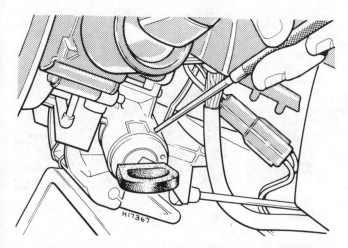

Fig. 12.29 Ignition switch removal using a pointed tool to depress the lock spring – 1986 models onwards (Sec 17)

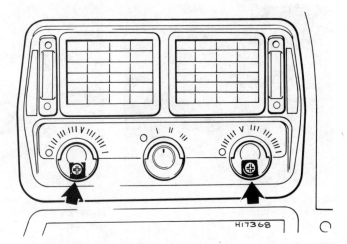

Fig. 12.30 Heater control panel retaining screw locations – 1986 models onwards (Sec 17)

spring depressed, and remove the switch. It may be necessary to move the key slightly to the left and right to align the key barrel and lock housing cam, so permitting removal.

Reversing lamp switch
38 Refer to paragraph 17.

Stop-lamp switch/handbrake warning switch
39 Refer to paragraph 20.

Heater blower motor switch
40 Carefully pull off the three heater control knobs.
41 Undo the two retaining screws and remove the heater control panel.
42 Undo the two switch panel-to-facia securing screws and withdraw the panel.
43 Depress the two tabs on either side of the switch and remove the switch.
44 Disconnect the switch wiring multi-plug.

Door mirror control switch
45 Using a thin screwdriver carefully prise the switch out of its location in the facia.
46 Disconnect the wiring multi-plug and remove the switch.

All switches
47 Refitting is the reverse of the removal procedure. Reconnect the battery and check for correct operation on completion.

18 Cigar lighter – removal and refitting

1 Disconnect the battery negative terminal.
2 On pre-1986 models remove the ashtray then undo the screws and withdraw the ashtray housing. On 1986 models onwards, refer to

Section 49 and remove the radio/cassette player.
3 Disconnect the wiring from the cigar lighter body.
4 Pull out the cigar lighter element.
5 Push the lighter body and illuminating ring out of their locations then separate the ring from the lighter body.
6 Refitting is the reverse sequence to removal.

19 Bulbs (exterior lamps) – removal

Headlamp
1 From within the engine compartment pull the multi-plug from the rear of the headlamp (photo).
2 Remove the rubber gaiter and rotate the bulb securing clip or release the spring clip arms according to type (photo).
3 Withdraw the bulb, taking care not to touch the glass with your fingers (photo). If the glass is touched, wipe the bulb with a rag moistened with methylated spirit.

Front sidelamp
4 The bulbholder is located on the side of the headlamp unit and is removed by twisting it anti-clockwise (photo).
5 Withdraw the push-fit bulb from the holder.

Front direction indicator lamp
6 Working through the aperture in the inner wing panel in the engine compartment, turn the bulbholder anti-clockwise and withdraw it from the lens unit (photo).
7 Depress and turn the bulb anti-clockwise to remove it from the holder.

19.1 Headlamp bulb multi-plug and rubber gaiter

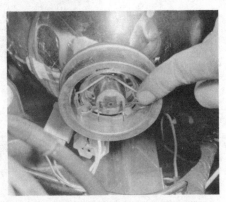

19.2 Releasing headlamp bulb spring clip arms

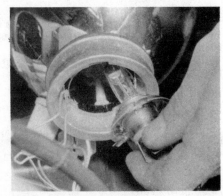

19.3 Headlamp bulb removal

19.4 Sidelamp bulb location (arrowed) in side of headlamp

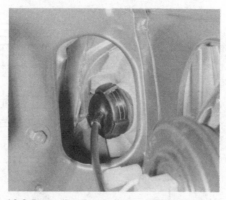

19.6 Front direction indicator bulbholder accessible through inner wing panel aperture

19.8 Front auxiliary lamp lens retaining screw

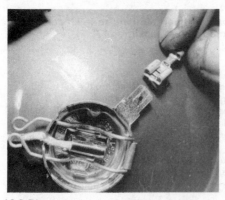

19.9 Disconnecting auxiliary lamp earth lead

19.10A Release the spring clip legs ...

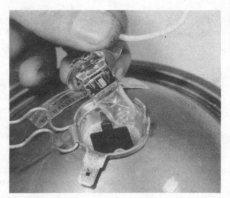

19.10B ... to remove the auxiliary lamp bulbholder

Front auxiliary lamp and foglamp

8 Undo the retaining screw at the bottom of the lens and withdraw the lens assembly (photo).
9 Disconnect the earth lead and remove the lens (photo).
10 Spring back the clip legs and remove the bulbholder, then withdraw the bulb (photos). Avoid touching the bulb glass with your fingers. If the glass is touched, wipe it with a cloth moistened in methylated spirit.

Rear lamp (Saloon)

11 Open the tailgate, reach down and depress the retaining tab on the side of the bulbholder. Swing the bulbholder outward to release the locating tag at the other end.
12 Remove the relevant bulb by pushing down and turning anti-clockwise (photo).

Rear lamp (Cabriolet)

13 Open the boot and pull the rear bulb cover open.
14 Push the upper and lower retaining tabs apart and withdraw the bulbholder.
15 Remove the relevant bulb by pushing down and turning anti-clockwise.

Rear lamps (Estate)

16 Open the tailgate and release the side trim panel by turning the four screws a quarter of a turn with a coin.
17 Push the upper and lower retaining tabs apart and withdraw the bulbholder.
18 Remove the relevant bulb by pushing down and turning anti-clockwise.

Rear lamp (Van)

19 Open the rear doors and remove the rear trim panel to gain access to the bulbholders (where applicable).

20 Remove the individual bulbholders by turning anti-clockwise, then similarly remove the bulbs from the holders.

Rear number plate lamp

21 Using a small screwdriver carefully prise the lamp out of the bumper.
22 On pre-1986 models turn the bulbholder anti-clockwise and remove it from the lens. Withdraw the push-fit bulb (photo).

19.12 Removing the rear lamp bulbholder for access to the bulbs

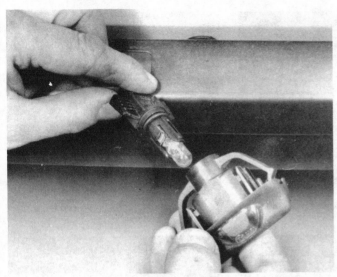

19.22 Removing the number plate lamp bulbholder from the lens

Fig. 12.31 Hazard warning switch bulb renewal – pre-1986 models (Sec 20)

23 On 1986 models onwards spread the retaining clips and withdraw the bulbholder. Remove the bulb by pushing and turning anti-clockwise.

All lamps
24 Refitting of the bulb and holder is the reverse sequence to removal in all cases.

20 Bulbs (interior lamps) – renewal

Pre-1986 models
Glove compartment lamp
1   This is simply a matter of gently pulling the bulb from its holder.
Heater control illumination lamp
2   Slide the heater control levers to the top of their travel.
3   Pull off the heater motor switch knob and then unclip the control trim panel from the facia.
4   Pull the bulb from the lamp socket.
Hazard warning switch lamp
5   Grip the switch cover and pull it off.
6   Gently pull the bulb from its socket.
Interior lamp
7   Carefully prise the lamp from its location and remove the bulb from its spring contact on the lamp body.
Load space lamp
8   Using a thin screwdriver, prise the lamp from its location (photo).
9   Remove the bulb from its spring contact clip.
Load space lamp (Cabriolet)
10 Open the boot lid and prise out the lamp with a thin screwdriver.
11 Depress and twist the bulb to remove it from the bulbholder.
All lamps
12 Refitting all bulbs is the reverse sequence to removal.

1986 models onwards
Glove compartment lamp
13 From inside the glove compartment undo the two switch assembly retaining screws and withdraw the assembly.
14 Using a thin screwdriver carefully prise out the switch and remove the bulb by pushing and turning anti-clockwise.
Heater control illumination lamp
15 Carefully pull off the three heater control knobs.
16 Undo the two retaining screws and withdraw the heater control panel.
17 From the rear of the panel, push and turn the bulb anti-clockwise to remove.
Hazard warning switch lamp
18 Refer to paragraph 5.

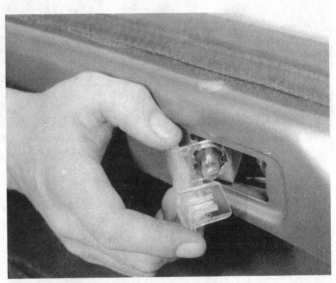

20.8 Removing the load space lamp

Interior lamp
19 Refer to paragraph 7.
Load space lamp
20 Refer to paragraph 8.
Load space lamp (Cabriolet)
21 Refer to paragraph 10.
Manual choke knob warning lamp
22 Remove the choke knob by depressing the pin located on the underside of the knob.
23 Withdraw the sleeve, then remove the bulb by pushing it down, then pushing down the bulb retainer using a thin screwdriver.
Fuel computer lamp
24 Remove the fuel computer as described in Section 28.
25 Using thin-nosed pliers, turn the bulbholder anti-clockwise to remove then withdraw the push-fit bulb.
All lamps
26 Refitting all bulbs is the reverse sequence to removal.

21 Exterior lamps – removal and refitting

Headlamp
1   On pre-1986 models, remove the radiator grille as described in Chapter 11.

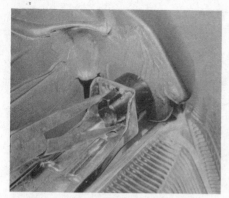

21.3A Releasing the headlamp side plastic retaining clip head

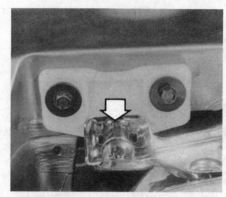

21.3B Headlamp upper plastic retaining clip head (arrowed)

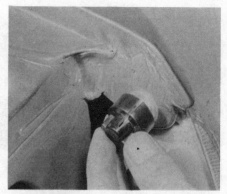

21.7A Removing the retaining clip head ...

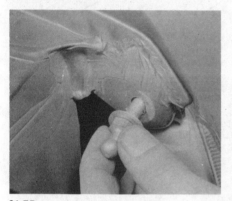

21.7B ... and the ball-headed bolt

21.8A Release the adjuster by turning the collar (arrowed)

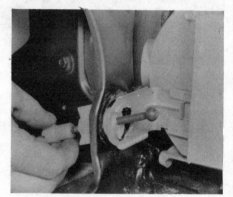

21.8B ... then remove the adjuster

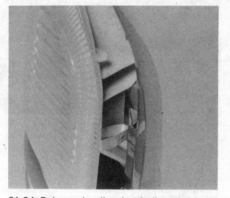

21.9A Release the direction indicator side spring clip ...

21.9B ... then pull the unit out at the bottom to remove

2   Working in the engine compartment, disconnect the headlamp wiring multi-plug and remove the sidelamp bulbholder.
3   Rotate the side and upper plastic retaining clip heads through 90° to release the headlamp mountings (photos).
4   With the headlamp unit released, pull it sharply forward off its lower ballstud.

Front direction indicator lamp
5   Working inside the engine compartment disconnect the indicator bulb holder from the lamp.
6   Remove the headlamp as previously described.
7   Remove the headlamp upper plastic retaining clip then unscrew the ball-headed bolt (photos).
8   Remove the lower adjuster by turning the collar (photos).
9   Release the side spring clip, then pull the lamp out at the bottom to disengage the upper tangs (photos).

Rear lamp
10   Remove the bulbholder(s) as described in Section 19.

11   Remove the lamp retaining screws or nuts as applicable, and remove the lamp.

All lamps
12   Refitting is the reverse sequence to removal.

22   Headlamps and auxiliary lamps – beam alignment

1   The headlamps are adjustable individually for both horizontal and vertical alignment from within the engine compartment. The auxiliary lamp adjustment is carried out by slackening the lamp mounting and moving the lamp as necessary.
2   Accurate alignment can only be carried out using optical beam setting equipment, and this work should be entrusted to a Ford dealer.
3   Holts Amber Lamp is useful for temporarily changing the headlight colour to conform with the normal usage on Continental Europe.

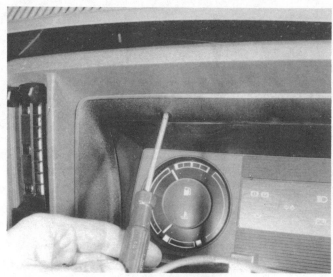

23.2A Extracting the instrument panel bezel screws

23.2B Removing the bezel

23 Instrument panel – removal and refitting

Pre-1986 models
1   Disconnect the battery negative terminal.
2   Extract the screws and pull the instrument panel bezel from the panel. The two clips at the base of the bezel will release by the pulling action (photos).
3   Extract the two screws which hold the panel to the facia (photo).
4   Remove the dash under-trim panel, reach up and disconnect the cable from the speedometer by depressing the serrated plastic ring.

5   Gently pull the cluster forwards and to one side so that the wiring multi-plug can be disconnected. Withdraw the panel.
6   Refitting is a reversal of removal.

1986 models onwards
7   Refer to Chapter 10 and remove the steering wheel.
8   Extract the two screws and pull the instrument panel bezel from the panel. The two clips at the base will release by the pulling action (photo).
9   Undo the four screws securing the panel to the facia (photos).
10 Pull the panel away from the facia and disconnect the wiring multi-plug and speedometer cable from the rear of the instrument

23.3 Removing the instrument panel retaining screws

23.8 Bezel lower retaining clip (arrowed)

23.9A Instrument panel upper retaining screw (arrowed)

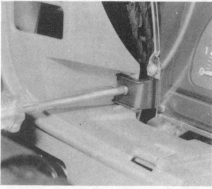

23.9B ... and lower screw removal

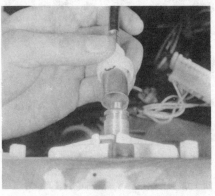

23.10 Disconnecting the speedometer cable

panel. It may be necessary to feed the speedometer cable slack through the bulkhead from the engine compartment to facilitate removal. Withdraw the panel (photo).

11 Refitting is a reversal of removal.

24 Instrument panel components – removal and refitting

1 Remove the instrument panel as described in Section 23.

Panel illumination and warning lamp bulbs

2 Turn the bulbholders anti-clockwise and remove them from the rear of the instrument panel (photo).
3 The bulbs and bulbholders are renewed complete, the bulbs cannot be removed from the holders separately.
4 Refit by pushing down and turning clockwise.

Printed circuit

5 Remove all illumination and warning lamp bulbholders.
6 Undo all the nuts and remove the washers from the printed circuit terminals.
7 Remove the wiring multi-plug retainers and carefully pull the printed circuit off the pins on the rear of the panel (photo).
8 Refitting is the reverse sequence to removal.

Speedometer

9 Undo the retaining screws around the edge of the panel at the rear and separate the two panel halves (photo).
10 Undo the two screws and remove the speedometer (photos).
11 Refitting is the reverse sequence to removal.

Tachometer

12 The procedure is the same as for the speedometer except that the unit is secured by three nuts.

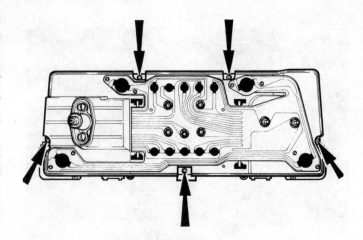

Fig. 12.32 Instrument panel assembly retaining screws – pre-1986 models (Sec 24)

Fuel and temperature gauges

13 Proceed as for the speedometer but remove the combined gauge assembly after undoing the four nuts.

25 Speedometer cable – removal and refitting

1 Disconnect the battery and remove the instrument panel as described in Section 23.

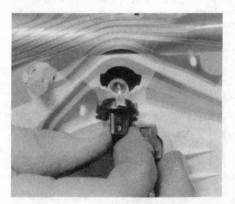

24.2 Instrument panel bulb renewal

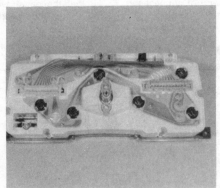

24.7 Component arrangement at rear of instrument panel

24.9 Instrument panel assembly upper retaining screws (arrowed)

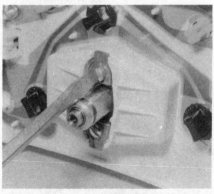

24.10A Extracting speedometer retaining screws

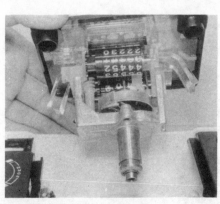

24.10B Speedometer removal

2 Disconnect the cable from the transmission and release it from its clips and grommet.
3 Withdraw the cable through the bulkhead.
4 Refitting is a reversal of removal. The inner and outer cables are supplied as a complete assembly.

26 Clock (facia mounted) – removal and refitting

1 Remove the instrument panel as described in Section 23.
2 Undo the screws around the edge of the instrument panel at the rear and separate the two panel halves.
3 Undo the retaining nuts and remove the clock.
4 Refitting is the reverse sequence to removal.

27 Clock (roof mounted) – removal and refitting

1 Disconnect the battery negative terminal.
2 Extract the two screws which hold the clock to the header panel.
3 Disconnect the clock and courtesy lamp wiring plug.
4 Detach the lamp from the clock.
5 Refit by reversing the removal operations. Once the battery is reconnected, the time must be set in the following way.
6 Turn the ignition key to position II. The clock will indicate a random time and the colon will be flashing at one second intervals to prove that the clock is running.
7 Using a ballpoint pen or similar, gently depress the upper recessed button. For each depression of the button, the clock will advance one hour.
8 If the clock indicates am instead of pm advance the clock through a full twelve hours.
9 To regulate the minutes, depress the lower recessed button. For each depression, the clock will advance one minute.
10 The colon will now be static and the set time will not advance until the stop/start button is depressed. This is a feature of great advantage when setting the clock accurately to a radio time check. Once the clock has started, the colon will flash.
11 To set the calendar function, again turn the ignition key to position II. Depress the function control once. The clock will now indicate a random date. Continue adjustment within four seconds of having depressed the function button.

12 Using a ballpoint pen or similar, depress the upper recessed button.
13 For each successive depression of the button the clock calendar will advance one day.
14 Once the correct day is obtained move the ballpoint pen to the lower recessed button and depress the correct month.
15 The clock automatically compensates for months of varying numbers of days.

28 Fuel computer – removal and refitting

1 Disconnect the battery negative terminal.
2 Undo the two instrument panel bezel retaining screws and ease the bezel out to release the lower clips.
3 Withdraw the computer module from the facia to the right of the instrument panel.
4 Disconnect the wiring multi-plug and remove the computer.
5 Refitting is the reverse sequence to removal.

29 Fuel computer speed sender unit – removal and refitting

1 Undo the retaining nut and detach the speedometer cable from the speed sender unit.
2 Unclip and disconnect the wiring multi-plug.
3 Undo the retaining nut and withdraw the speed sender unit from the transmission.
4 Refitting is the reverse sequence to removal.

30 Fuel computer fuel flow sensor – removal and refitting

1 The fuel flow sensor is used in conjunction with the fuel computer on fuel-injected models and is located on the fuel distributor at the front left-hand side of the engine compartment.
2 Disconnect the wiring multi-plug then undo the two banjo unions on the side of the unit. Note the position of the sealing washers.
3 Undo the two retaining screws and remove the fuel flow sensor.
4 Refitting is the reverse sequence to removal. Ensure that the sealing washers are correctly fitted.

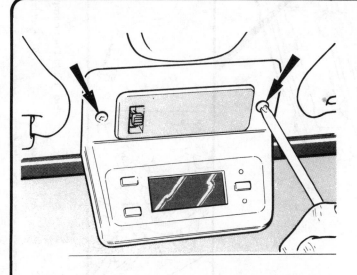

Fig. 12.33 Roof mounted clock removal (Sec 27)

Fig. 12.34 Setting roof mounted clock (Sec 27)

A Reset button   C Select button
B Adjust button

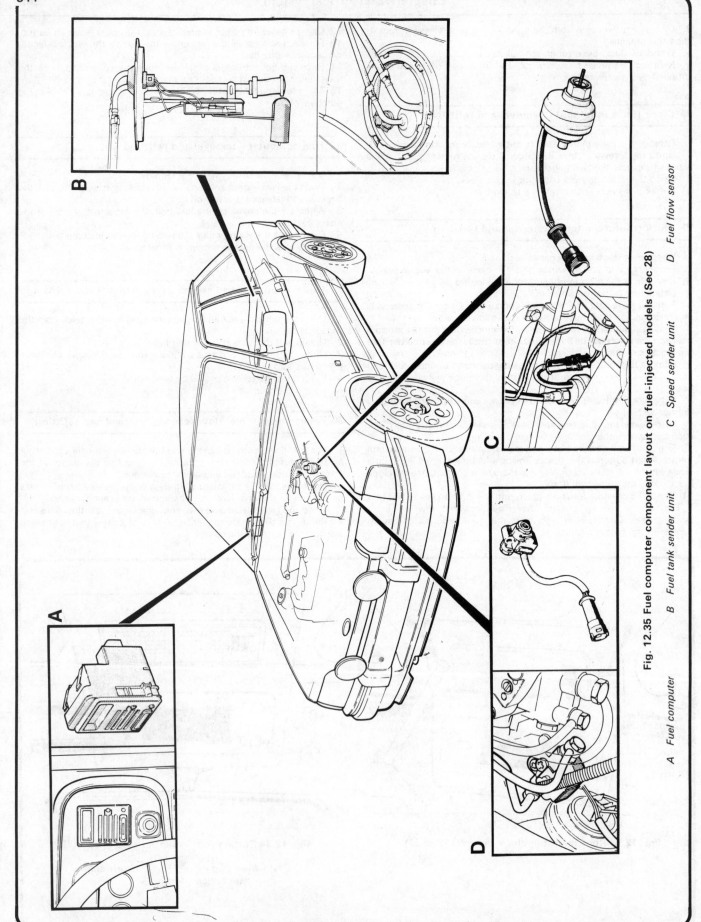

Fig. 12.35 Fuel computer component layout on fuel-injected models (Sec 28)

A Fuel computer   B Fuel tank sender unit   C Speed sender unit   D Fuel flow sensor

31 Auxiliary warning system – description

1 This system monitors the fluid levels and front brake pads for excessive wear. In the event of a fluid level dropping below the specified level, or the brake pads wearing down to the minimum allowable thickness, the driver is warned of the particular malfunction by means of a warning lamp.

2 When the ignition is first switched on, all warning lamps will illuminate as a means of verifying that all bulbs are working. This illumination period is of five seconds duration.

3 The system embraces the following components:

Fuel low level warning lamp. Activated by a sensor in the fuel level transmitter when the quantity of fuel in the tank falls below 7.0 litres (1.5 gallons).

Coolant low level warning lamp. Activated by a float-operated reed switch mounted in the expansion vessel.

Washer fluid low level warning lamp. A similar device to the coolant switch, it activates when the fluid is down to about 25% of capacity.

Engine oil level warning lamp. Activated by a dipstick whose resistance increases when its marked lower section is not immersed in oil.

Brake pad wear indicator. The sensing of worn disc pads is carried out by electrodes built into the pad. When the friction material has worn down to about 2 mm (0.079 in) thick, the electrodes cause the warning lamp to illuminate. In this instance the brake pads must be renewed at the earliest opportunity, as described in Chapter 9.

32 Auxiliary warning system – removal and refitting of components

Low washer fluid warning switch

1 Drain or syphon out the reservoir fluid then disconnect the switch multi-plug. Lever the switch away from the seal grommet using the flat blade of a suitable screwdriver. Do not allow fluid to enter the connectors.

2 Refit in reverse order of removal, checking that the grommet is correctly seated. On completion, check that the switch is operational and that there are no leaks around the grommet.

Low coolant warning switch

3 Drain the coolant from the expansion tank (see Chapter 2), having first depressurized the system if necessary.

4 Detach the switch multi-plug and then unscrew the threaded retainer. The switch can then be levered from the seal grommet using a flat-bladed screwdriver. Do not allow coolant to enter the connectors.

5 Refit in reverse order, and, on completion, check switch operation and, when reservoir is refilled to the specified level, that there are no signs of leaks from the grommet/retainer.

Warning indicator control unit

6 Remove the radio speaker grille and speaker from the facia.

7 Disconnect the multi-plug from the warning indicator/control assembly and then remove the two nylon fixing nuts which hold the assembly in position on the facia panel. Take care when withdrawing and handling the unit not to knock it, as the integral micro-electronics could be damaged.

8 Refit in the reverse order of removal. On completion check that the warning lights function for the initial period of five seconds after the ignition is switched on.

Low fuel sensor unit

9 This is integral with the fuel tank sender unit and is removed from the tank as described in Chapter 3.

Brake pad wear indicators

10 The removal and refitting of the brake pad sensors is described in Chapter 9.

Auxiliary system warning light bulbs

11 The auxiliary warning light bulbs are integral with the instrument panel and are welded in position. They cannot be individually renewed. To remove the instrument panel refer to Section 23.

33 Horn – removal and refitting

1 The horn(s) are located in the left-hand front corner of the engine compartment. Before removing, disconnect the battery.

2 Disconnect the lead from the horn.

3 Unscrew the single bolt and remove the horn and bracket.

4 Refitting is a reversal of removal.

34 Windscreen/tailgate wiper blades and arms – removal and refitting

1 Pull the wiper arm away from the glass until the arm locks.

2 Depress the small clip on the blade and slide the blade out of the hooked part of the arm (photo).

3 Before removing the wiper arms it is worthwhile marking their parked position on the glass with a strip of masking tape as an aid to refitting. Raise the plastic nut cover.

4 Unscrew the nut which holds the arm to the pivot shaft and pull the arm from the shaft splines (photo).

5 Refit by reversing the removal operations.

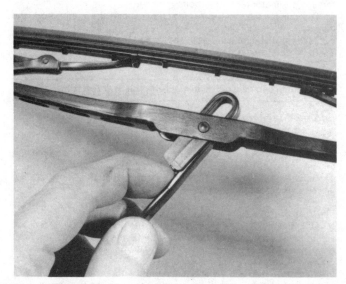

34.2 Disconnecting wiper blade from arm

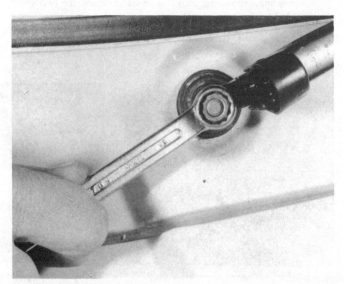

34.4 Unscrewing wiper arm nut

35 Windscreen wiper motor and linkage – removal and refitting

1   Remove the wiper arms and blades as previously described.
2   Disconnect the battery negative terminal.
3   Remove the nut covers, the fixing nuts, washers and spacers from the pivot shafts.
4   Disconnect the wiper motor wiring at the multi-pin plugs.
5   Unscrew the two fixing bolts and withdraw the motor complete with linkage from the engine compartment (photo).
6   Remove the spacers from the pivot shafts.
7   The motor can be separated from the linkage by removing the nut from the crankarm and then unbolting the motor from the mounting.
8   Refitting is a reversal of removal, but connect the motor crankarm when the link is aligned with it as shown in Fig. 12.36.

36 Tailgate wiper motor – removal and refitting

1   Disconnect the battery and remove the wiper arm/blade assembly.
2   Remove the pivot shaft nut, spacer and outer seals.
3   Open the tailgate and remove the trim panel (refer to Chapter 11).
4   Release the earth lead and unscrew the two, or on later models, three wiper motor mounting bolts (photo).
5   Disconnect the multi-pin plug and remove the motor from the tailgate.
6   Take off the pivot shaft seal, spacer and bracket from the motor.
7   Refit by reversing the removal operations.

37 Windscreen washer pump – removal and refitting

Engine compartment reservoir
1   Drain the washer fluid container.
2   Disconnect the lead and washer pipe.
3   Ease the top of the washer pump away from the fluid container and remove it (photo).
4   Refitting is a reversal of removal; check that the pump sealing grommet is a good fit.

Wing mounted reservoir
5   On some models the windscreen washer pump and fluid reservoir are mounted on the forward end of the underside of the left-hand front wing panel. It also incorporates the headlamp washer pump which draws its fluid from this reservoir also.
6   To remove the reservoir and pump units withdraw the level dipstick and syphon the fluid out of the reservoir through the filler neck.
7   Unscrew and remove the reservoir retaining bolts at its top end from inside the engine compartment.
8   Working under the wheel arch, unscrew and remove the two lower retaining bolts.
9   Withdraw the reservoir, carefully pulling its filler neck through the grommet on the inner wing panel. Disconnect the pump hoses.

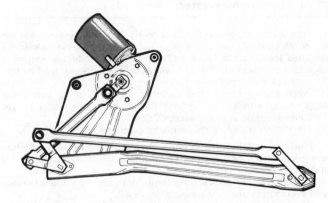

Fig. 12.36 Windscreen wiper crankarm alignment for refitting (Sec 35)

10   The pump and fluid level sensor unit can be eased away from their location apertures in the reservoir.
11   Refitting is a reversal of the removal; check that the pump and fluid level sensor grommets are in good condition when reassembling, and check for leaks on completion.

38 Tailgate washer pump – removal and refitting

Saloon
1   Remove the load space trim panel as described in Chapter 11.
2   Disconnect the pump leads at the multi-plug.
3   Unscrew the three reservoir mounting screws, and remove the resevoir until the fluid pipe can be pulled from the pump.
4   With the reservoir removed, pull the pump from its reservoir seal.
5   Refit by reversing the removal operations.

Estate
6   Open the tailgate, raise the spare wheel cover and disconnect the electrical leads and fluid pipe from the pump.
7   Extract the two securing screws and remove the pump.
8   Refitting is a reversal of removal.

39 Windscreen washer jets – removal and refitting

Single jet system (pre-1986 models)
1   Open the bonnet and disconnect the washer pipe from the jet.
2   If the pipe stub on the jet assembly is now pushed to one side, the jet retaining tang will be released and the jet can be removed from the bonnet grille slots.

35.5 Windscreen wiper motor location in engine compartment

36.4 Tailgate wiper motor retaining bolts (arrowed)

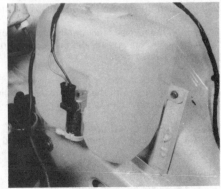

37.3 Windscreen washer fluid reservoir and pump

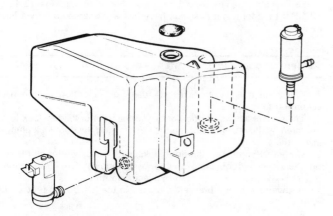

Fig. 12.37 Windscreen washer reservoir and pumps (Sec 37)

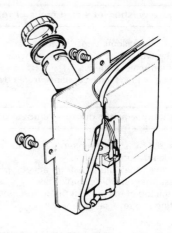

Fig. 12.38 Tailgate washer reservoir and pump (Sec 38)

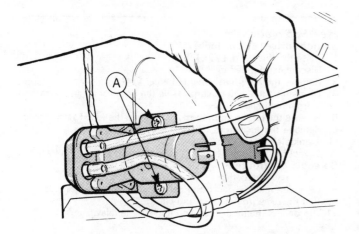

**Fig. 12.39 Tailgate washer pump retaining screws (A) –
Estate models (Sec 38)**

3 Refit by reversing the removal operations. The end of the plastic washer pipe should be warmed in very hot water to make it easier to push onto the jet pipe stub and so avoid breaking it.

4 Adjustment of the jet spray pattern can be done using a pin in the jet nozzle.

Twin jet system (pre-1986 models)

5 Later models are fitted with a twin jet windscreen washer system instead of the single jet type used on earlier models.

6 The jets are now located as shown in Fig. 12.40, one each side on the bonnet inner panel. The washer supply hose is connected to a central T-piece connector which directs the fluid to each jet.

7 The twin jets can be adjusted in the same manner as the earlier single type. They should be set so that the fluid jets hit the windscreen about 250 mm (9.8 in) from the top edge of the windscreen.

Twin jet system (1986 models onwards)

8 1986 models onwards are fitted with a twin jet system but using the same jet type as the early single jet system.

9 Removal, refitting and adjustment procedures for this washer type are therefore the same as described previously.

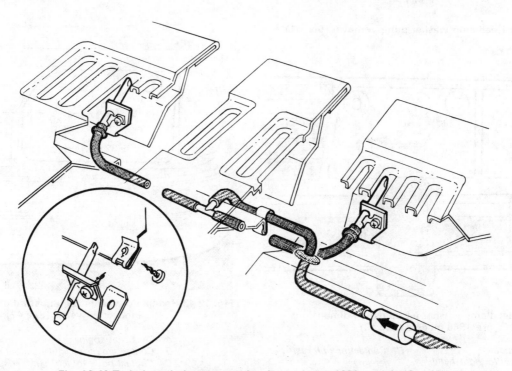

Fig. 12.40 Twin jet windscreen washer layout – pre-1986 models (Sec 39)

40 Tailgate washer jet – removal and refitting

1   Remove the tailgate wiper motor as described in Section 36.
2   Pull the washer jet off the tailgate wiper motor shaft, disconnect the hose and remove the jet.
3   Refitting is the reverse sequence to removal.

41 Headlamp washer pump – removal and refitting

1   Drain the washer reservoir by syphoning, and disconnect the electrical leads from the pump.
2   Disconnect the fluid pipe from the pump.
3   Release the reservoir clamp screw.
4   Ease the top of the pump from the reservoir and remove it upwards.
5   Refitting is a reversal of removal.

42 Headlamp washer jet – removal and refitting

1   The headlamp washer jets are an integral part of the bumper overrider and cannot be removed separately. If a jet is to be renewed for any reason the complete overrider must be obtained (see Chapter 11).

Fig. 12.41 Headlamp washer pump removal (Sec 41)

2   Adjustment of the jets entails the use of special tool 32-004. If this tool is available the jets should be adjusted as shown in Figs. 12.42 or 12.43. If the tool is not available have this work carried out by a Ford dealer.

43 Central door locking system – description

1   This system is available as standard, or as optional equipment according to model.
2   The system allows all door locks and the boot or tailgate lock to be operated by the driver by turning the key or using the door lock plunger inside the vehicle.
3   On pre-1986 models the door locks, with the exception of the one on the driver's door, are actuated by solenoids. On 1986 models onwards the locks are actuated by electric motors.
4   An overload circuit breaker is located in the fusebox to protect the system.

44 Central locking system components – removal and refitting

Pre-1986 models
Switch (driver's door lock)
1   Raise the driver's door lock fully.
2   Disconnect the battery.
3   Remove the door trim panel (Chapter 11).
4   Disconnect the wiring plugs inside the door cavity and release the wires from their clips.
5   Release the lock control rods and remove the lock fixing screws.
6   Remove the lock from the door interior by guiding it round the glass guide channel.
7   Extract the two screws and remove the switch from the lock.
Solenoid control relay
8   Disconnect the battery.
9   Remove the under-facia trim panel from the passenger side.
10 Pull the relay from its securing clips.
11 Disconnect the multi-plug and remove the relay.

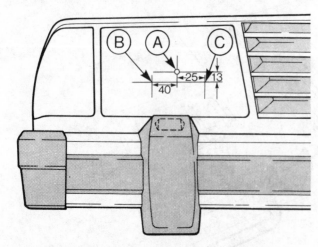

Fig. 12.42 Headlamp washer jet adjusting dimensions –
pre-1986 models (Sec 42)

A   Lens centrepoint
B   Contact point for right-hand jet spray
C   Contact point for left-hand jet spray
All dimensions in mm

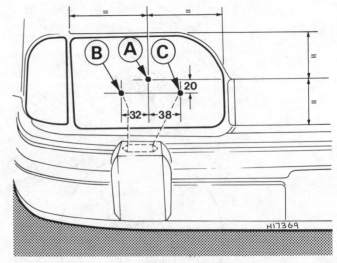

Fig. 12.43 Headlamp washer jet adjusting dimensions – 1986 models onwards (Sec 42)

A   Lens centrepoint
B   Contact point for right-hand jet spray
C   Contact point for left-hand jet spray
All dimensions in mm

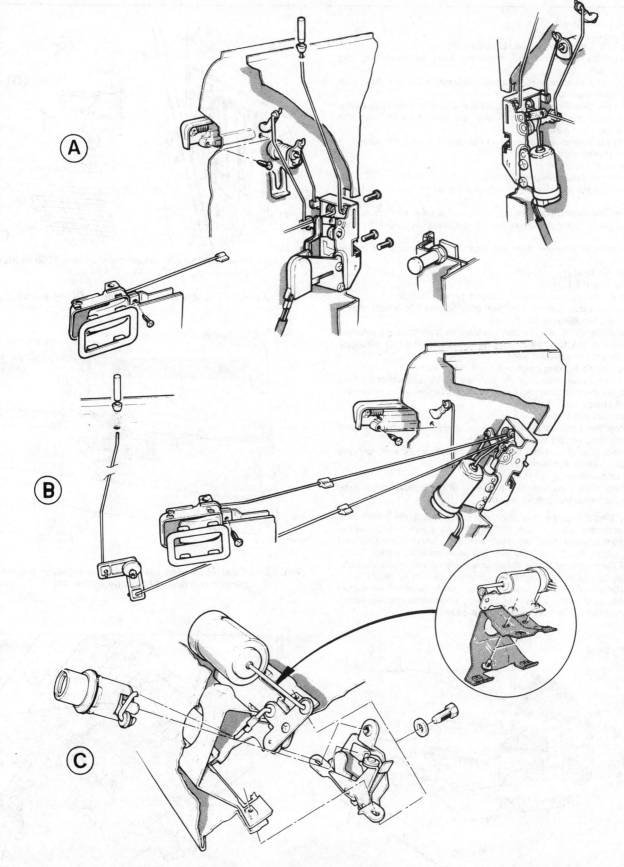

Fig. 12.44 Layout of the solenoid operated central door locking system as fitted to pre-1986 models (Secs 43 and 44)

A *Front door components*   B *Rear door components*   C *Tailgate components*

Solenoid (rear door)

12 Disconnect the battery.

13 Remove the door trim panel (Chapter 11).

14 Remove the bellcrank and operating lever by extracting the securing screws.

15 Release the operating rod rubber insulators from the door and disconnect the wiring.

16 Extract the lock securing screws, push the lock into the door cavity and then withdraw the lock with the operating rods through the cut-out in the door panel.

17 Extract the screws and disconnect the solenoid from the lock.

Solenoid (front door)

18 Disconnect the battery.

19 Remove the door trim panel (Chapter 11).

20 Disconnect the lock operating rods and extract the three lock fixing screws.

21 Release the wiring from the clips, manoeuvre the lock round the door glass guide channel and remove it through the cut-out in the door panel.

22 Separate the solenoid from the lock after extracting the fixing screws.

Solenoid (tailgate)

23 Disconnect the battery.

24 Open the tailgate and remove the trim panel (Chapter 11).

25 Remove the lock rod clip and then prise out the clip which retains the lock cylinder. Remove the cylinder.

26 Slightly lower the tailgate and working through the lock cylinder hole, move the lock lever away from its spring until the lock engages.

27 Disconnect the solenoid wiring.

28 Extract the lock fixing bolts and remove the lock.

29 Insert a screwdriver through the aperture left by removal of the lock and unscrew the two solenoid fixing screws. Withdraw the solenoid.

Solenoid (boot lid)

30 Disconnect the battery.

31 Remove the boot lid lock unit, as described in Chapter 11 and disconnect the solenoid wiring.

32 Unscrew and remove the two solenoid retaining screws, unhook the operating shaft and withdraw the solenoid.

System components refitting

33 Refitting of all components is a reversal of the removal procedure, but note the following special points:

(a) *When fitting the door lock solenoids, locate the guide lock assembly into position, but do not fully tighten the retaining screws until after the bellcrank and rubber operating rod guides, and the internal lock operating lever are fitted*

(b) *Check that, when the solenoid is in the unlocked position, the gaiter has an uncompressed length of 20 mm (0.78 in)*

(c) *Before refitting the door trim panel check that the wires within the door cavity are out of the way of the window regulating mechanism and secured by strap clips*

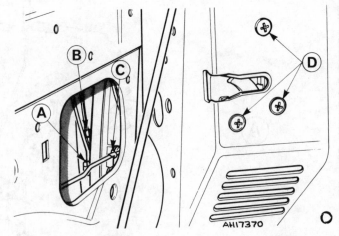

Fig. 12.45 Door locking rod attachments – pre-1986 models (Sec 44)

A, B and C Control rods   D Lock retaining screws

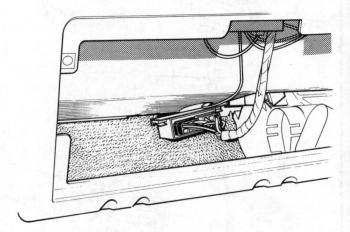

Fig. 12.46 Central locking solenoid relay location behind glovebox – pre-1986 models (Sec 44)

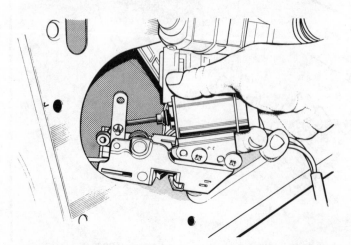

Fig. 12.47 Door lock solenoid removal – pre-1986 models (Sec 44)

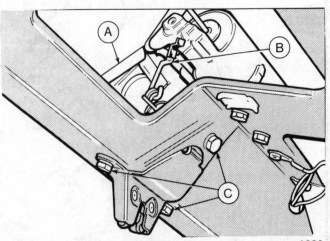

Fig. 12.48 Tailgate lock and solenoid components – pre-1986 models (Sec 44)

A Lock barrel clip   C Lock retaining bolts
B Lock rod clip

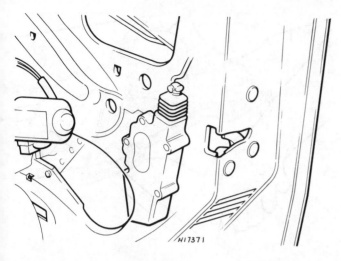

Fig. 12.49 Door lock motor location – 1986 models onwards (Sec 44)

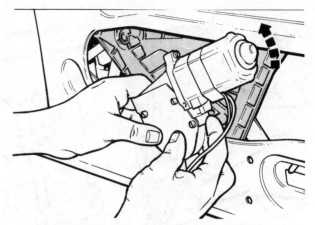

Fig. 12.50 Window motor removal (Sec 46)

Turn motor as shown to remove

1986 models onwards
Motor (front and rear doors)

34 Disconnect the battery.
35 Remove the door trim panel (Chapter 11).
36 Undo the two retaining screws, or drill out the bracket rivets, and withdraw the motor.
37 Disconnect the motor from the operating rod, disconnect the wiring multi-plug and remove the motor.

Motor (tailgate and boot lid)

38 Disconnect the battery.
39 Open the tailgate or boot lid and remove the trim panel where applicable (Chapter 11).
40 Disconnect the motor wiring multi-plug.
41 Undo the motor retaining bolts, disconnect the operating rod and remove the motor.

System components refitting

42 In all cases refitting is the reversal of the removal procedure.

45 Electrically operated windows – description

1 Electrically operated windows are available as standard or as optional equipment according to model.
2 The electric motor drivegear engages directly with the window regulator mechanism.
3 When the ignition is switched on, power is supplied through a relay mounted in the fusebox.
4 A circuit breaker type of overload protection is provided.
5 When a control switch is actuated the motor operates to lower or raise the window.

46 Electrically operated windows – removal and refitting of components

Switch
1 Disconnect the battery.
2 Carefully lever the switch from the armrest and disconnect the multi-plug connector (photo).
3 Refit by reversing the removal operations.

Motor and regulator
4 Lower the window fully on the door that is being dismantled.
5 Disconnect the battery.
6 Remove the door trim panel (Chapter 11).
7 Disconnect the motor wiring multi-plugs and retaining clips.
8 Remove the mounting screws from the motor and the regulator – three screws each (photo).

46.2 Electrically operated window switch removal

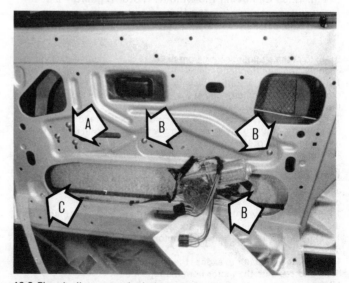

46.8 Electrically operated window mechanism
A *Regulator mounting screws*   C *Glass channel fixing screw*
B *Motor mounting screws*

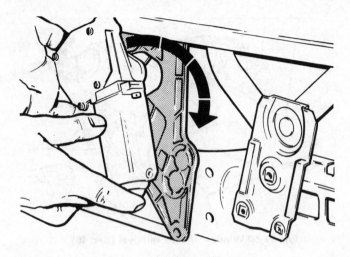

Fig. 12.51 Window motor rotation to clear door aperture (Sec 46)

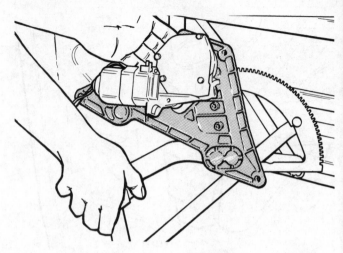

Fig. 12.52 Withdrawing the window motor and regulator from the door (Sec 46)

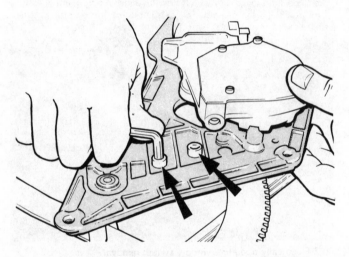

Fig. 12.53 Removing the window motor regulator travel stop (Sec 46)

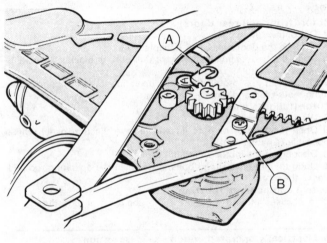

Fig. 12.54 Window motor driveshaft circlip (A) and gear guide retaining screw (B) (Sec 46)

9   Extract the retaining screw from the door glass channel. Detach the channel from the door and remove the door glass (see Chapter 11).

10 Grip the motor mounting plate in one hand and the regulator in the other. Raise the regulator and at the same time pull the motor towards the hinge end of the door.

11 Slowly twist the motor in a clockwise direction and at the same time fold the regulator over the top of the motor so that it comes to rest on the lock side of the door.

12 Rotate the motor mounting in an anti-clockwise direction until a corner of the mounting comes into view in the cut-out of the door.

13 Move the assembly so that this corner projects through the cut-out and then turn the whole assembly in a clockwise direction and guide it out of the cut-out.

14 Remove the two Allen screws from the regulator travel stop, and the single screw from the regulator gear guide.

15 Extract the circlip from the motor driveshaft and remove the drivegear.

16 Move the regulator to expose the motor mounting bolts. Extract the bolts and separate the motor from the regulator.

17 Reassembly and refitting is a reversal of the dismantling and removal procedure. Before refitting the door trim check that the wiring is secured out of the way of the window regulating system.

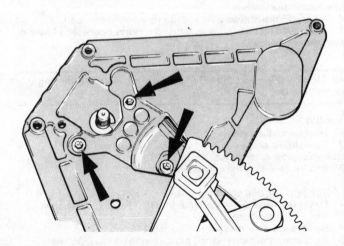

Fig. 12.55 Window motor mounting bolt locations (Sec 46)

47 In-car entertainment equipment – general

1   The following Sections (48 to 59) cover radio, radio/cassette player and related items of Ford manufacture as fitted in production either as standard or optional equipment.
2   Where equipment is to be installed at a later date and is not necessarily of Ford make, refer to Section 60.

48 Radio – removal and refitting

Early models
1   Disconnect the battery.
2   Pull off the control knobs, the tuning knob spacer and the tone control lever. Remove the cover panel.
3   Extract the four fixing screws from the front of the radio.
4   Pull the radio far enough from the facia to be able to disconnect the aerial, power supply and earth leads and the speaker wires.
5   Unscrew the two nuts which hold the receiver to the mounting plate. Remove the mounting plate.
6   Take off the rear support bracket and locating plate.
7   Refitting is a reversal of removal.

Later models
8   Disconnect the battery.
9   Remove the radio control knobs and withdraw the tuning knob spacer and the tone control lever.

10 Unscrew and remove the facia plate retaining nuts and washers, then withdraw the facia plate.
11 The radio retaining tangs can now be pulled inwards (towards the centre of the radio) and the radio withdrawn from its aperture. You may need to make a suitable hook-ended rod (welding rod is ideal) to pull the tangs inwards to release the radio.
12 With the radio withdrawn, disconnect the power lead, the speaker plug, earth lead, the aerial cable and feed.
13 From the rear of the radio remove the plastic support bracket and locating plate, then remove the radio from the front bracket.
14 Refitting is the reversal of the removal procedure.

49 Radio/cassette player – removal and refitting

Early models
1   The procedure is the same as for the radio as fitted to early models, and described in Section 48.

Later models
2   Disconnect the battery.
3   To withdraw the radio/cassette unit from its aperture you will need to fabricate the U-shaped extractor tools from wire rod of suitable gauge to insert into the withdrawal slots on each side of the unit (in the front face).
4   Insert the withdrawal tools as shown (see Figs. 12.59 and 12.60) then, pushing each outwards simultaneously, pull them evenly to withdraw the radio/cassette unit. It is important that an equal pressure is applied to each tool as the unit is withdrawn (photo).
5   Once withdrawn from its aperture disconnect the aerial cable, the power lead, the aerial feed, the speaker plugs, the earth lead and the light and memory feed (where applicable).
6   Push the retaining clips inwards to remove the removal tool from each side (Fig. 12.61).

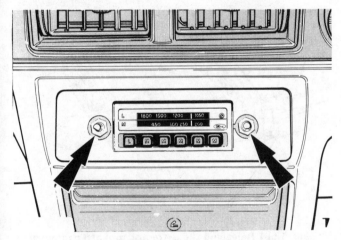

Fig. 12.56 Early type radio cover panel retaining nut locations (Sec 48)

Fig. 12.57 Later type radio retaining tang locations (Sec 48)

Fig. 12.58 Radio rear support bracket and slide (Sec 48)

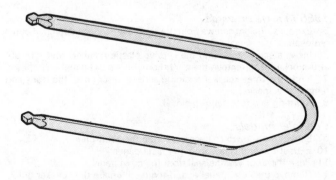

Fig. 12.59 Radio/cassette player extractor tool (Sec 49)

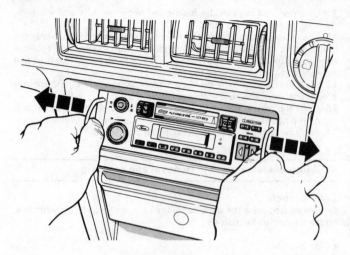

Fig. 12.60 Radio/cassette player removal using the extractor tools (Sec 49)

49.4 Using the removal tool to remove the radio/cassette player

7 Refit in the reverse order of removal. The withdrawal tools do not have to be used, simply push the unit into its aperture until the securing clips engage in their slots.

50 Graphic equaliser – removal and refitting

1 The procedure is the same as for the radio/cassette player as fitted to later models and described in Section 49.

51 Loudspeaker (facia mounted) – removal and refitting

1 Carefully prise up the speaker grille using a small screwdriver. Lift it from the facia.
2 Extract the speaker mounting screws which are now exposed.
3 Lift the speaker up until the connecting wires can be disconnected by pulling on their terminals. The wires have different connecting terminals to prevent incorrect connections.
4 Refitting is a reversal of removal.

52 Loudspeaker (cowl panel mounted) – removal and refitting

Pre-1986 models
1 Prise out the grille retaining clip.
2 Extract screws as necessary to be able to remove the cowl panel/grille.
3 Extract the four speaker mounting screws and withdraw the speaker until the leads can be disconnected at the rear of the speaker.
4 Refitting is a reversal of removal.

1986 models onwards
5 Extract sufficient screws from the scuff plate to facilitate cowl panel removal.
6 Insert a screwdriver into the captive plastic retainers and turn 90° anti-clockwise to remove them. Withdraw the cowl panel.
7 Undo the three speaker retaining screws, disconnect the leads and remove the speaker.
8 Refitting is a reversal of removal.

Cabriolet models
9 Extract the screws as necessary from the scuff plate.
10 Extract the end screw from the facia panel.
11 Prise the door weatherseal from the cowl panel.
12 Remove the cowl panel and, if required, unclip the speaker grille.
13 Extract the four speaker mounting screws and withdraw the speaker until the leads can be disconnected.
14 Refitting is a reversal of removal.

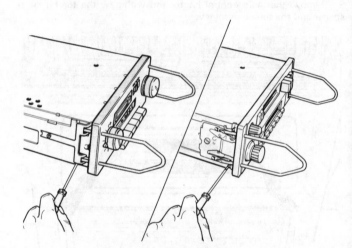

Fig. 12.61 Releasing the extractor tool after removal (Sec 49)

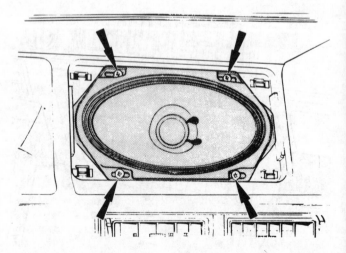

Fig. 12.62 Facia mounted loudspeaker retaining screw locations (Sec 51)

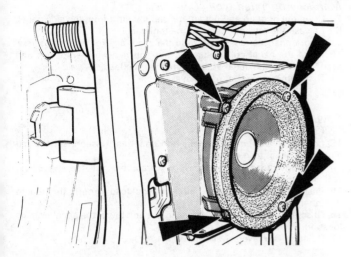

Fig. 12.63 Cowl mounted loudspeaker retaining screw
locations – pre-1986 models (Sec 52)

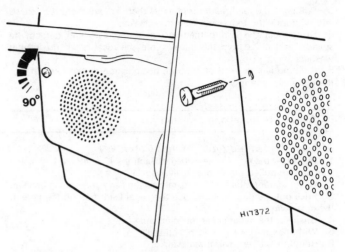

Fig. 12.64 Cowl mounted loudspeaker panel plastic retainer
removal – 1986 models onwards (Sec 52)

---

53 Loudspeaker (rear parcel shelf mounted) – removal and refitting

Note: *Refer to warning about loudspeaker fitment at the beginning of Section 60.*

1 On pre-1986 models, prise the loudspeaker cover free by inserting a screwdriver blade into the slots on the side of the cover.
2 On all models undo the four speaker retaining screws, pull the speaker away from the shelf and disconnect the wires.
3 Refitting is a reversal of removal.

---

54 Loudspeaker (rear parcel tray mounted) – removal and refitting

Note: *Refer to warning about loudspeaker fitment at the beginning of Section 60.*

1 Unscrew the collar and pull the wiring plug from the loudspeaker.
2 Remove the rear parcel tray then unscrew the four retaining screws and remove the speaker.
3 Refit in the reverse order to removal.

---

55 Loudspeaker (rear quarter panel mounted – Cabriolet) – removal and refitting

Note: *Refer to warning about loudspeaker fitment at the beginning of Section 60.*

1 Fully open the roof and lock it.
2 Pull off the roof release lever knob and remove the window winder.

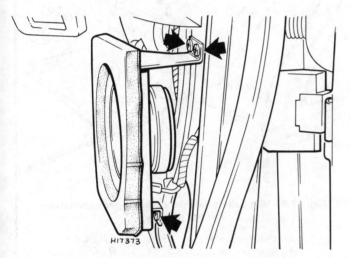

Fig. 12.65 Cowl mounted loudspeaker retaining screw
locations – 1986 models onwards (Sec 52)

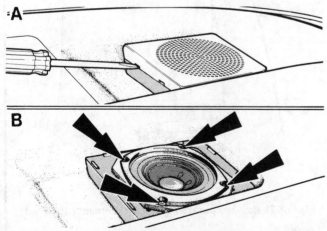

Fig. 12.66 Rear parcel shelf mounted loudspeaker removal –
pre-1986 models (Sec 53)

A   Prising cover open   *B   Retaining screw locations*

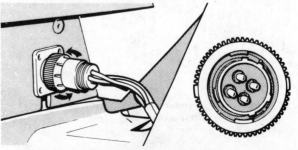

Fig. 12.67 Rear parcel tray mounted loudspeaker wiring
plug details (Sec 54)

3   Pull back the rear quarter trim panel then remove the three screws and withdraw the trim panel with the speaker.
4   Disconnect the wiring then extract the screws and detach the speaker and grille from the panel. Note the location of the rubber washers.
5   Refitting is a reversal of removal, but position the speaker so that the terminals face forwards.

56   Aerial – removal and refitting

Manually operated type (except Cabriolet)

1   Withdraw the radio as described in Sections 48 or 49 until the aerial lead can be pulled out of the receiver socket.
2   Working under the front wing, release the aerial inner wing bracket.
3   Prise out the grommet and pull the aerial lead through the hole in the inner wing.
4   Unscrew the aerial collar retaining nut.
5   Withdraw the aerial, spacers and seal.
6   Refitting is a reversal of removal.

Manually operated type (Cabriolet)

7   Open the boot lid and detach the support strut from the side panel.
8   Release the tabs and remove the trim panel.
9   From under the rear panel undo the aerial bracket retaining screw.
10   Undo the aerial collar retaining nut and remove the spacers and seal. Withdraw the aerial after unscrewing the lead.
11   Refitting is a reversal of removal.

Power-operated type (except Cabriolet)

12   Carry out the operations described in paragraph 1.
13   Lower the bottom facia insulation panel and disconnect the red and white aerial feed cables.
14   Working under the front wing, extract the self-tapping screw which secures the aerial lower bracket.
15   Prise out the grommet and pull the aerial lead through the hole in the inner wing.
16   Unscrew the aerial upper retaining nut and lower the aerial from its location. Take off the seals and spacers.
17   Refitting is a reversal of removal.

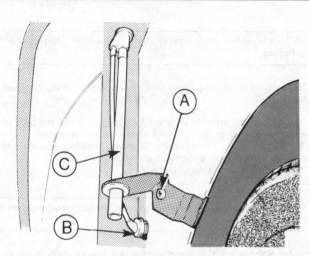

Fig. 12.68 Manually operated aerial attachments (Sec 56)

A   Inner wing bracket screw   C   Aerial
B   Rubber grommet

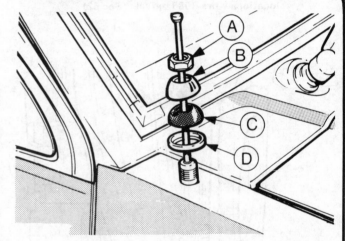

Fig. 12.69 Manually operated aerial upper attachment fixings (Sec 56)

A   Collar retaining nut   C   Spacer
B   Bezel   D   Seal

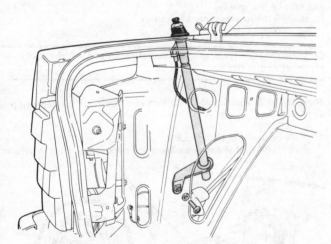

Fig. 12.70 Manually operated aerial location on Cabiolet models (Sec 56)

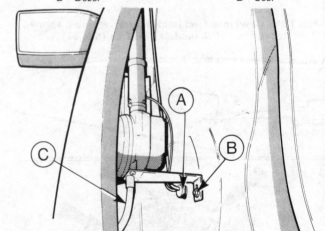

Fig. 12.71 Power operated aerial attachments (Sec 56)

A   Grommet   C   Aerial drain tube
B   Lower bracket screw

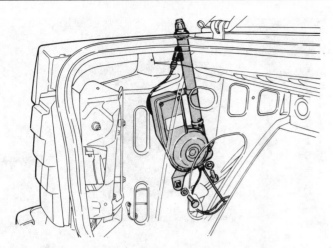

Fig. 12.72 Power operated aerial location on Cabriolet models (Sec 56)

Power-operated type (Cabriolet)
18 The operations are the same as for the Cabriolet manually operated type described previously, but in addition disconnect the power feed multi-plug before unscrewing the aerial lead.

All aerials
19 If a new aerial is being installed, it will have to be trimmed to the radio. To do this, tune in the receiver with maximum volume to a weak station near 140 kHz (214 m) on the AM scale.
20 Insert a thin screwdriver into the trim screw hole provided in the receiver and turn the screw until maximum volume is obtained.

57 Heated rear window aerial amplifier – removal and refitting

1 On some 1986 models onwards the radio aerial is incorporated in the heated rear window element, and to assist reception an amplifier is fitted. This is located in the tailgate adjacent to the tailgate wiper motor. Removal and refitting is as follows.
2 Remove the tailgate wiper motor trim panel and the adjoining trim panel.
3 Undo the two screws and withdraw the amplifier.
4 Disconnect the wiring and remove the amplifier.
5 Refitting is a reversal of removal.

58 Heated rear window element – general

1 The rear window heater element/aerial is fixed to the interior surface of the glass.
2 When cleaning the window use only water and a leather or soft cloth, and avoid scratching with rings on the fingers.
3 Avoid sticking labels over the element and packing luggage so that it can rub against the glass.
4 In the event of the element being damaged, it can be repaired using one of the special conductive paints now available.

59 Speaker balance control joystick – removal and refitting

Pre-1986 models
1 Disconnect the battery.
2 Use a screwdriver and carefully prise free the balance control bezel.
3 Pull free the cassette stowage box from its aperture.
4 Rotate the securing clip anti-clockwise to remove it and the balance control from the box. Detach the wiring multi-plug.
5 Refit in the reverse order of removal.

1986 models onwards
6 Disconnect the battery then remove the instrument panel as described in Section 23.
7 Carefully prise off the trim bezel using a screwdriver (photo).
8 Turn the retaining clip anti-clockwise and remove the clip (photo).
9 From within the instrument panel aperture disconnect the wiring mutli-plug and remove the unit.
10 Refit in the reverse order of removal.

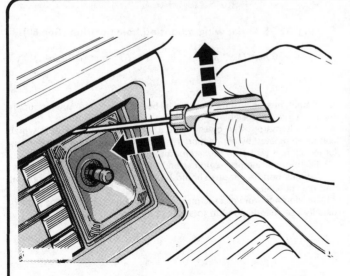

Fig. 12.73 Removing the speaker balance control bezel – pre-1986 models (Sec 59)

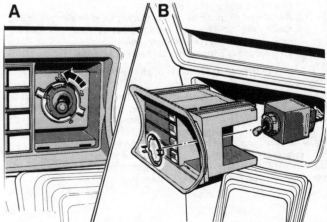

Fig. 12.74 Speaker balance control removal – pre-1986 models (Sec 59)

A   *Releasing the securing clip*
B   *Balance control removal from stowage box*

59.7 Speaker balance control bezel removal

59.8 Speaker balance control retaining clip

60 Radio equipment (non-standard) – installation

Warning: *The siting of uprated high powered speakers close to seat belt inertia reels can adversely affect the seat belt operation, due to the influence of the speakers' magnetic field.*

1   This Section covers briefly the installation of in-vehicle entertainment equipment purchased from non-Ford sources.

Radio/cassette player
2   It is recommended that a standard sized receiver is purchased and fitted into the location provided in the facia panel or centre console.
3   A fitting kit is normally supplied with the radio or cassette player.
4   Connections will be required as follows:

   (a) *Power supply, taken from the ignition switch so that the radio is only operational with the ignition key in position I or II. Always insert a 2A in-line fuse in the power lead*
   (b) *Earth. The receiver must have a good clean earth connection to a metal part of the body*
   (c) *Aerial lead. From an aerial which itself must be earthed. Avoid routing the cable through the engine compartment or near the ignition, wiper motor or flasher relay*
   (d) *Loudspeaker connections, between speaker and receiver*

5   Location of the aerial is a matter of choice. A roof-mounted or rear wing-mounted aerial usually provides the most interference-free reception but if a front wing position is preferred, mount the aerial as shown in Fig. 12.75. Cut the hole by drilling and filling or by means of a tank hole cutter. Paint the edges of the hole to prevent rusting.
6   If the radio is being installed for the first time, interference will almost certainly present a problem when the engine is running.
7   The ignition HT leads will have been suppressed during production, but a 1µF capacitor should be connected between the + terminal of the coil and the coil mounting bracket bolt.

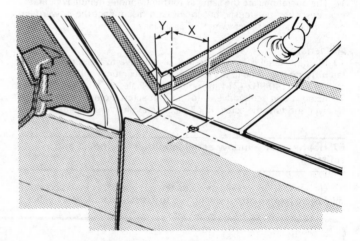

Fig. 12.75 Aerial wing mounting hole position (Sec 60)

   X   50 mm (1.97 in)   Y   18.5 mm (0.73 in)

8   Sometimes an in-line choke can be fitted into the power supply lead as close as possible to the radio to reduce interference.
9   The alternator often gives rise to a whine through the radio which can be eliminated by connecting a 1.0 to 3.0 µF capacitor between the large terminal (B+) on the alternator and earth.
10 Further interference suppression will be on a trial and error basis. Sometimes bonding straps should be connected between the bonnet and rear bulkhead.
11 Interference from electric motors, flasher units or front disc pads is usually not serious enough to suppess and can be tolerated.

61 Fault diagnosis – electrical system

Symptom	Reason(s)
Starter fails to turn engine	Battery discharged
	Battery defective internally
	Leads loose, or terminals corroded
	Loose connections at starter motor
	Engine earth strap loose, broken or missing
	Starter motor faulty or solenoid not functioning
	Starter motor brushes worn
	Commutator dirty or worn
	Starter motor armature faulty
	Field coils earthed
Starter turns engine very slowly	Battery in discharged condition
	Starter brushes badly worn, sticking or brush wires loose
	Loose wires in starter motor circuit
Starter spins but does not turn engine	Pinion or flywheel gear teeth broken or worn
Starter motor noisy or excessively rough engagement	Pinion or flywheel gear teeth broken or worn
	Starter motor retaining bolts loose
Battery will not hold charge for more than a few days	Battery defective, internally
	Electrolyte level too low or electrolyte too weak due to leakage
	Plate separators no longer fully effective
	Battery plates severely sulphated
	Alternator drivebelt slipping
	Battery terminal connections loose or corroded
	Alternator not charging
	Short-circuit causing continual battery drain
	Integral regulator unit not working correctly
Ignition light fails to go out, battery runs flat in a few days	Alternator drivebelt loose and slipping or broken
	Alternator brushes worn, sticking, broken or dirty
	Alternator brush springs weak or broken
	Internal fault in alternator

Failure of individual electrical equipment to function correctly is dealt with under the headings listed below

Horn

Horn operates all the time	Horn push either earthed or stuck down
	Horn cable to horn push earthed
Horn fails to operate	Blown fuse
	Cable or cable connection loose, broken or disconnected
	Horn has an internal fault
Horn emits intermittent or unsatisfactory noise	Cable connections loose

Lights

Lights do not come on	If engine not running, battery discharged
	Wire connections loose, disconnected or broken
	Light switch shorting or otherwise faulty
	Light bulb filament burnt out or bulbs broken
Lights give very poor illumination	Lamp glasses dirty
	Lamps badly out of adjustment
Lights work erratically – flashing on and off, especially over bumps	Battery terminals or earth connection loose
	Lights not earthing properly
	Contacts in light switch faulty

Wipers

Wiper motor fails to work	Blown fuse
	Wire connections loose, disconnected or broken
	Brushes badly worn
	Armature worn or faulty
	Field coils faulty
Wiper motor works very slowly and takes excessive current	Commutator dirty, greasy or burnt
	Armature bearings dirty or unaligned
	Armature badly worn or faulty

Symptom	Reason(s)
Wiper motor works slowly and takes little current	Brushes badly worn Commutator dirty, greasy or burnt Armature badly worn or faulty
Wiper motor works but wiper blades remain static	Wiper motor gearbox parts badly worn

Electrically operated windows

Symptom	Reason(s)
Glass will only move in one direction	Defective switch
Door glass slow to move	Stiff regulator or glass guide channels

Door glass will not move:
    With motor running
 	
    Motor not running
	Binding glass guide channels
	Faulty regulator
	Faulty relay
	Blown fuse
	Fault in motor
	Broken or disconnected wire

Central door locking system

Symptom	Reason(s)
Complete failure	Blown fuse Faulty master switch Faulty relay Broken or disconnected wire
Latch locks but will not unlock, or unlocks but will not lock	Faulty master switch Poor contact in pulse relay multi-plugs Faulty relay
One solenoid or motor will not operate	Poor circuit connections Broken wire Faulty solenoid or motor Binding bellcrank rod Binding driver's remote control lock button Fault in latch

Wiring diagrams commence overleaf

1980-86 Model

COMMON POINT	DIAGRAM/ GRID REF.
S103	1/H1
	2/H2
S104	1/J1
	2/J2
S105	1/H1
	3/G1
	4/H1
	4a/H1
S106	1/K5
	2/F6
	3/F6
	4/K5
	4a/K5
S107	1/K1
	2/K2
	3/K2
S108	1/A8
	2/B8
	4/A8
S109	1/A2
	2/B1
S110	1/J6
	2/J5
	3/J5
S113	1/H1
	2/G1
S120	1/A4
	4/A4
	4a/A4
S123	1/H5
	2/J5
	3/J5

COMMON EARTH POINT	DIAGRAM/ GRID REF.
G102	1/L5
	2/F7
	3/F7
	4/L5
	4a/L5
G103	1/A8
	2/B8
	4/A8
G104	1/A2
	2/B1
G105	2/M7
	3/M7
	4/M7
	4a/M7
G107	1/D3
	3/B4
	4a/D3

1986-89 Model

COMMON POINT	DIAGRAM/ GRID REF.	COMMON POINT	DIAGRAM/ GRID REF.
S116	3a/F6	S1025	1a/G3
	4/E6		2a/G3
S1002	1a/G8		3a/G3
	2a/H1		4/K5
	4/H1		4b/G3
	4b/H1	S1027	2a/M4
S1012	1a/F2		3a/M4
	2a/C3	S1032	1a/B2
	3a/C3		4/4A
	5/B8		4b/4A
S1014	1a/J2	S1043	2a/F5
	2a/E3		3a/F5
	5/C4	S1044	1a/H5
	5/D6		2a/C5
S1021	1a/A8	S1052	1a/H8
	2a/B8		2a/E5
	4/A8		3a/E5
S1024	1a/3D		5/C3
	3a/C4		5/C6
	4b/E2		5/D1

COMMON EARTH POINT	DIAGRAM/ GRID REF.	COMMON EARTH POINT	DIAGRAM/ GRID REF.
G1002	1a/F8	G1006	1a/D3
	4b/F6		3a/B5
G1003	1a/A8		4b/D3
	2a/B8	G1008	2a/M4
	4/A8		3a/M4
G1005	1a/G4	G1009	1a/K8
	2a/G4		4/M7
	3a/G3		4b/K8
	4/L5		
	4b/G4		

Wire Colours

B	Blue	Rs	Pink
Bk	Black	S	Grey
Bn	Brown	V	Violet
Gn	Green	W	White
R	Red	Y	Yellow

NOTES:
1. Feed wires are coloured red (black when switched) and originate from diagrams 1 and 1a.
2. Earth wires on all diagrams are coloured brown.
3. The above tables show where common connecting points and earths interconnect between diagrams.
4. Not all items are fitted to all models.
5. Brackets show how the circuit may be connected in more than one way.

Table of common points/earths, wire colours and notes.

ITEM	DESCRIPTION	DIAGRAM/ GRID REF.	ITEM	DESCRIPTION	DIAGRAM/ GRID REF.
1	ABS Warning Relay	1a/C1	40	Econolight Switch (amber)	1/F3
2	ABS Warning Switch	1a/B2	41	Econolight Switch (red)	1/F3
		1a/B8	42	Electric Choke	1/F5
3	Air Flow Potentiometer	4a/D7	43	Electric Mirror	3a/F1
		4b/D7			3a/F8
4	Air Temp. Sensor	4a/B7	44	Electric Mirror Control Switch	3a/H2
		4b/B7	45	Electric Window Motor LH	3/G8
5	Alternator	1/A3			3a/G8
		1a/A3	46	Electric Window Motor RH	3/G1
6	Antenna Module	3a/M2			3a/G1
		5/F2	47	Electric Window Relay	3/E1
		5/F5	48	Electric Window Switch LH 1980-86	3/H8
		5/F8	49	Electric Window Switch LH 1986-89	3a/H8
7	Auto. Trans. Inhibitor Switch	1/D7	50	Electric Window Switch RH 1980-86	3/H1
		1a/D7	51	Electric Window Switch RH 1980-86	3/K1
		2/B7		(LH window driver controlled)	
		2a/B7	52	Electric Window Switch RH 1986-89	3a/H1
8	Auto. Trans. Relay 1980-86	1/E1	53	Electro./Hydraulic Actuator	4a/E3
9	Auto. Trans. Relay 1986-89	1a/E1	54	Fader Control (4 way)	5/B4
10	Auto. Trans. Selector Illumination	2/J5	55	Flasher/Hazard Switch	2a/K3
		2a/J5	56	Flasher Lamp LH	2/A8
11	Auxiliary Air Device	4/F4			2a/A8
		4a/C7	57	Flasher Lamp RH	2/A1
		4b/C7			2a/A1
12	Auxiliary Warning System Module	1/K3	58	Flasher Lamp LH Side Mark	2/C8
13	Battery	1/F8			2a/C8
		1a/F8	59	Flasher Lamp RH Side Mark	2/C1
14	Brake Pad Sender LH	1/C8			2a/C1
15	Brake Pad Sender RH	1/C1	60	Flasher Relay 1980-86	2/D1
16	Choke Switch	1/K5	61	Flasher Relay 1986-89	2a/J3
		1a/K5	62	Fog Lamp Switch 1980-86	2/K6
17	Cigar Lighter	2/K6	63	Fog Lamp Switch 1986-89	2a/K6
		2a/K6	64	Fuel Computer	1a/L3
18	Clock	2/G5	65	Fuel Flow Sensor	1a/C8
		2a/G5	66	Fuel Injection Module	4a/J5
19	Cold Running Valve	1a/D5			4b/J5
20	Cold Starting Valve	4/F3	67	Fuel Injection Module Relay	4a/J3
		4a/F3	68	Fuel Injection Relay	4/J2
		4b/F3			4b/J2
21	Coolant Temp. Sensor	1/B7	69	Fuel Injection Relay	4a/J2
		1a/B7		(KE-Jetronic 1984-86)	
22	Cooling Fan	1/A6	70	Fuel Pump	4/L6
		1a/A6			4a/L6
23	Cooling Fan Switch	1/A7			4b/L6
		1a/A7	71	Fuel Sender	1/L7
24	Dim/Dip Relay V	2a/D1			1a/L7
25	Dim/Dip Relay D	2a/E1	72	Fuel Shut Off Valve	1/C7
26	Dim/Dip Relay L4/L5	2a/F1			1a/C7
27	Diode Block	4/J6	73	Glove Box Lamp/Switch	2/G7
28	Dip Beam Relay	2a/A5			2a/G7
		3a/A2	74	Graphic Equalizer	5/B7
29	Distributor	1/D4	75	Handbrake Warning Switch	1/K7
		1/D6			1a/K7
		1a/D4	76	Headlamp Unit LH	2/A7
		4/C3			2a/A7
		4/C6	77	Headlamp Unit RH	2/A2
		4a/C4			2a/A2
		4b/C4	78	Headlamp Washer Pump	3/A7
30	Door Lock RH Front	3/J1			3a/A7
31	Door Lock Actuator LH Front	3/J8	79	Headlamp Washer Relay	3/C6
32	Door Lock Actuator LH Rear	3/L8			3a/B4
33	Door Lock Actuator RH Rear	3/L1	80	Heated Rear Window	3/L4
34	Door Lock Motor LH Front	3a/K8			3a/M3
35	Door Lock Motor LH Rear	3a/M8	81	Heated Rear Window Relay 1980-86	3/C3
36	Door Lock Motor RH Front	3a/K1	82	Heated Rear Window Relay 1986-89	1a/1B
37	Door Lock Motor RH Rear	3a/M1			3a/C1
38	Door Lock Relay	3/K6			4/B1
39	Door Switch	2/H1	83	Heated Rear Window Switch 1980-86	3/H3
		2/H8	84	Heated Rear Window Switch 1986-89	3a/J6
		2/K1	85	Heated Windscreen	3a/F6
		2/K8	86	Heated Windscreen Relay	1a/H1
		2a/H1			3a/E1
		2a/H8	87	Heated Windscreen Switch	3a/J6

Key to wiring diagrams.

ITEM	DESCRIPTION	DIAGRAM/ GRID REF.	ITEM	DESCRIPTION	DIAGRAM/ GRID REF.
88	Heater Blower Illumination	2/G6	122	Radio Unit	3/H6
		2a/G6			5/D3
89	Heater Blower Motor	3/G6			5/D5
		3a/G6			5/D8
90	Heater Blower Switch	3/G5	123	Rear Wash/Wipe Motor	3/M5
		3a/G4			3a/M5
91	High Beam Relay	2a/A6	124	Rear Wash/Wipe Pump	3/M6
92	Horn	3/A6			3a/M6
		3a/A6	125	Rear Wash/Wipe Switch	3/G4
93	Horn Relay	3a/B1	126	Reversing Lamp Switch	2/C7
94	Horn Switch	3a/K5			2a/C7
95	Idle Speed Relay	1a/D1	127	Spark Plugs	1/E4
96	Idle Speed Valve	1/F6			1/E6
		1a/F6			1a/E4
		4/E3			4/D3
97	Ignition Coil	1/D4			4/D6
		1/D6			4a/D5
		1a/C4			4b/D5
		4/B3	128	Speaker LH Front	5/A2
		4/B5			5/A5
		4a/B4			5/A8
		4b/B4	129	Speaker LH Rear	5/F5
98	Ignition Module	4a/J7			5/F8
		4b/J7	130	Speaker RH Front	5/A1
99	Ignition Relay	1/D1			5/A4
		1a/D1			5/A6
		2a/C1	131	Speaker RH Rear	5/F3
100	Ignition Switch	1/K1			5/F6
		1a/K1	132	Speed Sensor	1a/D8
		3/K2	133	Speed Sensor Relay	4/J3
		5/D1	134	Spot Lamp	2/A3
		5/D4			2/A6
		5/E7			2a/A3
101	Instrument Cluster 1980-86	1/K4			2a/A6
		2/F4	135	Spot Lamp Relay	2/E1
		4/K4	136	Starter Motor	1/B5
		4a/K4			1a/A5
102	Instrument Cluster 1986-89	1a/K4	137	Stop Lamp Switch	2/C5
		2a/F4			2a/C4
		4/L3	138	Suppressor	1a/D5
		4b/K4			3a/B2
103	Interior Lamp/Switch	2/G4			4/D2
		2/K4			4b/H4
		2a/G4	139	Tailgate Lock Motor	3a/M5
104	Knock Sensor	4b/C3	140	Tailgate Release Actuator	3/M4
105	Licence Plate Lamp	2/M4	141	Temperature Sensor	4a/D6
		2/M5			4b/C3
		2a/M5			4b/D6
106	Light Cluster LH Rear	2/M8	142	Thermal Time Switch	1a/C5
		2a/M8			4/D5
107	Light Cluster RH Rear	2/M1			4a/D5
		2a/M1			4b/D5
108	Light/Dimmer Switch	2a/K4	143	Throttle Position Switch	4a/F5
109	Light/Wiper Switch	2/J3			4b/F5
		3/J3	144	Throttle Switch	4/E6
110	Low Brake Fluid Sender	1/E7	145	Warm-Up Regulator	4/F5
		1a/E7	146	Wastegate Solenoid	4a/C6
111	Low Coolant Sender	1/B1			4b/C6
112	Low Oil Sender	1/F4	147	Windscreen Washer Pump	3/C7
113	Low Washer Fluid Sender	1/B8			3a/C7
114	Luggage Comp. Lamp	2/L3	148	Wiper Intermittent Relay 1980-86	3/C1
		2a/L3	149	Wiper Intermittent Relay 1986-89	3a/D1
115	Luggage Comp. Lamp Switch	2/M3	150	Wiper Intermittent Speed Control	3/F3
		2a/M3	151	Wiper Motor	1/E2
116	Luggage Comp. Lamp/Switch (cargo)	2/L2			1a/E2
		2a/L2			3/C4
117	Multifunction Switch	2/J4			3a/C4
		3/J4	152	Wiper Switch 1986-88	3a/K4
118	Oil Pressure Switch	1/F5	153	Wiper Switch 1988-89	3a/K4
		1a/F5			
119	Over Voltage Protection Device	4b/J3			
120	Overrun Shut Off Valve	4/C7			
121	Pressure Actuator	4b/F2			

Key to wiring diagrams continued.

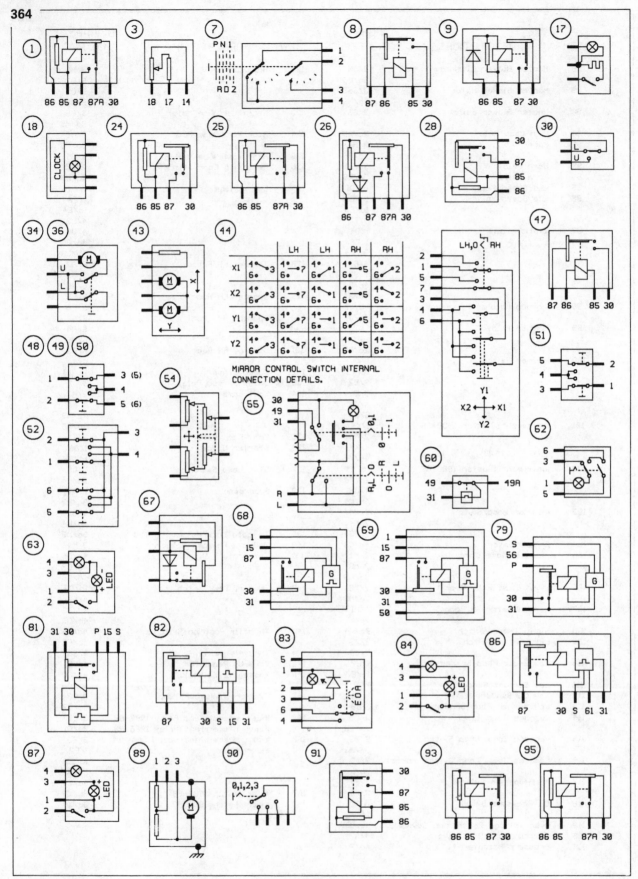

MIRROR CONTROL SWITCH INTERNAL
CONNECTION DETAILS.

Internal connection details all models.

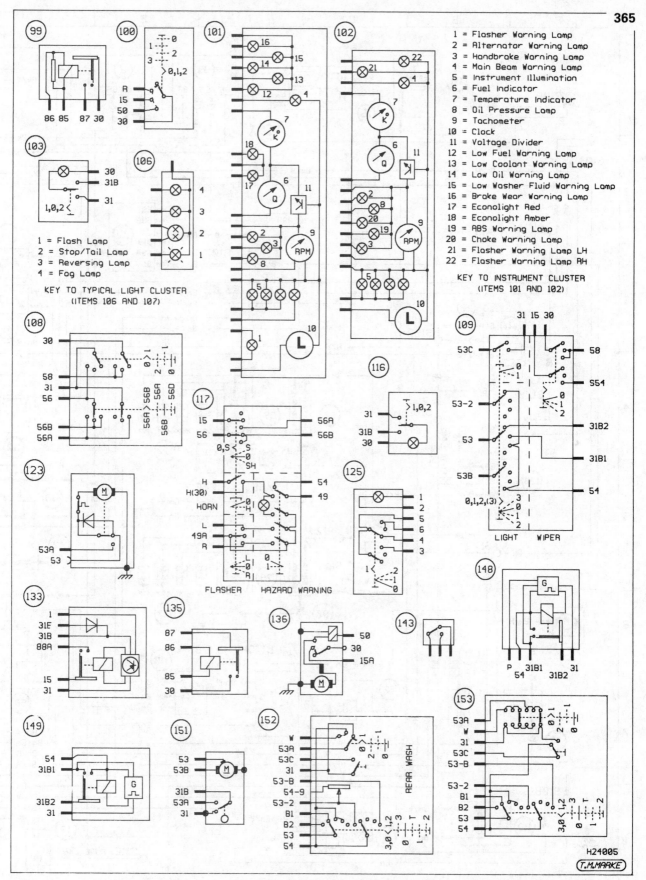

KEY TO TYPICAL LIGHT CLUSTER
(ITEMS 106 AND 107)

1 = Flash Lamp
2 = Stop/Tail Lamp
3 = Reversing Lamp
4 = Fog Lamp

1 = Flasher Warning Lamp
2 = Alternator Warning Lamp
3 = Handbrake Warning Lamp
4 = Main Beam Warning Lamp
5 = Instrument Illumination
6 = Fuel Indicator
7 = Temperature Indicator
8 = Oil Pressure Lamp
9 = Tachometer
10 = Clock
11 = Voltage Divider
12 = Low Fuel Warning Lamp
13 = Low Coolant Warning Lamp
14 = Low Oil Warning Lamp
15 = Low Washer Fluid Warning Lamp
16 = Brake Wear Warning Lamp
17 = Econolight Red
18 = Econolight Amber
19 = ABS Warning Lamp
20 = Choke Warning Lamp
21 = Flasher Warning Lamp LH
22 = Flasher Warning Lamp RH

KEY TO INSTRUMENT CLUSTER
(ITEMS 101 AND 102)

HORN

FLASHER   HAZARD WARNING

REAR WASH

LIGHT   WIPER

H24005

T.M.MARKE

Internal connection details all models continued.

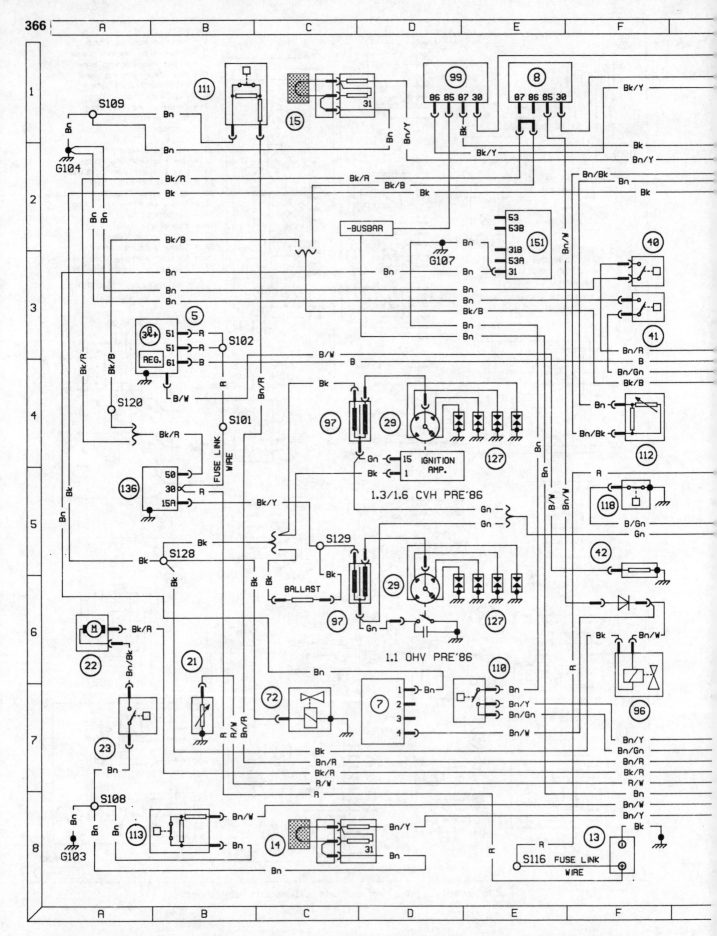

Diagram 1 : 1980-86 Starting , charging and ignition (except fuel injection) all models .

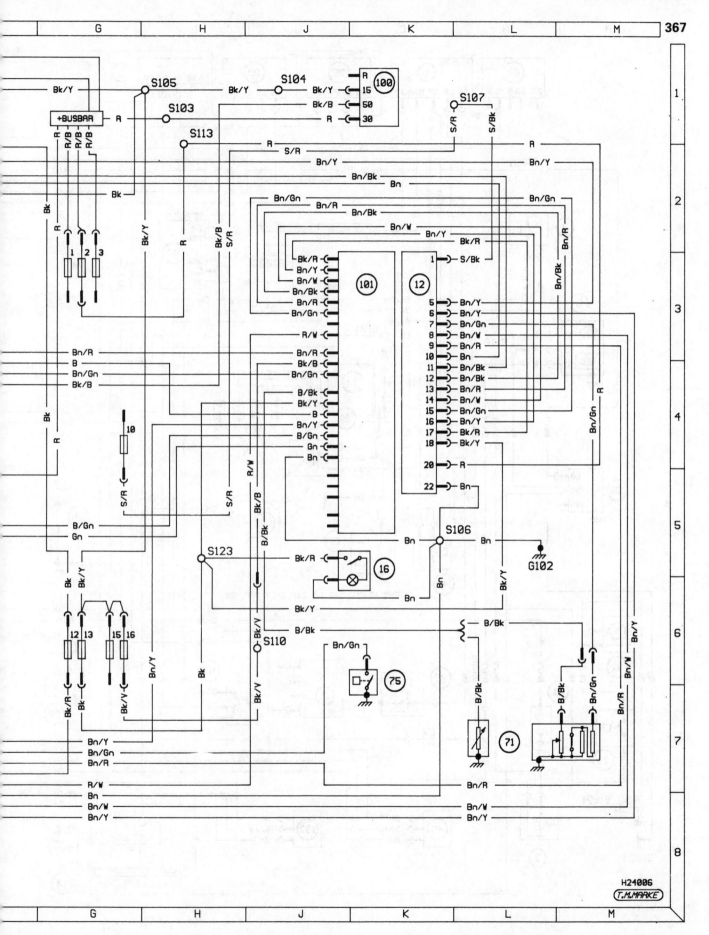

Diagram 1 continued .

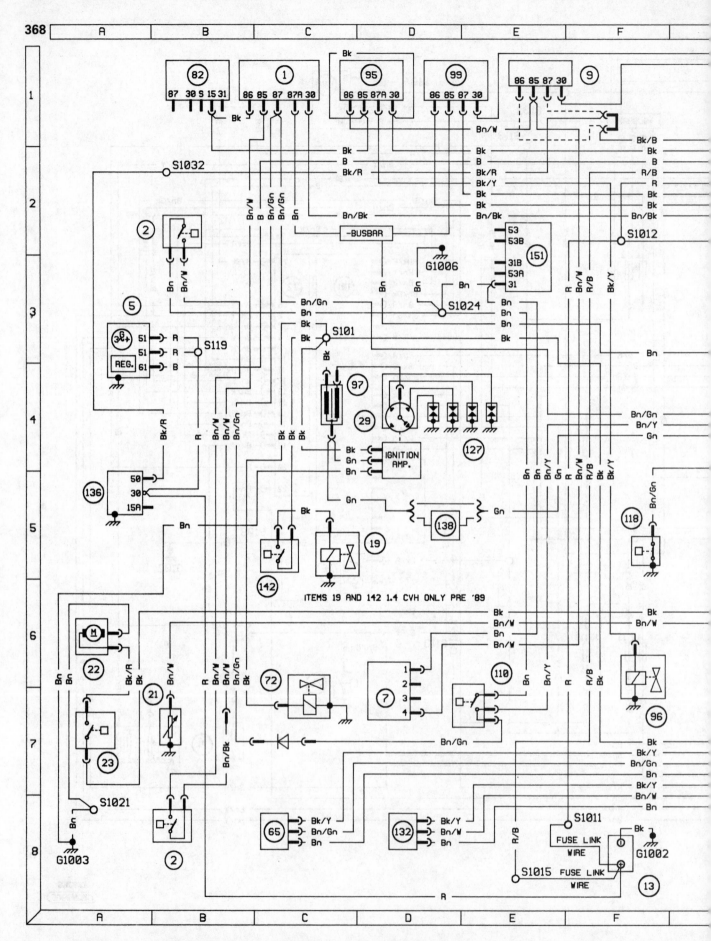

Diagram 1a : 1986-89 Starting , charging and ignition (except fuel injection) all models .

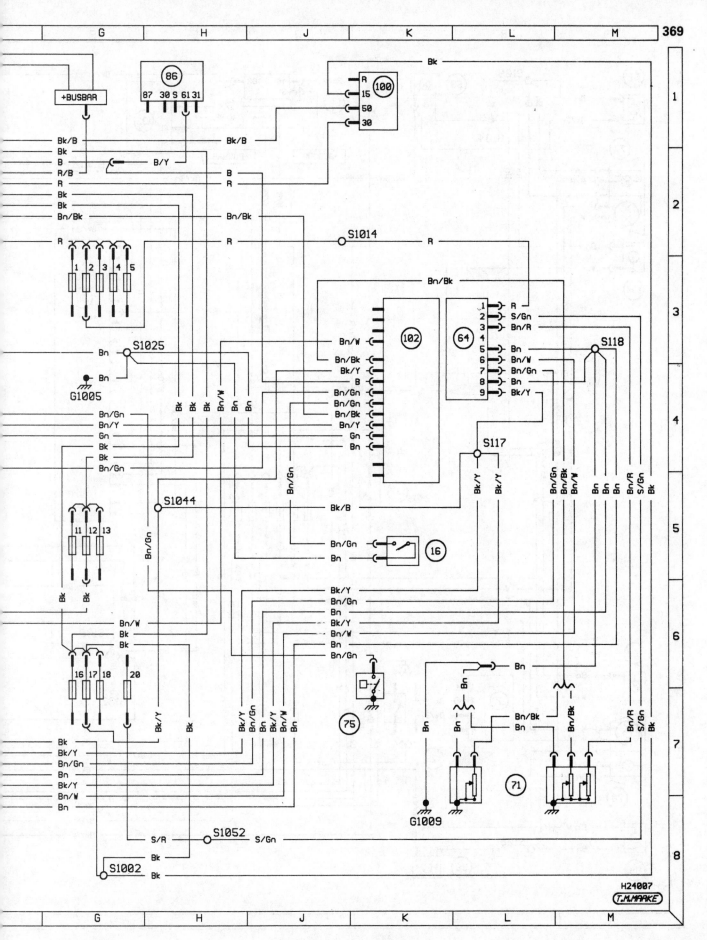

Diagram 1a continued .

H24007

T.M.MARKE

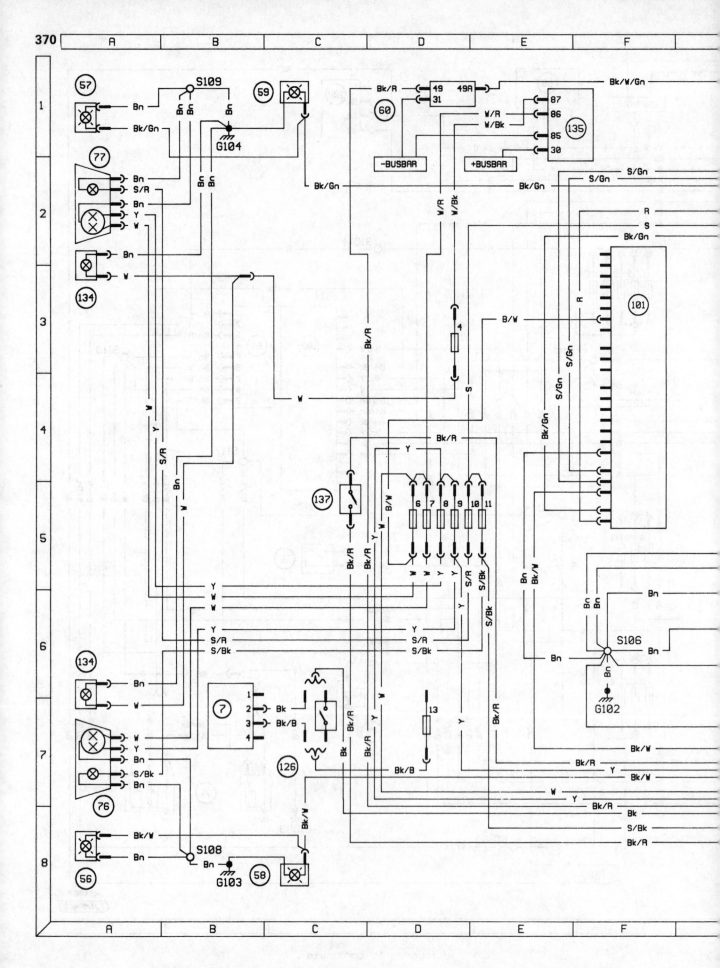

Diagram 2 : 1980-86 Lighting all models .

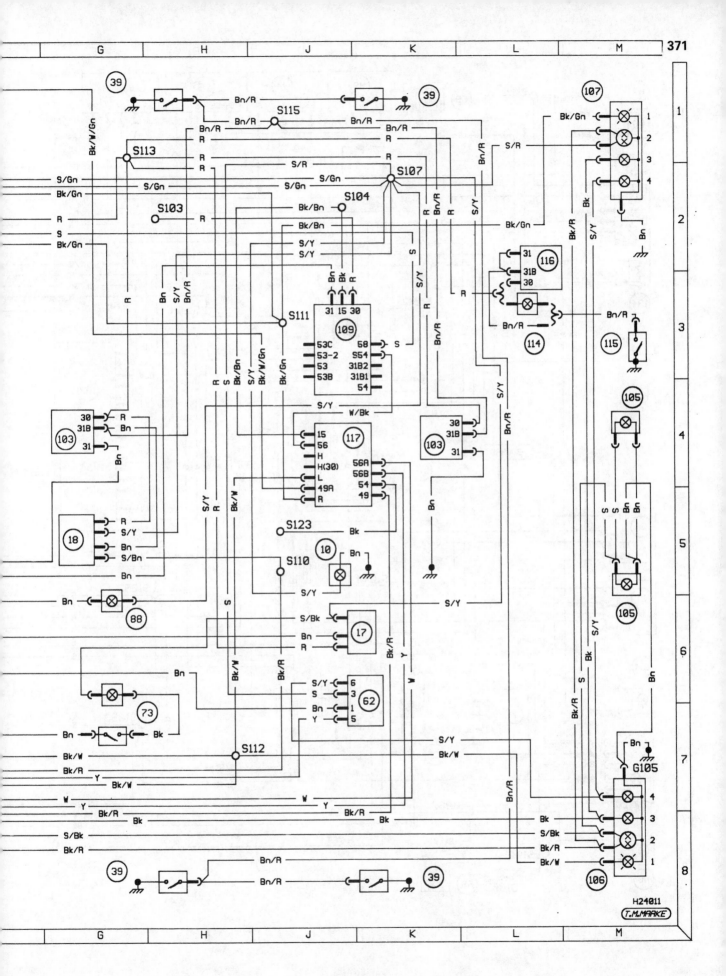

Diagram 2 continued .

H24011

T.M.MARKE

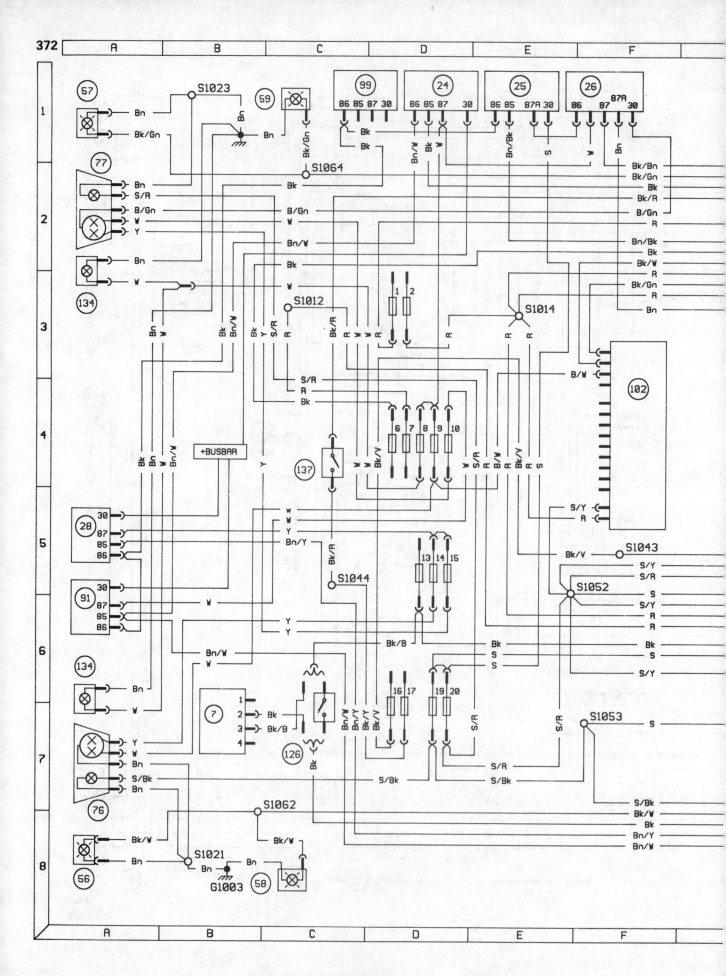

Diagram 2a : 1986-89 Lighting all models .

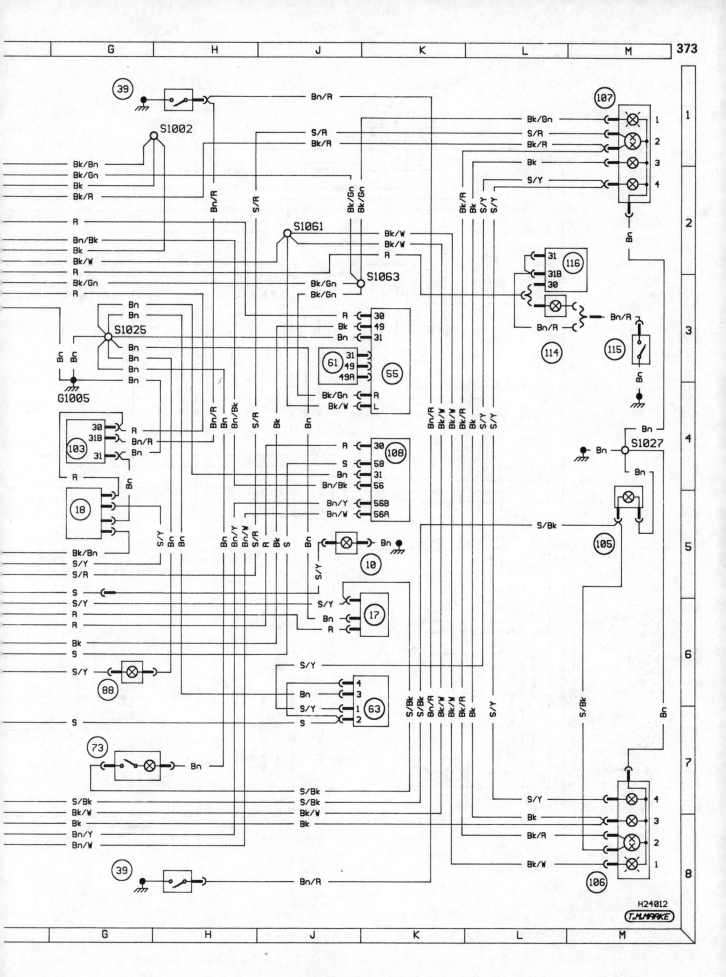

Diagram 2a continued .

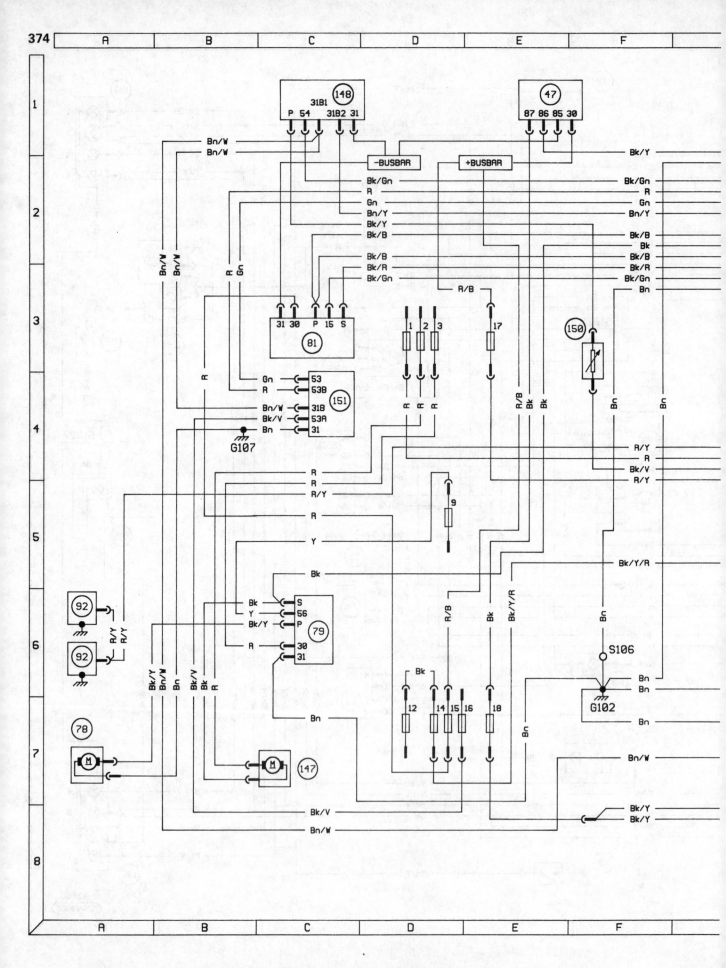

Diagram 3 : 1980-86 Ancillary circuits all models .

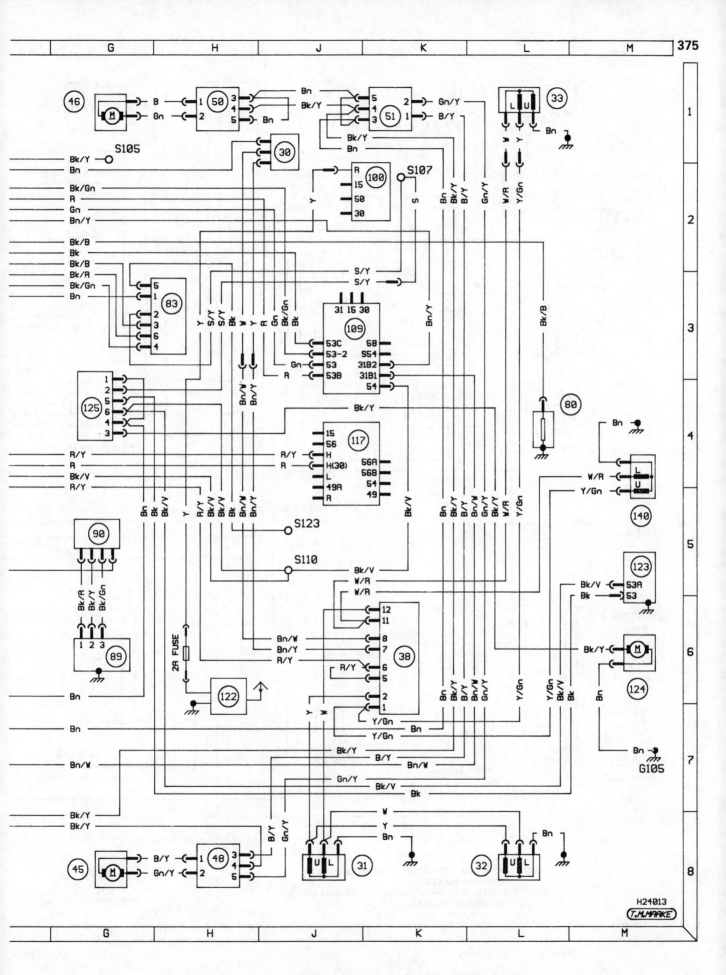

Diagram 3 continued .

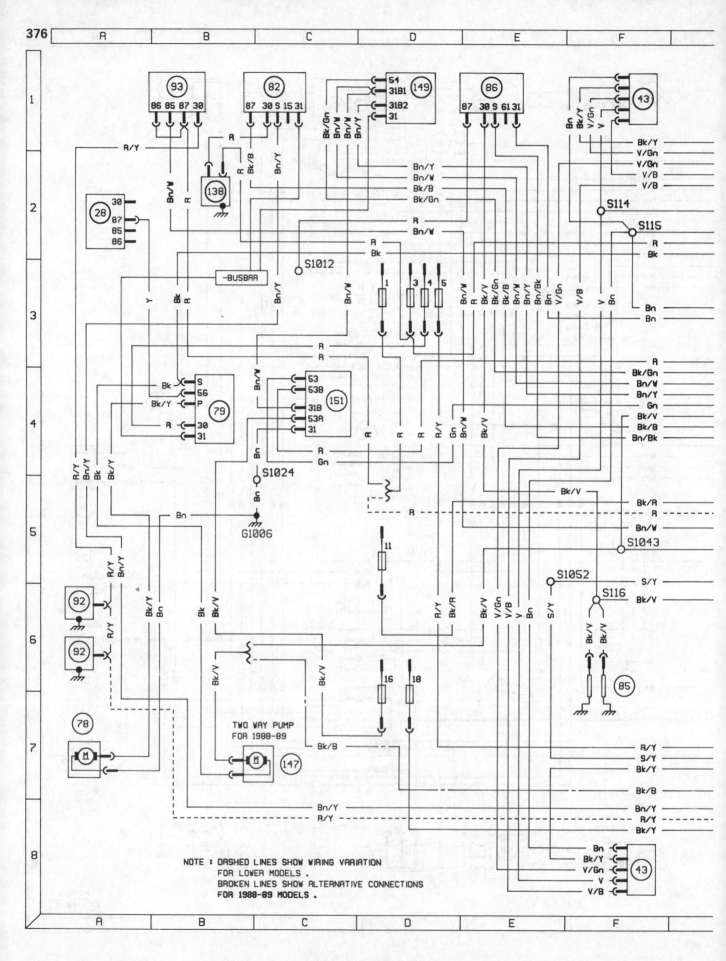

Diagram 3a : 1986-89 Ancillary circuits all models .

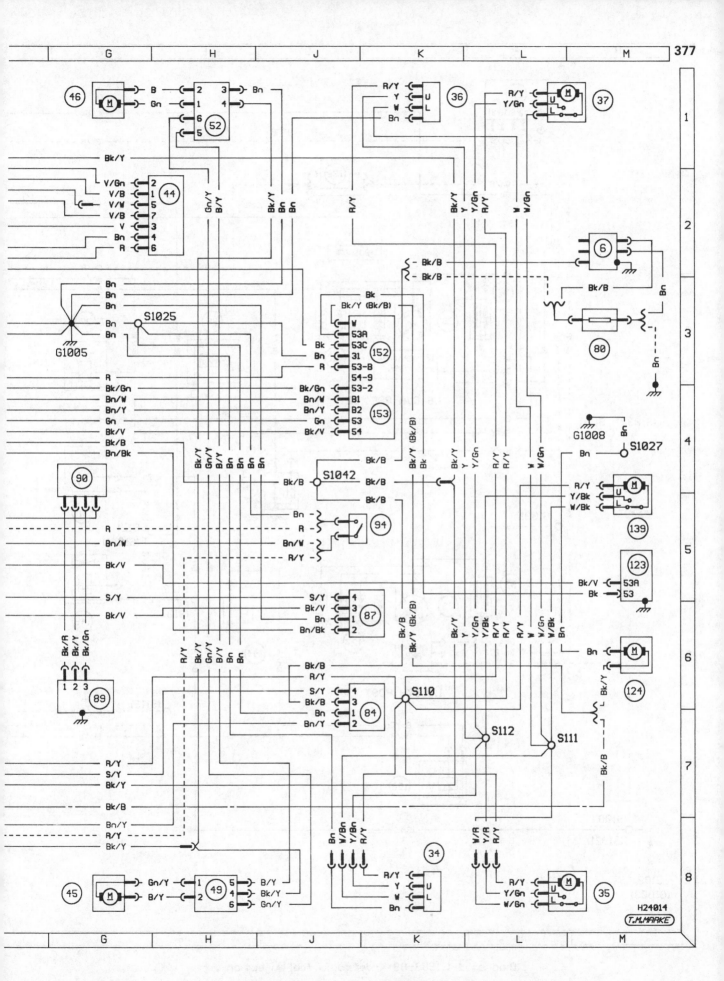

Diagram 3a continued .

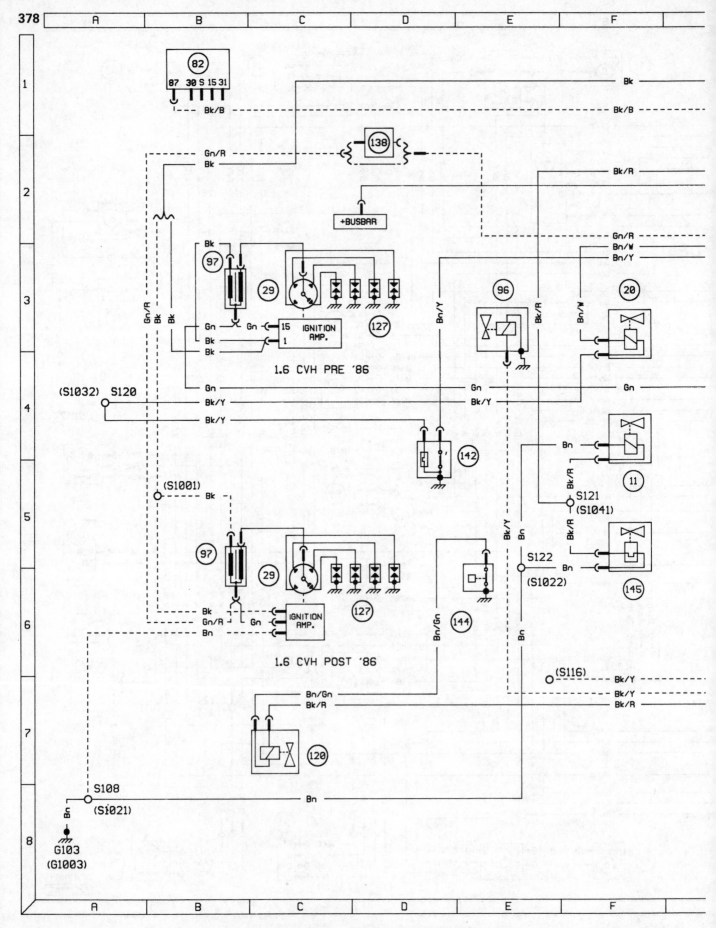

Diagram 4 : 1983-89 K-Jetronic fuel injection .

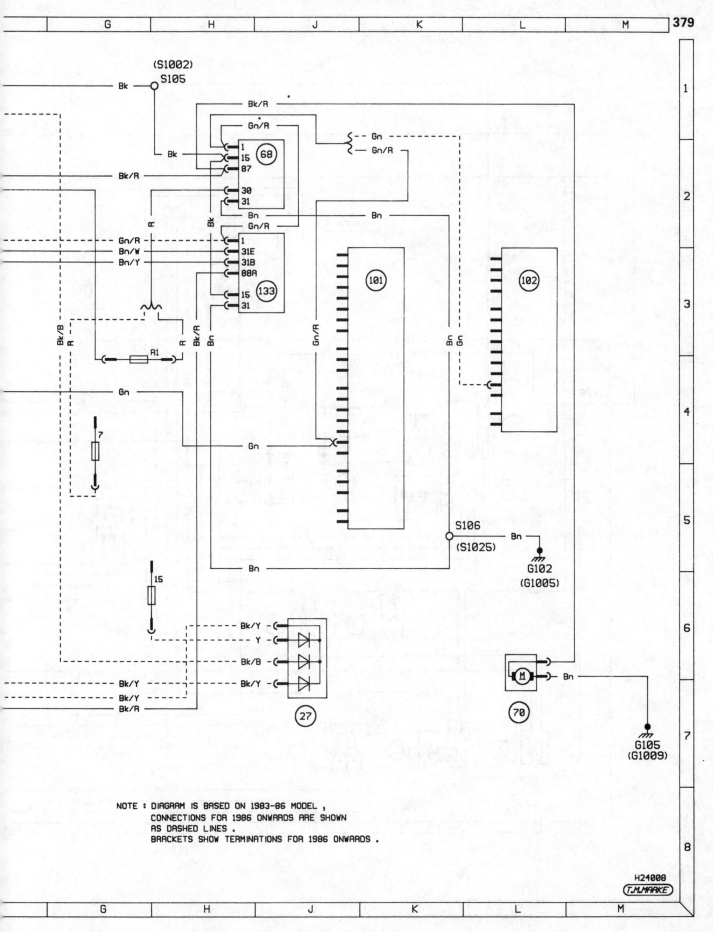

NOTE : DIAGRAM IS BASED ON 1983-86 MODEL ,
CONNECTIONS FOR 1986 ONWARDS ARE SHOWN
AS DASHED LINES .
BRACKETS SHOW TERMINATIONS FOR 1986 ONWARDS .

H24008
T.M.MARKE

Diagram 4 continued .

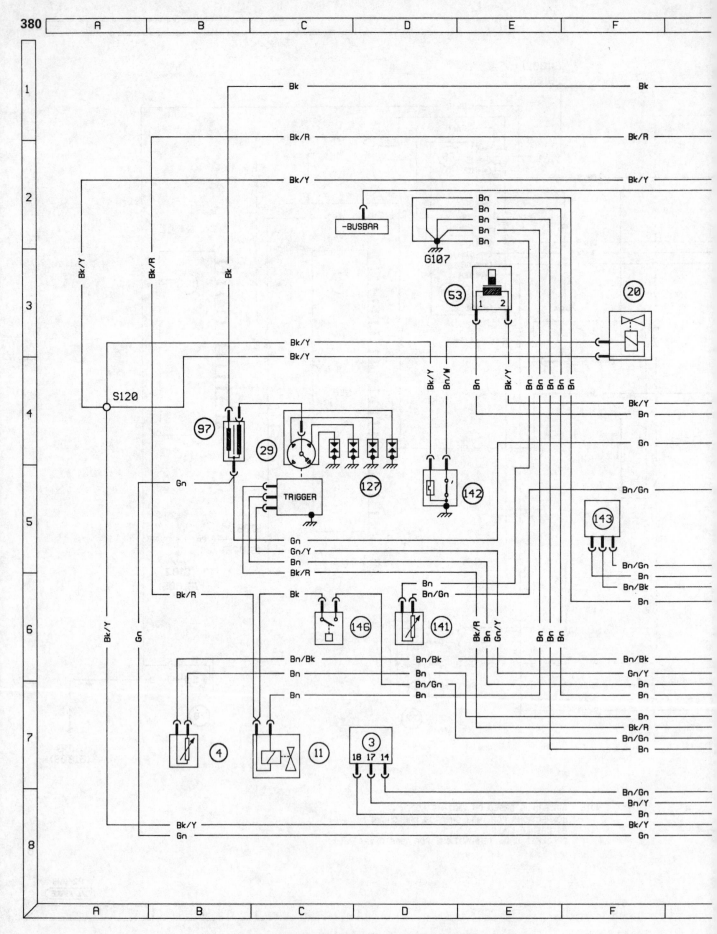

Diagram 4a : 1984-86 KE-Jetronic fuel injection .

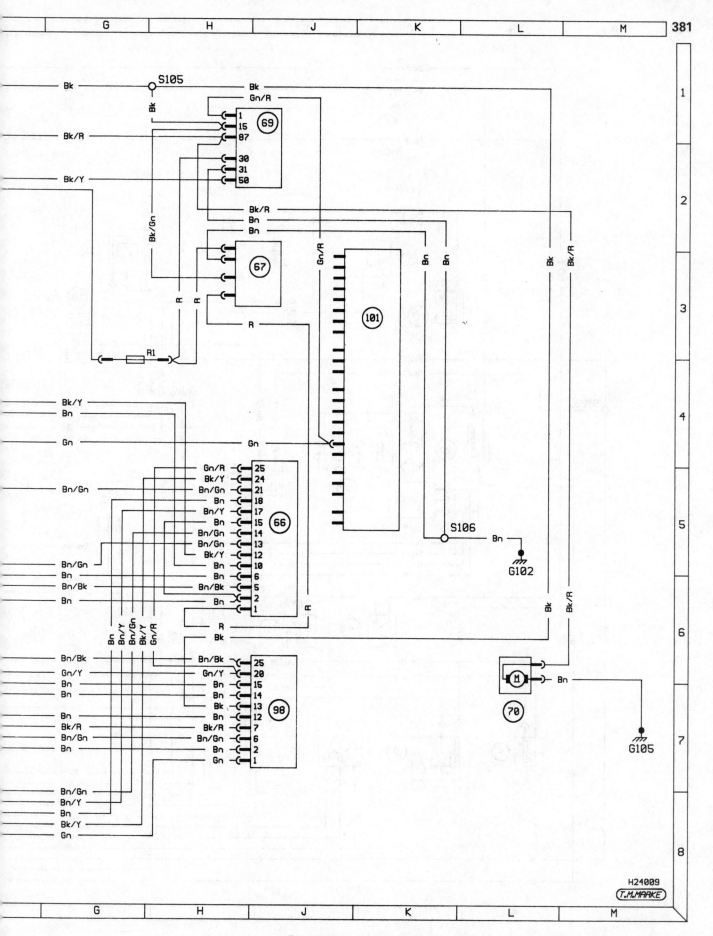

Diagram 4a continued .

H24009

T.M.MARKE

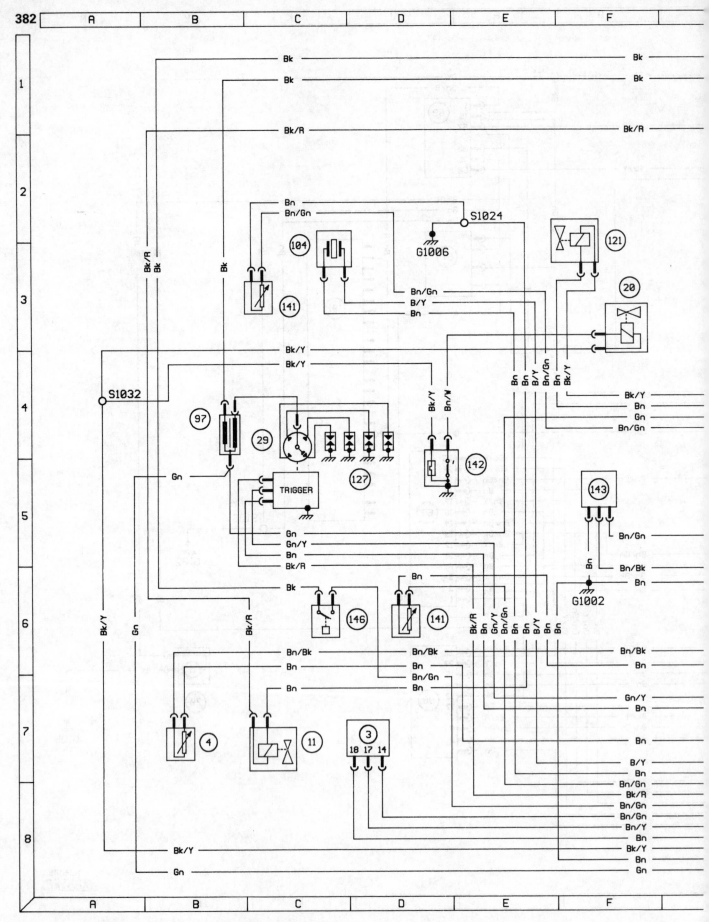

Diagram 4b : 1986-89 KE-Jetronic fuel injection .

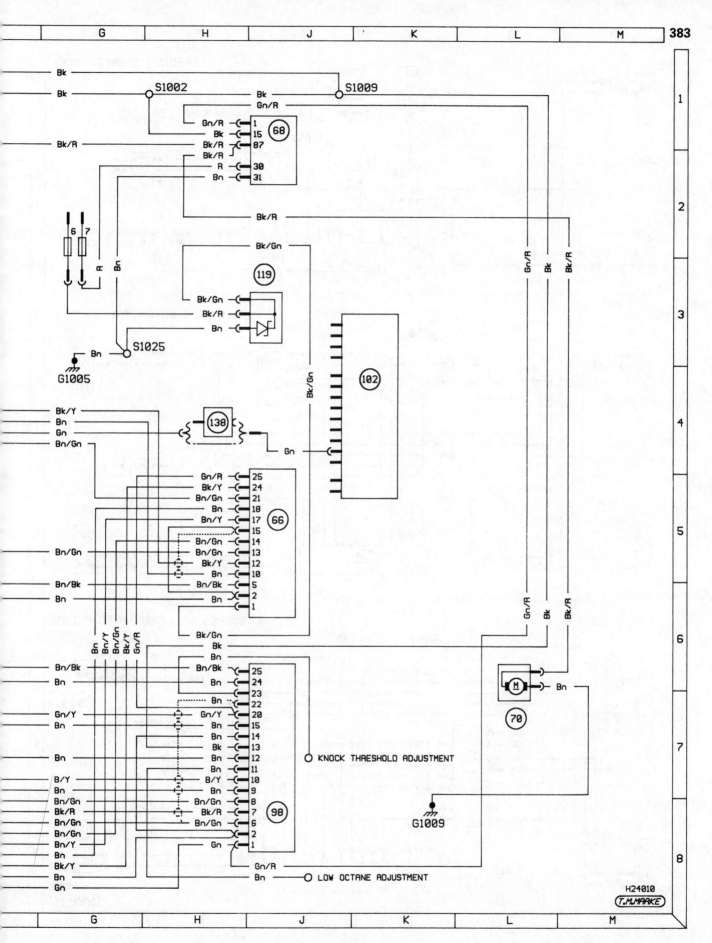

Diagram 4b continued .

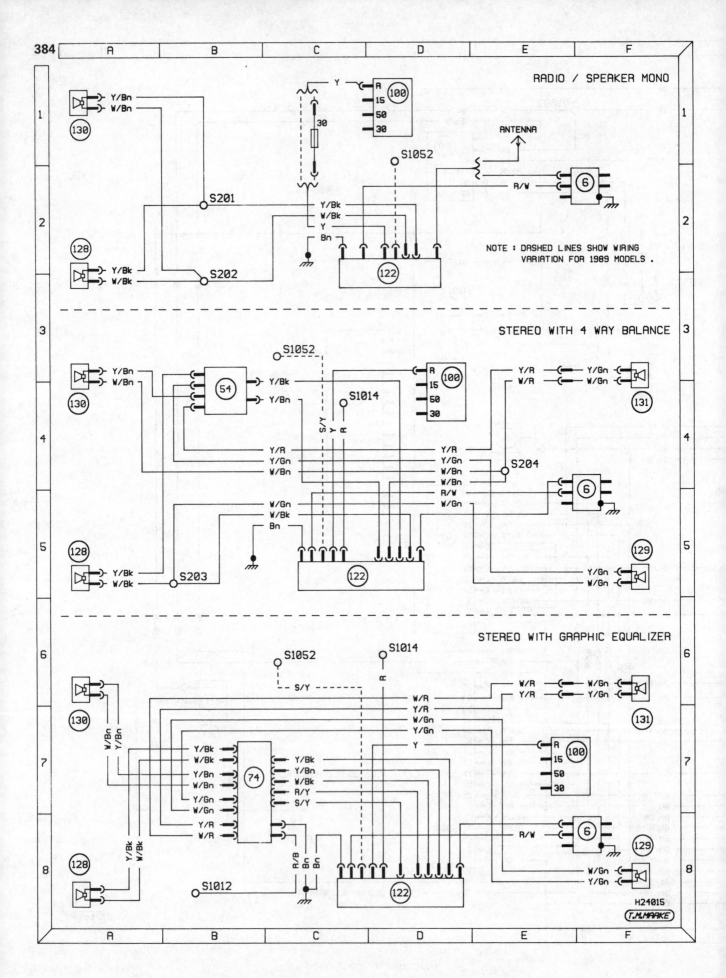

Diagram 5 : 1986-89 In car entertainment all models .

Chapter 13 Supplement:
Revisions and information on later models

Contents

1 Introduction

This Supplement contains information which is additional to, or a revision of, the information given in the first twelve Chapters.

The Sections in this Supplement follow the same order as the Chapters to which they relate. The Specifications are all grouped together at the beginning for convenience, but they too follow Chapter order.

It is recommended that before any work commences, reference is made to the appropriate Section(s) of this Supplement, in order to establish any changes to procedures or specifications, before reading the main Chapter(s).

The vehicle used in the preparation of this Supplement and appearing in many of the photographic sequences was a 1989 model Escort L, fitted with a 1.3 litre High Compression Swirl (HCS) engine.

2 Specifications

These Specifications are revisions of, or supplementary to, the Specifications given at the beginning of the preceding Chapters.

Engine – 1.1 and 1.3 HCS
(Specifications as for OHV engines given in Chapter 1 except for the following)

General

Designation	HC2V
Engine code:	
1.1	GUC
1.3	JBA
Capacity:	
1.1	1118 cc
1.3	1297 cc
Bore:	
1.1	68.68 mm (2.70 in)
1.3	73.96 mm (2.91 in)
Stroke	75.48 mm (2.97 in)
Compression ratio	9.5:1

Cylinder block

Number of main bearings	5
Cylinder bore diameter:	
1.1:	
Standard (1)	68.680 to 68.690 mm (2.7059 to 2.7063 in)
Standard (2)	68.690 to 68.700 mm (2.7063 to 2.7067 in)
Standard (3)	68.700 to 68.710 mm (2.7067 to 2.7071 in)
Oversize 0.5 mm	69.200 to 69.210 mm (2.7264 to 2.7268 in)
Oversize 1.0 mm	69.700 to 69.710 mm (2.7461 to 1.7465 in)
1.3	As for OHV engine in Chapter 1 but there is no 4th standard oversize

Crankshaft

Crankpin (big-end) diameter:	
Standard	40.99 to 41.01 mm (1.6150 to 1.6157 in)
0.254 mm undersize	40.74 to 40.76 mm (1.6051 to 1.6059 in)
0.508 mm undersize	40.49 to 40.51 mm (1.5933 to 1.5960 in)
0.762 mm undersize	40.24 to 40.26 mm (1.5854 to 1.5862 in)
Main bearing running clearance:	
1.1	0.009 to 0.046 mm (0.0003 to 0.0018 in)
1.3	0.009 to 0.056 mm (0.0003 to 0.002 in)
Big-end bearing running clearance	0.006 to 0.060 mm (0.0002 to 0.002 in)
Crankshaft endfloat	0.075 to 0.285 mm (0.0029 to 0.012 in)

Camshaft

Inlet cam lift:	
1.1	5.15 mm (0.202 in)
1.3	5.70 mm (0.224 in)
Exhaust cam lift:	
1.1	4.92 mm (0.193 in)
1.3	5.76 mm (0.226 in)
Inlet cam length:	
1.1	32.036 to 32.264 mm (1.262 to 1.271 in)
1.3	32.586 to 32.814 mm (1.283 to 1.292 in)
Exhaust cam length:	
1.1	31.806 to 32.034 mm (1.253 to 1.262 in)
1.3	32.646 to 33.874 mm (1.286 to 1.334 in)

Pistons

Diameter (1.1):	
Standard (1)	68.65 to 68.66 mm (2.7048 to 2.7052 in)
Standard (2)	68.66 to 68.67 mm (2.7052 to 2.7055 in)
Standard (3)	68.67 to 68.68 mm (2.7055 to 2.7059 in)
0.5 mm oversize	69.20 to 69.21 mm (2.7264 to 2.7268 in)
1.0 mm oversize	69.70 to 69.71 mm (2.7461 to 2.7465 in)

Connecting rod

Bore diameter:	
Big-end	43.99 to 44.01 mm (1.733 to 1.734 in)
Small-end	17.99 to 18.01 mm (0.708 to 0.795 in)
Connecting rod endfloat	0.10 to 0.25 mm (0.0039 to 0.0098 in)

Note: *the HC2V engine has four connecting rod weight classes, A, B, C and D stamped on the rod opposite the oil drilling*

Gudgeon pin
Pin length:
    1.1 .... 58.6 to 59.4 mm (2.308 to 2.340 in)
    1.3 .... 63.6 to 64.4 mm (2.505 to 2.537 in)
Pin diameter:
    White .... 18.026 to 18.029 mm (0.7102 to 0.7103 in)
    Red .... 18.029 to 19.032 mm (0.7103 to 0.7498 in)
    Blue .... 18.032 to 18.035 mm (0.7104 to 0.7105 in)
    Yellow .... 18.035 to 18.038 mm (0.7105 to 0.716 in)
Interference fit in connecting rod at 21°C (70°F) .... 0.013 to 0.048 mm (0.0005 to 0.0018 in)
Clearance in piston at 21°C (70°F) .... 0.008 to 0.014 mm (0.0003 to 0.0005 in)

Cylinder head
Minimum combustion chamber depth after skimming .... 14.4 ± 0.15 mm (0.567 ± 0.005 in)
Valve seat width .... 1.18 to 1.75 mm (0.046 to 0.068 in)
(**Note:** *No repair to valve seats using conventional tools is possible*)

Valves – general
Valve timing:
    1.1:
        Inlet opens .... 14° BTDC
        Inlet closes .... 46° ABDC
        Exhaust opens .... 49° BBDC
        Exhaust closes .... 11° ATDC
    1.3:
        Inlet opens .... 16° BTDC
        Inlet closes .... 44° ABDC
        Exhaust opens .... 51° BBDC
        Exhaust closes .... 9° ATDC
Valve clearances (cold):
    Inlet .... 0.22 mm (0.008 in)
    Exhaust .... 0.32 mm (0.012 in)
Valve spring free length .... 41.0 mm (1.615 in)

Inlet valve
Length .... 103.70 to 104.40 mm (4.085 to 4.113 in)
Head diameter:
    1.1 .... 32.90 to 33.10 mm (1.296 to 1.304 in)
    1.3 .... 34.40 to 34.60 mm (1.355 to 1.363 in)
Stem diameter:
    Standard .... 7.025 to 7.043 mm (0.276 to 0.277 in)
    0.76 mm oversize .... 7.225 to 7.243 mm (0.284 to 0.235 in)
    0.381 mm oversize .... 7.425 to 7.443 mm (0.292 to 0.293 in)
Valve stem clearance in guide .... 0.021 to 0.690 mm (0.0008 to 0.027 in)
Valve lift:
    1.1 .... 8.450 mm (0.332 in)
    1.3 .... 9.350 mm (0.368 in)

Exhaust valve
Length .... 104.02 to 104.72 mm (4.098 to 4.125 in)
Head diameter:
    1.1 .... 28.90 to 29.10 mm (1.138 to 1.146 in)
    1.3 .... 28.90 to 29.10 mm (1.138 to 1.146 in)
Stem diameter:
    Standard .... 6.999 to 7.017 mm (0.275 to 0.276 in)
    0.076 mm oversize .... 7.199 to 7.217 mm (0.283 to 0.284 in)
    0.381 mm oversize .... 7.399 to 7.417 mm (0.291 to 0.292 in)
Valve stem clearance in guide .... 0.043 to 0.091 mm (0.001 to 0.003 in)
Valve lift:
    1.1 .... 8.070 mm (0.317 in)
    1.3 .... 9.450 mm (0.372 in)

Torque wrench settings
As for OHV engine in Chapter 1 except for the following:

	Nm	lbf ft
Big-end bearing cap bolts:		
Stage 1	4	3
Stage 2	Tighten by a further 90°	Tighten by a further 90°
Crankshaft pulley bolt	100 to 120	74 to 89
Cylinder head bolts (M11 – necked):		
Stage 1	30	22
Stage 2	Tighten by a further 90°	Tighten by a further 90°
Stage 3	Tighten by a further 90°	Tighten by a further 90°

Fuel system

Air cleaner element .... Champion W225

Carburettor

Type .... Weber 2V TLDM
Application .... 1.1 and 1.3 HCS engines
Idle speed (fan on) .... 700 to 800 rpm
Idle mixture (CO content) .... 0.5 to 1.5%
Fast idle speed:
    1.1 .... 2800 rpm
    1.3 .... 2500 rpm
Float height .... 28.0 to 30.0 mm (1.10 to 1.18 in)

	Primary	Secondary
Venturi diameter	26	28
Main jet:		
1.1	92	122
1.3	90	122
Emulsion tube	F113	F75
Air correction jet:		
1.1	195	155
1.3	185	130

Fuel requirement

Fuel octane rating (HCS engines) .... 97 RON (leaded) or 95 RON (unleaded)

Ignition system – (HCS engines)

3-D Electronic ignition system 1989-on

Application .... 1.1 and 1.3 litre HCS engine
Type .... Fully electronic, distributorless ignition

Coil

Type .... High output
Output .... 37kV (minimum) open circuit
Primary resistance (measured at coil) .... 0.50 to 1.00 ohms

Spark plugs

Type .... Champion RS9YCC or RS9YC
Electrode gap .... 1.0 mm (0.040 in)
Firing order 1-2-4-3

HT Leads

Resistance .... 30 000 ohms maximum per lead

Clutch

Torque wrench setting

	Nm	lbf ft
Cover assembly to flywheel (all OHV engine models – 1987-on)	24 to 35	18 to 26

Driveshafts

CV joint lubricant type/specification .... Lithium-based grease to Ford specification A77SX 1C 9004 AA
(Duckhams LB 10)

Steering gear

Torque wrench setting

	Nm	lbf ft
Steering tie rod to steering rack (using locking fluid – see text)	72 to 88	53 to 65

Bodywork

Power operated roof fluid type/specification .... Brake hydraulic fluid to Ford specification SAM-6C-9103-A
(Duckhams Universal Brake and Clutch Fluid)

Torque wrench setting

	Nm	lbf ft
Hydraulic ram upper pivot stud (Cabriolet models)	16	12

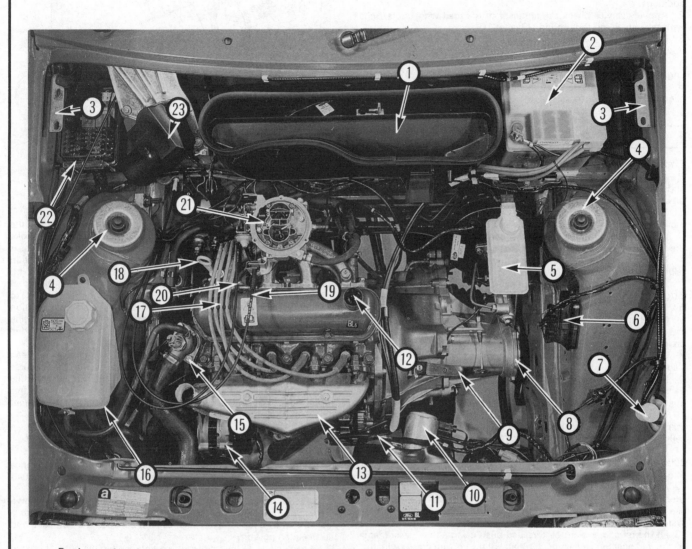

Engine and under bonnet component location on 1989 1.3 litre HCS model. (Air cleaner removed for clarity)

1 Ventilation air inlet duct
2 Battery
3 Bonnet hinge
4 Suspension strut upper
   mounting
5 Brake system fluid reservoir
6 Ignition system control unit
7 Windscreen washer reservoir
   filler cap
8 Transmission housing

9   Clutch release lever
10 Cooling fan motor
11 Starter motor
12 Engine oil filler neck
    (cap removed)
13 Exhaust manifold shield
14 Alternator
15 Coolant thermostat and
    fan thermal switch
16 Coolant expansion tank

17 Spark plug HT leads
18 Engine oil dipstick
19 Choke cable
20 Throttle cable
21 Carburettor
22 Fusebox
23 Windscreen wiper motor

3 Routine maintenance

1 The Routine Maintenance procedures given at the beginning of this manual are still applicable for 1989-on models, with the following additions.
2 At every service check the tightness of the road wheel nuts/bolts with the vehicle on the ground (Chapter 10).
3 On automatic transmission models only, check and adjust the downshift linkage every 6000 miles (Chapter 7).
4 On OHV and HCS engines, every 24 000 miles visually inspect the engine oil filler cap (see Section 4 of this Supplement).
5 At the same interval, on all models, check and adjust front wheel alignment (Chapter 10).

4 Engine

Engine oil cooler – general description

1 An engine oil cooler may be fitted to fuel injection, turbocharged and automatic transmission models (do not confuse with transmission oil cooler).
2 The cooler consists of a small heat exchanger type element mounted between the cylinder block and oil filter.
3 Oil passes through the heat exchanger, which is also connected to the cooling system by hoses.
4 Thus the coolant is used as the cooling medium, the heat transfer taking place in the heat exchanger.

Engine oil cooler – removal and refitting

5 Remove the engine oil filter (Chapter 1, Part B, Section 23).
6 Note the angle at which the coolant hoses are set, then disconnect the hoses and plug their ends to minimise coolant loss. If necessary, drain the coolant system as described in Chapter 2.
7 Using a ring spanner or socket, undo and remove the threaded sleeve.
8 Remove the oil cooler and its gasket.
9 Should the threaded bush come out with the threaded sleeve, or if it is removed for other reasons, it should be renewed.
10 Clean the threads of the female connection in the cylinder block, then commence refitting by screwing a new threaded bush into the cylinder block.
11 Apply Omnifit Activator 'Rapid' (to Ford Specification SSM-998-9000-AA) to the exposed threads of the bush and to the internal threads of the threaded sleeve.
12 Apply **one drop** of Omnifit Sealant '300 Rapid' (to Ford specification SSM-4G-9003-AA) to the threads of the bush. **Do not** use more than one drop, as there is risk of contaminating the oil system.
13 Fit the oil cooler over the threaded bush using a new gasket, and secure it in position (remember the angle of the coolant pipes) with the threaded sleeve, tightening it to the specified torque.
14 Fit the new oil filter (Chapter 1, part B, Section 23).
15 Reconnect the coolant hoses, top up the oil and coolant to their correct levels, and then run the engine to normal operating temperature and check for leaks. On completion, allow the engine to cool and recheck oil and coolant levels.

Timing belt and tensioner (1.4 and 1.6 CVH engines) – modification

16 From April 1988 (build code JG) a modified timing belt tensioner incorporating a larger diameter tensioner roller was introduced, and from October 1988 an improved timing belt is used. When renewal of the timing belt becomes necessary, only the latest, improved timing belt must be used (the older type will no longer be available). On models produced before April 1988 this will entail renewal of the tensioner roller.

Engine (1.1 and 1.3 HCS) – general description

17 The 1.1 and 1.3 litre High Compression Swirl (HCS) engines were introduced at the beginning of 1989 and fitted to certain 1.1 Escort models and all 1.3 Escort models, including the Van and Combi, replacing the previous OHV engine.
18 A further development of the Ford 'lean-burn' principle, the HCS engine is basically similar to the previous OHV engine, being of

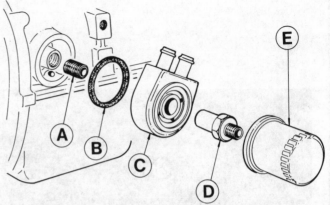

Fig. 13.1 Engine oil cooler assembly (Sec 4)

A   Threaded bush
B   Gasket
C   Oil cooler

D   Threaded sleeve
E   Oil filter

four-cylinder, in line OHV construction, but nearly every aspect of the engine has been re-designed. 1.1 litre versions have a longer stroke and five bearing crankshaft, but the major difference with both types is in the cylinder head, where the inlet valve ports and combustion chambers are designed to impart a high level of 'swirl' to the incoming fuel/air mixture. The valve arrangement is also different, being of 'mirror' design where the inlet valves of the centre cylinders are next to each other. Combined with the new 3-D fully electronic ignition system which has no moving parts, the result is an economical engine with cleaner exhaust emissions which can run on leaded or unleaded fuel without adjustment to the ignition system.
19 Although most components of the HCS engine have been redesigned, for the most part the servicing and overhaul procedures given in Chapter 1 for the OHV engine remain unchanged and only those differences affecting the procedures are given in this Supplement. Similarly, only those Specifications which are different are given at the front of this Supplement.

Cylinder head (1.1 and 1.3 HCS engine) – removal and refitting

20 The procedure is covered in Chapter 1 Section 5, but reference should be made to the relevant Section in this Supplement for details of disconnection/removal of individual components which differ.
21 Note the three stages for tightening the cylinder head bolts shown in the Specifications. This is applicable to M11 sized bolts with a necked shank (a reduced diameter section between the bolt head and the threaded portion).
22 At each stage all the bolts must be tightened in the order shown in Fig. 1.8 Chapter 1. **Note:** *Cylinder head bolts may be used a total of three times (including initial fit) and must be suitably marked to indicate each removal operation.*

Valve clearances (1.1 and 1.3 HCS engne) – adjustment

23 The procedure is as described in Chapter 1, Section 6 but note that the valve arrangement has been altered and is now as follows.

Valve No	Cylinder No
1 – Exhaust	1
2 – Inlet	1
3 – Exhaust	2
4 – Inlet	2
5 – Inlet	3
6 – Exhaust	3
7 – Inlet	4
8 – Exhaust	4

Engine (1.1 and 1.3 HCS) – method of removal

24 The engine can be lifted from the engine bay provided the radiator and certain other ancillary components are removed first to give room for manoeuvering. These are detailed in the removal procedure.
25 Before commencing work it will be necessary to make up two lifting eyes from $1/4''$ mild steel bar, approximately 3″ long and $1/2''$ wide, with two $1^1/2''$ holes drilled in them (photo).

Engine (1.1 and 1.3 HCS) – removal

26 Remove the bonnet as described in Chapter 11 Section 6, but additionally disconnect the earth lead between the bonnet and bodywork (photo).

27 Disconnect the battery negative lead.

28 Remove the air cleaner as described in Section 6 of this supplement.

29 Drain the engine oil (Chapter 1 Section 2).

30 Drain the coolant (Chapter 2 Section 3)

31 Remove the radiator (Chapter 2 Section 6) (photos).

32 Disconnect the heater hoses from the inlet manifold and the water pump.

33 Disconnect the lead at the anti-run-on valve solenoid on the carburettor.

34 Disconnect the throttle cable (See Section 6).

35 Disconnect the choke cable (see Section 6).

36 Disconnect the fuel inlet (blue clip) and outlet (green clip) pipes from the fuel pump (see Section 6).

37 Disconnect the brake servo vacuum hose from the inlet manifold by depressing the outer ring and pulling the hose out (photo).

38 Disconnect the earth lead from the inlet manifold.

39 Disconnect the following electrical connections;

    (a) *Cooling fan thermal switch on thermostat housing (photo)*
    (b) *Coolant temperature sender (photo)*
    (c) *Alternator*
    (d) *Ignition coil (see Section 7)*
    (e) *Oil pressure switch*
    (f) *Ignition thermal switch in inlet manifold (See Section 7)*
    (g) *Ignition TDC sender (see Section 7)*
    (h) *Reversing light switch (see Section 9)*
    (i) *Transmission housing earth lead*

4.25 A locally made-up lifting eye

4.26 Lifting off the bonnet

4.31A Radiator lower mounting bolt ...

4.31B ... and upper locating peg

4.31C Lifting out the radiator

4.37 Disconnecting the brake vacuum servo hose

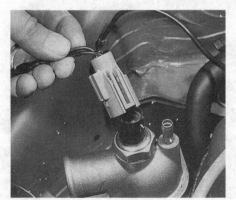

4.39A Disconnecting the cooling fan thermal switch ...

4.39B ... and coolant temperature sender

40 Disconnect the speedometer cable (photo).
41 Disconnect the exhaust downpipe from the exhaust manifold flange (photo). The nuts are easier to reach from underneath the vehicle and once undone support the exhaust on wire.
42 Disconnect the starter motor and engine earth lead which is under one of the starter motor bolts (Chapter 12 Section 12).
43 Remove the starter lead support bracket from the transmission housing.
44 Disconnect the gearchange mechanism (Chapter 6 Section 3).
45 Remove the driveshafts (Chapter 8 Section 5). **Note:** *On removal of the driveshafts push a length of wooden dowel into the hole vacated by the driveshaft in the transmission housing to prevent the sun gears of the differential becoming misaligned. A piece of broom handle is ideal, but will have to be turned down somewhat.*
46 Support the right-hand side of the engine on a trolley jack and just take the weight of the engine.
47 Remove the right-hand engine mounting by undoing the top nut on the wing panel, removing the bolt accessible from inside the wheel arch, and the three bolts securing the mounting bracket to the engine (photos).
48 Once removed, undo the Torx headed bolt securing the mounting to the bracket (photo).
49 Refit the bracket to the cylinder block and bolt one of the made-up lifting eyes to the bracket using one of the spare bolts (photo).
50 Fit the other lifting eye to the transmission housing (photo).
51 Secure suitable lifting gear to the engine and just begin to take the weight. **Note:** *If because of the angle of the lifting sling/chain the carburettor is likely to be damaged, remove the carburettor as described in Section 6.*
52 Remove the alternator (Chapter 12 Section 8) to give more room for manoeuvering the engine out.
53 Pull the transmission breather hose from inside the wing panel.
54 Remove the nut from the left-hand front engine mounting.
55 Remove the nut from the left-hand rear mounting and also remove the nuts securing the mounting bracket to the transmission housing and remove the bracket (photos).
56 Commence lifting the engine slowly, checking all round that everything has been disconnected and that the engine does not foul other components as it is lifted. Swing the engine and tilt it as necessary to clear obstacles (photos).
57 Once out of the engine bay, swing the engine clear and lower it onto a suitable work surface.
58 Remove the starter motor (Chapter 12 Section 12) and then separate the transmission from the engine (Chapter 1 Section 15).

Engine (1.1 and 1.3 HCS) – dismantling
59 Follow the procedure given in Chapter 1, Section 16, noting the following differences:
60 There is no coolant transfer pipe along the front of the engine.
61 Disconnect and remove the HT leads as described in Section 7.

62 There is no distributor to remove. The procedure for removal of the coil is given in Section 7.
63 The big-end cap bolts are Torx type bolts (photo).
64 Remove the ignition system TDC sender as described in Section 7 before removing the flywheel to prevent damage to the sender.
65 There are five main bearings, numbered 1 to 5 from the timing chain end. The caps have an arrow on them which points to the timing chain end (photo).
66 The crankshaft thrust bearings are still fitted either side of the centre main bearing.
67 The rear oil seal carrier is secured in place by Torx type bolts.

Engine (1.1 and 1.3 HCS) – examination and renovation
68 The procedure is as described in Chapter 1, Section 17.

Cylinder head and pistons (1.1 and 1.3 HCS engine) – decarbonising
69 The procedure is as described in Chapter 1, Section 18, noting the following.
70 When cleaning out the swirl ports, great care must be exercised not to damage the valve seats, especially if using power tools (photo).
71 The valve arrangement is different, being of mirror effect, where the inlet valves for number 2 and 3 cylinders are next to each other (photo).
72 When refitting the valve stem oil seals, tape the end of the stem to prevent damage to the seal as it is fitted, and use a double-depth socket or length of tube to push the seals fully down (photos). Remove the tape on completion.
73 The valve seats cannot be re-worked using conventional tools.

Engine (1.1 and 1.3 HCS) – reassembly
74 Following the procedure in Chapter 1, Section 19, noting the following.
75 Tighten the main bearing cap bolts to the specified torque (see Chapter 1) before fitting the oil pick-up tube.
76 When fitting the oil pick-up tube, use a spanner on the flats of the flange to line it up (photo).
77 The flywheel is dowelled to the crankshaft and cannot be fitted off-centre (photo).
78 The big-end bearing cap bolts are angle tightened after an initial torque load (see Specifications). Use the correct tool if it is available or make up a card template with the specified angle marked on it (photos).
79 Apart from lining up the camshaft and crankshaft sprocket timing marks (for valve timing), there is no ignition timing mark to worry about.

Engine (1.1 and 1.3 HCS) – refitting
80 The engine refitting procedure is a reversal of the removal procedure given earlier.

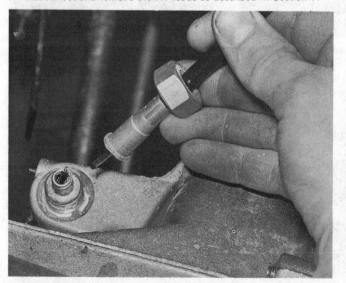

4.40 Disconnecting the speedometer cable

4.41 View of the exhaust downpipe from below

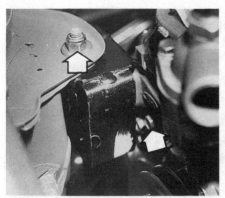

4.47A Right-hand engine mounting nuts/bolts (arrowed)

4.47B One bolt (arrowed) is accessible from within the wheel arch

4.48 Torx headed bolt (arrowed) securing the mounting to the bracket

4.49 Lifting eye bolted to right-hand mounting position ...

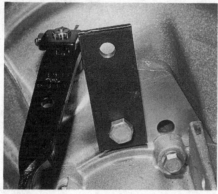

4.50 ... and on transmission housing

4.55A Mounting nut location A and bracket-to-transmission housing nuts B

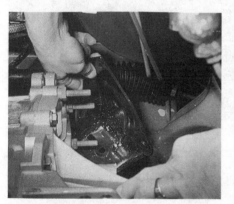

4.55B Removing the mounting bracket

4.56A Lifting the engine and transmission upwards ...

4.56B ... and out of the engine compartment

4.63 Big-end cap bolts are Torx type bolts

4.65 Crankshaft laid in position

4.70 View of the swirl chamber in the cylinder head showing the valve seats (arrowed)

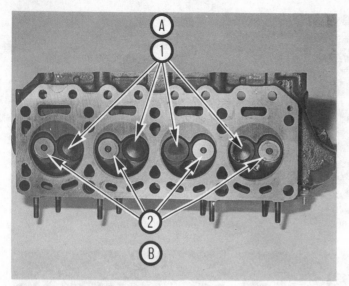

4.71 View of the cylinder head with valves fitted

A   Inlet side
B   Exhaust side
1   Inlet valves
2   Exhaust valves

4.72A Tape the end of the valve stem before fitting the valve stem seal

4.72B Using a double-depth socket to push the seal fully home

4.76 Line up the flange using a spanner

4.77 Fitting the flywheel to the crankshaft

4.78A Using the correct tool ...

4.78B ... and utilising a card template to angle tighten the big-end cap bolts

5 Cooling system

Water pump (1.1 and 1.3 HCS engine) – removal and refitting

1   The water pump is of slightly different design to that shown in Chapter 2, there being no transfer tube along the front of the engine and the outlet elbow being straight (photo).

2   Removal and refitting procedures remain the same as described in Chapter 2, Section 8.

6 Fuel system

Weber 2V DFTM carburettor (1.4 litre CVH engine) – refitting

1   When refitting this type of carburettor, the lead for the anti-run-on valve should be removed from the metal clip which secures it to the carburettor body, re-routed as shown in Fig. 13.3, and taped to the vacuum hose.

2   The metal clip should be discarded, and the securing screw refitted to the carburettor body, ensuring it is fully tightened.

Fuel pump (1.1 and 1.3 HCS engine)

3   The fuel pump on HCS engines has three connections and not two as on previous OHV units (photo).

4   The additional hose is the fuel return to the tank which was previously fitted on the carburettor, but is not used on the Weber 2V TLDM carburettor.

5   With this in mind, removal and refitting procedures are as described in Chapter 3, Section 7.

Throttle cable (1.1 and 1.3 HCS engine) – removal and refitting

6   To disconnect the cable for carburettor removal release the cable barrel end fitting from the throttle lever then remove the single bolt from the cable support bracket assembly (photo).

7   To disconnect the cable for renewal (as described in Chapter 3, Section 10), disconnect the cable from the throttle lever, pull out the securing clip from the support assembly (B in photo 6.6) and release the cable from the bracket.

8   Refit in reverse order.

Choke cable (1.1 and 1.3 HCS engine) – removal, refitting and adjustment

9   The procedure is as described in Chapter 3, Section 12 except that to disconnect the cable from the carburettor release the outer cable securing clamp and unhook the cable end fitting from the choke lever (photo).

5.1 View of the modified water pump with straightened elbow fitted to HCS engines

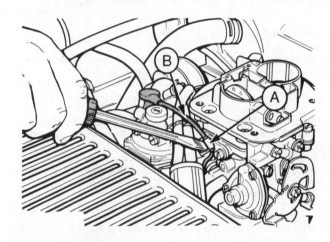

Fig. 13.2 Removing the metal cap (A) securing the lead (B) for the anti-run-on valve (Sec 6)

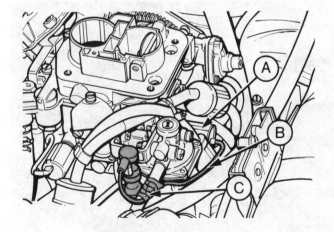

Fig. 13.3 Correct routing of the anti-run-on valve lead (Sec 6)

A   Anti-run-on valve
B   Lead
C   Lead taped to vacuum hose

Air cleaner filter element (1.1 and 1.3 HCS engine) – renewal

10 The procedure is as described in Chapter 3, Section 3, but only two screws secure the lid.

Air cleaner assembly (1.1 and 1.3 HCS engine) – removal and refitting

11 Remove the filter assembly as described earlier then unclip the fuel trap and vacuum hoses (part of the ignition system), from the side of the cleaner (photo).
12 Lift the air cleaner sufficiently to enable the crankcase ventilation hoses to be disconnected (see later paragraphs) then withdraw the assembly. Refit in reverse order.

Carburettor (Weber 2V TLDM) – general description

13 The Weber 2V TLDM carburettor is fitted to the 1.1 and 1.3 litre HCS engine and is very similar to the Weber 2V carburettor fitted to 1.4 and 1.6 CVH models.
14 It is a twin venturi, manual choke carburettor. The secondary venturi has a vacuum operated inhibitor which prevents the secondary venturi opening until the engine has reached normal operating temperature.
15 The carburettor is fitted with a new idle circuit, a power valve for high speed enrichment and an electrically operated anti-run-on valve. Carburettors for the UK market have no throttle kicker.

Carburettor (Weber 2V TLDM) – idle speed and mixture adjustment

16 Idle speed and mixture adjustment is the same as described in Chapter 3, Section 14, but the different adjustment screw locations are shown in photo 6.16. Note also that an Allan key is required to adjust the idle mixture screw (photo).

Carburettor (Weber 2V TLDM) – fast idle adjustment

17 Prepare the engine as described in Chapter 3, Section 14 paragraphs 1 to 6 then proceed as follows.
18 Remove the air cleaner assembly as described earlier.
19 Hold the choke valve fully open, start the engine and check the engine speed.
20 Adjust as necessary on the fast idle speed screw (photo).
21 Turning the screw anti-clockwise increases the fast idle speed, turning it clockwise decreases the speed.
22 On completion stop the engine, remove test equipment and refit the air cleaner.

Carburettor (Weber 2V TLDM) – removal and refitting

23 Disconnect the battery negative terminal.
24 Remove the air cleaner as described earlier.
25 Disconnect the throttle and choke cables as described in earlier paragraphs.
26 Disconnect the fuel inlet hose. If crimped connections are used cut them off and renew them with screw type clips.
27 Disconnect the lead at the anti-run-on valve solenoid (photo).
28 Remove the four Torx type through bolts securing the carburettor to the inlet manifold (photo).
29 Lift off the carburettor (photo).
30 Refit in reverse order using a new flange gasket (photo).
31 On completion check the idle speed and mixture settings as described earlier.

Carburettor (Weber 2V TLDM) – overhaul

32 The procedure is basically as described in Chapter 3, Section 25 (1.6 litre models, 1986-on) but use the specifications in the front of this Supplement and note the following differences.
33 The secondary venturi vacuum unit is mounted on the choke assembly bracket and is removed with the choke assembly after disconnection of the vacuum hose (photo).
34 The fuel inlet filter is a different arrangement and is inside the fuel inlet union (photo).

Operation on unleaded fuel – general

35 Continous operation on unleaded fuel requires specially hardened valve seat inserts, and in some cases the ignition timing needs adjusting to prevent detonation or 'pinking'.
36 All models with HCS engines can run on leaded or unleaded fuel without the need for any engine adjustment.
37 For all other models owners wishing to run their vehicles on unleaded fuel are advised to consult their Ford dealer for details of engine suitability, and of any ignition timing adjustment which may be required.

Crankcase ventilation system (1.1 and 1.3 HCS engine) – general

38 The crankcase ventilation system on HCS engines consists of two hoses, one from the engine oil filler cap and one from the crankcase, connected through an adaptor to the underside of the air cleaner element (photos).
39 Servicing consists of periodically cleaning out the hoses and the filter mesh in the oil filler cap (photo).
40 Renew the O-ring seal in the filler cap if it becomes damaged or worn.

6.3 Fuel pump connections on HCS engines

A   Inlet from tank   C   Return to tank
B   Outlet to carburettor

6.6 Throttle cable support bracket on 1.3 litre HCS engine

A   Securing bolt
B   Securing clip

6.9 Choke cable outer cable clamp (A) and end fitting (B) on 1.3 litre HCS engine

6.11 Fuel trap on side of air cleaner housing on 1.3 litre HCS engine

6.16 Idle speed screw (A) and mixture adjustment screw (B) on Weber 2V TLDM carburettor

6.20 Fast idle speed screw on Weber 2V TLDM carburettor (arrowed)

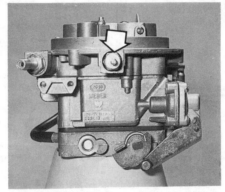

6.27 Anti-run-on valve on Weber 2V TLDM carburettor (arrowed)

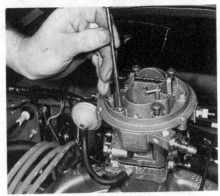

6.28 Removing the four Torx bolts on the Weber 2V TLDM carburettor

6.29 Lifting off the carburettor

6.30 Fitting a new flange gasket

6.33 Choke assembly mounting screws (arrowed) on Weber 2V TLDM carburettor

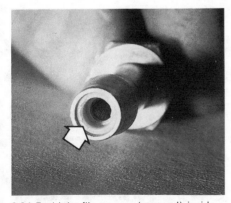

6.34 Fuel inlet filter gauze (arrowed) inside fuel inlet union

6.38A Engine oil filler cap and ventilation hose on 1.3 HCS engine

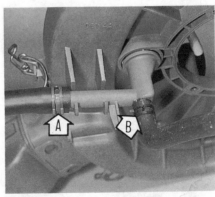

6.38B Adaptor on underside of air cleaner housing
      A   Hose from oil filler cap
      B   Hose from crankcase

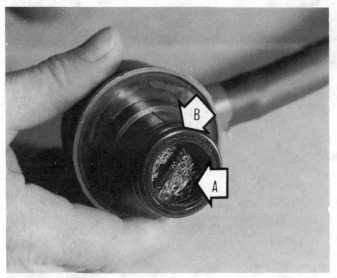

6.39 Oil filler cap on 1.3 HCS engine
A *Filter mesh*   B *O-ring seal*

7 Ignition system

3-D Electronic ignition system – general description

1   A fully electronic ignition system is fitted to all HCS engines.
2   The '3-D' system is so called because it computes a three-dimensional map of 256 calibration points drawing information from three sources – engine vacuum (load), engine speed, and spark advance. These form the X, Y and Z axis of the 3-D map.
3   The ESC module (control unit), mounted on the left-hand inner wing panel, monitors engine load, speed and operating temperature and computes the correct degree of spark advance under all engine operating conditions (photo).
4   Engine speed is monitored through the speed sensor mounted on the cylinder block, facing the flywheel. The sensor is 'triggered' by cut-outs in the flywheel. A larger cut-out in the flywheel denotes 90° BTDC for No 1 cylinder (photos).
5   As speed increases, so does the frequency and amplitude of the signal sent to the ESC module.
6   Engine load is monitored by a vacuum hose between the inlet manifold and the ECS module (photo).
7   Engine temperature is monitored through a thermal sender screwed into the bottom of the inlet manifold and connected electrically to the ESC module.
8   A DIS coil assembly is mounted on the cylinder block by number one cylinder. The coil has two primary and two secondary windings. It is connected to the battery and ESC module via a three pin plug.
9   The HT leads connect to the coil by 'quick-fit' type plugs and to the spark plugs by conventional connectors.
10 One coil supplies current to numbers 1 and 4 cylinders simultaneously, the other to 2 and 3 cylinders. Whenever either of the coils is energised, two sparks are released. One is routed (for instance) to number 1 cylinder on compression stroke, the other to number 4 cylinder on exhaust stroke. This spark is 'redundant' and has no detrimental effect on combustion.

3-D Electronic ignition system – servicing and overhaul

Warning: *Electronic ignition systems carry very much higher voltages when working on such systems. Refer to the Safety First Section at the beginning of this manual and always disconnect the battery negative terminal before working on any part of the system.*
11 No routine maintenance is required on the 3-D ignition system, there being no moving parts, apart from spark plug inspection, adjustment and renewal (see Chapter 4, Section 10 and later paragraphs of this Section).
12 Because of the need for specialist equipment to test the system and diagnose faults, the help of a Ford dealer will have to be sought should a fault occur.

3-D Electronic ignition system – component renewal

ESC module (control unit)
13 Disconnect the vacuum hose from the module.
14 Undo the central retaining bolt and pull out the multi-connector (photos).
15 Remove the screws securing the module to the left-hand inner wing panel and withdraw the module (photo).
16 Refit in reverse order.
DIS coil
17 Pull back the wire clip and pull off the multi-plug (photo).
18 Compress the clips on the side of each HT lead connection and remove the HT leads (photo).
19 Unscrew the three Torx screws securing the coil to the cylinder block and withdraw the unit (photo).
20 Refit in reverse order, pushing the HT lead connections firmly back into place (photo).
Engine speed sensor
21 Disconnect the electrical connection from the sensor (photo).
22 Remove the securing screw and withdraw the sensor (photo).
23 Refit in reverse order.
Engine temperature sensor
24 Drain the cooling system as described in Chapter 2, Section 3.
25 Disconnect the plug from the sensor.
26 Unscrew the sensor from the bottom of the inlet manifold (photo).
27 Refit in reverse order, being careful not to overtighten the sensor in the aluminium manifold. Refill the cooling system as described in Chapter 2 on completion.
Fuel trap
28 A fuel trap is fitted in the vacuum hose between the inlet manifold and the ESC module (see also Section 6).
29 When refitting a fuel trap, the side marked DIST faces the ESC module and the side marked CARB faces the inlet manifold.
Spark plugs
30 The spark plugs themselves are conventional and should be inspected and adjusted, the gap being set to that shown in the Specifications at the beginning of this Supplement, and renewed, at the intervals given in the Routine maintenance Section.
31 Disconnect the HT leads by pulling on the rubber cover and not on the lead (photo).
32 Brush out the spark plug recesses in the cylinder head.

7.3 3-D Electronic ignition system ESC module

7.4A Engine speed sensor mounted on cylinder block (engine removed for clarity)

7.4B The cut-outs in the flywheel – larger cut-out arrowed

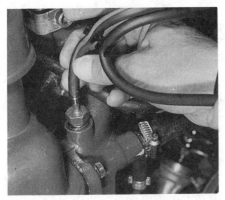

7.6A Vacuum connection on inlet manifold ...

7.6B ... and ESC module

7.14A Undoing central retaining bolt on ESC module multi-connector ...

7.14B ... and withdrawing the connector

7.15 ESC module securing screws (arrowed)

7.17 Showing wire clip on coil multi-plug

7.18 Compress the clips (arrowed) and pull off the HT lead connections (coil removed for clarity)

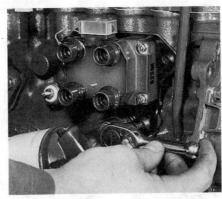

7.19 Removing the coil (engine removed for clarity)

7.20 Push the HT lead connections firmly back in place

7.21 Disconnecting the plug from the sensor

7.22 Sensor and securing screw

7.26 Engine temperature sensor screwed into bottom of inlet manifold

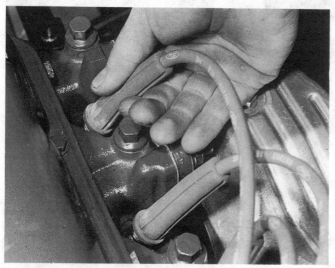

7.31 Disconnecting an HT lead from a spark plug

33 Use a double depth socket and ratchet to remove each plug in turn.
34 Refit in reverse, starting each plug off in its thread by hand to avoid cross threading them.

8 Clutch

Clutch (1.6 models, 1988-on) – Low-lift

1 From May 1988, 1.6 models are fitted with a 'Low-lift' clutch assembly. This simply means that the internal components have been modified resulting in reduced pressure plate lift.
2 The components of the 'Low-lift' clutch are not interchangeable with 'High-lift' clutches and the clutch driven plate and pressure plate are stamped, 'Low-lift' for identification.

Clutch fork (June 1988-on) – removal and refitting

3 From June 1988 (build code JC), all models are fitted with a one piece clutch fork assembly (photo).
4 These components are not interchangeable with earlier versions.
5 To remove a one piece fork assembly proceed as follows.
6 Remove the transmission as described in Chapter 6.
7 Undo and remove the pinch bolt and then lift off the release lever (photo).
8 Remove the rubber cover from the end of the shaft.
9 Remove the nylon bush (photo).
10 Remove the release bearing (photo).
11 Lift the fork assembly from the lower bearing then lower it out of the bellhousing (photo).
12 Refit in reverse order using a little lithium based grease on all pivot points.

8.3 One-piece clutch fork *in-situ*

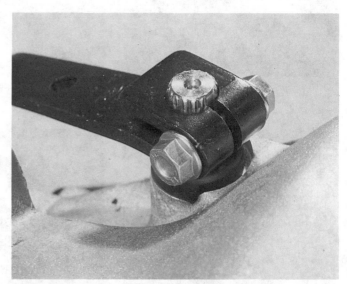

8.7 Clutch release lever pinch-bolt

8.9 Remove the nylon bush

8.10 Remove the release bearing

8.11 Lift out the fork assembly

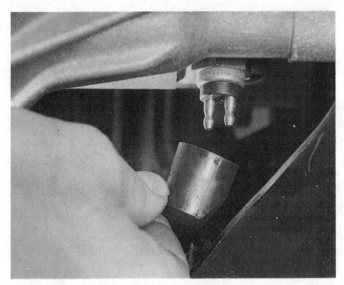

9.8 Disconnecting the reversing light switch

9 Manual transmission

Gear selector mechanism (1987 on) – dismantling and reassembly

1 On both four and five speed transmission units built after February 1987 (build code HK), the gear selector mechanism has been modified.

2 When dismantling or reassembling these units, the following procedure should be used.

3 Before the main selector shaft is removed, the gear selector gate, which is secured by two bolts, should be removed.

4 On reassembly, the selector gate is fitted after the main selector shaft, and before the guide levers.

5 The boss on the selector block must engage in the gate, and on five speed units, the reverse gear lock should face downwards towards the selector shaft.

Reversing light switch – removal and refitting

6 The reversing light switch is screwed into the side of the transmission housing.

7 To remove the switch, first disconnect the battery negative terminal.

8 Disconnect the electrical connections to the switch (photo).

9 Unscrew the switch from the housing.

10 Refit in reverse order.

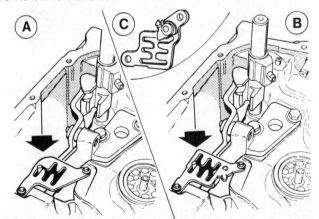

Fig. 13.4 Modified gear selector mechanism on 1987-on models (Sec 9)

A 4-speed transmission C Reverse gear lock on underside of gate
B 5-speed transmission

10 Automatic transmission

Automatic transmission starter inhibitor – renewal

1 All models with automatic transmission have a starter inhibitor relay mounted in the fuse/relay box.

2 When renewing the relay, only the correct relay obtainable from Ford dealers must be fitted.

3 An incorrect relay can allow the engine to be started in any gear selector position and also allow the starter motor to continue turning after the engine has started.

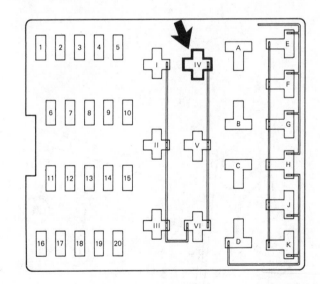

Fig. 13.5 Starter inhibitor relay location in fusebox (Sec 10)

11 Driveshafts

Outer constant velocity joint bellows – renewal

1 On the larger diameter right-hand driveshaft, there is no alternative but to detach the driveshaft from the hub carrier as described in Chapter 8, Section 5, in order to renew the outer joint bellows.

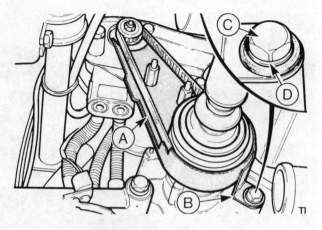

Fig. 13.6 Modified right-hand side modulator drivebelt cover (Sec 12)

A Latest level guard	C Bolt
B Additional support leg	D Washer

12 Braking system

Anti-lock brake (1987-on) – modulator drivebelt cover
1   From November 1987 the right-hand side modulator drivebelt

cover has been modified to include an additional support bracket secured by a bolt, see Fig. 13.6.

13 Suspension and steering

Steering gear – overhaul
1   When overhauling the steering rack, (see Chapter 10, section 28) the following method of securing the tie-rod may be used in preference to staking the balljoint.
2   Before fitting the tie-rod to the steering rack, coat the threads of the tie-rod with Loctite 270.
3   Fit and tighten the tie-rod to the specified torque. Note that this torque should only be applied where Loctite is employed as the locking medium.

Steering rack (1988-on) – description
4   From September 1988 all Escort models are fitted with a new 'variable-ratio' steering rack.
5   The system gives greater response at high speeds and makes for easier parking.
6   The procedures covering the steering rack given in Chapter 10 remain unchanged.

Steering column (Cabriolet) – removal and refitting
7   On Cabriolet models produced after January 1987, an additional steering column brace is fitted as shown in Fig. 13.7.
8   This brace may be fitted to earlier models to stiffen the steering column and reduce vibration.
9   The necessary parts and fitting instructions are available from your Ford dealer.

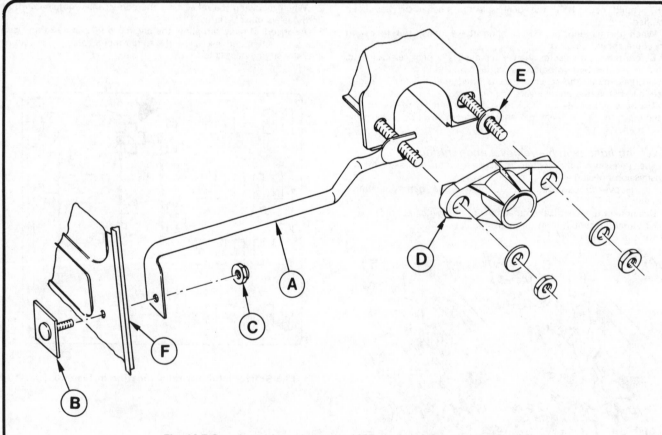

Fig. 13.7 Steering column brace on 1987-on Cabriolet models (Sec 13)

A Brace	D Support bracket
B Special bolt	E Spacer washer
C Nut	F Bodywork

14 Bodywork

Bonnet (1988-on) – removal and refitting

1 The procedure is basically as described in Chapter 11, Section 6, but the earth lead between the bonnet and bodywork must also be disconnected.

Radiator grille (1988-on) – removal and refitting

2 The radiator grille is integral with the bumper moulding and is removed with the bumper (see next paragraph).

Front bumper (1988-on) – removal and refitting

3 The procedure is basically as described in Chapter 11, Section 12, but if more access to the nuts in the wheelarches is required, remove the wheelarch liners.

4 Note also that the windscreen washer reservoir is now located in the front left-hand wheel arch, but the bumper retaining nut can be reached without removing the reservoir (photo).

Door trim panel (1988-on) – removal and refitting

5 From 1989, a new foam watershield is fitted under the door trim panel, secured in position by a strip of butyl.

6 To remove the watershield, the butyl strip must not be touched with the hands or subsequent adhesion will be impaired.

7 If the foam watershield is damaged beyond re-use on removal, all traces of it, and the butyl must be removed from the door inner skin. The butyl can be removed by 'rolling' it up on its self to form a ball.

8 New butyl strips can then be applied and a new watershield fitted. Use a roller to press the shield into contact with the butyl strip.

9 Alternatively, an alkathene sheet can be used, which is secured in place with double sided tape.

Door locks (1987-on) – removal and refitting

10 From August 1987 all models are fitted with 'Tibbe' high security locks to all doors, ignition lock and fuel filler lid.

11 Repair/overhaul kits are available for these locks from Ford dealers, and locks can be re-built to any key combination code.

12 The removal and refitting procedure for the high security locks is as described for normal locks in Chapter 12, Section 24.

Boot lid (Cabriolet) – removal and refitting

13 Open the boot and prop it open using a length of wood.

14 Pull out the clips securing the gas strut and remove the strut.

15 Working inside the boot, undo the nuts securing the hinge assemblies to the framework.

16 Ease the lid rearwards to disengage the studs, and lift the lid away.

17 The hinge assemblies can be removed from the lid by prising off the plastic covers and undoing the bolts securing the hinges to the lid. One is accessible from the outside and one from inside.

18 Refitting is a reversal of removal, but do not fully tighten the bolts until the lid has been lined up and closes properly.

Electric windows (Cabriolet) – removal and refitting

19 Proceed as described in Chapter 12, Section 46, paragraphs 1 to 7, then lower the window so that the window securing channel can be seen through the lower opening in the door. It may be necessary to temporarily connect the wiring to do this.

20 Remove the regulator securing bolts and nuts (Fig. 13.9).

21 Release the regulator mechanism rollers from the window securing channels and remove the glass from the door (see Chapter 11).

22 Release the wiring loom and remove the regulator mechanism from the door (refer to Chapter 12, Section 46).

23 Begin refitting by locating the regulator mechanism loosely in position in the door.

24 Refit the wiring loom.

25 Refit the window glass and insert the rollers of the regulator mechanism into the window securing channel.

26 Fit and tighten the regulator securing bolts and nuts.

27 Fit the inner and outer door weatherstrips.

28 Raise the window fully and check that the edge of the glass is in alignment with the roof seal.

29 Adjust the height and alignment of the glass using the screws indicated in Fig. 13.10.

30 Refit the door trim panels etc, as described in Chapter 12, Section 46.

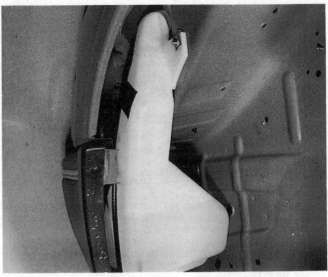

14.4 View of windscreen washer reservoir in wheel arch (liner removed)

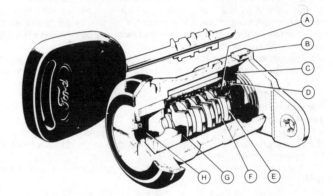

Fig. 13.8 'Tibbe' high security lock (Sec 14)

A Housing	E Tumbler
B Lever	F Spacer
C Bush	G Retaining ring
D Barrel	H Shutter assembly

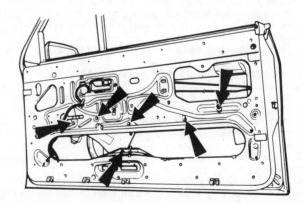

Fig. 13.9 Electric window regulator securing points (arrowed) on Cabriolet models (Sec 14)

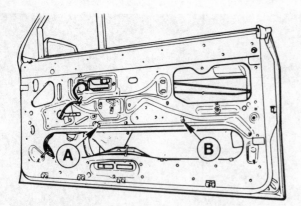

Fig. 13.10 Adjusting points for electric windows on Cabriolet models (Sec 14)

A Glass weight   B Glass alignment

Power operated folding roof – general description

31 As from 1987, a power operated folding roof is available as an option on Cabriolet models.
32 The roof is operated hydraulically from an electric pump located in the left-hand side of the boot. Hydraulic rams, mounted on each side of the vehicle by the rear wheel housings, actuate the roof folding mechanism. A control switch is mounted on the centre console. In event of failure, the roof can be operated manually by opening a bypass valve on the side of the pump.
33 The system is sealed and requires no regular maintenance apart from periodic checking of the fluid level.

Power operated folding roof – fluid level checking and bleeding

Level checking
34 The level should be checked with the roof **open**. With the roof in the closed position, the level will be lower due to the displacement of the hydraulic rams.
35 Pull down the trim panel/pump cover on the left-hand side of the boot.
36 Check that the fluid in the reservoir on the end of the pump is between the MIN and MAX marks on the sight glass.
37 If the level requires topping-up, remove the filler plug from the top of the pump reservoir and fill the reservoir with the specified fluid until the level reaches the MAX marks.
38 Refit the filler plug and trim panel.

Bleeding
39 Open the bypass valve on the side of the pump body.
40 Open, close and re-open the roof manually.
41 Fill the reservoir to the MAX mark, then fit the filler plug loosely and close the bypass valve on the side of the pump.
42 Open and close the roof several times using the power mode.
43 When all air has been bled from the system, the roof will operate smoothly without jerking, and the level of noise from the pump will be steady.
44 Top up the system, tighten the filler plug and refit disturbed panels.

Power operated folding roof – component renewal

Hydraulic rams
45 Remove the rear wheelhouse covers as described in Chapter 11, Section 33.
46 Mark the two hoses connected to the ram for reassembly, then remove the circlips securing the ram to the two studs on the framework.
47 Release residual pressure in the system by opening the filler plug on the pump body.
48 Loosen the hydraulic unions on the ram, then remove the ram from the studs and lay it in a suitable container in the boot. Undo the unions and catch the hydraulic fluid in the container.
49 If the unions are to remain disconnected for any length of time, cover the ends to prevent dirt entering the system.
50 Fitting a new ram is a reversal of removal, noting that the large circlip is fitted to the lower stud.
51 On completion, fill and bleed the system as described earlier.

Hydraulic ram upper pivot stud
52 Should the hydraulic ram upper pivot stud break in service it can be renewed as follows.
53 Open the tap on the hydraulic pump then manually open the roof halfway.
54 Using a mole wrench remove the broken end of the pivot stud from the framework. If the remaining stud is too short it may be possible to remove it using a proprietary stud extractor kit.
55 De-grease the threads on the new stud, apply locking compound to them, then fit the stud and tighten it to the specified torque.
56 Refit the hydraulic rams as described earlier.

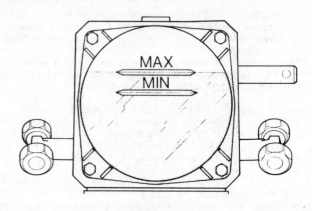

Fig. 13.11 Fluid level sight glass for power operated folding roof (Sec 14)

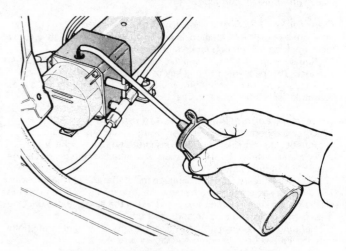

Fig. 13.12 Filling the reservoir (Sec 14)

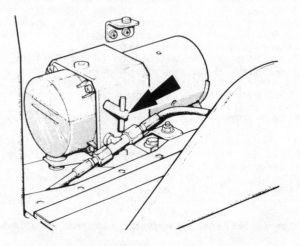

Fig. 13.13 Bypass valve on side of pump (Sec 14)

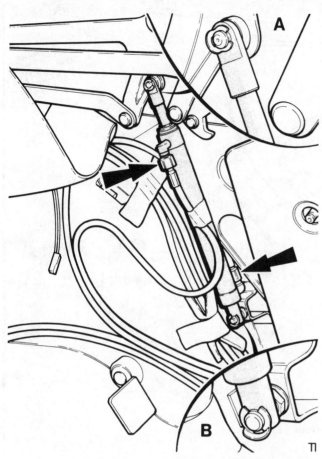

Fig. 13.14 Hydraulic ram assembly – hose connections
arrowed (Sec 14)

A and B Upper and lower clips

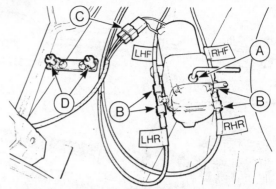

Fig. 13.15 Showing pump removed from mounting and hoses
marked (Sec 14)

A   Filler plug   *C   Connector*
B   Hydraulic unions   *D   Pump mountings*

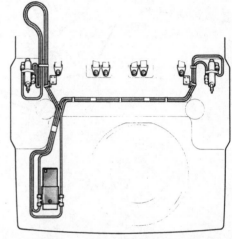

Fig. 13.16 Routing of hydraulic hoses and location of tape at
clips (Sec 14)

Pump

57 Disconnect the battery, then pull down the pump cover in the boot and open the bypass valve by 90 to 180 degrees. Do not open it any further.

58 Open the roof manually.

59 Remove the floor panel and left-hand wheelhouse panel from the boot. This involves propping open the boot lid and disconnecting the supporting gas strut from the lower balljoint.

60 Release residual pressure in the system by opening the filler plug on the pump. Tighten the plug when the pressure has been released.

61 Disconnect the electrical lead to the plug.

62 Remove the nuts securing the pump to the boot floor, and place the pump in a suitable container to catch the fluid which will be spilt when the pump hoses are disconnected.

63 Mark the hoses for reassembly, then undo the connections. Cover the open ends if they are to remain disconnected for any length of time.

64 Refitting is a reversal of removal.

65 On completion, fill and bleed the system as described earlier.

Hydraulic hoses

66 Renewing the hydraulic hoses involves disconnecting the relevant hose connections from the pump or ram (see earlier paragraphs), noting its routing, and when it is clipped or taped to other components. Refit in the reverse order to removal.

67 On completion, fill and bleed the system as described in earlier paragraghs.

Demister nozzle – removal and refitting

68 Disconnect the battery earth lead.

69 Remove the dash lower trim panels.

70 Remove the shrouds from the upper part of the steering column. The upper section of the shroud is secured by one screw while the lower one is held by three screws.

71 Remove the instrument panel (see Chapter 12, Section 23).

72 Pull the hoses from the demister nozzles and then detach the hose from the right-hand side vent.

73 Unscrew and remove the four fixing screws from the demister nozzle assembly.

74 As the upper fixing screw of the crash pad also secures the demister nozzle, the crash pad must be removed by extracting four screws. One screw is located under the ashtray, one screw at each windscreen pillar and after pulling the crash pad forward the last screw may be extracted, also releasing the demister nozzle.

75 Remove the demister by drawing it downward and to the side with the front door wide open.

76 Refitting is a reversal of the removal procedure.

Face level vent (right or left-hand) – removal and refitting

77 Remove the dash lower trim panels.

78 Reach up behind the facia panel and pull the hoses from the vent nozzle.

79 Apply pressure to the rear of the nozzle to eject it from the front of the facia.

80 Refit by reversing the removal operations.

Face level vent (centre) – removal and refitting

81 Prise up the loudspeaker grille and remove it from its spring clips. Extract the speaker mounting screws and withdraw the speaker (if fitted) until the leads can be disconnected and the speaker removed.

82 Pull the hoses from the centre vent assembly by inserting the hand into the aperture left by removal of the loudspeaker grille.

83 Extract the screw which secures the rear of the centre vent and push the vent out of the front of the facia panel.

84 Refitting is the reverse of the removal procedure.

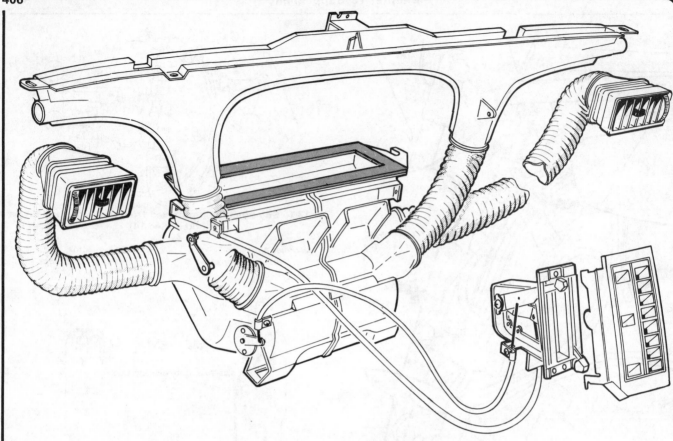

Fig. 13.17 Heating and ventilation system – Base models (Sec 14)

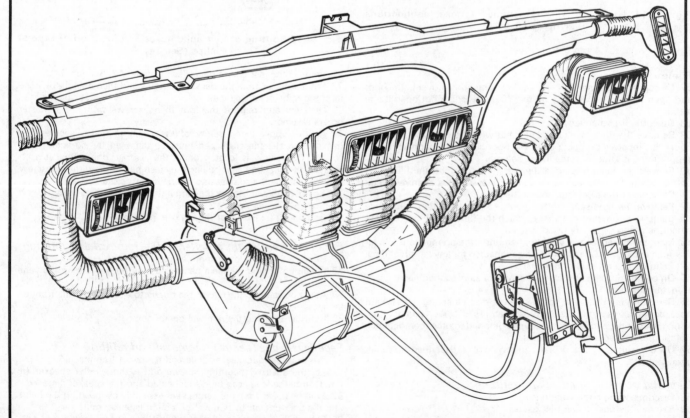

Fig. 13.18 Heating and ventilation system – All except Base models (Sec 14)

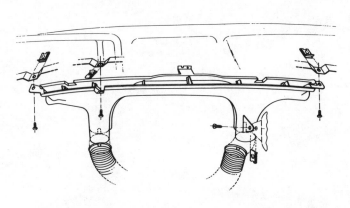

Fig. 13.19 Demister nozzle fixing screw locations (Sec 14)

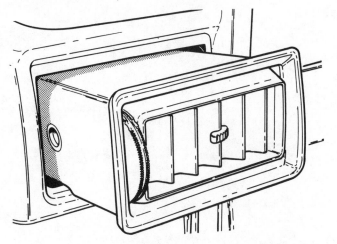

Fig. 13.20 Removing a face level vent nozzle (Sec 14)

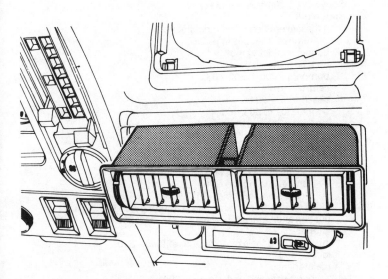

Fig. 13.21 Removing the face level centre vent (Sec 14)

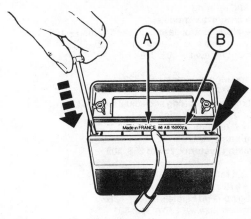

Fig. 13.22 Removing the rear cover of the roof mounted clock
(clips arrowed) (Sec 14)

A   Country of origin   B   Part number

15 Electrical system

Side indicator repeater lamp – bulb renewal

1   Reach up behind the front wheelarch and locate the back of the repeater lamp holder.
2   Depress the two clips on the holder body and push the assembly outwards and out of the wing.
3   Twist the bulbholder anti-clockwise to free it from the lens.
4   Pull the bulb from its socket.
5   Push in a new bulb and refit the assembly in the reverse order to removal.

Clock (roof mounted) – bulb renewal

6   Remove the clock as described in Chapter 12, Section 27.
7   Remove the rear cover from the unit by depressing the two clips at the top outer corners of the cover (Fig. 13.22)
8   The bulb, now accessible, is a bayonet fix in its holder.
9   Refitting is a reverse of removal.

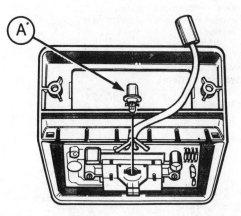

Fig. 13.23 Removing the bulb – A (Sec 14)

Index